# bulletproof diva

## also by lisa jones

Uplift the Race: The Construction of School Days
(with Spike Lee)

Do the Right Thing (with Spike Lee)

Mo' Better Blues (with Spike Lee)

# bulletproof diva

## tales of race, sex, and hair

## Lisa Jones

**doubleday new york london toronto sydney auckland**

PUBLISHED BY DOUBLEDAY
a division of Bantam Doubleday Dell Publishing Group, Inc.
1540 Broadway, New York, New York 10036

DOUBLEDAY and the portrayal of an anchor with a dolphin
are trademarks of Doubleday, a division of
Bantam Doubleday Dell Publishing Group, Inc.

The majority of the pieces herein originally appeared in *The Village Voice.* "Is
Biracial Enough?" "She Came with the Rodeo," and "Looking for Mariah"
appear here for the first time.

We gratefully acknowledge permission from the following:

From the book *Three Pieces* by Ntozake Shange. Copyright © 1981 by
Ntozake Shange. Reprinted with permission from St. Martin's Press, Inc.,
New York, NY.

From the poem "Zoom," which appeared in *All the Renegade Ghosts Rise* by
Thulani Davis. Reprinted by permission of the author.

From *The Venus Hottentot* by Elizabeth Alexander, the University Press of
Virginia, 1990.

Book design by Gretchen Achilles

Library of Congress Cataloging-in-Publication Data

Jones, Lisa.
    Bulletproof diva : tales of race, sex, and hair / Lisa Jones. — 1st ed.
        p.   cm.
    1. Afro-Americans—Drama.   2. Afro-American women.   I. Title.
PS3560.05144B85   1994
814'.54—dc20                                                                    93-40749
                                                                                        CIP

ISBN 0-385-47122-X

April 1994

First Edition

10 9 8 7 6 5 4 3 2 1

## for the ladies

Hettie Jones,
Kellie Jones, Cora Coleman, and the gentlewomen Rice,

and in spirit,
Kimako Baraka
and
Anna Lois Russ Jones

# contents

## one
## how i invented multiculturalism

## two
## bring the heroines

## five
# the hair trade

# acknowledgments

Most of the bits and pieces collected here come from a column I began in 1990 at the *Village Voice*. "Skin Trade" (which won out over "Hot Comb," "Booty & Soul," "Reckless Eyeballing," and "Mules & Men") was given a loose mandate: a column on the politics of style. I thank Donald Suggs for suggesting such a beat in the first place, and many others at the *Voice* for their support: editor-in-chief Jonathan Larsen, managing editor Sarah Jewler, and editors Mary Jo Neuberger, Joe Levy, Vince Aletti, and Amy Virshup, though most particularly Thulani Davis and Doug Simmons. My gratitude to columnist-in-crime Leslie Savan for nearly a decade of lipstick tips, and to my research assistant, Mia Mask, and Omoronke Idowu, my intern. Arts editor Lisa Kennedy, prime editrix of "Skin Trade," gets all the thanks in the world. To my colleague Greg Tate, the same.

Shouts to the ancestors (literary and otherwise) and Malaika Adero, the Baraka family, the late Sylvia Ardyn Boone, C & C Computer Tyme, Cesar Cacho Jr., William Calhoun, Gordon Chambers, Nicholas Charles, Faith Childs, Barron Claibourne, Uncle Darryl, Michaela Angela Davis, Peyton Beaumont Farley, Uncle Flat Top, the Glamorous Grandmas of Newark, Cheryll Greene, Kevin Griffith, bell hooks, Sherrilyn Ifil, Jon Jon, Mr. Coyt L. Jones and the Archie family, Stephanie and Suzanne Jones, Katrinia Karkazis, Peter Lau, the late Wyn Loving, the Loving-Cortes family, Slick Mahoney, Manhattan Theatre Club, the late Eduardo Mejia, the New York Joneses, Percidia Alice Norris, One Way Productions, Susan Osorio, the Playwrights' Center, Perez and Associates, Evette Porter, Renée Raymond, Rodeo Caldonia, Alva Rogers, Uncle G. L. Russ, Coreen Simpson, Linda Villarosa, and William Byrd Wilkins.

Big thanks to the Doubleday tribe and to my editor David

Gernert and his assistant Amy Williams. Also to the folks at Lowenstein Associates and to my agent, Ms. Barbara Lowenstein herself.

In her usual way, my lawyer and best friend María Peréz saw
this book coming long before I did. Please note, all the hair issues
discussed within are hers. I myself have none.

# bulletproof diva

# introduction

This is a book of tales.

It may be the ravings of a madwoman who loved having her hands in other people's hair, and who should have gone to beauty culture school and owned a wig shop like her great-aunt, or moonlighted as a barber like her grandfather, but by happenstance became a writer.

Or it's a catalog of American obsessions in the nineties—race, sex, and hair, and the marketing and consumption of race, sex, and hair—that includes close encounters with brown plastic Barbie dolls, corporate boys, polygamists, hair traders, biracial entertainers, skeezers, supermamas, and cowgirls.

Or, more likely, it's a continuous reenactment of my defining moment as experienced in a movie theater in London, England, during a Saturday matinee of *Imitation of Life*, the 1934 version. The year is 1983 and I have just turned twenty-two. I sit in the back of the dark theater thrilled because I am about to see, for the first time, a big-screen version of myself and her name will be Peola. But as the film progresses, I notice that this Peola isn't me at all, she's a remake of Frankenmulatta, that character from *The Octoroon Concubine of Frankenstein,* one of Mary Shelley's lost sequels.

These are funeral rites for the Tragic Mulatto.

Warning: This may also include shameless acts of soapbox politicking toward the cause of politicizing multiracial identity in the nineties. Say that again two more times fast.

This is a passing novel. Guess who's passing? You.

Certainly this is a search for heroines.

Here's a quiz: Why did African-American girls who came of age in the seventies convince themselves they had to be the perfect composite of Angela Davis and Diahann Carroll as Julia? You will be graded.

Perhaps I should tell you this is a sorrow song for my aunt Kimako who was knifed to death by a stranger in her Manhattan high rise because her doorman assumed that any man who was black like her and requested entry was automatically a friend.

This is a cover of *Upscale* magazine showing Janet Jackson, her skin lightened to the tone of Marilyn Monroe's.

Herein is an extended nappy-hair conspiracy theory as proven by remarks made in *U.S. News & World Report* concerning Lani Guinier, the law professor whose nomination as assistant attorney general for civil rights was withdrawn by President Clinton in 1993: "Strange name, *strange hair,* strange writing—she's history" (emphasis mine).

A fact, as documented by the television series "Eyes on the Prize, II," the fifth episode, *Ain't Gonna Shuffle No More (1964–1972):* The black consciousness movement at Howard University began in October 1966 when Robin Gregory became the first homecoming queen to sport an Afro. The writer Paula Giddings, interviewed in the documentary, offers this account of the homecoming coronation: "The curtains opened . . . the lights began to come up at the same time. Well, before you saw Robin, you saw . . . the silhouette of her Afro. . . . The audience exploded. . . . It was a wonderful moment. People started jumping up and screaming. Some were raising their fists. Then spontaneously a chant began . . . 'Ngawa Black Power! Ngawa Black Power!' . . . a chain was created and people started to march to the rhythm of 'Ngawa Black Power!' . . . [they marched] all the way around the auditorium and out the door and into the streets of Washington, D.C., past the campus, still chanting 'Ngawa Black Power!' and that was really the launching of the movement." The following school year students occupied an administration building to demand that Howard adapt a curriculum that incorporated, as it had not done before, black culture and history.

Believe it or not the following headline appeared in the *New York Times* on March 3, 1993: FOR A BLACK WOMAN, SPACE ISN'T THE FINAL FRONTIER.

Consider this a narrative in which we invent our own heroine, the Bulletproof Diva. A woman whose sense of dignity and self cannot be denied; who, though she may live in a war zone like Brownsville, goes out everyday greased, pressed, and dressed, with hair faded and braided and freeze-dried and spit-curled and wrapped and locked and cut to a sexy baldie (so she is all eyes and lips) and piled ten inches high and colored siren red, cobalt blue, and flaming yellow. She is fine and she knows it. She *has* to know it because who else will? Perhaps she is Marian Anderson singing her Easter concert on the steps of the Lincoln Memorial after the Daughters of the American Revolution prevented her appearance at Constitution Hall, because opera singer or no opera singer, no colored woman was gonna open her lungs and blow in their hall, not in 1939, no, no, no. Anderson, of course, became in 1955 the first Negro to sing at the Metropolitan Opera House in New York City, where she appeared in Verdi's *The Masked Ball* and blew. But you *know* that.

A Bulletproof Diva is not, I repeat, *not* that tired stereotype, the emasculating black bitch too hard for love or piety. It's safe to assume that a Bulletproof Diva is whoever you make her—corporate girl, teen mom, or the combination—as long as she has the lip and nerve, and as long as she uses that lip and nerve to raise up herself and the world.

This is also a search for home.

So I lied. It's an appreciation of several homes.

Accept this as a manual: How to survive a Jewish mother who thinks she knows how to cook collard greens better than you do and happens to be right.

This is what happens when you grow up listening to your father recite poems like "Beautiful Black Women . . ." and preach Sunday sermons at "Soul Session," where folks talk about revolution in between playing James Brown, the Temptations, and Billy Preston, and get to standing up, swaying, and clapping just like church. You develop, to borrow a phrase from Patricia Williams, "feelings of exaggerated visibility," which, later on when you attend an Ivy League university, are countered by feelings of exaggerated invisibility.

Evidently this is the result of having an aunt whose repertoire includes "black folks love Chinese food more than orgasm"; "They need to free Mike Tyson and put that Desiree girl in jail for rape"; and "America's a great country, but whitey's doing his best to mess it up."

This may contain a series of photographs of my handsome grandfather. Dark Gable, they call him. And these are his bowling trophies, his cigars, and his Negro League stories.

At last, here find a collection of love letters to my grandmother, who while she lived loved a good Snoopy cartoon as much as she did the Race; an Americanist who had not a blind faith but an intellectual engagement with democracy, who believed black folks built this country; an internationalist, lover of all who presented themselves to be loved.

Hello my name is Lisa Victoria Chapman Jones. Victoria after the queen, Chapman after my great-great-grandmother Delphia Chapman who was once enslaved in America, though she lived on past Emancipation until she was 105 years old, whereupon she died. But only because her house caught fire.

Welcome to my America.

# one

# how i invented
# multiculturalism

# how i invented
# multiculturalism

It was easier than you think. First I arrived, fatter than an A&P chicken, just another black child in New York City born to a Jewish woman and a Negro man. Before race became my passion and my battle cry, the only thing I wanted in life was to be joined at the hip with my older sister. At the wee age of three I followed her to the Church of All Nations school on the Lower East Side. For many years I thought the entire world was a band of Latin, black, and Chinese children dancing around the maypole and singing "Que Bonita Bandera" and the few Ukrainians who served us lunch.

Picked up my first curse word, *maricón,* from Jesús,

born in the Dominican Republic, which was an island, he showed me, just across the river from our playground on Avenue D. Twenty years later I moved there, but someone had changed the name to Brooklyn.

Endured my first Toni home permanent at age six to have an Afro like Angela Davis. This continued for four years, then thanks to chemical overload or natural progression, my hair napped up enough to make a 'fro on its own.

Ate potato kugel and boiled chicken with Aunt Fannie, the only Jewish relative who didn't disown my mother for marrying a black man. Eighty-year-old Aunt Fannie stayed in Flatbush through the Caribbean migration and was known to have made only one comment about her niece's interracial marriage: "How do you wash that hair?" she said, leaning over her grandnieces, still in grade school, and their enormous globes of nappiness.

Metamorphosed, in the late sixties at age seven, as a nationalist poet. Appeared in the poetry revue *In Praise of Black Women* on stage at the Negro Ensemble Company Theater wearing seventeen braids and reading, in the style of the Last Poets, "Fried Chicken and Collard Greens/Gramma." My grandmother had me recite this masterpiece for her friends the social workers and other silver-haired belles of black Newark whenever we came across the Hudson to visit.

Named my cat Huey Newton. Named my dog Ho Chi Minh.

Grew dreadlocks at Methodist summer camp in New Hampshire. The camp counselor couldn't comb my hair. Hung out on a nude beach in Nantucket another summer realizing how black people's bodies put the fear of God in some white folks. Most memorable summer: 1969. Spent two blissful months in a cabin on the Jersey shore with a household of very opinionated and well-dressed black women—my grandmother, several aunts, scores of cousins, and my sister—riding bikes six in a row and lip-synching to Aretha. The townies thought we were some lost tribe of Amazons.

Went to high school in Chinatown. The yearbook lists my two favorite books as *Wuthering Heights* and *Native Son.*

Endured chemical relaxers to slay my Afro and curling irons in homage to Farrah Fawcett.

Gave up my cherry in Babylon, Long Island, in a trailer home owned by the Italian drug dealer. My first boyfriend was his son, a black kid with an orange Afro who sold reefer on the weekends in Washington Square Park. The kid introduced me to Jimi Hendrix and sushi. I gave him Chaka Khan and Caporel's Spanish-style fried chicken.

Took hustle lessons in the mid-seventies from a Polish DJ who grew up around Puerto Ricans and had a black Panamanian girlfriend. Became a regular at the Paradise Garage. Thought the "disco sucks" movement was a racist ploy backed by the Ku Klux Klan to keep folks of different cultures from dancing together.

Traveled to Trinidad the summer of junior year in high school at the invitation of seventeen-year-old pen pal Jenny Paul. Jenny's best friend Wendell was Chinese, East Indian, and African. Didn't bring back much Trini twang, though did learn how to wine like a Trini at Saturday night jump-ups in Port of Spain.

Worked in Greece as a mother's helper. Stumbled on a shrine of one of Europe's many black Madonnas on a tiny island off the coast of Crete.

Found my soul sister/best friend on an Ivy League campus in the late seventies wearing a red bandanna, booty-tight jeans, and five-inch heels. Once she cursed out the entire rugby team for advertising a "slave auction" fundraiser. "Puerto Rican" wasn't inclusive enough for Miss Two and a Half; she called herself "black Latino" or "Third World Woman."

Read Wole Soyinka, William Carlos Williams, and Gloria Anzaldua. Led a boycott against the campus store for tracking black male customers like prison escapees.

Cofounded the We Waz Girls Together Off-Campus Collective. Threw "After the Revolution" parties with Ghanaians educated in Britain, white women in "Warhol does Mao" T-shirts, Nuyoricans in Izod polos, white guys from Chicago who spoke "black English," black women from Compton who became prison lawyers, and Cubans in deck shoes who wanted to be rich whites and, in fact, were.

Lived in a North London squat with African-American rock & roll expatriates and a Scottish skinhead motorcycle gang.

Returned to New York in time for the premiere of *Purple Rain.* Wondered if black women—especially browner-skinned black women—would be missing from Afro America's new media facelift as sculpted by fellows like Prince and Michael Jackson.

Refused to endure a "California curl" so my hair could bounce, as promised by a stylist, just like rainbow-baby actress Rae Dawn Chong's.

Dug Jessica Hagedorn's collection *Pet Food and Tropical Apparitions,* about a Filipino-American woman coming of age to black music and California kitsch. Discovered the multiculti in me and loved her fiercely. Knew that cultural pluralism was more than a performance piece for well-heeled art house patrons, but an everyday life led by thousands of Americans, black, yellow, brown, red, and yes, even white.

Reborn as a race woman after Howard Beach. Joined the Make Black Film movement. Made Black Movies.

Reread Zora Neale Hurston, Kafka, and Nella Larsen. Rediscovered my mentors, Thurgood Marshall, Fannie Lou Hamer, Che, and Ida B. Wells. Have plans to revamp Dr. King's Poor People's Campaign in crack capitals across the country. But first I have to write my version of *Bonfire of the Vanities.* Instead of scratching each other's eyes out, everyone does what everyone has wanted to do all along: has sex.

Eventually I'll make it to the Motherland when I raise the cash. It's been a wonderful life, really.

*1991*

# hair always and forever

We ate lunch, the tape recorder was rolling, and now the legendary jazz singer would tell me her life story. This was her preface: "When I was a little girl, about thirteen or so, they told me that a woman's pride and glory was her hair. Then they told me mine wasn't any good. I guess I went to war to absolve myself of this grief."

Not, "Back when I used to gig at the Five Spot . . ." or "Coleman Hawkins sure could blow . . ." but, everything I've done with my hair explains everything I've done with my life and my art. This wasn't an epiphany for me as much as a confirmation of something I've believed for a while. Hair is the be-all and end-all. Everything I know about American history I learned from looking at black people's hair. It's the perfect metaphor for the African experiment here: the price of the ticket (for a journey no one elected to take), the toll of slavery, and the costs of remaining. It's all in the hair.

People, mostly men, tell me I'm too strung out on hair. That hair is not political, that it doesn't matter what we do to our hair, that there's more to life than hair. But this is just not true. Like Jamaica Kincaid, who writes only about a character named Mother, I've decided to write only about hair: what we do to it, how we do it, and why. I figure this is enough.

Which is how I happened upon Charlene's, a place where women can go twenty-four hours a day to get their hair done. Now twenty-four hours really means Monday through Thursday till midnight and twenty-four hours on the weekends, but it doesn't matter. The idea still titillates me to no end: a place where you can go just about any time of day or night if your hair "turns back," which means, in case you didn't know, returns to its natural state.

Last year Charlene's, lit up in green and red like a Christmas tree, became the newest neon landmark on Flatbush Avenue, the Broadway of Brooklyn. Lest you thought twenty-four-hour hair was peculiar to the fashion victims of downtown Brooklyn, it's not. With eleven shops, three in the New York area, Charlene's is one of the largest black-owned salon chains in the country. Charlene's Fifth Avenue, in midtown occupies a swanky office building across the street from Lord & Taylor. If you're hair obsessed like me, you'll get a thrill from the familiar perm aroma that drifts down to the lobby from the salon on the second floor. Former model and football player Troy McSwain, now general manager of the New York–area shops, looks straight off the pages of *Ebony Man:* a fade with a crown of "texurized" curls—yet another euphemism for chemicals. (Yes, I identify everyone I meet by hairstyle.) Troy gives me the grand tour: twenty-two hair stations, five waiting rooms with burgundy velveteen chairs, and a supply room where hair products are doled out to stylists, depending on the job, by the ounce. Inventory control, says Mama, keeps costs down.

Mama is owner Charlene Miles, the Charlene of Charlene's. It's a tight-knit family business. Troy and the other salon general managers, who are the same age as Miles's oldest son, the company president, call her Mama. He wants me to speak to Mama herself because she is, after all, the inventor of twenty-four-hour hair.

While Troy calls Detroit, I check out the photos: Ms. Miles with Oprah, Ms. Miles with Jesse, Ms. Miles with Nancy Wilson, Ms. Miles in a new mink coat. Ms. Miles's soft voice on the phone reminds me of my grandmother, who took me at age six to get "straightened and curled" for the first time at the hair salon atop Bamberger's in downtown Newark.

Before cosmetology school, Miles did all kinds of work—"from cotton chopping on up the line." As a young woman in the 1950s she spent most of the decade on the road styling trade shows for Posner's hair products. With six chairs and three thousand dollars, Miles opened the original Charlene's salon in Buffalo, New York. The year was 1960. Her first employees were black beauty-school grads on welfare. White salons refused to hire them.

Spiritual daughter of Madame C. J. Walker, purveyor of the hot comb, Miles was an early champion of chemical relaxers at the dawn of the sixties. Later she boycotted the Afro. ("I lost money. In this business you gotta change with the changes.") Years of styling hair showed her how difficult it is for working women to make it to salons during the day, hence the twenty-four-hour hair concept. Late-night customers aren't sleazy, Miles will testify, just "family people; lawyers and housewives who leave the kids with their husbands."

And so went my night at Charlene's: I arrive just after nine on Saturday, and stylist Eddie Ogletree, a receptionist, and a janitor are the only folks around. Eddie has styled hair going on thirteen years; in the eighties at salons like Black Hair Is and Soul Scissors. He offers to give me a "blow-curl" while I wait for the games to begin. Late-night business at Charlene's Fifth Avenue has been slow since the city shut down half of its dance clubs a few years back, but the salon does have its after-hours regulars: "Your club crowd comes in from eight to eleven," Eddie breaks it down. "From two to seven, you have your postal workers" (from the main post office on Thirty-third Street). Wedding parties show up after three ("I do the bridesmaids, Jerome does the bride"), the church ladies after four. Then the sun comes up. Every Friday, for a few months running, Eddie saw a woman whom he believes was carrying on an affair: "She had a Mercedes, Jersey plates. I saw the car from the window. She'd come in around one. Her hair was always a mess. I'd curl it, but she'd style it herself. She didn't want to look too 'done.' "

Night manager Jerome Shavers rolls in with a bald head and ample panache to match his job title. In addition to his salon gig, Jerome does hair for musical revues like *Chitlin' Circuit,* now playing at Sweetwaters, a supper club near Lincoln Center. On the last day of every month, twenty wigs from the traveling sixties revue *Beehive* are shipped to him UPS. He has one day to style them and ship them back.

Jerome regales me with tales of "his nights at Charlene's," which he pronounces in an exaggerated lisp, as if recalling some infamous cabaret or brothel. He always asks new faces what brings them to the salon so late at night. One woman said she just couldn't sleep. Another swore her husband wouldn't let her back in the house unless she got rid of the "Afro beads" on her neck.

When Jerome the hair griot gets on a roll, he'll take you anywhere. Tonight it's back to Missouri, where he was "Curl King of St. Louis." As a young stylist he "pumped" two dozen curls a day for an old-school salon owner by the name of Master Metcalf. Jerome is ready to swear that Metcalf did cold waves on black hair to create a loosely curled effect twenty years before the Jheri curl. She sold fried chicken and fish out of the salon and would curse you out in a minute. Once a woman threatened to bomb the shop because her hair "went back" too fast. Metcalf cursed her under the table. It was Metcalf who kept Jerome off the streets when he was a teenager by giving him a job in her shop. Every time he twirls an iron, he thinks of her.

Charlene's is still empty at 2:00 A.M. Hours have gone by listening to Jerome. He's talking now about being "called" to do hair and why: to save his Mama and her girlfriend, Miss Orphelia, from being bald-headed. (The two burned each other's scalps regularly with head-over-the-sink perms.) This is where I belong forever, in Charlene's twenty-four-hour hair joint, listening to Jerome's war stories. Bury me under a hair dryer, Jerome can deliver the eulogy: "Here's she rests—fried, dyed, and laid to the side."

*1991*

# my slave
## name

My name is owned by so many other people, I often think

that I have not a name but a group moniker: the Free-

masons, the Moonies, the Lisa Joneses. Ever notice that

every year there's an *Ebony* bachelorette named Lisa

Jones? (I hope to make the list in 1995 as Lisa Jones

number 52.) My mother has this story she tells: When I

arrived there was only one other Lisa in Manhattan—the

very slender wife of a famous conceptual artist. Zillions

of American mothers in the early sixties must have

dreamt up the same story. The Lisa population, as you

know, now outnumbers laboratory rats.

As *Ebony* bachelorette Lisa Jones number 52,

I would say, names are among my obsessions, or as girlfriend Dean-dra would say, my "issues." What's life without African-American names, nicknames, and naming rituals? Without folks calling other folks "out of their names"? Or of wondrously mythic stories involving names—like that of a friend's cousin who since grade school had gone by "Niggerman." He died in the electric chair. His crime? Shooting a white man for calling him "nigger."

The jazz dynasty is proof alone that names are divining rods: Mingus, Thelonious, Ornette, Coltrane. Even with all their urban newness, hip-hop names in rhythm and word play are reminiscent of the blues: Big Daddy Kane meets Blind Lemon Jefferson. And what of that gold mine of names as metaphor in Afro-Am lit? Bigger Thomas, Shug Avery, Milkman Dead, Jesse B. Semple, and Sula—possibly derived from the West African name *Sule*, meaning adventurous. New black cinema aches to be in the grand name tradition: *She's Gotta Have It*'s Mars Blackmon gets his name not from the candy bar, but from the filmmaker's great-grandfather. Here's the real question: The stank-breath character in *House Party* named Billal—is that a Muslim name or just a pun on bile?

We writers raid our family trees for names (Uncle Bubba, Aunt Gottlieb, Uncle Flat Top), then scavenge our friends'. (My friend Byrd—real name—has an uncle named Duck—real name.) But no one, I thought, could beat my great-uncle G. L. Russ. (G period, L period. Period.) Come to find that initial names were common among black men, like my uncle, born around the turn of the century. The Black Muslim "X" (signifying the absence of ancestral name) and hip-hop's initial as exclamation point (as in Chuck D.) join in to make another tradition: The name implied.

The field of names that young African Americans in the nineties draw from begs of excavation. A good friend teaches black studies to Ivy League freshmen. Her students, born in 1974, have names like Kenyatta, Rhasaam, Zuwena, Shakinah, and Rondai. Some are "movement babies" whose parents gave them African and Muslim names at the height of black cultural nationalism. Some converted from Anglo names as recently as the Afrocentric eighties. And there are those, like Shakinah and Rondai, whose names reach to Africa, if not for content, then for sonic inspiration.

Naming/renaming has been an "issue" for black folks on these shores since the slave ships docked. Following Emancipation, not only did families seek to reconstruct their ranks, but their names as well. Sixties nationalism made an expressive though shrill link between slave names, slave hair, and slave mentalities. It wasn't just Cassius Clay, Abbey Lincoln, and Stokely Carmichael who took African and Muslim names, but thousands of regular folk. While hippies baptized their kids Moon Unit and River Phoenix, folks named their's Kwesi and Latifah. Even Clarence Thomas's son, born in 1975, was christened Jamal.

Afrocentricity has brought back African name books, a fixture in black bookstores of the nationalist days. The slave-names-for-slaves doctrine is now gone; these new books appeal to spirituality rather than politics. They discuss African philosophical ideas about naming and offer names that reflect the continent's diversity, whereas the old books gave just Swahili names, or names identified only as "Afrikan."

I've seen over ten name books on the shelves recently. Four were published last year, including *Senkha-sen Ren-a (May They Mention My Name)*, a handbook of names in the ancient Egyptian language Metu Neter. (I chose the name *Amaumeru*, meaning, "I remember the heroes.") There's the popular *Book of African Names* by Dr. Molefi Asante, who coined "Afrocentricity." Asante's mission: to provide alternatives to the rash of African-inspired names that reflect, so he deems, "a half-understanding of the culture." His most colorful example is of a girl named Rhodesia after the former stomping grounds of strident racist Cecil John Rhodes.

Sheniqua, Twanda, Lakeisha—I call these the Watts, Africa, names; they sound African to some ears, yet they're made in chocolate cities like Detroit. Mattel's new African-American fashion doll line has two dolls with Swahili names and one named Nichelle, which falls in the "Frenchified" category of the Watts, Africa, aesthetic (along with names like Chante, Saute, Tanqueray). There's a R&B/pop category too: A friend just became aunt to nieces named Shalimar and Cameo. I admire the invention of these names, how boldly they announce themselves, how they aim for the singular quality of royalty. I try to imagine the world that they conjured up for the parent. Tanqueray, say, must have been less a brand of a gin made in England than a place like Tangier, with beaded curtains and sandalwood incense.

Watts, Africa, names don't get much respect from the intelligentsia. *Essence* ran an opinion piece a few years back dismissing them for being "cumbersome," "phonetically incorrect," and, presumably, low class. A buppie couple in their early thirties, asked recently why they chose an Anglo name for their child, said, "At least we didn't name her Toyota Corolla." (Some lump the contemporary African name movement, over twenty years strong, in with more fanciful Watts-Africanisms.) Then there are others, like Gordon Chambers, a twenty-five-year-old jazz musician, who sees himself as part of a "postmodern George Wolfeian generation of young boho and buppie African Americans." Black cultural awareness, he believes, is an "assumption that doesn't necessarily have to be proven anymore. We don't have to wear it as much."

I made peace with my slave name only recently, and have even found a measure of tenderness for it. Truth is, life would be empty without folks singing to me, "Me and Mrs. Jones" or "I got a love jones for you baby, oohoohooh." And how could I wean myself from spectacular nicknames like "Worm the Phi Slama Jama Hermaneutic" that compensate for the *Ebony* bacheloretteness of my name?

A tidy coda came last summer. Since I was eight I have considered taking an African name; more, back then, as a badge of blackness than to escape the baby-girl femininity of my given name. This is an irony to me now, given that all along I've had one of the most indelibly "colored" names in the book. I was late to work one day when a very skinny brother missing a few teeth asked me to sign a petition. As I signed it, he looked me over, "What's your national-lee-tee?" "Negro," I said, with plenty sarcasm. He had such a good laugh that I was nearly two blocks gone before his comeback. "With a name like that," he yelled out louder than anything on Flatbush Avenue that morning, "you just ought to be."

*1992*

# never "auntie"

The perverted love letter from Jim Crow America that unnerves me most was white folks' fondness for calling mature black women "auntie," a keepsake from slavery days. One translation of this is that even a total stranger could stand in as a wet nurse and be good for a forgiving embrace; and that, somehow, though no longer cattle slaves, black folks were still the emotional property of whites, still to be counted among their personal effects. Like many African Americans of my generation, I first came across such expressions, and the images that accompanied them, in a history book. Having no firsthand reference, these words seemed camp and almost fantastical. Did white folks really say this stuff with a straight face?

You couldn't put a red bandanna, see, on my favorite aunt, Cora, with a ten-foot pole, or for that matter have her suckle Massa or brats. Damnation would be yours. This conviction I guess is a little like Eddie Murphy's gleefully ignorant joke about slavery being for those other nigras. Yet whatever auntie was, historical reality or figment of white folks' imaginations, Cora has never been. Of course most women weren't the stereotype either, weren't that auntie, even if they did auntie work. Still, I bring it up because the distance my aunt's life has measured from auntie's life continues to feel uncommon and extraordinary. I could watch television for a day and not know that women like my aunt really exist and have existed. At a time when portraits in American entertainment of black women as caretakers of white folks have resurfaced with creepy popularity, it's worth repeating: My aunt has never been your auntie. I will never be your auntie. Auntie yourself.

Tailored to the nines, the coif always in place, my aunt, Ms. Cora Coleman to you, cuts a mean figure even at sixty-five. Her tongue is a very sharp instrument, somewhere between a switch-blade and a chainsaw. There's always that point in a conversation with her in which she'll have you grabbing your gut, bent double 'cause you can't laugh anymore. It usually falls halfway through one of her famous missives to America. Cora is among God's children who will never forget the African Holocaust or forgive the white man for poot, though she admits having known some "decent white folks" in her time. On the other hand, she is profoundly patriotic and might even be considered something of a jingoist.

The sitcom based on her life is still too hip for television: the closet Elvis fan who plays Nat King Cole when company comes; the retiree whose Scrabble partners, all lady retirees, meet each week to debate whether the latest injustice against black folks is indeed that or just the misdoings of the race's more triflin' members. Every episode, she ends up kicking the ladies out because they get too loud, tear up her house, and wake up her white neighbors. Then she sends the neighbors to bed with a piece of her mind, stays up for the national anthem, prays "To Whom It May Concern" (the God who looks out for colored folks when no other God will), and says good night till next week.

We are not related by blood or marriage, my aunt and I, but by friendship. Aunt Cora and my grandmother were best friends. Gramma passed six years ago, though the family that she and my aunt created has remained. Cora Coleman met Anna Lois Jones when Gramma was taking donations for the Red Cross in the Colonade Apartments, the newly integrated high rise in downtown Newark where my grandparents moved in the early sixties. Cora, a court reporter for Jersey's Essex County, lived down the hall. My grandmother worked for Newark's housing authority, was a lobbyist for education, and did trench work for many civic causes. The two became old friends immediately.

Beyond their involvement in Newark black politics (like holding fundraisers for future mayor Ken Gibson), grandmother and aunt shared an ethos about children—that they should be loved abundantly, exposed to everything, never stifled. Childhood upsets kindled this. My grandmother was a champion runner at Tuskegee on her way to the Olympics the year Jesse Owens competed. Her father, a stern race man and business owner, had to leave the South after threats from the Klan. He forbid my grandmother from entering the qualifying races, believing track was not proper race work for the daughter of a pastor.

Aunt Cora grew up in Depression-era Newark in an extended family led by her grandmother Cora Lee Helen Struther Rogers, a "beautiful, evil woman who sat on her hair and ran a tight ship." Too proud for Relief, Cora Lee had little Cora and her brother do their homework by gas lamp when the light bill couldn't be paid. Even in the hardest times, the children were sent to the junior museum to study natural history. Backward folks mumbled that Cora Lee was raising them white. My aunt recalls never wanting for anything except affection. When her mother died young of congenital heart failure, Cora, a sheltered eighteen-year-old, left her grandmother's house and joined the military. She visited Cora Lee once before shipping off for duty in Japan. Grandmother told granddaughter she was "allowed" one kiss, and pointed to her wrinkled cheek; it might have been the first and surely was the last.

Cora made it her life business that no little girl be without a doting aunt. Her "kids" now number close to twenty. Cora's auntship also brought with it an extended family: Her brother Oscar, a career marine who taught in inner-city schools after the service, became our Uncle Flat Top. An old friend, Alice, took the mantle of sweet Alice, the aunt whose hugs went on forever. Our Jersey cousins were Alice's nieces and Cora's many kids.

The summer of 1969, the cousin-nieces were rounded up for a month at the Jersey shore with Gramma and Aunt Cora presiding. Every morning us recruits fell in line for inspection by Sergeant Cora. The day began with her marching orders: "Look alive, *tafadali!*" By using the Swahili word for "please" in such a context, my aunt both endorsed and poked fun at the nationalism of the day. Cora has always been one of those folks who can't help but signify.

Easter, Christmas, Fourth of July, we shuttled between houses. The family embraced relatives from four or more blood-family groups, friends, the single and divorced, the gay and straight, a few conventional nuclear families, and a few white folks (including my mom who, missing an older sister-friend, found one in Cora). "We don't choose our mothers or fathers," Aunt Cora told me once, "but we can choose our families"—wisdom that sounds New Age, yet properly in line with her up-South, old-school preachifying.

*The history you save may be your own.* When I was holed up in Minneapolis, Minnesota, last summer, my aunt came to cook me succotash. I knew as a girl that Cora was "in the service." Though a photograph of Aunt Cora in uniform stands guard above my writing desk, the details were still hazy. Almost thirty years after we were united as aunt and niece, I asked Cora about that photo.

I come from a family of Negro Historymakers, so it didn't surprise me that my spirit aunt would be one in her own right. Cora was a Black WAC. Truman signed an executive order in 1948 to integrate the armed services. The deed wasn't done, it turned out, until four years later. When my aunt enlisted in 1949, she found herself in the last segregated company of the Women's Army Corp. Company B was a no-mess bunch from up North that placed first in the marching band competitions. They almost served some scalps one night in Camp Lee, Virginia, when the white women in Company C broke into hateful southern swan song ("In the moonlight you can hear those darkies singing"). Cora remembers the black female captains and lieutenants who looked out for the recruits. These career officers joined the service in the early forties before it became the Women's Army Corp; often they were nurses who enlisted because civilian America wouldn't give them jobs.

Trained as a court reporter, Cora was sent to Yokohama, Japan. There she earned three medals and stayed on for a year as a reporter in the army's civilian employ. Occupied Japan she describes as a surreal place with its fog and rickshaws and its American-imported racism (nightclubs with signs that forbid "niggers and dogs").

Black Americans, it's been said, are the true patriots. Still it's always disarmed me that my aunt's patriotism could coexist with a sublime hatred of all that whitey is and all that whitey does. (I use the arcane "whitey," because she means it in the sense of whitey, the great institutional animal.) I finally made sense of Cora's marriage of the two through stories of her life in uniform. This is her remembering retreat:

"You're walking alone in a lonely field when retreat blows and there could be nobody around you for miles. You could just be out there picking straws, but when you hear that bugle, you salute. There's such a pride you have standing there. It's a very secret pride. You could still go back to the base among your peers and say, 'I'm only in here for what these honkies can do for me,' but you had your moment in that field. You forget everything that's wrong and have this sense of belonging to this great society called America. If you think about it, what else do we have to belong to?"

Also in Minneapolis, I had the unsettling opportunity to stand up to one of my heroes. The City of Lakes, Minneapolis is advertised as a liberal oasis between the coasts. Naturally when my aunt shows up it is anything but. In one week she is treated like a suspect while shopping at a progressive-chic *parfumerie;* she witnesses a black man getting beat on the head by four white cops; and she sees enough Debbies curled up with Sam to let loose an avalanche of historical memory about Debbie's debauchery and psychosis being the true root of the race problem. The Debbie thing was shaking me up. I too had seen enough Debbies curled up with Sam in Minneapolis to last two lifetimes. Then again, if one Debbie hadn't curled up with Sam, I wouldn't be on this planet. I had a headache.

At a restaurant one night we argue. It's great cinema that in this restaurant of cloth napkins we are the only black folks. Aunt Cora's position has racism defining everything: that whitey's massa plan rules the world. Mine is that whitey holds the purse strings, though racism isn't the only way of explaining the universe. I raise my voice, it cracks, I steer it steady. This is not casual rebellion. I am my mother's, still, I am very much my grandmother's child. I was willed this sense that your elders are your gods on earth. I would have walked behind my grandmother carrying an umbrella if asked. This voice raising is not easy, but I want her to know about my inheritance. How this power is only made possible by her life and what she endured—the grace and intelligence with which she endured it and the anger and history she never forgot. If I feel more mighty than whitey, it's her bequest. Aunt Cora taught me that knowledge works. That it could get you, like the Isley Brothers sing, to the next phase.

It feels good to have spoken up. But the next day's headlines drive nails into my little victory: lockout of Haitian refugees, forced famine in Somalia, Nazism's new clothes in Europe. Maybe my elders know something I don't. Perhaps in the massa plan my doormat days are fast coming.

*Do you know who speaks through you?* Early in my aunt's career as a court reporter she was assigned to a judge who thought it appropriate to sentence a man on his hospital deathbed. Aunt Cora doesn't remember the details, the man's plea or the severity of the crime he was charged with, just the venom of this white judge as he castigated this black man who lay motionless, tubes connecting him to an oxygen tank. Cora stood beside the judge and silently took the record. For several days afterward she was sick. Her own muteness, she said, had poisoned her.

"You can imagine a person like myself, sitting there, recording the facts. Being seen, but not heard. All we could do was sit there and burn. Our hands were tied. We were trying to make a living. We were proud to be court reporters, doing the best job we knew how, and then we had to watch our people get railroaded time and again. During the riots, when blood was running down Springfield Avenue like a waterfall, black folks were coming into court with their heads split open, looking at us like we were traitors—we burned then too. Either you became cynical or you just didn't hear. You wrote words, not sentences; it helped you do your job."

My aunt would have been a writer, my grandmother too. My mother is a writer who came to it later in life after raising and supporting children on her own. All three indulged me, I realize now. Aunt Cora has been announcing my profession since I was seven and carried a pad and pencil to record family conversations. My mother typed my poems. Summers at my grandparents' house Gramma set up a desk and called it "Lisa's office."

Those who don't know me assume that I write because of my celebrated writer father or my less celebrated writer mother. Or that I do it in spite of them or to spite them. But when I sit down, the voice that stays in my ear is my aunt's. It's merciless, it laughs a chill up my spine, it never forgets. It's taken me years to know that voice was my aunt's. The voice that never got to speak in court. I listen for her now. She urges me to speak with her, through her, and, when necessary, back at her, to get to the truth that the day demands.

*1993*

# mama's white

Just another rainbow baby on the IRT, that's me, handing out flyers modeled after Adrian Piper's seminal art piece, "My Calling (Card) #1" (1986):

Dear Fellow Straphanger:

My mother is white. And I, as you may or may not have figured out, am black. This is how I choose to define myself and this is how America chooses to define me. I have no regrets about my racial classification other than to lament, off and on, that classifications exist period.

Actually the mystery of my background is really

not much of a mystery at all, despite those taboo-love-child stories you read in *People* or *Jet*. If you boned up on your world history, you'd know that unions between people of different racial classifications, such as my (white) mother and my (black) father, are not a recent phenomenon. Entire countries in South America are peopled by the offspring of such relationships. Even our own country is more of a creole outpost than we are ready to acknowledge.

Are you still staring? Let me guess. My white mother presents a different set of enigmas to you based on your own racial classification. Those of you who are black might find "evidence" of my white parent reason to question my racial allegiance. For those of you who are white, evidence of my white lineage might move you to voice deep-seated feelings of racial superiority. You might wonder why I would choose to identify as "fully" black when I have the "saving grace" of a white parent. I have no time for this sort of provinciality either. I realize both sets of responses display an ignorance of our shared cultural and racial history as Americans.

I'm sorry you're still staring. If you care to, I'll gladly engage you in a lengthy conversation about this subject at another time. But right now I'm having just another "attitudinous"-black-girl day on the IRT, and if you keep staring, I'll just stare right back. I regret any discomfort my presence is causing you. Just as I'm sure you regret the discomfort your ignorance is causing me.

Yours (More Truly Than You Think),

**L.J.**

This is the story of Emily Sohmer Tai and Hettie Jones, two women who don't know each other and whose only connection is the melanin count of their skin.

Recently Emily Sohmer Tai, who describes herself as the "white female half of an interracial marriage," wrote a letter to the *Village Voice*. The letter is worth returning to as an example of the closeted superiority trip I mention above. And what I mean by superiority trip is the type of thinking that assigns whiteness highest value (and upholds white people as the only viable arbiters of experience), though this thinking may at times be draped in the gauze of liberalism.

I had written a sentimental tribute to my sixty-five-year-old Aunt Cora for a series the paper ran for Black History Month. In one section I recount my aunt's visit to Minneapolis, where I was living at the time, her brushes with racism there, and her reaction to the large number of white female–black male couples that coexist there alongside this racism. I sized up these couples as "Debbies curled up with Sam"—to allude to the lady-stud legend that burdens them and, at the same time, to pry it apart. I was sure to note, in the same breath, that if one Debbie hadn't curled up with one Sam, I wouldn't be around. Clearly I was saying that these duos tangle up my emotions; I look at them as a child of an interracial marriage, but also as a black woman who has witnessed the market value put on white femininity.

Tai seems to have got stuck on one word, "Debbie," and looked no further. Her letter responds to my entire essay as if it were merely a personal attack on her and other white women in interracial relationships. Tai never once mentions my aunt. In effect, she completely erases Cora's story. What I got from this is that there is nothing I could say about my aunt, her amazing life, and our feelings as black women about interracial relationships—some shared, some not—that could be as important as Tai's outrage as a white woman measuring herself against a stereotype. Nothing, simply, was as worthy of readers' consideration as Tai's story, Tai's version of history.

There's a shrillness to Tai's letter, and it seems to come from the fact that I don't accept her view of what interracial identity means. She rather smugly assumes, in fact, that she can define this experience for me. To Tai, this identity is a haven from racialized society; to me, it's not. And Tai assumes again that such a safe house is indeed something I have political or aesthetic interest in embracing. I've been called "nigger bitch" more than once in life, and I wonder if Tai would advise that I handle it by shouting back, "Actually, guys, my mom's white, so call me half-white bitch, or how about mongrel bitch, since it's better rhythmically?"

Left unsaid, though lurking in the margins of Tai's letter, is this amazement that I, as a woman, would claim "black" over "interracial" or "white." The implication being that choosing black was somehow a settlement, a compromise following a personal identity crisis, and not a much larger cultural-historical calling or even just sheer love, romance, and respect for blackness (in all its permutations), for better or for worse, amen. Would Tai's mouth hang open if I told her my story? That, among others, it was my (white) mother who raised me to think politically about being a black woman?

Could Tai picture this complexity as well? That I'm a writer whose work is dedicated to exploring the hybridity of African-American culture and of American culture in general. That I don't deny my white forebears, but I call myself African American, which means, to me, a person of African and Native American, Latin, or European descent. That I feel comfortable and historically grounded in this identity. That I find family there, whereas no white people have embraced me with their culture, have said to me, take this gift, it's yours, and we are yours, no problem. That, by claiming African American and black, I also inherit a right to ask questions about what this identity means. And that chances are this identity will never be static, which is fine by me.

Tai's reaction to this "racial persona" of mine is nothing I haven't come across before. White women in particular have trouble seeing my black identity as anything other than a rebuff of my mother. Deep down I wonder if what they have difficulty picturing is this: not that I could reject, in their minds, my own mother, but that I have no desire to be *them*.

Friends of mine, who are also rainbow babies pushing thirty, have had similar run-ins, and sometimes we sit around and compare notes. We're not disinterested in our white "heritage," even though most of us don't know our white relatives (apart from the parent who raised us), or we were given up for adoption by a white biological parent and have never had white family. In my own case, my mother's parents, first-generation American Jews, disowned her for marrying black. When she announced she was pregnant, they begged her to have an abortion. On hearing that in her third year of marriage my mother was pregnant with a second child, again they begged her to abort.

We of the rainbow persuasion joke about whites' inability to imagine why we would want to see ourselves as people of color and as African Americans—how connected this makes us feel. What could they possibly think is *in it* for us to be white people? Would it extend refuge or protection, provide moral directive? If it helped us get better jobs and higher salaries, would it offer spiritual community? Would it bring us family?

Forget everything that the Emily Sohmer Tai example tells you about race, and meet Hettie Jones, author, poet, teacher, and my mother. Her memoir, *How I Became Hettie Jones*, revisits her life as a woman among the Beats as the starched-collar fifties gave way to the guns-and-roses sixties. It also tells of her marriage to my father, writer Amiri Baraka, and of her own coming of age as a writer. If you want to know more, the book is in paperback. I will share this: The most dreadfully cute fact about my mother is that she has taken to checking "other" on her census form. In the line slotted for explanation she writes, in her flowery longhand, "Semitic American mother of black children."

Fans of *How I Became Hettie Jones* include young African Americans, many of them women, who seek me out at public events to express how the book touched them. They are moved by the woman-finding-herself-amid-the-ruins story, but they relate also to the story of Hettie, the white woman who *stayed behind*, or *stayed on*, or was just plain *there*, raising the black children while the brothers went where their muses took them. They know women like Hettie. These women live in their neighborhoods. These women are the mothers of friends. Sometimes these women are their own mothers. They're pleased someone is telling this story.

Her literary endowments aside, my mother is my mother, and I'm very protective of her and of our relationship. I find myself in this amusing little bind at times, which reminds me over and over that what I am, I guess, for lack of a more sexy and historically complex word, is a humanist. This is the bind of explaining that my mother is white, though I am black, then getting pissed when people reduce dear Mom to the calling card of "your white mother." Negotiating all this continues to be one of the challenges of my intellectual life. I'll crib from Greg Tate on this one: "The world isn't black and white, it just feels that way sometimes."

I owe Mom a couple of solids. One for being strong enough in her own self to let me be who I was gonna be. My pride in being a black woman actually brings me closer to my (white) mom. This identity gives me a stronger sense of history and self, and I can come to my mother as what the New Age folks might call a "fully realized person." If I called myself "interracial" (in my mind, and I know others see this differently), I would need her presence, her "whiteness," to somehow validate my "half-whiteness."

Another solid. Mom's bohemian from way back. The journey she's made as a woman, as an artist, making herself up in America, has been useful to me as a black woman living outside of society's usual paradigms of femininity. Mom knew that we—my sister and I —needed black female relatives and role models, and she made sure these ties were in place. She never tried to substitute for these; what she gave instead was her own DNA, her own boho Mama-in-the-black-stockings self, and she trusted that this would be enough.

Solid number three. My mother, more than anyone I know, has taught me difference as pleasure. Not as something feared or exotic, but difference as one of the rich facts of one's life, a truism that gives you more data, more power, and more flavor. These are the sort of things you needed to get by: a black South Carolinian grandfather who did the Moon Walk before Michael Jackson (though he called it the Camel Walk), a mother who speaks Yiddish and jazz, a

Caribbean boyfriend to make you rice and peas, and a sister who's a Latin American art scholar so you won't lapse into thinking you're God's gift to all knowledge as a North American Negro.

Today my mother is in town from Wyoming, where she's teaching for a stint. We hug, I cook her tofu and collard greens, we swap clothes, watch TV evangelism for a goof. We talk about race as the world places it on us. We argue sometimes, but we don't stumble on it. When our differences in age and race make themselves felt in how we see the world, it doesn't butt against our love, our trust.

I've got my pad and pen out and she's laughing at my official-ness. Mom, not *how,* but *why* did you become Hettie Jones?

"After the breakup of my marriage," she explains, "people asked me why I didn't change my name, why I didn't, quote, 'go back to the Jews.' There was no going back to something that denied you."

And why was it important to you that we be black and not "biracial"?

"I was not about to delude you guys into thinking you could be anything different in this country. And, frankly, I didn't think that being anything other than black would be any more desirable."

Mom, what you say in the book about black people's anger in the sixties being necessary to America, how did you come to this?

"Some people think that I'm dishonest and that I'm a martyr for saying that, but there's a certain time in your life if you're a white person and you have black children that you have to see that the world is ready to take them on. I love my children and I just sensed that the world had to go through this period in order for it to be a better place for them."

Motherhood has been more than a domestic chore or emotional bond for my mother. It's a political vocation—one she's taken seri-ously enough to go up against the world for. She always stands ready to testify about how her children and blackness have broad-ened her own life. In the music—jazz, blues, the language—she found her own.

Mom's headed back to Wyoming. The cab driver offers to put her backpack in the trunk. "May I take your parachute?" he asks. People of all ages and backgrounds say fetching things like this to my mother. She's led, as she wrote once, a "charmed life in the middle of other people's wars," and it comes through in her smile. When Mom sends the mojo his way, the cab driver lights up like New Year's Eve on Forty-Deuce. I'm reminded, right then, that there is no place that I'm ever gonna go (by way of geography or ideology) where I can't bring my mother, and where I can't bring myself, which she has in large part made possible. And, as Adrian Piper would have me ask, what are all you—black and white— gonna do about that?

*1993*

# video soul
# (and salsa)

You used to go to clubs with names like Buttermilk Bottom and Paradise Garage. You used to wear very short skirts and, when you danced, move your rear end in such a way that many people who didn't know you at all would want to get to know you right away. You would do this until eight in the morning. Afterward, you'd go eat French toast on Second Avenue, catch the F train to Coney Island, and sleep all day in the sun. This was known as a night on the town.

Now you have a job. Maybe you have two jobs. Maybe you have two jobs, a very small apartment you pay lots of money to rent, and heavy philosophical questions to consider like, "How come my man doesn't answer his phone at nine o'clock at night?" Because of all this, it is quite likely that the only going out you want to do on Friday night is to a video store. And this is how you meet Tony Smith, who owns Tompkins Square Video on Avenue B near Tenth Street, and Carmen Montalvo, who runs the joint when Tony's not around, and all the folks who hang out there.

If you're lucky one Friday, you might catch Tony and Carmen working the store together. Tony and Carmen make you feel like multiculturalism was born on the Lower East Side, and is alive and doing quite well, thank you. Tony's slim with a crooked smile. He's got a Nuyorican accent, though he's black, as in black American. Carmen's healthy figured and Puerto Rican. In a former life she was a Jewish mother. Carmen's motto is: "Once you go black, you never come back" (except don't tell her I told you).

Tony used to be a deejay. He made a vow to leave club life before he turned thirty, so a year and half ago he opened his own video store, where you can rent movies like *Black Orpheus, Diary of a Chambermaid, The Jetsons Meet the Flintstones,* and *Cleopatra Jones.* The distribution outfits that supply Tony told him that mixing "black and Puerto Rican videos" with "white videos" wasn't good business. Tony didn't care too much what they thought, that's why you can go into Tompkins and find *Slaughter's Revenge* displayed next to *My Dinner With Andre.*

A typical Friday night around nine: Tony's playing house music at club volume. The TV's on with no sound, and Michael Jordan and the other guys in Chicago are making one last push against Detroit. Instead of viewing a new arrival like *Crack House* ("Getting in is easy, getting out is hell"), everyone in the store—a dozen people at the moment, Latinos, blacks, and whites—is leaning on the counter as if they're in some sports bar, witnessing the Bulls get played. Above the counter is a movie-marquee-style signboard that Tony's carpenter installed this afternoon. It's supposed to list new arrivals. Instead JESUS WAS HERE is printed out in neat block letters. "Who's Jesus?" a customer asks Tony. "Oh," he says, "that's my carpenter."

"Sexual harassment is not a problem here, it's one of the benefits," reads a sign behind the counter. If there's anyone harassing people, it's Carmen. "We're up to nine hundred customers now," Tony boasts, "and Carmen still remembers all their names and their numbers." "Like Roman, 1504?" she bats her eyes at Tony, "you know that guy?"

Classic Carmen: She barks, with hands on hips, at full lung power, "I HAVEN'T SEEN YOU IN AGES!" at some guy who just came into the store. You think he's her man or something, but he's just another customer. An Asian punk, in a T-shirt that warns us "A Mind Is a Terrible Thing to Waste," returns *Beverly Hills Brats* and *Paperhouse.* Carmen hollers politely, "Thank you, Mama." This is Carmen addressing a favorite customer: "You know your girlfriend brought someone in here who looked just like your brother. I think she's playing you dirty."

"What kind of mood are you in?" Tony asks a customer, "Suspense, action, or horror?" He sends Luis to pick a few titles. Luis, the third man at Tompkins, could be a hard rock if you go by his broad shoulders and scowl, but he's just a shy sixteen-year-old kid. Tony and Luis cut a deal. As long as Luis stays in school, there'll be a part-time job for him at Tompkins. *Total Recall* opened today, and Tony, Carmen, and Luis have announced that after they close the store, they're headed to the midnight show. Twenty minutes later, six people from the neighborhood stop in to ask if they can go too.

"My mother calls me Mr. Public Relations." This is Tony talking. "If anything happens on the block, I know about it. The other day, a white customer was being followed, so he came in the store, and I had someone walk him home. . . ." You can't hear the rest of Tony's story because Carmen is shrieking, "DON'T LET IT HAPPEN AGAIN!" at some brown-skinned cutie with long eyelashes who's returned *Switchblade Sisters* a couple of days late.

Near closing time, Tony performs Operation *Harlem Nights* on a copy of the Eddie Murphy movie that got stuck in a customer's

VCR. A half dozen people are still wandering around the store looking for the perfect nighttime companion. A kid in a "Ninja Turtles Rule" T-shirt flips through the Nintendo file. "You got any new games, Tony? I'm sick and tired of what you got."

"What's your problem, Seymour? There are 130 games—what about *SuperContra?*"

"Oh, I didn't see *SuperContra.*"

"That's 'cause you're buggin', Seymour. Now go outside."

"I can't go outside, Tony, it's boring outside."

It's Luis who gets to scream now: "THEY TOOK JORDAN!" The entire store gathers around the TV to say good-bye to Chicago. Carmen then ushers customers out with their videos and their very own dose of tough love ("GET OUT ALREADY!") so that the Tompkins crew can make it to *Total Recall* in time.

After exceptions are made for latecomers who use creative tactics to gain entry, like swishing their faces against the store window, Tompkins Square Video is finally, officially closed for the evening. Carmen counts receipts. Tony counts money. Together they pull down the iron gate, on which one of the Lower East Side's many muralists has spray-painted a portrait of a lone videocassette. Carmen paces the sidewalk. "I hope we can get a cab to the movies. Tony, do you mind changing your skin color, so we can get a cab, PLEASE." Tony puts his keys in his pocket and lights a cigarette. "Sure Carmen, anything for you."

*1990*

# east river's edge

No one has a name for it, but it's been going on every summer, every Sunday, for ten years. And for the last three of these ten years, DJ Louie and DJ José have lugged their fourteen crates of records and fifteen stereo speakers to East River Park, just across the overpass at Tenth Street and FDR Drive. They suspend a piece of green tarp between the limbs of a sturdy tree and a play-ground fence, and set up their turntables underneath. DJ José spins records, mostly salsa and merengue (with one hour of "English music—you know, standard disco—and classics from the fifties") and DJ Louie sweet-talks into the mike. People come from all over Loisaida, even

Brooklyn, East Harlem, and Jersey, to cram into the small space between the playground and the ballpark, which becomes an open-air dance hall lit by two street lamps. This goes on from one in the afternoon until sometime after midnight, every Sunday, every summer, without fail.

Some come to eat (vendors sell homemade rice and beans, *pasteles,* and *alcapurrias*). Some come to drink (*cerveza fría* sold from garbage pails filled with ice). Some come to bet on dice and cards (under single, naked light bulbs in makeshift tents nearby). But most come to dance—under very few stars, the smog, the heat —to what DJ Louie (a bright-eyed human cannonball) and DJ José ("the guy in the long hair who looks like Jesus," says Louie) have to play for them. All ages and shades of brown pack in together. Mothers leave strollers on the sidelines and partner up with their babies. Old ladies missing a few teeth stand alone rotating their hips like clockwork. Young men in long shorts and baseball caps dance together without touching. Couples grind furiously as if all things to come depended on this one good sweat. The Tenth Street overpass becomes a balcony, the best view in the house.

Even though the DJs try to keep things even—50 per cent merengue, 50 salsa—the battle between *salseros* and *merengueros* rages all night. "I don't want to be racist," confides Louie, a native Nuyorican, "but Dominicans and Puerto Ricans are always fighting. Puerto Ricans are mostly salsa people, and Dominicans are merengue people. See, salsa is like soul and merengue is like rock and roll. I give Dominicans credit for their music, but they try to act too macho about it, like it's the best."

Louie and José aren't on salary. "What I make here is what the people give me," says José, who's been spinning records since the "days of the 45s." Vendors pass the hat for the DJs and dancers give them money to announce their families or dedicate songs. Miguel Maldonado pays to hear "La Soga" by V. Rogue and La Gran Manzana because he just turned seventeen: "I want to dedicate it to my own self 'cause I love this record so much."

*"Llegó la hora,"* Louie announces. "What will it be, *una*

*salcita?"* Half the crowd yells "No!" "Or *un merengue?"* "No!" the other half calls back. José plays *"Devórame Otra Vez* (Devour Me Again)" and after the first few beats, objections from the merengue corner die down. A woman selling sodas dips a handkerchief into her ice bucket and squeezes it over her head. Then she grabs a man by the neck and forces him into a kiss. A middle-aged man with a mustache, and a tattoo on his arm showing two hearts pierced by a knife, watches his wife dance with a young bodybuilder.

The last dance is not a merengue or salsa, but Frank Sinatra's "New York, New York." Some folks line up like the Rockettes. "I want to wake up in a city that never sleeps," Franks sings, while a sleeping man near the turntables cuddles a can of Budweiser between his thighs. Someone standing in the middle of the overpass waves the Puerto Rican flag in time to the music. "It's time to say so long," Louie croons, pressing his lips against the microphone, "but we'll be back next Sunday. Even if it rains, I love you."

*1990*

# the outback

The gospel of cultural pluralism brings me to Utah. I've been speaking at colleges around the country as a journalist and coauthor of "Spike Lee books." Once I live through the pure terror, I'm glad to do the talks. Glad to be that beam of color for p.o.c. youth roughing it in the still snowy white collegiate outback. Glad to be a diversity moment for others. Better me than Professor Griff. Better me than Patty Buchanan.

In Utah I find what one finds when one travels in any direction or looks under any rock: people of African descent and variations on that theme. Four meet me at the airport; a surprise because a college rep warned on

the phone, "We don't have many minorities and stuff like that
here." And what a bushy-tailed "them" they are, full of questions
such as, "Should history books be rewritten?" and "What do you
think, as a *sister*, about the *Jungle Fever* phenomenon?" Or the
usual, "Did you have an identity crisis growing up *interracially
mixed?*" (which, put that way, sounds like inbreeding Pan-American
style).

I dub them the Fab Four in honor of Michigan's spunky Five:
Melanie, twenty-one, student senator, zoology major, future chiro-
practor, has lived in Utah since grammar school; Dennis, twenty,
from "somewhere near Tupelo," Mississippi, came to Utah to study
automotive design ("before there were women, there were cars");
Belva, nineteen, moved in junior high, and now studies respiratory
therapy, and is, among other things, an albino who wears her plati-
num-blond "black hair" in a permed wedge cut; and army brat
Zack, twenty-two, known as "DJ Ivory," but is changing his name to
"the Visionary" to get away from "all that mighty-whitey business."
Before college, Zack did time in the Gulf. Even in Colin Powell's
armed forces, Zack will tell you, white guys like him still get called
"nigger lover" for hanging black.

The Fab Four's repertory of black media culture is as up-to-date
as any hipster's from Brooklyn Tech. They've got the latest Queen
Latifah, watch *A Different World*, admire Oprah and Toni Morrison.
Zack plays Farrakhan's speeches on his radio show. Dennis, who
plans to design his own line of cars one day, relates to Ice Cube's
take on black self-reliance. Arguing about new black cinema is a
favorite pastime. They question whether air-head comedies like
*Livin' Large* "trivialize the black experience." I wonder just what
black experience they mean? The one they see in music videos or
the one they live in Utah?

It's spring at Weber State University, a large commuter school
just outside of Salt Lake City, and the young Republicans are
leafletting the quad. Their dramatic backdrop, the Utah mountains,
sharp white peaks against a true-blue sky, is very close to the illustrated rocks of ages you see in hymn books; the Mormons couldn't
have ended up anywhere else.

Weber is courting diversity, and with numbers as low as 150 students of color out of fifteen thousand, it still manages to have the most realistically "all-American" student body in the state. A poster announces the Miss Indian of Utah pageant ("contestants must have at least one-fourth Indian blood"), and style around campus—big hair, suntans, zoot-suit jeans—makes everyone look Hispanic-by-Hollywood. Student-run KWCR touched more than a few racial nerves when it switched formats to become the only rhythm and blues–based station in Utah, with a full Sunday of hip-hop programmed by Zack. ("Geez," said a student, "don't you think it's getting *too* black?") Belva got sick to her stomach in a faculty/student meeting when a professor argued that a rhythm and blues–based station "wasn't multicultural enough" and went against Dr. King's dream.

There's my speech, a luncheon, then the Fab Four and I go for an opinionated tour of Salt Lake City and surrounding territories. We drive through the one-drag town of Ogden, home to Weber State, Hill Air Force base, and most black Utahans. African Americans migrated to Ogden for railroad work starting around the turn of the century. Alberta Henry, the spry seventy-two-year-old president of Salt Lake's NAACP, came from Kansas in 1949. Henry says, "Utah kept all the black codes of the South" until the late sixties. The state still has no unified civil rights bill and was the last in the union to pass hate crimes legislation. The Fab Four have their own stories of race hate in Mormonland. Rocks and "nigger calling" welcomed Belva and her twin sister to public junior high in the mid-eighties. Dennis has come to accept regular harassment from cops for "being the wrong color."

Twenty minutes on the thruway and we're in Salt Lake cruising the campus of Weber's competition, the University of Utah. The Fab Four play the old game of "Look, There's a Black Person." We pass a honey in a four-by-four. Belva's not impressed: "That's an athlete, you can tell from California plates, but they usually date only the white girls." Lounging on the grass are a black man and woman, a rare sight in Utah, to hear Melanie, our driver, tell it. She almost swerves off the road to get a good look.

Our last stop is the Crossroads Plaza mall in downtown Salt Lake. The Fab Four say it's a typical Utah mall—department stores, food court, movie theater (playing *White Men Can't Jump*)—still, nods to the cultural rainbow, at least in consumer items, would get a rise out of even the most jaded East Coast multiculturalist. Filipino fast food, Latin American textiles, a Japanese gift shop. We stop at an African art shop that also sells "African trade beads" to kids who see them on models in *Elle*. Asian and Latino teens parade around the mall. In Salt Lake, you'll find gang members from the Samoan Crips transplanted from L.A. and upwardly mobile Mexicans who prefer to be called Hispanic.

On the plane back I'm trying to fit my Fab Four into all this talk about post–soul culture and fragmented black communities of the nineties. Nothing, I think, will define their sense of black community more than the ideological battles to come around interracial relationships and mixed-race identity. What they've come to call the "*Jungle Fever* phenomenon" is setting off Scud missiles in their psyches. All seem torn; it sorta feels politically incorrect, but they've got too many ties to white folks to believe it's flat wrong. Belva is most opposed to interracial relationships, though she takes heat from blacks for being albino, is engaged to a Mexican American, and has many white friends. Zack criticizes men whose "rhetoric celebrates the black queen, while they sleep white," but his own race complicates his critique. Dennis has no apologies for dating across race ("Who's the sellout, me or the guys selling drugs to your little sister?"), yet he'd consider adopting "endangered" young black males before having babies with the woman he lives with, who is white. I was taken with how honestly they spoke of their conflicts, their choices. The Fab Four are not members of a race-ambivalent middle class growing up alienated outside of the hood. They belong to an expanding body of young Americans, race identified but grappling with new definitions of community.

"Do you still want to change the world?" Zack asks, as we pull into the airport. In my speech, I talked about being their age and on my way to law school to become the next Morris Dees, exterminate the Klan, and change the world. Then I read Gayl Jones's *Corregidora*. Jones, equipped with nothing save lyrics and her own version of the American story, disarms the psychological vise grip of slavery. I was driven to rethink my tactics. I'm lost in a thought bubble, taking in the fertile cultural moment that brought me to Utah to talk about my grandmother, my mother, Thurgood Marshall, Chuck D., cultural pluralism (without racial apathy or loss of community), and Shades of You makeup.

But I'm thinking also of Charlayne Hunter-Gault, who returned in 1988 to deliver the commencement address at the University of Georgia, which she and fellow student Hamilton Holmes integrated more than a quarter century earlier. Hunter-Gault was the first black person to deliver the address in the university's 203-year history, and resisting the comforts of tokenism, she urged those assembled not to pretend that "the events of the past twenty-five years, even my presence here today, have transformed our peculiar world into one that is beyond recognition." African trade beads in the Salt Lake City mall? Cute, but not even close, and no cigar.

"Well, do you . . . ?" Zack's sounding worried now.

"What?"

"The world . . ."

"Yeah. Definitely"

*1992*

# tragedy
## becomes her

*Don't hate me because I'm still tragic and beautiful (after all these years). Isn't it true I work best for you as a tragedy? You have your moment of showy guilt, then I'm out of your hair for another decade, until the next movie. You never have to face that this Frankenstein of yours is you also, is us, is America. Yet how could you? That would render even you impure. So let it remain just me and my tragedy. The toxic mix of my blood.*

Somebody get an exorcist! I'm being haunted by a miniseries that aired months ago—Alex Haley's *Queen*, as scripted by Hollywood screenwriter David Stevens.

Caught up, as we were, in the questions of authenticity and plagiarism surrounding *Roots*, Queen snuck by without a hard glance. The series was such a monument to a nineteenth-century brand of racial determinism, those who did brave the six hours of flagellation still have the shakes. Perhaps Black History Month should be renamed Black Future Month, so we won't be subjected to any more TV fodder that, rather than presenting ground-breaking interpretations of history, feels like an excuse to see black people lynched, raped, or chased by the Klan on national television. America's racial violence is reenacted without any new way of understanding it, absent any hint of black folks' resistance or agency. The moral here? History tells us black Americans were run to the ground like Georgia mules, why should the future hold anything different?

*Queen* follows the life of Haley's grandmother, Queen, daughter of a master and a slave. The miniseries was marketed as a work of New Age racial healing, out to probe miscegenation with sensitivity and frankness. Turns out it was more akin to American film's tragic mulatto narratives of yore—a foreboding parable of race mixing and the race mixed. Skim off the melodrama and these films are cautionary tales about interracial sex and, more acutely, integration and black parity. In these days of furious cultural commingling and mixed-race scholarship and activism, *Queen* plays as an endorsement of an older racial order.

At the same time *Queen* romances the past, it manages to be cock-and-bull revisionism of the cheerful sort. Picture Halle Berry as the rosy-cheeked Queen, a formulaic house nigra so devoted to the plantation she volunteers as an overseer during the hard times of the Civil War. Leave it to Queen to have the mistress in the fields picking cotton as she, Queen the slave, eggs her on with a whip! Is this priceless moment meant to suggest that the Africans who became slaves were just as abusive to whites—and therefore just as culpable for slavery?

In fact modern day plantation dramas like *Queen* seem intent on erasing from our minds that there were such things as masters and slaves. We were just one big happy family back then, with a few codependency issues to work out, but no big deal. Slavery days were some of the best days of our black lives, these tales suggest. We were well fed, we didn't have to compete in the job market, we got to prance around in those off-the-shoulder plantation sundresses. And certainly we didn't worry much about the black man shortage, 'cause, like Queen's Mama, Easter, Massa was always willing to slip us some, all we had to do was holler. What *Queen* boils down to is *Roots* for the self-help generation: Racism is and has always been just a black self-esteem problem. If black folks would get over their demons already, so says *Queen,* America would treat them just fine.

Back to the tragic mulatress text: Not only does *Queen* drag out mulatto clichés from every B movie and paperback, it luxuriates in them with eerie aplomb. The trailer described Queen as having "raging blood" that tore at her insides in the same way that the Civil War was tearing at her country. *Queen* producer Mark Wolper, whose father David Wolper produced *Roots,* told *Entertainment Weekly* that the hardest part about filming the miniseries was finding an actress "who is as white as [I am] but yet is black. And she had to be a hell of a f———ing actress"—as if there weren't scores of chillun who fit the bill running around Hollywood. One can only guess that Wolper and the other creative types behind *Queen* weren't up on the tragic mulatto genre, so much so that they were hell-bent on reinventing the wheel.

Vessel of desire and pity, martyr or redeemed heroine, the tragic mulatto has been a Hollywood standard since the silent era. (*The Octoroon,* made in 1913, may have been her earliest screen appearance.) Each decade she resurfaces with a new wardrobe: the postwar "moral mulattos" (seen in *Pinky* and *Lost Boundaries),* who taught white America compassion for the Negro Problem, gave way to the island half-breeds of the 1950s. (Dorothy Dandridge carried the weight of this imagery in movies like *Island in the Sun.)* That the tragic mulatto is almost exclusively a woman isn't hard to unravel. A man might work his tragedy out through violence, whereas a woman can be plain doomed, attractive, and worthy of clemency.

As relief from the conservatism of the eighties, the tragic mulatto was resurrected yet again in films like *Angel Heart* and *Mona Lisa,* where she appears as the predictably tortured exotic. In the nineties she has been less of a cipher and more of a player in the likes of *One False Move* and *The Crying Game.* Though now front and center to the narrative, the character remains true to blueprint —a lost child. She no longer seeks to pass, yet she still hasn't found a home.

Apart from being such a throwback, there's a reason why *Queen* is still squatting in my psyche. It's a paragon of the lessons the mulatto and her tragedy oblige and why America clings to her so dearly:

Miss Tragedy is the morbid personification of integration. Those raging bloods of hers will explode one day, as will America's if it keeps mixing up bloodlines. Mono-race communities are the only place to find love and shelter. Don't cross the tracks.

The mulatto's alienation is ultimately her own psychological illness—neither socially constructed nor shared—and she should bear it in silence. Or, in the case of the latter-day pop mulattoes, she must market it as a fable of caution, like the warning label on a pack of cigarettes.

Miscegenation is still black folks' problem, best dealt with across the tracks and behind closed doors. While Queen ends up in the loony bin, rejected by her slave-owning family, the whites never suffer a moment of remorse. Far from addressing miscegenation with any new complexity, *Queen* did the usual and let white folks off the hook. Like satisfied johns, they're allowed to put their jays back in their pants and sneak back to the big house. The "stain" remains within black folks.

Tragic mulatto has two choices: get black or die. And her redemption—because all this is really her own fault for daring to be born—is only possible when she admits she's a Negro (which, in *Queen,* is like owning up to your codependency). Queen doesn't decide who she is in any way that embraces African-American culture, or even her African and Irish roots. She accepts where she belongs—which is vastly different. Her sense of self is not truly addressed, just society's pressure.

If you dig deep beneath the melodrama and the psychosis, the tragic mulatto on film has been a tangled metaphor of black resistance. The dissatisfying thing, at least on the symbolic tip, about her being "returned" to the black community, as she is in *Queen* and most of the other narratives, is she is stripped of her rebel spirit. She loses her power to rock the racial boat, to question race-based class hierarchy, to expose both the white and black world's creole underbelly. And like any other po' plantation chile, she's left singing what Michele Wallace calls the invisibility blues.

*How do you like me now? I could be heroine, I could be healer. I talk back. I refuse complicity with any of you if I can't speak the truth that is mine. On my body is inscribed the future. I'll keep my hands around your throat until you claim me. I am yours. I am yours. I am.*

1993

# is biracial enough?
# (or, what's this about
# a multiracial
# category on
# the census?: a
# conversation)*

*Who are you, what are you, where are you from, no, where are you really from, where are your parents from, are your grandparents Americans? Are you from here, what's your background, what's your nationality, where do you live? Are you black, are you white, do you speak Spanish? Are you really white, are you really black? Are you Puerto Rican, are you half and half, are you biracial, multiracial, interracial, transracial, racially unknown, race neutral, colorless, colorblind, down with the rat race*

* This was a speech given to "Common Differences," a conference of interracial student groups sponsored by Wesleyan Interracial Pride (I-Pride) and held at Wesleyan University in May 1993.

*or the human race? Who are you? Where are you coming from? Who are your people?*

THE IDENTITY FAIRY: Excuse me, before you get all up in my business, don't you want to know my name?

Should we keep it simple or run the extended-play version? I hail from the Afro-rainbow tribe. Papa's black by way of Newark and South Carolina, Mom's Jewish by way of Brooklyn and Eastern Europe. Ethnically I'm African American. Politically I'm a person of color. My résumé: Womanist-theater producing circa the eighties; day jobbing at an alternative newspaper, looking to define the role of race woman in the multiculti nineties. My faith is strictly rhythm and blues. Still hung up on soul music, poetry and jazz, sixties girl groups. Air guitar to the Isley Brothers and Living Colour. Marley heals my soul. Al Green and Sting wake me up in the morning. I go to Aretha and Joni Mitchell when I need to cry.

I know a Panamanian-American computer technician who is deep brown as a Senegalese and ethnically Latino. He speaks Spanish and Brooklyn-Italian blue-collar English. Ask him what he is, he'll tell you black Hispanic. I know a Caribbean-American architect who has lived on three continents, calls soccer football, and has a white great-grandfather and a Chinese great-grandfather, though he himself is gingerbread brown. This guy is from Grenada originally, though he identifies politically as African American. I also know a music promoter, black, who was raised by his mother, Jewish, in the suburbs of San Francisco. But from the way this guy swaggers and curses you'd think he was gangsta straight out of Compton. Trust me, all three guys are cute.

Say I marry one of these guys, will our children be multiracial, multiethnic, African American, black, people of color? Will they be called "niggers," "cocos," or "spics"? Will they live in an America where race, as Cornel West reports, still matters? Will they live in a war zone like Bosnia, where ethnicity, culture, and religion still matter? Or will AIDS and toxic waste cut their lives short before they can begin their pontificating, philosophizing, awfulizing, agonizing, rejoicing, preachifying, and signifying over just who they are in this shaky home we call the Americas?

Last night I had dinner with a group of friends who are Asian, Latino, and African American, and combinations of the above mixed with European. I love us dearly. We take David Dinkins's gorgeous mosaic quite literally and we aren't alone. We value the ethnic histories, rituals, stories passed down to us from our families of origin, from our families of choice, and from our book learning. We swap these traditions, make up new ones. At home, we identify each other by turf: Peter is Miss Mott Street, I'm Miss Bowery, Miss Dorado Beach is Maria. Yet we'd probably be more comfortable with the public monikers black, Latino, or Asian, than with "biracial" or "multiracial."

Most of us just hit the big three-oh. We saw the sixties as grade-school kids. We memorized TV pictures of dogs sicced on black folks in Mississippi and stories our grandparents told of Japanese internment camps out West. We can tell you about the years before English-as-a-second-language programs, when little girls like María, Margie, and Gladys were thrown into English-only class-rooms and left to sink or tread water. We got to Ivy League colleges thanks to affirmative action programs. Corporate America hired us under diversity initiatives.

The idea of a "multiracial" category on the census fills us with ambivalence. Is this just one more polite, largely academic game of identity hopscotch folks are playing while Los Angeles burns? Still, we're keeping our ears open.

*What do you know about the groups that are behind this census movement? Are they a multiracial, interracial Mafia? Biracial Rambos and contras? Are they white parents of mixed-race bambinos bartering for a safety zone for their café-au-lait kids? Or are they regular folks searching for a new way to identify their families?*

THE IDENTITY FAIRY: This is what I know so far. There's the Association of MultiEthnic Americans (AMEA), a nationwide confederation of interracial/multiethnic support groups based in San Francisco. And there's Project RACE (short for Reclassify All Children Equally), a lobbying organization out of Atlanta that campaigns on the local level. As of May 1993, due to the labors of Project RACE, three states have passed and two are reviewing legislation that adds the category "multiracial" to school forms.

AMEA and Project RACE are at the forefront of the census movement. This June these groups and several others will converge on Washington at hearings before a subcommittee on the census. If their efforts pay off, "multiracial" will replace "other race" on census forms in the year 2000. What this will mean, no one's sure. Could there be a massive flight from the categories Hispanic and black? Will the 9.8 million Americans who checked "other race" in 1990 switch over without a hitch to "multiracial"? By the turn of the new century, will the numbers in the "other race," now "multiracial" category, have multiplied dramatically? Will America have become the brown stew pot that *Time* and *Newsweek* have been warning us about since the mid eighties? And call them black, multiracial, or Hispanic (another ethnic appellation concocted by politics), will the majority of these brown ones still be poor folks? Or might all Americans check "multiracial," finally recognizing their heritage for what it is?

*Give us your off-the-cuff take on this census movement.*

THE IDENTITY FAIRY: I haven't been to any meetings, but I did speak at length with several organizers and foot soldiers, including, among others, Carlos Fernandez, president of AMEA, Susan Graham, executive director of Project RACE, Kendra Wallace, Project's vice president in California, and Michelle Erickson of Chicago. Erickson pulled her five-year-old son out of the public school system rather than choose between existing racial categories. (She identifies Andrew, her son, as biracial.) Instigated by Erickson's letter-writing campaign and the lobbying of Project RACE, the state of Illinois is now considering the "multiracial" category.

Many in the census movement see the bottom line of their

crusade as a fight for the self-esteem of their children. Graham of Project RACE, who is a white mother of two, as she calls them, "multiracial kids," says children are psychologically healthiest when they have accurate racial labels at their disposal. But what on earth constitutes an accurate racial label? And if the census movement is ultimately out to do away with such sacrosanct labels, will creating new ones accomplish this?

Beyond the children's self-esteem issue, the movement's larger agenda and philosophical goals registered blurry. Race is configured as choice, as a category on a school form. Race is not seen as a political/economic construct, a battleground where Americans vie for power and turf, but a question of color, a stick-on, peel-off label. If there *is* an end goal to the census movement's efforts, it appears to be assimilation. I don't mean this in the didactic sense of chiding others for wanting their piece of American pie; I mean it as finding a place to fit in, creating a space of comfort for self, away from the choke hold of race. The business as usual of discrimination, against the have-nots, who are usually shades of brown, and in favor of the have-sos, who are usually shades of pink, is left undisturbed.

When I heard that all state legislation for school forms would remain symbolic until the Congress and the Office of Management and Budget vote to add multiracial to the list of official categories, I scratched my head. And when I heard that the activists couldn't agree on whether those who checked the "multiracial" box would be considered a disadvantaged minority deserving of federal protections under the Voting Rights Act, I scratched some more. Why was this movement—potentially a vital movement for the acknowledgment of hybrid cultures/lives—being tied to a kite that no one could steer?

*Do you have other concerns about the census movement?*

THE IDENTITY FAIRY: Let's look at a few:

*Is race (and racism) left intact?* Instead of fighting for a new racial category, if the end goal is, as census activists say, to do away with the biological pseudoscience of race, why aren't they in the trenches casting stones at institutional racism? Anna Deavere Smith's *Fires in the Mirror* quotes an interview the playwright did with Angela Davis. Davis says she feels tentative about the meaning of race these days, but not tentative at all about racism. People of color, whether they call themselves biracial, Swirls (as they do in Fostorio, Ohio), or zebra Americans, are disproportionately members of America's underclass. Here's a meaningful contrast: Ohio became the first state last year to adopt the multiracial category on school forms. This year, Ohio saw a bloody uprising at the Lucasville state prison. Almost 60 percent of prisoners there are black men, though African Americans make up barely one quarter of the state's population. Will the symbolic recognition of multiracial identity reverse numbers like these?

I was struck that the census movement had no alliances with progressive organizations representing other people of color. None of these organizations had staged a teach-in or protested over the miscarriage of justice in the Rodney King case. Was biraciality being constructed as a less progressive stance than identifying as a "person of color," that catchphrase invented in the eighteenth century, then popularized in the seventies, as an expression of solidarity with other p.o.c.s worldwide?

*Cape Town, U.S.A.?* It's been asked before, and until I hear a good comeback, the question stands: Would "multiracial" be akin to South Africa's "colored" caste created under apartheid? Carlos Fernandez of AMEA believes that an "in-between" racial category isn't racist in itself, it is how such a category is used. Yet why wouldn't multiracial/colored by mythologized or positioned politically any differently in America?

*Are we special?* The census movement and its "interracial/biracial nationalists," as I refer to them playfully, claim biraciality as a mark of "racial" singularity, one that in America (where most racial groups are multiethnic and multicultural) has little grounding. Their insistence on biraciality's unique status borders on elitism. They marvel at the perks of biraciality: That biracials have several cultures at their disposal. (Though don't we all as Americans?) They say things like "biracial people are free of bias because they embody both black and white." Can you fight essentialism with essentialism? Are we to believe that all biracials are chosen people, free of prejudice, self-interest, and Republican Christian fundamentalism?

By proclaiming specialness aren't biracials still clinging to the niche of exotic other? "How could we not love them, they're so cute," boasted one white mother active in the census movement of her biracial children. Minus butter-pecan skin and Shirley Temple curls would they be less of an attractive proposition?

*The nationalist vibe.* The writer Kristal Brent-Zook calls nationalism a search for home, for family, and for sameness. Young movements of any kind are prone to nationalism, yet it's hard to forgive the biracialists for indulging. A large part of why they disassociate themselves from traditional ethnic communities is just *because* of their hybridity, their lack of purity.

Is there now to be a biracial party line to tow and a biracial lifestyle to upkeep? *Interrace,* a magazine chronicling the census movement and interracial and biracial social life, called the actress Halle Berry's choice *not* to marry interracially a "cop-out." (One guesses they made this judgment about the race of Berry's husband, baseball star David Justice, based on photographs. A few issues later, when *Interrace* found out that Justice happened to be "Afro-European," they laid out the biracial carpet.) Are those of us who marry the same, "mono-race" partners now retro, antiprogressive? Have the interracial/biracial police determined that the only way to change the world is to breed a "new race?" "Like it or not," read a letter to *Spectrum,* the newsletter published by Multiracial Americans of Southern California (MASC), "racially mixed people are the most beautiful people of all." The new Stepford people.

*What's history got to do with it?* As black/white biracials, when we distance ourselves from the African-American freedom struggle, from aging, though historically critical, ideas like "black power" and "black community," do we fail to honor a history that brought us to where we are today? Is biraciality political sedition? And if it feels that way, and it shouldn't, how can we make it feel less so? Are there ways to be responsible to a history that we are indebted to without being imprisoned by it?

I found the generalizations the census movers made about African Americans disturbing. Resistance from some blacks to the multiracial category was translated into resistance from the entire African-American population. Aren't some of the parents involved in the census movement African Americans? The bills to add the "multiracial" category on the state level have all been introduced by African-American legislators. The census initiative has garnered support from local chapters of the NAACP. *Essence* magazine and other black publications spread the word about AMEA and fellow interracial groups long before their white counterparts.

To say that biracials have been cold-shouldered by African-Americans throughout history, as some activists suggested, is selective ignorance. Black communities have always been shelter to multiethnic people, perhaps not an unproblematic shelter, yet a shelter nonetheless. Black folks, I'd venture, have welcomed difference in their communities more than most Americans.

*Nothing but a photo-op?* Watching biraciality gobbled up so eagerly on the Donahue and Oprah circuit makes me pause. If it weren't such a fashionable and marketable identity these days would so many folks be riding the bandwagon? (And like the hip-hop club, media darlings of the late eighties, the biracial lobby comes across on television as having have no agenda other than its own pride politics.)

Are biracial people being offered up as the latest market ripe for exploitation? *Interrace* magazine sells T-shirts inscribed with Webster's definition of biracial. The ads urge buyers to "Wear the Right Thing" or to "end racism . . . advertise in *Interrace.*" *New People: The Journal for the Human Race* hawks ceramic wedding figurines in your choice of complexions. Not unlike trade or hobby magazines, both publications look at the world through one prism: biracialism.

*Are we family?* Shouldn't we ask what makes biracial people a community? What holds us together other than a perceived sense of our own difference from the ethnic mainstream? Consider if the Mexican-Samoan kid in San Diego has the same needs as the black-Jewish kid from New York's Upper West Side? Maybe politically as people of color, but do they share a definitive mixed-race culture? And if they do, should we call it "biraciality" or should we call it "American culture"?

*Does blackness remain a stigma?* As my telephone travels made clear, the census camp is not minus attitudes of: "If you had a choice you'd be anything but black." Biraciality was posited by some as an escape from the "blemish of blackness." Chicago mother Michelle Erickson asked me quite innocently if I knew how degrading it was "to be attached to categories like black or Hispanic." Kendra Wallace, a biracial woman in her early twenties, pronounced rules of membership in the black community to be too stiff —based, she feels, on such criteria as "hair texture and whether one speaks proper English or not." (Is African-American diversity still that invisible to the world? One could have come away with a picture far more complex by watching a week's worth of sitcoms.)

A moment of cruel and unusual irony took place in a conversation with Project RACE's Susan Graham. During Black History Month, Graham's son returned home with some materials on Langston Hughes. Graham was disappointed that the school had failed to focus on "Langston Hughes's biraciality." I reminded Graham that African Americans as a whole were a multiethnic and multiracial folk, and that Hughes never hid the fact that he had white family, yet he "cast his lot," as the expression went back then, with his darker kin. Hughes's writing, one can safely say, celebrates, if not romanticizes African-American culture. Graham seemed irritated. The one-drop rule was the only thing that kept him in the black community, she insisted. If Hughes were alive today, he would choose to be multiracial, he would identify first with mixed-race people and the work of her lobbying group.

People of all races and cultures should feel free to claim Hughes as an idol, but wasn't Graham aware of a rather painful history? One where black people have had their every gift confiscated and attributed to others? Would this now happen in the name of multiracialism?

*Seems like you've exhausted the critical tip. Did you happen upon anything constructive in your telephone encounters with the biracial movement?*

THE IDENTITY FAIRY: Carlos Fernandez said something that made sense. Official recognition of multiracial identity may not end racism; it is, however, a necessary step. If we refuse to recognize that any material reality exists between black and white, we do nothing except enshrine these social boundaries—and enshrine the political divide that upholds them.

Certainly the daguerreotype of mixed-race people as freaks of nature could use a long overdue slashing. If the biracial lobby can help in this regard, bless them. Says Kendra Wallace: "We're invisible or our identities are always problematized and sexualized." Our "bloods" are at war inside of us. If mixed race were made normal, we could look forward to the comic mulatto, the introspective, the slovenly. We might one day come to miss ye olde tragic mulatto, the world's pet mule.

As much as I found myself resisting the biracial nationalists, to deny a group the right to identify as they wish to seems equally reactionary. In October last year the San Diego Unified School District, known for its conservatism, balked at admitting a little boy to grammar school until his mother, Patricia Whitebread, who is black, assigned him an "appropriate race." (Unlike many school forms nationally, San Diego's has no "other" designation.) Whitebread refused. The school district admitted the child anyway. Later the district classified her son as black without Whitebread's permission.

The activists I spoke to framed their cause as a civil rights movement. Perhaps one not as transparently vital as a movement for equal opportunity in employment or fair access to housing, but certainly one consummate with religious freedom or freedom of expression. In *Interrace,* psychologist Francis Wardle, director of the Center for the Study of Biracial Children, a clearinghouse in Colorado, makes a passionate appeal for interracial family networks not to been seen as a threat to African Americans:

"We are so aware of the need to improve conditions for so many blacks in this country that we are very puzzled some high profile blacks spend time and energy fighting us.

"We are not the enemy. . . . Don't insist we must raise our children to belong to a distinctive (and arbitrary) racial or ethnic category. Don't say that history and society must define who we are and what we want our children to become."

Perhaps the arrival of the biracialists might finally drive home to traditional ethnic communities the need for more proactive coalition politics. Kendra Wallace thought biracial organizing would allow people to leave racial enclaves, build bridges, and in time, return. In the lore of the passing novels, those who "passed for white" (or in this case "stood for colored") always found their way back to the black hearth. Of course the black hearth, as we approach the twenty-first century is more fragmented and scattered than ever.

At the dinner table last night we gathered, not to discuss the dainties of identity politics and the census, but to remember a close friend who died a year ago from AIDS. I could tell you that AIDS is an equal opportunity killer and I'd be telling the truth. I could also tell you that more and more of those who die from AIDS are people of color; that would be true too. This speaks reams about race and the very real equation of power, poverty, and privilege.

I like to think of Eduardo Mejia, the friend we lost, as a multiculturalist and global citizen cut from the cloth of a W. E. B Du Bois. To Eddie, unlike Kendra Wallace, *black* embraced every ethnic community that wished to claim it (a belief he shared with the Pan-Africanists of the sixties and the British Asian-Caribbean-African coalitions of the seventies). Would it surprise you that Eddie was a fair-complexioned Puerto Rican? A gay man and nurse, "the Queen," as we called him, was a street-shrewd philosopher who studied race all his life. He identified as a black, as a person of color, as Latino, as Puerto Rican, as a New Yorker. No one identity canceled out the other. Knowing Eddie, "biracial" would have been a label either too precious or sterile. He would have told you in one breath that he was "a Puerto Rican from a Haitian block in Brooklyn, who stands for gay rights and the freedom struggles of people of color around the world" before he would describe himself as biracial. It wouldn't have been fierce enough, specific enough, or ultimately progressive enough for Eddie in his day. But that would've been Eddie's choice; you may decide otherwise. Eddie, I'm sure, would have loved you and claimed you just the same.

*What's your idea of art and scholarship that politicizes multiracialism?*

THE IDENTITY FAIRY: Certainly the visual art and writings of Adrian Piper provides keen example. Piper works genius at demystifying the political economy of what she tags "racial classification." Her call to American whites to face up to their black heritage (and to blacks to do the reverse) takes multiracialism/multiculturalism beyond politically correct arts programming and into the realm of configuring a new American identity.

The work of writers and media artists Guillermo Gómez-Peña and Coco Fusco also stands out. In her contribution to the anthology *Black Popular Culture* Fusco tells us that in Cuba, where the black people in her family come from, there's an expression that goes *"Chivo que rompe tambor con su pellejo paga,"* which translates literally, "The goat who breaks the drum will have to pay with his skin." The phrase has another meaning as well: "The troublemaker turns him- or herself into the instrument to continue the music." Fusco argues that "black popular cultures, especially musical cultures, have generated an abundance of archetypes that embrace dissonance and contend with internal difference; these [are] semantic residues of histories of contradiction and conflict. Maybe one of these days our intellectual debate will catch up with our popular cultural ability to engage dissent, without the defensiveness that continuously rears its head."

Gómez-Peña's work takes on America in the "intercultural crisis." Writes critic Richard Schechner: "Interculturalists [such as Gómez-Peña] refuse utopian schemes, refuse to cloak power arrangements and struggles. Instead, interculturalists probe the confrontations, ambivalences, disruptions, fears, disturbances, and difficulties when and where cultures collide, overlap or pull away from each other. Interculturalists explore misunderstandings, broken messages, and failed translations—what is not pure and what cannot successfully fuse. These are seen not as disasters, but as fertile rifts of creative possibilities."

*Any last words of advice to those swimming in the identity pool?*

THE IDENTITY FAIRY: As you get older, chances are you will define yourself by your alliances with a multitude of communities. No one community will speak for you completely and no one community should be so static as to not let you share in others.

As for the biracial nationalists and their movement: Check them out, debate them, start your own. Don't accept any position—be it biracial/multiracial/interracial/African/Asian/or Latin American—as a political catchall.

Challenge all your communities to live up to you. The late poet Audre Lorde, African American, Caribbean American, feminist, gay, and supporter of the global causes of people of color, always spoke as a member of all her many homes.

In coming to self, balance individual identity with a responsibility to and critical eye on history. I'll never forget visiting the Afro-American Cultural Center at Yale as a prefreshman. I wandered around the building looking at the posters and murals, remnants of the late sixties, of the days when black students were admitted to mainstream universities in sizable numbers, of student protest for admission and retention initiatives, of sit-ins for ethnic studies departments. Alone, I walked the rooms of the House, as we call it, and felt the spirits of those students. A priceless moral and intellectual inheritance was being passed to me. On the train back home, I wept all kinds of tears: angry tears, tears of pride, gratitude tears. Later I would move away from the House and find other homes, but I always took the House and that inheritance with me.

Welcome to America. It ain't as airbrushed as a Benetton ad, but it's a happening place. Hope you brought your Rollerblades *and* your Air Jordans.

# two

# bring the heroines

# bring the heroines

*Wanted: Women, single, married, with kids/without, lovers of men, lovers of women, generous hips and butts preferred; to lead housing rights movements, voter registration drives; to be inventors, blues legends, moguls, vigilantes, soothsayers, mystics. Hair not an issue. Method actors or naturals okay. Call immediately for a screen test.*

Film and TV may have taught us a black heroine ain't nothing but a sandwich; still, we hope on. Picture our anticipation last month when the previews for *Stompin' at the Savoy* hit the decks. Rare—monumental even—

for the lives of black women, four in this case, to make prime-time, network viewing. A "motion picture for television" (ooh, just the sound of that evokes progress). Set in Depression-era Harlem. And, yes, the women were, you guessed, domestics, but we deserved a catch: life outside of Missy Anne's hot kitchen.

We holed up in front of tubes across the nation, with our combs and hair pomade, our bottles of Clearly Canadian, our checkbooks to balance, our knitting. All's aglow at first. A luscious cornucopia of skin tones from stars Lynn Whitfield, Vanessa Williams, Jasmine Guy, Vanessa Bell Calloway. Nice camera choreography from director Debbie Allen in the opening scene. Nice acting from Jasmine Guy in a speech that plays against the tragi-mulatress type. Nice near minstrelsy when Allen, doing a cameo as an "attitudinous" prostitute, is threatened by Whitfield brandishing sizzling curling iron. Nice, nice, nice for television.

Then the ending—and our defeat. Guy finds herself a fine yet poor black man, only to drop dead soon after from tuberculosis. Calloway gets her own pad downtown and a white lover; then he ditches camp and she goes crazy. Williams, an aspiring singer, loses her nightclub-owner sugar daddy to Whitfield and is reduced to gigging at pit stops in Jersey. Whitfield, the most driven, sees all her material dreams come true, yet is left alone. So we sit back, once again, and wonder when black girls on screen are gonna get something other than a bum deal on life. (Excuse us, 'cause we got the sassy-catty-black-women-alone-again blues.) Whitfield is warned: "You want too much and you're gonna be disappointed when you don't get it." And, by hook and crook she gets it all, except she ain't happy. Nothing like a fashionable postfeminist coda.

*Savoy* fits a trend: pop images that depict black women's ambition as solely materialistic and ill serving the community. We've seen it in the "boyz" movies. Professional women—a/k/a working women—are too busy to raise kids right, says *Boyz 'N' the Hood*. The selfish, scheming buppie chicks of *Strictly Business* lose their empathy for black men, along with their "soul," in bed. A neat companion legend was at work in the vilification of Anita Hill: Flash cards provided by Clarence Thomas crony John Doggett III at the hearing drew Hill and black professional women like her as desperate lunatics who live that *Fatal Attraction* life.

So we hear that success will turn you bitch, turn you antimale/family/race, turn you crazy, turn you *white*. Quite a fallacy if you crack some history books. Black women's ambition, I'd wage, has been linked primarily to community uplift. Look at all the social workers, teachers, antilynch campaigners, antipoverty workers, the church activists. The field hands of every black political movement, the editors and typists of every black arts movement. Now suck some teeth.

In the world of *Stompin' at the Savoy* even sisterhood is bankrupt. Whitfield is left not just without a man, but sans friends. Williams goes back to distrusting women after Whitfield shimmies away with her man. And only after the fact do the girls find out Guy caught TB and was buried a pauper. Director Julie Dash said once that she sees no reason to make films about black women hating each other. It wouldn't involve any tasty dramatic risks for her as an artist and intellectual. Others have done so well with backbiting she-devils, why impose?

Watching *Savoy* brought back shades of *Mahogany*, the Diana Ross–fest of 1975, directed by Berry Gordy. La Ross stars as a fashion model/designer who risks losing her man—and her Black Card—by frolicking as the glamorous Negress in Europe. *Mahogany* is out on video now, and recently I found myself at a brunch where it was playing on a big-screen TV as a stylishly retro background visual. The whole room groaned when Bille Dee delivered the film's famous line: "Success is nothing without someone you love to share it with." Another struggling woman artist and I were loudest; nervous perhaps, deep down, that we'd be gagged one day with the same scenario. *Mahogany* ends with Ross running home to Chicago and Billy Dee the grass-roots politician. (But not without that white mink coat.) Not retro at all, so it seems. Almost twenty years later, *Savoy* tugs the same motto: Nothing you will ever do matches what a man—very specifically a black man—can bring to your life. In this day and age, art that tells us the only solution is a good man is way simplistic, detached from our lives, and plain lazy. As for many of us—by choice or the numbers game—this is not an option, nor should it be a requirement.

I know a successful art dealer in her late twenties who admits to being a closet cult fan of *Mahogany;* she owns two video copies and the soundtrack. Dana's middle-class parents wouldn't allow her to see blaxploitation-era films. They made the exception for *Mahogany,* since it featured that cinema rarity, a glamorous black woman who wasn't a prostitute. Never before, says Dana, did a brown-skinned woman have so many costume changes. Though now she has a problem with the moral, that a woman's success happens at the expense of a man, Dana often crawls into bed and loses herself in the film on a PMS day. In what other movie can Dana see a black female character travel around the world, start her own business, and never wear an apron? When it comes to black women on-screen, *Mahogany* is still better than most. The pickings continue to be that slim.

Panning *Savoy* was not my assignment here. It's encouraging that the gigs went to director Debbie Allen and screenwriter Beverly Sawyer. The piece actually helped me clear up some thoughts on how art functions in my own life. Not fond of the rigid "positive-image" approach, I still crave heroines. In art and fantasy I want to win. I want power, even as I ride off a cliff. I want art to show me what I can do, not what I can't. And I don't want to waste seven bucks to be told that my tragic flaw is that I am a woman, I am black, and I have expectations. I can get that in the street for free.

*1992*

# venus envy

I take butts very seriously. And butt theory too—from actress/comedian Phyllis Stickney ("Power of the Boo-tay") to Audre Lorde ("Uses of the Erotic: The Erotic as Power," her manifesto on pleasure and black female agency). So seriously, that a few weeks back I was roused, for the first time, to express my two cents via the *Voice*'s letters page. But one sarcastic little stab at fashion writer Anka Radakovich—for pitching girdles to those of us who are cursed, she feels, with "bulbous rear end[s]" and "big ol' butt[s]"—wasn't enough. Radakovich's butt baiting needs to be "read," as we say in the vernacular, some more.

More interesting than Radakovich's history-blind tribute to a girdle's ability to "flatten your fanny" was the juxtaposition of her piece with an ad for padded underwear that appeared on the following page. No more "flat, sagging" buns, the ad promised; these briefs can simulate what "nature may have neglected." Here stands another example of the Eurocentric aesthetic's attraction/repulsion to the buttocks. (Ooh, says Freud, look at those tushes; females are more anally inclined, more, yikes, primitive!)

A veritable butt revolution has swept America in the last two decades—brought to you by black music, designer jeans, and MTV. (Once you've seen Janet Jackson gyrate to "Black Cat" can you really go back to Twiggy?) Could it be the rump is edging out legs and boobs as the preferred female fetish commodity in the eye view of mainstream white culture? Butts, yes, but just a champagne-glass full, *s'il vous plaît.* Listen to the alarms that sound right before swimsuit season: Butt alert, hide those heinies! (Even in a hotbed of correct sexual politics like the *Voice*, large derrieres have been likened to cows' asses.) What's all the hullabaloo? Fear of the big black butt?

A recent spread in *Elle* caught my eye (and those of a few male friends who announced benevolently that they had discovered, at long last, "the butt of life"). Most black models you see in *Vogue* and *Elle* et al. have pouty, little, pocket-size booties not much different from their Caucasian sistren, or if they do have some butt, it's not featured. Enter sixteen-year-old Beverly Peele, dashing solo around an eight-page layout styled like an English country garden. (My, times have changed, no chain-mail midriff, no bone through her nose?) In one drop-dead photo she stands, in profile, clutching flowers to her breast; a beaded jacket rises above her waist, exposing gently poked-out belly, arched back, and skimpy bikini thong. All eyes are led to her near-nude rump, which really *is* taking no prisoners. Breathtakingly endowed, Peele's cheeks seem to stretch horizontally for more than a foot. Hers is what's known as a "high butt," an outie, a shelf, and she wears it with an expression that mixes solemn pride and innocence.

*In profile.* Mmmm. Haven't I seen this image before, another time, another place? In an anthropological textbook, maybe, as an illustration for an ideologically charged concept known as "steato-pygia." Webster's calls it "an excessive development of fat on the buttocks esp. of females that is common among the Hottentots and some Negro peoples." Mercenary scientists and cultural theorists, whose fascination with the trait dates back to when Europeans first hit the shores of southwest Africa, called it "abnormal," "genetically base," "malformed." Nineteenth-century etchings of Hottentot women were rendered in a style that's purposely cartoonish—as if the subjects were she-devils, Loch Ness monsters, missing links. There's a sense of alchemy at work, stretching truth for profit.

Isn't Peele lucky to be a young black woman posing for a fashion spread in America circa 1991—while Negro bodies and self-expression are in vogue, marketable, and represent some vague notion of visual equality, in lieu of political and economic power? With a resplendent derriere like hers, in another era, Peele could have been the legendary Hottentot Venus herself: the twenty-five-year-old woman from the Cape of Africa, known in Dutch as "Saartjie" (little Sarah), who in 1810 was exhibited naked in a cage in London and Paris. When Saartjie died five years later she was the subject of a famous dissection that was used to support almost a century's worth of myths of white racial superiority. Today you can find the revered "Hottentot apron" (her pendulous labia minora) in Paris's Musée de l'Homme. Her genitalia float in a jar of formaldehyde, a shelf above Broca's brain. In a country where we can crown three black Miss Americas but almost fail to pass a civil rights bill, perhaps Peele is the Venus's twentieth-century incarnation.

The Hottentot Venus became the dominant icon of black femininity in the nineteenth century, reduced in the European imagination to her two sexual "attractions"—butt and apron. (And her disembodied buttocks live on. Peek at the album cover photo of 2 Live Crew's *Me So Horny*—black women don't have faces or souls, just big ol' butts.) Representing sexual deviation and disease (the Hottentot apron was compared to the syphilitic vaginas of European prostitutes), she was an allegorical deterrent to the Continent's rising tide of miscegenation. Maintaining this notion of the black female sexual "other" became crucial to doctrines of racial purity in both Europe and the antebellum South. Fear of big black dick? Public Enemy and others want to keep this bit of race lore fresh in our minds, but what about fear of big black ass? Wasn't the rape of African women during slavery a form of castration, of conquering the "sexual beast"?

Among the young African-American womanist intelligentsia, the Hottentot Venus is being resurrected as a cause célèbre and bestowed with a Frida Kahlo–like martyrdom. Last year visual artist Renée Green did an installation at Clocktower Gallery in New York based on Saartjie's story. (Observers were invited to stand on a platform and be displayed.) Patricia Hill Collins's *Black Feminist Thought* (1990) argues that the treatment of black women's bodies in nineteenth-century Europe and America (a most chilling example being the Hottentot Venus) became the blueprint for contemporary pornography's objectification and dismemberment of women's bodies.

The title poem of Philadelphia-based writer Elizabeth Alexander's first poetry collection, *The Venus Hottentot* (1990), begins with the voice of Georges Cuvier, the man who dissected the Venus ("Science, science, science/Everything is beautiful/blown up beneath my glass"), then segues to Saartjie's ("Since my own genitals are public/I have made other parts private"). Not only does this Venus have a point of view, but Alexander as the modern black woman artist/translator holds court, navigating through these two versions of history. As horrific and oppressive a symbol as the Hottentot Venus became under Cuvier's knife, she is now reclaimed and offered as an homage to black female resistance. When I called Alexander recently to talk shop, she told me that legend has it that the African women exhibited as Hottentot Venuses—there were many—were the inspiration for the bustle. (*Fairchild's Dictionary of Fashion* tracks down the bustle to 1830, just fifteen years after Saartjie's death. Could be!) Alexander says the legend rings true to her: "That which you are obsessed with, that you are afraid of, that you have to destroy, is the thing that you want more than anything. Black culture has been expropriated in this manner for centuries. Those who have expropriated it have utter contempt and disregard for the people who represent this culture. Detached from those who inspired it, culture is siphoned off as 'style.' I daresay European women walking around in bustles weren't thinking about the Hottentot Venus, just as American women in 'Bo Derek braids' weren't thinking about cornrows."

*1991*

# gold digging
# the skeezers

A young woman we know writes:

There was a time in my life when I too derived power from using my body to manipulate men. This was in the late seventies, a few years before the second coming of the miniskirt, when being naked in public still meant something. Nowadays, it's just one big meat market out there. Even on TV, a tit here, some ass there, nothing registers on the Richter scale. I blame crack. In the crack ecosystem, women's bodies are the lowest commodity. You can try to make a cute statement like Madonna and walk outside in your bra and panties, but the irony will be lost on the guy who offers you a dollar for a blowjob. Every day I'm surrounded by hateful images of women and hateful language—*gold diggers, skeezers* (women who screw for status), crack hoes (women who screw for a fix). Is it my imagination or are women playing along with it? I mean, has anyone stood up and said this devaluation of our bodies and our humanity has got to stop? No, we just get on "The Party Machine" with Nia Peeples and gyrate to the beat. I'm a feminist, or a womanist, or pro-woman whatever, but I swear, I'm about to borrow an Uzi from my neighbor the crack dealer and shoot the next traitor I see in a Lycra mini. Surely this is misplaced anger. Can you help?

First of all, don't annihilate any innocent young black women—AIDS and teen pregnancy are doing that work for you. You're right about one thing: These images are everywhere. They reign in hip-hop, which brought us the word "skeezer." In the tabloid circuit, if it isn't Sandra Miller Reese called a gold digger for pressing charges against Mike Tyson for fondling her in a club, it's Vicki R. Long, called a skeezer for bedding an archbishop. You'll even find them in that cutting edge of creativity—black cinema: not just in a newfangled *Superfly* flick like *New Jack City* (where a skeezer named Uniqua gets between the brothers), but in a family movie like *Five Heartbeats* (where a skeezer named Tanya gets between the brothers).

The woman-as-gold-digger image is as old as the hills. The *Oxford English Dictionary*'s first reference is this from 1920: women who "dig for the gold of their gentlemen friends and spend it on being good to their mothers and their pet dogs." By way of rap etymology, skeezer comes from the verb *to skeeze* (to fornicate; particularly a rap entourage with groupies on the road). An early cite would be UTFO's single "Skeezer Pleaser" from 1987. In the concert film *Raw*, also 1987, Murphy's paranoia about crafty American dames and "bush bitch[es]" taking half of his empire became a standard for nouveau-riche hip-hop's depiction of women. And if a clothes hanger–abortionist gangsta rapper like Ice Cube weren't enough to stop the stream of women trying to stymie men with sex, we now have male-produced female decoys like H.W.A. (Hoes Wit Attitude) and B.W.P. (Bytches With Problems) to pass off bite-the-bullet negativity as empowerment theory.

As a black woman, you may be particularly sensitive to the skeezer image and not know why. This might have something to do with its affinity to another age-old stereotype, the black female as Jezebel, the sexually loose and aggressive figure who justified rape by white men during slavery. Later this delightful image was transmuted into the parasitic welfare mother (who feeds on the system) and, finally, the skeezer/gold digger (who feeds on brothers with bank). What might make the skeezer an even more painful thorn in your side is that, unlike its forerunners, this type is manufactured primarily by black men. And just as Coco Fusco questions whether *Mambo Mouth*'s John Leguizamo is "Broadway's latest primitive . . . stomping verbally on the women he shares an ethnicity with" for ticket sales, one wonders too whether the misogyny so rampant in skeezer imagery and black male pop product in general is also a kind of primitivism milked for consumption by the white mainstream. (The pop success of records like N.W.A.'s new offering of gangsta rap—featuring such beauties as "One Less Bitch" and "To Kill a Hooker"—is one of many clear signs that the market for this music is larger than just young black men.)

When you dig behind the skeezer/gold digger character you find a storehouse of male fear and insecurity. Men deal with women they can "buy" presumably so they can control them, though when "bought women" exploit the situation, men, caught in the logic of their own game, cry victim. Music videos that feature skeezers are more successful as portraits of male ineptitude than paeans to machismo. EPMD's "Gold Digger" begins with the rappers in a group therapy session with a white shrink. Later the guys twiddle their thumbs while axe-toting women, spray-painted in gold, work the EPMD gold mine.

A typical defense of skeezer imagery is that it speaks to "real-ness." But whose realness? (Clearly this is realness as defined by certain individuals and not by natural law.) And why the assumption that realness equals good art? Unfortunately life mimics bad art too: Could N.W.A.'s Dr. Dre have taken their song "One Less Bitch" a little too seriously when last January he allegedly beat up Dee Barnes, host of Fox's rap show *Pump It Up!*, for giving the group bad press?

If this all depresses you, let me recommend an empowerment pill: Hunt down a copy of the feminist film journal *Camera Obscura*, number 23, and read Tricia Rose's "Never Trust a Big Butt and a Smile." Rose positions women rappers like MC Lyte, Salt-N-Pepa, and Queen Latifah as important feminist cultural critics. "By expressing their sexuality openly and in their own language," Rose writes, black women rappers challenge their male counterparts to address women as equals. And by conducting their dialogue with men in the open, they move an issue once characterized as domestic into the public, hence political, arena. Rose recalls an MC Lyte video where the rapper reads her man in a subway car in front of his boys, i.e., the community.

I called Rose recently to swap skeezer stories. (Rose: "How does a skeezer let you know she 'did' Al. B Sure!? By mentioning in passing that the brother has flat feet.") The saddest thing about the skeezer/gold digger character, Rose pointed out, is that it reminds us how in a market society we are all commodities. But it's also a twisted testament to female power.

If you pursue this thought, then Robin Givens—according to her commodity value—is the most powerful woman in America. She "took out" millionaire Mike, the most lethal man in the world. Dogged for being a gold digger when she divorced Tyson after nine months of marriage (and alleged physical abuse), Givens went on to redeem herself in the eyes of some of her critics with *A Rage in Harlem*, in which she plays a character very similar to her media persona, though does it on-screen, in a tight Lycra dress, for every-one to consume. After seeing the movie, a friend—an intellectual man, I thought—said, and I quote verbatim: "Givens is not a bad person after all. And her ass! She was pretty talented. This gave the Tyson thing a context. She deserved the conquest. And she didn't even have to go ten rounds with the brother."

*1991*

# **super**mamas
# revisited

You pink-ass, corrupt honky judge, take your little wet noodle the hell
out of here. And if you see a man anywhere, send him in, 'cause I do
need a man.

—*Pam Grier as Foxy Brown*

If you're looking for heroines in all the wrong places
—like your video store—check out the gun-toting,
karate-kicking, sass-spitting supermamas of the seventies blaxploitation flicks. It's "bad black chicks"
like Pam Grier *(Coffy, Foxy Brown)*, Tamara Dobson
*(Cleopatra Jones)*, and Jeanne Bell *(T.N.T. Jackson)*
up against crooked white cops (pigs), crooked black
politicians (sellouts), and lecherous drug dealers of
all races (the pushermen). The black girls serve
justice the American way, vigilante style, with bare
breasts and sawed-off shotguns. When a pimp called
Doodle Bug finds out Cleopatra Jones is back in

town, "Man," he whines, "that broad is just ten miles of bad road."

Of course these films are "negative image" superfests. All we do in these movies, and by inference life, is sell drugs, sell our bodies, and shoot each other. For home-video release, they should come with labels. "Warning: This film contains oppressive images of blacks that may be unsuitable, unpleasant, and downright unfit for some viewers." But even a label wouldn't prepare you for this scene from *Foxy Brown:*

"Crawl over here, you no good nigger bitch," demands a European heroin dealer of Foxy Brown, who's posing as call girl Misty Cotton. "I know I'm not good enough for you, but let me have your precious white body just once," pleads Foxy. When the dealer spits on her, Grier pulls out a .45 and points it to his temple: "You want to spit on me and make me crawl, white motherfucker? I'm gonna piss on your grave tomorrow." She does.

Supermamas have their share of personal problems. Coffy's relatives are all druggies, dealers, number runners, or in the hospital with brain damage. Cleopatra Jones is forced to leave behind Rufus, a righteous black man with a vast Afro (played by Bernie Casey), to go on special assignment in Hong Kong. T.N.T. Jackson's new man (Stan Shaw) turns out to be her brother's murderer. Foxy Brown shoots her brother's ear off because he has her man set up by pushermen. (Says a white pusherman in *Foxy Brown,* "maybe these people don't believe in family loyalty.")

Blaxploitation's favorite pusherman pimp is Antonio Fargas. Fargas, as Link, Grier's no-good druggie brother in *Foxy Brown,* sums up the genre's male problem this way: "I'm a black man and I don't know how to sing and I don't know how to dance and I don't know how to preach to no congregation. I'm too small be a football hero, and I'm too ugly to be elected mayor. I watch TV and see all them people in those fine houses they live in and all them nice cars they drive, and I get all full of ambition. So tell me, what am I supposed to do with all this ambition I got?" Star in blaxploitation flicks, naturally.

In their own contorted way, roles like Cleopatra Jones and Foxy

Brown raised Hollywood's threshold of black female visibility. Whatever you say about Cleo and Foxy, they are not shuffling mammies, teary-eyed mulattoes, or boozy blues singers. They talk back. They are political in that they are about ridding "the community" of drug slavery and corruption. They take the law into their own hands (vigilantes Foxy and Coffy) or they *are* the law (special narcotics agent Cleo). *Get Christie Love!,* a supermama spin-off that ran for one season in 1974, starred Teresa Graves as television's first black female cop.

Despite the confines of genre—dim-witted plots and motivations, racial stereotypes, and slaphappy nudity—these actresses have moments of transcendence, of "attitudinous" rebellion; moments when they win the image war. When a crooked cop calls Cleopatra Jones "dark meat," she chuckles at his insolence: "Baby, I think you'll find this meat rather tough."

Life as a supermama isn't gonna be easy. But consider the advantages:

*What you'll get to wear.* Low-cut silver maxidress with a cropped white-mink jacket, red-plaid bell-bottoms, seashell choker, beige knit mini with beige, high-heel, thigh-high suede boots, eight-inch curly Afro wig, twelve-inch nappy Afro wig, mane of loopy, processed curls, feather halter, black leather bells and matching jacket with wide lapels, powder-blue maxidress with ruffled split up to the crotch, sunshine-yellow pantsuit with brown piping and canary-yellow applejack, and the classic combo: rabbit fur jacket, red turtleneck, and black bells.

*What you'll get to do:* Shoot a man while his pants are around his ankles; become a pimp's leading lady by fistfighting with his stable of whores; hide razor blades in your Afro wig; shoot your boyfriend, a right-on politician, in the nuts when you catch him with a white woman; tell a pusher, "There's no such thing as light shit, brother Snake," and flush his stash down the toilet; castrate a pusher and present his software in a pickle jar to his old lady; ride a motorbike; burn a thirty-million-dollar poppy field in Turkey; and fight (and beat) a tribe of ninjas in Hong Kong.

*Things that will happen to you:* All the righteous black men in your life will get shot in the back while you watch. Then you'll meet some brothers from the Anti-Slavery Society, a neighborhood antidrug group, who'll help you get revenge.

*Songs they'll sing about you:* "Coffee is the color of your skin/ Coffee is the color of the world you live in" *(Coffy);* "Baby, you're so fine, loving you just blows my mind" *(T.N.T. Jackson);* "Sweet as a chocolate bar/No one knows who you are/Such a rare black pearl in a very big world filled with tragedy and tears" *(Coffy).*

*Who will write these songs:* Willie Hutch, Roy Ayers, Joe Simon, and Millie Jackson.

*The names men will call you:* Black trash, chocolate, darkie, goddamn nigger cop fink, goddamn black bitch, big-jugged jigaboo, nigger bitch, lucky nigger junkie broad, crazy black bitch, spook, sweet pickaninny, jive jungle freak.

*The names you'll call men:* Lousy stinking pig, white motherfucker, ugly prickless white faggot, whitey, super honky, fatso.

*How they will market you:* "A one-woman hit squad on a trail of vengeance lined with hitmen, prostitutes, and thugs"; "In the bedroom and out in the open, she revs up the action so no one is safe from her wrath"; "She's a one-mama massacre squad."

Why wait?

*1990*

# girls on the strip

The comic strip that is my life might be perfect material for Barbara Brandon's "Where I'm Coming From," if it weren't so, damn, excuse me, X-rated. Like Brandon's strip, mine has a dozen *dames de couleur* ("the girls," Brandon calls them) who run around with piled-high hairdos and argue all day, usually on the phone, about racism or sexism on the job, what a dog boyfriend has been this week, and whether Clarence Thomas will suffer a nervous breakdown by the year 2000. Why my girls won't play well in the *Des Moines Register* is because, when it comes to boyfriend's p-size or beating the yeast monster, they find it hard to hold their tongues. I tell them, you girls won't play in Albuquerque until you wash your mouths with Lysol. But who listens to me?

Barbara Brandon, however, has been playing in Albuquerque, Harrisburg, Pennsylvania, and a dozen other cities. As of last November, Brandon became the first black woman cartoonist to be syndicated nationally so she's getting plenty ink. *Glamour, People,* and *Time* have all descended on her little studio in Brooklyn's Fort Greene to have a peek.

Brandon has mixed feelings about being, in the nineties, a "first black something." Though with the prospect of seeing her characters on T-shirts, calendars, and greeting cards by fall, thrill is winning out. "Girl," she says, in stylish outer-borough girlfriendese: "Don't we just *need* greeting cards? I'm tired of coloring in those faces."

The girls have been making noise in Brandon's head since college. *Elan,* a black women's magazine, bought the strip in the eighties, only to fold soon after. Her next stop was *Essence,* where they needed a fashion writer more than a cartoonist. Brandon took the writing gig, as it beat dressing mannequins for JCPenney. Eventually she sold the strip to the *Detroit Free Press,* where it has appeared weekly in the life-style section since 1989. Getting by on seventy-five dollars a week from the strip and the odd freelance job, she left *Essence* to devote 24-7 to her girls.

Cutting a syndication deal, Brandon's next move, was no weekend at Virginia Beach. The strip was criticized by potential buyers for its Feiffer-style talking heads. Put the girls in real environments, they said, draw some male characters, make it a daily. Brandon stood ground, and finally signed with Universal Press Syndicate, where she's in good company with "Doonesbury" and "The Far Side," and is encouraged to be as political as she can get away with.

Fifty papers have signed on so far, yet some, like the *Minneapolis Star Tribune,* may have done it to beat the local competition— they've yet to run the strip. "Where I'm Coming From" is as far north as Calgary, Alberta, and as south as Houston. New York City papers, though they serve a majority nonwhite population, are holdouts. Is it a question of space (an old cop-out) or are Big Apple dailies not ready for women who talk loud about pregnancy out of wedlock, affirmative action, and racial identity?

"I'm personally insulted," says Brandon, "if a paper is not interested in the strip because it only features black women. Does that mean my existence can't teach anything? Hey, I didn't grow up with a community of ducks, but I read 'Donald Duck.' And I don't live with a dog, but I read 'Marmaduke,' and I understand it too."

The girls of "Where I'm Coming From" are twenty- and thirtysomething and have names like Lekesia, Nicole, and Alisha. Lydia, who owns a business, named her new baby Aretha. Judy wants to be a novelist. You won't see "cleavage or hot pants" here, says Brandon; the emphasis is on minds for once, not rumps. As single women, the girls are inevitably compared to "Cathy," queen of the coffee mug and greeting card set. With due respect to creator Cathy Guisewite, this is Brandon's comeback: "Buying a bathing suit and worrying about when we'll be size six again, we all trip like that, but I don't want to in my strip. I think I have more of a responsibility." Instead of one character being the repository of every stereotypically female neurosis, Brandon offers a balance. If a strip shows Nicole going on about boyfriend, then Lekesia is on the other end of the phone rolling her eyes.

Brandon's critique of hetero relationship-obsession is an ongoing theme. She takes digs at women who have blinders on when it comes to everything but their man. That men appear in the strip only as voices on the telephone speaks to their complicated presence and absence in the lives of black woman of Lekesia and Nicole's generation. These male phone voices, disembodied and shown in blownup and cluttered type, remind me of the adults in "Peanuts," who are represented only as high-pitched garble.

Brandon is a walking library of black comic-strip history, having grown up putting in Letratone (the dots that suggest Negro skin) for her father, Brumsic Brandon, Jr.'s strip "Luther." In 1969, the year Barbara turned eleven, "Luther" became the third black feature to go national. Images of blacks in American comics have paralleled those in film: Step-in Fetchit characters ruled until pioneer strips by black artists, like Morrie Turner's "Wee Pals" and Ted Shearer's "Quincy," won syndication in the sixties. By the eighties, newspapers lost interest in efforts to integrate the comics. After fifteen years in newsprint, "Luther" was dropped. Brandon traces her lineage to Jackie Ohms, a black woman cartoonist whose character Torchy Brown, a girl reporter, ran in black newspapers like *The Chicago Defender* in the 1930s, ten years before the debut of "Brenda Starr." Torchy dealt with "sexism, racism, and her man," so Brandon preens, and was way ahead of her time.

A *Mad* magazine kid who didn't care much for the Archies, Brandon kept a Feiffer strip tacked above her bed in junior high. In a house that doubled as a gallery for her father's comic art, she was never at a loss for black images in the medium. I, on the other hand, remember combing newspaper strips, cartoon shows, and comic books for little black girls—and drawing a blank. It seemed we couldn't be imagined on screen as live characters or on paper as illustrated ones. I ask one of my foul-mouth friends to confirm this, and she comes up with "Josie and the Pussycats," a 1970s television cartoon that followed the escapades of a female rock group. Remember Val, she asks, the black girl who played drums? Didn't you feel liberated by Val?

Brandon's strip and the commercial recognition of other women whose humor has intelligence and political bite, such as comedian/ actress Phyllis Stickney, performance artist Rhodessa Jones, and novelist Terry McMillan is more than welcome. (You have to make it to Stickney's live show at the new Cotton Club in Harlem just to hear her call Clarence Thomas the "jungle fever judge.") In mainstream comedy, black women have been familiar whipping posts. We are the female image, says bell hooks, that everyone is allowed to show contempt for. It's about time girlfriends get out there and return the compliment.

*1992*

# soldier in the style wars

You're a smart girl, concerned individuals tell me, write about the Gulf war or Lee Iacocca shooting spittle on Japan or how a gang in L.A., the Crips, got tight with some dictators in Latin America, the Medellín drug cartel. But why style? Isn't it . . . too . . . *fem* for you?

I've always admired the way the Crips did a leveraged buyout of the color blue and would shoot in cold, red blood anyone found wearing the rival gang's color—red—on Crip turf. This conjunction of style, power, desire said so simply, so precisely, everything one needed to know, really know, about the human tribe. Style is political, of course:

It's about danger and choices, who is made family and who is made slave.

Put race in the mix and you've got (mis)representation (who gets to take the pictures) and the now heated, ever muddy waters of appropriation (who gets paid). Madonna cashes in on a dance style created by black and Latin gay men, frames it as a homage to white, female glamour queens, and the dance originators are left without a wooden nickle. Do we ignore this and wiggle our butts to her music, smack her, or applaud her marketing genius? And why do the critics who salivate over Madonna and her womb of symbols never mention Josephine Baker? With her body, style, and the adulation of her white fans, Baker wrote entire treatises on how the "primitive" functioned to the repressed who invented it. What of Grace Jones? You can talk about gender and power when you're dressed in Marilyn Monroe's garters, sure it's safe, yet what if, like Grace, you throw gender to the wind as a uselessly polite, bourgeois restriction, and dare all of us—no, command us—to want you still? Now *that's* signifying chutzpah. In a magazine recently I read Grace Jones described as "the woman Jean-Paul Goude invented." Yeah, and the Greeks gave birth to Egypt.

Style is where I want to be right now. I feel like I'm listening at the bedroom door of all your psyches. Feminism puts me there, too. For black women without access to the room of one's own to make leisure-time art, our bodies, our style became the canvas of our cultural yearning. It has been, in recent history, not just a place of self-mutilation, but a place of healing. Racism wounds us in gender-specific ways. Men, an elder once told me, are made to feel stupid, and women to feel ugly. Claiming beauty (and the power in that), and the dissemination of it to the young women who follow us, is serious, in my mind, serious as boys pointing cannons at oil wells.

I get these large ideas about style from visionaries like Coreen Simpson. At the threshold of womanhood and in search of a God, I happened on one of Simpson's photographs: a cook, a black woman with an expanse of hip and breast, standing in the kitchen of a restaurant. The face she presents is regal and unexpectedly sensual.

American cinema's pictures of mammy as mere bosom for white woe, mammy as woman with no personal stake or ambition, were dashed right there. I realized how important one's own eyes, Simpson's in this case, were to transformation. Just in a gesture, this woman's hand on her hip, I found a reservoir of cultural history—a history of pleasure and a history of self-defense—and it was all so close to home.

Coreen Simpson, for those who haven't seen her shuttling around New York City with her cameras and sack of treasures, is a visual artist—a fine-art photographer and jewelry designer—known on the international fashion scene as the midwife of the Black Cameo. Simpson is doing her usual quota of three things at a time: adding a new item to her accessories line (the Black Cameo Scarf, a pattern that combines the original Black Cameo ancestress, cowrie shells, and sea horses), having dental surgery, and preparing for a solo show of her photo collage, inspired by hip-hop style and Romare Bearden's jazz paintings. As we unravel her life, I take pictures in my head; not photos, because she moves so fast, I take music videos: of Simpson rushing between life locations, with her melting-pot voice—Brooklyn black, been-to-Europe, Upper West Side Yiddish—as narration.

The photographer and her younger brother were foster kids growing up in the 1950s. At age six and five they were removed from a middle-class home on Long Island and placed in a Manhattan orphanage. The two were eventually taken in by a family in Bed-Stuy. Simpson recalls the trauma of being uprooted, but also how she was "floored by the style, bravado, aura of the people in Brooklyn. There was this guy who walked around in an orange suit; everyone was outdoing each other with these outrageous ensembles. At the orphanage, you never had your own coat, you had to pick one from the community closet. So I was always aware of clothes." A visit from a social worker in "mink pom-pom balls on her suede boots" is still vivid: "I had never seen a black woman like her before, and I was enchanted."

Simpson "took the back door" to photography, first writing lifestyle pieces for small magazines like Vy Higgensen's *Unique NY*. She brought along a camera to control the look of her stories and soon was known more for her images. In the eighties Simpson became one of the first black female photographers to cover the European fashion collections. Impressed, she was not: "You did see black representation on the runway. Iman was working. All the *girls*, but fashionwise, there's more on the street."

For her hip-hop series, begun in 1982, the photographer set up a portable studio in downtown clubs, Harlem barbershops, and braiding salons in Jamaica, Queens. "I knew there was more to it [hip-hop] than these cute little dance steps that were being played up in the media," she says. "The style element was very important; very African and very American at the same time. I connected it to the way people dressed when I was growing up in Brooklyn. Black folks, as far as style goes, we're the leaders. I think it's important to document this. That's why I did the hip-hop photos so big, because I wanted viewers to confront that black America originated these styles."

Simpson has had a jewelry jones since she can remember. She went to Puerto Rico as a teenager to study Spanish and ended up selling costume jewelry door-to-door. As an adult, Simpson came to jewelry design to supplement her income as a freelance photographer with two children to raise. After three years of selling her one-of-a-kind pieces on New York streets, her work was picked up by retail shops and featured in fashion magazines.

A futile search for a black cameo led Simpson to design one of her own in 1989. Later research told her that the art of cameo making was thought to be inspired by Egyptian glyptics, carvings on precious stones. Likenesses of black women were made in the seventeenth century by Italians, who were the first to mass produce cameos. These cameos are rare, many are in European collections or museums.

"If you look at most white cameos, the model holds her head down in a demure way or seems vulnerable," Simpson explains. "With all the problems we have as black women, I knew this cameo had to look up." Demand for the cameo has been so steady that Simpson continues to expand the line. I went to a dinner party in Minneapolis recently where the hostess's Black Cameo was displayed on the table as a centerpiece, right next to the gourmet black-eyed peas.

In my fantasy music videos of Simpson, one location is the factory that manufactures her cameo. It's her first visit and she explains to factory managers, all short white guys who ressemble Rick Moranis, the importance of getting the features right—long neck, twisted locks, and full-bloom lips—since, Simpson stresses, this will be the "first American cameo of a contemporary woman of color." Later for Lee Iacocca or the Medellín drug cartel, this is history. The soundtrack is the Isley Brothers' "Who's That Lady," the 1964 version with the wild samba feel. Simpson profiles an asymmetrical hat that would have Catwoman at her knees and bangles on each arm up to the elbow. No one can keep their eyes off of her.

*1992*

# this is faith

The college boys are trying to make sense of all the leg and thigh rising and rising above them. Seems like Christo has staged another environmental art hoax: the Twin Towers smothered in black Lycra. This ain't the World Trade Center though; these are the gams of Felice Rosser, a six-foot-tall black woman with a bass guitar. And this ain't two miles from CBGB; this is Toad's Place in Ivy League New Haven, a frequent stop for big money tour buses.

Tonight's bus belongs to headliners Living Colour. But back to the woman with the bass guitar, not that we could ever lose her, as she's nothing short of magnificent with that river of dreadlocks cascading past her shoulders and that cocoa belly exposed to the wind; locked as she is knee-deep in a groove that says all at once, quite loudly, rock/reggae/funk/you-guess/does-it-matter, and standing, as she is, at the very edge of the stage, just straddling and straddling that groove until hell or kingdom come. In the face of this Cleopatra electric, the college boys are backing up, bewildered, straight-up lost in a collision of fear and desire. This bass woman is by no means fitting their picture of band leader, bass guitar player, lead singer, date, hairdo. What do their eyes see? Death or a warm wet place, or both? And what are they forced to confront? Their mothers, their guitar gods, their country?

Standing on a bar stool in the back, I'm lost too. It's that rush that hits the clit of your very soul when you're witnessing something for the first time that will define you for years to come. Where can I buy this, where can I see this again, where can I bathe in this? The vocal harmonies are working the Middle East, the I-Threes, and Laura Nyro duets with Labelle. The music is getting hard and soft in all the right places. And all this image/text/sound is being mainlined straight to my brain, my crotch, and that pumping thing under my T-shirt.

Who are these urchins of the diaspora? The keyboard player/vocalist might be a rare Ethiopian miniature or just an East Village fashion plate in leather hot pants and sturdy shoes. The drummer has the long neck of a Masai and is slamming the bass drum upside the head like a metal-head's mama. And the tiny guitar player with that cabbage of dreads sprouting over his head is giving me all-blues. He cradles his axe to his pecs as if it's his woman, not his johnson, then fingers it till it wails pleasure. The college boys have no more room to back up.

Living Colour plays a powerhouse set, complete with a spine-numbing "Amazing Grace," perhaps to lay a little church on the redneck vibe fogging up the club. I'm still with the new kids who call themselves Faith. You can see why. With their instruments held together with gaffer's tape, it's probably all they have. It's October

1990. I had come to New Haven trailing a man, but ran into something a little more lasting, an aesthetic. I found a band called Faith, and I'm head over heels involved.

### this is a photograph, 1992

The view up Broadway from Soho to Harlem is all water towers and gargoyles, those details the aerial shots in movies don't catch. A photo session is about to begin on this eleventh floor loft around the corner from the Time Cafe, hanging post of the glam and glamy paid. Writer Malu Halasa, Felice's girl since college, and her husband, Andy Cox of the Fine Young Cannibals, live here, though as usual they're offering it to Felice and her band. The loft has seen much of Faith, from after-gig parties to baby showers, and everyone's nostalgic today because Malu and Andy are giving it up for London. The bass lady herself walks in pushing an empty stroller, all flustered 'cause she lost her rock & roll costume bag on the D train. Her old man and manager, Buzz, brings up the rear with the kid and that constant smirk of his: That Felice, if she weren't so talented, if I didn't love her so goddamn much.

Felice Rosser has a lot on her mind these days. Drummer Garry Sullivan is on the road *without* the band. Poached a few days ago by the B-52s, he'll be gone for six months, or maybe for good. The other Faithfuls aren't here, either, and may not be; something about a tiff last week. Though soon they file in; anything for the band. Guitarist Rene Akan, last, is full of ginseng and happenstance: His clothes are missing, his cat's sick, he wants a Bob Marley tattoo. Keyboardist Diana Baker rolls her most deadly weapon, those Ethiopian poster-child eyes. Rene plays uncle, lullabying the kid with James Brown tunes, then takes his place in the frame.

They decide against sunglasses and in favor of natural light. Leaning against each other to balance Felice's gift of height, they look like who they are: a Brooklyn family of choice, not some folks out to storm the rock citadel, though they are that too. Malu, just another Arab-American rainbow baby, be-dreaded Buzz with his Coke-bottle specs, the drooling kid, and finally, the skinny British photographer, are dragged into the shot too. Aside from the drummer, the only missing person is comanager Nicole Payen, who compares her day job of human-rights work for Haitian refugees to managing a black rock band in search of a record deal. Click.

## dance for the industry

Like any number of New York local bands hard up with dreams, Faith has a sizable following and a name with club bookers in the city for putting on a feisty live show. From their first gig in 1988 at a squat in Alphabet City, things had inched forward, for the most part, though now they feel they're circling the runway. Joining the Black Rock Coalition (BRC) and playing Coalition-produced showcases in 1989 was a turning point. Living Colour guitarist Vernon Reid asked them to take part in a benefit concert for homeless New Yorkers at the Beacon Theater that summer, along with Stevie Ray Vaughn and John Cougar Mellencamp.

So in their first working year as a band Faith had played a two thousand–seat theater. Soon they were opening at clubs like Wetlands for every big act that came through, "but only on the black side," says Buzz. Industry scouts began slinking around after the Beacon benefit. Showcase hell followed, as the band strutted, usually early evenings in the dark hole of CBGB, for independents like Pow Wow records and majors like CBS and Epic. These were funhouse events: maybe twenty people in the audience, along with perplexed record company folks. And our four African Americans on the auction block rocking until they bled. Pure funhouse, but no deal.

Other doors opened and closed. Faith passed on chances to contribute to small-label compilation discs, holding out for major-label deals that hobbled along, then never happened. Word came back from the sniffers: This band's not ready (though how to be "ready" was never outlined). Or the songs aren't there yet. (An odd one: You go to a Faith gig and what you get *is* songs. "Felice has that camp-fire ability," says a BRC member. "Anyone can sit down with an acoustic guitar and sing along to her music.") Or, the most frustrating: We don't know how to market this band. This is usually a code for "weird, unclassifiable black folks don't sell; there's no audience for them," which American artists have had to prove wrong time and again. The question was fast becoming not whether Faith was ready for the industry, but whether the industry was ready for them.

## tribal grunge

Brand naming their music has always been a problem for Faith. "I don't know what we call it, tribal grunge, or something?" pipes Rene, followed by a laugh track. Felice uses "rock" to shock people who assume she plays reggae because of her locks. The term "black rock" doesn't work for anyone in the band. To Rene, it's as redundant and insulting as "Jamaican reggae." Ah, the lovely semantics you do battle with as an African American aching to stretch outside of market trenches and gimmicks and just do some art. Let's all move to London.

You'll hear the odd novelty-reggae song from black American artists. For Faith, reggae informs everything they do, including their "rock" songs. Their reggae palette sets them apart too. Not the fad of the moment, dancehall, it's a softer-edged groove that recalls the seventies. Even at their hardest, Faith seems to come from a peaceful, wise place. Though Rene says he's "addicted to distortion," his sound is not aimless industrial noise; it's closer to a primal human voice. Faith's cover of Funkadelic's "Cosmic Slop," say, comes off less as guitar pyrotechnics than the mating call of leopards.

Then you have the image wall. (Unless, of course, you are, know, or live with people like Faith, and you take your/their identity as "normal" for granted.) The locks alone set off a series of puzzlements: Felice, Diana, and Rene are neither the fashion-dread adolescents you see in Sprite ads these days, nor are they practicing Rastafarians. The Faith women have long locks well matched to their womanly bodies. Just the act of wearing locks uncovered sets them apart from most women working in reggae, who wrap at least the crown of their heads for spiritual reasons.

To boil it down, you have a major style war happening on stage: Says BRC cofounder and longtime Faith enthusiast Greg Tate, "Faith doesn't fit any of the clichés of what it means to be a rock band. It's fronted by a big sister with dreadlocks who plays bass. The music is very soothing vocally, then they rupture that. They're about as comfortable with being benignly psychedelic as they are with being straightforward dubwise. Basically, they shatter all conventions of what genre is."

"Yeah," says Diana. "A & R people try to figure us out and they get a big headache."

### pow wow soundbite

Eight days into January 1991 and it's cold as a witch's tit outside and not about to let up. Onstage at CBGB though, we're frying pork rinds. This must be a showcase because the feedback is so vicious it stings. Tonight is for Pow Wow Records, who are close to making an offer. The band's apologizing for tuning up onstage, while Garry tries to cover with nervous fill-ins on the high hat. The bass lady doesn't make it to that knee-deep groove of hers until the final song. Then she's *on* stage, legs spread, humping each bass note, her locks doing a mad Krishna dance of their own. She takes a lyric up like Chrissie Hynde, then oozes it down like Nina Simone. The posers glance up from their beers and dig, at last. Felice never looks at them. "This morning I had no money to pay the van, no clothes to wear to the gig. This ain't no glamorous shit, this rock & roll. But I believed, I prayed, and I'm here." The small audience claps hard for an encore. Felice finishes in grand rock decadence, her body exhausted and bent over like a rag doll, her locks coiling around the power cables on the floor. But the moment is lost. God at the lighting board has aimed the spotlight somewhere else.

### the bass lady

Felice Rosser's mother recorded a 78-rpm record at a Woolworth's in Detroit in the 1940s, then put it in the basement for thirty years. She types letters for a judge now. Her father, a real estate broker, and her grandfather, a factory worker, only listen to country music. "Sunday nights my mother always had the radio preachers on," she says. "I told my grandmother I wanted to be a preacher, 'cause I loved the way those preachers talked. Jesus, ah huh, Jesus. They'd make those Bible stories come alive, like Elijah going up in a flaming chariot and Moses. The magnificence of it all. Then the Beatles on Ed Sullivan was the next big thing, and of course Kennedy got shot. I went on a Beatles quest for the next ten years."

Home was Russell Woods, a black middle-class enclave in Detroit. Being a too tall, too smart black girl in public school made you an easy target. Felice was shipped off to Roeper City and Country in the suburbs, where it was "okay to be smart and like rock music." At Roeper she hung out at bar mitzvahs, sang in a madrigal group, and met her first black beatnik. A first guitar came next, and at night Felice locked her bedroom door and taught herself to play Joan Baez songs.

"In 1968, the hippie movement started, and of course you didn't send your daughter to an expensive private school so she could freak out, but that's what was happening. After ninth grade I was back in public school—and just continued freaking right out. There was a whole contingent of black people who were freaking out, and white people too. We'd go see concerts a lot.

"Jethro Tull played six nights in Detroit and we went every night. Saw Zep, Sly, name it, we saw it. Only thing, we didn't see Hendrix, but we did see the Moody Blues the night he died. Hitchhiked to the Toronto Jazz and Blues Festival 'cause I was getting into the blues. I was struck by the Wolf. Something about him, he laid a vibe on me.

"At the Michigan Palace, this big rock club in Detroit, the New York Dolls changed my life. David Johansen had on these clear plastic pants and some big old clogs, and Johnny Thunders had on these really tight pants, and all this hair. It was more aggressive and glitter. Everybody was styling hard. The bass player, Arthur Kane, had broken his arm, and he was just standing on stage with this cast looking really mean, while somebody else, the roadie or something, was playing the bass. They played only two or three songs, then the P.A. broke. We were hanging around the backstage door, of course. The Dolls were long gone, but their manager was around. He said, 'Where can you get a drink in this fucking town?' It was 12:30, and I remember thinking, he wants to get a drink! I'll never forget that. I *had* to go to New York."

Anthropology, Faulkner, and reggae awaited Felice at Barnard. Her literary magazine, *Upstart*, published classmates Jim Jarmusch, Luc Sante, and Darryl Pinckney. (Pinckney's novel, *High Cotton*, has a character etched allegedly from Felice's life: The black girl in Paris with the white boyfriends.) She remembers being "totally unconscious on a black tip. I just wanted to have fun and go to concerts. I didn't know the world was such a racist place until I started going on job interviews." Felice made her way downtown eventually, to Indian food on Sixth Street and new kinds of rock, mainly Patti Smith and Television. Rock in Detroit had meant large arenas. At CBGB she found out the music could be personal (though still loud, fast, and guitar based). And punk was saying anyone could do it.

Felice took punk at its word. But first, senior year abroad (digging Arabic music in Paris and London punk) and dead-end secretarial work for CBS Records (she was "passed to black music" because the rock music department wouldn't hire her). Then she headed downtown for good. Felice jammed with fellow East Villagers like painter Jean Michel Basquiat, who made clarinet music into "pure noise." Deerfrance, a good friend who worked the door at CBGB's, played guitar, so Felice picked up bass. The bands piled up: Cargo, V. (after the Thomas Pynchon novel), the Blue Picts, the Wild Wild West. In between all this came a book contract with Simon & Schuster and a move back to Paris to work on her novel. The novel is still unfinished—the music snatched her away.

By 1987 Felice had done two years in a "real musician's gig," an all-women reggae band based in Brooklyn. She was exploring Rasta, letting her hair dread, and learning more about her instrument. The band was nurturing and she loved the music, but those power chords were calling. After being told for years she couldn't sing, that she had a "sixties voice," Felice made three brave moves: ignored everything, allowed her musical souls to copulate, and started her own band.

### fem-rock, not

A Marshall amp is dressed in a Marcus Garvey scarf and a belt of cowrie shells. Botanica candles are burning onstage. Faith the rock band is honoring Malcolm X this evening, February 21, 1991, on the twenty-sixth anniversary of his murder. There's no announcement. This is just something between the man and Faith. Felice has other concerns to get loud about. Tonight's gig at the Knitting Factory made the *Village Voice* as a weekly choice, though the band is close to livid about its assigned moniker. The bass lady grabs the mike close as a security blanket. "Contrary to *Village Voice* opinion, we are not a fem-rock band. We've got two very handsome young black men up here. And I'm not a fem, I'm not a butch, and I'm not a bitch. I don't know what I am." Rene stomps the pedal and lets loose a Molotov cocktail of distortion. Faith is gonna play hard tonight.

What fem-rock is, we don't know, but Felice has made it clear it's not her cup of goldenseal. There's friction within Faith about what a band led by a woman should symbolize. (Diana thinks it's "unfortunate" that a woman leading a band should be seen as exceptional.) This isn't so much ambivalence about feminism, though womanism would probably be the preferred term, as it is a feeling that the band shouldn't be colonized by any flag.

Leaving behind straight reggae in the eighties, Felice also left the concept of an all-women unit. It'd be easier to get a deal if Faith were a girl group—there's a market niche for that. But Faith's gender balance is something all the musicians revel in and want to uphold. Rene talks about the "perfect chemistry" of the band in terms of male/female, lightness/heaviness, soft vocals over hard guitar and drums—and how the soft/hard dynamic doesn't always break down by gender.

This symmetry certainly sets Faith off from the rigid gender divide in black popular music. Arrested Development breaks through this too, but band leader Speech still stands as the father figure/swami of the hip-hop commune. In Faith you have a strong woman, leading a band of men and women, and no one's energy is diminished because of it. We may assume the reality of this in our own lives. In pop imagery, though, it's a new moving picture, and a statement in itself; one that counters all sorts of au courant artifacts of black men and women lunging at each other like cannibal pit bulls.

The gender breakdown is also the root of the band's under-stated but rushing sensuality. Malu Halasa, president of the unoffi-cial Faith fan club, is still trying to nail it: "It's not lick-my-dick rock. It's not the Victoria's Secret catalog. It's more the kind of sensuality and sexuality that real people have. 'Earthy' sounds too much like Janis Joplin. It's earthy and steamy too. I mean, look at Rene. If that's not walking hot sex, I don't know what is. Look at Felice: She's wild, she's beautiful, she's distinctive. They drive ev-eryone insane with their adrenaline. It's almost like they can see the future."

The yin yang of Faith notwithstanding, the music is pushing some womanist science, whether band members articulate this off-stage or not. Women in the audience connect with obvious, loud pleasure to Felice running the show. (Songs are dedicated to Blanche DuBois and Winnie Mandela, but also to Magic Johnson and the "brothers in prisons.") They get happy over Diana and Felice's between-song call and response. This is typical: Rattling her bracelets, the bass lady coos, "I got to take some of this shit off. If you're a girl you've got to have this stuff. It happens all the time, your heels get stuck in the street. We women gotta do what we gotta do." Diana answers with a line from the black girl's canon of nurs-ery rhymes, "Bra too tight, booty shaking from left to right." Women also hook into the songs, most written by Felice: about affairs with younger men, self-reliance, being in love and in power struggle, and the wear and tear of love games on your ego. These offer up a complex portrait of black femininity. Usually we come off as all powerful or all vulnerable in pop music. Felice seems to say we negotiate both verities.

In the band's rehearsal space, with a wooden bass on her thigh, Felice talks about bringing a new sensuality to the pop panorama, where the ruling black female icons are the sequined R&B queen or the desexed folk singer. Felice doesn't find the focus on sadomasochism in music these days to be transgressing any taboos, or even much of a turn on. She's after a "comfortable, mystic sensuality" that she finds in the imagery of "southern blues," a legacy from her grandmother, who eloped to Detroit from Georgia. But this doesn't mean gingham dresses: "I want to rock, and I want to rock hard, so I'm not gonna be wearing flimsy outfits and fancy clothes. I just want to wear pants 'cause you can rock hard in pants. I can't stand there with no dress on and my legs open. You know, I gotta do stuff with my legs."

"My whole life I never thought I was beautiful," Felice continues, her voice quieter now. "I was too tall, too dark, nose too big. But musicians are always talking about rectifying past lives. This is what I'm doing, I guess. This music makes me feel beautiful. I love how sexy the bass sounds. I'm finding out more and more, it's nothing you can buy. Before these shows I used to run around the Lower East Side, going crazy with my little twenty dollars 'cause I had to get a shirt or something for the gig. But now I realize that there's nothing you can buy, 'cause I bought everything, and it didn't work for me."

Rene joins Felice in the studio and the two trade off images of black women in music like baseball cards. Rene: "What about Chaka Khan, Aretha, Billie Holiday?" Felice: "Yeah, Billie Holiday. There was that sense of her own self-exploration. Chaka Khan has that too, but Billie Holiday! To a society that denies that we as black women have an inner life, Billie Holiday said, This is how I think, this how I speak, this is how I look. She wasn't just a natural sister, she was *magic.*" Watching Felice move (with the awkward grace of an antelope), and speak (in that Detroit, up South, "ed-ju-macated," Village-hipster drawl of hers), and sing (with that richly textured voice of blues and triumph), you get some of that magic too.

### the man from sulfur-8

Into the Chinese restaurant on lower Broadway came walking hot sex. Rock imp Rene Akan is picking at his egg foo young and reminiscing about superheroes. The homemade kind, with names like Supersonic, the Human Fly, and Sulfur-8 (after the hair pomade). These were his confidantes, growing up in the Williamsburg section of Brooklyn, an oddball, gifted kid in a family of Jehovah's Witnesses. Rebellion snuck up with adolescence. Soon he was hanging with white kids from Brooklyn Heights and hopping trains bound for Washington Square Park.

"I started cutting school to check out the street musicians. There was this one wicked guitar player with a lazy eye playing Hendrix stuff and Santana. Since forever, I have been into Santana. That tone on 'Black Magic Woman'! From the time I was seven, I knew that was the way a guitar was supposed to sound. You hear one note, and that becomes your note for life."

Rene made it through high school and went to work for the phone company. Nights he studied political science at Hunter College. At twenty-one and still sheltered in many ways, he happened upon *The Autobiography of Malcolm X*. The raging had only begun. It continued with the Michael Stewart and Eleanor Bumpurs murders, and the Move bombing in Philly. Arrested for standing on the wrong street corner with the wrong attitude, he spent three days in jail: "I knew I needed another outlet. I got into guitars in a heavy way, lost my job." Slapped with probation for playing "Voodoo Chile" on the roof of Hunter, Rene split college too. He was drafted into a reggae band fronted by a bass player who was once a roadie for the Bad Brains. Rene stayed for a while, then moved on to East Village hardcore.

"I was playing with this band of Ukrainian guys, then went to one guy's house and found out he was a Klansman. That was bizarre. I was doing this hardcore thing, but getting into all sorts of other music: Fripp, Eno, African music, the blues. What I dug about hardcore is that it's visceral. Something about that fuzz and that chunky sound. But in terms of the content, I thought it was kinda stupid. I wanted a voice for the guitar that could pull together all the different types of music I heard in my head."

Wanted: Guitarist for a reggae-rock band. Rene answered Felice Rosser's classified ad in the *Voice* in November 1987. "An hour after auditions were supposed to begin, time I was paying for, Rene comes strolling in with his ripped-up clothes and a little hat," Felice remembers. "Everyone else was dressed nicely. I said, Who is this person, he's late and all. Well, Rene plugged in and started playing the blues like Muddy Waters. Four notes in, I said, that's my guy."

Rene's in full regalia today: a magician's top hop (missing the top, so out sprout, very coyly, his dreads), his metal-boy and Afro-chic talismans, combat boots, and tuxedo tails. On the iron horse to Brooklyn he's railing about the image politics of rock & roll. You should look at the musicians-wanted classifieds sometime, they all say "image important" or "long hair a must," he yells. "Not only is Faith out here, not really playing reggae and not really playing rock, but we don't look the part. Not just Felice and Diana as women, but me as a guy. I'm not blond. I don't look like Slash or Lenny Kravitz either. I'm a dark-skinned man. How are they gonna package me as a guitar god?"

### nubian soundbite

The Gods, the young ones from the Five Percent Nation (and those who like to style as if), are being frisked with metal detectors. They've come to see their boys, Brand Nubian, rising sons of East Coast hip-hop, at Wetlands in lower Manhattan. This is Black History Month, 1991.

With Gods packed in so tight, there's little breathing room in this small club. The opening band—yet another lost tribe of aboriginals—files onstage and jaws drop like dominoes. Felice and Diana have their locks crimped. It's a look that melds love child Lisa Bonet and Medusa, and it leaves the baby-faced Gods scratching their baseball caps. When Felice straps on her bass, a God shrieks, giddy with disbelief, "Oh, shit!" His boys in the back fall out.

Having started rowdy, the crowd keeps it up. (One God blows smoke straight at Felice's throat for the entire set.) But the music creeps up on them. Bodies are moving, just a bit, as if Gods don't want other Gods to know they're really down with such weirdness. Before "Cosmic Slop," Faith's parting anthem, Rene, who rarely talks on stage, grabs Diana's mike and shouts, "Rock & roll is black music!" The Gods, who can dig nationalism packaged in any torch song, roar.

Rap shows being short, the club asks Faith to play a second set following Brand Nubian. The crowd is down to a handful; most are Faith junkies, bohos of all creeds and colors, though a few Gods are hanging too. Felice, who never sways from under her constant halo of light-love-humanism, prefaces her younger-man song with a smile and story. "A little God," yes he did, tried to rap to her between sets. Diana isn't impressed. Introducing "Cosmic Slop," she plays a nursery rhyme on the keyboard. "Hey, Mommie," she whines along, doing her best God imitation, "What's a Funkadelic?"

## on keys

Diana Baker's got a bachelorette pad in Alphabet City. She calls herself "an African woman living on the Lower East Side," so you'll know the difference between her and everyone else slumming in their renovated flats. Hers in an old building on a block known for crack traffic. A sign in the hallway warns tenants not to let their kids eat the rat poison.

Like the rest of the band, Diana comes from middle-class or aspiring folks who preached hard work and education—and had fabulous record collections. And same as the others, she did higher education, East Village rock & roll, and, along with Felice and Rene, Rasta. Diana grew up in Pontiac, Michigan, and South Plainfield, New Jersey, the only child of a schoolteacher and a jazz musician. (Her father, who passed when she was young, played tuba in the Air Force One band. They flew around the country with the president and played whenever he landed.) In high school she made all-county, then all-state choral groups. Her dream was to go on the road with a modern, black-boho version of the Andrews Sisters.

Back in Michigan, music wasn't as "segregated" as Diana finds New York radio to be. "Parliament-Funkadelic was the standard. Groups like Parlet and Brides of Funkenstein were enormous. We listened to jazz like folks listen to Hot 97. There was even a black radio station that played rock. That's how I found out about the Bus Boys. I thought they were huge nationally, then I came to New York."

Diana transferred from a Jersey college to the New School in Manhattan to be closer to the downtown club scene. Her family freaked out when she left school to play music and started locking her hair: "First I cut it all off. I went over to my grandmother's house. She told me how cute it looked short, but then she looked closer and said, 'But you're not combing it!' I know what Grandma was thinking, 'My God, she left college, she's not combing her hair, she's probably not bathing. The child's going to the dogs!'"

Rene brought Diana in as a singer shortly after his audition. Drummer Garry Sullivan, raised up in local Bronx metal bands, came next, answering another of Felice's classifieds. The four got on so well, they edged out their keyboard player and gave Diana the job. Faith is Diana's first band; she'll tell you every road story: from the broken-down vans to almost getting killed that time Faith's driver fell asleep at the wheel en route to Virginia for a gig with fellow rockers, also black, the Good Guys. Once Faith played a private party in Darien, Connecticut. When the music got a little loud for Darien, cops showed up to cart off the band, not the family who hired them.

Asked whether there is any image of black women in pop music that she identifies with, Diana screws up her face: "They're all Whitney Houston clones. There's not even a black woman out here with her own hair. No one is comfortable with or can sell her own image. That's the beauty of Faith, it's just us up here, we're not gimmicks in miniskirts. That's why the record companies are so scared of us. The independence we project is even scarier than the strength. They don't have any precedents for us." How about Tracy Chapman and Joan Armatrading? "They're solo artists and their music is mellow and palatable; as folk signers they're easier to package."

And what of the long line of black women "in rock": Tina Turner, Betty Davis, Pauline Black of Selecter, Rhoda Dakar and the Body Snatchers, the women of the Family Stone, Poly Styrene of X-Ray Spex, Neneh Cherry in her punk phase; and bands like Labelle and Isis; or Chaka Khan, the women of Graham Central Station, Merry Clayton, Taka Boom, Joyce Kennedy from Mother's Finest, Nona Hendryx, Grace Jones, D. K. Dyson of Eye & I? (Felice's list includes Bessie Smith and Memphis Minnie, who wrote "When the Levee Breaks," covered on *Led Zeppelin IV*). Foremothers, yes, but few and far between. Largely they've been ignored by rock criticism as innovators in the genre, and are thought of as anomalies. No one has bothered to chart lines of influence, or note that their audiences have included like-minded boho chicks. Even the BRC's revision of rock history, as quoted and mythologized by the pop-music press, leaves them out.

**mystery soundbite**

We're back at CBGB, and it's spring now. Faith is in showcase mode again, this time for Forty Acres and a Mule Musicworks, Spike Lee's new company, distributed by Columbia Records. Label director Lisa Jackson fell for the band and has brought Lee to see for himself. On stage Faith is dishing their sexy best. Felice introduces Rene as "our guitarist, the cute guy over there showing his nipples." But tonight it's the songs that really stand out. Felice's younger-man tune, "What Should I Do About You," is sweating up the bar stools. "It's a strange, strange acid life," she sings, "He was 19/She was 35/ . . . He came so quick the first time/Then they tried a second time." The band debuts a new piece, "Race," which Felice describes on mike as "the sad story of the pulling away that happens between black and white friends": "Your reality is so dif-

ferent than mine/See, they follow me around in stores/And I've
never had a job where I could use my mind/ . . . Now you call me
long distance to ask how New York City has been/But I've got
nothing to tell you/Because when we talk about race, you don't
understand."

Felice is working the hair overtime tonight, swinging it 360
degrees around her head, like Marley always did. So busy watching the hair show, some folks missed the main event. "My God,"
screeches an A&R type at the bar, "what's that growing under her
blouse?"

### heavy with child

And somewhere in between, our heroine gets pregnant. Not unlike
your period, it always happens in the middle of some painfully
important, big male moment, like standing on the verge of a record
deal after you've busted your butt for four years. Think about the
courage it took Felice to stand on that stage at CBGB, black and
pregnant, playing rock & roll, the sacred text of white-boy angst,
and being gaped at by A&R suits and skirts. And doing it in a black-
lace tunic and Lycra pants, and having the gall to announce, "Lately
I've been exploring my sensuality."

All comanager Nicole Payen had to say was, "It's lucky big tops
and leggings are in this season." The pregnancy, though unplanned,
was welcomed. Felice and Buzz had been together as a couple since
the band was born. And Felice, over twentysomething and counting, felt it was her time. The summer of 1991 was turning out to be
Faith's busiest yet. Averaging three or four shows a month, the band
stayed onstage through Felice's eighth month.

For Felice this meant not only performing, but dropping tapes,
renting vans, rehearsing, booking shows, sales clerking at HMV
Records, prenatal checkups, Lamaze classes, cleaning, cooking,
bass practice, working on songs after midnight, and combing the
city for rock & roll maternity wear.

Seth Malik arrived December 20, 1991. Seth was the third son
after Cain and Abel, a gift to his mother after hard times and trag-

edy. Malik, an Arabic name, is Buzz's contribution. It had been a long year.

## let's make a record deal

The summer of '91 also had promised a miracle. After seeing the band live, Spike Lee and Lisa Jackson were ready to sign them to Forty Acres and a Mule Musicworks. Then a snag: The A&R attachés at Columbia saw a Faith showcase shortly after and were dead against a signing. Musicworks pitched Columbia a low-budget deal, but after nine months of wrangling, it fell through too.

Lee wasn't pleased with the outcome. Faith, in Lee's opinion, "deserved to be signed." Apparently word came from as far up as Columbia president Don Ienner's office that the band had, among other things, an image problem. Says Lee, "They just didn't like the way the band looked." Lisa Jackson, who has a mane of locks herself and has been in the record business for a decade, backs Lee up: "I can't say I got this verbatim from Columbia, but this is my feeling: Columbia's biggest objection to Faith was the fact that this was a rock band led by a black female. And not only is it led by a black female, but not your typical petite rocker. They weren't prepared to promote it."

Everyone staggered back to their day jobs: Felice to the record store, Diana to teaching nursery school, Buzz to his messenger gig, Nicole to human-rights work, and Garry to playing drums in the subways and passing the hat. Rene got a new "slave," musician slang for day jobs, as a model at the Art Students League, where Charlton Heston and Madonna once bared their torsos too. The lady retirees who paint him often linger after class to inquire if he's a musician. Sometimes they even ask to touch his hair.

"One of the wildest moments," Felice remembers, "was when I read that Sinéad O'Connor was pregnant when she got signed. She actually made her record during her pregnancy. She was so glad it happened that way, she said, 'cause she felt so powerful and creative. When we started talking to Forty Acres, I was pregnant. I was thinking, great, I'll be pregnant, make my record, and have some money in my pocket. When the deal fell through, here I was with this baby coming, scrambling, thinking, how am I going to live, how am I going to survive?"

The A&R factory workers who checked out Faith must have wondered how they could sell the band as a rock rebellion fantasy to the white adolescent market when Faith's image didn't involve them. Felice, the consummate humanist, would probably disagree. Once she opened a set with a very polite, "Fuck racist white America." A white guy yelled back, "Right on!" Black folks in the audience kept silent.

Why was it easier to sell Ice Cube's letter bombs to white America these days then a band like Faith, who grew up in the college boys' backyards, went to school with them, and speaks their language? "The face of black rebellion now is KRS-One and Ice Cube," a colleague reminds me. "The powers that be have decided that that's our safe space. Even in our rebellion, motherfuckers want to ghettoize and contain us."

### faith ever more

The phone rings, it's Felice. She doesn't want the band to be portrayed as black artists victimized by the system when she herself doesn't feel like anybody's victim or anybody's cliché. The record industry isn't most people's idea of an equal opportunity wonderland, but she knows what she's up against. It took six years for Vernon Reid to get a deal for Living Colour. (Of course Reid had to be a virtuoso guitarist, make friends with Mick Jagger, and start a political movement first.) Even Funkadelic and the Beatles, Felice reminds me, were turned down many times. Hendrix had to go to England. Punk and hip-hop snuck in on small labels. It's a racist, sexist, corporate migraine, but she can handle it.

Faith has decided, in the do-it-yourself tradition, to put out their own seven-inch single and see what bites: Maybe the majors will come sniffing again, maybe more gigs, a tour. While Felice and Rene are auditioning drummers, Buzz is running around town with Seth on his back, having their DAT mastered and pressed. With

Garry's exit and deals falling through, Rene felt like the band was "hemorrhaging." This isn't just a record, says comanager Nicole, "this will be our Grammy. We're giving it to ourselves. We needed it."

"Not too many things come around in life that you really believe in." We're in Brooklyn today at Nicole's place, close to the projects in the less chic rump of Fort Greene. A Haitian-American boho in her twenties, Nicole is talking about hooking up with Faith, though she knew nothing at the time about managing a band. She saw one Faith gig and pledged her life.

"Excuse me if I'm not blond or blue-eyed, but I'm a rock & roll chick. If someone would sit down and talk to me and see who I am, it wouldn't seem so farfetched. My experience isn't the project girl, but it isn't the black middle-class girl either. And En Vogue doesn't represent me as a black woman. In fact, they represent something that I'm trying to get away from.

"Hendrix, the Doors, the Yardbirds, that's part of my culture too. All this stuff about Malcolm X is cute, but people like Faith, we're products of integrated schools and integrated neighborhoods. The civil rights laws changed the country completely. Certainly they had to expect changes in the music, which is what American popular music has been about from the get go. And we represent some of those changes.

"There's more than a record deal at stake here; this is about our lives. Are you saying my life, my experience, isn't a valid as Nirvana's or Ice Cube's? Whether or not the industry is ready to deal with *this* America, we're here. Whether or not they're ready to play it on the radio, it's being felt. And it's not gonna go away just because they don't understand it."

## subway to heaven, october 1992

"Unity and peace is pussy and soft/Black people don't like white people/And white people don't like black people/And I guess that's the way we want it." This is a warning from Bushmon, a post–Fishbone, post–Living Colour type of crew on stage at Space at Chase, a bar near NYU's village campus. They look just out of high school, these guys, some with dreads, some not. The drummer's Asian, another kid's a rainbow baby. Quite the new world order rock band.

Bushmon is sharing the bill tonight. Faith is like an old guard to this set, and there's a sadness to that, given the band still hasn't made it to the promised land yet. This gig is something of a test. It's their first since Garry's departure and they're anxious. When Felice makes it to her knee-deep blues, the worries pass. The groupies are worshiping at Rene's wah-wah pedal. Diana and Felice's harmonies wrap over and around each other like silk ribbons. Faith tonight is larger than the missed record deals and the lost drummers. Much, much larger.

The band is on my mind, as usual, on the train back to Brooklyn. There's an ad for Virginia Slims across from me. It pictures a petite rocker, in the Bananarama vein, with a flashy new red guitar, not like Felice's muddy brown thing patched with gaffer's tape. "Life's like rock and roll," the ad tells us. "It's more fun when you take the lead." I want to deface it and write, "Rock supremacist pigs and your impossibly slender-hipped, female mirrors DIE." But I don't. I've got Faith.

*1992*

For information on Faith, contact Lionhearted Management, 17900 Goddard, Detroit, Michigan 48212.

# the invisible ones

The silent witness I carried with me throughout the Thomas/Senate/Bush *v.* Hill showdown was the judge's sister, Emma Mae Martin. In Pin Point, Georgia, that Moon River township we now know so well from the legends told of her brother's great escape, Martin still lives in poverty. She supports three of her four children and one son's pregnant fiancée on her salary as a hospital cook. Her run-down frame house has a hole in the roof.

You might know the judge's sister through his now infamous public castigation of her as a welfare dependent ("She gets mad when the mailman is late with her welfare check"). He used sis as an example of all-gone-wrong with liberal handouts and civil rights leadership. Serving up such a portrait of his sister turned out to be a shrewd career move for Thomas. It was this speech, made to a conference of black conservatives in 1980, that caught Reaganite ears and led to Thomas's quick ascent in the Reagan/Bush new American order. Though his comments came back to haunt him briefly during the confirmation process, they were buried under the pile of issues dug up by Hill's harassment charge.

In the scramble to get to the bottom of Thomas, a few journalists talked to his sister. Not surprisingly, the story of Martin's life as told by Martin offered quite a different picture from Thomas's soundbite. No welfare addict, Martin was forced to seek assistance during a family crisis, a common scenario for women. Married with kids right out of high school, her man walked out on her. While Thomas was at Yale Law School in the early seventies, Martin worked two minimum-wage jobs to support her children. When an elderly aunt who minded the kids suffered a stroke, Martin left work to care for both aunt and children. With her meager income and no child support, she found, as many women do, she couldn't afford a nursing home and child care. Welfare was a last resort. After four and a half years on public assistance, Martin returned to the work force. She reports to her hospital job most days at 3:00 A.M.

Martin's story becomes an even more telling parable of women and the poverty cycle once you find out that her life has mirrored her mother's. Leola Williams was also left by her husband with three young children to support. She got by picking crabs at five cents a pound; then came a crisis—fire destroyed her home and possessions. With an extended family in place, Williams was able to manage without welfare. She sent Thomas and his brother to live with their grandfather, Martin to stay with her aunt, and worked as a live-in housekeeper for rich whites. Today she's a nurse's aide at the same hospital where her daughter cooks.

Martin isn't a typecast welfare queen sucking the nation dry, as Thomas seemed to suggest, but a single woman like his own mother, who worked low-paying jobs without benefits to support her family and turned to relatives for help. (Where was Thomas, the lawyer, the federal agency chair, when his sister fell on hard times?) Thomas's distortion of his sister's life says a lot about him, yet it says even more about America. No child- or health-care system, dead-end jobs, dysfunctional schools, yes. But what of the political and media value put on the lives of women like Martin? Especially black women like Martin. The Martins of this country are pigeon-holed as sub-American, subfemale, and often—in renditions of the new crack-addicted underclass—dangerous and subhuman.

It's not just women like Martin who are ignored, stereotyped, and often scapegoated, it's families like Martin's. Among African Americans, single women head nearly half of all families. And over two-thirds of all black children under eighteen are being raised in these households below the poverty line. Poverty figures come not just from income, but from an individual's "dependency burden." Less discussed than the cost of children is the cost of care for elderly relatives. When old ones fall sick, it's the women of the family who care for them at the expense of their own personal ambitions. (And in most African-American families, for financial and cultural reasons, this care-taking happens at home.) It's the Emma Mae Martin syndrome. While Thomas was pulling himself up by the bootstraps, *self*-helping himself, Martin took care of auntie, because who else would? And for this, he calls her a welfare queen.

Law professor Patricia King was among those who gave testimony opposing Thomas at the confirmation hearings. King's statement centered around Martin and Thomas's ignorance or willingness to overlook the compounded hardships faced by women like his sister. Her remarks were treated summarily by the committee. Others raised the Martin issue, but it fell on deaf ears. Legal scholar Kimberlé Crenshaw made the point in a roundtable discussion in the journal *Tikkun*, only to be countered by Catharine McKinnon, who argued that gender shouldn't be the only factor in the Left's criticism of Thomas. This was a month before Anita Hill and sexual harassment, perhaps to some a more appealing "middle-class" women's issue than welfare rights.

Mainstream media circulated Thomas's nasty cliché of his sister as ammunition against his nomination. For the most part, though, the cliché was left undisturbed. The failure to look behind the stereotype sanctioned it. Scarier than the idea that Martin and women like her are disregarded—by Thomas, by the country, by the press—is how easy it is to disregard them. Who pickets, who lobbies, who screams? Used as a cutout for both pro- and anti-Thomas arguments, Martin remained just that.

As Emma Mae Martin was rendered invisible, so was Anita Hill, though in a more enigmatic way. Hers is the "postmodern variation on black women's 'silence' " Michele Wallace names in *Invisibility Blues*—in the frame, yet only when uncritical or mute. This is ironic when you realize that in the last month Hill has been the most visible and discussed African-American woman since Tawana Brawley. (This shows you, more representation, more screen time, doesn't always translate into more power.) Discredited for speaking as a woman and as a black person, Hill was rendered invisible as both. Looking for positive fallout from the hearing, many said that the black professionals on parade made appealing role models. And Anita Hill—shunning victimhood, though somewhat reluctantly—is admirable. Yet what happened to Hill sent a more forceful message than her face on the tube: Speaking out doesn't pay. A harassed woman is still a double victim, and a vocal, critical black woman is still a traitor to the race.

Despite his loud and repeated insistence that he was being persecuted by stereotypes, Thomas and the committee did more than any gangsta rapper to refocus attention on rancid formulas of black femininity. The stereotypes that blanketed Hill were far more insidious and destructive than the Big Black Dick myth that Thomas shouldered, a comic image kept alive by the pornography that he allegedly consumes. Try the Black Bitch—the emasculating matriarch, calculating and bitter. Or her younger sister, the male-deprived black professional woman caught in a "fantasy," as if the reality of a relationship with a man like Thomas, his sexual interest in her, or potential to be threatened by her were beyond her intrinsic worth.

Or the Handicapped Intellectual. Often Hill's legal education, powers of reason, and ability to articulate herself were on trial or the source of curious, as in disbelieving, interest. Or the Black Woman With a Color Complex. You might not have caught this stereotype as it zoomed by so fast. Thomas went so far as to speculate at one point in the hearing that Hill's motive for depriving him of his natural right to sit on the Supreme Court was her jealousy that he dated a light-skinned woman and promoted one at the EEOC.

There was also the Sexually Available Woman prototype, the one we can't shake. After all it was practically legal to rape a black woman up until the second half of this century, and still remains, as recent New York cases and media coverage attest, less newsworthy a crime. In an exquisitely backward op-ed in the *Times,* sociologist Orlando Patterson defended the alleged harassment as a "down-home style of courting" done while Thomas had his "mainstream cultural guard down." Thomas, Patterson argued, "may have done something completely out of the cultural frame of his white, upper-middle-class work world, but immediately recognizable to Professor Hill."

The battle of Hill/Thomas also taught us how invisible we (black) women are as black people. It's always been our burden: The community depends on our silence, and "race" is often used by our brethren to keep us from speaking critically. When we do, we're tagged as agents of the oppressor, devaluing anything we have to say as coming from a black perspective, from black people. Among its many achievements, what the Thomas/Bush lynch strategy did was promote male experience as the only black experience. (More working black folks saw prime-time Thomas than daytime Hill. And after Thomas's lynch speech, support for him among African Americans, according to *Time,* jumped from 60 to 70 percent.) But if we wanted to reduce history likewise: Was not the "rape" of Anita Hill by this process a definitive black experience?

A young civil rights lawyer confided to me recently that the Thomas hearings were the source of the most painful experience in her professional life. A month before Hill, she did an anti-Thomas teach-in on WLIB along with influential black New Yorkers, among them *Amsterdam News* publisher William Tatum and State Senator David Patterson. Callers were supportive of her. A day after Hill's allegations were made public, she was invited on WLIB again, this time with three other female lawyers. The lawyers didn't say unequivocally that Hill was telling the truth, only that she deserved to be heard. The tone of the call-ins changed radically. The panel was vilified. The word "feminist" was a curse worse than "bitch" and associated with female shame and the betrayal of black men. The last caller, a woman, said that the community should be happy that Thomas went after a black woman.

Some of the most virulent anti-Hill voices I heard during the hearings came from black women. But this hostility is easy to trace: Who loves or abhors a black woman more than another black woman? The little value we have for one another is yet another enabler of our invisibility. What's the source of this? We rarely see each other in positions of power, know few role models. For those of us who are heterosexual, media images have us fighting over what statistics warn is a dwindling supply of black men. The old "I'll cut you if you look twice at my man" posture is trotted out in every film from *Pinky* to *Livin' Large*. (At Thomas's swearing in, John Doggett III, the man you'd think would be every black woman's worst enemy, was pounced on by young women after his autograph.)

In the middle of the Hill/Thomas live-action morality play, I accompanied a friend to an abortion clinic. The assisting nurse, a black woman, chatted on as she hooked my friend's legs into the stirrups. She disagreed with Thomas's politics, yet didn't believe Hill one iota. Why? Just didn't trust her. Certainly lingering beyond the hearings is the stench of our distrust for one another. Those who know how sisterhood saves have a heavy responsibility to pull women of the "Video Music Box" generation up by the garter straps. Raised on video's business-as-usual violence against women, they have, as a shield, internalized distrust of other women in ways that seem unparalleled in my adult life.

Black women need feminism more than ever. Who else, after all, has a stake in our visibility—in an affirming community, in our power and representation—but ourselves and all those children we're raising? The cost of blind race loyalty will be our lives. With the Thomas nomination and hearings, Bush has set an ugly new standard for cunning manipulation of race and the black community. No doubt he'll continue to do the slick thing, vetoing legislation like the Family Leave Act and an unemployment benefits bill while pulling the wool over our eyes with opportunistically black politicos like Thomas.

That Anita Hill spoke at all, despite efforts made every step of the way to deny her voice, despite the mud or the consequences, was in the spirit, I'd like to think, of an older, more valiant generation. How many more African-American women, though, share Emma Mae Martin's story? Educational and economic barriers and the weight of family responsibility keep us silent, keep us from challenging the political process and discourse that boxes in our lives. Though absent from the harassment proceedings, at the confirmation hearing Martin sat behind her brother, head bowed. Whatever personal hurt she felt from his public smear of her was submerged, as she closed ranks with the family. Martin's family loyalty seems analogous to what race loyalty often means for black women: protecting the honor of men and the race before self.

What we have to realize as African-American women is that gender is not just a "self" issue. We are the community. (With the great numbers of female heads of household living below the poverty line, we definitely are the underclass.) It's on us to challenge the community with our concerns. Given the state of civil rights organizing now—its vacuum of leadership, lack of agenda, and loss of target constituency—this is an ideal moment for black women to create a popular movement to fill the void.

Working through existing channels could be a start. Last July the National Association of Black Journalists elected its first woman president, as well as four women to a five-member executive board, through the clout of a two-thirds-female membership. In her acceptance speech, new president Sidmel Estes-Sumptner, an Atlanta television producer, told the group she was putting the newsrooms of America on notice about their hiring practices. "They haven't heard from a black woman before. Especially not a black woman from the South," said Estes-Sumptner, bringing the women in the convention hall to their feet, hands in the air and far from silent.

*1991*

# she came with the rodeo

I come with a dowry. Four boxes of props, most notably a construction hat, plastic pork chops, and several unused diaphragms poked with holes. Two boxes of costumes, among them a half-dozen pairs of black leggings well worn at the crotch. One box of faded press releases announcing the Rodeo Caldonia High-Fidelity Performance Theater. An album of photographs showing young women outfitted as urban witch doctors in faux-leopard skirts, lace veils, and the occasional cowrie-shell ankle bracelet. A black leather motorcycle jacket brought brand-new for twenty dollars from a junkie on Astor Place—its side pockets now caked with bits of Jolly Rancher water-

melon candy and missed birth control pills, its breast pocket permanent home to a small tin of rum raisin lip gloss, a New York City
subway token from 1986, and a crumbled copy of the last page of
Shange's *Spell #7*. The play's final line is circled in red: "crackers
are born with the right to be alive/i'm making ours up right here in
your face/& we gonna be colored & love it."

I am a Caldonia and these are some of my personal effects.

We decided against the Warm Leatherettes and took Caldonia, fancying the inheritance of B. B. King and sundry blues songs that told
of "hardheaded" brown girls with pretty lips. Caldonia, B. B. sings,
why is your big head so hard? A rodeo brought folks together to stir
up dust. Shange herself had moved to Texas and was riding bare-
back. We were impressed. Rodeo Caldonia, it was. Twelve women,
sometimes more, in our twenties and giddy with our own possibility. We were gonna do theater. Performance pieces we were calling
them. We didn't care much about genres and structures and things.
Our need was to get out in public and act up; to toss off the
expectations laid by our genitals, our melanin count, and our college degrees. Rodeo heralded our arrival: young, gifted, black, and
weird (so we thought), and in search of like souls.

*We splurge on a cab to carry props. Me, Celina, Derin, and our
caravan of shopping bags and backpacks. First stop at a drugstore to
buy spray paint and Tampax, then to Sweetwaters to do Carmella &
King Kong in the basement. We have nerve to knock egos with R&B
supper club legend Arthur Prysock. His people get mad at us for
taking up too much dressing room space. In the hallway we run lines
as the guests arrive. Suited-up black folks from the upstairs, up-class
Sweetwaters come watch our show, along with our dread and Lycra
friends from downtown. The Uptowns snicker and squirm. But we
are hardly studying them; this is for us. After the show Prysock's
henchmen ban us from the dressing room, so we gather instead in the
tiny ladies john. Wasn't Sandye's eye rolling absolutely brilliant?
How did Candace manage to give La Josephine and valley girl all at*

*once? We are the most beautiful women in the world. Art, says Nan
Goldin, is about leaving a record no one can revise. We are not
thinking of hereafters. Art is how we love ourselves now.*

In the summer of 1985 I took a trip with my sister Kellie to the
Virgin Islands, where we had some meaningful exchanges with local
gigolos on the beach. My sister's a curator and art historian and she
suggested I write a piece based on our encounters, a performance
work to go along with the latest exhibition she was organizing, this
one at an old schoolhouse turned alternative art space in the Bronx.
The exhibition, "In the Tropics," was to examine the Caribbean's
image as playpen of the Americas for some, and as hometown for
others. At the time "my writing" consisted of a few record reviews
and a short story published under a pseudonym in a college literary
magazine. Kellie kept insisting I had that elusive thing called a
"voice" that would lend itself to more ambitious work. I doubted
this, though I took her invitation anyway, and came up with something that didn't quite fit the bill, but was what I had on my mind at
the time. *Carmella & King Kong,* billed as "an act of jungle love," is
the story of pagan goddess Carmella who falls in love with Sepia
dawg Kong and loses, among other things, her mind.

*Carmella* became a performance piece, whatever that means, a
play with photographs, shown as slides projected on a screen above
the stage. The stage in this case happened to be the hallway of the
old schoolhouse. I got together some actresses and singers I knew,
or really young women aching to be, and put the thing on, which
meant directed, carted props, cleaned up, and played financier on
my two-cents-above-minimum-wage salary as a copy editor. The
exchange of energy and kinship had to continue, so us young
women aching to be proclaimed ourselves a group and kept going.

For such a grand name, Rodeo Caldonia High-Fidelity Performance Theater, we had a small repertoire: two theater pieces written by me, *Carmella & King Kong* and *Combination Skin,* and one
poetry revue, *Welcome to the Black Aesthetic,* that never made it to
the stage, though was quite the out-of-body spiritual experience to

rehearse. Probably our most significant contribution to the world of performing arts was us roaming the streets as a pack, showing up at parties, and talking race, sex, and hair into the night over Celina's barbecue wings and Donna's guacamole. A kind of traveling conceptual art piece on black female representation, in which Diana Ross's whine matters as much as Mary McLeod Bethune's institution building. We kept the Rodeo together for two years, from 1986 to 1988, then hit the road alone.

*With my body on fire. We are now booked at Sweetwaters' basement for the entire month of August. Tonight is my birthday. The Caldonias bring out a plastic gag cake and the whole basement sings. Look at me, smiling and sweating; me, ravenously horny with cheeks flush red. We hide our props in a utility closet hoping no one will notice and trash them. We head downtown. There's a surprise party at Mom's. The gold earrings from Derin mean so much, I know how tight money is these days. We are always going someplace else, with our pedal-pusher pants and naps on display, and our dangling earrings and men's oxfords. Head further downtown. The secret lover has thrown a party at a squatter's loft in my honor. The Caldonias dance together in a circle, laughing loud and showing off. Lover eyes me from a corner where he works the turntables. Can there be another, another, just another night, I say, please.*

Presenting, the Caldonias. The empress of 'tude Celina Davis, dancer/writer/director, runs ground control and protects us from wolves in sheep's dreads. Derin Young, singer/songwriter, is 100 percent adrenaline uncut. Our resident coquette, Candace Hamilton, does Marilyn mopped up with a biscuit and a side of collards. Lorna Simpson is simply the most beautiful woman west of Dakar and north of Papeete. Her photographs, with their silences and whispers, inspire us to bring our own secrets to the art. Donna Berwick translates big ideas into costumes with little explanation. A trained actress with a capital T, Sandye Wilson gives us a healthy dose of grief for being laissez-faire about theater form. We adopt sixteen-year-old actress Amber Villenueva as our baby girl. Kellie

Jones, advance squad, cooks a mean fried porgy and spreads the word about the shows. Actress Raye Dowell and her ingenious sense of style (Negress flower child roams the diaspora while reading biographies of Frida Kahlo) are the impetus for many a Caldonia to practice dress-up as daily performance art. (A look Raye made classic: a Black Power button stuck on a floppy, resort-wear hat. The effect: Baps do revolution too.) Our most accomplished craftsperson onstage, Pamala Tyson, gives big sister and class clown. Alva Rogers becomes our mascot. Her haunting indigo beauty is "ancient to the future," like the arias of Art Ensemble of Chicago. Alva's sheer presence and her singing, a blend of opera, jazz, blues, and nursery rhyme, always explain us better than any motto.

We are joined at times by artist Alice Norris, hat designer Suzanne Kelly, and actress Daphne Rubin-Vega, and later by Stephanie and Suzanne Jones, twin turks of parody. But we remain a constant: Smart-ass girls with a sense of entitlement, who avail ourselves of the goods of two continents, delight in our sexual bravura, and live womanism as pleasure, not academic mandate. Ten years earlier, when most Caldonias were just graduating junior high, Shange had told black women to find God in themselves. We are the prodigal daughters come home to roost. Lots of lip and shorter hemlines.

*Derin's mom taught her Yoruba songs in their apartment in East New York. Derin went to Stuyvesant, the brainy-kid public high school. She majored in political science like I did. Thought she was gonna be lawyer too, but ended up singing. Vicious Deenie I call her, 'cause she talks as fast as she thinks: subway vibrations as music; hidden messages of cartoon theme songs; a racist master plan coded in Social Security numbers; the splendor of black velvet against brown skin. Ironman calls her the Last African Virgin. It's her eyes. The eyes of a princess sold by her tribe to the slavers. Old eyes.*

A cherished keepsake of Rodeo is that it was, without premeditation on our part, a walking tableau of diva complexity. Each eccentric self and artistic point of departure—from the composer of fabulist slow jams (Derin) to the collard Marilyn (Candace)—made possible one's own. We didn't come together around a rigid ideology or fixed notion of black identity. We came simply to break bread and share our yearnings. And in this common space, each found her own voice, her own funk.

Black men had jazz and athletics, places where dignity, auteurship, and creative exploration were possible despite the barbwire elsewhere. Where were such collective spaces for black women? African Americans have a regal history of solitary divas. Pick any number of great artists—Josephine Baker, Billie Holiday, Adrienne Kennedy—they made amazing work in isolation or under the wing of white patronage or in a community of men. And, yes, there were the quilting circles and the club meetings and the antilynching activist groups and Madame C.J's cadre of beauticians. The girl groups of the sixties made their mark (though as a whole, they were more prefab vehicle than acts of woman genius). The literature had its own matrilineage. But where were the women who made mad, reckless, and twisted music, dance, and theater together? Who told of longings other than the arrival and departure of characters called "my man"? Or invested these arrivals and departures with a deeper echo?

Later on we found out about the International Sweethearts of Rhythm, *dames de couleur* in a blazing swing band from the forties; and the social protest folk of Sweet Honey and the Rock born in the seventies; and the poetry-theater jam sessions of Jessica Hagedorn, Thulani Davis, and Ntozake Shange in the early eighties; and found contemporaries, like choreographer Jawole Willa Jo Zollar and her company Urban Bush Women, who slam-dance to the squeaky dream songs of writer/performer Laurie Carlos. So "we the wild girls," as Alva Rogers called us in her swan song to Rodeo written in 1989, were not alone after all.

Critics were convinced that women responded to *For Colored Girls* only because it spoke loud about black male sexism and ended with a man throwing his children out the window, which said critics read as a declaration of war against all black men. But the real thrill, the visceral thrill of *For Colored Girls,* was those seven women characters, in their matching dresses, each in a color of her own, carrying on in their girl language in their all-girl space. Have you ever stomped with a drill team? Played jacks? Jumped double dutch? Or been grateful enough just to turn the double-dutch rope? Put on makeup in a bathroom crowded with Kabuki dolls? Out-switched and out-sang the Supremes, the Ronettes, or the Vandellas, casting yourself as Diana and your two best girlfriends as Flo and Mary? If not, you just haven't lived. Men end up by default of imagination being the justification for these acts of bliss. Like they say in jazz, "He thought it was about him." And he was wrong.

*Donna and Lorna together. Friends for ages from Queens who found their way to the Rodeo. Their sign language is all raised eyebrows and pursed lips. They converse in an intricate syncretic dialect of Queens b-girl, art criticism, and haute couture–speak known only to sets of Silent Twins. Them giggling and leaning against each other expresses all that I love about being a colored girl. They are always in conspiracy; a whisper, a poke, then Lorna's belly laugh and Donna's tee-hees. Lorna's skin is seamless brown silk, Donna's all cream. Their difference in color is minus the familiar divide of privilege and shame and seems to exist just for our looking pleasure. They must know how beautiful they are side by side; they cannot contain their good fortune to be, as Nel longs for Sula, girls together. Thick as thieves, rushing boys' hearts with a glance. If we all could be like Donna and Lorna, girls together.*

With Rodeo I was able to dig out that voice Kellie was so certain I had. It surprised me when I did find it. It is a laughing voice, impudent, at times even sinister. Not at all, some say when they meet me, like me, a short girl who is polite to old people and painfully shy. In the company of the Caldonias I become a rogue. Our call and response is lusty and loud. I begin to write thinking of Rodeo as my audience, not, as I had done before, the gray bosses at work, gray professors at university, gray poets of the textbooks. This frees me, I feel at the time, to say and do anything.

*Talk about blue lights in the basement. We were witnesses tonight. Saw this power hovering above, we actually saw it. A blue magnetic field. Freaky-deaky. A visit from ancestresses or something. Alva, as Carmella, and Sandye, as Torch Singer, took the spirit and rocked. Had a table reserved for Gramma and Aunt Cora. They got stuck in Jersey traffic and missed the show. Sweetwaters agreed to let us do the entire thing all over again just for Gramma. Must've been her silver Afro and the way she strut into the joint like it was a meeting of the Phillis Wheatley Literary Society. I did hide behind the bar while Derin and Amber, as Beautietta and the Twilights, set up the voodoo pyre with those diaphragms next to that Alice Walker datebook and those plastic watermelon harmonicas, but Gramma and Aunt Cora laughed for days. Those Sweetwaters people must think we're très weird. Our boyfriends don't comb their hair. Derin's running around calling herself the reincarnation of Lieutenant Uhura. Alva mainly stays to herself munching on blue corn chips and reading* Black Women in Nineteenth-Century American Life. *And there's Candace, always trying to sell the bartenders antique jewelry or Jamaican cupcakes, then getting onstage as Princess Pamela the restauranteuse in those polka-dot spike heels, waving plastic pork chops around and talkin' 'bout the affair she's having with Idi Amin.*

Satire was a large part of the voice I found in Rodeo. As I saw it back then, satire made possible both a celebratory and critical dialogue with one's self and the world. I got to disarm the pain and dance away triumphant. I never studied it formally, but found it in steady supply in my Rodeo cronies. Pamala Tyson's *Soul Train* locker-dancer interpretations told a minihistory of black gesture and dance, of coonery in bed with racial pride, of elegance and the persecution of those who measured uncool. Alva Rogers's nursery rhymes were either theme songs of horror films or vestiges of a "Brady Bunch" childhood in the South Bronx or more likely both.

The Rodeo got taken to task for our humor and enjoyment of it. One memorable occasion was on a late-night talk-radio show. How dare we, the host was anxious to know, call a black male character King Kong? Had we forgotten how scorned black men were in America? How could we, as we did in the slides that accompanied *Carmella & King Kong*, show photos of bare black breasts alongside Fannie Lou Hamer trudging through the southern dust? Was Pam Grier worthy of being named in the same breath as Coretta Scott King? There was this assumption that being black and a woman carried with it a responsibility to be dire and remorseful. Or mystical and abandoned. Or issuing proverbs from the rocking chair. You-all are having too good a time, said the stares we got from the host, you don't want folks to think you girls are hoes. As if there was no identity between that of the girl who wanted the bluest eyes and that of the grandmother who had learned to love her brown ones, except that of a ho.

*He tells me the play is all wisecracks, one-liners. Not as smart as the first one. Midnight somewhere downtown, on a side street empty except for cabs shooting from the dark like comets. I sit on a stoop and stare at my hands. Then get tough, shake a finger in his face, throw a punch. Finally I cry. So it had mattered what he thought. Rain falls and I go on crying like the movies. Unlike the movies, he stands there guilty, twenty-eight years old and still unable to put his arms around a woman in public. Years later he tells me I was postmodern without reading up. Way ahead of my time. That good. After all.*

Growing up, the Caldonias inhaled the parody so evident in blaxploitation flicks and saw, through the rose-colored glass of childhood, the Black Arts movement's celebration of everything Afroed and black. The renaissance of fiction by black women that dawned in the seventies, we caught that too. These books made us feel less invisible, though their stories were far from our own lives as big-city girls; girls who took ballet and were carted off to Planned Parenthood in high school so as not to risk that baby that Mom, not Mama, warned would have "ruined our lives." College was expected. The southern ghosts of popular black women's fiction, the hardships and abuse worn like purple hearts, the clipped wings were not ours. We had burdens of our own. Glass ceilings at the office and in the art world, media and beauty industries that saw us as substandard, the color and hair wars that continued to sap our energy. We wanted to hear about these.

*I travel to New Orleans. For sale, for sale, get your mammie figurines, for sale. Stout blackened women with red bubbles for lips and starched white aprons. No resemblance to my grandmother or great aunt. Women with width, but women whose mothers made sure their baby girls never had to step foot in the big house with a rag and Murphy's Oil Soap ever again.* CONTEMPORARY REPLICAS OF A BELOVED AMERICAN CLASSIC, *says the sign in the curio shop. I buy two. Back home I chop off their heads and put the torso mammies in a performance piece.*

There was talk in 1986 of the arrival of a new way of looking at the world by young black artists. The new black aesthetic it was called by those who christened it, namely Trey Ellis and Greg Tate, and those who spread the word such as Michele Wallace and Henry Louis Gates, Jr. This aesthetic was described as being wide enough to contain everything from Spike Lee's Hollywood-financed dramedies, to Lorna Simpson's photo-text and its landscape of female symbols, to the revamping of the classics by Armani-clad jazzbos who had no use for the avant-garde, to hip-hop's deification of Malcolm. It was said to embrace, among other things, irreverence, profit-making, an elastic view of "black" art, ideas of integration and nationalism, a yen for tradition (or at least the apparel), and the usual questions about who we are and where is our home. Rodeo was named as one of upstarts of this aesthetic. Such a lofty goal was the furthest thing from our minds back then, I can testify. Though reflecting on those performances of ours—really rites of self-discovery staged in supper-club basements, church sanctuaries, and bars—it's clear to me that our take on blackness and femaleness did trumpet the cultural explosion that followed.

Two photographs of Rodeo, one that appeared in *High Performance,* a magazine covering performance art, and one in *Interview,* scorched through the available portraits of black women and caused a stir at the time, this being 1986. In the *Interview* photo we pose in party dresses from the fifties and African-print lapas. Alva holds a flower. Lorna wears glasses. We are not selling sex or pain, but we are sensual. Our skin color variations make a lush fresco, and our jumble of hair textures and styles is throwing curveballs at correctness. There we are, breathing intelligence, mischievousness, and triumph (that word again). There's also something pampered about us and fancy-free. We're not career girls or call girls or Bess or Beulah. We seem to be urban intellectual bohemians or art school grads or some such diva. Miles from naturalistic. In 1986 this was still a brand-new image. Had young black women been presented this way before in the mainstream? Apparently not.

Julie Dash called. She was in preproduction for a film called *Daughters of the Dust* and wanted Alva Rogers as her lead. Cinematographer Arthur Jaffa was equally spellbound. There were calls from Hollywood agents and production companies. Letters from young bohemians from Iowa to Teaneck. We became a metaphor for a new generation by standing in front of a camera and being ourselves, with a little stardust courtesy rags from Donna's bottomless closet. In the *Interview* photo, I am wearing a red silk bathrobe. A white baby doll is pinned to my temple like of one of Billie's gardenias. (Who knows what look I was going for—Lady Day reincarnated as a womanist kitchen-table surrealist playwright?) I remember the day well. After the photo session the Caldonias walked around downtown, where we continued to act out and take photos of ourselves. Look at us, we were saying, acknowledge us, commit us to memory.

*Nellie throws a fundraiser for us in his new brownstone duplex in
Fort Greene. Filmmakers and cartoonists and hip-hop enfant ter-
ribles show. Everyone takes their shoes off at the door so as not to
mess up Nellie's polished wood floor. This reminds me of the old
days when Papa B. was a Moslem, no shoes in the house and no
bacon. The Caldonias cook trays and trays of chicken. We stand
beautiful and strong and explain our mission: to carry Hansberry's
legacy to the twenty-first century. The men compliment us on our
chicken.*

Everyone was forming tribes. The Black Rock Coalition. Forty
Acres and a Mule Filmworks. The nations of hip-hop. The Hudlin
Brothers. George C. Wolfe assembled a team of collaborators that
would eventually bum rush the American theater. At Irving Place, a
club in Manhattan, some Caldonias and our lovers saw for the first
time a band called Fishbone that manages to set our racial angst as
black-teens-in-the-buttermilk to giggling power chords. The
Caldonias held a benefit for *Diva DeKooning*, a magazine we
planned to publish on the subject of black women's style as high art.
(Our funders pulled out at the last minute, but the magazine remains a provocative idea.) At the benefit Robbie McCauley, Laurie
Carlos, and Jessica Hagedorn debuted their new performance collective, Thought Music. Comedian Phyllis Stickney declined our
invite; Hollywood beckoned. There was this feeling that we were
living a movement marked by particular hairstyles, catchphrases,
and T-shirts. The (white) American imagination had shifted. To be
alive, young, and this new thing called African American suddenly
made one relevant and commercially viable. Folk art, be gone. And
so entered the vultures of commerce.

*We help Derin move the rest of her stuff from her mom's place in
Brooklyn to her new studio in Sugar Hill. She swears to us she lives
underneath Butterfly McQueen, who may be mad and may zoom
around her apartment all day on roller skates. Her man is up in the
loft bed writing songs on acoustic guitar. Derin and I go stand in line*

*for fish sandwiches. Fish "sangwiches" remind me of fried whiting in Newark. "Fried whitey," as it was called, which you ate with ice-cold watermelon. While Rodeo rehearses, sometimes I think of Papa B. Of Sterling Street, Spirit House, and the Spirit House Movers; of Papa B. rehearsing plays in the theater on the first floor of his house, Spirit House. How a dozen of us, adults and children, piled into a broom closet one night to record sound effects for* Slaveship. *Recreating the entire Middle Passage in a broom closet. I was not more than seven, but I remember women crying and men moaning and someone holding me very tight, as if the ship and the water that Papa B. had told us to imagine were right there. I remember a flood of terror. The shackles and chains. The heave of the ship. The rocking.*

One night at Sweetwaters Sandye Wilson, who played Torch Singer in *Carmella & King Kong*, thanked Greg Tate for hanging. He had not come to lift props or lend some cliché version of emotional support; he was there to dig the art. Tate came every weekend of our run, along with other male artists-in-arms. It meant a great deal to have black men respond to the work. I was excited by the possibility of belonging to a community of artists where women and men could engage each other's minds with candor and the assumption of equality. Given the hostile divide in black literary circles, stoked to boiling point by the media, such an alliance seemed all the more meaningful. Though Rodeo and the male artists we moved with never did realize this community in any organized way, there was definitely an exchange of ideas going on, and a potent one.

Rodeo connected with black men who knew our art was woman-centered and were drawn to it for just that reason. Marc Brown, our makeup artist, lavished the work with the drama of opera and enthusiasm of a chocolate fiend in Nestlé heaven. (Marc's death from AIDS in 1988 was the loss of a true friend and a collaborator who I had hoped to work with for eons.) Steve Williams designed our flyers and was a loyal fan. Al Blue spread the word and helped on the technical end. Lewis "Flip" Barnes was a familiar beaming face in the crowd. Vernon Reid took part in an early work-shop of *Combination Skin.* Brothers, all.

*We carry crates of records to Harlem as the sun comes up, then make love all morning on a bare mattress on the floor. He tells me stories about Indian reservations in Florida and bars in Brooklyn called Dirty Bud's Recovery Room. He calls my clit a little old woman in a boat. At four in the afternoon we surface finally, but then only to take photographs of signs:* WHITE HOUSE OF BEAUTY. MUSEUM OF COLORED GLASS AND LIGHT. SPACE ANGLES MYSTERY SOLVED.

The Caldonias were in relationships with men who were any-thing but "sitcom brothers." Young schemers like us, they were conversant in black politics and culture and had passed on job security for creative freedom. They too were exploring "out" texts of blackness—from minstrelsy to the dread hardcore of Bad Brains. Though I chose women as my primary subject, these brothers hit me with a challenge to make art that could also upend stock effigies of black men. Arguing, busting up, chowing down, and partying with these guys, I often felt during those days that the brother-sister thang glorified in black folk talk was a genuine, nourishing part of my life. It strikes me now how only one of those relation-ships survived the ain't-nothing-going-on-but-the-rent eighties; and how the men and women artists I knew from that period had wild-monkey passion but rarely ended up together; and how the men went on to marry women who were supportive, but not artists, while the women were still searching for love from a like mind.

*I squint at the mirror. All my life I felt I was too big down there. I always covered up. Now I have calf muscles from climbing flights of stairs to the train, to my apartment on the fifth floor, to work, carry-ing props, journals, cameras, but still hips and still ass. Show that butt, wear tighter clothes, flaunt those hips, Donna says. It's Donna who dresses us and tells us how fab we look. Alva does our hair.*

*These two roommates know all the beauty secrets for black girls. Use this. Don't use that. Their elaborate rituals at the quest of beauty amaze us. They take this very seriously. Like Madame C.J. inventing a wider tooth hot comb. You will love yourselves by any means necessary.*

The portrayal of feminism as some sort of game sport of man hating or pulpit of crunchy-granola correctness has always read to me like some impossibly cartoonish send-up. It remains so far from the feminism that I have lived, particularly the one I knew in Rodeo. I'd count Rodeo as my defining feminist experience, even though I've been calling myself the f-word since high school. In Rodeo I learned that feminism was to me, stripped to its intimate essentials, a passion for the creative culture of women and a belief that communion with other women was a bread-and-water necessity. Outside of debates on employment rights, abortion, child care, and whether feminism serves women of color—and the other big politics of the movement—what has kept me interested in feminism and *identifying* is the pleasure. The pleasure in women's voices, our dozens, our ways of caring and getting mad, and above all, in the way we love deeply. As some call it, *hard.*

Give me a girl gang, a crew. A zillion sisters ain't enough. To be a girl among girls, I feel as if I am at the height of courage and creativity. As an adult I am continually trying to re-create these spaces of safety and unconditional love. Like my grandmother's house, where Gramma, Aunt Cora, and Mom addressed the world's ills with a little Johnnie Walker Red and a clean dishrag. Like Mom taking her daughters out of the city in her geriatric car, us three singing love songs from the forties like belles of the ball. Like the We Waz Girls Together Off-Campus Collective at Renee, Myra, and Maria's, where we took character names from black women's fiction and imagined ourselves divas of myth. Renee was Willy Chilly, after the Wild Child of *Meridian;* let Desdemona keep stepping. Like Rodeo.

Lorna's photographs are in museums across the country now.

Amber is a rap star. Pam was an Ikette in *What's Love Got to Do With It?* The Jones Twins' crossbreed of theater and music, "be-bop muzak," can be seen around New York. Derin just got back from Japan, touring with French pop star Vanessa Paradis. She's gigging now with her own band in Parisian nightclubs. Alva is workshopping her play with music, *The Bride Who Became Frightened When She Saw Life Open,* and studying toward a masters in musical theater. Raye's living and working in L.A. Donna designs costumes for film. Celina's still directing. Kellie's exhibition, "Malcolm X: Man, Ideal, Icon," is touring the country. Candace, the relentless romantic, found love, made a baby, and now runs a small press with her husband. We never officially disbanded, just moved on. I went off to film school, a trade mill that frowned on the word "art", a drastic change from the feel-it, do-it aesthetic of Rodeo. The trade mill succeeded in convincing me not to trust that voice of my own, so recently found. Eventually I did get her back and I don't plan on letting her go any time soon.

There are times when I mourn Rodeo's passing on. Our grand schemes still beg to be realized. Imagine if we had launched, as we dreamed, an institution or two: a center to finance and stage work by black women in the theater arts regardless of waves of commercial interest, a multimedia production complex devoted to collaborations between African-American women across disciplines. Or think of what we could have done just as a theater collective, touring the country as ambassadors of kitchen-table surrealism, hauling our conceptual art piece on black female representation around the world. If we had gone national, Greg Tate is sure we could have done for womanism what Public Enemy did for black nationalism—made it pop. The next generation of Caldonias will have to take up that flag. Perhaps the young women of hip-hop, groups like T.L.C., have already begun.

*Tonight's our reunion. We sit around 'til late (not so late this time) talking about days present and past, over Donna's guacamole and Celina's wings. Everyone's radiant and full of gossip. I ask for old*

*Rodeo stories. Celina, C. as we call her, goes first. Hers is about our gig at Blackbyrds, a little bar downtown that's long gone. Some young white gentlemen were using the stage as a chaise lounge. Our show was going up in an hour, but they weren't moving. I had arrived first and they flat ignored me. C. came next; they weren't having her either. The two of us sat there all frustrated with these white gentlemen. But soon the other Caldonias floated in. Just these women setting up slide projectors, throwing clothes, fixing hair, talking about last night's date and who would come to the show let loose a stream of energy that swept the white gentlemen off the stage; which is what spirit bound together should do, move mountains or, as here, molehills. After C.'s account, there's silence around the table. C. lets the silence lie. After a while she says, "That's my story."*

My dowry: a motorcycle jacket and a mammie doll missing its head. Plastic pork chops and New Orleans amulets. Diana's whine, Josephine's wiggle, the roll of Nina Mae's eyes, Fredi's demons, Bessie's stomp, Billie's fruit, Adrienne's ghosts, Julia's wig box, Pam Grier's gun, Shange's God. A Caldonia girl. Swollen with dreams, fearless and fine. I came with the Rodeo.

*1993*

# three

# the blackest market

# 1-800-wasp

If you dropped dead tonight and were reborn in a mail order catalog, you'd say, "Please Lord, let it be J. Crew." So even in the next life, you could be seen, says the new fall catalog, "placing bids at Christie's" or "huddled in the stands at the Army-Navy game." Nouvelle prep, it is. Roll-neck sweaters dyed java ("the new black"), flannel blazers in basil or dijon. Working in the city, though bound for Cos Cob. Not as straitlaced Yankee as L.L. Bean, but urbanely WASP (more a state of dress, a wallet size, than a rigid racial criterion). Even Afrocentric iconoclast-bohème-girl writers hunger for some version of it. We mix the felt bowlers and peg-leg wool pants with kente knapsacks and MAKE BLACK FILM T-shirts. It's a look we can't resist: Zora Neale Hurston meets George Sand and Jessie Fauset at Emily Dickinson's cabin in Amherst. Our kind of weekend.

Catalogs are mighty image banks these days. The top trendies —Lands' End, Tweeds, and J. Crew—together mail millions of books each year to potential customers in fifty states. One quarter of J. Crew buyers are college students. (The catalogs are dropped in dorms by the pound.) Like MTV, these designer advert-zines arrived in the eighties; they seemed to enter our lives in a new way (in the mail and largely unsolicited) and they fed our national lore. We look for ourselves in their cultural display cases. When people of color are missing as models—and they are for the most part—they're "disappeared" as ideal consumers, as sample citizens.

J. Crew, born in 1983, is not really a catalog at all, but a lifestyle guide with full-page photos and commentary (low boots to take you from "Park Ave. to Patagonia"). Stores and magazines have lost their point of view, gloats company creative director Jim Nevins, but not J. Crew. What that p.o.v. is is not too hard to suss out: Class. The name's a dead giveaway: "Crew" for the Ivy League trademark sport. And "J.": possibly borrowed from J. G. Hook, which packages "well-bred, classical apparel for women with an upscale lifestyle," recites a company spokesperson. One of J. Crew's retail stores arrived in New York City two years ago at, where else, that yuppie theme park, South Street Seaport.

J. Crew sells its WASP fantasies not from a converted farmhouse in Greenwich, but from Manhattan, a few blocks above Fourteenth Street. (Their warehouse, in Lynchburg, Virginia, has a prefab elite address: One Ivy Crescent.) Perhaps it's a small irony, but Crew's customers are 60 percent urban, and California is one of their strongest market bases. Being a WASP these days may carry some modest stigma in name, though not in name brand. Everyone, so it seems, wants to wear WASP clothes. Or, more to the point, fill their shoes, confiscate their myth and power.

Flipping through J. Crew's aisles this fall, you'll notice more black models peppered throughout. More, but not many: four—three women and one man—out of more than fifty total. (One black model per catalog had been their running standard.) September's male model has an eerie resemblance to actor Courtney Vance in John Guare's *Six Degrees of Separation.* (The play's based on the true story of a young black man who—armed with nothing but an oxford shirt—ran a con game on rich whites.) With so much banking on image, since the consumer can't touch or try on, every choice designers make is carefully considered. The decision to use black models, especially in a catalog like J. Crew that oozes Anglo out of every 100 percent cotton pore, must be no exception. Were J. Crew's black models a nod to the racial rainbow seen in fashion mags or liberal window dressing? Or, better yet, a conscious effort to attract African Americans in what may be the waning days of the catalog boom? With annual postal rate hikes, catalogers can't afford to prospect randomly for new customers, why not target blacks?

"We don't do race-oriented marketing," said Adrienne Perkov, J. Crew's director of new market development. "We try to make the product available to everyone." That's an old standby: We don't market to a particular racial/ethnic group (i.e., whites, when we use all-white models), we sell a life-style. As if whites are "everyone," because it's assumed they have no race, and blacks can't signify this "everyone," because we do have one. "We always use a few," offered creative director Nevins, but he didn't have a clue why there would be more black models this fall. Although the company did a customer survey last year, according to Rae Slyper, director of marketing, race wasn't queried. "We wouldn't think of asking anything like that," Slyper yelped, nearly horror-struck. "Is this article about MINORITIES?!?"

"Invisible People" is the title of a new study of "minorities" (whatever that means in these times of shifting demographics) in magazine ads and mail-order catalog, compiled by New York City's Department of Consumer Affairs. The meager representation of nonwhites is supported by two industry myths: that blacks in particular don't have disposable income (black consumer spending, the study says, will max out at four hundred billion dollars this year); and that when blacks appear in ads, companies experience "white flight" (a falsehood disproven by market studies since the sixties. If anything, putting black models in ads increases sales because blacks identify with them and buy more). Of the 157 catalogs reviewed, blacks made up less than 5 percent of 22,685 models pictured, despite the fact that blacks buy from catalogs at nearly the same rate as whites. (And a disproportionate number of the black models used were juveniles or light-complexion adults.) Several high-circulation catalogs, such as L.L. Bean and Laura Ashley, were whites-only.

Courting black consumers could mean better business for a catalog like J. Crew than the company might realize or be willing to acknowledge. Black people spend a good deal of their disposable income, says African-American consumer-market specialist Persephone Miller, on "image-enhancement" products, which include designer-label clothing from "upscale retailers." We tend to have poor images of ourselves, and through these products we seek to belong, to be accepted.

For those of us who don't "belong" in stores, the idea of shopping in the privacy of our own homes has a double meaning. Mail-order catalogs—toll-free, twenty-four-hour hotlines—are a racially stress-free shopping encounter, no more hassles, no more watchful eyes. All you need is a major credit card (which you might not have, since a lower percentage of black folks have them), and you're guaranteed unconditional acceptance. No one has to know your race, just buy. Or as some might say, buy in.

*1991*

# a doll
# is born

This is my doll story (because every black journalist who writes about race gets around to it sometime). Back when I started playing with Barbies, there was no Christie (Barbie's black friend, born in 1968) or black Barbie (born in 1980, brown plastic poured into blonde Barbie's mold). I had two blondes, which I bought from girls at school with my Christmas money.

I cut off their hair and dressed them in African-print fabric. They lived together, happily polygamous, with a black G.I. Joe bartered from the Shepp boys, my downstairs neighbors. After an incident at school, where all of the girls looked like Barbie and none of them looked like me, I galloped down our stairs with one Barbie, her blonde head hitting each spoke of the banister, thud, thud, thud. And galloped up the stairs, thud, thud, thud, until her head popped off, lost to the graveyard behind the stairwell. Then I tore off each limb and sat on the stairs for a long time twirling the torso like a baton.

Do little black girls still grow up slaughtering or idolizing pink-fleshed, blue-eyed doll babies? Even after two cultural nationalist movements, four black Miss Americas, and integrated shelves at Kiddie City and Toys 'R' Us? In 1987 Dr. Darlene Powell-Hopson, a clinical psychologist, replicated a landmark study done by a team of black therapists in the forties; a study that was later used to argue *Brown v. Board of Education.* When asked which doll is the good doll, which doll is the right color, a large percentage of children, black and white, still chose the white doll. Powell-Hopson's twist was intervention. Before kids were asked to choose, they were told stories about the black dolls, stories that presented them as great beauties, as heroines. The percentages reversed.

Powell-Hopson got a call last summer. Some folks at Mattel toys had read her book, *Different and Wonderful: Raising Black Children in a Race Conscious Society.* Would she be interested in consulting them on a new product, a line of African-American fashion dolls to be introduced in fall of 1991? A number of black women were involved: There was Mattel product manager Deborah Mitchell and the principal designer for Mattel's fashion doll group, Kitty Black-Perkins (who outfitted the first black Barbie eleven years ago). And Alberta Rhodes and her partners at Morgan Orchid Rhodes running the PR train. Powell-Hopson did a little research on Mattel. Her main criticism: Like many large toy companies, Mattel had put few marketing dollars behind their black dolls. "Christie was always in the background in group ads," Powell-Hopson remembers, "and kids pick up those messages." But eventually she did sign on.

These women midwifed "Shani," whose name according to Mattel means "marvelous" in Swahili. (My Oxford University Press Swahili-English dictionary says "startling, a wonder, a novelty.") Shani's being touted as the first "realistically sculpted" black fashion doll, though small black-owned companies have been making fashion dolls for years. (And black-owned doll companies have been around even longer, perhaps even before Marcus Garvey's Negro Doll Factory run by the United Negro Improvement Association). Shani's debut at the American International Toy fair last month was an extravaganza fit for a bap in miniature. Mattel threw a party in her honor, complete with En Vogue singing the Negro national anthem.

Mattel calls Shani "tomorrow's African American woman" (one-upping *Essence*'s "Today's Black Woman"). She has a new body ("Rounder, more athletic," Mitchell giggles into the phone. "Her hips are broader, but she still can fit Barbie's clothes"); a new face (fuller lips and broader nose); and new clothes ("Spice tones, ethnic fabrics," glows Black-Perkins. "Not fantasy colors like pink or lavender"). And her new skin alludes to the range among African Americans: Shani, the lead doll, is berry-brown; Nichelle, deep mahogany, and Asha, honey, are her two friends.

I carry around a photograph of Shani and her playmates to show the girlfriends, who are single and childless and have no idea of the hard time black parents have tracking down culturally affirming toys, as do Powell-Hopson and Black-Perkins, mothers both. Not so fast, the girlfriends snap. "Why can't they make one with dreads?" whines Susan, who wears extensions and works for the U.S. Attorney's office. "They must be from D.C.," observes honorary girlfriend Alejandro, eyeing their loud costumes and sculpted hair. "That light one, Asha, is gonna sell out and leave poor Shani and Nichelle on the shelf," comes the usual grunt from the ever color-struck Tamu. Deandra is most upset: "It's the hair."

All three dolls have hair past shoulder length. Powell-Hopson had hopes that one of the dolls would have shorter hair, "an Afro, an asymmetrical cut, something." Mitchell admits that Mattel heard similar concerns in the focus groups: "To be truly realistic, one should have shorter hair. But little girls of all races love hair play. We added more texture. But we can't change the fact that long, combable hair is still a key seller." (When I relay this to Deandra, she sucks teeth: "More chicken-before-the-egg theories.") Fantasy hair or not, Powell-Hopson holds that the Shani doll shows "social consciousness on Mattel's part."

More like marketing savvy dressed up, nineties style, as social consciousness. Mattel knows that African Americans will make up nearly 20 percent of the population by the next century and that we have more disposable income than ever before. Sales of black Barbie doubled last year, following an ad campaign in black print media. Mattel decided to advertise after research showed most black consumers didn't know the doll existed. Black Barbie had been around for ten years (twenty-one years after Mattel introduced what it calls the "traditional, blonde, blue-eyed Barbie"), yet Mattel had never given her a major marketing push. The doll had only appeared, as part of a group of other Barbies, in a few adult-directed TV spots; kids had never seen her on the tube on Saturday mornings.

Fashion dolls aren't born every day. At least not at Mattel. There's Barbie, her friends, boyfriend Ken, and a few celebrity dolls now and then. Shani is Mattel's first "non-Barbie fashion doll." The women behind Shani, like Mitchell and Powell-Hopson, want her to be more than just a Barbie in blackface. Shani's "character sketch" (the doll's publicity fact sheet) matches her, dare we say, ethnically correct physique. ("She's not just a pretty face . . . she's very conscious of her culture.") In 1992 Shani gets a boyfriend. What about a play set? How about "Community Center," where Shani can teach black history to inner-city youth? Or "Corporate America," where Nichelle can argue with her boss about whether her braided hair is really appropriate in the boardroom?

*1991*

# faded
## attraction

I've got some crazy friends, I'm telling you. Now, Tamu is big humor. Tamu's thing is skin color. My girl is as high-yella as they come, or "light, bright, and damn near white," as goes another expression from the archives. Yet if a Negro is not pushing blue-black—complexion and politics—she won't give him the time of day. You've heard of reverse discrimination, well, she's reverse color struck. But don't blame Tamu, she's just a Black Power baby. In junior high in the early seventies she heard tapes of Malcolm X lamenting how the rape of black women during slavery deprived him of his rightful pigmentation. Well, she pitched her tent right there and hasn't changed camps since.

If poor Tamu had been in *The Wizard of Oz* she'd be the one singing, "If I only had some melanin." Naturally, anything folks do to lighten their skin gives her the heebie-jeebies. Mention Michael Jackson, she screams genocide. Skin peels and nose jobs are acts of treason. Her latest pet peeve: fade cream, also known as skin-tone cream, bleaching cream, skin whitener. Check *Ebony, Jet,* or *Essence* for the advertisements.

To remind me of the pain, the wounds, the subtext that these products carry with them, Tamu carts me off to the Schomburg Center for Research in Black Culture ("in Harlem, U.S.A.," as she would say) to scan back issues of *Ebony* and *Sepia* for fade-cream ads. Alongside ads for Sweet Georgia Brown Hair Dressing Pomade and Alaga Syrup, we find some beauties:

Nadinola Bleaching Cream (1952): "Few men can resist the charm of a honey-light complexion," says a fair-skinned model with a wink. Palmer's Skin Success Cream (1956): "Works to help your skin look clearer, fairer even when neglect and the sun of passing summers have made it hopelessly dark." Black and White Bleaching Cream (1949): "Those moments when he tenderly draws you closer for your triumph before his admiring eyes, that's when shades lighter skin becomes a priceless treasure."

The marketing and product identity of fade creams have kept up with the times: A 1966 ad for Nadinola, a skin-lightening cream first manufactured in 1899, reinvents it as a cosmetic that "brightens away skin discolorations." Fade creams kind of laid low in the seventies (in *Jet* they were replaced by ads for Raveen and Duke grooming aids for Afros). They made a comeback in the eighties, which saw a return to "lighter, brighter" standards of African-American beauty. (Dark and Lovely, a line of hair products born in the black-is-beautiful seventies, proclaimed in 1986: "Dark and Lovely Lightens!") Some of the recent print ads Tamu loves to hate:

Porcelana Medicated Fade Cream's 1989 campaign featured an early period Lisa Bonet look-alike, giving second-generation Spelman or Smith bap attitude. The kicker: "The faded beauty of Marlénne Kingsland." (This made Tamu's blood boil. How dare a product with such a dark—I mean, white—past try to be so damn upscale?) Ultra Glow Skin Tone Cream made it to the Afrocentric nineties this way: In African-print headwraps, models representing three shades of black beauty stare ahead defiantly. Ultra Glow, the ad boasts, keeps "women of color radiantly beautiful."

Tamu and I hop over to a department store down the street from the Schomburg to examine their fade-cream collection. A salesclerk named Verona, who's worked there three years, tells us that Dr. Fred Palmer's Skin Whitener is the most popular cream ("People come in and try to buy up the whole supply; we need to order more"). Verona reports that customers use the creams to fade dark marks left by blemishes. She herself stays clear of them: "I tried to use a fade cream once, but it changed my face different colors." What kind of different colors? "Dark black and blue." Blue? *Blue?* Tamu's on a mission.

Back home Tamu calls Dr. Claudette Troyer, a dermatologist at Harlem Hospital. The active ingredient in over-the-counter bleaching creams is hydroquinone, Troyer says, "a melanin-inhibiting" agent. Doctors prescribe it to even out skin color after pregnancy (hormonal changes can cause spotting) or to lighten dark scars after injury. Maybe two times a year Troyer gets women who want to be prescribed hydroquinone to bleach their skin a lighter shade, but most are out to get rid of dark spots. Is this stuff harmful? Even the over-the-counter products (which by law contain only 2 percent hydroquinone) can cause adverse reactions. When used too often, Troyer warns, dark blotches can appear on the skin.

Tamu discovers that the Food and Drug Administration (FDA) is reviewing O.T.C. bleaching creams, though the review (a general review that includes many other O.T.C. products) is a very slow process that has been underway since the seventies. In 1982 the FDA banned all bleaching products containing mercury. Until the review proves otherwise, those with hydroquinone are still considered safe. The American Academy of Dermatology faxes Tamu some articles published in medical journals in the late eighties that document cases where skin developed dark spots or was discolored blue-gray after prolonged use of bleaching creams with hydroqui-none.

Then Tamu happens upon the most amazing fact of the day. The Dermatological Society of South Africa has documented thousands of cases of black women who were disfigured by hydroquinone-based skin lighteners. Last December the government banned the products altogether. South African anthropologists believe one rea-son skin lighteners have been so popular with black women is that beauty standards in the country are influenced by notions of racial superiority. *("I* could've told you that," snorts Tamu.)

To report the horrors, Tamu immediately gets on the phone with another friend, a Puerto Rican doctor who also dates only blue-black. "Yes, child," says Alejandro, "I remember Miss Skin Success Cream [referring to a man he used to live with]. Miss Thing had about six jars of it; I thought it was on sale. But no, girl, that was about self-*hatred*, yes! My college friends came over once and liber-ated the stuff out of the medicine cabinet. Didn't they read him, girl? "Miss Thing, you better get to the Clorox, 'cause it's not gonna work!"

*1991*

# make self-love

A young woman we know writes:

Lately in the mirror I am visited by an extraterrestrial with a Brillo pad for hair, a butt bigger than the land mass of North America, and toothpicks for legs. Has there ever been an uglier black child? Am I suffering from "self-hatred," that infamous and slippery condition pinned to black folks, or have I been in the Midwest too long? And what is this self-hatred stuff, anyway? Is it an accurate description of how Eurocentricity makes folks feel about their bodies, skin, hair, intellect? Doesn't it sound a bit severe? I mean, I don't *really* hate myself, do I?

Can we talk self-hatred? Maybe I know a lot of confident, in-the-positive black folks, but this idea of *hate* just rubs me wrong. The cultural renaissance and kente-youth movement aside, I've been all over the country and to Canada this year and have witnessed plenty of African Americans loving themselves (sometimes to sheer abandon!). You can see it in their pride, style options, right on down to the way they walk. And what about whites emulating us? Yesterday on the bus in Minneapolis I noticed five, count 'em, five white guys with dreadlocks. X-tension Generation, a hair salon in town, does nothing but dreadlocks and African-inspired braids for Caucasians. Does anyone talk about whites hating themselves when they do cross-cultural bonding, borrowing, or highway robbery? Of course not.

Before we buy the concept wholesale, seems to me black folks could benefit from a vigorous discussion of self-hatred on all fronts —in academia, media, the mental health community, at house parties. And, for once, can we put aside positive/negative image arguments, and what's black and what ain't arguments, and listen to what living, breathing people have to say about their choices and cultural balancing acts? Thank you very much.

You're not the only one all caught up with this self-hatred question. I've been devouring bell hooks's new essay collection, *Black Looks: Race and Representation.* You know hooks is my girl; she always gives a most fierce reading of race/sex conundrums. In "Loving Blackness as Political Resistance," hooks tells us that obsession with self-hate eclipses dialogue around loving blackness. The question she asks is not as obvious as it might seem: What would it mean to replace the discourse of self-hatred—rooted in victimization—with one based on loving, as the Batson Brothers say, "the Africa in you"? I'm right there with hooks. Thing is, hooks never challenges the notion that there are masses of folks out there hating themselves. I don't think there are myself, not exactly, at least. Then again, I live in the nation of Brooklyn, where switching butt, hair freestyling, dress-up, noses in the air, and black folks enjoying each other's bodies are national pastimes, so maybe I'm biased.

A couple of years back I clipped an article from *Essence*'s twentieth anniversary issue. I saved that thing in plastic, carry it with me everywhere. Audre Lorde, Octavia Butler, and other literary foremamas talk about surviving the last two decades. One piece came from Louise Meriwether, author of *Daddy Was a Number Runner* (which, along with *The Soul Brothers and Sister Lou* and *The Street*, were this girl's *Catcher in the Rye*). Meriwether says this: "I dislike the term 'self-hate,' which often is untrue. Disliking certain aspects of yourself is not the same as hatred. I prefer to describe the condition as a lack of self-love. I emphasize love, because whatever we focus on expands." The Meriwether approach speaks to me, okay? Let's contemplate and learn from how we got ovah, instead of dwelling on how we stay under. Can I get a witness?

But I know. It ain't as simple as all that. The lack of love for and devaluation of black bodies, black selves, is all too close. Just the other day, this woman pushing thirty comes up to me at a party talking about what "good hair" I have. I wanted to smack some sense into that child. Problem was, girlfriend had blue contacts on and I would've risked dislodging her retina. Then this friend, Jewish, who has a niece, Afro-Brazilian, told me about taking the eight-year-old to an exhibit at the Smithsonian on sixties fashion. In front of the Afro wigs, dashikis, and Black Power buttons, black niece asks white aunt: "Is black still beautiful?" Black is always beautiful, my friend coughed up between tears. She questioned later how many others could be counted on to give her niece this message, including the little girl's own mother, who is black. In *Black Looks*, hooks asks that we take a hard look at black children before engaging in "some new-age denial" of self-hatred.

Self-hate or not self-hate? I took the question to some mental health professionals, you know, black headshrinker types. The consensus was that the term wasn't appropriate or exact enough, although the "symptoms" are prevalent and exist across class. Psychologist Darlene Powell-Hopson prefers the term "low racial self-esteem." Often, she says, people, particularly children, "compartmentalize": They have race-based animosity toward other blacks, yet feel they're fine.

Psychiatrist Joseph Brewster, in private practice in Manhattan, tells me that what constitutes the "self" is the biggest debate in his profession, so "self-hate" is amorphous when it comes to any cultural group. Arguing race politics off the time clock, however, Brewster does use the term because it's familiar. More often than not, he says, black people, not the white power structure, are one's first channel of self-hating impulses. Brewster recalls some precious dirt he heard on an entertainment exposé show. Apparently it wasn't crossover success that drove Michael Jackson to a nose job, but taunts from his siblings about the width of his schnoz. The most cleverly disguised form of "self-hatred," according to Brewster, is the blame-whitey-hate-all-whiteys syndrome, which offers a false sense of comfort and superiority. Like a professor of Pan-African studies who told him as a college student that the white man was the devil, though not to bother majoring in math because "we didn't do well in it."

Of the dozen folks, young and old, that I got nosey with on the subject, all were vehement that they did not "hate" themselves, past or present. They did describe, at one time in their lives, disliking shape of nose, skin color, booty size, or hair texture. Denial, semantics, or evidence of the complexity of the issue, you choose. The only person who actually admitted to feelings of self-hatred was a very dynamic sister named Nora Hall. In her work as an organizational consultant Hall repackages the idea of self-hatred as shame. She says most people find ideas like psychological oppression, racism, and other "isms" so depressing they'd rather not deal with them at all. Shame makes it more intimate—and surmountable. Though whatever wordsmithing we do to dress up or dress down the matter, it's near impossible to grow up black in America without running smack into it.

I don't know if any of this is of use, but to hear hooks and others tell it, awareness is crucial. There's a body of evidence that speaks to our subjugation and one that speaks to our triumph. It's your choice which cloak you wear. In "Loving Blackness," hooks begins with Malcolm: "We have to see each other with new eyes." Girl, what can I say? Find yourself a new pair of eyes.

And would you please, in the jargon of self-help lit, stop awfulizing? You don't hate yourself, you've probably just come down with a bout of *Eurocentricity Blues*. Try dancing naked in front of a mirror to Sir Mix-A-Lot's "Baby Got Back" or Labelle's "Going Down Makes Me Shiver." Marvel at the magnificent soft sculpture of your cheeks. The fruit, the flower, of it all. Ask yourself, can a butt be too big? Then repeat after our patron saint of desire, Shange: "I found God in myself . . . and I loved her fiercely." If all that don't work, call me in the morning.

*1992*

# profiling

Before Madonna discovered vogueing—and gay men gave birth to it in Harlem Elk lodges—there was profiling. Profiling is about being the high priestess of the moment. The feature presentation. It's about walking into a room, anywhere, anytime, and owning it. People of African descent are the kings and queens of it. Like my friend Alejandro, the doctor, who sashays into my apartment without a hello, sits at the table (as if waiting for the maid to wipe up the crumbs), crosses his legs, gives a half glance my way, and says, deadpan as hell, without missing a beat, "Here it is, Miss Two, just for you."

Profiling has a zillion and one meanings: To

know you look good or *think* you look good; to dress or behave in a way that attracts attention. Depending on the speaker's tone and delivery, it could be cut or compliment. My friend Percidia remembers the word from her high school days in Virginia in the late sixties: "There were two all-black schools in Richmond—Armstrong and Maggie Walker. And when these two played each other in football, nobody would be in their seats, everybody would be profiling *down*. People would walk from end line to end line and back, showing off their outfits, their hairdos, and talkin' 'bout other folks and their outfits and hairdos. Didn't see a play on the field."

Lately, profiling has been on my mind, and not just because of *Paris Is Burning.* (Do the dispossessed make mockery of the affluent when they master the pose, or do they reaffirm the vise grip the pose has on their psyches?) A few Saturdays ago I took part in a bare-bones spectacle of profiling. I haven't indulged in such shameless profiling since girlfriend Kim and I dressed in matching camel-color pantsuits to see the Commodores sing "Brick House" at the Garden. Because we were sitting in the boonies—second to last row —we felt obliged to sing, at the top of our lungs, along with every word out of Lionel Richie's mouth.

I'm here to confess.

Desperately in search of Negroes, my friends the Twins dragged me to a house party the Brownstone Underground was hosting at a Manhattan loft. The BU is a group of cousins in their twenties—the Jellerettes and the Griffiths—who work in media. They went to white Ivies (Cornell, Brown) and black Ivies (Morgan, Howard) and among the four of them they know just about every on-the-verge young specimen in the city—filmmakers, lawyers, writers, investment bankers, TV producers.

We rode by in a rusty sedan from El Barrio Cab Service, but had the driver drop us off one block west, so as not to be seen ducking out of such a skanky ride. Then we joined the mass of well coiffed, color coordinated, and casually upscale inching their way into the building. Even celebs were doing time outside (anchorwoman Rolanda Watts, with new long, blondish tresses, exchanged pleasantries with actor Kadeem Hardison). After an hour and a half on a line that wasn't moving, the Twins and I started acting out: the verbal component of profiling, engaging in loud and bodacious commentary to call attention to ourselves. Can you blame us? How could we justify waiting on line to get into a house party? Don't we have more juice than that?

Okay, so I led the pack by obsessing on the anchorwoman's supernatural hair color. But like all successful profilers, a scene began around us. Conversations flourished, most involving our favorite topics, race and sexual politics. "If black folks really want to control our culture, we're gonna have to come out our pockets," said a performance artist with corkscrew dreads. "To be perfectly honest," whispered a woman in a Ralph Lauren shirt, "I go home every night and play with myself, what do I need a man for?"

Our group left the herd pushing to get in and leaned against cars. At three in the morning newcomers were still arriving, and they had to decide whether to queue up with the desperados or lounge with us. Somebody rolled down a car window and turned on an AM-only radio. ("Oooh," one Twin moaned, "that's so ghetto, I love it!") The other Twin said she felt like pulling up a lawn chair and downing a cooler. She reminisced about the good old days at Howard, when Negroes would cruise the cul-de-sac facing the student center, all slow, showing off their rides. Once a guy drove by in a car, hitched to, yes, a boat.

The profiling high point, I must admit, did not originate with our group. You-know-who, an outside linebacker for a New York team, allegedly the most dominant defense player in football, arrived in a white limo. No, let me restate that: The folks driving the gentleman's limo backed it onto the sidewalk. Well, out comes the Hulk and, what, he can't get in. Even *he* doesn't have enough juice. (Or he hadn't profiled it successfully.)

An act of profiling justice arrived in the form of Ray Hands. A hatmaker who gives rent parties in his Bed-Stuy loft, Hands is no millionaire, unlike the Hulk. But, so says Miss Roj in George C. Wolfe's *The Colored Museum*, "God created black people and black people created style." And Hands is one of those folks God put on earth to throw together some style. Well, didn't Ray Hands pull up in his own white limo. (I saw those "Z" plates, Ray, don't lie, a friend must've cut you a deal for the night.) And didn't he emerge wearing a plaid Nehru jacket with matching shorts and, get this, the largest applejack I ever saw in my life. (Move over Lawrence-Hilton Jacobs.) Don't ask if the hat matched, you know it did. That damn hat was so big, one Twin dubbed it an "actual-size" applejack. Need we say, Ray got in. Swiftly.

*1991*

# color therapy
# by deandra

Love, peace, and hair grease, this is Deandra, coming to you live from Minnesota. What do you mean you don't know where Minnesota is? Get out your map, I'm talking Midwest and then some. Malls, snowblowers, jumbo thruways, a Lutheran church on every corner. Don't talk to me about sixty-below wind chill factors and hail the size of deer turds. I will tell you one thing. Hell is *not* about fire.

You know my best friend, Miss Columnist? She's here for nine months to explore the kinder, gentler America, where they don't run folks out of the neighborhood with baseball bats, they just burn a cross on your lawn—

your private property—and call it free speech. Girlfriend asked me to do the column this month, being that she's wrapped up in a severe case of culture shock. It started on the plane with the announcement of connecting flights to Dubuque (where they burn lots of crosses) and Milwaukee (where they eat lots of blacks). Never mind she was on her way to that happening, politically progressive town, Minneapolis, home of the Save the Earth movement and the purple Prince. What if she wandered into some Aryan Nation booby trap? What if Nazi yuppies chanting WELFARE SCUM! ate her for lunch? Poor diva hasn't left the house in two weeks and I'm nothing but an errand girl: Buy me Tampax, buy me blue corn chips, buy me *Essence* magazine.

Now girlfriend is picking up creepy vibes from the wheat field–theme Contact paper in the kitchen, the liver-colored tile in the john, the gerbil-beige carpet in the living room. The color scheme, she's convinced, is sending her subliminal white-supremacist messages. She yells, why didn't I pack her Nelson Mandela and Frida Kahlo T-shirts? She threatens to hang herself with the shower curtain if she doesn't see someone wearing faux kente cloth in the next forty-eight hours. Get to the couch, I tell girlfriend, it's time for color therapy by Deandra.

We begin slowly. I have her read aloud passages from Jean E. Patton's *Color to Color: The Black Woman's Guide to a Rainbow of Fashion and Beauty,* published this year. *Color to Color* is "Afrocentric color analysis" that brings racial uplift work to the closet and makeup counter. Patton claims Charleszine Wood Spears and Ella Mae Washington as godmamas in the struggle. Spears and Washington were African-American home economists who, as early as the 1940s, self-published manuals on selecting colors for skin-tone enhancement. Like "bad hair," Patton preaches, there is no such animal as "bad color." Purge your psyche of old race tales about hussy red and other "loud" hues that call attention to lusciously endowed Negro bodies. Don't take refuge from the hard eye of status quo aesthetics in muddy colors that "recede" you into the background.

Too hip for the "four seasons" approach, Patton arranges black folks in four "palettes" drawn from the diaspora and ancestral cradle. (Miss Columnist, you take the "spice" palette, which makes your celebrity models Tina Turner and Malcolm X.) Skin color variations are christened with references to sensual fabrics and high-caloric foods. And that enduring affliction of being "color struck," the preference for or hatred of complexions dark or light? Patton gives it joyous, new meaning just in time for Kwanzaa. Revel in the rainbow, *struck by color,* praise the Lord! Ssshh! says girlfriend, can't you hear the wallpaper whisper, "white power"?

I try the historical approach. We discuss culture and color research. The "color revolution" of the 1960s (psychedelics, anything-goes brights, the sophistication of monotone black or white) wasn't spontaneous generation but the by-product of nothing less than global political upheaval—the surge of youth culture, feminism, African independence. Before this, the Euro-American tableau had shunned colors associated with darker-skinned peoples (the African indigos, the hot Spanish reds), with a few departures, except as costumes. The enduring symbolism of evil, menacing "black" and innocent, clean "white" has its roots in nineteenth-century Europe's scientific racism. The "blackness" of Africans was seen as a disturbance of nature. (Were babies born black, French anthropologists who traveled to West Africa in the early nineteenth century wanted to know, or did they turn that color from too much sun or being kept in smoky huts?)

Color theorists in the seventies were quick to conclude that using "black" as a racial identifier would only hinder the social acceptance of people of African descent. Patton jumps on this in *Color to Color,* asking, what makes black-as-negative so fixed when the "values" of color change? Black, featured boldly in many flags of Africa and revered there as a symbol of power, health, and strength, has been in transition on Euro-American turf since the color revolution. By the eighties, Real Men Wore Black: It was out of mourning, it was "daytime." And though in clothing and design "all-black" is getting kinda tired, what's it being replaced by? High-energy color. Diaspora color! Girlfriend's still distracted. She throws every white towel, every curtain, every sheet into the middle of the room and yells, WESTERN, CHRISTIAN VALUES; EUROPEAN HERITAGE!

I walk girlfriend back to a chair and dump a pile of magazines and CDs on her lap. Look, I tell her. As they dominate the pop eye, isn't it arresting, inspiring, titillating to see young African Americans shake up colors—their iconography, their appeal? How these musicians, actors, and models saturate the cultural canvas with a prism of skin tones and the way they wear and present colors— Queen Latifah in warm pumpkin crowns, Arsenio in cobalt-blue suits, Living Colour, the band, throwing paint like Pollock, its Brit spelling shouting out to diaspora blacks: We are living, we are everywhere, we look good in fuchsia.

Girlfriend throws the magazines on the floor. She misses Brooklyn. She misses sisters in tangerine lipstick, stoops in Park Slope painted red, black, and green, nose rings, Isaac's purple high tops, faux kente shoulder bags, baby jumpers, evening wear, and place mats.

I give her a new box of Crayola crayons. Listen to this: In the eighty-eight-year history of Crayola, only two colors have ever had their names changed. One was "flesh," which became "peach" in 1962, "a result of the civil rights movement," says the official company fact sheet. (The color "indian red," lowercase to keep it consistent with other crayon names, still remains in the line.) Crayola has been spurred on by American teachers to test-market a "Skin Tones of the World" collection. You'll love the sticker on the pack: "A multicultural assortment . . . plus black and white for blending." Go ahead, I tell girlfriend, draw Brooklyn. She pouts.

Come on, you need a walk. We battle snow in search of cappuccino. We pass buses, billboards. Hey, isn't this a trip, we're in a state with a tiny, 6 percent population "of color," but all the outdoor ads we've seen feature black people: The Virginia Slims Afro-chic model in electric-blue kufi, Oprah in a different color low-cut sweater for each day her show airs, Joey Browner of the Minnesota Vikings in an ad for Zubaz workout wear uses a globe for a footrest. What does it mean? I'll tell you what it means, girlfriend snarls, they don't lynch Negroes here, they just put our faces on pancake mix. Obviously, I tell her, this color therapy stuff isn't doing you any good, maybe you're just PMSing. She sucks teeth: You have twenty-four hours to find faux kente.

In the coffee shop we meet a young man who says things like "my beautiful Nubian princess" and has, thank God, his very own faux-kente kufi. Walking home, Miss Columnist buys the latest *Ebony Man* with chocolate cover boy Wesley Snipes in, all at once, magenta pants, a goldenrod-and-hot-pink vest, and persimmon blazer. She tacks it above her computer.

I think she's gonna make it after all.

*1991*

# dirt and overness

This is Brooklyn, there *are* no secrets. And if you can't take the heat, Miss Nine Months in the Midwest, call U-Haul to carry your wide-load receiver back to the cornfields, and don't expect me to visit.'' That's Deandra, of course, ever demure, ever tactful, ever too fabulous for her paycheck. Her advice: Give up hope for a private life now that I'm back in the borough. But didn't we all move from trigger-happy Sugar Hill and the overhip Lower E. to the maple groves of Fort Greene and Prospect Heights for sanctuary? So that no one we know or care about would see us in raggedy plaits pushing ten tons of dirty panties and humming our favorite laundry song, Phyllis Hyman's "Don't Wanna Change the World (I Just Want To Be Your Girl)"?

Well, I hate to break it to you, as Deandra broke it to me, but brush those teeth, take off those mammy-for-a-weekend headrags. You're being *watched* and your outfits are being *rated!* Didn't we find out that Miss Brooklyn is the most fabulous Negress of all? So fabulous, she makes a Pedro Almodóvar movie look like *The Muppets Go to Ibiza.* Know why? 'Cause we're all here! So and so, the songwriter-producer, and so-and-so, the model-actress turned cosmetic saleswoman, and we all live within five blocks of each other. You know what that means, don't you? What those polite little *New York Times* profiles on black, artsy Fort Greene won't tell you. Dirt! Dirt for days, years, centuries. Who's boning whom (or whatever the hype word of the week is), who left whom, who should've left whom, and who is "in euphemism" with whom, as in, "seeing," "friends with," or the least subtle, "talking to."

And overness? Self-absorbed, self-conscious, self-righteous, that's us. *Over*come with ourselves. We're too grand, aren't we, with our mud-cloth top hats and kente parasols? (Accessories really help us strike that balance between African and American, don't they?) And too fabulous, with our three-picture deals, European subsidiary rights, and our jazz-pop albums stretched out on the R&B tip, platinum-bound, no question. Johnny Kemp was a sage, wasn't he? It's about getting paid, because after all, getting paid *is* a black issue, isn't it? Naturally, there's concern that so-and-so is getting paid more for being black and fabulous than we are, but there's enough to go around—isn't there?

So when Deandra called last night to say meet me at Two Steps Down, one of those Fort Greene hangouts where the dirt flies fast and furious, I wasn't exactly rushing the door. Nothing against Two Steps, fine establishment, good food, but truth is, I wasn't ready to make my Brooklyn debut. I was two paychecks away from that kind of wardrobe. But Deandra has this way of twisting your arm, leg, and upper thigh, so I found myself on the D train, DeKalb bound. Along for the ride was a white woman in violet lip gloss holding a kitten and a black man in shades holding a fat, oily snake. They seemed to have just met, by chance, on this train car. Another woman was dressed head to toe in gold, to match a fifteen-inch gold beehive and nails, twenty-four-karat plated. Sitting next to the Flo-Jo lady was a young black guy with jeans way past his butt, a Mötley Crüe scarf tied on his head like the rock boys do, and his nose deep in the Holy Koran. I felt very much at home.

Two Steps, on the other hand, was full of mannequins from the Armani A/X sample sale. Deandra's friend, the young jazz-hybrid singer Gordon Chambers, was gospelizing his precious heart and soul out, yet the Fabs, having to choose between catching the spirit or striking the pose, chose the pose. Sucking down Kir Royales at a table front and center were Deandra and her crew, their heads bent together in weighty cultural exchange.

"I want to make it with Chris Rock, Wesley of course, fine Kevin Jackson last seen in *Caucasian Chalk Circle,* Sinbad but only on the cover of *Essence,* Cynda Williams's in need of a comb in *One False Move,* but did you get an invitation to the Jean Michel Basquiat opening, I did, it's a shame that *Vanity Fair* article tries to discredit Basquiat's work, white jealousy if you ask me, and by the way, should I name my dog Richard Wright or Wilfredo Lam?" said Deandra.

"Wilfredo Lam. Lam was a race man too, but he was an absolutely more sexy one than Wright 'cause he was a surrealist, and if you name your dog after him, more people will appreciate him, but really, I've got to figure out a title for my new book, obviously I need something womanist, something colored, and something to express my hybridity, but before that, I must talk for a moment about how guilty I feel sitting here drinking five-dollar champagne coolers when Fort Greene has the highest infant mortality rate in the city, and babies in the Walt Whitman projects two blocks away are being raised on a strict diet of Hawaiian Punch and Devil Dogs, and fine young men in Bed-Stuy shoot each other for recreation, but honestly the only bad thing about being a notorious black woman writer is that the current side pieces of all my ex-Negroes come up to me at literary events and try to run these weird power moves by announcing, in front of as many innocent bystanders as possible, that they are now screwing my ex-Negroes, then they look at me solemnly like I should care," said another dear friend, Tamu.

I used to care (about middle-class negritude and identity angst, that is), though lately I've been questioning my market niche. A job at *PC Magazine* is sounding real good. I met some nice guys at Cables & Chips the other day. I bet they could teach me a thing or two about ports and circuits. When I left Two Steps Down, Tamu and Deandra had their arms above their heads playing freeze tag. Deandra explained later that indeed they were not playing freeze tag, but attempting to be more colored, more fabulous, and more paid than anyone else in the room. And the only way to do this was to assume Diana Ross's I-Am-the-World pose, so vividly preserved on celluloid in *Mahogany*. But why were they doing this? Because Deandra's new Negro's ex-ex had just walked into the room and someone had to throw shade first. I headed straight for the pay phone downstairs. Forget the D train, get me a gypsy cab. Is this Black Pearl? Take me to Manhattan quick, Brooklyn is just two steps *over*.

*1992*

# school
# clothes

The white children on the back of the White Pages are smiling. They all have freckles and warm flannel shirts. "Can You Find the Drug Pusher In This Picture?" the caption asks, since this is an ad for the Partnership for a Drug-Free America. Read on, and in small type you'll be assured that none of these cherubs sell crack because, after all, "We all know what drug pushers look like. We've seen them often enough on television." The pushers are the guys in the baggy jeans with their baseball caps turned around, right? But wait, not *those* guys in the caps; the *black* and *brown* guys! Shucks, under those caps these days it's so hard to tell.

Our favorite storybook of the supernatural, surreal, and painfully real, *Jet* magazine, recently sampled black educators on the
value of dress codes at inner-city public schools. All saw codes and
uniforms as bait to get poverty-cycle kids to focus on academics
and as an effective deterrent to school violence. Sobering tales were
told of kids getting shot for wearing the wrong color or the right
Nikes. And even of a rash of homicides in Chicago called the Starter
Jacket Murders after the to-kill-for sports-logo jackets. Oddly
enough, or not so for *Jet*, there was an item in the same issue on the
rap duo Kris Kross and their oversize sports-logo clothes worn
backward—a form of "Kross" dressing *Jet* found inventive and
charming.

There's something sadly ironic about endorsing dress codes in
city schools to curb violence, while Madison Avenue, Hollywood,
and Afro-chic entrepreneurs ride the jock of young black male style
straight to the bank. A recent sighting guaranteed to induce nausea
is Mattel's "Rappin' Rockin'" Barbie and Ken, Vanilla Ice clones
who come with thick gold chains and a boom box: Hip-hop style
repackaged and safely distanced from the black subject/suspect. So
we see: It's not the gold chains, the Starter jackets, or the Nike high
tops that are inherently criminal, it's what George Bush likes to call
"the little brown ones" wearing them.

Though you could argue that policing style is just another form
of policing those doing the stylin', some parents and folks who run
schools in New York City would disagree. They see it as a means of
protecting kids in war zones. As of last year, close to twenty city
public schools, backed by parent-teacher associations and district
offices, have instituted voluntary dress codes.

Parents say they favor the codes primarily to cuts costs. (Most
codes call for a white shirt and simple black skirt or pants.) In the
age of BabyGap, GapKids, Nike baby shoes, and so on, it's no small
expense keeping the young ones up-to-date in the hype gear. (With
40 percent of black children living below the poverty line in families headed for the most part by single women, it's more like a
serious hardship). Parents also agree with *Jet* that school codes help

stop the theft of high-status clothing that they say happens in and around their neighborhood schools.

Teacher and mother Isabel Cacho leads a class of bilingual fifth graders at a school in Bedford-Stuyvesant that adopted a dress code this year. To Cacho, "right" and "wrong" clothes are a source of unhealthy anxiety for her students, even at eleven years old. She describes how painful it is to see children in threadbare pants sitting next to others decked out in Ralph Lauren Polo. Though not Catholic, Cacho says she sent two of her own children to a Catholic school in the eighties to cut down on clothing costs and steer them clear of the "deadly" sneaker and leather wars. She's glad her younger son, O'Neil, eleven, is able to attend a dress-code elementary school, P.S. 308. O'Neil, who can tell you anything you want to know about Cross Colours and Marco Polo pants though he doesn't own any, says the dress code instituted at his school last year makes kids "prouder to be from our school." Still, sometimes, he feels, "you want to make a look that's you, but the principal is saying be somebody else."

At his comical and patronizing best, Ed Koch unveiled in 1988 a plan to improve the quality of public education in the city: dress codes. The mayor made a deal with a manufacturer to donate uniforms to one Harlem school. That's as far as he took this educational initiative. Board of Education official policy on the codes is that they must be voluntary, as the federal Department of Education has suggested that restricting dress could be a violation of the First Amendment. The surge of interest in codes began a few years back. Principal Carole Foster of P.S. 175 in Central Harlem claims uniforms tripled enrollment and upped reading scores there. With over one thousand public schools spread throughout five boroughs, it's doubtful that codes will ever be a citywide movement, yet more schools are opting for them, including, this fall, Brooklyn's J.H.S. 265 in Fort Greene.

You'll find Susan Smith McKinney Junior High underneath the long arm of the elevated Brooklyn-Queens Expressway. Boxed in between the Brooklyn Navy Yard and the Walt Whitman projects, it's a modern prison of white brick and wired-in windows. The school has been getting press of late due to its new principal/crusader. Henry Pankey is out to turn one of the city's most infamous war-zone schools into a photo-perfect model of inner-city pride. A former actor, the fifteen-year vet of the public school system thinks educators could stand to learn something from theater and advertising.

Armed with nothing but high ambitions and a deep voice, Pankey has refinished 265 with the title of "prep school," complete with academic goals and uniforms to reflect "Wall Street–style success." The seventy-three-dollar outfits combine a preppy blazer with a vest or tie of an African-inspired print. Pankey resents that articles on the school have focused on the uniforms; they're just the first step in his plan to raise up a school once known for absenteeism and assaults on teachers.

With portraits of Mayor Dinkins and Malcolm X holding vigil, eight McKinney preps file into Pankey's office to discuss the uniforms. These are young adults not likely to be cowed by the conformity that school uniforms represent. They have other questions for Pankey: What if the kids from the shelters can't come up with the money? Why should seniors pay for uniforms? Isn't the African print "kind of played"?

When I tell certain colleague friends about my trip to 265, they aren't as romanced as I was by the African-print vests. Cultural critic/hip-hop observer Tricia Rose likens dress codes to airlifting swimsuits to Somalia, but no food. "What about more counselors, a lecture series, a book reading drive?" Rose reminds me. "Can't we do anything besides tell kids if you look like the white middle class everything will be okay?"

In the lobby of J.H.S. 265, there's a sign: NO WEAPONS, NO BEEPERS, NO RADIOS. The eight kids in Pankey's office voiced real fears about the violence around them. Tyrone wanted to know why the girl on his block who got killed over a pair of earrings didn't make the six o'clock news. Lisa swears that Pankey is the only principal she's met brave enough to wait with his students at the bus stop. These kids know their immediate predator isn't the amorphous white system chipping away at their civil liberties, it's the little knucklehead next door with the semiautomatic.

On the train at DeKalb Avenue, the closest stop to 265, there's a public service ad that kindly reprints Emily Dickinson's poem, "Hope is the Thing with Feathers." Someone has crossed it out and written: "Hope is making it off this fucken train and not gettin kill [sic]."

*1992*

# **mandela** diary

They said he was tired. They said he spent twenty-seven years of a life sentence in jail for treason (a fancy way of saying he fought for the right to vote in the country he was born in; a right, it was said, over and over again, he still doesn't have). They also said the man who had the sense to release him from prison should be rewarded for his foresight.

They said the man who had been in prison would visit eight cities in America, the land of the free, and that the first city would be New York, the city of opportunity, where most of the people in prison are black, and most of the people who run the prisons are white. Others said for a country like America to welcome this man with open arms (so much so that he would declare during his visit, "I am a Yankee") was the biggest hypocrisy of all. Because back in 1962, the Central Intelligence Agency, an organization, some people say, America uses to spy on and even kill people who live in other countries, may or may not have had a hand in putting the freedom fighter behind bars.

Yet he came anyway, the freedom fighter (which is easier to say or has fewer complicated implications than deputy president of the African National Congress). At the airport he was met by the governors of three American states. And the flag of the once banned African National Congress, not the "official" flag of South Africa, was flown next to the American flag (which is so sacred, it soon may be legally protected from fire).

Some people, many of them black, thought the high points of freedom fighter's visit were his pilgrimages to Brooklyn and Harlem. Others weren't satisfied; they said he spent too much time nuzzling with the mayor and affluent New Yorkers than communing with those people in New York, many of them black, who had supported his cause all along. But in Brooklyn and Harlem, most people who greeted the freedom fighter and his wife, also a freedom fighter, opened their arms without question.

At times their visit felt like the most joyous and historic reunion in years; a time akin to the early sixties, when the newly independent nations of Africa led black Americans to rethink their culture and politics in relation to the continent. The visit of the freedom fighter positioned us, for a minute, at the center of world politics. It made us the First Family. It gave us, once again (and perhaps for longer than a minute), an accessible past, so that the African part of the equation suddenly made a lot more sense. And we bought, the T-shirts to prove it.

What becomes a legend most? Nelson Mandela.

*Day One:* Bedford-Stuyvesant, Brooklyn. Where this morning, and it's not even eight o'clock yet, you wake up to African drums. Police barricades and vendors hawking T-shirts line Fulton Street as far south as you can see. Families pack into the athletic field of Boys and Girls High School (which bans students from wearing gold jewelry, shearling coats, and miniskirts). There's no shade in the field at all, and in the middle, surrounded by more blue sawhorses, is a small, open-faced trailer draped with the banner BOYS AND GIRLS HIGH WELCOMES NELSON MANDELA. Not counting the airport, this will be Mandela's first stop on American soil. An hour earlier, 1010 WINS news radio said he was tired, that he'd scrap the trip to Boys and Girls in Bed-Stuy, dubbed the "Soweto of New York," and proceed directly to Manhattan and ticker tape. Still, the assembly at Boys and Girls, which is mostly black and under twenty-one, is confident.

Homages to sixties nationalism beam from every corner. Important young men in Malcolm X glasses and important young women in African-fabric headwraps scurry back and forth. These are students from Boys and Girls and the Central Brooklyn Youth Coalition who planned the program. An ANC youth leader, who will later have the honor of introducing Mandela himself, arrives on the trailer's makeshift stage to "share with [you] a few of our slogans." "All the power," he calls, and the congregation answers the usual, "To the people!" Next, a man who doesn't identify himself goes on mike to "thank the sisters for their support of the warriors up here."

Television crews scout photo ops amid the sea of brown children. NBC approaches a seven-year-old boy with a headful of dreads as he straddles a police barricade. The blonde newswoman taps the kid on the shoulder with a pencil to get him to face the camera. He does, but refuses to smile. Elders wait patiently in the hot sun. Anna Nicholson, eighty, who worked for twenty-five years in the garment district, says she's here to see Mandela because, "They didn't break his spirit. My grandfather was a slave, and he used to say, 'If you got an education, they can take everything, but they can't get it out of your head.' "

*11:35 a.m.:* It's CNN's point man in Bed-Stuy, natch, who breaks the news: Mandela's plane has touched down. But is he coming to Boys and Girls? Day-Glo yellow FREE SOUTH AFRICA signs are distributed to the crowd, which has doubled. Police helicopters begin flying over the field every ten minutes.

Two hours later than expected, two hours of hot sun later, the motorcade graces Bed-Stuy. Though sweaty and thirsty, the crowd is still good for a rock-star's welcome, complete with catcalling and tears. An elevated subway line looms above Boys and Girls's field, and a train passes just as Mandela appears at the rickety podium, its sound drowned out by the crowd. For three minutes straight they yell for him. Mandela smiles widely and seems so young. His silver Afro frames his face like a halo. A woman says out loud to no one in particular, "Look at him, look at him! He looks just like my grandfather." (This woman, our reporter realizes a few seconds later, is herself.) Winnie glows in traditional purple-and-white dress. This is a truly religious experience, a man back from the land of the dead to lead the living and an authentic African queen. (Winnie is not really a queen, though she was the first black medical social worker certified in South Africa.) Mandela brings the crowd back to earth with comments on the quality of education in the Natal province: "Our education is not controlled by our people, but by whites." The people respond, surprisingly in unison, "Same in Brooklyn."

As the ringside photographers pack their gear, a girl in a long, green satin dress and veil, wanders into the press area selling buttons. She says her name is Adashina, that she's nine years old and a member of the African Islam mission on Bedford Avenue in Brooklyn. She says, "The imam of the mission makes the buttons, and we sell them and give half of the money to him." One button insures that ISLAM IS THE ANSWER. Our reporter buys one with the legend SHE WAITED FOR MANDELA.

*The township outside City Hall, 3:20 p.m.:* Some 350 people have the privilege of sitting on the dais (including ninety-two-year-old black reparations activist Queen Mother Moore, who in the second row is three seats down from Bella Abzug, but behind Dick Gregory, who is front row right). Most who came to see the FREEDOM MAN (says a button with his picture) claim his key to

the city are in the street just beyond City Hall. The "townships" is what a passerby coins the area where folks stand in the
street, hoping for a glimpse of Mandela but contained by barricades.

A dozen teenage boys stand on these barricades trying for a
better view. For support, they lean on a parked Channel 2 news
truck. Correspondent Reggie Harris, who is black, sits atop the
truck pecking at his laptop and following the dais on portable moni-
tor. Harris warns the kids to stop leaning on the truck. "Hope your
ass falls off," one kid yells back. Before wandering away, the boys,
all black, give the truck a good push.

Noise from the sidelines has quieted down a bit, and we hear
Dinkins make his proclamations: "Mr. Mandela, I am proud to
present to you the people of New York, a gorgeous mosaic of races,
religions, national origin, and sexual orientation." A twenty-five-
year-old Nigerian man, also in the townships section, holds up a
sign as Dinkins speaks. "Criticize black Africa," the sign reads, "as
you do apartheid, it's a human rights issue." The Nigerian explains
that he's not here to protest, just to let people know that "atroci-
ties going on in black Africa are virtually ignored by the Afro-
American elected officials and activists. Why is it okay for black
Africa to kill other Africans, and not okay for apartheid to kill black
Africa?"

*4:30 p.m.:* The City Hall ceremony ends, though not too many
people in the townships seem to notice right away. Michael McIntyre, director of the Queens Independent Living Center, an advocacy and resource center for disabled New Yorkers, was of the
chosen who sat on the dais, and he's suited down for the occasion.
As McIntyre talks about how the civil rights movement of people
with disabilities is related to the struggles of blacks in South Africa,
Jesse Jackson is making his exit. Though many people want an
audience with the reverend, Jackson spots McIntyre and hurries
over to offer his hand. In the hustle, McIntyre's wheelchair is sent
careening down the sidewalk. Jesse rushes off and doesn't seem to
notice. "I've been outshined," says McIntyre with a coy smile. He

puts his chair on course and continues in a quiet voice discussing "the apartheid of the disabled."

*Day Two, Harlem, 2:30 p.m.:* The number 2 train stops at the corner of Martin Luther King Jr. Boulevard (125th Street) and Malcolm X Boulevard (Lenox Avenue), one block east of Africa Square. Near the train entrance is a book vendor, a golden-skinned woman with blond dreads who asks first if she is speaking to a "sister" before launching into a tirade about police harassment: "I've been out here since eight in the morning. The cops tried to tell us to move. Meanwhile, you've got some white folks around the corner supposedly selling ANC T-shirts. That money ain't going to no ANC. This is our event, this our community. This is the only time we get to make money."

Nearby another vendor, selling copies of *The Blackman's Guide to Understanding the Blackwoman* by Shahrazad Ali, complains that she's been hassled by the cops all day: "They tried to stop us from selling, but they couldn't because vendors make a program. It's not enough to see an event, you need souvenirs." Another, who calls himself "Watermelon Man," peddles chopped watermelon. "Bensonhurst gave watermelon a bad name," he says, "but basically it's good business."

*3:15 p.m.:* Smack in the middle of 125th Street, in front of the state office building, an impromptu drumming session is drawing a group of dancers and shouters. "Do that dance, sisters!" urges a man in a construction hat, who later yells at the cops, "Your wickedness can never overpower the goodness here." Cops arrive to break up the dancing. They need the space to park police cars.

In African Square, the same spot where Malcolm X, Adam Clayton Powell, Fidel Castro, and Martin Luther King once addressed Harlem, the masses are gathering for Mandela. The dais is set up in the intersection of African Square itself, while the streets that lead into it serve as holding pens for the crowds. On the south side of ACP Boulevard the horde extends to 123rd Street. On every floor of the former Theresa Hotel people lean out of windows and hang banners. A group sitting on top of a bus shelter waves red, black, and green flags. Spotted in the sea of faces: a man strutting a large gold medallion in the shape of the African continent. In the middle of the continent is a mirror.

Jesse arrives earlier than the Mandela motorcade to get an early piece of Harlem. The dais fills up: Congressman Charles Rangel (in kente strip), sour-faced city pol Denny Farrell, Flavor Flav (with clocks), and Chuck D. (with Raiders cap). A tree that is supposed to be planted in African Square in honor of the children of Soweto is moved by forklift in front of the dais, where it obscures all the profiling happening on the dais platform. Folks are most upset. The call goes up: "Move the tree!"

*7:15 p.m.:* "We want Mandela," comes the chant from way down on 123rd Street. Some folks say they've been waiting in African Square since eleven in the morning. Fainting people are being carried out left and right. Those in the way back see the motorcade first. The screaming, the cheering, the flag waving ripples to the front. A black Secret Service agent appears on stage with a large object hidden behind a raincoat. Harlem's favorite widow introduces herself as "Mrs. Malcolm X" and, as if on cue, an elderly woman near the stage rises to her feet and waves a white handkerchief. There's a shock of recognition from Winnie, then she embraces widow X, a/k/a Betty Shabazz (an image bite that makes evening news). Winnie, in Western dress tonight, notifies Harlem that "we have no reason to trust Mr. de Klerk yet. . . . We want to know if you're with us when we go back to the bush." "Teach," says Harlem. "Tell it," says Harlem.

Dhoruba Bin Wahad, an American political prisoner for nineteen years, speaks almost intimately to Mandela from the podium: "You were the symbol that helped sustain me." Wahad cautions him that the same people who "helped convict you now want to befriend you." Dinkins shifts in his seat.

Nelson Mandela finally walks, slowly, carefully, downstage to address the "working people of Harlem." He recites the names that have been called so often in the last couple of days: Sojourner

Truth, Paul Robeson, Rosa Parks, Marcus Garvey, Fannie Lou Hamer, Malcolm X. "Harlem symbolizes strength, beauty, and re- sistance," Mandela caresses. Later, in a firmer voice, he contradicts his wife: "We do not doubt the sincerity of Mr. de Klerk." Not once does he acknowledge Wahad, his empassioned words or his cau- tions.

After the Mandela motorcade pulls away it's announced that ten thousand dollars was raised by passing the hat; cranky, jaded, un- derpaid New Yorkers, Harlemites mostly, passing bills from hand to hand, had given the ANC ten grand. As the tired and maybe the spiritually fed make their way home, a man sets up a cardboard box to sell Mandela books and biographies. He shows off a rare photo. "This," he says, "is a picture of Mandela as a baby being washed."

*Yankee Stadium, the Afterparty, 11:15 p.m.:* The speeches are over. Last act, KRS One and Boogie Down Productions, has steam still to share: "Everything you see is not rosy, it's not happy, and it's not hand clapping. What you see here today is called revolutionary- ism. We, here in America and in South Africa, we have got to get together under one roof and say we are sick and tired of the bullshit!" Not the perfect evening news sample, but the crews are long gone, knowing perhaps KRS would be too saucy for the harmony-fest broadcast news is staging out of the Mandela visit.

"Fifteen to twenty years from now," KRS bellows to a nearly empty Yankee Stadium, "there'll be a totally different story about what went on here tonight. Tell your children the truth! Apartheid ain't over yet." The music kicks off. KRS starts rapping: "Mandela's not free, Mandela's not free." A young white woman in a "Black Pride, Providence College" T-shirt grinds her hips to the beat. "He can't even vote in his own country."

*Day Three:* Winnie in Brooklyn. Driving over the Brooklyn Bridge, the cab driver, age thirty-five and African American, ex- plains that he "objected to Jewish leaders objecting to Mandela calling the PLO comrades in arms. As far as I'm concerned, Israelis are doing the same thing to the Palestinians that white South Afri- cans are doing to black South Africans." After dropping two black passengers at their destination, the next ride he picks up is an Orthodox Jew.

House of the Lord Church in downtown Brooklyn is the site of a "women's leadership symposium" with guest of honor Winnie Mandela. Distinguished ladies in Sunday church clothes and plumed hats, or African gowns and tucked headdresses, line up on this brilliant spring afternoon outside of the church, which, like everything else in the city, is surrounded by police barricades. Ladies like writer Paula Giddings, Jewel Jackson McCabe, president of 100 Black Women, and Assemblywoman Helen Marshall from Queens. And ladies who usually don't have to line up, like Mother Hale, *Essence* editor Susan Taylor, and the NAACP's Hazel Dukes. So many of them sport the Black Cameo, the cameo for the women of color created by artist Coreen Simpson, it looks like the seal of a new order.

When Winnie Mandela walks into the church, everyone rises. There are many black women journalists covering the event, including the *New York Post*'s Pamela Newkirk, and they and other members of the press rise too. The response is the most heartfelt yet: Women whoop, cry, holler, throw their hands in the air. Anything anyone says at the podium after that gets a "That's right," "Yes!" or "Umm hmm." Betty Shabazz introduces Winnie once again: "This sister's presence in our midst is enough. She shouldn't even have to speak ["That's right" "Uh humm" "Yes"]. To have gone through what she has gone through ["That's right" "Uh humm" "Yes"], and to see her present, so composed! There must be a God. There's got to be a God."

Winnie stands in the pulpit with her fist raised, her upper arm tucked near her temple, in the way she does, turning the Black Power salute into a comfortably feminine gesture. "My sisters, my sister Joyce [Dinkins] over there," Winnie bows her head. "I will not address the gentlemen, they have no business being here." Thunder from the audience. Then not in jest, "If women were at the forefront of our struggle, it would have been won long ago." Mrs. Mandela goes on speak of projects for which the ANC needs to raise money; this is the first concrete example of the ANC's works that we've heard in three days.

After the House of the Lord, we all rush up the block to the Brooklyn Academy of Music to hear more Winnie. BROOKLYN'S AFRI-CAN DIASPORA WELCOMES NELSON AND WINNIE MANDELA, reads a banner outside of the academy. Master of ceremonies Cicely Tyson is full of quips for this audience of mostly black women and their children (Empty baby carriages are left in the lobby). "Oh, the joy," she testifies, "of knowing who you are, what you are, and where you're from." Cicely tells a story: Winnie was detained in 1958 for her involvement in a demonstration against passbooks for African women. She was pregnant at the time and later was banned from the courtroom for wearing traditional dress. Apparently Winnie told the court: "Of the few rights I still have in this country, Mr. Prosecutor, I still have the right to choose my own ward-robe!"

For the ladies here at the academy, Winnie adds a glittering green-and-gold headdress to her outfit. Yes, she did say, "We know you will be there to take up arms with us." And yes, we did say we would. But more moving was her simple reminder that the people who die in South Africa, and die often, are children. There's blood everywhere, and mothers like Winnie are tired of mopping it up. It was something that with all this talk of foreign relations, diplomacy, and merchandise, we had plain forgot.

*On the D train back to Manhattan:* A young black woman, around eighteen or so, wears a Simpsons family T-shirt with the moto FAMILY BONDING. She has a black eye and bruises on her arm, and stares off into space. Next to her is a young black man, around eighteen or so, sporting a thick gold chain and white leather warm-up suit. He glares at other passengers as if daring them to say something. In the entire car, not a single Nelson Mandela or Win-nie Mandela button or T-shirt in sight.

*1990*

# forty acres and a holiday

There are three legends told of how enslaved Africans in the Texas territory came to know of their freedom, and why the word didn't get to them until two months after the Civil War ended, which was a good two and half years after Lincoln's Emancipation Proclamation. Or, to make it plain, rather late. One legend says the messenger, a black Union soldier, was murdered. Another says he arrived, but had been delayed by mule travel. (A variation on this is that he had stopped to get married.) The third and favored is that the news was withheld by white landowners so they could bleed one last crop from slave labor. What *is* held as fact is that June nineteenth—the day that federal troops rode into Galveston with orders to release those kept as slaves—has been celebrated for 127 years, in Texas and beyond, as Emancipation Day, as Jubilation Day, as Juneteenth. The day the last ones heard.

Juneteenth, the name, is one of those fab African-Americanisms, functional, rhythmic, at once concise and not too concise. It fuses the month of June with the number nineteen, and eludes to the fact that the holiday was held in adjoining states on different days of the month as folks got the word. Early emancipation rituals were not exclusive to Texas (South Carolina and Mississippi's fall in May)—or to the South. What may have been the first emancipation ceremony was held in New York as early as 1808 to mark the legal cessation of the slave trade.

No state comes close to Juneteenth in Texas, the black folks' Fourth of July, with its parades, feasting, pageants, and preachifying. Emancipation day organizations in Texas date back to the turn of the century. The most powerful image from the early days must have been former slaves themselves, who, according to tradition, marched together at the end of parade lines. By the 1950s Juneteenth Day came to be linked with, not freedom from slavery, but segregation. On Juneteenth, Texas's Jim Crow cities would allow blacks to be citizens for twelve hours a year by granting them entry into whites-only parks and zoos. With the passage of civil rights legislation in the sixties, refined black Texans abandoned Juneteenth to their country cousins and took to celebrating Independence Day in July along with their white brethren.

A Juneteenth renaissance has been gathering steam since the mid eighties, spurred by the Afrocentricity crusade. Beyond being a hootenanny for black Texas (the condescending folksy portrait favored by the local press), it's become a holiday eagerly adopted nationwide by African Americans in search of cultural signposts. Not to mention one that offers, as is required these days, a dramatic tube-and-T-shirt–friendly soundbite of black history.

The J-Day momentum is due in large part to the efforts of a man you might call Daddy Juneteenth, state representative Al Edwards from Houston. Edwards sponsored the bill that made Juneteenth an official Texas holiday thirteen years ago, a feat in a state that still closes banks for Confederate Heroes Day. Juneteenth U.S.A., Edwards's organization, tracks J-Day rites across the country and is fundraising for a national educational headquarters. To Edwards the holiday has tremendous secular and sacred promise. He sees it as an economic vehicle for African Americans, as well as a day that should be observed with almost holy remembrance: "The Jews say if they ever forget their history, may their tongues cleave to the roof of their mouth. . . . Let the same happen to us."

You can find Juneteenth rituals in all regions of the country now. States like California, where Texans migrated en masse, have held Juneteenth festivities for decades. The New York area's largest is in Buffalo, tapping into upstate's rich history of antislavery activity. Wisconsin counts at least five, including Milwaukee's, where Juneteenth has been celebrated since 1971 and is the best attended single-day cultural event in the state. Far from being family picnics, these festivals sometimes last for days, made possible by the legwork of community groups, city cooperation, and private sector donations. Juneteenth in Minneapolis, now in its seventh year, is building a rep as one of the most progressive and trendsetting J-Day celebrations in the Texas diaspora. What began as a poetry reading in a church basement is now two weeks of programming, including a film festival and an Underground Railroad reenactment. At these celebrations old world often knocks against new world, when Miss Juneteenth pageants (inherited from towns like Brenham, Texas, which crowns a "Goddess of Liberty") share the stage with Afro-chic street fairs ablaze in faux kente.

There are those who think Juneteenth is an embarrassment. That the holiday tells more of our ignorance and subjugation than of an inheritance that predates slavery in the Americas. Or that it's "too black" because it promotes a separate but not equal Fourth of July, or "not black enough" as it's often funded by white purses. And of course that it's far too symbolic and doesn't solve anything. What does a Juneteenth celebration mean anyway when the Freeman's Bureau never gave us our forty acres and a mule? (Not thrilled about news of the state holiday, one former Texas legislator had this to say: "Dancing up and down the streets, drinking red soda water, eating watermelons. . . . I grew out of that.") But Juneteenth critics haven't put a dent in the holiday's grass-roots popularity.

Folks are hungrier than ever for rituals that enshrine our identity as hyphen Americans. Kwanzaa's metamorphosis in the last few years speaks to this need. And merchandising opportunities are never far behind: Evolving in two short decades from cultural nationalist position paper to mainstream ethnic festival profiled in the *Times*'s Living section, Kwanzaa has spawned its own designer cookbook and Santa surrogate, Father Kwanzaa. Now Juneteenth spreads like spring fever. Also gaining steam are rites of passage ceremonies for young men and women that are based on ancient African models and seek to address modern urban ills. (The National Rites of Passage Organization held its fifth annual conference this year.) And spotted last year in *Sage: A Scholarly Journal on Black Women:* plans for a Middle Passage memorial holiday that would fall near Thanksgiving.

Buried in their shopping ethos, we tend to forget holidays were once holy days that defined us in more profound ways than what Nintendo jumbo pack we got for Christmas. Michael Chaney, an arts activist in Minneapolis, believes that Juneteenth rituals could be more than acts of racial communion; they could have a role in redefining America: "We have to realize our own role as historians. We need to ascribe our treasures and offer them to the world. Juneteenth should be a day for all Americans to get in touch with the Africanism within."

Juneteenth does have great possibilities as a new American holiday. Along with reuniting blood relatives, the families that emancipated slaves made embraced family beyond kin, family as community. In this tradition, modern Juneteenth doesn't circumscribe any Dick-and-Jane paean to the nuclear family. You can be a single parent, gay, from D.C. or Ann Arbor; it's a history that includes you. You can read the Emancipation Proclamation out loud or drink some red soda water if you damn please. Or just take a moment out of your day to think about all the folks that laid down nothing less than their lives so that you could see the twentieth century.

*1992*

# looking
# for mariah

They came to see the nose. The nose never lies. Even the missing nose of Egypt's great Sphinx tells a story. Legend has it that Napoleon gave the Sphinx a nose job in the eighteenth century during the Battle of the Nile—too Negroid, too strong? An Egyptologist friend of mine told me it wasn't Napoleon after all, but Egyptian pharaohs, who made a practice of smashing noses off the statues of their predecessors so the old kings couldn't "breathe," meaning exert influence from the afterworld. Murphy's Law: You can never find a good racial conspiracy theory when you need one.

The nose in question is Mariah Carey's. The twenty-year-old pop singer with a seven-octave vocal range. Mother sang with the New York City Opera. At six, little Mariah could do *Rigoletto* in Italian. Later she discovered gospel, then rhythm and blues, Aretha, Minnie Riperton, and things have never been quite the same. Just before Thanksgiving, two dozen media types gathered at an invitation-only luncheon to meet Carey. The singer's debut album, released last June on Columbia/CBS, was now double platinum. Two singles, "Vision of Love" and "Love Takes Time," had topped the pop and R&B charts.

At the luncheon, held at Lola's, another vibe cafe hovering just above Fourteenth Street, all the guests save two or three were black. Seated at linen-clad tables were folks like Janine McAdams, *Billboard*'s black-music editor, *City Sun* arts editor Armond White (who said, on record, he came to see the nose), and a writer from a dance music trade publication who admitted that "for once race wasn't an issue," he had come for the food. (Fried chicken was served.) Apparently the guest of honor was most interested in meeting writer Nelson George, who had sized Carey up in *Playboy*. George's comments, having nothing to do with her body, had all to do with her soul, or more specifically, her marketing profile. George had dubbed Carey a "white girl who can sing."

It was all over the press that Columbia/CBS had rolled out hordes of money for the Carey project. One questions whether the company would have made the same investment in a black vocalist of comparable talent working in the soul idiom. Take Carey's labelmate Regina Belle. Critically acclaimed voice. But Columbia had waited for a good response from the R&B sector on Belle's debut record before selling her, second time around and without fanfare, to the pop market. Carey, on the other hand, was put out as pop product from jump.

Columbia certainly didn't, for Belle, scrap a video and shoot a new one, putting the combined cost of both at $450,000, or so an inside source told Rob Tannenbaum for *Rolling Stone*. (This figure was later dismissed by the company as "total bullshit.") Or give Belle, as they gave Carey, a "promotional blitz equal to the push given Bruce Springsteen in 1975," says Tannenbaum, securing her an appearance on "Arsenio" even before the CD was released. ("We don't look at her [Carey] as a dance-pop artist," Columbia prez Don Ienner told *Rolling Stone*. "We look at her as a franchise.")

Did it matter that Regina Belle is a brown-skinned black woman sans weave? Did it matter ultimately, in Columbia's decision to go all out like this for a new artist, that Carey looks the way she does (long blondish hair, pale skin), and that she is what the press had said she is—white? But is she really?

Though at times Carey's voice on her CD is swallowed by a virtual solar system of twinkling synthesizers, it does have its own guttural integrity. Not the life-experience soul power of a Miki Howard, but Carey is young yet. No question, it's a voice with more emotional grip than Lisa Stansfield's, the white Brit, who *Entertainment Weekly* had crowned the new queen of soul. The girl really *could* sing.

And what *about* that nose? In the CD's cover photo, one curly strand of auburn-blonde hair is strewn across Carey's plump nose, casting it in high relief. Shot from another angle, the nose might have been fuller still. Sign of the tar brush? Said a friend, framing the CD box in his large brown hands, "Saw her videos, but honestly, I can't call this one. Don't know if she's dating Negroes or what, but I tell you one thing, if she herself is not a Negro, there's definitely a Negro component up in there." *Maybe she isn't white, or all white, or . . . ? What is she, or what isn't she?* And since Carey's record company hadn't found it worth mentioning, did only her hairdresser know for sure?

Turned out Mariah Carey was ready to answer just this question at the Mariah Carey luncheon. A vision of loveliness in, how apropos, a two-tone cat suit (black from middrift down, white up top), Carey appeared even taller and leaner than on video. She planted herself opposite George and calmly set the record straight. "My father is black and Venezuelan. My mother is Irish and an opera singer. I am me." The *New York Post*'s gossip page added some spice the next day. Below the caption, CAREY: MIXED ANCESTRY, it was reported that "rocker" Carey wanted to "sock" George for calling her a "white girl who can sing." As I was sitting at the next table, I can confirm: Things weren't dramatic as all that.

The *Post* managed to bungle up Carey's mixed-race résumé, calling her half "black-Brazilian" instead of half "black-Venezuelan." *USA Today* carried the story the following week with the caption MARIAH CAREY, MISUNDERSTOOD. Courtesy information supplied by a Columbia publicist, it was noted that the *Post* had "blown out of proportion" Carey's anger at George and that George and Carey were friends. Before leaving Lola's, George did stop to pose for a photo with Carey, but the luncheon was the first time the two had met.

How's this for a racial conspiracy theory?: Had Columbia/CBS been engaging in a little nineties-style "passing" of Carey? Did the company profit, especially in the first few months of the record's release, from having Carey's racial dossier remain under wraps? (White soul singers being more lucrative pop meal tickets than black ones.) And now that Mariah's background was the source of speculation, was the company interested in smoothing out the edges so as not to alienate any market group? Carey conducting her mixed-race confessional at a fried-chicken confab with George, Mc-Adams, and other influential black-music journalists played like a media maneuver of high order. Soon stories embracing Carey and her biracial identity appeared in the black press. And compared to her first music videos, those that aired post-luncheon showcased a decidedly black presence. (Black bit players, missing before, were cast in endearing roles.) Perhaps higher-ups in Columbia marketing had decided it was time to "come out" with the Carey story before the company was charged with running some sort of cover-up.

I had frustrating conversations with two publicity reps in Columbia's pop division and two in black music. (Ever wonder how offices are set up at these record companies? Is there the pop big house, and then, a few flights down, the black music shanties?) All were adamant that no attempt had been made to mask Carey's background. Though not one wanted to address this on the record, and not one would comment on who had organized the shindig at Lola's and why.

Each conversation I had became twisted in the cobwebs of racial semantics. One publicist said the label had never pronounced Carey "one hundred percent white or one hundred percent black"; that "Carey's heritage has nothing to do with her voice." And why should Carey have to "broadcast her racial background"? When asked, Carey "will answer, but she's not gonna bring it up."

Another suggested that the record company wasn't responsible; "It's a personal thing, not a label thing." And that, if Carey's race wasn't as important to her as it was to other people, this was not a political issue, but a testament to her marketing savvy: "All entertainers like to be viewed as universal."

One told me I was the only person in America interested in Carey's race (or lack of one) and the connection between her look and her marketing budget: "Mariah had a number one black single and a number three black album. Obviously, the black population is identifying with this woman. So is the white population. White or not, no one cares what her background is."

All judgments about Carey's race, said yet another publicist, came from the press based on photos. Both the *New York Times* and *Musician* had fawned over Carey as a "white soul singer." Nelson George told the *Post* that he judged Carey white based on information supplied in a press release from Columbia and the CD photo. When *Voice* critic Vince Aletti described Carey as a white singer who could "pass for Whitney Houston," he received the following letter from a reader:

> *Yo! Vince,*
>
> *You'd better take another look or get yourself some glasses. Not only can Mariah Carey pass for black, she is black! She's just a lighter Whitney Houston. You can't claim this one.*

Aletti says he came to his conclusion from the "gungho marketing" of Carey: "It doesn't happen as often with black artists. Especially coming from a company like Columbia."

Last August Rob Tannenbaum arrived at a rehearsal studio to interview Carey for *Rolling Stone*. Tannenbaum asked the publicist on the scene if Mariah was black, because the "way she's photographed, it's hard to tell what her background is," and in person, he was getting a less ambiguous picture. According to Tannenbaum, the publicist "assured" him that Carey was white. Tannenbaum questions why, when the press started calling Carey "the white Whitney Houston," no one from the company came forward to correct this, to mention that she's half black, if not black period. "If they [Columbia] didn't deliberately create a misimpression," says Tannenbaum, "they didn't go out of their way to clear one up."

As the Carey luncheon was wrapping up, the singer posed with two journalists, deep brown and dashing in black suits. Set against them, the darker hues of her skin seemed all the more prominent, seemed to glow. (I remembered the photo of Carey on her CD's inner sleeve, her ample nose hidden behind song credits.) In person, Carey came across, quite clearly, as a rainbow baby of African descent, skin toasted almond and hair light brown. The ivory-airbrushed, blonde-hair-blowing-at-the-beach fantasy on view in her publicity shots appeared to be entirely a studio creation.

So Carey has declared herself to be a person of color. Whether or not there is a political dimension to that identity in her mind is a different story. Is she, as Nelson George had tagged Renee Tenison, *Playboy*'s 1990 Playmate of the Year, another not so much color-blind, but "race-neutral," mixed-race child? Carey was born in 1970, which means she didn't turn ten years old until 1980. She might well be ignorant of the political importance of affirming a black identity, of the role this has played in the African-American freedom struggle.

Along with her declaration, Carey said this: "It seems that most people don't know much about interracial children." What don't people know? I itched to ask, at this most polite of gatherings. That they exist? That they have options? That they can't be blamed for

America's subtle and not so subtle forms of apartheid? That they are the solution? That they *just want to be me* until America forces them to declare an allegiance?

Several months before the Carey luncheon, an article titled "Who's Black and Who's Not?" appeared in *Ebony*. Penned by Lynn Norment, the piece was illustrated with snapshots of actress Jennifer Beals and singers Paula Abdul, Jody Watley, and Prince. Under each photo, readers were invited to check boxes labeled "black" or "white." *Ebony* and *Jet* are known for their campy coverage of interracial identity (geez Louise, look at those half-white, half-black twins!), but this piece had critical gut: "The issue . . . is not mixed parentage and the increasing number of children from such unions. The issue is the downplaying or a denial of a Black parent or Black heritage for economic, social, or career gain by a descendant of mixed or even unmixed marriage." What makes the current trend so "fascinating and provocative," Norment continues, is that "media and moguls, particularly in the entertainment industry, seem to be encouraging crossoverism, especially by *ethnically ambiguous females*" (emphasis hers).

Walking home from Lola's, the questions piled up: By marketing themselves as anything but black, do light-complexioned entertainers such as Carey become, in the eyes of most Americans, de facto whites? And do Carey and other people of color who feel more at ease representing themselves by their combination ethnic heritages, and not by race (making use of a privilege to remain outside), teach the world how to be "raceless"? Or are they are positioning themselves as a separate class along the lines of South African "coloreds"? And why aren't Carey et al., if they know or care how racism operates, more willing to take a racial stance? Or have we arrived at a point in history when "black" and "white" have become, to quote bell hooks, "definitive no-nos, perpetuating what some folks see as stale and meaningless binary appositions"; a time when such stances/affirmations/commitments serve little purpose?

*Ebony's* known for trafficking in paradox. Two months after chiding racially ambiguous entertainers for hauling tail to the bank without paying their black dues, the magazine published a piece by the same writer, Lynn Norment, on Paula Abdul. Norment praises Abdul for giving "expanded definition to the term 'multiple,'" for being "multitalented, multifaceted, and multiethnic." "Syrian-Brazilian-Canadian-American" is how the singers describes herself. Norment tells us that Abdul acknowledges African-American culture as her most profound influence and is often mistaken for black and Hispanic (or accused of passing for anything but). Yet the singer refuses to be badgered into declaring for any race, for "she is what she is [Syrian-Brazilian-Canadian-American], and stardom will not change that." This time around, Norment has turned multiculti cheerleader, and she congratulates Abdul for working her hybridity for a bigger market share. Why does racial ambiguity get applause in this case? Apparently, to read *Ebony*, what makes the difference is who orchestrates the sell. If it's people of color, it's about *getting paid*. If it's the entertainment industry, it's a sin of omission. Keep that in mind.

I'm on the other side of the spectrum from race-neutral rainbow babies who claim a multitude of heritages but no race. My older sister and I, born in fifty-nine and sixty-one respectively, never explored an option other than black, never wished to. Blackness has always been this wide and miraculous world of people and places and passions and histories and *stances*. Of course, stances. Honorable stances that gave you dignity, that made you part of a much larger world. By all means, stances.

Race politics, the us versus them of it, were spelled out for us early. Growing up on the ethnic Lower East Side (before it became the fashionable multiculti East Village, and New York the gorgeous mosaic), kids from the Ukrainian school on Sixth Street threw evil looks at us and eventually bottles. To be half white, in my mind, in 1965, meant being half *them*. And why should I claim something that wanted no part of me?

There were the aesthetic and intellectual dimensions as well. After seeing Sly and the Family Stone at the Fillmore East just as puberty hit, who didn't want to be Cynthia Robinson, the funky light-skinned sister on trumpet? Later my idols became "high-yella" race women like Angela Davis, Kathleen Cleaver, and Nikki Giovanni. I joined the post–civil rights generation of collegians who took Afro-American history and lit and fashioned ourselves black leaders on campus. We remembered at least the chorus of "Say It Loud—I'm Black and I'm Proud" and clung to fond memories of African dance classes at the New Afrika Houses of our childhood. These signposts stuck in our minds, even when Bakke struck a match under affirmative action and radio melted rhythm and blues down to urban contemporary. And black became less "political vocation" and more "ethnic option."

What does this have to do with Mariah Carey? To value freedom and liberty is to respect the choices others make in identifying themselves, be it by sexual preference, culture, or race. Yet the Careys of the new world have shown me the weight history lays on my open mind. I can't resist comparing them to bisexuals swinging on the closet door in an America in which an "out" gay identity still means a helluva lot. Perhaps I haven't yet figured out what "I am me" solves more than "I'm black and I'm proud." One thing I'm clear on: If we can't find a way to make *multi*ethnic stand for *anti*racism, then I'll pass on it.

The ironies of racial identity and cultural province in the nineties are making popular culture the best sideshow in town. Cultural mulattos (Prince, Madonna, George Michael, Michael Jackson) rule the marketplace. Rainbow baby girls (Mariah, Sade, Jasmine Guy) rule the mirror. Ethnicity is often presented as an open-invitational participatory sport (Vanilla Ice, New Kids on the Block, white female rapper Tarrie B. from Compton). "Separated from a political and historical context," bell hooks writes, "ethnicity is being reconstituted as the new frontier, accessible to all, no passes or permits necessary." Hence my anger when a publicist told me that Mariah Carey's voice had nothing to do with her heritage. I like to think it does, so that people of African descent might still have some sort of title to black culture. Yet this might be romantic, even retrograde, of me in an age when exchange cross culture, cross race happens at a dizzying pace.

The politics of race somersault all around us: More talented-tenths, middle-class blacks, are coming of age in integrated neighborhoods, being educated at majority-white institutions, and laying down roots outside of African-American communities. Pop culture positions blacks center frame as racially motivated violence chokes urban America; President Bush vetoes civil rights legislation as Miss America 1990, a black woman, passes the crown to Miss America 1991, also a black woman; illiteracy, teen pregnancy, and drug slavery dog the underclass, while a new black conservative lobby gains power by showing little sympathy for poor blacks.

How will the expanding pool of mixed-race people figure into this new world? On one hand, our presence could force all Americans to take a hard look at race as political construction, its utilities and its dead ends. On the other, mixed-race people could remain invisible, our numbers having little impact. The white world invites us to be privy to white privilege. In the black world, specifically in black intellectual communities, we shy away from challenging stereotypes of "the black experience" with our particular histories. These days the race-neutral Mariah Careys seem to be multiplying faster than the heirs of Davis, Cleaver, and Giovanni.

I wonder what message the cautionary tales of the passing novels could send to rainbow babies of the nineties. These novels were written by African Americans in the early part of the century. For all their melodrama, tinny plots, and soapbox politicking, they've always resonated with me. The costs of abandoning black culture and community is one of the genre's central themes, and it's a theme that hits me, as they say, where I live. Though for reasons you might not expect. When my mother married my father, she was deserted by her white family and embraced by his black family. I have always been made to feel, in part because of her stories, that black communities and black cultures are a steady home. A home that is still quick to remind me, in ways material and ethereal, that it keeps the lights on for me. To abandon this home, as my mother's stories whispered, would mean to swim with sharks.

James Weldon Johnson's *Autobiography of An Ex-Coloured Man* (1912) is often called the thinking-colored person's passing novel, as it speaks its truth minus the violins. The closing passage hits deepest. Not because it describes an experience I have lived, but because it tells of one that I ache to believe in, despite how the world around me splinters in ways I don't recognize.

The ex-coloured man goes to hear Booker T. Washington speak at a benefit for Hampton Institute. Though Mark Twain and others share the podium, Washington has the audience in his hand:

"Not because he so much surpassed the others in eloquence, but because of what he represented with so much earnestness and faith. It is this that all of that small but gallant band of coloured men who are publicly fighting the cause of their race have behind them. Even those who oppose them know that these men have the eternal principles of right on their side, and they will be victors even though they should go down in defeat. Beside them I feel small and selfish. I am an ordinarily success-ful white man who has made a little money. They are men who are making history and a race. I, too, might have taken part in a work so glorious.

". . . I cannot repress the thought that, after all, I have chosen the lesser part, that I have sold my birthright for a mess of pottage."

Is it true what those labels say, NO SALE IS EVER FINAL?

*1990*

# four

# genitalia and the paycheck

# corporate boys

Deandra, my crazy friend the photographer, is scoffing down rice and beans at a Cuban restaurant on Flatbush Avenue and talking about Negroes. Most of my straight women friends in their late twenties are grumbling about the one-in-four problem (one out of every four black men in this city is in jail, to which we add: number two is on drugs, number three prefers gentlemen or blondes, and number four already has ten women), but not Miss One and a Half. She always has a Negro or two on hand. Girl, *let me tell you* (Deandra loves to milk it), I've got myself a corporate boy. I drop my fork.

In college, Miss Bohemia wouldn't have been

caught dead with a Negro in an alligator shirt and Levi's, and now she's dating corporate boys? I still believe in revolution, Deandra assures me, it's just, Che Guevara doesn't turn me on anymore. Revolution or no revolution, Deandra's attracted to power, so her taste in men changes with the political forecast: Today Huey Newton, tomorrow Ron Brown.

Deandra confesses that she's been watching corporate boys for a while. The ones who ride the iron horse into the city from buppie enclaves like Fort Greene, Prospect Heights, and Park Slope. They went to the right schools, and now they have the right jobs and the right cars (though between student loan payments and Amex bills, repossession is around the corner). And, of course, the right suits. (They work those suits, don't they? It's not about the suit making the man, it's about how the man is filling out the suit.) Something about their swagger and confidence started ringing my bells, Deandra says, Girl, forget about the dreadlocks and the dashikis, just give me a clean head and a Brooks Brothers charcoal gray (or even a Cricketeer, I'm not a purist).

Deandra goes on about corporate boys and how the suit is such a loaded symbol in their lives. It's their badge of honor (stamps their professional degrees on their sleeves), their passbook to the white-collar world (even gets them a cab sometimes), and immediately "neutralizes" their skin color in the company of what corporate boys call their "majority brethren."

And, Deandra tells me, they have such a way with language. In familiar company they speak a creole of King's English and blacker-than-thou neologisms. You know, girl, they have to prove they're down all the time (lest we think they're sellouts), so they come up with the most endearing homeboyisms. Check out hommie's wig, my corporate boy said to me the other day, why doesn't he comb it? Looks like Nipsey Russell got lost in the African rain forest. It's that fascinating mix of extreme self-love and seething self-hatred that middle-class blacks do so well. Enough already, I tell Deandra, fix me up with some of your corporate boy's friends.

Lunch with bachelor number one is in the corporate dining

room of a major commercial bank. Needless to say, he and I are the lone spots of color in the place. The only son of a large West Indian family from Bedford-Stuyvesant, Keith Browning (names changed to protect corporate identities), twenty-four, went to an Ivy League school to learn how to be a banker. Keith's staid blue and black suits are custom-made by his father, a tailor, and he is quite proud of how they fit him, unlike the "off-the-rack polyester jammies" worn by the lower level management types who work a couple of floors below him. Being a "custom man" is not so much a question of ego. Like many black men, he's a hard fit. "If you have a high behind," Keith says, "pants will ride up on you and ruin the line of the suit." As we nosh on our bow-tie pasta, I can't help staring at the knot of Keith's paisley tie, which is slightly askew. "You can't look too good," he tells me. "Then you're perceived as a threat. You already stand out as a minority. And I definitely do because I'm six-foot-four and most of the majorities I work for are Lilliputians."

Bachelor number two receives me in his Prospect Heights duplex: exposed brick, Levolor blinds, every electrical appliance known to mankind. The walk-in closet I pass on the way to the john is a virtual gallery: creamy leathers, mossy suedes, and a few dozen or so Cosby-style sweaters. And this is the *casual clothes* closet, mind you. Wonder where he keeps his suits. Damon Givens, twenty-eight, grew up in the South Bronx, went to college out of state on a basketball scholarship, and is now a second-year attorney at a Madison Avenue firm. He tells me that going to college with fifteen pairs of sneakers and checking out his wealthy white roommate's closet (loafers, snow boots, and a pair of track shoes held together with duct tape) taught him a lot about priorities. Instead of high tops, now he collects Italian suits. Damon says his Armanis ("Manies," he calls them) and Hugo Bosses ("Hugues") make him something of maverick at the firm, but they're a better fit. He can get a way with a lot more in terms of cut than color because in the corporate world "it's about avoiding anything threatening. And color is threatening psychologically."

In his Toyota Celica ("just lean back and pretend it's a 280 SL"), bachelor number three takes me on a tour of the Brownsville housing project where he spent the first thirteen years of his life, before winning a scholarship to a Massachusetts prep school. After B-school, Michael Geffens, twenty-eight, worked at an investment bank until last year when he was laid off in the crunch. This is how Michael bought his first suit: He took the annual report of a company he wanted to work for to Barney's and matched a suit in a photo with one on the rack. Today he wears custom jobs by a guy named Rock out of California. Rock comes to Manhattan several times a year to hold fittings at the Waldorf Astoria, then sends the measurements to Hong Kong. The suits come back with the label: "designed exclusively for Michael Geffens." Michael and his boys share this same tailor and they refer to their suits as "rocks."

Michael describes the cockiness he feels as a young black man in an expensive suit. He savors the reactions he gets. Older black women smile at him like he's their son; young guys in kente-cloth kufis size him up, he feels, like "Who's the wannabe in the suit? Doesn't he know that he's still a nigger?" At work once, Michael changed to sneakers and jeans in the bathroom. A co-worker, one of his majority brethren, was shocked to run into him in such an altered state: "Gosh," his co-worker marveled, "if I saw you in the street with that on, I'd never think you're as intelligent as you are."

Deandra calls later in the week to ask how I did with the corporate boys. They talk a good game, but girlfriend, how do you get past the elitism? One bachelor kept going on about "mutants" (any "homeboy in a Gumby fade who's not rolling nine to five") and "perpetrators" who hang out in buppie watering holes like Honeysuckle's and B. Smith's but have to go home first to change into a suit. Deandra wants me to meet her corporate boy because, naturally, he isn't like that. (Not only does Deandra get the Negroes, she gets the exceptions.) Dodd Hicks treats us to a Thai meal on the Upper East Side.

Rising close to six-foot-three with the beginnings of a paunch and back-set hairline, Dodd reeks power. He humors us by engaging in the type of mock self-deprecation that only the truly confident can afford. Dodd tells us about the "who's-that-other-nigger-in-a-suit look" he gives and gets from other young black men on Wall Street. "White people have done a good job of convincing us that opportunities extended to others limit our own," Dodd says, fingering the lapels of his Hugo Boss. Deandra looks up at him like he's the best thing since the Afro pick. What could be more attractive than nationalist rhetoric from a boy in a suit?

*1991*

# open letter to a brother

I'm not gonna lie. I have an attitude right now. It has something to do with: witnessing a "domestic" tragicomedy on Flatbush Avenue; an ad for Smirnoff vodka on a bus shelter; and thinking of you, and how you equate freedom and power with the ground you can cover with your johnson.

What I'm talking about, brother, is the Dog Syndrome. Gotta have more than one female, or "piece," as we're known in some circles. Take pride in declaring that no woman alive has shackles, rings, or papers on you. Don't mind profiting from the dire black male/female ratios out here (in this city, we outnumber you and are more likely to have a higher level of formal education, while one in four of you is in jail). And, so says the rap anthem of moment, you're "down with O.P.P.," that's "other people's pu . . . ," let's call it pudendum. (Nowadays, see, it's not even enough to have a couple $p$'s of your own, you have to be all up in somebody else's $p$.) It's not a class thing, or a regional thing, or necessarily an African-American thing, but it seems to be, the way you flaunt it, quite the in-style thing. "Who's down with O.P.P.?" is the call. And the chorus comes back: "Every last homie."

The latest contest over authenticity (who gets to market the race) is particularly ironic given the fracas between black men and women. You've seen the books: From Shahrazad Ali's *The Blackman's Guide to Understanding the Blackwoman* (a sister points the finger at sisters) to Nathan and Julia Hare's *Crisis in Black Sexual Politics* (a brother and sister point fingers at the white power structure). The battle is not just over who's to blame for what's being called the crisis in black male/female relationships. It's also over "oppressed within the oppressed" status—who suffers most from racism, whose issues will top the racial agenda. ("Babies making babies" has been eclipsed in the last year by the "endangered black male.")

So it's clear everyone's coveting the soapbox. Yet how many of us really have an investment in togetherness beyond the neat platform of race? I mean this in the largest sense, not just heterosexual coupling, but as a community of individuals with shared interests. A cultural communion based on right here, right now, not on some glorious polygamous past in a storybook Motherland. The brawls being so ugly and constant, lately I've been thinking *black people* is just a polite misnomer for a bunch of folks with guns to each other's heads.

Back to the bone I'm picking with you, brother. The reason I feel entitled to bring "us" up in public is because of that old mantra, "the personal is political." This is what I've found: Who we sleep with, how we dress, and the music we listen to define us politically in a more immediate way than who we vote for, what dogma we espouse, and which racial box we check on the census.

I have this theory, brother, that the Dog Syndrome is more than a rite of sexual passage for you; it's your very own liberation politics. Quiet as it's kept, I know very few of you who yearn to dismantle the Mandingo myth. (Hell no, party over here.) Truth be told, you're out here getting mo' and mo' *p* like your very being, and your very *blackness,* depended on it. Like AIDS is something that is happening to other people and not to us (in fact, more and more, it's happening primarily to us). Or like you can have little or no responsibility for what fucking can reap: babies. When over 60 percent of African-American children are being carried financially by women alone, one wonders where the men are at. Getting O.P.P.?

This comes at a time when black female life is assigned—in the infotainment industries, in popular language, and on the avenues—such little value, despite the gains of the civil rights movement and feminism. It's a time when Andre Young, Dr. Dre of N.W.A (who sells a zillion CDs preaching "One Less Bitch"), can assault—as in punch, kick, and body slam—television host Dee Barnes and get tapped on the wrist with a petty fine and probation. It's also a time when, to follow the example of the St. John's acquittal, the victim's race—black—may have made the rape less of a heinous crime, in the minds of those who tried the case and a largely indifferent media, than the Central Park rape.

You'll find the print ad I spoke of playing larger than life-size at your local bus shelter. Not a shot glass in sight, it shows a woman on the arm of an Armani-suited brother whose neck is wrenched back in an obvious and quite awkward manner so he can scan the anatomy of another woman. Poor urban districts have a disproportionate number of ads for liquor and tobacco, and now this, which hit me in my "positive image" weak spot. What's the sales pitch here for young black men? Disrespect a sister today, it's perfectly cool, and downright stylish?

But listen, brother, I'm looking to talk to you, not the ad industry. We black folks hide, like everyone else, from our demons. No historical guilt, no sense of personal accountability. Wrong. Brother beware, this Dog Syndrome is one mean, undercover demon. If your access to power in the real-world arena is limited, there's always the power of the johnson. And what a cheap fix it is. When I see a brother all caught up in the Dog Syndrome, I see the tragedy of black male impotence masquerading as power. Sad truth is, those who traffic in impotence/ignorance—like the harder-than-thou Dr. Dre, who takes on "nigger" as an honorific and favors a woman for a punching bag—are hightailing it to the bank.

Imagine an entire generation of young males coming of age and modeling themselves on men of means like Dr. Dre or finger-happy Mike Tyson. Will they live forever as adolescents, clutching their bozaks like teddy bears, hiding under their N.W.A caps, and being as hard as they wanna be, or they claim they have to be, O.P.P.'ing their demons away? Sorta like Prince, stroking his way through "Lady Cab Driver": This is for the Middle Passage, umhh, this is for chattel slavery, umhh, this is for Howard Beach, umhh, yeah, that's the one.

About that domestic scene on Flatbush: A man chases a woman down the street. He grabs for her pocketbook, she resists. "Give it to me, bitch," he yells. "That's why I dogged your ass with Tanya. You ain't worth shit, bitch." Finally he corners her, takes something from her pocketbook, and shoves the pocketbook back in her arms. He shuffles away with the object of all the fuss: a twenty-cent pack of Bon Ton corn chips.

Yours in love and trouble,
**Lisa**

*1991*

# drop-dead fine

*Bloodcurdling* was a word without a case history before this scream. This scream traveled two rooms to lodge itself in the girl's aorta. She ran, half naked, half asleep, from her bedroom to the front window. A knife fight was happening down below in the street involving two men, one knife, and a woman in the middle, screaming to put all screams to shame.

Operator 911 took the address and asked for a description of the man with the weapon. The girl hesitated; it was dark, she couldn't make out details. True to routine, Operator 911 pressed ahead: "Is he a male black?" Then raising her voice, strangely insistent: *"Is he a male black?"* The girl was suddenly wide awake. She had been dreaming, before the scream, of frolicking with a "male black" in a celestial sea. Now she was standing barefoot in America, watching a knife fight on a Brooklyn street corner, and being force-fed racial stereotypes by a 911 operator.

No coincidence. Everywhere the girl looked, paper tigers like the endangered male black and the suspect male black stared back at her. She worried about who was labeled endangered, and therefore worthy of protection (young men), and who was not worthy (young women), and how anyone could make this distinction. In music and films, she saw the prey/predator role embraced, as shield perhaps, but also as badge, and saw it sold proudly, almost gleefully, to the masses, most of whom were eager to consume large quantities of male black without getting anywhere near where male blacks might live. Always statistic, always suspect, where did male black exist outside of this?

*Is he a male black?*

The night after the scream the girl went downtown to hear poetry and jazz. Poet Carl Hancock Rux came to the stage backed by gospel singers. Though a young man, Rux talked the talk, his voice, way deep, the voice of preachers and Last Poets past. He opened with a piece he called "Save the Animals": "I got a name/Call me nigger/Negro/negritude/black boy/ bastard child/African/Afro American/afrodisiac/young buck super stud . . ./So how do you make love to a Negro without getting tired?/You don't make love to him at all."

*Is he a male black?*

Always, but not by way of danger, by way of pleasure. The girl was looking to uncover the meaning of an ancient stricture known as "fineness." This was an important project. Only fineness, she reasoned, being as romantic and esoteric as she damn pleased, could help her break through the male black's sloganized endangerment. In fineness, there was wisdom. Fineness was no pseudoscientific black essence, it was critical inquiry. It was, as a fellow finewatcher had schooled her, a "specifically, culturally black means of appreciating someone's black aesthetics in a way that no other word captures." Fine, to hear another fine-watcher tell it, was the motivating force behind most if not all activity. "That man was so fo-ine, he made my car run into a tree," and so on. And by virtue of being so lusciously onomatopoeic, it had to reveal something precious, hidden, and old.

The girl recalled her first intellectual encounter with fineness. She was maybe six years old, at her father's house in Newark, lucky to be hanging with some very grown teenagers who had a new portable record player and one 45, Marvin Gaye and Tammi Terrell's "Ain't No Mountain High Enough." They played the song for hours straight, and each time, these young women would fall to their knees and lament that Marvin was oh-so-fine. What was this fineness that it could possess the grown like hard liquor or religion?

Raised within earshot of sixties' Black Arts poetry, the girl would become even more intimate with fineness. Sonia Sanchez laid praise for all things lanky, fine, and committed to the struggle. A major text was Nikki Giovanni's "Beautiful Black Men (With compliments and apologies to all not mentioned by name)," which sung of brothers with "they afros" as "the same ol' danger/but a brand new pleasure." The girl came to think of fineness as an exalted state that would be realized after the Revolution. Later, to poets of the seventies' loft-jazz scene, the observance of fineness could produce a spiritual trance capable of healing sexism, racism, colorism, and any other 'ism that might be bothering folks. Here the girl was thinking of work such as Ntozake Shange's "lotsa body & cultural heritage" or Thulani Davis's "Zoom (the Commodores)," which engaged fineness as rhythm and blues: "Zoom you Commodores/maybe you are the best of us/that can love & believe."

Webster's take on "fine," the girl was surprised to find, matched fineness as a state of physical grace ("hardened close to the limit of efficiency . . . superior in conception"). An example, in the girl's mind, might be a clean head with a hairline shaped with diligent—almost painful—precision. To others, fine was a code that meant, precisely, big thighs, big butt, no exception.

Beyond the visuals, fine carried with it a sense of coolness, defiance, brilliance of gesture, a signature walk, a devastating smile, slyness, nobility, wit, uplift of the race, and, without question, a particularly African-American poetics with the English language. Fine was not *fly* (a material judgment that had something to do with the way one's clothes hung and how one's attitude tended to match). And fine was not necessarily handsome. Fine was handsome with a story. Like Deandra describing Michael Jordan as a "bird in the mythological sense. Like when you read about dinosaurs and wish you were there." Or Cheryl saying that when she was young, fine had meant "wavy-haired, bow-legged, and tall, but this was changing now." When asked if fine would one day become as mainstream and uniformly Caucasian as the high five, she sucked her teeth, "Honey, fine ain't going nowhere."

A sweetness of the girl's life had been to share in the ritual of naming fineness. It was among those stolen moments of communion that Cornel West might call black joy. The dissection of fineness was art obviously, specifically art that healed. The girl and her cohorts imagined Fine Studies to be, not some double standard of male objectification, but a way they recouped black men from the ugliness of their surroundings. Anointing male black with fineness put him in a magical world where he wasn't the hunter, the hunted, or the fossil. (Fineness was plentiful.) It redeemed and elevated, often beyond the fragility and hollowness of love relationships. Fineness was fantasy too.

The quintessential, nouveau-classical moment of fineness is still Denzel Washington in the Civil War drama *Glory*. Removing his shirt to take a whipping from the Yankee captain, Denzel bares scars that suggest he was a runaway before joining the Union army. The actor gives us real teardrops here, not born of pain, but in steadfast pride and remembrance: Pure race-man fine. A lost and now exhumed text of fineness that the girl is fixating on lately is a photo of Huey Newton in Elaine Brown's memoir of the Black Panther party. Brown paints Huey as a psychotic misogynist of genius stripe. (He punished and humiliated women, then named one to lead the party during his exile.) Of the drop-dead fine canon, Huey is photographed at home, shirtless and surrounded by books, pulling Bob Dylan's *Highway 61 Revisited* from its record sleeve. Was Huey's world a ghetto rebellion fantasy that hid boho aesthetics? Ah, fineness, ain't it deep?

*Is he a male black?*

The girl surrounded herself in this fineness, this aroma, much like Calvin Klein's Escape. Eau de Fine. No one would ever take male black from her and her sentimental self, ever again. Not all the 911 operators or the male blacks themselves, with their loves unrequited and deferred. This fineness belongs to her and to those who do the ritual. In her chest, split open like an Alison Saar sculpture to reveal trinkets and talismans, are all the fine ones. And there they stay, talking shit and playing ball, as Marvin sings "Ain't No Mountain High Enough" to Tammi, over and over, and over some more.

*1993*

# brother jon

Jon Jon is this guy I met in Minneapolis. I stopped by Applause Records one Saturday and working the counter is this brother who could be the son of Valentino or Eddie Kendricks, but dressed up sixties mod, like Cosby circa "I Spy." He scans my choices and asks if I'm hip to Me Phi Me, Ephraim Lewis, and other young black musicians, post-Fishbone, who have deals with major labels and whose work resists industry race prisons. (Yes, most of the artists who hold this pass card are men.) Chitchat about apartheid marketing in music leads us to the blue-green swamps of race, class, and sex. Customers are waiting to buy Stravinsky and Tom Jones. Jon and I are having a town meeting about stagnant images of black masculinity and quadroon balls in nineteenth century New Orleans.

Like many young folks who work record-store plantations, Jon makes music himself. In the late eighties he sang with a band out of Chicago, Hot Sauce, which he describes as the "psychedelic side of Fishbone." Hot Sauce followed the Purple rainbow to Minneapolis in search of a deal with an indie record label. The group broke up soon after, though Jon stayed in the Twin Cities tinkering with various bands, including his latest, Dope Fiend, "a pretty noise thing with a big beat to keep the brothers interested." Jon lives in music, it's his political party, his religion, his family of choice, his take on blackness.

I tell Jon about this story I've been writing called "All the Boys were Hendrix," riffing on my days as a groupie to young black rock bands caught between King Jimi and the void. This was in the seventies, a few years before Prince and Living Colour. Hendrix's own image fused drag queen and pimp Mack Daddy, and the brothers I knew who worshiped at his throne had a male energy different than Funkateers and gangsta rappers; one that often acknowledged its woman self and had its own erotic cool. I wondered how a twenty-six-year-old like Jon, who flips through record bins that include (rainbow baby for peace) Lenny Kravitz and (hip-hop's hardest) the Geto Boys, chose what kind of man to be. Jon's model, it turns out, isn't a dead president like Hendrix or Sly, it's Fishbone's Angelo Moore—equal parts blues archivist, rock scientist, minstrel, race man, ambassador of integration. Heavy on rhythm and pictures, Jon has a songwriter's way with words that is savored best raw. So here I bring you Jon, and "his own self's thing," just about unadulterated:

"Jon Jon, the alternative Negro, is what my friends call me. That boy *al*-ternative, they always joking around, 'cause I like to debate black stereotypes, what people say black is. They say black folks don't be listening to that shit you be listening to, Jon. You better turn that Dinosaur Jr. off, motherfucker, you're with the brothers now, listen to some brother shit.

"I got this friend who's always boasting about being from the hood, from Brew City, where brothers get capped day and night. That I'm-from-the-ghetto attitude really gets me. Somehow we're not *real* unless we're ghetto enough. I went to live with my grandmother for a year in Chicago after high school. The lady's eighty-fucking years old, drinking every day. Some of my friends thought I was cool because my grandmother's place was so crazy; 'cause the house got roaches and kids going crazy; and the TV's up loud; and everybody's hollering at everybody, drinking and smoking; and somebody's shooting up in the back room; while my frub uncle's twirling around downstairs listening to his stereo. Ain't that some shit?

"Growing up in Chicago was "Good Times" and "The Cosby Show" at the same time, 'cause Grandma was up in the ghetto and my parents lived in some kind of good section, at least it stayed good for a while. I'm adopted. Wonderful home, great fucking family values, and then they got divorced. Dad hooked up again, this time to a woman he met on tour as road manager with the Delfonics. He came home one day and said he wasn't gonna work for the white man anymore. So I said, what man are you gonna work for? He told me he'd figure that out later. Dad joined the Nation of Islam, and from seventy-three to eighty-one we followed Islam from Elijah Muhammad's perspective. Me and my brothers and sisters went to Muslim schools and the whole bit.

"I was on a little free-base journey before I put a band together. Cam, my best friend, went to the air force for a year after high school. That's when I really fucked up, 'cause it's Cam that keeps me alive when I'm out there too foul. When Cam came back, me and him had an agreement that if he caught me basing he could knock the shit out of me. I could always hear his noisy ass car pull up in the driveway, so I could've thrown the shit under the bed and played like I was watching *Superfly* on TV, but I didn't. That's how I stayed straight.

"After Cam's adventure in the air force we started reading these cute *Id* and *Face* magazines and doing a London hipster trip. We had been to every house party on the Southside and had used that up. We hit gay discos for a while, which was cool, but it wasn't our scene, we were into guitars. That took us to the Northside and put us in this integrated environment. I got hip to politics on a global scale hanging with white kids who talked to me about the shit. I had white kids schooling me on Malcolm X, even though I grew up a Muslim. Trip.

"I used to make excuses for dating white girls; I went through that whole period. Sometimes I do still feel that by hanging out with girls who aren't black, I'm messing up on a responsibility. I was chilling with my friend Star the other night, and Star says, 'Hey man, we live in fuckin' Minnesota, everywhere we go there's fuckin' white girls. If we run into a black girl, that's cool, I'm sure we're gonna talk to her, but if we don't, we're not gonna just sit back and wait.' That's true. If you go to First Avenue on weekends when they play rock, there aren't that many black girls there. What you gonna do? Go on funk night or 'black night' just to meet the black girls? My friends in Chicago still give me shit, though. Jon Jon, you got a black girlfriend yet? When I do get with a black girl she has to be down with Tribe Called Quest *and* the Cocteau Twins, that's all I know. And when I make it to London or New York, I'm gonna scoop me one up. I know y'all out there.

"I don't refer to women as 'bitch' or 'ho' any more; my friend Iyanna told about myself, though growing up in the hood, you hear girls say 'bitch' all day; it's almost as natural now as 'nigger.' Lots of girl buddies of mine talk to me about their problems. Like, girl buddies call to ask if they should get an abortion. I tell them, it's on them. Basically I'm against abortion, being that I was adopted. If my mother had aborted me, I wouldn't be around to talk as much shit as I do, so I'm biased! But since I don't have a vagina and a womb and all that, it's not my right to tell a woman her business. So when it comes down to it, I believe in choice. My sister's twenty-one and she has a one year old. Sometimes she says shit like, 'Fuck this ugly-ass baby, I wish I never had the motherfucker.' Mama thinks she's talking out of her head, but no, no, sis means it. It's incredible that someone would feel that way about a child. Society looks at little black girls with babies and says, foul, so maybe my sister picked up that message. To me, though, it's birth, and birth is positive.

"In junior high school I started listening to rock accidentally 'cause my bedroom was in the attic and I could only get AM stations. I dug Led Zep and shit they call 'rock that will never die,' then metal, then shit that was cooler than that, like the Cure, your Smiths, Sonic Youth. Then Fishbone opened for the Beastie Boys in Chicago in eighty-five. I forget how my hair was looking at the time, but we said, Wow, here are some brothers that look just like us, brothers who didn't grow up listening to R&B radio. Brothers who probably grew up outside of the city, went to school with white kids, and spent a good amount of time listening to the Butthole Surfers. Cam had been writing music and he said, Jon come over and scream on some of these tunes, we can do this kind of punk thing. Three months later we were playing shows.

"When you see bands like Bad Brains or Fishbone, they're saying, I'm just as much man as you are even though I don't play basketball or wear gold chains. It's about being a man with another type of edge. There's rowdiness, but it's playful rowdiness, it's not a 'niggers killing niggers' rowdiness. You hear about police brutality, but in Fishbone and 24-7 Spyz songs you also hear about racial harmony, probably because some of the guys have interracial relationships and they need to let folks know that it's okay.

"Brothers who are coming up now, brothers younger than me, the first band they saw playing instruments, period, not rapping, was Living Colour. Seeing Living Colour changed their ideas about what black guys are supposed to be doing. But is it a sign of social change that brothers are allowed to express their complexity in music and get bankrolled? I dunno.

"To me, we need to stress individualism right now. We all make individual choices and these choices go beyond skin color. Brothers don't get a break from me just because they're brothers. Like, I can't buy the line that it's the white man's fault that we're doing crack. Sure the white man put crack in our communities, but the white man didn't put the pipe up to your mouth. That's your dirty work, my brother."

*1992*

# the signifying monkees

FORT LAUDERDALE, FLORIDA—Though the state of Florida's case against hip-hop lewd boys 2 Live Crew has been front-page news here since June, the dailies can't print the charge itself—too many dirty words. When the Crew's leading *mensch,* Luther Campbell, hears Judge June Johnson read it aloud for the first time to the original jury pool of twenty-five—twenty-two whites (who turn pink) and three blacks (who turn gray)—he bolts from his seat in the small county courtroom and storms out. Campbell probably pictured himself doing a year of solitary confinement, and here's why:

. . . as live persons before an audience, [they] did knowingly conduct, perform, or participate in, by words and/or conduct, a show or performance which was obscene . . . [which] included . . . an apparent version of [2 Live Crew's song] "Me So Horny," consist[ing] of verbal depictions or descriptions of sexual conduct . . . deviate sexual intercourse, as defined in Florida Statue 847.0011, and actual physical contact with a person's unclothed buttocks, examples of which are: "Let me stick my dick in your behind," [and] "I'll be fucking you and you'll be sucking me, lick my ass up and down, lick it till your tongue turns doo-doo brown" . . . and in the course of said performance . . . did simulate an act of deviate sexual intercourse as defined in F.S. 847.0011 . . . examples of which are: placing the face of a woman into or in very close proximity to the groin of one of the performers, Luther Campbell, and through the acts of another performer, Mark Ross, uncovering and exposing the breast of another female.

In the court hallway, in front of a dozen television cameras, another dozen scribbling reporters, Campbell yells at his attorney, Bruce Rogow, "What the fuck is this shit? You told me the shit was gonna be played on tape!" Rogow explains that what he's just heard is called an "information," and though issued by the state, it's not evidence, just an accusation. The judge, who has long blonde hair, blushed herself as she struggled to get through the awkwardly worded statement. The overall effect: Heidi reading porno confessions to a classroom of retired grade-school principals.

### condoms and microcassettes

In the Safeway supermarket parking lot on Las Olas Boulevard one car's bumper sticker reads BEAM ME UP, LORD, another's CENSORSHIP SUCKS. Both have Broward plates. That's Broward County. Home to the county seat, Fort Lauderdale, known as "Fort Liquordale," until media darling Sheriff Nick Navarro and the FLPD kicked out spring break a couple years back. Their goal: to attract a calmer breed of tourist and eventually remake Spuds-MacKenzie-by-the-Sea into the "retirement capital of the retirement capital" to compete with Miami next door in Dade County.

Broward has been better known lately as home to Hollywood, Florida. As part of an ongoing crusade for "family values," Hollywood mayor Sal Oliveri recently proclaimed "Pornography Awareness Week," corresponding with the final week of the 2 Live Crew trial. (Oliveri's crusade has included painting over a beach-side mural of the Coppertone Girl's nude buttocks.) 2 Live Crew made history here last June when they were arrested for performing songs from *As Nasty as They Wanna Be*, the group's third album, ruled obscene by a Florida federal judge earlier that month. Club Futura, where the bust took place, now sells T-shirts with the legend BROWARD COUNTY: CENSORSHIP CAPITAL OF THE WORLD. Birth of a tourist attraction?

But that bumper sticker isn't for sale at the Safeway in downtown Fort Lauderdale, a couple blocks away from the Broward County courthouse, where 2 Live Crew is standing trial. On the display rack closest to the cash register, instead of copies of *Family Circle*, you can choose from five types of condoms and microcassettes sold by the three-pack. Remember that: condoms and microcassettes.

### two live jews

"Two live Jews, kosher as they wanna to be." It's day one of the trial, and the first one-liner comes from a legal eagle in the spectator pews, one of many young attorneys and prosecutors who flock to the courtroom for a piece of the action. "I'm a Jew," he says, "so I can make fun of them all I want." The eagle is describing defense lawyers Bruce Rogow (representing Campbell) and Allen Jacobi (in for Mark Ross, a/k/a Brother Marquis), who have just arrived in court.

The two do cut an odd pair: Jacobi a rock-&-roll lawyer whose clients have included Eric Clapton, Peter Max, and the Church of Scientology, was raised kosher in Miami Beach, though with his deep tan and longish black hair, you might mistake him for Greek. Rogow, professor at Nova Law school in Fort Lauderdale and former president of Florida's ACLU, represented Mississippi civil rights workers in the sixties and has taken a half-dozen cases to the Supreme Court. If it weren't for the distinctive schnoz, Rogow's Ivy League suits and narrow bow ties could label him a WASP from Connecticut, where he grew up.

The prosecution, surprisingly enough, is also awash in the melting pot. Leslie Robson, born in Hong Kong and educated in England, finished her law degree at Nova and is now assistant state attorney in charge of Broward County's vice division. With her slight British accent and Eurasian features, Robson doesn't fit the stereotype of the Southern cracker fundamentalist after an improper acting colored boy like Luther Campbell. Neither does her coprosecutor, assistant state attorney Pedro Dijols, a supervisor in the misdemeanor division. Dijols, a black Puerto Rican from New York who went to law school in Florida, describes himself as a "fan of rap music." He tells female reporters about the tattoo on his left bicep: Underneath a Cheshire cat in a fedora is the inscription, in Latin, "Let the thing speak for itself." The motto turns out to be the prosecution's losing strategy in the case.

Then there's her honor June Johnson, who the press pool refers to affectionately as "Judge June," a Louisiana native with a dry wit, whose sideline remarks in court evidence a concern for matters affecting women and children. The judge, who usually tries DUI cases, even brings her mother to court one day.

"If you think of Miami as Los Angeles," Jacobi explains, then Broward is the Orange County of Florida." And though everyone from Florida, says a reporter, "is from somewhere else originally," it's amusing that it is this group of "outsiders" who will struggle over this case that represents, in the minds of some, the Wonderbread majority versus the "others."

It's these outsiders who will instruct, in the case of the judge, and interpret, in the case of the lawyers, Florida's obscenity law, modeled after the Supreme Court's 1973 *Miller v. California:* "The average person applying contemporary community standards, would find that the work, taken as a whole, appeals to prurient interests, . . . describes, in a patently offensive way, sexual conduct . . . [and] lacks serious literary, artistic, political, or scientific value."

These outsiders—and the fifty Broward County citizens who they sift through to pick a jury of six—will raise complicated questions: What constitutes a community, and is it acceptable that the standards of some people in the community are different from others? And just what, if anything, is obscene? As well as, what is art and who decides?

### the signifying monkees

And what about the defendants? Multimillionaire Campbell, twenty-nine, president of Luke Records, from (as the media lathers it up) the "hard-core Miami ghetto of Liberty City," who can choose whether or not to wear a custom-made Italian suit to court. Ross, twenty-three, 2 Live's primary lyricist, originally from Rochester, New York, dresses in baggy clothes and beads and is fond of "cultural rap like De La Soul and Tribe Called Quest." (Says Ross, people probably think the group is a bunch of "backwards niggers and geechees who don't know how to do anything but cuss, but that's not the case.") And Wongwon, twenty-six, a Trinidadian of African and Chinese ancestry, who grew up in Brooklyn and founded the group five years ago on an air force base in California with David Hobbs (Mr. Mixx, the Crew's DJ). Mixx was not charged because detectives didn't consider his contributions to be an integral part of the performance. Another strike against the state.

In a case that is all about 2 Live Crew's words (or, as the defense points out, their "lyrics"—making us pause to consider if there is a difference), it's strangely symbolic that we never hear the three speak in the context of the proceedings (the law says they don't have to, it's the state who must prove its case to the jurors "beyond a reasonable doubt"). The jurors watch them like one-eyed hawks. Their body language: Ross often slumps in his seat and chews on a toothpick. When the state plays an audiotape of the group's infamous concert, Wongwon, who has a disabled left arm, taps out the beat on the table with his right hand. Their clothes: Campbell doesn't wear a suit during jury selection because he doesn't want the "white, blue-collar workers who may get on the jury to think I'm uppity." Their every gesture: Ross blows his nose often; Campbell hands his cellular phone to his bodyguard, who sits, every day, right behind him. It must be a strain for these guys who sell shock value to sit still for so long and be so silent. But they do—like See No Evil, Hear No Evil, Speak No Evil—they sit through the eleven-day trial while words are slung back and forth all around them.

At one point a detective who testifies for the prosecution translates "Marquis's babies"—a line from a song performed the night of the bust—into "monkey's baby." Ross (whose rapper's ID, Brother Marquis, comes from the Marquis de Sade) sits through the botch in the courtroom but complains bitterly during a break. After Henry Louis Gates, Jr. (whose works include *The Signifying Monkey,* a collection of postmodern criticism of black literature) testifies that the music of 2 Live Crew has artistic value, I tease Ross that the group should change its name to "The Signifying Monkees." The joke doesn't go over well; no room for sarcasm in a court of law.

After all, there is a trial going on. And even though Dennis Barrie and Cincinnati's Contemporary Art Center were acquitted the week before in an obscenity trial involving the exhibition of photographs by Robert Mapplethorpe, this is Broward County—a lot further away from New York than Ohio is. This isn't a collection of silver-print photographs exhibited in museums; this is rap music performed in a nightclub. In fact, Campbell never once refers to his music as art, though he often calls it "entertainment" and is quick to tell you it has "artistic value." ("Rap music is not on trial" is a constant refrain—initiated by the prosecution and carried by the defense. Repeated so often, as an argument for and against the artistic content of 2 Live Crew's music, it becomes a hollow slogan.)

This isn't work with a large critical following; this is music that received scant critical attention until it ended up as a free-speech mantra. And these aren't "righteous rappers" like Boogie Down

Productions's KRS One (quoted in the *New York Times* as spokesman of a new black youth culture), but the Miami-based nasty boys of rap, whose rude snipes on record about other rappers have lost them friends in the hip-hop community. (Kid N' Play and Salt-N-Pepa are called "faggots" and "dykes" on *Banned in the USA.*) The creator of this work is not a dead white man but three living black men; "young and virile," as they're often referred to in the press, perhaps perceived by those who wish to see them prosecuted, as capable of violence, rape, or miscegenation.

The pipes squeak so loudly in courtroom 354, where the trial takes place, they often interrupt the proceedings. In this small, aging county courthouse, which is connected to a brand-new, very large county jail, prisoners are handcuffed together in twos and led back and forth by deputies. Most of these deputies are white, and most of the men in handcuffs are young and black. On their way to lunch during the trial's first week, the Campbell entourage runs into a group of prisoners and their keeper on the staircase. The men call out "Luke, Luke, Luke Skyywalker" (a name George Lucas sued Campbell to drop), hailing the rapper as a hero. He looks a bit embarrassed, but gives them a "Hey, what's up," and continues down the stairs.

Symbolism aside, this is a trial. A real trial, say Brother Marquis's eyes. If convicted the three could be charged with a misdemeanor, fined one thousand dollars, and slapped with a year in jail. When the state asks a detective on the witness stand to confirm that Campbell, Ross, and Wongwon did indeed perform songs ruled obscene, and that they did so that night in Hollywood as "live persons," Judge June adds, "that's their problem. They're too live."

## motion sickness

The first day of the trial is all motions—each side attempting to get evidence admitted and procedural questions answered in a manner that will advance their case. Rogow, the trendsetting constitutionalist, argues that selecting a jury pool from voter registrations lists, the method in Florida and most states, is unconstitutional in obscenity cases. Obscenity is the only charge, he holds, that requires jurors to bring their knowledge of "community standards" to bear on the decision.

In a county where 13 percent of the population is black and only 5 percent is registered to vote, black people are automatically underrepresented in the jury pools, as are young people. This, Rogow contends, gives the court a narrower frame of reference with which to judge community opinion.

Rogow's motion is a sweeping gesture that feels at first too grand a consideration for a county court. The judge rules against it, but it turns out to be an effective framing device for the trial: establishing the importance of a diverse jury and of looking at "community standards" as more than just the dominion of middle-class whites from Broward suburbs like Plantation. Rogow's challenge even makes it to page 16A of the *New York Times* with the amusing pullquote, "Middle-aged whites aren't representative, the court is told." Campbell schools reporters during a break that the only way he can foresee a fair trial is if "the judge lets us have black people on the jury." And "young people," Jacobi pipes in. "And young people," Campbell repeats.

Later in the day Campbell signs autographs for three white teenagers—hillbillies in high-waters who sport fresh hickeys on their necks. The teens shout in court, "2 Live Crew, doing the right thing!" Campbell tells them to watch out, "Y'all might wind up here with us."

### suicide mission

Assistant State Attorney Dijols, whose usual beat is DUI cases, eventually admits toward the end of the trial that when he first heard the state's only piece of evidence—a barely audible microcassette recording of the performance in Hollywood that night—he knew the case was a "suicide mission." This is an odd admission from a prosecutor who made it very clear that he had volunteered for the case, and was not, as Campbell had charged early on, a "token" brought in by the state attorney to lend "ethnic credibility" to the prosecution.

The state makes every possible move to postpone the case and bolster its scanty evidence. They ask that a "transcript" of the performance prepared by the Broward County sheriff's office be admitted as evidence, to "assist" the jurors in judging whether the performance is obscene. This amuses Rogow at first, who says "no one gets a transcript of the performance when they go to see *My Fair Lady.*"

The prosecution does manage to get four songs from *As Nasty As They Wanna Be* admitted as evidence, despite high-pitched objections from the defense ("This record is not on trial!"). Judge Johnson is given the opportunity to review the songs before potential jurors arrive. "Are they talking or singing?" The judge wants to know. Rogow beats out the prosecutors to answer her: "They're rapping, your honor." "DO YOU BELIEVE IN HAVING SEX?" blares from the speakers set up in the middle of the courtroom. "HELL YES," the speakers call back. "Is this like an act you see in Las Vegas?" Judge June asks. "No," Rogow assures her, "rapping is music that engages in call and response with its audience."

### twenty questions

Time for jury selection. First, the prosecution and defense take potential jurors through voir dire (from the French phrase, "to speak the truth"), the question and answer session attorneys use to determine which jurors will best advance their case. Jurors are quizzed about explicit language, oral and anal sex, their tastes in music, and what they know about 2 Live Crew.

Dijols questions jurors if they can stomach "offensive language" like "anal sex, oral sex, and ejaculation" that will be dredged up in this case. One woman replies that, as a teacher, she hears worse every day. "What grade do you teach?" Dijols asks. "Kindergarten" (the evening news's soundbite of choice). A middle-aged man with thick red glasses says he heard the group's music was "promiscuous." When Rogow grills the would-be jurors if they consider oral or anal sex to be morbid or shameful, they all shake their heads "no." No one bothers to remind them that oral and anal sex are illegal under Florida's sodomy law.

Rogow is approached during a break by a French television

crew who inquire if all sex is obscene in America. Rogow chuckles, "No, but in America good sex is illegal." Later that afternoon, two fifteen-year-old white girls in Catholic school uniforms scurry over to the defense table to get Campbell's autograph.

## race is not on trial

Assistant State Attorney Dijols is shaking his head. (There's a silent style war being waged in the courtroom between Dijols's loosely curled hair, cut into a seventies-style shag, and Campbell's closely cropped fade.) "Race has reared its ugly head again in this trial," Dijols rants. You get the feeling that Dijols is the kind of person who would like to leave race out of it. He's referring to the case of Bernard Kinnel, one of three black people in the original twenty-five-person jury pool.

Kinnel, a truck driver, wears a gold earring and a beeper. (Campbell has two beepers.) In voir dire Kinnel admits to liking rap music, and even to hearing the clean version of 2 Live Crew's "Me So Horny" on the radio once. "What did you think?" the judge asks, genuinely interested. "I didn't give it a rating," he shrugs, and the courtroom snickers. Later, when Dijols presses Kinnel on whether he considers himself a fan of 2 Live Crew, he hesitates a bit, says yes, but adds that he is also fan of other rap groups. Rogow asks Kinnel later if he could be a fair juror despite his interest in rap. He can, he says, because his real love is "slow music," not rap. (Might Kinnel have been using the word "fan" differently than Dijols? Which speaks to yet another subtext of the trial: How words and their meanings are so speaker- and context-specific in this age of cultural relativism.)

Dijols moves to eliminate Kinnel as a juror based on the fact that he referred to himself a fan of 2 Live Crew. Rogow then charges that Dijols is striking Kinnel because Kinnel's black. Follow the twists: Here you have a white defense attorney (a progressive, free-speech advocate) calling a black prosecutor (a registered Republican) a racist. (Campbell is with Rogow all the way on this one; he nods his head up and down furiously.) Dijols is livid. He jumps from his seat and yells at the judge: "I want the record to state this prosecutor is a black prosecutor, a member of Mr. Kinnel's same race!" The judge strikes down Rogow's challenge; Kinnel doesn't make the jury.

When the trial ends for the day, reporters rush over not to Campbell, but to Dijols: "The basic premise behind this is that blacks can somehow relate to this music more, and therefore have lower moral standards. This music is obscene. It would be obscene if it was country western, reggae, or rock & roll. If they were so concerned about the black and white issue, why isn't Campbell using black defense attorneys?" On his way out, Mark Ross, in a pair of exaggerated "field-hand" overalls that belong in a high school production of *Huck Finn*, walks by Dijols chewing a tooth-pick.

### translating from the crew

"Cultural translators" are a crucial part of this trial.

Exhibit A: The witnesses for the prosecution, Detective Eugene McCloud, a heavyset black man with glasses, fourteen years with the Broward Sheriff's Office (BSO), and Detective Debra Werder, a heavyset white woman with frosted blond hair, married to Sheriff Navarro's chief of personnel.

The BSO had the detectives prepare "transcripts," which are their interpretations of the garbled microcassette recording of 2 Live Crew's concert that night at Club Futura. According to Campbell and defense attorneys, these transcripts are quite inaccurate—rife with misnomers and editorial comments. But the state wants to introduce the transcripts as evidence; it could be the only opportunity for jurors to read 2 Live Crew's dirty words and finally be shocked. (After hearing the judge's first reading of the "charge," the jury has been largely unruffled by 2 Live Crew's language arts.)

Robson's numerous attempts to get these transcripts admitted as evidence, as reading material for the jury, are denied by Judge Johnson. What the state manages to do in lieu of this is have the detectives translate the "remixed" performance tape line by line. So the tape plays a bit, then is stopped by Assistant State Attorney Dijols, who works a mixing board from a corner of the courtroom. Detective McCloud then "translates" what he's heard (refreshing his memory with his "transcript"). This goes on for two-and-a-half days.

The effect of McCloud's translations is pure pathos. Here's a thirty-eight-year-old man in a suit repeating lines like a trained parrot—some he flubs intentionally. It's as if he's translating from the Jive (remember that long-lost lingo?). The tape blares: ALL HOS SUCK DICK. McCloud translates: ALL WHORES SUCK DICK. Or sometimes McCloud narrates action in the club: "Ross [Brother Marquis] approached the girl from the back and embraced her. The girl's breasts came out."

Assistant State Attorney Robson: "The breasts that came out, were they the breasts nearest to you or away from you?"

McCloud: "Away from me."

At one point Robson has McCloud in the middle of the courtroom demonstrating how the dancers moved on stage. Campbell bitches loud during a break: "People are supposed to be judging our concert in its entirety—as a whole, like the law says. But the state keeps stopping the tape and they got a man up there narrating! Worse part about it is you got to listen. You can't say nothing. That lying motherfucker!"

At a coffee shop across the street from the courtroom, the Campbell entourage eats lunch. Debbie Bennett, Luke Record's publicity director, brings Campbell a plate of soul food from a Liberty City greasy spoon. Campbell is so mad about the McCloud performance that he blows up at lawyer Allen Jacobi in the middle of the luncheonette. Why aren't the lawyers butting into McCloud's testimony if it's so inaccurate? We've got strategies, the lawyers say. "This is some nigger shit, isn't it?" charges Campbell, not used to delegating authority. "I may be a nigger," he belts at the top of his lungs, "but I ain't a dumb nigger." He storms out. Word comes back to Debbie, forget about the soul food, order him a turkey sandwich.

After lunch there's a breakthrough. The jury has sent a note to Judge Johnson asking if they are allowed to laugh. It's a deciding moment in the case. Campbell calls it as soon as he can speak, which at the advice of his lawyers is only outside of the courtroom: "That's your verdict, right there." He grins like the Cheshire cat tattooed on Dijols's arm.

Like I said, cultural translators are a crucial part of this trial.

Exhibit B: Witnesses for the defense, Duke University professor and literary critic Henry Louis Gates, Jr., and *Newsday* music critic John Leland.

I have an amusing encounter with Gates and Leland in the lobby of the Riverside Hotel, down the street from the courthouse, the night before they testify. This is my first time meeting Leland, and when he arrives at the front desk, Gates announces him: "Ladies and gentlemen, this is Luther Campbell." Certainly one could say, for the day they spend in Broward, Leland and Gates are Luther Campbell. They explain his music, his "entertainment," his "artistic value," whatever it is he does, better than he ever could. But then, says Gates, Campbell's an artist, so that's not his job.

Leland's an old hand, having testified on the Crew's behalf on three occasions, the first in February 1990, at an obscenity trial in Alexander City, Alabama. He gives an entertaining, annotated history of hip-hop, which includes a stop in Miami for the birth of ghetto bass, as originated by the Ghetto Style DJs, of which Luther Campbell is a founding father. Jurors' eyes widen.

Gates defends the artistic value of 2 Live Crew's music to the jury by establishing it as part and parcel of a black oral and literary tradition that is twice as old, and then some, as the courtroom they sit in. He breaks down big words, for these parts, like "signifying," "hyperbole," and "parody," and explains why works of art are rarely to be taken literally. 2 Live Crew's music, he argues, takes one of the worst stereotypes about black men—that they're oversexed animals—and blows it up until it explodes. The jurors study him carefully: the suit, glasses, cane. When Gates compares 2 Live Crew to Archie Bunker, buzzers go off in the jurors' heads. The two black women in the jury, Gertrude McLamore, a retired cook, and alternate Wilma Williams, a retired school principal, beam at him, as if to say, finally someone to vindicate these ignorant colored boys.

Dijols spends most of his cross-examination attempting to put literary criticism on trial, a losing battle to fight against Gates, the dean of the signifying monkees. Dijols asks, "Does this work advance black culture?" "Yes," Gates answers with a straight face. Dijols continues: "Are you saying that this is part of fighting for civil rights and fighting for equality? Are you equating 2 Live Crew to black leaders like Martin Luther King?" Gates hesitates; not even he can go that far. "I never equated the two. There is a difference between a civil rights march and exploding a stereotype."

Something Gates tells the court sticks to my head like Velcro: "There is no cult of violence. There is no danger at all that these words are being sung." I wonder if he's seen 2 Live Crew in concert and watched them push women to the stage floor, pour water on them, and chant, "Summer's Eve, Massengill, bitch wash your stinky pussy!" I've been watching Brother Marquis around the courtroom. With his signifying, double-entendre way of dressing and speaking, I wonder if he can answer some of the questions I have about 2 Live Crew's "entertainment":

"We recorded 'Throw the D' in Eighty-Seven. It was kinda X-rated and it was a hit. Common sense told us to follow up on our hit. We put our minds to work and came up with this whole thing here: being the nasty boys of rap. We knew we had to talk about something. At the time, L.L. Cool J was talking about how bad he was, and the Fat Boys were talking about how fat they were. Since Miami is up on sex—anything nasty these cats go for around here—we said, let's talk about sex.

"The bottom line is getting dollars and having your own. It's really a black thing with us. Even though people might say we're not positive role models to the black community, that if you ask us about our culture, we talk about sex, it's not really like that. I'm well aware of where I come from. I know myself as a black man. I think I'm with the program, very much so. You feel I'm doing nothing to enhance my culture, but I could be destroying my culture. I could be out here selling kids drugs.

"The women come on stage on their own. Sometimes we do grab a girl. The water-fighting thing, that's not for me, but that's our job. We go out there and do it to the best of our abilities, then we go offstage and carry on like regular men. I'm not really like the way I talk on records and act onstage.

"I'm not gonna try to disrespect you and call you all those names like I do on those records. I would never do that to a young lady, especially a sister. I'm degrading you to try to get me some money. Richard Pryor was degrading you on record. And besides, just let me do that. You got pimps out here who are making you sell your body. Just let me talk about you for a little while, you know what I'm saying? And make me a little money."

### campbell's souped

I'm in a black BMW convertible heading towards Miami from Fort Lauderdale on Interstate 95. This is not my car. I couldn't even rent this car. This is Luther Campbell's car. Luther Campbell is talking on one of his two car phones. The audio outfit where the state attorney's office had the infamous concert tape remixed is a place where Luke Records *used* to do business. Campbell's pulling the plug at this very moment. First he's got to yell in the owner's ear for a while.

I notice a copy of *Fortune* magazine on the backseat. We're speeding fast now. Campbell thinks he spots a cop car in the rear-view mirror. This is all I need: To get busted in Broward County with Luther Campbell, I'll never live this down. My friends think his music is nothing but "misogynistic smut." They compare it to "farting" and say it "defiles an entire culture." They'll disown me and I'll have to move to Miami and work for Luke Records. Okay, no cop car, relax.

Campbell is bitching about how many people are serving him with lawsuits these days. ("They see a nigger making money and they want to jump on the bandwagon.") He has a child on the way from his current lady, Tina, and an eight-year-old daughter, Shane-tris. (Campbell just arrived at a child-support settlement with her mother, Terry Brinberry.) Another woman from Miami is filing a paternity suit against him.

I share my theory with Campbell that he probably grew up

middle class and, through his music, lives out some rough-riding homeboy fantasy. He doesn't appreciate this theory at all. 2 Live Crew is just a gig, he says tiredly. Luther Campbell is the businessman, the president of Luke Records, the scrupulous investor, the property owner, the little-league team sponsor, the man whose net worth, rumor has it, is over five million dollars. The man whose office is dominated by framed portraits of Martin Luther King and Malcolm X.

Campbell talks about his childhood in Liberty City, growing up in a two-bedroom house with five brothers. The Campbell brothers are all superachievers: one's a physicist, another's an executive chef. Luther is the youngest, the spoiled one, the only one who didn't go to college. Now he makes more money than all of them. And no, he was not in a gang. And yes, he did get started selling records out of his car.

"Two bedrooms, you know what that means?!," he says. "All of us were in one room, and *they* were in the other." Campbell's father, Charles Sr., born in Jamaica, is a custodian. His mother, Yvonne, who is under five feet tall, was a hairdresser until her arthritis got bad. The Campbells have been in court with their son for the last four days. They say they're "extremely proud" of their son's accomplishments. A reporter in court tells this story: Apparently Campbell would prefer that his parents not see his adults-only act. Once they did slip in. He spotted them in the crowd and refused to do any more dirty songs. The audience wanted their money back. Another story: When asked if he planned on getting married anytime soon, Campbell said, no, because the only woman he had ever thought of marrying was already taken. His mother.

### mr. america

"What's happening?" Brother Marquis asks Mary the bailiff, the court's unofficial court jester, whose tiepin is pair of miniature handcuffs. "Nothing yet, you just keep smiling. You want some water?" she offers in a thick Southern drawl. "Here's your last glass."

Gates and Leland had helped, but Rogow's thorough cross-examination of the detectives put the case to rest. The odds for acquittal are at three to one; reporters take bets in the court hallway. Campbell's family and most of the twenty-five staffers of Luke Records pack the court. The court clerk is a young black woman with extensions who cracks a big smile when she reads the verdict, "Luther Campbell, *not guilty.*"

Campbell kisses his mother first.

Outside of the Broward County Courthouse palm trees are blowing in the wind. TV cameramen are jogging backward to get a frontal shot of Campbell as he jaywalks across the boulevard. Campbell is the tallest man in the crowd, he is the brownest man in the crowd. His girlfriend, Tina, very pregnant, is two steps behind him. Campbell's parents, on the sidewalk, watch him disappear in the distance. This is a Norman Rockwell painting.

One consensus in the 2 Live Crew trial is that the only thing obscene in America is spending money the wrong way. Another constant refrain was "it's a job." Lots of people seem to do work that requires that they separate what they do from themselves. It suddenly hits what an American phenomenon Luther Campbell is. He's sold us soft porn as music, he's sold us the First Amendment as entertainment *(Banned in the USA)*. And he goes out of his way to let you know that he is not what he sells.

As much as we think he doesn't speak for us (me, you, your grandmother), he speaks for our country. As American as Pete Rose, McDonald's fried apple pie, and Luther Campbell.

*1990*

# pussy
# ain't free

Remember the Roxanne wars of '85? U.T.F.O. cut "Roxanne Roxanne," cold dissing yet another "stuck-up, devi-
ous, and sinister" homegirl. Along comes fourteen-year-
old Roxanne Shanté from the Queens Bridge projects,
Long Island City, the unauthorized rapper behind "Roxanne's Revenge." Shanté (real first name: Lolita) tells
the U.T.F.O. crew to "suck my bush." Requests for "Roxanne's Revenge" pour into black music stations before
Pop Art Records even presses it. U.T.F.O., after threatening to sue, answer with "The Real Roxanne," sung by the
Roxanne of their choosing. Shanté takes it to the stage,
namely the Roxy–Red Parrot club scene in New York,

and wins the battle with fierce freestyling. In 1986 she drops out of sight.

After having a kid (Kareem), Shanté surfaced last summer when producer Marley Marl convinced her to record "Have a Nice Day" (Cold Chillin'). She came back Ali-style, proclaiming in her trademark squeak that she's "the mike's grandmistress . . . the queen of the crew with the juice"—laurels that, in her absence, MC Lyte, Salt-N-Pepa, Queen Latifah, and others have dibs on. (These contenders are so young, the title in question should be princess; if there's a queen in the house of rap, it's Millie Jackson.)

Shanté's three singles to date deliver their share of quick draws, but improvising live is where Shanté has most rappers beat; given an inch, she'll read any man in the audience faster than a snap queen can raise his right arm. On the subject of male rappers and their female problem, Shanté, who's seventeen now, has no use for any oppressed-other politics. She accepts what rap boys have to say about girls, for the most part, with a shrug and a smile. Yet her freestyle "The Pussy Ain't Free, You Gotta Give Up Money" isn't about acceptance. It's much closer to Janet Jackson's idea of control, and seems more sound advice to Shanté's young female audience than Madonna's promo for teen pregnancy "Papa Don't Preach." Just who owns the means of reproduction? I'd like to hear someone answer Shanté on that.

*Tell me about your live show.*

ROXANNE SHANTÉ: They turn off the lights. My MC says, "Are you ready for Roxanne Shanté? Well, here's the queen!" I go out there and say, TELL 'EM WHO I AM! My DJ cuts in Heavy D and The Boyz's "The Overweight Lover's in the House." Again I say, WHO AM I? Then the DJ cuts in "Payback." I rap freestyle to that, do my new single "Have a Nice Day," and end with another freestyle.

*How do you work a freestyle?*

Usually I start with, "The Pussy Ain't Free." And more [ad-libs] about guys. My language is very vulgar, and that's bad, because I have little kids who come see my show and they go home quoting me. I had somebody's mother call me up. Her kid is four and she took her to see me at a stadium in New Jersey. For the past two weeks this kid's been going around the house saying, "The pussy ain't free, you got to give up money." Some people tell me, "Listen, don't you think you oughta cut it down?" If I did cut it down, what would I do—"One-two, one-two, what we gonna do?"? My audience is used to hearing me say things like, "See that guy right there? He makes me sick. Always wanting the blank, but ain't got no blank." You can imagine what goes in there. [Whispering] "Always wanting the pussy, but ain't got no dick."

*You can say that in this paper.*

Really? I must sound like I'm terribly nasty. I'm not.

*If you use explicit language, there must be a reason for it.*

Some people say I use it just to be known, 'cause I had to work so much harder than men did. L.L. [Cool J] can go out there and say, "Rock the bells," and the crowd yells.

*And when you use explicit language . . .*

They love it. If they didn't love it, I wouldn't use it. When I pick a guy from the audience and start dogging him 'cause he said something smart, the crowd goes wild.

*You bring him up on stage?*

No, he stays right there in the audience, behind the guards, 'cause he might get mad and try to punch me. If he yells something like, "Yo, fuck her," I'll be like, "What? Fuck your mother," and such and such. I'm a little nicer now. I don't get that many hecklers 'cause don't nobody wanna get cursed out and be embarrassed the next day in school. "Ahh, I seen Roxanne curse you out." Though some guys like it 'cause they think it makes them popular. They be like, "Talk about me, talk about me!"

*So you get out there and you really dog 'em, but these guys get off on it?*

Guys like me; it's the girls who don't. The guys be looking forward to getting the drawers. [In a sexy male voice] "Yo baby, you need such and such." They be giving me all that coon-neckedee-neckeedee talk. They be looking forward to gettin' some so they can say, "I got Roxanne!" Now, girls, they roll their eyes, act like they don't like me. Some girls I meet are nice, they'll say, "Yeah, I like your records." But most will be like, "I coulda done better." Well, bitch, if ya coulda done better, why am I up here and you're down there? Why you waste your fifteen country dollars to come see me, if all you gonna do is stand there and stick your lips out? Me and girls never got along.

*Is that why you started rappin', because you hung out with guys?*

I hung with guys. Never with girls. Girls cause problems. I'd say guys encouraged me to rhyme. Guys like Hakim, MC Shan, and them. You know, beating on tables and stuff like that. They inspired me a lot.

*When "Roxanne's Revenge" came out, you were fifteen, right?*

Fourteen. Tasting success. I would go to the park with my friend Sherron and the fellows wouldn't want to give me the mike. How dare they? When I got it, I'd start with, "You right there in your mock neck and Lees/Scratching your ass like you got fleas." The crowd would go crazy 'cause I was so little, with a high-pitched voice.

*In songs by male rap artists it seems all women are hoes or bitches out to steal their seed or, in the case of Dana Dane, run with all their Gucci stuff. What's up with this?*

See, there's no such thing as an "in-between girl." Even the homeliest girl wants. She wants gold earrings, chains, et cetera. Anyway, guys pamper girls and make them want these things. So what makes a girl a ho? Because she won't give you none? I walk down the street and guys say, "Yo baby, yo baby, I'm talking to you, yo Trooper." (I wear a Troop jacket.) And when I don't speak, they say, "Yo, fuck you 'cause you ain't fly anyway." I'm the type to turn around and say, "Then why the fuck was you chasing me?"

Guys dis girls for the stupidest reasons. They want the kind of girl they can just slap up. No nigger slap me. I haven't been slapped yet. Let somebody slap me . . . Wait a minute, I have. So I lied.

*You told me you don't like "Dumb Girls" [Run-D.M.C.], but "Dear Yvette" [L.L. Cool J] you like. Don't they both dog women?*

To me, "Dumb Girls" had no meaning. What's the sense in

making a record called "Dumb Girls"? Girls aren't dumb. If you think about it, a dumb girl can get more out of a guy that a really smart girl can. 'Cause the dumb girl could be playing dumb. It was a stupid, dumb record. I started to make a record called "Dumb Guys," but I didn't want to do anymore answer records.

I didn't find anything wrong with "Dear Yvette." L.L. was talking about one girl. Her name was Yvette. I know a lot of girls like Yvette. He wasn't downing her, he was trying to get her to better herself. So he wrote her a letter telling her what she should do—get a GED and stuff like that.

*Are you saying you don't mind the records male artists are making about women?*

Rap is about using fighting words, instead of fighting. Instead of saying "Let's fight," people say, "Let's battle." I bet rap shows have saved a lot of lives. Even though there were shootouts afterwards!

Half of it is about people getting so dressed up for the shows. Not in regular suits, but in stuff that cost more that: leather, Gucci suits, Fila suits and sneakers. We're talking expensive shit here. So if somebody steps on homeboy's sneakers, of course he's gonna break and wanna fight. Especially if the other guy got on Pro-Keds, flair-leg jeans, and a mock neck. There used to be this guy going around called the Slasher. He'd slash leather jackets at parties and concerts. Do you know how ugly a leather looks after it's been cut?

*As long as you're able to defend yourself with words, you don't care what they say?*

Exactly. But sometimes I do feel hurt about records made about me. I have had records made about me that have gotten deep-down dark and dirty. I've been called "project ho" by niggers who never got a bit o' pussy. One guy was talking about "Roxanne Shanté is only good for steady fuckin'." How long he been knowing me? Turns out he never even met me. I could've bugged out, ran up to him and killed him, and he wouldn't have known what I looked like.

Regardless of how hard I play on the outside, I'm still a woman. I'm still sensitive. I don't like to see dogs get hit by cars. I don't like to see children get beatings.

*What do you think of the other women rappers?*

There's enough room for everybody. I'm not against no female rappers, just as long as they don't get in my way.

*How about a battle between women rappers?*

That would have to be a Don King promotion, because it would be a strict fight afterwards! That's something you'd want to put on before a Tyson fight! Let everybody get in the ring, let all the mikes come down, and let everybody go for theirs! I think girl rappers are more fierce than guys. I can't rate myself. I might not be the last one standing, 'cause girls can get down and start writing, and I'm the kind of person to do mine off the top of my head. I'd be so nervous, I'd be downright vulgar. I'd say the kind of stuff that makes people's mothers climb into the ring.

*What do you wear when you go on?*

Anything I have on. I walk out there, get a seat. I look like a female Bill Cosby. I have my legs crossed and I just talk. I don't get dressed up, 'cause I find it fake. A hip-hopper is a regular street person, so I wear my regular clothes. If I was doing a show tonight, I wouldn't wear this hat, but I'd wear these jeans, these sneakers, this shirt, and put curls in my hair or throw on a Gucci hat. I'm not a dressy person. That's why when I go out, people see me and say, "That ain't her, look what she got on."

*1988*

# reckless igging

A peculiar little crime called "reckless eyeballing" cost Emmett Till his life one hot summer night in Money, Mississippi, back in 1955. The fourteen-year-old boy visiting from up North allegedly ran his eyes over a white woman and let out a whistle. Till turned up in the Tallahatchie River with a bullet in his head and the motor of a cotton gin tied to his neck with barbed wire. No one ever found his testicles.

Fast forward twenty-seven years and several hundred miles to Minneapolis, Minnesota. Folks whose only reference to interracial relationships is the Spike Lee film like to call Minneapolis "the *Jungle Fever* capital of middle

America." This liberal oasis in the Republican Midwest has, estimates say, the highest number of mixed-race unions per capita. Yet wander the Minne-Apple and you won't strike color-blind nirvana (the economic divide between the races, as elsewhere, is glaring). You will find something closer to *Purple Rain*'s Romper Room of black male–white female desire, especially on the nightlife scene. In clubs like Prince's new digs, Glam Slam, you'd think black women were prehistoric mammals that didn't make it through the Stone Age. Just us fossils holding up the wall.

A local musician tells me that he can accept institutional racism, but what bothers him most—really, really bothers him—is still not feeling safe walking the streets with a white woman. Is the pinnacle of personal freedom and power for him, I wonder, unfettered access to what the lynchers saw to it Emmett Till would never have?

If I don't sound my jolly, multiculti self, it's that seven months here and the Rodney King verdict have replaced my New York–melting-pot/interracial-family-of-origin questions with what you might call a simple dose of black women's rage. Miss Columnist has been touched by a common phenomenon for sisters in these parts: She's been recklessly igged, which is to say, in the vernacular, ignored, disrespected, tossed off.

In the week after the L.A. uprising there were three hits in a row. At a cocktail party, a woman, white, came on to the man I was with, in my very presence, like I was the rug on the floor. A few days later, at a restaurant, my quick trip to the john provided enough time for the waitress, also white, to proposition my dinner date. Then, the finale. On the street, a close friend, with an X cap on his head and a blonde on his arm, would have passed me by without a hello if I hadn't flagged him down like a traffic cop. Mr. X had guilt plastered all over his face. He's a buddy of mine and I could give two ideological shits about the race of his partner. I *did* mind being disposed of so cavalierly as a thinking person, as a friend, as a *real* sister. But hey, maybe fossils just aren't visible in broad daylight.

These events sent me to get the tea on *Fever* issues in Minneapolis. For young African-American women here the stylishness of black male–white female coupling is a thorn in their side deeper than what one woman called "the polygamy issue." The women I spoke to consider themselves multiculturalists. They are not opposed to interracial relationships. A couple even have white parents. What vexes them is how little value they're assigned in a sexual marketplace where white femininity still has tremendous currency. Walk around town some days, they say, and you'd think Afrocentricity and rhapsodies to the Nubian Princess never made it past Cleveland.

An actress who's lived in Minneapolis and Chicago, Tina, who's twenty-seven, tells me that her black male friends say they're attracted to white women for their sexual bravado. Yet these same men are turned off by hers: "A white woman's aggressive, but I'm a slut, a skeezer, or a ho." Nandi, twenty-three, from a mixed-race family in Canada, is a senior at the University of Minnesota. Her parents are happily married, she assures me, though looking at interracial couples at the U, she thinks, "these relationships have no integrity. The brothers lower their eyes when they see me. Sometimes, in all my anger, I have to remind myself that my own mother is white."

Then there's Lynn, a singer who grew up in Minnesota and returned after graduation from Spelman. Lynn spent her young adulthood in social situations where it was all the rage for men to date exclusively white. Spelman helped her disengage this fact from her sense of self-esteem and belief in black political community. Lynn has "stopped walking into Glam Slam wanting to kill every white woman with a brother," yet sometimes she asks herself why the black men she knows "don't see what is beautiful as me? If you have a problem with my hair, don't you have a problem with yours too? Isn't us being together what binds our culture and community? By favoring white women, aren't you saying that your idea of our community is not dependent on me? How can you not want me and still want my politics?"

"The Debbies are bold in Minnesota," is a mantra that Sasha, twenty-six, a publicist and Minneapolis native, teaches me. "Brothers give them big juice," she reports. "They know the advantage is theirs and they milk it." We work out as much frustration as we can with Debbie Lingo ("Debbie-free zones," "invasion of the Debbies") without choking on our own bigotry. After hanging out with Sasha, I'm left with the old questions of where white women have stood in America's coiled legacy of racism and race mixing.

In Minneapolis's feminist circles one hears the party line of white women as racial innocents. Sasha et al. are quick to disagree. Tina tells of a white coworker who thought she was humoring Tina with lusty details of her black-male conquests. It was hard for Tina to imagine that the woman could be so blisteringly ignorant of black-relationship politics that she would carry on so thoughtlessly. Tina's convinced the coworker was flexing her muscles. What stake would she have in dismantling a pecking order of femininity that puts her at the top?

New York–based playwrights Laurie Carlos and Aishah Rahman were in the Twin Cities recently to talk about their work. There they sat in high-art diva wear: a mix of African- and Japanese-inspired prints, kitsch scarves, basic black, and the odd bolero hat thrown in for drama. A young woman in the audience asked Rahman why she'd "said good-bye to naturalism" as an artist. There was a lot bubbling behind the question. She seemed to be saying, how do you blossom when the guns are against you, how do you speak your stories when everyone calls you a liar, how do you stay beautiful to yourself when every mirror tells you otherwise? "Well, my dear," said Rahman, batting her eyes, "I didn't have to say good-bye to naturalism, because I never said hello to it."

*1992*

# it's racier
# in the bahamas

We found out a long time ago that everyone masturbates and that everyone wants to be rich. The new truth is that everyone is consumed with the same racial mythologies that made this country so great:

Blondes have more fun if they're sleeping with black men; black women of all complexions prefer dark-skinned black men; white men love themselves exclusively, they invented masturbation; Puerto Rican women in Hartford have the hots for black men; women who love women want to make it with women of color; white men in leather want black men, also in leather; Asians of both sexes adore whites of both sexes; Jewish women from all countries want it bad with everyone; light-skinned black American women with money think they invented pussy; light-skinned Latin men, especially Colombians, love and marry dark-skinned women from all Latin countries; progressive black American men with money say color isn't an issue, yet are only seen in public with women with "good hair"; progressive, dark-skinned black American women who get no play from color-struck brothers are experimenting with white men; the finest men in the world are all black and are usually from Zimbabwe, Atlanta, or Brooklyn; the finest women in the world are from Brazil, come in all colors, but usually have hair like Troy Beyer, Diahann Carroll's daughter on *Dynasty*. And if you think you don't fit into all this, you're lying.

Two things happened recently that convinced me these allegories are held to be self-evident:

One: Last year before it got too cold, two friends and I were drinking beer one Sunday at an outdoor café on Bleecker Street. Sucker for heated discussion, I suggested that instead of sexual fantasies, we trade race fantasies (which would lead us to class and sex anyway).

First on the chopping block was Idris, a Latina from the Bronx, who confessed that her race fantasy was to be rich, like Donald Trump, and to marry a man who was even richer, like Howard Hughes. Though it was not crucial that her husband be Howard Hughes—after all, he was dead—it was most important that he be white, and for all practical purposes, impotent. She would jet around the world giving her husband's money away to people of color fighting wars of national liberation. She would take lovers at every port. These lovers could be of either sex, but would always be of color.

Up second was Patrick, black and gay from East New York. Pat said his race fantasies involved that idea of uplift as well. He wanted to be very rich, like Rockefeller, and run a home for young black and Latino homosexuals. He would be an idol of desire, father figure, and priest to these young men, but take none as his lover, preferring to date rich white men exclusively.

I am a child of leftist bohemians, so my fantasy involved the American dream. I'd bury my racial impurities forever by marrying into an old black family of race men, mother five heirs to the mantle, live in a huge house in the suburbs of a thriving black metropolis, vacation in Sag Harbor, and solely by virtue of my virtue as a black woman, be involved in changing the world every moment of my life. Some who know me well say this scenario is not true, and others say it's true without a doubt; which I guess gives it credence as a fantasy.

Even funnier than our three-hour conversation was that during the course of it we each witnessed an ex-flame of ours actually pass by strutting his fantasy. (Pat's, an intense middle-aged black man in a beret, was strolling close to a young blueblood.) Was Bleecker Street really the crossroads of the fantasy world or had we been in New York too long?

Two: I went to the Bahamas.

You know about the blue waters, as in gems, and the white sands, as in powdered platinum, and the trees that tower like dinosaurs and bear fruit. You know about the bright drinks with too much rum, and the Isles of Perpetual June, where you spend petite eternities on the beach, toasting your body and reaping your soul. You know about the music. "Hot, Hot, Hot." You know peas and rice go with conch fritters, and that crawfish walk backward and taste best with lemon and butter. And that "Purple Haze" is not about an acid trip, but the way the sun sets in the Caribbean, clinging to the sky like a scorned lover. These things you know.

But consider this ad for a film released through United Artists in 1958: " 'Island Women.' The Whole Ripped-Bare Story of the Beach Babes of the Caribbean! White-hot off the blazing beaches of the Carib sin-ports. . . . The story of excitement-mad 'nice' girls looking for 'kicks' in the luxury isles. Everything you've heard about them is TRUE!"

So it's been going on for a long time. And thirty years later, on the sin-port of Eleuthera—the Bahamas's Beauty Queen, as it's called; one hundred miles of exquisite scenery and beaches, rolling hills and farmlands, white cliffs and seventeenth-century villages, once home to the world's premiere pineapple plantations—it's in full swing.

I'm here for a wedding. My oldest friend, a white woman, gave up painting a couple of years back and went to live in the Bahamas. She is now to marry a local gentleman of reputable family who was educated in North America. They will tend bar together, he will build her a house on a majestic cliff overlooking the aquamarine abyss, and she will find reason to paint again.

The wedding party arriving from stateside includes my friend (I'll call her Sarah) and her three college chums: a Jewish woman from California, a black man from Massachusetts (accompanied by his fiancée, a white woman), a brown-skinned Cuban woman with "good hair" (accompanied by her fiancé, a light-skinned brother with an M.B.A.); along with, Sarah's sister (married to a black man), her mother (once married to a black man), and me (looking for a black man). We will spend a week together, including Thanksgiving Day, and share many things, race fantasies not among them.

Traveling in foreign countries is the only time I truly feel like an American. I'm middle class, more or less, and Ivy League–educated, though I'm still ranked as a perpetual minority (read: underclass) by belonging to a caste of people who, worldwide, even in their own countries, are disenfranchised. What this means in my own country is that I am never quite a citizen; or I don't feel like one; or more often than not, I'm not treated like one. One reason I do feel like an American when I travel is that I carry a verification of my citizenship. Even so, I usually spend my entire trip lugging my American baggage—the Howard Beach "accident," the ghost of Eleanor Bumpurs. And just when I've set all this down—it's time to go home.

But this is not home. Here I am in the islands. The sky is blue. The sun is shining. And everyone who is an American—minority, majority, whatever—belongs to one class, the foreigner class. And it is through this identity that I happen upon the curious sensation of being under the skin of a white girl, or at least, under the skin of the stereotype; the one who voyages to Carib sin-ports, meets handsome men who look something like Calvin Lockhart or the young Belafonte, and is wined and dined (though she may often pick up the tab) and made to feel like the most desired woman on the face of this earth.

This is an experience you are not often privy to as a black American woman, even if you are light-skinned and heterosexual like me and have a certain amount of privilege in your own culture. There is always a woman who is lighter, brighter than you are, has longer hair, and lighter eyes than you do, and is willing to give up more to get to that brother in the suit. Yes, despite *Elle* magazine–style affirmative action and rap nationalists talking good-brother talk on your radio, the most desired woman on the face of this earth is still a Breck Girl.

And for most of my trip to Eleuthera, I am reminded of this. Perhaps even more so because my beach-side reading material is the copy of *Invisible Man* that I bought at the LaGuardia Airport bookshop before the flight down. (They had an impressive selection of books by black authors. Though I have a copy at home, I chose *Invisible Man* to send a message to the buyers that sacred black texts sell at airports.) *Invisible Man,* even on the beach, even on this beach, which is silver and littered with weeping palms, puts me in a mood: dark, brooding, and very colored (or, should I say, very judgmental?).

Over and over I read the passage in which two crazy men, on a bus bound up North, discuss the fate of our young hero: "Most of the time he'll be working, and so, much of his freedom will have to be symbolic. And what will be his or any man's most easily accessible symbol of freedom? Why, a woman of course." Then I instant replay a couple of scenes in my head:

One: Drinking at a local bar plastered with photos of the foreigner class in various states of debauchery, I encounter a young Bahamian who greets me with lust in his eyes. When I don't respond, he moves immediately to the woman on my left, a full-bodied brunette with blonde ambition. She arranges herself, with a deep breath, to receive his look, her cup size expanding by two letters. The fantasy I assigned the scene: a queen lapping up the sweat of a slave. The way they saw themselves may have been a different story.

Two: Sarah's father, who owns a furniture business in Latin America, tells me at the bar one night that, not only is he giving his daughter to her husband, he is giving her to the entire island. It's an offering the white man's burden requires him to make.

The well-to-do ladies of Eleuthera—the most dizzying array of light-skinned black women in polyester ever assembled under a thatch roof—throw Sarah a bridal shower. The women of the American wedding party, myself included, arrive late and are ushered to a table in the middle of the room where we sit by ourselves surrounded by red and pink streamers. As we file by the local women shoot us with looks that could raise the dead. I know these looks well because I am usually not on the receiving end, but dishing them out.

I realize that this is the first time in the five days that I've been here that I have spent more than five minutes in the company of black women. On the beaches and in the bars, it's women of the foreigner class and island gigolos. Here I am relieved to be setting eyes on them finally, and they're looking at me like I've got honorary white status. And I'd get more scorn for that than the other Americans would get for being white. And what about the white Americans? How do they see me down here? While Sarah is opening her gifts, the Jewish woman from California whispers to me, "I'm so glad they did this for her. Sarah's busted her ass for *these* people," as if Sarah had spent ten years doing missionary work on the island.

One day we drive out to Savannah Sound, the poor Eleuthera. Goats and chickens cross the roads casually. The sun seems brighter on this part of the island, as in no rest for the weary. Here the trees really weep, the wind makes their branches bow to the ground. Sarah has taken some of the American wedding party to visit her husband's poor relatives. They live in a little rectangle of a house that looks like a train car, worn at the edges, yet tended with love.

In the back room sits a pretty young woman in glasses, brown-skinned and petite, surrounded by ten children, two of them infants. She tells me that with two kids of her own, she is too poor to work outside of the home, so she minds neighborhood kids instead. The white women rush to the children, who are mostly boys, all pretty and brown with holes in their clothes, and pet and coo over them as if they were small animals. These are children who in the States would be passed up for adoption, who as young men would be seen as angry and without options—and by routine feared. I turn away to avoid shooting looks at anyone I have to share a hotel room with later.

In bed that night I read about the other Bahamian islands in a guidebook called *Welcome Bahamas.* "San Salvador: This island is preening for its Big Moment, October 12, 1992, the 500th anniversary of the arrival of Christopher Columbus in the New World. . . . Cat Cay: Posh, Yachts, millionaires, and fishing tournaments . . . the Prime Minister has announced plans to increase per capita income to $10,000 annually. This is the primary criterion for entering the First World, a goal sought for the Bahamas by the twenty-first century." I write in my journal: "The way Sarah walked through the shack her new relatives live in; how grand she must feel living among such humble, appreciative people who treat her like royalty, make much of her otherness, gladly step and fetch. What security that yields, what accomplishment, what an affirmation of her femininity, of her class position, of her self worth."

What about Sarah? In grade school we took modern dance from a vampire on the Bowery; at fourteen, we were groupies to a black rock band; at eighteen, we did Europe by backpack. What could a nice bohemian girl like her want with a Cinderella fantasy like this? And why did she have to travel to the Caribbean to find it? For one thing, she didn't have to dress up like an investment banker and work overtime; or beg, borrow, and steal, like Sherrie Levine, for a loft in Tribeca. In America, these days, even a white woman has to work hard to get to that brother in the suit. Down here, all Sarah had to do was be. The natives took care of the rest. I am reminded of the woman at the bar with the expanding cleavage: Who can affirm a queen, but a slave?

The wedding is a grand opera of color. The road, jet black from last night's rain; the trees, fragrant and moss green. As our car approaches the church, wedding guests overtake the road, and we must drive behind them forming a slow, almost lazy procession. The healthy brown of their skin sparkles red in the noon light. And the clothes: pink satins, every imaginable blue, from busy royal to powder pure, hot orange coupled with lace, reds that scream (as in hibiscus), and reds that moan (as in burgundy). The church, pastel green trimmed with vanilla, sits on a hill, earth green, and spread out below are fifty perfectly whitewashed steps. The groomsmen, magnificent in a white even brighter than the steps, their bow ties and cummerbunds scorching aqua; the groom himself, all in white, could be off to his first communion. The gold piping on the bibles, the purple stained-glass windows, the little chestnut-skinned flower girl whose hair glistens as orange as flying fish eggs. The bride, like a pearl, her dress shimmering under the sun, tells me later that she was completely naked underneath. When the reverend reads the objection clause, the packed church holds its breath. The groom's legs shake violently. I expect an old girlfriend of his to come running into the church and lay a baby at the altar. No one is safe in paradise, I think. Not even a white girl.

  The reception is held at a country club facing the Atlantic Coast of the island. It was built in the fifties and hasn't been used for years; its white-painted verandas and gazebos blistering under the rays, its paths and gardens in need of grooming, all adding to the old-world elegance of the place. (Oh colonialism, such a style war.) After the toasts, the reception turns into an island jump up. At the bar, men in tuxedos place colored potions before me: Bahama

Mama, Torpedo Sunsplash, Lone Wolf (crème de menthe, vodka, amaretto, with a garnish of rhubarb), Castro Libre (a Cuba Libre with 150 proof Bacardi). A drug kingpin, who now owns hotels, a regal black man in a navy blue jacket and white colonial kickers, asks to ride me back to New York in his six-seater. A customs officer I met at the Nassau airport offers me a job as his mistress. To my right and left, I hear lines like: "God bless America, she lookin' fine,"; "This package wrapped nice, mon,"; and "Gimme a beautiful sister like you, I'll cut the white girls loose tomorrow."

For the first time in the seven days I've been here I realize how black women of the foreigner class fit in. It seems we have an even higher currency in these parts. The experience we offer is like traveling to China and buying a Coca Cola T-shirt. And what does the experience offer us? If you had no ambition other than to feel like an heiress on the run from Mommy and Daddy, being ogled over by brown-skinned men with wide white smiles and large hands (playing Shirley Temple to his Bill Robinson or Fredi Washington to his Paul Robeson, however you see yourself, ladies, this is the islands, no one is judging), you could have stopped the clock, stood right there, with one eye on the ocean, the other on the subject at hand.

But me, I'm sightseeing. Just want to look. Yes, I'm just here for the sights. The breeze off the ocean, ninety degrees in the shade. Just a little look see. "Nice girl travels to sin-port meets carefree island hunk. Everything you heard is true" is not my fantasy. My fantasy, the consummate race man, is only a reality. In fact, that's his problem. He's back in America giving it to some undeserving babe and giving it to her good: He calls it freedom. Oh the horrors. The tide has turned; I'm indignant. Someone has the nerve to request "Hot, Hot, Hot" for the third time. Two beach blondes, burned golden and flaunting it in white minis, walk into the country club and are carried aloft, like figureheads on a ship's bow, by five Bahamians gyrating to an R&B ode to Casanovas. This is a freaking minstrel show. I'm calling Delta tomorrow, change my flight goddammit. No, I don't want another drink. Don't even think about putting your hand on my thigh. I'm a black American, goddammit, and I'm not impressed.

The only person who could get a rise out of me at this moment is Denzel Washington—the closet thing Hollywood has to offer to a young race man. And, sure enough, he walks in. Not really, but there's enough of a resemblance to prompt a full-body rush. He appears under a gazebo, materializing from thin air, like Denzel did when he played Steve Biko in *Cry Freedom*. When you see a man like this, you realize why white men had to convince themselves colonialism was a God-given right. Michelangelo's David ain't got a thing on this. This is God's idea of Development. If blue collar is your fantasy, you've got the wrong number. This is the lost Nubian prince hotline. Never mind the class wars, give us a king, but make him dark skinned. The sculpture of the head and always the dialectic: blackness of hair against brownness of skin. Every gesture, done as if to music, and the eyes, the brown eyes. Later for Cupid's bow, this boy is throwing javelins from across the ballroom, and they're aimed straight at the groin.

I went back for Christmas.

*1989*

# genitalia and the paycheck

Remind me that Deandra is in love again and therefore not to be trusted. Before euphoria arrived, this time wrapped in dreadlocks and mud cloth, old girl and I would kick womanist ballistics any time, be it four in the morning, whenever. Lately, all I get is an answering machine with Aaron Neville wailing, "Love came out of nowhere/ baby/just like a hurricane." You do realize, I tell Deandra when I finally catch her, that you've committed a cardinal sin in the girlfriend canon. When I say, girl, we need to talk, you don't say next week. The appropriate response is, *Jump?,* sister, how high? The womanist-guilt card still works; Deandra grants me an audience.

It's about that Terry McMillan book again, and the Mike Tyson case again, and a sitcom called "Martin," and something some guy said to you on the street, am I right? Deandra can guess me a mile away. Sister, she offers with the heavy sigh of a Baptist missionary, you have Deandra's permission to unload.

MISS COLUMNIST: I see this guy reading *Waiting To Exhale* on the D train, so I ask him what he thinks. Now we all owe Miss McMillan a million pounds of gratitude for upping the stakes for black women in publishing. But wasn't the book a Harlequin romance minus the blonde woman on the horse? Turns out this guy loves the book because, I quote, it tells *the* black woman's perspective on relationships. I happen to be a black woman, as you know, and I am *not* spending my life waiting to exhale until brother in the Prince Charming suit pulls up in the Range Rover, okay? (Not this week at least.) Why does every last character suffer from the same brand of BMW materialism? And must *Exhale* regurgitate the fable of black woman as insatiable hyena of the boudoir? Between rappers turning "ho" into a national chant and *Exhale* telling African Americans that our real problem is the shortage of brothers who are both well hung and well paid, I'm getting to think that all we can offer each other as black women and men is genitalia and the paycheck. Assuming it is, we might as well move into separate armed camps surrounded by those bulletproof partitions you see in candy stores in Washington Heights. Then we can exchange the goods in generic Pathmark baggies. Pussy: weight fifteen pounds. Though contents may shift in packaging.

DEANDRA: Who needs stodgy white men when we can look forward to folks like you as the high-art police? You just wish two books of yours were being made into major motion pictures starring a matinee Negro like Wesley Snipes so you could play Queen to his Chicken George out back in the trailers. And let me get this straight: Are you recommending that black artists be limited to presenting sociological position papers? *Exhale* doesn't pretend to be a floor plan of the psyche of every black woman in America. This is a novel about four middle-class women in the suburbs near Phoenix who buy teddies from Victoria's Secret and are waiting for that brother in the Prince Charming suit. This is not about you, me, or the homicide rate in Detroit. And as I know quite a few details about your personal life, perhaps I don't need to remind you that waiting to exhale in Phoenix (as it is in Brooklyn, last time I checked) is also an S.B.E. (Significant Black Experience). I myself was not above learning from *Exhale.* It helped me identify very clearly the kind of woman I don't want to be, and for this I'm grateful. It also made me realize that this longing I have for black men is far deeper than dime-store romance. It's how I gather lost family, love brothers I never had, make peace with the father I barely knew, make a home out of ashes. The ceasefire begins with you, sis. So, how's Mike Tyson bothering you today?

MISS C.: Groupies like Pamela Des Barres who ride the axes of the white guitar gods and live to write memoirs about it are celebrated as cultural heroes. Their bed jumping and their peekaboo minidresses are called creative expression and rarefied performance art. When a black woman goes to some famous guy's hotel room and tells the world what happened there, she's called a two-dollar ho looking to get paid. Meanwhile, brothers have elevated pimping into not-too-rarefied performance art. Rappers like Big Daddy Kane compose songs such as "Pimpin' Ain't Easy" and Negroes with Ph.D.s chuckle and add the line to their repertoires. Black girls don't go into hotel rooms looking for heroes or black men to tell them they're beautiful. Pimps, on the other hand, are just misunderstood father figures from dysfunctional families who become the inspiration for great soundtracks.

DEANDRA: Your point again?

MISS C.: Tyson will walk on appeal, a nouveau riche brother who could afford to buy himself some William Kennedy Smith–style justice. Sad thing is that no one (black folks, the media, Baptist ministers, feminists) is really interested in justice for Tyson the man or Desiree Washington the woman. This is all about the boxer and the beauty queen, windup toys for Nielsen families. Would anybody have commissioned a documentary on any old black man who raped any old black woman? If you noticed, Barbara Kopple's film did little to question the image of Tyson as brute minus brain cells, as Cus D'Amato's nigra Frankenstein. There was no attempt to show Tyson as a man who acted intelligently on any front. This is a champion, mind you, one who apparently knows boxing history inside out. To be great at anything requires a mind. Don't tell me Tyson doesn't have one. Listen to this: One woman interviewed in the documentary actually recommended clemency for Tyson because he's from the hood; that his anger is ultimately created by the white power factory, and therefore he can't be held responsible for it. That there's nothing any man from Brownsville or Compton can do to hurt us that we shouldn't excuse him for. Including rape. Well, sorry, that's just not in my program. I cannot accept rape as one of the occupational hazards of being a black woman. And tell me, what maxim says Tyson's crime is endemic to the ghetto? Certainly not statistics on rape and domestic abuse, which run the gamut of class. There are plenty of men from mean streets who don't make a habit of pummeling and raping women. I say keep Tyson on ice.

DEANDRA: It amazes me that you can call for another black man to rot in prison when something like one quarter of the population, more in some cities, is doing just that. Do you think prison qualifies as reform? Do you think a black man—or any man—learns gentleness and respect for women in prison? And where is it written in the womanist rule book that we must exonerate every woman, including Desiree the beauty queen, because we share genitals? Why should the media dictate my call to arms when I could be writing screenplays about Ida B. Wells? So, where does poor Martin and his sitcom fit into this?

MISS C.: Poor Martin, my rump shaker. I loved that show. Martin Lawrence is a funny Negro. I adore the way his ears stick out and how humor occupies every part of his body. So why does "Martin" go break my womanist heart? Last week, Martin's girl Gina, played by Tisha Campbell, leaves work in the middle of an important presentation that could win her a promotion. Why? To take care of Martin, who has the sniffles. The episode ends without us finding out what happened to Gina's promotion or indeed to girlfriend's job. Here we have this adorable sitcom in which the O.P.P. generation gets cozy with monogamy. Then we are shown that for women, monogamy probably equals poor job ratings and/or indentured servitude. A seductive payoff if there ever was one. For a break, I turn to talk TV, where the hottest act in the big ring is the face-off between black men and women. Watch Bubba and Bertha strut and slobber like Dobermans. They're so colorful when they're mad at each other, we could laugh at them forever. Gag me with the remote! Finally, yesterday I nearly lost it when on Houston Street in broad daylight I hear a young man say, and verbatim I quote, "I wouldn't even rape that skank ho." He wasn't reciting Ice Cube, he was asking for my number. Rewind?

DEANDRA: Don't tell me you're still waiting for commercial TV and angry man hip-hop to affirm you? Broadcast your own fairy tales. Why aren't you writing about me? Nubian American Princess meets Nubian American Prince. He cooks her omelettes. His Valentine's cards have charming nationalistic soundbites, like, "Black-love, struggle love, reciprocity love. Our ancestors quake with our power." Once he left a message on her answering machine with these four words: "I love you, sis." To be his sister, to be his lover! Revolutionary petunias were blooming everywhere and it was only March. Write about *that*, girlfriend.

MISS C.: Not enough genitalia, and not enough paycheck.

*1993*

# five

# the hair trade

# planet hair

I haven't read J. A. Rogers's *100 Amazing Facts About the Negro* yet, so I wonder if it tells of any amazing triumphs over Bad Hair. Like our patron saint of Good Hair, Madame C. J. Walker, who made a small fortune off the scalps of Negro women who had so little time to "Fix that Mess" (says a recent ad for Le Kair's Black Satin Cream Relaxer). Or of the incredible balancing acts of Tamara Dobson ("Run your fingers thru my nine-inch 'fro if you want to, daddy, I got a gun to your jugular") and Miss Ross ("I need twelve inches or more")?

Is there mention of Harlem's Hair Station on 125th Street (owned by Koreans, Rogers would have pointed out)? Or of its manager, Alexis Smith, a black man, who for the past nine years has made his living putting that heifer Mother Nature in her place?

It's a just-got-paid Friday, just after five. You can see the sign from Lenox Avenue:

HAIR STATION

MANUFACTURE

100% HUMAN HAIR

BRAIDING & WEAVING.

Near the IRT entrance on Lenox and 125th, Rastas selling bootleg shearling are blasting Marley's "Could You Be Loved" ("Don't let them change you/Or even rearrange you/Oh no"). The sound trails down the block to Hair Station's small storefront, where hair, real human hair, hangs in neatly coiffed horsetails from every inch of wall space. Some is displayed, like scalps, in glass cases.

The after-work crowd works the counters. A half dozen young women in black shearling (real) and leather (real) hover over one counter petting a length of "Bone Straight." (Which may take its name from the new relaxer by TCB. "Not just straight," the ads promise. "Bone Straight.") They compare it to "French Refined" (European stock: bouncy, silky, with a hint of curl), which Alexis says is tied with "Bone Straight" for best-seller: " 'Bone Straight' is hot right now, but the most versatile hair out is 'French Refined.' It doesn't condemn you to one style."

CAUCASIAN STRAIGHT, KINKY STRAIGHT, KINKY AFRO. Whose hair was this before? Hair Station imports it in bulk, mostly from Asia, where poor women sell their long, straight locks for money. The hair is "retextured" in a secret heating process ("bogus places use chemicals," says Alexis) to match black hair types, permed, Jheri curled, or untreated.

"There's Chinese hair and hair from Italy," adds the Korean owner, a stocky man who asks not to be identified. "The European hair is more expensive because it's rare. One or two people a year come to us off the street to sell their hair, some Spanish girls, but we can't do that. That little amount doesn't help us."

You choose from unlimited blends of brown, black, and blonde, or novelty colors like neon yellow (Phyllis Diller), deep purple (circa George Clinton's Brides of Funkenstein), and siren red (Chaka Khan). "We don't dye like everyone else," Alexis confides. "We have a secret way of dyeing."

PRICES ARE SUBJECT TO CHANGE WITHOUT NOTICE. "Price depends on texture and color," Alexis will tell you. "I got hair, twenty-two bucks, good hair. Places try to sell you the lower quality stuff for more money. Buy bad hair, after a couple days, it tangles, it itches. If you sweat, the chemicals go to your scalp.

"Big-time salons, downtown and Fifth Avenue, buy our hair. They condition it before they do the weaves or the braids and charge their clients two and three grand. Places in California make it four or five."

WEAVING THREADS AND NEEDLES SOLD. Alexis holds up to my temple the most expensive item in the store, a thirty-inch auburn length of "Kinky-Straight." It passes my knees. The owner nudges Alexis in the ribs. "Tell her about the bald ladies with the bald hair. That's funny. They don't want to show it to you."

Alexis explains: "Women come in, you know what they need, everybody knows what they need. But you have to find a way to tell them, without saying your hair is bald, whatever. Without offending them. Because people are very offended. Their hair is thin."

What would you say to a woman who doesn't have a lot of hair? That she needs a wig?

"*No!*"

The faux pas is mine. Wigs, you see, to a midwife of manes like Alexis, are a last resort, a lazy way out. "There are many different methods of weaving or braiding hair in." Alexis counts off on his fingers as if addressing a group of preschoolers. "You can glue it in, you can sew it in, do box braids. There's a new system called interlocks. It's so good, a guy could run his fingers through your hair and nothing could happen."

HEADS WITH HUMAN HAIR AVAILABLE FOR BEAUTY SCHOOL USE. Let me ask you this, I say to Alexis. Some people say, uhm, some people think, that it's not right for black women to wear hair, you know, weaves, and maybe they should just wear their own hair and be natural. What do you think about that? Uh, the politics of that?

Alexis rolls his eyes. "Most women who buy hair for weaving actually don't have short hair. It's the convenience of it. If the weave enhances them in the process, so be it. By all means use the hair. But if the black man really likes you, he's gonna like you for you, not because of your weave."

SUPER WAVEY, EUROPEAN WAVEY, KINKY AFRO. A mature woman in Blackglama mink slaps Alexis's cheek when he tries to have a look under her matching hat. He can only smile.

"Me dealing with women, I really understand. When you wake up every morning and you gotta hot curl, press, comb everything, *and* go to work? It's not gonna happen.

"My customers see guys walking past the door and they go 'AAAAyyyye!'" Alexis hides his face in his hands. "But me, they don't care. When I first started working here I was like a male looking in. You're coming to a whole new world. I can't say I'm a woman now, but I got a pass card."

DEEP WAVEY, BODY WAVEY, JHERI CURL. This is a blood bank. Hair types A, AA, B. Bad hair, warns Alexis, the kind that Hair Station doesn't sell, the kind tainted with chemicals that irritate the scalp, is a bad transfusion.

"They sell low-quality hair all over the city," Alexis tells me. "Places have even started carrying the yak hair, which is animal hair."

You mean they try to pass it off as human hair?

"Yeah, yeah, this is New York," says Alexis. "I won't get egotistical and say we sell the best hair in the city, but we're the leaders. When we deal with hair, it's a personal thing. Our customers trust us like they trust their doctors."

It's almost seven now. With fifteen minutes to closing, women pack the store so there's scarce breathing room. They push between counters in search of the perfect weekend piece. A young woman in purple shearling pounds on a display case, her sights on a length of "Bone Straight" protected behind glass.

They forbid me from coming back Saturday. Alexis keeps shaking his head: "It's a madhouse." I want to stay behind the counter some more with Alexis. Watch him watch us get close to the mirror, real close, painful close. Like this: You hold a length of hair up to your face and you squint. Give us profile, straight on, squint some more. Picture your man's hands in your hair or "hair that moves" (says an ad for TCB No Lye Relaxer) or fifteen minutes of extra time in the morning. Then Alexis saunters over, hand on your shoulder. That'll work. Remember, he cares, he's not here to play you. And when the time is right, when you've decided, *really* decided, he sends you home, with the real you, wrapped up neatly in a brown paper bag.

*1990*

# the hair
# trade

In my personal stash of obsessions, hair rules (though Elvis as the Antichrist and chicken wings with Alaga syrup run close seconds). So when I say cracking the hair trade was on par with making that hajj to Mecca, you'll understand where I'm coming from. No offense meant, just my jones talking. Besides, the hair trade had all the Mecca prerequisites: mystery, an obstacle course, the sacred inner core. It was a pilgrimage bound to uncover a solidly American hash of race, kitsch, and commerce. But to 'fess up, I had no theoretical master plan, I was just plain nosey. Who were these alchemists, and how did they turn bushels of straight hair nappy?

So I set out to find *that* factory. Such a factory, or so I imagined, was in Brooklyn, perhaps tucked away on a Flatbush side street, near the bustling Afro-Caribbean stretch of Church Avenue, and most certainly above a fruit stand that sells okra and salt beef. In this factory, "raw" hair would be magically, or not so magically, transformed from "Bone Straight" (straight out of the Liaoning province) to "French Refined Wavy" (a/k/a African-American hair under the influence of a perm). Korean supervisors would keep watch over poor Haitian and Salvadoran women as they tended boiling vats of hair with long wooden sticks. Mecca would be a place that mocks nature and makes a pretty penny at it. Mecca would be a hair factory.

Of course, this took a minute because, so it goes, Mecca ain't about to find you, you go in search of it. My odyssey carried me first to shops that sell the finished product, 100 percent human hair for braiding and weaving, textured to match black hair types, untreated and permed. For looking too long and hard at labels, I was chased away, or shopkeepers would murmur things that made perfect sense like, "We don't know where it comes from, we just sell it," and nudge me to the door. When the dependable creatures who work in hair salons were asked to direct me to . . . (having no name for it, I made one up) a *hair factory*, they ditched the subject quick. "Trust us," they said. "We provide the hair," which I translated as: Something bad will happen if you step foot in such a place or, child, don't go stirring up no dirt, especially if it's gonna affect my personal livelihood, thank you.

The official information machine was of little help. The health departments, trade commissions, barbershop licensing offices, and regional customs bureaus of the world passed me back and forth. No one had clue one, and I became a quack for asking. Was this . . . (the name problem again) *hair product* a vegetable, mineral, or human appendage? Like a single strand of hair, it floated through the cracks.

———

The use of human hair extensions for weaving and braiding boomed in the seventies, yet it's a practice no doubt as ancient as Jerusalem. Herbert Feinberg's *All About Hair,* a short history of hair replacement, reports unequivocally, though without supporting detail, that hair weaving—the attachment of hairpieces to beget length and volume—was invented by black people a century ago. (I'd take it back another two.) The contemporary American trend seems to have piggybacked from the Motherland-inspired braid styles exhumed in the sixties. Ancient cornrow braids—often adorned with beads and cowrie shells—had their renaissance. By the next decade, braids were being elongated to Gidget-glam lengths with synthetic and human hair extensions. With the advent of buppiedom and *The Cosby Show*'s blow 'n' curl vision of America, permed tresses came back strong in the eighties. Weaving was an obvious next wave. Weaves are best done with human-hair extensions called "wefts," so human stock, as opposed to the synthetics that flooded the market in the seventies, returned en masse to corner wig shops.

The importing and processing of human hair is a tiny, tight-lipped business. In this country, very few companies actually process hair—convert it from straight to curly/kinky textures. Most "raw hair," as the trade calls it, is processed abroad, in Korea primarily, and sold prepackaged here at Asian retail shops like Folipa International Imports on Fulton Street in downtown Brooklyn, a stretch known as "weave row." The smattering of American companies in the processing business, most in New York and California, have showrooms where they retail by the pound, though the bulk of their work is in supplying salons and shipping mail order around the globe.

A small hair world, it is. The processing companies—call them hair factories—are a closely tied, though intensely competitive, pack. These are family outfits, Jewish and Italian, that have intermarried employees and managers over the years. Old names in the business are the De Meo Brothers, the Tucciarones, the Rubins. (AlKinco Hair Company, run by the Rubins, has been in what the industry tags the "Afro side" of the business for ages. Trade gossip has it that the name "AlKinco" is a polite version of "El Kinko," code for, he who processes kinky hair.) Several of these companies have been up and running for close to eighty-five years. Processing techniques have remained the same over time and are treated as family heirlooms. Employees outside the family take vows of silence. When asked about her processing methods, one company president would volunteer only this: "Does Sylvia tell you how she cooks her collard greens?" Case closed.

Even harder to track down than the hair factories are the import firms. Only a handful of companies do this end of the business full-time. No import license is needed to transport human hair Stateside, and more and more, storefront businesses are shipping in their own product. (These days hair arrives primarily by UPS and Federal Express.) Older hair factories express concern about a budding cottage industry where shady retail operations process hair out of bathtubs and have the public convinced they're selling the same fussed-over hair goods.

Just as Korea came to dominate wig production worldwide in the late sixties, it has moved on the braiding and weaving market. Americans once bought most of their raw product from China, Korea, and India; now Koreans buy from the same sources, process it themselves, and ship to their own retail networks in the States. The Jewish and Italian hair factories say Korean-made goods are mass produced and of cruder quality. (Quality is a big word in the hair business and is used in ways arcane and racially demeaning, but more on that soon.)

"Foreign" hair is imported to the States for two main uses: human hair for wigs and hairpieces; animal hair—goat, pig, and horse—for paintbrushes and hairbrushes. The hair trade buys raw stock in bulk by the kilo. In most cases it's treated abroad first in an acid bath to kill bacteria. Processing companies "refine" the raw hair, a process that involves, among other things, removing the roots, as they mangle easily. Refined hair is then chemically or steamed processed to hold curl. The end product is called "commercial hair." After all these conversions, commercial hair maintains a top and bottom and must be braided or attached accordingly. Treated and processed hair lives forever, making it congruous perhaps to an embalmed corpse. (Though if given the chance, silverfish and moths could devour an entire warehouse.)

The Census Bureau assigns every imported product a fixed description and commodity number, and you might be yearning to know that "human hair, dressed, thinned, bleached, or otherwise worked," is commodity number 6703.00.3000. Last year hair came from eleven countries, all in Asia and Europe. Top on the list were Korea and China; Indonesia, which hair traders consider be an "up and coming hair market," ranked third. Through the seventies, stock imported from Europe was the only hair product sold to what the industry calls the "Caucasian trade." Now that the European market is drying up, Asian hair goes to all races, in most cases, unless specially ordered. When you buy human hair in lengths for weaving and braiding, in wigs, and as male hair-replacement product, what you buy nine times out of ten is Asian hair.

The trade also peddles animal hair, used mostly for braiding, as it can stand in for very tightly curled, "wooly" hair. (Often dreadlock extensions are made from animal hair. Animal stock is bleached and sold as human gray hair as well.) The animal of choice is yak, a long-haired wild or domesticated ox found in Tibet and central Asia. Yak hair is sometimes mixed with angora (from angora goats) to soften it. There are those who balk at mixing animal with human (animal), yet it happens to be an old practice. In the sixteenth and seventeenth centuries, hairpieces were commonly made from animal and human hair. And until synthetic wigs became so common and cheap, the theatrical market always relied on animal hair, particularly yak wigs.

Many in the trade are worried that the seemingly abundant supply of raw hair from Asia could be on the wane. Most raw stock comes from China, though it's processed in Korea, and the concern is that the supply will dry up as China is gripped ever tighter by the long arm of the West. (Apparently beauty shops are sprouting up in

China that promote ye ole magic Western elixir—the perm.) Adorable Hair-Do, in Manhattan's design district, has been importing Chinese hair since 1910 and isn't worried too much about the China supply. Despite westernization, Adorable believes population growth will zoom on, and the manes will be there to cut, especially in the rural provinces.

But what of the Italian story? Italian hair, once thought to be an ever plentiful source, has diminished to nearly a custom-order operation. Says one importer, every month he used to bring in twelve cases of Italian hair at 110 pounds each. He can't even get a fifth of a case today, and the costs are out of bounds. (Adorable bills an item they advertise as "Italian First Quality Human Hair" for ninety-five dollars an ounce.) Another importer is convinced that the product known as Italian hair is no longer. A good percentage of the hair processed in Italy, he says, is "cut" with raw hair from Spain and India.

Asking industry types where raw hair comes from, and how the business is organized abroad, is to knock up against a covenant of silence. From a dozen conversations you might end up with this: In China, hair is much like a crop. There are hair farms, where hair is collected and packaged for shipment abroad. In India, women cut their hair and offer it to the church as a sacrifice. Allegedly the church supplies exporters, who then ship raw goods to Korea or directly to the States. Factories in Italy that collect and process hair have been in business since the nineteenth century. Before the war, peddlers supplied these factories by crisscrossing the Italian countryside to buy hair from poor women. Ponytails were bartered along with "combings," from combs and brushes, which women stored in glass jars. With Italian hair now scarce, and white American buyers ever in search of Cortez's fountain—pure European stock—Russian hair has been flown in as a substitute. The fall of the communist bloc has paved the way for a busy black market in Russian hair.

An old rating system operates in the hair trade. Italian stock is the number one European hair import, despite how much the supply has declined. It's still referred to as "first quality" hair and is gobbled up by custom-wig makers and the men's toupee market. Labeled as "second quality" hair, Asian and Indian hair costs less and at one time was sold only to what old-timers in the business call the "colored trade." Among salons that specialize in weaving and cater to a black clientele, there's another rating system: "Good hair" is human hair, period; "bad hair" is prepackaged hair that's been cut, or mixed, with synthetic or animal hair.

Asian retailers are adamant about not rating hair. They insist that all the hair they sell is "best quality," which of course is as much a feel-good strategy aimed at consumers as it is a reversal of the rating system's racial hierarchy. Still, the old rating system predominates. A throwback to nineteenth-century racial codes, the system is augmented symbolically by the industry's overall race schema. In this country, white and Asian-American men sell commercial hair for braiding and weaving, which is bought and worn primarily by black women. The one black company in the processing business in the New York area might very well be the only one in the country. A black salon owner who buys hair wholesale in Brooklyn sizes up the race dynamic like this: Tensions between those who buy and those who sell aren't expressed overtly, yet resentments are bubbling near the surface. The owners of an established hair factory made sure to note several times during my visit that they sell to the Afro trade "by default, not by design," as over time the more lucrative side of the business has shifted from white to black. Meaning, one assumes, if they could pitch Ferraris to nouveau riche whites in Ramsey, New Jersey, they might feel better about their line of work.

After hiking much pavement and nosing my way into shops, I found two hair factories in the most obvious place, the Yellow Pages, under the banner of "hair replacement, goods and supplies," and, small wonder, they invited me down. It didn't matter that ten others slammed the phone in my ear, convinced I was out to steal their processing secrets. Mecca was near.

A hair factory might often attempt to camouflage itself behind the more respectable label of "designer of hairpieces" or "supplier of hair." Their sales pitch, on the other hand, is a dead giveaway: "Manufacturers of 100% Human Hair," they boast, in phone book ads and on street signs. Lugo Hair Center in Brooklyn is of the boastful. (Lugo, it turns out, *is* in East Flatbush, though it's run by Hispanics, not Koreans.) The company claims to manufacture "First Quality Caucasian Hair in All Colors & Textures." This might translate as: We process straight hair to curly textures, but all our raw product is imported from Europe. Prepare: Even before you step foot into a hair factory, you are required suspend reality. They *make* human hair. This is not a grammatical error; this is a way of life.

Welcome to Harlem. Where 125th Street meets Fifth Avenue, look for the McDonald's billboard framed in a kente-cloth design, as it's a stone's throw from W.A.J. Wigs. In the hair business for thirty-one years, W.A.J. predates the nouveau-kente generation by a couple of decades. W.A.J.'s second-floor factory/showroom/salon shares space with a business called "The Miracles of Rev. James," which offers the services of a spiritualist who guarantees results in twenty-four hours. Jean Church, niece to company president Verlie Wyche, runs the showroom desk, where traffic never lets up. Women in search of the perfect match pull wefts of hair out of shoulder bags like dead rabbits, or juggle adjectives to describe the hair of their dreams. ("It's like black dirty blonde that's a little nappier than French.")

The seventy-year-old Verlie B. Wyche and other Harlem salon owners will tell you that W.A.J. invented the Afro toupee and was the first hair company to process raw Asian hair into permanent kink. Other hair factories hotly dispute this, claiming they've made straight to kinky conversions since the forties. As a maker of custom-fitted Afro toupees, W.A.J. is well known nationally on the black salon circuit. And Mrs. Wyche did originate in the early seventies a widely used method of weaving. But the title of inventor of straight-to-kinky-weave stock remains up for grabs.

Adorable Hair-Do ("Human Hair Manufacturers Since 1910") inhabits a floor of an upscale office building in Chelsea. Like

W.A.J., based on word of mouth rather than advertising, Adorable ships their texturized hair product worldwide. Adorable's showroom is a shrine to celebrity clients, with posters and signed publicity shots plastered like wallpaper. En Vogue thanks Herbert generously, profusely, lavishly. Company president Herbert Teitelbaum, ensconced in his office, reaches his son Gary, the V.P., by intercom in the showroom. Mr. Herbert (so he's called in the company brochure) reports that Patti Labelle's stylist just called from the tour bus to say how pleased she was, really, absolutely, better-than-before pleased, with the hair Adorable sent overnight rush. Gary blushes. On the way to the factory itself we pass a fashion spread with the models Cindy Crawford and Naomi Campbell. Campbell wears a pout and an ankle-length weave. Adorable has taped its own legend on the photo: "Both women are beautiful, but only one is Adorable."

It's at Adorable that I first enter Mecca. Rhyme, reason, and order seem clear only to the initiated. After a month of searching the city, there are boxes of raw hair wide open before me. This hair, in lengths of roughly eighteen inches, is wrapped at the top in twine and fans out below like a whisk broom. It's as still as a movie prop, a scalped ponytail from a spaghetti western. And it's bone, as they say in the hair world, straight. (When I asked Mrs. Wyche of W.A.J. if "Bone Straight" was shorthand for "born with straight hair," she said quite earnestly, no, "straight as a bone.") In another area of the factory, women, Salvadoran perhaps, uncoil hair product from dowels. It then joins a large pile of stiff coils for transfer to the next stage. Men, Dominican perhaps, pull the coils back and forth through upright stationary combs called "hackles." The hair comes out in a bushy mound, soft like a six-year-old's Afro puff before a lifetime of relaxers. Several more women, Honduran perhaps, take this crinkly hair and run it through a sewing machine, which attaches a thick seam on one edge. This seam, as you can learn in W.A.J.'s how-to-weave video, is used to anchor, with thread or glue, your living hair to the commercial hair.

I am led into the Kaaba, the sacred shrine, the inner sanctum, where straight is brewed kinky. I see dye buckets, shampooing machines, vats of bleach labeled DANGER POISON. I leave the room dizzy with fumes, as if I had spent the night at the old Paradise Garage riding the moon on poppers. Mecca at last, yet the mystery, like the smell, lingers.

Touring W.A.J. fills in gaps. Raw hair is washed, then wrapped on dowels. Dowel width determines kink. (In W.A.J.'s closet-size "wrap room," two West African women wrap hair as methodically as metronomes while they chew gum and listen to Afro-pop on the radio.) This hair on dowels is dyed and processed chemically (smells like an industrial-strength version of a home perm). Processed hair goes through hackles to loosen curl and blend colors. Weft seams are made on a special machine that creates a stitch as intricate as an eyelash. Finally, lengths of commercial hair are sealed in small, clear plastic packs (dead ringers for bagged narcotics), then shipped in white gift boxes. During my tour, a Hasidic man delivers a large rectangular box. I ask President Wyche if there's raw hair in the box, and if so, if it's from China or India. She gives me one of those looks: Girl, you're far too grown for your age. Mrs. Wyche has quite deliberately evoked the archetypical black godmama with the eyebrows-raised legend spirit. Quite a power move. Mecca was only letting me in so far.

Hair factories are a storehouse of kitsch beauty culture, but they can also hip us to that unwritten chapter of American social history, the hair trade.

In the 1970s, its prime, W.A.J. was a prominent Harlem institution. (The company sponsored two Miss Black Teenage America pageants. Actress Sheryl Lee Ralph, in an elegant short Afro, was a runner-up one year.) Wyche tells stories about traveling to hair shows in the South to demonstrate W.A.J. hair goods, and of the informal networks of salons run by black women, which, in the tradition of Madame C. J. Walker's beauty colleges, also functioned as community centers and counseling offices. As a memento of my tour, Mrs. Wyche and her sister, Ella "Terri" Dufau, the factory manager, present me with a copy of a W.A.J. flyer from the early sixties advertising "kinky wigs and toupees for the Negro woman and man." The flyer was autographed by Mrs. Martin Luther King, Sr., on a visit to W.A.J.'s showroom.

With a name as suffocatingly cute as its product line, Adorable Hair-Do was founded in 1910 by owner Herbert Teitelbaum's great-uncle, a Jew who emigrated from England. Until the seventies, the company maintained its original showroom above the Baby Grand Nightclub on 125th Street. (The Teitelbaums say "race riots" pushed them downtown.) Adorable claims to have done the original research on the machine-wefting process and has papers to prove it. (Before machines became standard in the late forties, hair was sewn into wefts by hand, strands at a time.) Gary the V.P. will also show you the company's 1942 catalog, where yellowed newsprint illustrates hair for weaving. "Crimpy hair transformations," as they were called, fit around the head with an elastic band, the whole apparatus resembling a theatrical beard. By Mr. Herbert's account, Adorable, called Howard Tresses at the time, began processing straight to nappy in the early forties, stewing hair in crocks on the roof of its Harlem showroom.

The Tucciarones are the most picturesque historians of the hair trade, no contest. That's Biagio ("Bill") Tucciarone of B.T. Hair Goods, established in 1969 (taking the name of his grandfather's company, founded in 1910), and his father, Joseph, now retired, of Accu-Hair International Consultants, opened in 1949. Joseph Tucciarone sold his business in the eighties to a woman who crafts *sheitels,* religious hairpieces, for the Hasidim. These days B.T. Hair Goods is a small custom-order sample-matching operation run out of Bill's mother's cellar in the Bronx, though at one time five generations of Tucciarones worked the Manhattan factory. Being a Tucciarone means you can name different "grades," really nationalities, of hair in the dark (i.e., Russian: "dead straight, but also tends to be lumpy"; Belgian: "more durable, better food"). The family has always sold "first quality" hair to the Caucasian market—and still upholds the old rating system. But Bill Tucciarone will assure you "taking care of the colored trade" is not beneath him. "Don't get me wrong," he says, "if they want good hair, they can come to me. They just got to want it first." (Alas, if us coloreds would only aspire to "good hair," it would be within reach.)

The annotated and subjective chronicle of hair trade to the Americas as told by the Tucciarones goes something like this: Outside of medical and theatrical uses, early markets for commercial hair in this country were married Hasidic women and Chinese women (who, following ancient practice, embellished styles with add-on hair). During the Second World War the Italian connection dried up for a spell, sending American hair factories scurrying, like they are today, after black-market Russian hair. Supply from Italy has never returned to its original volume, as after the war Italian hair donors discovered two American imports: the beauty parlor and the haircut. "Second quality" hair goods have always been steered to Negro consumers. (Hair traders consider Asian hair to be a coarser stock that lends itself to curly conversions.) The only change is, by the seventies boom in black-hair extensions, Asians got rid of their middlemen.

It's clear that the manufacture of wigs and hairpieces for black women has been an active industry since at least the turn of the century. The business picked up steam during the war, an event that corresponds with the second great migration of African Americans to the urban North. Gary the V.P. from Adorable puts it this way: "More black people came to the cities to work in the forties, and therefore they needed hair for style." "Style" or social necessity, the manipulation of black hair has been key to the assimilation equation since square one.

And so ends the Tucciarones's saga, and so we peck at the surface of the hair trade as American social text.

Humanitarian spirit manifests itself in the oddest places: hair factories. Factories are often approached by people whose need for hair has little to do with lipstick vanity: burn victims, victims of leukemia and alopecia (sudden, in some cases unexplained, loss of hair).

Hairsmiths treasure these cases, especially when children are involved. It lends a certain largesse to what they do; not only do they manufacture human hair, they're in league with the tooth fairy. The elder Tucciarone has his story about the little leukemia victim who was able to go to school without shame wearing a wig he made from her own hair. She died nine months later. Mrs. Wyche has hers about the dog-bite victim so grateful for his Afro toupee he showed up at the factory with a Christmas present every year for twenty years straight.

In W.A.J.'s case the hair doctor–medical rescue worker role is supplemented by an even greater mission: race work. When Verlie Wyche talks about why she "invented" the Afro toupee it's with the righteous tone of one who has undertaken to uplift the race, despite how the world and the race may resist the effort. (Mrs. Wyche found it "ridiculous and demeaning" to see the black and hairless walking around with "Caucasian toupees.") Early photographs of Mrs. Wyche show a remarkable resemblance to the young Diana Ross. Not just looks; the aura of self-invention floats around both women like expensive perfume. Mrs. Wyche made kinky hair, those raised eyebrows are quick to remind you. What did you do for the race today?

With Mecca and my tour of the Kaaba behind me, I am feeling less wooed by the kitsch mystique of hair factories. I have my concerns. Given the hush-hush nature of the trade, do we know what we're getting? Commercial hair undergoes so many chemical processes, could it be caustic? And what of a particular rumor that dogs the trade like the smell of rotting flesh? If this rumor is true, should we pull the commercial hair from our heads right this moment and beg the higher power for quick forgiveness? *Is* cosmetic hair kosher product? You decide:

Poor labeling is rife. A common problem users encounter at the smaller retail outfits is that human hair is cut with synthetic. (Kanekalon, the synthetic that's made into wig and braiding stock, is the same fiber used for Barbie doll hair. Apparently Barbies exhaust more of it than the sum total of human wig wearers.) Though in some cases hairpiece makers combine human and synthetic for durability rather than for rip-off purposes, consumers feel that labeling should be required and monitored. Another typical complaint: Yak is cut with human, which is something to watch for, being that allergic reactions to yak are not uncommon.

False advertising is business as usual. Retailers and hair factories routinely trump up an item they call "French Refined" hair. This is no special feature. All commercial hair has been refined—it is by definition. ("Refined" merely refers to the chemical process that de-roots hair.) The French component is also meaningless, along with being inaccurate. Very little hair is actually imported from France; that which is, according to several importers, is probably Spanish or Indian hair that was processed within French borders. The French angle is so widely exploited, though, that most hair factories and retailers carry "French Refined" as a standard hair texture. Adorable, for instance, advertises five standard textures, including "French Refined Wavy," "European Straight Look," and "Spanish Wavy" (a "texture style" that they claim to have originated). All are made from Asian hair.

Human hair, the import, isn't governed by special regulations from any government agency, including customs. It's classified as a cosmetic (a product applied to the body to promote attractiveness), so it falls under the jurisdiction of the Food and Drug Administration. Customs and the FDA took my queries about the bacterial or health risks that might be associated with commercial hair with amused patience. "Not a high enforcement priority," customs compliance officers and FDA cosmetic specialists offered with a chuckle. (Did this response fall into the category of "We are sorry, your problem is not male enough or white enough to rate serious discussion"?) *If* customs opens boxes of raw hair they'd be looking for lice, but there's only a slim chance they would, because hair, I repeat, is not a PRIORITY.

The open-door policy on human hair is curious at first glance. Hair is human tissue—but dead cells. Of the body, bodylike, and, to quote shampoo ads, "full of body," yet not a body part, at least so says Western science. This doesn't stop hair from being an intimate and certainly sexual "personal object" that calls out for cleansing, grooming, vigilance. Hair product (embalmed hair), since it no longer grows, is classified as an inanimate object. It's sold as "human" in the same way leather is sold as animal hide. What all this amounts to is that no one worries. Certainly customs and the FDA aren't losing any sleep.

The health concerns I have about cosmetic hair don't rate an international crisis, mind you. Nevertheless, mostly women make use of it—particularly women of color, particularly women who aren't heard from as consumers—so it's worth raising the questions. Hair factory queen bees told about the mysterious acid baths hair receives abroad to kill bacteria. Okay, so what kind of acid? Does this acid go away when the hair is washed? Or does a wearer continually absorb it into her skin when she perspires? Raw hair is by routine bleached and dyed. Is the cosmetic-hair wearer also absorbing bleach? Dyes, too? Allergic reactions to hair bleach are common. Certain coal-based dyes are toxic and no longer allowed in over-the-counter hair dye products. Could a storefront industry out to cut costs be using cheap, unapproved dyes?

Tucciarone Jr. of B.T. Hair Goods, who's worked with hair since he was thirteen, believes the acid treatment performed on raw hair could be harmful to wearers if not washed out properly. He questions if most hair factories bother to do a thorough job. Dr. Deborah Simmons, an attending dermatologist at Harlem Hospital, frequently sees patients with skin problems brought on by extensions. Most of these involve braids that are too tight (which can lead to alopecia) or scalp conditions from not washing braided hair adequately. Simmons hasn't come across an allergic reaction to processing chemicals, though she believes the potential is certainly there.

Which brings us to, what if? What if cosmetic hair was recognized one day as a bad-boy product? An unlikely event, but let's consider it. Would consumers rush to kick the habit? There's an expression in the salon world, relayed to me by stylist Brenda Davis: "I'll wear extensions until they cause cancer, or a bit longer." Like the breast implant ban—some users would go kicking and screaming, if they went at all. The most common anxieties clients have about commercial hair, according to stylists, don't involve health risks at all. They worry about the cost of hair and what will happen to it in the rain.

Fables of the hair trade could make a flamboyantly stereotypical, international spy thriller set in Milan, New Delhi, and "the Orient," starring Mata Hari's great-granddaughter as a British-raised, black Eurasian agent in the employ of Her Majesty's Secret Service. A black belt in Goju-Ryu Karate, Kenya Hari sets out to crack the hair trade, then is lovingly derailed by American hair-care scion Wesley Snipes. Legend has it, as passed down by the hair trade's more colorful historians, that in China before communism, hair was cut as an offering to the gods. This hair was then stored in caves for hundreds of years. At one time, caves in China were brimming with perfectly preserved hair, and for a good part of this century, hair traders made do on this back stock.

Another myth conjures up an underground market in *American* hair. During the war period, from 1941 to 1949, B.T. Hair Goods actually did process American hair. Founder Biagio Tucciarone solicited the hair by putting ads in newspapers across the grain belt. Tucciarone couldn't turn much of a profit on the slim pickings here (a length of hair must be at least eight inches long to process, and Americans weren't producing the length), so he went back to the import business.

Finally, there's that smelly rumor the hair trade can't shake: Some in the salon world are convinced that raw hair comes primarily from cadavers. Factories and retailers deny this with great passion. How could it? they object. Raw hair must be in excellent shape to undergo processing. The Tucciarones, however, will tell you otherwise. When Bill Tucciarone was a teenager working at his grandfather's hair factory, he regularly saw pieces of scalp mixed in with the hair. His father Joseph will swear to you that at one time at least 85 percent of the hair was cut from dead folks.

Interestingly enough, from the FDA's point of view, the sale of cadaver hair, if it is taking place, isn't illegal. There are no medical warnings against it and no agency regulations currently forbid it. In the 1980s, anti-abortion groups were riled up about collagen-placenta beauty care products, which they thought were being concocted from aborted fetuses. These objections were never substantiated, yet there was no law on the books at the time that prohibited the use of "fetus-derived products." So fetuses or no fetuses, these products could have remained on the market.

All my gallows-humor illusions about the hair trade and the warehousing of "dead" hair were shattered by a very brief conversation with dermatologist Claudette Troyer of Harlem Hospital. Hair by definition is not exactly a bundle of life. "The thing is dead, medically speaking," says Troyer, "when it comes out of your head." Hair, like nails, is made from keratin. The growth activity happens below the skin. So, dead or alive, hair donors are created equal. Consumers can object to the sale of cadaver hair on spiritual grounds, but that's about it.

Enter a voice of lucidity: Braid designer Ruth Sinclair. Sinclair tells me I've been crawling up the wrong tree. The hazard of cosmetic hair, she says, doesn't strike the body, it eats at the soul. Sinclair is of the new school of Afrocentric cosmetologists who surfaced in the mid-eighties at salons such as Tulani's Regal Movement in Brooklyn and Cornrows & Company in Washington, D.C. With partner Annu Prestonia, Sinclair owns the braiding salon chain Khamit Kinks, which has shops in Atlanta and Brooklyn. ("Khamit," an early name for Egypt, means "land of the blacks." By adding "Kinks," Sinclair explains, "we've taken a word perceived as bad and made it good.") Sinclair has been braiding hair for eighteen years, and to her, the real concern isn't the possibility of chemical emissions from commercial hair (no more a risk, she says, than perming one's own hair). It's a beauty industry especially oppressive to black women. Sinclair's rap is a familiar one. Although it neglects two vital points, women's personal agency and hair as a creative turf, it still has currency:

"Black women are told that in order to be attractive and successful, we must emulate a European image of beauty. The damage this does to us subconsciously has never been studied. Just the daily pressure. Caucasian women will never have to live with the stress of taking their hair from straight to kinky on a daily basis just to be visually accepted in society.

"We are told as black women to assume an image that goes against what most of us are born with. Basically, the industry is saying that there's something wrong with us. And that this something must be controlled with artificial means—with their help. The industry will continue feeding us this line because it makes money off of us. Of course, the industry is not about to give up the revenue that comes from [commercial] hair, chemicals, and rider products. If they could find a way to make more money off of natural hair, believe me, they'd be selling that."

Hair extensions were the black-hair coup of the eighties, even more than the short-lived, vilified Jheri curl. They are more "yours" than a wig, if only by virtue of being more securely attached. They sell convenience and cultural versatility. In April you can wear a weave, invent an entire mane of processed curls, and carry forth like Diana Ross. By May you can put in braids and make a statement of racial pride—or not make one. Hair is still corporeal, except now it isn't necessarily biologically determined. But the real social innovation is that, unlike costly wigs with few styling options, extensions have made hair affordably disposable. *Disposable hair*—the postmod answer to racial difference. Disposable skin can't be too far behind.

Which is not to suggest that the racial allegories of the hair trade are so cut-and-dried. If anything the trade throws a curve ball at assumptions of racial difference. First look at the trade route. Hair is dispatched from Asia, processed in the States, and sent to points in the diaspora. (Take Paris, where hair for weaving and braiding is sold from kiosks in the Metro.) You have companies like W.A.J. Wigs, which buys hair from New Delhi, refines it in Harlem, and ships to, among other places, West Africa—a journey that suggests a gumbo of transcontinental influences.

In West Africa, braided extensions and weaves are "huge," to quote a frequent traveler to the region. Older women even wear them—in elaborate, braided styles that resemble hats. For little girls in Nigeria, it's the rage to have your braided extensions curled in Shirley Temple ringlets, a style called "the darling." So while African Americans are looking to Africa for cultural affirmation, Africans are hopping on the bandwagon of a "Europeanized" standard of beauty symbolized by wavy, loosely curled extensions. Or let's be more critically expansive, to advance the ideas of critic Kobena Mercer, and call it "New World": a syncretic beauty culture born in the diaspora.

If hair is the key racial signifier after skin, then the trade makes a fine mockery of it. Processed Asian hair passes as black hair. Italians allegedly blend hair from the Third World and it passes as European. The hair of yaks (the "black sheep" of the ox family) passes as nappy hair. As well it's worth remembering that most of what the hair trade sells is not dead straight hair—it's "texturized" hair; hair that is quite particularly African-American/African-diaspora hair, hair that is emulated in perms by European women worldwide. So toward the close of the twentieth century, what we have is a whole industry devoted to selling black hair (or, let's not get too excited, a particular type of black hair). Though black hair nonetheless: hair that was once demonized. Hair that was downcast. Hair that was "no good."

The Afrocentric braiders are on to something. They avoid the political swamp of extensions as European imitation by using synthetic stock. The likes of Khamit Kinks and Cornrows & Company design styles that are not simply hairdos; these are elaborate constructions, with hair piled high, woven with ornaments and shaped like fans, wedding cakes, hourglasses, and halos. Maybe they're crowns, maybe they're altars. Extensions here are used not to showcase length or "naturalness." This is hair as textile, fiber art, as nothing less than sculpture. What links the African-American/Africa-diaspora cultural practice with African traditional cultures is not the naturalness of the braids, it's the idea of construction. Hair in both traditions suggests spectacle and pageantry. It's always handled and adorned; hair is never left "as is." Hair exists to be *worked*.

Those wise ones, the ancient Egyptians, played their own game with hair: They cut it all off. They thought it barbaric, scholars say, or maybe just too damn hot. Egyptian-designed hairpieces used materials like palm leaves and wool that suggested hair, yet didn't try to duplicate it, allowing much room for creative play. (By the sixteenth and seventeenth centuries, Europe was hip to headpieces, and they were being worn there as tokens of class privilege.) Perhaps there's a cave full of Egyptian hair, perfectly preserved, waiting for us in the Nile Valley. Given the war of historical interpretation, it could be Nappy by Nature (to borrow the name of a hair salon just opened in downtown Brooklyn). Then again, it could be "Bone Straight." But ask Verlie Wyche. I bet she'd know.

*1993*

Hair grease has revealed itself to be the cesspool of racial politics that those of us who take hair seriously always suspected it was.

This is why: A profitable, white-owned company, in the business of selling what the industry calls "ethnic hair-care products" to the African-American consumer, is waging a legal battle with a smaller black-owned company over the trademark and product likeness of grooming aids that use an Afrocentric theme. The white-owned company is also claiming title to "African" as the first word in a hair product's trade name. A federal court in Atlanta will soon decide whether to lay a preliminary injunction against the black company. This injunction could prevent the black company from distributing its current product line, and possibly from using the opener "African" on any new merchandise until the case comes to trial.

On one side is the white-owned Shark Products of Brooklyn, New York, which makes hair-grooming potions and lotions under the trademark African Pride; on the other, B & J Sales of Fayetteville, Georgia, with its product African Natural. Both lines are aimed at the X-appareled, braided, and faded crowd of young and recently Afrocentric consumers. And both offer the same types of hair goo: leave-in conditioners, braid sheen spray, and so on. The two-year-old African Pride came out of the gate strong; this year selling nearly $2.5 million in the first quarter. African Natural, on the other hand, had been distributing for only three months when this controversy hit. Though to Shark, African Natural was enough of a financial threat and a "colorable imitation" of their line to hire a lawyer.

It's akin to grand larceny to some folks that African Pride is a white-owned product given its name, but also its Afro-chic packaging—red, black, and green—and high profile in the black press—full-page ads in *Ebony* and *Essence*. And what did Shark choose as the signature fragrance for African Pride? Watermelon.

Until a court rules otherwise, both Shark and B & J Sales have legal trademarks on their products. Still, Shark believes that B & J Sales is trying to capitalize on what it considers to be its unique success story. With African Pride, Shark is convinced it invented a whole new segment of the black hair-care industry, one defined by an African heritage concept. Plainly, Shark thinks it owns the Afrocentric sell and wants competitors to have no part of the booty.

Shark has had one scrimmage so far. It sued the California-based Walbert Laboratories, a company that makes the hair grooming aid Mother Africa, for copying its "trade dress," which included the use of the word "African" in the same color that it appears on Shark products. Walbert insists it chose red, black, and green, the colors of the African nationalist flag, independent of the African

Pride label. The case was settled out of court, with the smaller company abandoning the nationalist color scheme. Shark plans to sue Bronner Brothers of Atlanta, a black-owned company forty-seven years in the business, for marketing its new line, African Royale. Several black manufacturers and distributors are so outraged by Shark's bum rush they're weighing a boycott. "How the heck can he [president Brian Marks], a white man, try to patent the word 'African'?" one company manager snapped. "What's next? We'll have to ask his permission to call ourselves African Americans?" Marks refuses to comment on any of the court cases. All phone calls concerning Shark's legal disputes are referred to the company's public relations rep, who happens to be black.

Do a federal trademark search and you'll find scores of products that use "African" as a prefix (like African Queen cologne) or a derivative (Afroshave shaving products or Afro Sheen, hair dress, circa 1971). These include nearly a dozen hair tonics, some registered long before African Pride. African Formula, a line well known to health-food store patrons, has been on the market since 1983.

Put aside for a moment this bit of lunacy: that one person or company—white or black—could declare ownership of "African," just as one might own Subaru or Pepsi or any number of brand names. Or the idea that a white-owned company could have legal sanction to prevent black-owned companies from using their continent of heritage as a means of drawing black consumers. But just think of Shark claiming that it masterminded the Afrocentric sell when, long before African Pride's debut in 1991, or even African Formula's in 1983, Black Muslims hawked African-inspired hair concoctions on city streets. And decades before that black hair entrepreneur Madame C. J. Walker's products were sold using buy-black themes and Madame's own mahogany-skinned, broad-nosed image. From any angle, Shark positioning itself as the grandfather of Afrocentric hair grooming is a caper lifted from a blaxploitation flick.

Expect more of the same. With women of color recognized as the beauty industry's new frontier, mainstream companies are scurrying after their share. In the case of the $1.5 billion black hair-care industry, now dominated by white-owned companies, the challenge is not to enter the market but to rule. And Afrocentricity has become the sales ticket de rigueur. Revlon cashed in this spring with Kente Kreations—grooming aids named for African tribes. Try Masai™ Polishing Mist or Fanti™ Moisturizing Hairdress.

The kente pitch is in such high gear, in fact, that black companies are being forced to "out-Afrocentricize" the white competition, says Geri Duncan Jones, president of the American Health and Beauty Aids Institute (AHBAI), which represents the leading black manufacturers. Kemi Laboratories makes Kemi-Oyl, one of the many hair-skin multiuse oils you'll find at your local drugstore chain (where hair products are still segregated by ethnic category). To cut through the kente glut, Kemi and other companies are now advertising that they're black owned. But is this enough, with companies like Kenya Products in the mix? Kenya, a white-owned manufacturer based in New Jersey, sells an Organic Hair Skin & Scalp Oil that promises on the bottle to be a "remedy" of "exotic oils" drawn from the "darkest region of Africa."

If a black hair-care product is popular with consumers, does it matter, as Michael Jackson might chide us, if the company that makes it is black or white? AHBAI calls white companies' use of Afrocentric marketing "deceptive" to black consumers, who often assume these companies are owned by blacks and that their revenue goes back to African Americans in the form of jobs or community programs. (Often white-owned black-hair-care companies, which make 98 percent of their profit from black folks, don't employ equally high numbers.) Viewpoint of Chicago recently published a brand-awareness survey that showed black consumers were unpleasantly surprised and downright disturbed to find that major black hair-care products such as African Pride, All Ways, TCB, Dark & Lovely, Right-On Curl, and Let's Jam are not made by black businesses. Most customers surveyed said now that they know which brands are black made they'd show a preference for these in the future.

One ebony shopaholic wondered what all the ruckus was about.

Black folks, she said, were gonna buy heavily advertised products like African Pride and Cream of Nature's Kente Oil anyway, no matter who owned the plant. Wasn't it good tidings to see, at the very least, a healthy reflection of black culture in the packaging of these products, rather than a bunch of golliwogs pulling the wool off their scalps and talking about "Fix this Mess!" (to quote an ad for LeKair Styling Gel)? Elayne McClaire, marketing director of Creme of Nature and a black woman, spoke of the letters that have poured in from black patrons commending the company for "embracing African culture," as they believe Revlon did when it swaddled its product in kente and trademarked the names of African tribes. Perhaps to some folks, how many African Americans aren't getting the sales and manufacturing gigs in these mainstream corporations, or how many smaller black-owned companies are being edged out of business, or even the politics of a white enterprise trademarking the term "African Pride," aren't issues of concern; kente *is* enough.

The African Pride case shows how detached words and symbols like Africa (just a hair practice), black pride (a marketing pitch), and kente (a *Good Housekeeping* seal) have become from their cultural beginnings. Ethnicity, as the postmod watchers warned us long ago, is emerging as nothing more than a market niche, a field of products ripe for anyone to sell or consume, and the hair trade is leading the way to the mountaintop. What is Africa to me? Countee Cullen might have waxed in 1993. Just a hair grease.

*1993*

This article appeared in the *Village Voice* in August 1993. Shark dropped its case against B & J Sales three months later. The court, however, denied B & J's request that Shark reimburse the company for the considerable amount of money spent in attorney fees. Both companies have maintained their trade names and both continue to manufacture hair grease.

# hair again

Hair issues are among us. We must tease them out, hold them up to the light, and coax them into art.

The girl thought she had figured it all out. Hair was just hair, not a badge of correctness. And thanks once again to modern technology, which brought us no-lye relaxers and such, chemically altering your tresses was now a process somewhat removed from antiquated notions like self-mutilation and disfigurement, and was just as innocent as a five-dollar nail job. Jewish women iron, Asian women perm, WASPs highlight. So what if black women burn and fry? After all, isn't it impossible to tell where society's force-feeding leaves off and we begin?

Notice black women are dyeing blonde in droves? This is probably because it warms our souls and brings out the chestnut in our eyes. Be assured, it has nothing at all to do with Christie Brinkley.

Besides, we were at a magical interlude in black hair history. Lord have mercy, hair seemed practically depoliticized! At least in the New York City subway, where you could see every possible configuration, from curly permed shags to dreadlocks ablaze with purple henna. Revisionist hair theory was surfacing too. Kobena Mercer's essay "Black Hair/Style Politics" in *Out There: Marginalization and Contemporary Cultures* (MIT Press) puts the hair police out of a job. Mercer reads curly perm and relaxed styles not as white imitation, but "New World creolization," in the same vein as a diasporan miracle like jazz. Then the moment we'd all been waiting for: *Essence* invited men to comment on women's hair practice. Men gave thumbs-down to weaves and drippy curls. Women wrote back telling the men to mind their business. As if to say, this ain't about y'all and this ain't about The Man, this is our creative space, best you stay out.

So, yes, it was a wonderful time. Then, out of nowhere, massive hair drama took hold. The girl's hair was getting gray, prematurely mind you, but gray. This was a fact, and she planned to deal with it like a womanist with a capital W, by telling everyone she was practicing to be old, fine, and silver-haired like Camille Cosby. She had not planned, however, on such strange occurrences as having men she barely knew run across the street and exclaim, no, EXCLAIM, over her gray hair like it was a national tragedy on par with the Clarence Thomas confirmation.

Or, on the response she'd get from a good friend upon revealing plans to have her hair cropped short in pursuit of life as Camille. The friend recommended, without a dime of irony, that she reconsider because "girls like us need hair to balance hips." The girl had been under the impression that girls like us with college degrees and trips to Africa and Europe only need brains. She realized now she'd been gravely wrong.

What ensued was a tailspin of epic proportions. The girl plain lost her mind. Not only did she *not* cut her hair, she went and got more. Taiwan hair that is, lots of it down her back, the ends seared with a Bic lighter to keep them from unraveling. This produces a smell that can only compare to fumes from a crack pipe. When the girl looked in the mirror, she saw Milli Vanilli. She didn't scream, she just calmly found a scissors and started cutting. The hairlike substance landed on the floor in a decorous mound, looking not unlike conceptual art by David Hammons. Just add a chicken wing, some Gucci bags, and a snowball.

How the girl managed to spend a third of her paycheck on synthetic hair, then cut it off five hours later, is still a mystery. But the torture didn't stop there. Minutes after the scissors ordeal, she was on the phone with another hairstylist. It was late afternoon Saturday, the worst time to be up in anybody's salon, yet she had to get her hair streaked "brick brown, not red" or she'd die by morning. The stylist heard the edge in girlfriend's voice and had mercy. In the salon, with the "dye cap" on, having her scalp gorged with knitting needles, the girl freaked again. She pleaded with her stylist to rinse out the bleach. The stylist cursed her out in Spanish. The girl went home with half a head of streaks.

The girl's best friend told her to get to the couch on her hair issues. This is a woman who recently traded in her short natural to become a John Atchison Salon gal. She goes around saying things like "I love the respect I get because my hair moves," in jest, but you know she means every word of it. Why listen to her?

Suddenly everything was symbolic. Audre Lorde passed. The girl remembered a line from one of Lorde's poems: "Is your hair still political/tell me/when it starts to burn." This was surely a message from God that hair was the true battleground. The girl thought of how much was still done to placate polite white, black, and Hispanic society by keeping kinks in the closet. She thought of the girls in D.C. who sued to wear braids to the office. Of the girl rap stars who preach nouveau nationalism, but favor "bone-straight" tresses. Of the rainbow babies who fear loss of their pedigree ringlets more than loss of life. She thought of her friends with short naturals who work corporate gigs and are constantly being asked if they are chemotherapy patients, as if no one living or dead should parade around with so little hair. She thought of children's formula relaxer kits for girls age six to twelve. And of her great aunt the hairdresser who took a five-month-old grandbaby on her knee and declared, "I need to get to this head right away."

She remembered the horrors. Of hot combs dropped on necks. Of sisters almost going out like Van Gogh. Of scalps lined with keloids from countless no-lye, no-lie perms. Of entire heads of hair lost. And of a friend, Inez, whose father decided to relax her hair himself. He left her, at age nine, naked and shrieking, almost blinded by lye, while he went out for a beer.

The men she thought of most. Their fetishes always got the better of their politics. Like the boyfriend who spoke of how proud he was of his girlfriend's short natural, though he called her a "bald-headed black bitch" in private. Or the boyfriend who slapped her for cutting her hair, then apologized in tears. She imagined that heterosexuality was the source of all her hair issues. Yet she knew better, or did she?

Just as suddenly, the hair drama passed. The girl was at peace with her silver strands again. Bless Camille Cosby, bless Susan Sontag. It became clear that she had "racialized." Racialize is a cute new word that means "make everything about race" (which of course it is, even if some folks like to pretend it's not). In the end, though, she came to see that what had happened to her was not race-hair drama at all. It was PMS, overtwentysomething, holiday-hair drama, which, as her mother reminded her, happens to women of all races, colors, and cultures.

Damn, and the girl thought she had an angle.

*1992*

# Praise for Stephanie Dray and Laura Kamoie's
## *My Dear Hamilton*

"*My Dear Hamilton* is a superbly written, meticulously researched homage to the birth of America as seen from the eyes of a woman who helped bring it to life. Eliza Schuyler Hamilton is much more than a Founding Father's wife; she's a passionate patriot who finds the strength to steer her tempestuous husband away from his own worst instincts even when he betrays her. At once a wartime drama, a woman's coming-of-age, and a lesson on politics that resonates in today's world, *My Dear Hamilton* is the book of the year."

—Kate Quinn, *New York Times* bestselling author of
*The Alice Network*

"Not since I read Erik Larson's *Dead Wake* have I had such an edge-of-my-seat immersion into historical events. Eliza Hamilton is a remarkable heroine, depicted here with gorgeous prose and heart-tugging realism. No study of Alexander Hamilton would be complete without reading this book and learning the true source of the great man's strength—his wife. Full of history, engaging characters who shimmer on each page, and a tremendous love story, this is a book for everyone."

—Karen White, *New York Times* bestselling author

"Following their stunning success in *America's First Daughter*, Stephanie Dray and Laura Kamoie have penned an unforgettable story of the woman behind Hamilton. Combining treachery, lies, and the fate of those present at the birth of a nation, *My Dear Hamilton* is a masterpiece that is both intimate in detail and epic in scope—a triumph!"

—Pam Jenoff, *New York Times* bestselling
author of *The Orphan's Tale*

"*My Dear Hamilton* is a fascinating work of historical fiction, beautifully crafted and richly detailed. If you think you already know Eliza Schuyler Hamilton, her role in the founding of our country, her marriage, and her heartbreak, you'll marvel at the woman you meet in this compelling novel."

—Jennifer Chiaverini, *New York Times* bestselling author of
*Mrs. Lincoln's Dressmaker* and *Enchantress of Numbers*

"From the first pages of *My Dear Hamilton*, the words 'In the secret seethings of my discontented heart,' I was pulled in and swept away by this epic tale. Beautifully written and meticulously researched, this stunning novel captures the courage, strength, and kindness of the remarkable woman behind Alexander Hamilton. A fascinating read!"

—Ellen Marie Wiseman, internationally bestselling
author of *The Life She Was Given*

"Did you ever want your own private window on the past? Stephanie Dray and Laura Kamoie provide an intimate look into the life of one of our most intriguing Founding Fathers, as well as a front-row view of the ups and downs of the early days of the Republic. If you've ever wanted to banter with Hamilton or share a dish of tea with the Marquis de Lafayette, open the covers of *My Dear Hamilton* and step right into Eliza Hamilton's parlor. . . . The gang's all there!"

—Lauren Willig, *New York Times* bestselling
author of *The English Wife*

"Eliza Hamilton assumes her rightful place as one of America's founding mothers as she guides first her husband and then her fledgling nation into the annals of history. *My Dear Hamilton* is historical fiction at its most addictive!"

—Stephanie Thornton, author of *The Tiger Queens*

"An incredible, surprising, and altogether lovely tribute to the woman who stood beside one of the most unknowable, irascible, energetic, and passionate men who contributed to the foundation of this nation."

—Lars D. H. Hedbor, author of
*The Path: Tales from a Revolution*

# MY
# DEAR
# HAMILTON

Also by Stephanie Dray & Laura Kamoie

*America's First Daughter*

# MY
# DEAR
# HAMILTON

## A NOVEL OF ELIZA SCHUYLER HAMILTON

## STEPHANIE DRAY & LAURA KAMOIE

piatkus

PIATKUS

First published in the US in 2018 by William Morrow,
an imprint of HarperCollins Publishers

First published in Great Britain in 2018 by Piatkus

1 3 5 7 9 10 8 6 4 2

A CIP catalogue record for this book
is available from the British Library.

ISBN 978-1-408-71118-7

Printed and bound in Great Britain by Clays Ltd, St Ives plc

Papers used by Piatkus are from well-managed forests
and other responsible sources.

Piatkus
An imprint of
Little, Brown Book Group
Carmelite House
50 Victoria Embankment
London EC4Y 0DZ

An Hachette UK Company
www.hachette.co.uk

*Semper Fidelis*

# Note to the Reader

ALEXANDER HAMILTON LEFT us with more than seven thousand letters, essays, proposals, and other papers. Of his wife's letters, only a handful remain. Whenever possible, for Hamilton and other historical figures, we quote directly from primary sources, which reflect the biases, prejudices, and political opinions of the time period.

However, because the language of the eighteenth century was so stilted and opaque, we have taken the liberty of correcting spelling, grammar, and otherwise editing, abridging, or modernizing the prose and terminology in the interest of clarity.

We have also adopted some conventions for the purposes of familiarity and simplicity. For example, we refer to the Haudenosaunee Confederacy as the Iroquois. And what Hamilton gave the snappy title *Observations on Certain Documents Contained in No. V & VI of "The History of the United States for the Year 1796," In Which the Charge of Speculation Against Alexander Hamilton, Late Secretary of the Treasury, is Fully Refuted. Written by Himself* is referred to in this book simply as the *Reynolds Pamphlet*. For clarity in discussions of early national politics, we have largely used the terms federalists and antifederalists, and the political party names Federalists and Republicans to denote the two main political factions that dominated Hamilton's life, despite the fact that Republicans, Democrats, Democratic-Republicans, and Jacobins were all largely synonymous at the time. (The latter we occasionally use, because the Hamiltons themselves did, to disparage their Republican opponents.)

Finally, this novel's portrayal is skewed by our protagonist's biases. Whenever the historical record was in doubt, we have unabashedly, and occasionally uncritically, adopted the slant most favorable to the American revolutionaries, Eliza, and her family; it's her story after all. For a more complete understanding of our choices and changes, please consult our *Note from the Authors* at the back of the book.

Though the natural weakness of her body hinders her from doing what men can perform, she has a mind as valiant and as active for the good of her country as the best of us.

—PLUTARCH

# Prologue

*Spring 1825*
*The Grange*
*Harlem, New York*

T HE PROMISE OF liberty is not written in blood or engraved in stone; it's embroidered into the fabric of our nation. And so is Alexander Hamilton.

My husband. My hero. My betrayer.

Though Hamilton is more than twenty years dead now, his memory lingers where I stand in the garden of tulips, lilies, and hyacinths we once planted together. He is inescapable in even the smallest things. I cannot buy a pouch of seeds for this garden without money from the mint that he established. I cannot pass a newsboy on my walks through the city without seeing the paper he founded or without reflecting upon the freedoms for the press he helped guarantee. I cannot cast my gaze at the busy ships in the harbor without seeing the trade he assured, or the coast guard that he founded, or the industry and opportunities he provided for the people who now flock to our shores in search of freedom and a better future.

In short, there is not a breath in any American's life that is not shaped in some way by Alexander Hamilton. Certainly not a breath in mine. His memory, which I must honor for the sake of our children if nothing else, is impossible for me to escape.

Though I confess I have tried.

In the secret seethings of my discontented heart, I've searched for a life that is my own. A life not consumed by the questions he left in his wake—riddles I will never solve about our marriage, our family, and the suffering to which he exposed us. I've searched for a meaning to my existence not swallowed up by Hamilton's shadow. By his genius. By his greatness. By his folly.

And by his enemies.

For in the battle for history—a war for truth, fought against time—I am a veteran. I've been fighting that battle for decades, and perhaps never more ferociously than now, within myself, as I stare at the paper in my hand.

Squinting beneath my bonnet against the sunlight, I see a calling card, unremarkable but for the single name etched in the center with bold ink.

### JAMES MONROE

At the sight of it, an unexpected pain stabs beneath my ribs, where my heart picks up its pace. My basket of purple hyacinths lies forgotten at my feet as I stand up, a little breathless. For the only thing more astonishing than the name itself is that the card is folded at the corner, indicating the former president personally delivered it, rather than sending a servant.

I should feel honored.

Instead, I'm incensed that James Monroe has darkened my doorstep. And before I can stop myself, my voice drops low, as it always does when I'm angry. "What has *that man* come to see me for?"

"Couldn't say," my housekeeper murmurs, straightening her apron. "But he's waiting for you in the parlor."

It's not the protocol for a gentleman to present a card and wait, except when presuming upon familiar acquaintance. And though Monroe definitely *is* a familiar acquaintance—and more than an acquaintance besides—he has no right to presume upon our old intimacy. No right at all. Not after everything that has passed between us. Especially not when he's caught me out in the yard, in my gardening gloves and black workaday bombazine frock.

He should not expect, even under the best of circumstances, that I would receive a man of his rank and stature on a moment's notice. But then James Monroe has always been wilier than anyone gives him credit for, and I imagine that he's counting on the element of surprise to work to his advantage.

"Doubtless he's come to pay his respects to you," the housekeeper says.

And I give the most indelicate snort of my life, because I think it more likely Monroe has come to collect my surrender. For years now, to promote his so-called Era of Good Feelings, a popular President Monroe cut a swath through cities and towns, using his southern drawl and amiable manner to smother every last vestige of dissent. And charmed, no doubt, by that infernal dimple in his chin, everyone has genuflected.

Everyone but me.

Which is why I suppose he cannot retire in complete victory until he can boast of having been reconciled with the wife of Alexander Hamilton. But there are no good feelings here. And even though I'm not completely reconciled with Hamilton myself, I have no wish to become Monroe's final triumph.

As I clutch the card, much perturbed, the housekeeper prompts me. "Ma'am, you wouldn't want to leave the gentleman waiting."

Oh, but I do want to. I'd happily leave Monroe standing on the stoop of the house Alexander Hamilton built until the Virginian is bent with age and crumbling to dust. But Monroe has already invaded my parlor so I must deal with him. And I must deal with him myself. To do otherwise would be to discount a lifetime of lessons from my father, a general who taught me that when faced with the specter of defeat, one must meet it swiftly and with as much dignity as possible. So I remove my garden gloves, scoop up my basket of hyacinths, and say, quite grandly, "I will see him."

After that, I don't so much *walk* into the Federal-style yellow house as *march* into battle. I find Monroe in the old, faded parlor, sitting on a dark sofa I embroidered to hide where it has become threadbare. The gentleman rises to his feet to greet me, his familiar expression grave, hat clutched in now aged hands.

And from ten paces, I take the measure of him.

Six feet tall, square-shouldered, and rawboned as ever, Monroe is wearing antiquated black velvet knee breeches, long since gone out of fashion, which leads me to imagine the silver in his hair is powder from a bygone era. A showman when it comes to reputation, Monroe must be pleased, I think, to count himself in that pantheon of presidents my countrymen now venerate.

Washington, the father of the country. Adams, the mastermind of independence. Jefferson, the voice of the revolution. Madison, the father of the Constitution.

And Monroe, the last of the founders.

Or so they say. But if Monroe must be counted as the last, then by my reasoning, my husband was the *first*. For not one of these men would have ever become president without Alexander Hamilton, the architect of our very government.

Yet Monroe doesn't even glance at the portrait of my husband that hangs where the piano used to be—long since sold off to keep a roof over my children's heads.

Perhaps I cannot blame Monroe for avoiding the eyes of Hamilton's portrait. After all, even for me, the likeness still churns up a noxious stew of resentment, guilt, and loss. And I am not the only person in this world who loved the man and hated him, too.

So I nod to Monroe.

I should invite him to sit. I should serve tea. A thousand niceties are dictated by social grace when a president—even a former president—comes to call. But I observe none of them.

Instead, I wordlessly wait for him to deliver the first volley.

Finally, with a formal bow, Monroe drawls, "Mrs. General Hamilton."

Why does it suddenly bother me to be addressed this way? It's the title by which I've been known for almost thirty years. A title in which I've taken pride. A title some would say has opened as many doors as it has slammed shut. But somehow, hearing myself addressed as *Mrs. General Hamilton* by James Monroe feels as I'm being forced by him, for a second time, to loyally claim Hamilton as my own.

And Monroe—as much as any person still alive—has cause to know just how much that loyalty cost me.

Now Monroe rises up from his bow with the hint of the smile I once found so charming. He clears his throat and begins, haltingly. "It's been many years since we first met . . ."

Oh, after everything, is he truly appealing to our *history*?

As if I've forgotten. But I haven't. Not for a moment. Especially not recently, when the approach of the fiftieth anniversary of our independence reminds me daily of how my life has been entwined with the creation of this nation.

Monroe's, too, I must, in justice, admit.

At the start, I was a general's daughter and he was a handsome war hero. And now I stare at Monroe, wondering if he still has that bullet lodged in his shoulder, or if a surgeon ever managed to dig it out . . .

But I don't ask. I don't say anything. In truth, I take perverse pleasure in the pained yearning I imagine I see upon Monroe's face as I force him to founder against the wall of my silence. Silence is often the only weapon available to ladies. And I wield mine expertly.

In the thick awkwardness, Monroe clears his throat and continues what seems a rehearsed speech. "Yes, it's been *quite* a long time since we met. I find that the lapse of time brings its softening influences. Now we are both nearing the grave, when past differences can be forgiven and forgotten."

*Forgiven and forgotten.*

I nearly scoff, but I'm determined to hold my tongue as an act of resistance. After all, despite what Hamilton believed, I am no angel.

But Monroe seems not to realize the war I'm silently waging against him, and his gray eyes are hopeful. Why shouldn't he be hopeful? Napoleon Bonaparte once said that history is merely a set of lies agreed upon, and I know it would advantage me, and my family, to go along with all the little lies this new nation has agreed upon with regard to Alexander Hamilton. My sons will more easily find advancement if I do. My daughter might be courted by more respectable beaus. I myself might more comfortably mingle in society, if I so please.

All I have to do is surrender to James Monroe's wish for reconciliation.

And I should. I know that I should. I have every reason to put the past behind me.

But as I stand here, trying to form conciliatory words, I am over aware of my husband's portrait in its gilded frame, his extraordinary eyes looking down upon me. I turn my head toward the arched entryway, where his ghostly marbled bust has beckoned me, each night, like an intimate and a stranger. And I glance past that, to the doorway of the little green study in which I can still remember him toiling at his mahogany and satinwood cylinder desk, leather-bound books piled high on either side of him, ink smudges upon his hands, his quill scratching and candle burning late into the night.

*Forgiven and forgotten.*

If I am famous for anything, it's for being a *forgiving woman*. And as for the forgetting . . . there are so many things I should like to forget. Forgetting would lift the weighty cloak of the past from my shoulders and make the present so much easier. But memory unalterably sets our compass, and guides us down paths we might have preferred never to have walked at all. And my path goes back all the way to the start. To the fathers of this country who fought and bled beneath a starry banner of red, white, and blue. To the mothers who were the menders, the sewers of flags, the darners of uniforms, the binders of wounds. And, in my case, the quilter of the torn scraps of old paper that remind me why we ever fought in the first place . . .

# Part One

## A War for Independence

# Chapter One

*You have called together a host of savages, and turned them loose to scalp our women and children and lay our country waste.*
— ANONYMOUS AMERICAN SOLDIER TO
BRITISH GENERAL JOHN BURGOYNE

*October 17, 1777*
*The Pastures*
*Albany, New York*

I WAS *SOMEONE* BEFORE I met Alexander Hamilton.

Not someone famous or important or with a learned philosophical understanding of all that was at stake in our revolution. Not a warrior or a philosopher or statesman.

But I was a patriot.

I was no unformed skein of wool for Hamilton to weave together into any tapestry he wished. That's important for me to remember now, when every thread of my life has become tangled with everything he was. Important, I think, in sorting out what can be forgiven, to remember my own experiences—the ones filled with my own yearnings that had nothing to do with him.

I was, long before he came into my life, a young woman struggling to understand her place in a changing world. And torn, even then, between loyalty, duty, and honor in the face of betrayal.

*Torn* as I stood in my family's potato field surrounded by wounded soldiers, debating a choice that would never have given me pause before. Should I tend to the injured Redcoats while under the gaze of mistrustful American soldiers?

"Water, please, Miss Schuyler," croaked a British regular, lying in a furrow beneath one of our orchard trees.

He'd been evacuated here to Albany with at least a thousand others from Saratoga, where a brutal battle had been fought ten days earlier. Our hospital, churches, and pastures were now overrun with casualties from both armies and we struggled to care for them all. The least I could do was fetch the Redcoat a pitcher of water.

Instead, I hesitated, a knot of anxiety tightening in my throat, for I was now the daughter of a disgraced American general who had been relieved of his command under suspicion of treason.

Facing court-martial, my father already stood accused of taking bribes from the British and surrendering an American fortress to the enemy. For his daughter to be seen caring for the same enemy now . . .

I feared for anything I might do to worsen Papa's situation, so even as my face heated with shame, I turned away from the Redcoat to help others, forcing myself to remember that these British had been ravaging the whole of the Hudson Valley for months and terrorizing my countrymen.

*They are the cause of this bloodshed,* I told myself.

For the king's men had captured and occupied New York City, burned our state's first capital at Kingston to the ground, and during the fighting upon the plains of Saratoga, they had set fire to our summerhouse, leaving it in ruin. From here in the relative safety of the Pastures, we'd seen only the faintest glow of battlefield fires against the distant evening sky, but even now the acrid smell and taste of soot carried to us downriver. And I thought, *We've set the whole world on fire.*

Two summers before, our thirteen colonies declared independence from the British crown, but now our celebratory bonfires had given way to the flames of war. I hoped, following this American victory at Saratoga, that we were finally winning it. So I tended to a Continental scout who held a gory wound on his scalp that had reopened since a doctor last saw him.

"How bad is it, Miss Schuyler?" he asked, grimacing against the pain as I washed the wound and pulled my needle through the gash at his hairline.

"Fortunately, your brow is cool and it does not look to have festered," I replied. Fresh red blood oozed warmly over my fingertips. "Try not to pull it open again," I told the young soldier as I finished my stitches and cut the thread with a hunting knife.

While my father taught me to ride, fish, and know my way in the wild, my mother had trained me in rudimentary medicine while tending tenants, Indians, and one frontier army or another. And since I couldn't fight in this war, I contributed the way women could. I sewed. Uniforms, socks, flesh. "If all goes well, you'll be left with a battle scar to prove your bravery."

He grinned. "Thank you."

As a general's daughter, I knew what soldiers liked to hear. But it seemed, these days, I never knew what to say to please my mother.

"*Betsy*," she snapped from where she stood at the back gate removing an apron she'd dirtied helping soldiers in the nearby pastures. "Go in the house with the other children and clean up. Your father is expected shortly from the surrender at Saratoga. We must prepare to receive his guests."

I winced, fearful the scout beside me would misconstrue her words. For we were not expecting *guests*, but British prisoners. Nor was I one of the children. In fact, I'd just turned twenty. But I knew better than to point any of this out to my mother, a stern Dutch plantation mistress who'd been exceedingly vexed with me for months now.

*You're the sensible one, Elizabeth*, she'd said in the heat of our quarrel. *I expected better.*

As if I could stop the tides of change any more than she

could. I didn't say that, either. I merely wiped my hands, bobbed my head, picked up my skirts, and went. Broken oyster shells crunched underfoot on the drive as I passed the stables and made my way to my father's handsome brick mansion, which stood upon a bluff overlooking the majestic Hudson River.

The house was a flurry of activity as I hurried past kerchiefed Negro slaves moving the heavy mahogany table into the grand entry hall and went up the stairs to the bedroom I shared with my sisters. Well—just one sister, now, since Angelica had run off to marry a mysterious suitor against Papa's wishes a few months before. Now it was just me and eighteen-year-old Peggy who shared the spacious pale-green room with its wardrobes, armchairs, and canopied bed.

"Why can't General Gates take these prisoners?" Peggy cried, yanking on a pair of stockings. "He took Papa's victory, after all."

"That's true," I said. It was bad enough that a rival had pushed our father out of command. Worse that we were now saddled with the captives. We'd shown courtesy to imprisoned British officers before, in the early years of the war, most notably to the dashing Lieutenant John André, a clever and genteel officer who'd charmed my sisters and me with his sketches and accomplished flute playing.

But my father wasn't under suspicion then, and General "Gentleman Johnny" Burgoyne was no André—he was a monster and no gentleman at all. How was it going to look to the Continental soldiers in our fields, not to mention our tenants and neighbors, if we wined and dined the very same British general who sent Mohawk Indians to terrorize them?

But as our black lady's maid, Jenny, swept into the room and unfastened my apron and frock while fretting about the bloodstains, I reminded Peggy, "Even if you're right about Papa's victory being stolen out from under him, you cannot say such things lest you rub the salt of injustice into his still-raw wounds. And you especially cannot say it in front of the British, lest they sense disunity amongst our generals."

"That's no secret, is it?" Peggy asked.

Thankfully not, because Peggy was never very good with secrets. Indeed, Peggy had the habit of speaking aloud what others left unspoken. In fact, she'd quite nearly given away Angelica's plan to escape the house and run off with her beau, though now I sometimes wished she had. I wished we *both* had.

"I just hate that we must go to all this trouble for the same lobsterbacks who burned our Saratoga house," Peggy grumbled, rummaging in her tall oak wardrobe amidst taffeta, frilly petticoats, gauzy fichus, and embroidered stomachers.

On a sigh, I stepped into the petticoats Jenny held for me. "I hate it, too."

I hated that I couldn't be as happy about our American victory as I should have been. Hated that our Saratoga house was in ashes. Hated that Papa faced court-martial, his reputation in tatters. Hated that Angelica was gone and our mother blamed me for it. And hated most of all that it might be, at least in some small part, my fault.

Peggy harrumphed, admiring her dark glossy curls in a looking glass. "Well, we'll at least remind these king's men that we're not paupers. Wear the blue robe à la Française. Oh, and the blue earbobs. I know what you're going to say, but they're *not* too showy."

They were, for me. Angelica was the sophisticated one. Peggy the pretty one. And I was Philip Schuyler's *practical* daughter. The one who, as the second child in a family as large and prominent as Philip Schuyler's, was sometimes apt to be overlooked. There was even a story told in my family that when I was a babe, Mama was so distracted by her many responsibilities that she accidentally left me bound up in my cradleboard, hanging from a tree in the way of the natives. So it was that from the smallest age one can conceive of such a thing, I considered it quite natural to be overlooked.

And I never minded, because it allowed me to slip away to swim in the river, or stay up past bedtime without anyone noticing, and tag along after my father on adventures that were forbidden to other girls. Besides, people said very interesting things in front of girls they didn't notice . . .

But the blue paste earbobs *drew* notice. They sparkled like sapphires—exactly the sort of jewelry that I did not carry off well. Still, I treasured them for their sentimental value.

"I don't know," I said, studying my reflection as Jenny held them to my ear.

My younger sister met my gaze in the mirror. "Angelica left them for you. She *wanted* you to wear them."

Almost as one, we both sighed for her absence. *Angelica*. My brilliant sister. My closest friend and confidant. I sank down into the quilted wingback chair by the window where Angelica used to read her books, hoping in vain to catch a lingering scent of my sister's rosewater perfume. And I reread the little note that had accompanied the gift.

*I love Jack with all my heart, but that will never diminish my first and best attachment to you, Betsy—Angelica*

I hadn't wanted to help Angelica elope with Jack Carter, a commissary supplier of armaments and other goods, who had courted her in a whirlwind and stolen her away to Boston. I'd begged my sister not to run off with him. But she'd argued. *"Love is a thing beyond control. Passion is a thing beyond reason. It can't be denied."* Her eyes had nearly glowed with fervor. *"It's a thing almost . . . predestined."*

That still sounded like perfect nonsense to me. I'd thought her scheme foolhardy, dangerous, and disobedient. Not to mention *selfish*, for all the trouble it would give my parents in the midst of a war. And, if I am honest, there was also a childish part of me that despaired Angelica was to break the vow we once made to be spinsters together like the Douw sisters who lived on Court Street.

In this world on fire, her marriage was one rebellion too many for me, too. But in the end, I loved Angelica too much to deny her. Even though the elopement had put our mother into a fury and beset Papa with worry and embarrassment at the precise time he could least afford it.

"I think the earbobs will look quite fine on you, Miss Betsy," Jenny said with a shy smile upon her dark-skinned face. Jenny always knew the right thing to say. Maybe it was because, as was the custom on plantations in the Hudson Valley, she'd been given to us when we were little children still playing together, and now we couldn't manage without her. So I let her fasten them and powder me, even though powder always made me sneeze.

Just then, the sound of horse hooves clattered on the drive. Glancing out the window, Peggy announced, "Papa's home with the British prisoners." She all but dragged me down our grand staircase, with its rope-patterned balusters, past the papered walls painted with gray murals of ancient Roman ruins, and into the front hall, where our little brothers and sisters had gathered. Looping her arm in mine, Peggy gave a spiteful grin. "I'll bet this wasn't what *Gentleman Johnny* had in mind when he said he'd be eating Christmas dinner in Albany. Now he hasn't so much as a twig for a stew pot."

"*Peggy*," I warned.

Papa appeared from the back door near to where we all gathered to greet him. I scooped my baby sister Cornelia into my arms, and stood beside our brothers, twelve-year-old John, nine-year-old Jeremiah, and four-year-old Rensselaer, who, like a charming boy soldier, saluted Papa with a chubby hand.

"I do hope Papa seized Burgoyne's champagne," Peggy whispered to me, undeterred. "Spirits may be the only thing to see us through this indignity."

Papa's stern gaze cut to Peggy, silencing her at last.

Tall and dignified even in his traveling clothes, my father was the portrait of a cultured gentleman. But he was more than a gentleman; he was a general. So it pained me to see him out of his blue-and-buff uniform with its gold braids. Even more so when he frowned and said, "I expect each of you to show the utmost hospitality to our captive British officers."

Peggy crossed her arms in protest. "But, Papa, that man doesn't deserve—"

"It's not a matter of deserving," my father admonished. "The British think we're uncivilized people living in these wilds. If you'd seen the poor Baroness Riedesel *tremble* with fear of what we might do to her and her children . . ."

That image softened me because I knew the sad plight of women caught up in this war. Girls killed and scalped. Old widows robbed by marauding soldiers of every last thing they owned. Young wives abandoned and caught on the wrong side of enemy lines.

My father's voice took on the strength of conviction. "The British think we're children incapable of governing ourselves. It is in service to the cause of our independence to show them otherwise." Peggy opened her mouth to argue, but Papa stopped her short. "There will be no moment, in word or deed, from any of you that should make the prisoners feel anything but honored guests. I care not what others may say or do; as for me and my house, we will serve my country."

In saying this, he spoke as if giving law. But he was also encouraging us to see our own small contributions in this cause. So while others might rebel against him, I would not, even as I feared that the many watchful eyes around our house might see our hospitality as treason. "I'll help Dinah bring refreshments in from the kitchen," I said.

And in the end, everything was *almost* as my father wished it.

Redcoat officers filed glumly into the house, and Mama greeted them with her chin held high as befit her lineage, which she traced back to the first Dutch patroon to settle this colony when it was still called New Netherlands. She always said that a general's wife should show no fear, and neither should his children, so I forced myself to smile sweetly at each and every Redcoat. Not that they looked twice at me. Nor did I wish them to. Especially since I could well imagine them marching into our house under far different circumstances had the battle gone the other way.

After Burgoyne was settled in the most elegant and comfortable accommodations, I took his men pots of strong tea with Mama's short-crust biscuits and the preserves we'd been putting up for autumn made from Papa's prize yellow plums. All the while, I wondered which of our guests might have set fire to our country house or given leave to the Mohawks to scalp our settlers.

That night, our hostess duties continued in the kitchen. "Some prison this is!" Peggy exclaimed, eyes rolling as she took in a long table laden with silver platters. "They should be lucky to get stale bread but they're getting a feast."

Our cook, Dinah, had spent the day preparing local delicacies under Mama's supervision. All the servants were so busy catering to the needs of our *guests* that Mama had enlisted us and Dinah's daughter, our Jenny, to help. Like her mother, Jenny had a petite stature, but where our lady's maid had always been shy, Dinah issued orders like a battlefield commander.

Even to us.

"Miss Betsy and Miss Peggy, we'll start with the oysters. Take in the trays. Jenny, go fetch the butter." Peggy wrinkled her nose even as Dinah gave us a look that brooked no argument.

We did just what she said.

Burgoyne and his officers joined Papa at the long banquet table while the womenfolk of the household served them oysters followed by a course of striped bass our servants caught fresh from the river, along with seasoned cabbage and carrots, all to be washed down with Papa's best claret and Madeira wine and finished with a dessert of spiced bonnyclabber made from soured milk.

And if I'd not been a Christian, I'd have wished that they choked on it.

It was no small trouble to keep the British officers and their wives and children fed, especially since some rascal was milking the cows before our servants could get the cream. And though I tried to keep my little brothers from trouble, the next morning Jeremiah flung open the door to the room where Burgoyne and his officers slept. "You're all my prisoners!" he cried, then slammed the door again, laughing like the arch little fellow he was.

Prince, our butler, was not amused.

Carrying himself with a royal demeanor that defied his enslavement and justified his name, Prince was a dark, stately man, who was the most trusted servant in the household and whose disapproving tone was almost more intimidating than Papa's. "It would reflect best upon you, Miss Betsy, to keep your brothers in better order. And tell Miss Peggy I have my eyes on her."

I swallowed. "What's Peggy done?"

Prince tilted his head in the direction of the main hall. "She's flirting with the Redcoats. Flashing those dark eyes of hers. Don't either of you girls get in your heads that you can play the same trick on me twice."

I bit my lip, remembering how we'd lured Prince from his bed near the back door so that Angelica could slip away to meet her beau. He hadn't forgotten, and might have been angrier about it than either of my parents. Trying to reassure him, I said, "Don't worry. Neither of us have any use for these lobsterbacks."

So imagine my surprise to find my pretty sister sitting next to Burgoyne, the monster himself. The two of them, just sipping coffee there amongst Mama's silver, glass, and candles!

Peggy was laughing, having somehow charmed the British general into giving her his silver shoe buckles as a token of esteem. Worse, only a moment later, an unmarried British officer asked if Peggy might take him for a turn in the nursery where we grew Papa's plums, and she agreed.

Pulling my sister aside under some pretext, I asked, "What can you be thinking?"

"Papa said to be kind," she replied, clasping the general's sparkling shoe buckles with no intention of giving them up. "Besides, I don't remember you shunning that handsome Lieutenant André when he was here."

"The war was different then." More civilized, it had seemed. And farther away. Besides, I didn't have to shun men; they never noticed me with my sisters flitting about. But André was the sort of man who seemed to notice everything, and when he'd commented favorably on my drawings, I'd beat down the stirrings of attraction by reminding myself he was an enemy.

"The war is no different now," Peggy argued. "After all, we've only won a *battle* at Saratoga. If we should still lose the war, one of us might have to marry a king's man to save the family."

I sputtered in exasperation and more than a little astonishment. She should've known better than to behave in a way that might confirm suspicions that our family sympathized with the British. And as a general's daughter, she should've known better than to speak openly about defeat. But I was most horrified by her apparent willingness to wed an enemy, no matter her reasons. "I'd sooner marry a Barbary pirate!"

"Well, I wish you would," Peggy called over her shoulder as she flounced off. "Because I fear Papa will never consent to let me marry until you do."

I would've been more cross with her if it weren't for the fact that the kinder we were to the prisoners, the more it shamed them. A lesson I learned that evening as we gathered in the blue parlor near the fire and the British general offered my father an apology.

I wanted to think Burgoyne meant to apologize for the poor people who had the misfortune to be caught before his advancing army. Or even that he might apologize for the king, who had forced us all to this war. But instead he said to Papa, "Your hospitality is too much for a man who has ravaged your lands and burned your home. I regret the event and the reasons that occasioned it."

All eyes turned to Papa, who regretted the loss of life and his command more than the loss of his house—*all three* of which were occasioned, in part, by this man. And yet my father forced himself to a nod of acknowledgment. "It is the fate of war. If I had thought it necessary to save the lives of my men, I'd have done the same. Say no more about it."

This was, I thought, what it meant to be *noble*.

Not a title conveyed by a king. Not by birth or blood. But through a learned and practiced strength of faith and character. And insofar as our revolution was to teach that lesson to the world, I prayed it would succeed.

I wished to be as noble as my father. And I was shamed anew as I remembered the wounded Redcoat's face. The one who had asked me for water. The one from whom I had turned away. I'd been wrong—worse, driven by fear, I'd been *cowardly*.

And now I determined to be brave.

PAPA'S LITTLE STUDY at the back of the house, with its emerald flock-papered walls, and its books, maps, and calculations arranged in orderly fashion, was a place forbidden to my younger sisters and brothers. They never dared interrupt Papa's work, but because I had mastered the art of sitting with him without disturbing his thoughts, he sometimes indulged me to stay while he wrote his letters. So, bracing for the reprimand I deserved, I took the liberty of knocking upon the door.

Papa summoned me inside, and I closed the door behind me. But instead of slipping quietly into the window seat where I liked to read, I waited for him to finish his letter.

Finally, he poured a circle of wax upon the folded page and stamped it with his seal, then glanced up at me quizzically where I leaned with my back against the door. "What is it, my child?"

"What are you working on?" I asked, not quite finding the courage to tell him why I'd come.

He didn't press me on the matter. "I'm preparing my defense for the court-martial."

"*Good*," I said, guilt souring the dinner in my belly. "Then your name can be cleared of wrongdoing once and for all."

Papa wasn't always a calm man—he'd once threatened to dash the brains of an incompetent underling upon the ground—but he strove to conduct himself as a gentleman. And one of the ways he attempted to discipline himself was by the working of mathematical problems. He must have been struggling with something now, because he absently scratched figures into a notebook before saying, "Unlike you, my dear child, I am not entirely confident that I *will* be exonerated. But at least I will have a consolation which no one can deprive me of: the conscious reflection that I have done my duty, even if I am to suffer unjustly for my country."

I followed his gaze as it cut to the silver falcon coat of arms affixed above the fireplace.

*Semper Fidelis.* Always faithful. Always loyal.

That was our Schuyler family motto, one that had been flung in my father's face by our Tory neighbors when, in '75, Papa had exchanged his red officer's coat for a blue general's uniform and declared himself a soldier for the American cause. And now, because of me, he found himself accused of treason by some patriots, too.

I swallowed around a knot in my throat and finally said what I should have said months before. "I'm so sorry, Papa."

When my mother discovered that we'd helped my eldest sister run off, she'd said some *very* unhandsome words to Peggy and me, in both English and Dutch. And yet, my father had never let one word of blame pass his lips. Which somehow made it worse.

Tears now blurred my vision as I blurted, "I'm so sorry for what I helped put in motion with Angelica . . ."

For my sister's elopement had given the fractured and fractious soldiers of the Northern Department yet another reason to distrust Papa. My father should have been celebrated for cobbling together an army of fur-trading, river-going New Yorkers and un-ruly New England backwoodsmen. He should have been hailed as the general who staved off the invasion by felling trees over roads, destroying bridges, blocking rivers, and burning whole fields of golden wheat so as to leave the British with nothing but scorched earth. Instead, he'd been belittled as a general who could not command his own daughters, much less hold Fort Ti-conderoga. I worried that my role in Angelica's elopement had cost Papa the confidence of his men, allowing them to believe the very worst about his loyalties and competence. Perhaps it had even cost him his command.

So I expected, at long last, that with my apology, my father would bring down his wrath on me. But instead he simply said, "That was Mr. Carter's doing."

As much as my father had resented his new son-in-law, at least at first, I resented Jack Carter more. That's why I wasn't as startled as I should have been when Papa added, "I considered dispatching him with pistols, but I couldn't kill a man your sister saw fit to love. It also wasn't in my heart to disown her. So, at the end of the equation, there was no undoing this Gordion knot. And, as you will find is so often the case in life, my dear Betsy, the only prudent thing to do was frown, make them humble, and *forgive*."

I realized that he was frowning now.

That I was humbled.

And that I was also forgiven.

At least by Papa. And the love I felt for my father in that mo-ment was eclipsed only by admiration. Because I realized that it was *love* that allowed my father to set aside the injuries done to his reputation, security, and pride. For love of his family, and his country, he swallowed down indignity as if immune to its poison.

And I wished I could be like him.

But if there is anything that marks my character, it's that I have never rested easily in the face of injustice. My father might have been able to bear it, but I simply could not. If I'd been born a son, I'd have joined the army to see our family honor restored. I'd have trained to become an officer, testing my bravery and seeking glory upon a battlefield in service of the cause. I'd have challenged his detractors to a duel.

But how, I wondered, could a daughter make a difference?

# Chapter Two

*There is a spirit of dissatisfaction prevailing*
*among the soldiers and even the officers.*
—MAJOR GENERAL LAFAYETTE TO GEORGE WASHINGTON

*February 19, 1778*
*Albany*

MEN THINK STITCHERY the most demure of occupations—all they see is gently bred girls, their heads bent in domestic pursuit, their hands kept busy and out of mischief. But my mother knew sewing circles for the wheels of conspiracy that they actually are. At least amongst sisters. Which was why Mama wasn't about to leave us to our own devices.

Papa might have forgiven me, but my mother was still wroth. "You girls are dallying," she accused from her rocking chair in the yellow parlor, her own knitting needles clicking and clacking under her experienced hands. "Especially you, Betsy."

I pressed my lips together without offering a defense of myself, intent on not losing count of my stitches. But Peggy lifted her pretty head of dark curls to complain. "We've been knitting since sunrise; if we don't take a rest, we're going to split stitches and ruin the stockings."

"There's no time to worry about workmanship," Mama snapped.

Her special urgency was because the Committee of Safety and Correspondence was offering eight shillings to the first family in Albany to produce three pairs of two-threaded stockings for the soldiers billeted in our town.

Being one of the wealthiest families, we would not take the money, of course. But because we were beset by recent scandals, and Papa's court-martial had not yet been convened to clear his name, Mama wished to burnish our reputation by knitting stockings for the cause. After all, with Albany consumed in a near hysteria of suspicion and accusation, our jail was currently filled with formerly prominent citizens accused of being *enemies to this country.*

I was still desperate to do something to redeem myself and my family—something more than knitting stockings in a warm parlor with frost on the windows. Fortunately, an opportunity presented itself when my father emerged from his study and called for Prince to fetch him his hat and coat.

"I'm going to the hospital," Papa announced.

He was restless. For years, urgent letters from General Washington had come to us day and night, under seal and from riders on frothing mounts, but once the British were gone from our home, we no longer received any word from headquarters at all.

And the silence was deafening.

In what seemed almost a fit of defiance, Papa rebuilt our Saratoga house in a mere twenty-nine days, salvaging nails and hinges and knobs. Then he paced at the windows, staring beyond the fine trees to a country that was still at war . . . without him. He was a general without a command. A soldier without a battle to fight.

And somehow, I felt that way, too. As my father stooped to kiss Mama on his way out, I quickly finished my stocking and asked, "Can I go with you, Papa?"

I think he knew that I shared his restlessness and discontent, because Papa rescued me from my mother's withering glare by asking, "Can you spare Betsy? She'd be a help today. Peggy doesn't have the stomach for it, but Betsy's good with the soldiers. And Arnold likes her."

*Benedict Arnold,* he meant. The Hero of Saratoga.

Having led a charge in the battle amidst a hailstorm of grape-shot and musket balls, General Arnold had taken a bullet to the leg that shattered his bone. And his patriotism was so unimpeachable that his friendship bolstered Papa's badly bruised reputation.

It was probably for that reason that Mama agreed to part with me. I was a little sorry to abandon Peggy, who feigned the long-suffering look of a wounded soldier left behind. Still, Papa wasn't wrong about Peg's delicate stomach; she'd retched at the sight of a soldier whose face had been half torn off by a cannonball and none of the doctors wanted her back, whereas I knew how to make myself useful.

"Hurry while the horses are being brought out," Papa whispered. "Before your mother changes her mind."

I grinned. It was a grin that faded when we neared the barracks and passed a small gathering of patriot soldiers huddled together around campfires upon which they made paltry cakes of nothing more than water and flour.

These men did not salute.

One of them even spat as we passed.

*Green Mountain Boys,* I thought. Rude backwoods riflemen Papa once commanded who adored General Gates and had spread the rumor about Papa's supposed treason. Dr. Franklin famously said we must all hang together, or we would surely hang separately. Well, I wished he'd told the militia.

But if Papa feared them, he didn't show it.

Instead he rode on, contemptuous of the insult. Still, I knew he felt it, because he said, "I spoke for independence when I served in the Continental Congress. Now, blood has been spilled, widows made, children orphaned, and soldiers left half-naked, sick, and starving. I count it my duty to do for them what I can, whether I am in uniform or not, with rank and dignity, or without. Whether they spit at me for it, or not."

Letting go the reins of my mare for a moment, I reached with one mittened hand to touch him on his mount beside me, to let him know how much I felt pride in being his daughter.

And I hoped to make him proud of me, too.

When we reached the piazza at the two-story hospital, I dismounted like a soldier and collected a parcel of shirts and bandages from the saddle, tucking it under my arm. Then I took a deep breath, knowing the hospital air was often putrid.

And yet, those lingering in either of the hospital wings were the lucky ones. They had a roof and walls to protect them against the snowfall. The hospital could only accommodate five hundred beds—and even the floor of our church at the center of town had no more room, so many wounded soldiers had to make do with tent covers. And there weren't enough of those either.

We'd scarcely gone through the front door before a grizzled veteran with a bloodstained bandage tied about one eye actually had the temerity to shout in Papa's face, *"Where's our pay?"*

I wanted to say that he should ask Congress. But I was not tart by nature. Not like my sisters. I wasn't pretty enough to get away with it. So I held my tongue.

Fortunately, we were spared of a reply when Benedict Arnold limped over and shoved the angry man with his crutch. "Shut your bone-box and mind your manners around Miss Schuyler," Arnold growled at the veteran. "You're not the only one who can complain about not being given his due . . ."

In the face of the Hero of Saratoga's disapproval, the veteran went from steel to milk. "Yessir," he murmured.

Not giving the surly veteran another moment of attention, Arnold turned to me. "Miss Schuyler. Always a pleasure."

I bobbed my head, not put off by his growling, especially not when it was in defense of my papa. Arnold was simply gruff by nature, and it was a trait I knew the pain of his injury had worsened. "General Arnold."

But as Papa took Arnold aside into a little room the hero had fitted for himself as an office, I heard the veteran behind us grumble, "Guess it don't matter when the pay comes, since we're all soon to die on some snowy cliff in Canada."

I didn't blame the soldiers for their fear of the forthcoming winter campaign. The least we could do to encourage them was put warm clothes upon their backs, so I asked, "General Arnold, is there somewhere we can put these bundles of shirts to distribute to the men?"

"Leave them with Dr. Thacher," Papa replied. "That's not why we have come."

I blinked. "It's not?"

In answer, Papa turned to Arnold. "I thought you might like to borrow a horse and join me at the barracks in greeting my latest replacement as commander of the Northern Department."

At this, Arnold barked out a bitter laugh. "Washington's pet Frenchman? He's not due for a week yet."

Papa's mouth quirked in the way it sometimes did when he had a secret no one else knew. "My scout spotted a group of horsemen and sleighs, French uniforms, some of them. My guess is that Lafayette will be at the barracks within the hour, if he hasn't arrived already."

Arnold rolled his broad shoulders, sighing ruefully. "I'm sorry, Schuyler. To think we must fete and flatter and give your command to a damned boy soldier of *just twenty years* in the hopes he can deliver us an alliance with King Louis . . ." He glanced at me and reddened. "I beg your pardon, miss, for coarse language."

"Think nothing of it, sir," I said, quickly. "I'm accustomed to soldiers."

But inside, I railed at the very idea that the new general was my very same age. It was bad enough when they gave my father's command to Gates. Why should Congress now entrust the entire Northern Army, and perhaps even the fate of the war, into the hands of an untested young foreigner? This was *my father's army*. I could not be convinced otherwise.

And maybe Papa felt the same way, because he said, "If we get to Lafayette before anyone else, maybe we can talk sense into him about this campaign."

The bull-necked Arnold scowled, leaning on his crutch. "Lafayette's a lost cause. The lad was still in swaddling when you and I saw blood in the French and Indian War—but he thinks he'll win laurels throughout Europe for chasing his death in Quebec, taking our soldiers with him. A vainglorious French stripling isn't going to listen to reason."

"Washington trusts him," Papa said, simply.

"Lafayette is a titled *nobleman*," Arnold barked, as if he didn't hear Papa speak. "He'll think we're insolent inferiors trying to undermine him."

Seeing that Arnold was not to be convinced, my father gave a curt nod. "I understand if you want nothing to do with it; still, I must make the attempt. I'll invite Lafayette to dine tonight. You're welcome, too. Betsy, come along."

I should've nodded and meekly followed my father out. But I'd taken what Arnold said very much to heart. The army was, officially, no longer my father's responsibility or duty. There was a good argument to be made that he should simply return to his plantation and pull the gate closed until the war was over. Instead, he was taking what seemed to me a large risk. For a man under suspicion of treason and neglect of duty to speak against the new general's plans for attacking the enemy . . .

If this Frenchman must be set straight about the folly of marching in winter, it would be better for Arnold to do it. The Hero of Saratoga would risk much less.

*Betsy's good with the soldiers*, Papa had said. *Arnold likes her.*

That was true, in a fashion. Arnold had taken a liking to me—not, as my mother might have hoped, for any feminine charm—but for the same reason that most soldiers liked me; having spent most of my childhood tromping about the frontier, I carried myself with just enough boyishness to put them at ease. All the doctors complained that the thirty-six-year-old Arnold was a fractious patient, but I'd once helped to distract him from his pain with a game of backgammon. And I suddenly felt certain that Papa had taken me along with him to help convince Arnold to attend what might be the most important dinner of the war.

Because if we couldn't stop this doomed winter campaign, all the soldiers I'd helped stitch back together in autumn might be dead by spring.

"Oh, but General Arnold," I rushed to say, "I'd be so disappointed to miss you at dinner. I haven't had a good game in ages, and you did promise me a rematch, sir." Arnold's scowl lifted only a bit, and I wished I knew what else I could say to convince him. I'd never learned the art of wrapping a lock of hair around my fingertip and flashing my eyes at a man. That was the province of my sisters. But emboldened by what I took for encouragement in Papa's eyes, I quite shamelessly added, "And my sister Peggy has been asking after you."

The bachelor broke into a slow toothy grin. "Miss Peggy asked after me?"

Of course, my sister Peggy asked after every handsome soldier with the same interest and constancy she asked about ribbons, hats, and hair combs. But I nodded.

And Arnold seemed intrigued. "All right, then. I hate to disappoint a lady. But I fear Lafayette will not accept the invitation and we'll dine alone."

A happenstance I fretted about on the ride—which was mercifully short, given the difficulty Arnold's injury gave him in staying upon his mount—through our greatly disordered town.

Before the war, winter in Albany had been a thing of enchantment. Pristine snow-covered hills sloped gently to a frozen river, where skaters had frolicked amongst sleds and sleighs. And up from the river stood a cluster of about three hundred Gothic New Netherlander houses, their windows frosted and glistening icicles ornamenting the gables that faced the neatly kept streets.

But our once bucolic paths were now trodden to slushy brown mud, with milk cows roaming the streets for want of a pasture, and we were desperate for everything: meat, money, firewood, doctors. The circumstances were so dire that only a selfish or sadistic commander would force these soldiers to march.

And I feared this young upstart Lafayette might be both.

We'd scarcely arrived at the barracks when a commotion erupted from the direction of the river. I turned to see a procession of sleighs carrying soldiers, their white infantry uniforms embroidered with the fleur-de-lis of French heraldry. But at their head, wearing American buff and blue, rode a lanky young officer, borne upon a majestic mount like a conquering Caesar.

*This must be Lafayette,* I thought. And I didn't know whether to laugh or weep at the ridiculous sight of a baby-faced general who'd apparently traversed a wilderness in rain and snow, all while properly powdered and ornamented with gold braid and dainty lace. I confess that my first glimpse of him with one hand upon his hip, the other upon his sword in martial pose, was enough to convince me that he was exactly the young fool that Benedict Arnold supposed him to be.

But when my father moved forward to make introductions, Lafayette seemed to know him already, and snapped off a very correct salute. "Major Général Schuyler."

The respectfulness softened me a little.

When Lafayette dismounted and greeted General Arnold as well, Papa said, "I present to you my second-eldest daughter, Elizabeth."

Given the increasingly rigid revolutionary sentiment at the time, I was uncertain if I should curtsy to a nobleman like Lafayette lest I be thought a secret Tory. Before I could decide, Lafayette took my hand and pressed upon it an audible kiss. "*Enchanté,* Mademoiselle Schuyler. I am Marie-Joseph-Paul-Yves-Roch-Gilbert du Motier, the Marquis de Lafayette." My eyes must have widened because Lafayette laughed and added, "It is not my fault, all these names. I was baptized like a Spaniard, with the name of every conceivable saint who might offer me protection on the battlefield so that I might be invincible."

I could not help but smile at Lafayette's jest, though I disliked the word *invincible*. I'd known too many soldiers who thought themselves invincible in this war and now found themselves moldering in graves. And if Papa couldn't talk sense to this Frenchman, he was going to put many more into the ground besides.

Before Lafayette even inquired about quarters for his half-frozen men—or meeting the mayor who was, no doubt, scurrying out of his house now at the surprise arrival—he asked my father, "Report to me, please, the conditions of the forces here at Albany and their readiness for a winter campaign."

This was the news that we wished to broach slowly, over a good meal and in front of a warm fire, with Arnold vouching for all Papa had to say. But the Frenchman was already demanding a report, and looking to Papa to give it. Oh, how I *cringed* to see my father make *a report* to Lafayette, a now superior officer, one much his junior in age, and a foreigner at that!

Still, the important thing was that the Frenchman heard the truth. Not enough gunpowder, muskets, or bullets. Too few provisions of every kind. Men without shoes, without coats, without medicines. It was an army that could scarcely defend the river, much less mount an invasion.

Lafayette listened to all this with a half-lidded, nearly *insolent* gaze. It seemed to me that he didn't believe my father, or perhaps didn't wish to believe him. And rather than see Papa subjected to the further indignity of being dismissed, I was now eager to go.

Pretending at a chill I didn't feel, I rubbed my hands together. "I'm quite cold, Papa."

Knowing me to have the hardiest constitution of all his daughters, my father glanced at me with surprise, then back at Lafayette. "I should very much like to discuss this further, sir.

I extend my hospitality to you and your officers for dinner this evening. And with that, General Lafayette, I take my daughter and my leave."

But Lafayette's gaze skimmed over the encampment of miserable soldiers, and he actually dared to arrest my father's movement with a gloved hand tight upon his elbow. "I cannot let you go, Schuyler. For I see now that I am betrayed."

# Chapter Three

W HAT IS THIS hell of blunders, madness, and deception
I find myself involved in?" Lafayette shouted, having
herded us into a large tent he commandeered in the
field next to the barracks.

The Frenchman removed his hat, revealing a prominent forehead, and drew my father and a hobbling Arnold toward the
back, where they congregated around a table. Meanwhile I was
left to warm myself near a small camp stove, quite anxious about
the marquis's demeanor.

Lafayette gesticulated wildly, shouting in French—a language
I didn't know well—and imperfect English. "It was promised me
three thousand troops fit to separate Canada from Great Britain
and make her our fourteenth state. Instead, I find disarray."

*This is not my father's fault,* I thought. And even if our soldiers
had been in perfect order and well equipped, only a madman
would think to assault Canada in winter. It had already been
tried before and failed miserably.

Even I knew that, and I was no soldier.

I wasn't impressed or overawed by Lafayette's titles, or wealth,
or ridiculously long list of names. He didn't know our country,
our winters, or our river. He was too young and inexperienced to
know better, and I wanted desperately to say so.

"Please don't be alarmed, Miss Schuyler," a young officer whispered as he joined me near the stove, busying himself warming a pot of coffee. "General Lafayette—well—he can be . . . most passionate in his moods."

The fellow attempting to soothe me was a tall, hulking soldier, with gray eyes and a dimple in his chin just like mine. He tilted his head in a quick bow beneath his frosty tricorn hat, then returned to the stove and courteously poured me a cup. "My apologies, miss," he drawled. "It seems to be the dregs without sugar. In fact, I'm not even entirely sure it *is* coffee. But it's all we have."

I took the steaming tin cup warily as my father stood before a seething Lafayette and Arnold gingerly lowered himself into a camp chair, extending his injured leg. My drink was horribly bitter, but if it was good enough for our soldiers, I would just have to choke it down. "I appreciate it just the same, Major . . ."

"Monroe," he whispered with the kind of shy, blushing smile that men usually gave my sisters, never me. "Major James Monroe."

In spite of our situation, I found myself smiling a little, too. And under my breath, I said, "Have you served Lafayette long, Major Monroe?"

"Not precisely. I'm only here in my capacity as an aide to General Stirling, sent to deliver some confidential missives. It was a happy coincidence that he could send someone to accompany the French who knew the land, the language, and, well, Lafayette."

"How did you come to know our lands?"

"I served in the Hudson Highlands last year."

"And French?" I asked.

"My family is French Huguenot stock."

I sipped at the coffee and tried not to make a face. "And Lafayette?"

"I was with him when he took a bullet at the Battle of the Brandywine." Monroe smiled at a memory that should have made him frown. "He fell almost at my feet but somehow got up again to lead his men to safety. I stayed with him that night while the doctor tended him. So I know Lafayette is somewhat . . . irregular . . . but I think you'll find that he's brave and fair-minded."

Eyeing Lafayette, who was still gesticulating wildly at my father to articulate some point, I was not much reassured by Monroe's faith. A frigid wind gusted through the tent's flap, and when the major saw me shiver—this time without exaggeration—he removed his own coat and wrapped it around my shoulders. It was a small gesture, one I should have absolutely refused, since he'd already ridden so far in the cold, but one so gallant that I was charmed.

It's strange now, after all these years, to think how easily I was won over by James Monroe's soft southern accent and courteous manner. Stranger still to realize that if I'd been told in that moment that one of the men in that tent would betray us, another would become my enemy, and a third would win my heart forever—I not only wouldn't have believed it but would have guessed wrong as to which man on every score.

Thumping his fist on the table, Lafayette shouted, "This makes me wish I had never set foot in America or thought of an American war! All the continent knows where I am and what I am sent for. That I am to lead a great northern army. The world now has their eyes fixed on me. If I abort this campaign, men will have a right to *laugh* at me."

At this, my father's patience came to an end, and he delivered a stiff, cold defense. "I will remind you, General Lafayette, it was not my decision to send you here. I have been against it from the start."

Lafayette tilted his head in apparent confusion. "*Oui, oui.* But of course." He waved a hand. "That is what I am saying, my dear *Général* Schuyler. I have read your reports. I have seen what you have been forced to endure. I wish to take into my confidence you and General Arnold. Men loyal to Washington. Men I can trust."

I was so surprised at Lafayette's words that I nearly spilled what remained in my cup. My father appeared equally surprised and unsure how to react.

"In coming here," Lafayette explained, "I go very slowly, sometimes pierced by rain, sometimes covered with snow, and not thinking many handsome thoughts about the projected incursion into Canada. I think now this is a scheme to have me out of the way."

Papa took a moment to recover.

Benedict Arnold was quicker. "A scheme?"

"This plan is too stupid to be anything else," the marquis insisted. "I have seen such machinations in a royal court. It is an unmistakable pattern, no?" When no one answered, Lafayette went on, "It is a plot against Washington or to replace him. You cannot strike a powerful man until you first remove his allies. This is why his rivals must discredit you, Schuyler. And it is why they send me to perish on some icy ledge."

Even with all the plotting against Papa, I was loath to believe anything so diabolical could have been envisioned. But Lafayette was a nobleman from the most sophisticated court in the world, and possibly wiser in the ways of backstabbing politics than any of us.

So I believed him when he said, "Without Washington, there is nobody who could keep the army and the revolution for six months. We must give him a victory to bring back to the Board of War. If not in Canada, then somewhere else."

Papa agreed, renewing his invitation to dinner where a plan could be devised with the other officers. Lafayette accepted this invitation, but cautioned against speaking too freely, even with the others in his entourage, explaining why he'd taken us into the privacy of the tent in the first place. "I wish for the happiness and liberty of this country, but now I fear that she could be lost by her own sons. My friends, I fear a traitor amongst us."

～⁓

*You know Monroe to be a man of honor,*
*a sensible man, and a soldier.*
—LIEUTENANT COLONEL ALEXANDER HAMILTON
TO LIEUTENANT COLONEL JOHN LAURENS

We'd endured British officers in our house, but now we made ready to *welcome* the French.

"I worried Mama wouldn't leave us time to *dress*," Peggy complained, throwing herself down upon the damasked canopied bed we shared.

For our mother had not been warned to expect guests—much less a French general and twenty officers. If my father had a blind spot, it was his assumption that my mother was always ready to graciously entertain at a moment's notice. Even when noticeably pregnant, as she was now. Papa had, unwittingly, thrown her into a frenzy of preparation. With keys jingling at her hip, she marched from kitchen to larder to washhouse and back again, issuing orders to the servants and to us until the very last moment.

While I hurried to dress, Peggy propped herself up on her elbows to ask, "Are any of these French officers handsome, Betsy? Because if not, I'll wear my old flowered frock and leave my best brocaded gown for a better occasion."

"Wear the brocade." Then, a little guiltily, I added, "And please sit next to Benedict Arnold tonight."

Peggy groaned. "Why can't *you*? I'd rather sit near someone who isn't twice my age."

I dared not meet her eyes, especially as I scarcely acknowledged to myself that I wished to sit beside Major Monroe. Slipping into dainty blue heels with bright rose ribbons, I confessed, "I told Arnold that you asked after him."

"I only asked after his recovery," Peggy grumbled, rising from the bed so that Jenny could brush her curls up into a tall coiffure.

"Well, don't say anything to him about his slow recovery or his leg," I told her, because Peggy was the sort who needed to be told such things. Sometimes more than once. "Arnold is very sensitive."

Peggy merely shrugged in answer.

Fastening the blue paste earbobs, I was reminded again of my older sister. "We've still had no letter from Angelica in Boston . . ."

Sighing, Peggy nodded. "I suppose someday we'll become accustomed to not having word from her."

I didn't think so. I could never add up all the ways in which our painful separation imposed its scars on me. A part of me felt guilty for feeling this way when I had yet another sister at my side, but I sometimes thought I could never be happy without Angelica's protectiveness and the way she'd made me feel a needed part of her schemes. For as long as I could remember, we'd had a bond based on sharing confidences and sisterly advice. But my relationship with Peggy had never run as deep. I had *fun* with Peggy, and she made me laugh. But without Angelica I was left to figure out who I was—as a woman and a sister.

And since her elopement, I'd begun to think of myself differently.

No longer the middle sister, trying to mimic and falling short. Now, as the eldest daughter in the household, I felt a greater responsibility and confidence. So I pushed away the notion that the dazzling jewelry didn't suit me and made for my father's table.

Downstairs, beneath the chandelier and gilded portraits of my ancestors, Lafayette supped at one end of the glittering table next to my father. My mother presided at the other end near Baron de Kalb. Peggy squeezed between General Arnold and Major Monroe, which led to the happy circumstance of a space next to the latter for me.

It was surprisingly restorative to have *friendly* soldiers again in our home, and I listened intently for anything else Lafayette might reveal either about a plot against Washington or a suspected traitor amongst us. My attentions were so riveted on the Frenchman, in fact, that Peggy felt the need to twit me. "I thought perhaps a certain British Lieutenant André had already captured your affection," she whispered. "Or have you finally set your cap for a French nobleman?"

I forced down a swallow to keep from choking on my buttered bread and embarrassment. If she'd been closer, I'd have kicked her beneath the table. As Major Monroe was sitting between us, he only stopped shoveling food into his mouth long enough to interject, "Alas, the marquis already has a wife. I'm afraid you ladies will have to aim a little lower."

Peggy laughed. "To you?"

Reluctantly slowing his efforts to wolf down what might have been the first good meal he'd had in ages, Monroe blushed. "That would be more than *a little* lower. When it comes to marriage prospects, from the marquis to me, is a drop from a cliff."

I smiled at the major's self-deprecating nature.

Meanwhile, Peggy mused, "Lafayette is so young to be a general . . ."

"A year older than me," Monroe replied, loyally. "And in any case, I think we're better off under rising young officers than we are under Granny Gates."

*Granny Gates!* It was a highly insubordinate thing for a junior officer to say of a general. We should have upbraided Monroe for it. And yet I don't think he could have found any words that would have sounded sweeter to the daughters of Philip Schuyler.

I liked Monroe. I liked him very much. And that was even before Prince served our dessert course, when I noticed Monroe wincing as he rubbed at his shoulder.

"Are you injured, Major?" I asked.

"I was. It's all healed up now."

"Whatever happened to you?" Peggy batted her eyelashes at him.

Monroe flushed. "I was foolish enough to get myself shot at the Battle of Trenton."

We'd read newspaper accounts of that battle, and Peggy all but squealed. "Are you the one who seized the cannon shouting *Victory or Death*?"

With endearing humility, Monroe swirled a silver fork upon Mama's floral china plate. "Well, I don't remember what I shouted. All I heard was the whiz of a ball as it grazed my chest."

Now this was entirely too much humility. "*Grazed!*" I exclaimed. "Why, I read that it hit an artery and blood bubbled up like a geyser through your uniform. Or wasn't that you?"

Peggy's pallor turned a little sickly green at my vivid description and Monroe's eyebrow shot up, as if he couldn't fathom that a lady might say such a thing at the dinner table. He stammered, "That—that was me . . ."

I started to explain that I took a keen interest in medicine but was saved from myself when Peggy raised a glass, as if it were proper for her to propose a toast. "To the Hero of Trenton!"

I started to raise my glass, but in catching the darkening jealous gaze of Benedict Arnold, I quickly added, "And the Hero of Saratoga!"

Mama frowned at our antics from her end of the table. But from the other, Lafayette raised his glass, too. "While we remember our worthy brothers-in-arms, I toast Mrs. General Schuyler, our gracious hostess, whose husband must soon be acquitted of these ridiculous charges made by stupid men who, without knowing a single word about war, undertake to judge."

A more temperate man might have hedged his support, but Lafayette threw in for my father with his whole heart. And it thrilled me even as I looked round the table for those who might disagree.

My father nodded gratefully, as if humbled.

Then Lafayette stood and addressed me and Peggy. "Ladies, I am sad to abandon you now so I may hear wise advice from your papa and General Arnold."

With that, the servants cleared the plates and the most trusted senior officers closeted themselves away. Monroe was too junior to join them, so while Mama entertained the Frenchmen, we took Monroe into the blue parlor, where Peggy kept refilling his wineglass and I bested him in a ferocious game of backgammon.

"I *declare*, Miss Schuyler," Monroe drawled in defeat, his accent stronger the more wine he drank. "You take advantage! But I suppose I ought not feel unmanned by a game of *chance*. Who taught you to play?"

Still holding the dice, I boasted, "Dr. Franklin taught me when he visited to treat with the Six Nations. Besides, backgammon is only partly a game of chance. It is also a game of math and perseverance. You're forced to learn patterns and choose the best move, even if it is only a choice between evils."

Monroe dropped his gaze. "Is it in the nature of all New York belles to deprive a man of even his fig leaf?"

I blushed, because I knew what a fig leaf was meant to cover. Because Monroe was the first gentleman, since Lieutenant André had visited, who seemed to prefer talking to me than to flirting with my sisters. And because I believed he was calling me a *belle*. Pretending as if this were not a rare compliment, I asked, "Are we New York belles so very trying to your Virginian sensibilities, Major Monroe?"

He had the temerity to pause in thinking about it. "Any trial is compensated for how you ladies keep me from missing home. After all, if a man is so stupidly insensible of a belle's charms as to devote his attention to an absent ideal, she cannot receive a higher insult."

"I shall not be insulted if you pine for home." To prove it, I asked, "What do you miss most about your Virginia?"

I thought he'd mention his family or farmland or horses—or really, just about anything other than what he actually said. "My mammy's waffles, hot from the fire, slathered in melting butter."

I laughed, expecting that Peggy would laugh, too, when I realized that she'd somehow grown bored and left us alone. She'd later tell me that she thought Monroe a bit too unpolished and simple for her tastes. But he seemed to me as a still part of the river, where it sometimes runs deepest.

And he confirmed that impression when he confided, "As much as I miss home, I am curious about the world, and wish to see as much of it as I can."

"We're kindred spirits, then. As a girl, I used to gaze westward at the horizon with a strange yearning, wondering how far the land went, imagining what it would be like to see and explore everything."

He eyed me with curiosity. "That seems an unusual yearning for a belle."

I flushed, much less pleased to be described as a *belle* now. "Not for one who has come of age at the frontier."

"Albany is hardly the frontier," he said, with an indulgent smile. "At least, not compared to where I grew up."

"I'm speaking of Saratoga," I argued. "Before the war, that's where I felt most at home."

Our home at Saratoga had always seemed to be a mysterious gateway to a world I could scarcely fathom and longed to explore. I'd climb rocks and wade in creeks, and come back late with wildflowers in my hair, all brown from the sun. And Papa would tease that perhaps when my mother left me hanging in a cradleboard from that tree, I'd been switched with an Indian child.

When I told Monroe as much, he chuckled. "And *were* you switched? You can tell me. I'll always keep your secrets."

He leaned closer, and for the first time in my life, a flutter of *real* romantic interest stirred within my breast. Monroe was a patriot. A war hero, even. And possibility sparked between us. "Perhaps I *was* switched," I teased. "But I'd rather you tell me a secret."

"Oh?" he asked, swirling the claret in his glass.

"Do you think there's *really* a conspiracy against General Washington?"

"I know it," Monroe answered, draining his wineglass like a man who preferred beer. "It was within General Stirling's little family that we discovered the evidence."

Rapt, I leaned closer. "Who is the villain?"

"It's a cabal of villains. Inspector General Conway is involved for certain and . . ." Monroe trailed off there, as if aware that perhaps he'd said more than he ought to have.

But I pressed him. "Gates? Is it Gates?"

Monroe peered over his shoulder, then met my gaze and nodded, slowly. "Gates is trying to replace Washington as commander in chief of the military."

"Outrageous. Gates is a scheming bumbler," I hissed, though I knew my father would never approve of my saying so. But it was true. Gates would have lost even the Battle of Saratoga were it not for Benedict Arnold's heroics.

But as indignant as I was at the idea that the New England darling would ever be commander in chief, that wasn't as awful as my other fear. "Is there anyone close enough to Washington to do him harm?" I asked, because two years before there had been a plot to assassinate him and the culprit had been amongst his own bodyguards. And given that Gates had already used rumors of my father's treachery to oust him from command, and seemed willing to condemn Lafayette and the whole Northern Army to an icy death in Canada, what else might he stoop to in clawing his way to the top?

"No chance of that," Monroe assured me. "Not since Colonel Hamilton joined Washington's family as aide-de-camp. My good friend Hamilton is too cunning to let an assassin get close again. He would sniff it out at a mile."

I knew the name *Hamilton* already, of course.

We'd all learned about Alexander Hamilton's military exploits in the gazettes we read each morning at the breakfast table. In fact, when my sisters and I were away visiting our Livingston relations, Hamilton had even stopped to see my father—briefly—in passing through Albany.

But my clearest memory of ever hearing Hamilton's name was from the mouth of James Monroe. And spoken so fondly, too.

It *hurts* now to remember how fondly.

"It's the politicking in Congress and the Board of War that will do General Washington in," Monroe said, with more shrewdness than I might have expected. "Lafayette is right. We need to give Washington a win to bring back to Congress—even a symbolic one. Or Gates will get command and there goes the war."

At length, as if to fight off the effects of a large meal and the lateness of the hour, Monroe stood and shook himself like a giant hound caught in the rain. And when I saw him rub again at his shoulder, I asked, "Should it still hurt you?"

"Don't know," he replied. "The bullet lodged in my shoulder just likes to remind me of its presence sometimes."

"I know a little nursing. If you should like me to—"

"Oh, no, miss," Monroe said, nearly tripping over my mother's lace-covered sideboard table in his hurry to back away, as if I'd suggested something very untoward.

I'd only meant to offer some of the precious willow bark powder that Mama kept as a remedy for pain, but Monroe almost seemed to think I meant to undress him. "I wouldn't hazard being shot again. By your father this time."

*Virginians are preposterous creatures,* I thought for the first, but not the last, time. Thankfully, the farce was brought to an end because Lafayette emerged from my father's study, and the officers made ready to take their leave. I was sorry to see them go, especially because I did not wish to leave Major Monroe with the impression I was a coquette.

But when Lafayette came into the parlor to retrieve Monroe and say farewell, he noticed a *wampum* belt upon a table with Papa's outgoing parcels and letters, and tilted his head in apparent curiosity. "Mademoiselle Schuyler, your papa says you have accompanied him to treaty conventions with the Six Nations. Can you tell me of this?"

Flattered that Lafayette wished for *me* to explain it, I answered, "It's a wampum belt; they served as a form of money, once." At least until my Dutch ancestors began manufacturing *wampum* in such quantity as to make it worthless as currency. "Taken by themselves, the beads are merely white, purple, and black shells, sanded and drilled. But string them together and they can tell a story, seal a treaty, or serve as a badge of authority."

If you knew the patterns and the symbols. And I did, having

learned them at a very young age from the native women who bartered with Mama at the back door of our Saratoga house, and with whose daughters I sometimes played in their nearby village.

"What message does *this* belt convey?" Lafayette asked, peering at me from the corner of his eye.

"It's an invitation." For though Papa was no longer in command of an army, he'd long served as Indian commissioner, an important position he still held. "My father arranged to have this *wampum* belt and others to be delivered throughout Iroquoia to call for a meeting of the Iroquois Confederacy."

The young marquis seemed enthralled. "Do you know why?"

We could never emphasize enough to outsiders that the Iroquois were *not* to be confused with other Indians. The People of the Longhouse were a democratic nation, and a powerful one, represented by statesmen who had skillfully played the British and the French against one another for decades. "Because if we can convince the Six Nations to remain neutral, we'll deprive the British of their Indian guides and war bands."

Lafayette's smile turned sly. "May I?" he asked, and when I nodded, he took up the belt to inspect it. "These symbols, do you know what they mean?"

"Well that," I said pointing, "that is the tree of the Onondoga nation—the Keepers of the Central Fire, the custodians of records."

"And this?" Lafayette traced an open rectangle.

"The Oneida," I said, overcome by the sudden impression that he was testing me like a schoolmaster, and had been doing so since the start of the conversation. "People of the Standing Stone. They're friendly to us."

"Your father has invited me to go with him to Johnstown for a conference with the Six Nations."

I saw my father's strategy at once, and I warmed with hope. Despite the Six Nations' vow to remain neutral, many of them had sided and fought with the British against us. We couldn't hope to get them to join us instead, but in light of our victory at Saratoga, there might now be an opportunity to make them honor their vow.

*If* they would come to a meeting.

General Gates had turned a deaf ear when Papa urged him to pursue a diplomatic course with the Iroquois. There was no glory in that for Gates. But, thus far, the marquis had proved to be as fair-minded as Major Monroe claimed. Maybe we could convince *him.*

Iroquois neutrality could change everything. It could help win the war.

And it might be just the victory Washington needed.

"I hope you'll accept Papa's invitation to go," I said, because if Lafayette presided over the treaty convention, the Six Nations might attend for that reason alone.

After all, Lafayette had one thing Papa did not. He had the King of France behind him.

"Indeed, I will go, *mademoiselle,*" he said. "But given your knowledge, perhaps you should go, too."

"*Yes,*" I said, before my mother could even lift a disapproving brow. Before, even, I could discern whether or not it was an invitation made in earnest or jest. I knew only that it was the moment, in all my restlessness, I had pined for. And I was sure my father would understand that restless longing. "Oh, yes, I intend to go."

Angelica was not the only Schuyler daughter, after all, who could forge her own path.

# Chapter Four

WE WERE HEADED into Iroquoia.

The snows were still so deep we were obliged to go by horse-drawn sleigh, my father leading the way beneath gnarled tree branches that bowed, encased in glistening ice. Our slow pace frustrated the hard-charging Lafayette, who was eager to rendezvous with the Iroquois Confederacy.

And I was nearly as impatient, for so much was at stake—not just the Indians' neutrality, but the war itself. I'd once asked myself how a daughter could make a difference. Now I might have the opportunity. Though I'd attended Indian conferences before, never one like this—in the company of soldiers, as if I, too, were a warrior in a fight I believed in.

Bundled in a fur cloak, I rode nestled beside Major Monroe, who I suspected had been tasked to watch over me. "Are you warm enough, Miss Schuyler?"

It was the fourth time he'd asked.

"I am. Thank you, Major. Are you always so attentive?"

I didn't even have to look at him to know he was blushing. "I try to be attentive to ladies, who are so delicate."

This made me laugh, because he said it through chattering teeth. "I daresay the weather seems to go harder on Virginians. Perhaps I should be the one to offer you my coat this time?"

I regretted pricking at his pride because he scolded, "Ladies of Virginia would not go out in this weather. Nor would their fathers condone their presence on such an adventure . . ."

I couldn't tell if Monroe was jesting or if he truly disapproved. My father had never discouraged my sisters and I from taking an active part in his affairs; before she eloped, Angelica had dutifully sent Papa military intelligence reports from Albany, and I had sometimes accompanied him on his travels. I would later learn that the daughters of New Netherlanders expected to enjoy a bit more independence than other American women, but at the time it seemed only natural. "Why shouldn't he condone it? I have lived alongside the Six Nations all my life." When that didn't seem to convince him, I added, "Besides, when I was thirteen, I was adopted by the Iroquois."

At that last remark, Monroe's shy smile disappeared. Beneath his dark wavy hair, his gray eyes went wide and he looked so startled that I feared he might fall out of the sleigh. "Whatever can you mean? You're telling fibbery."

"You insult me, sir," I cried, like a man ready to challenge him to a duel. Laughing, I explained, "It's true. I remember well how all the chiefs, clan mothers, and greatest warriors, row after row, stood silently around an open space where green grass gleamed." Major Monroe now seemed enraptured, so I continued. "I dressed in white and they in the splendor of war paint. And I held tight onto my father's hand when, with much pomp and ceremony, the chieftains put their hands upon my head, commented on my black eyes, and gave me an Indian name." I pronounced the name in their language. "It means 'One-of-us.'"

Though Monroe could not seem to decide if he ought to be awed or horrified, Lafayette, riding beside the sleigh, turned to marvel. "Then, *mademoiselle*, you know not only the symbols but the language of the Iroquois League?"

"Some." I nodded, for I'd been raised in a home where Dutch, English, and Mohawk were all spoken.

Lafayette rubbed at his reddened nose. "Ah! We have the company of a pretty lady and the blessing of her knowledge. Pity, Monroe, you must leave us soon."

Monroe had come with us as far as he could. Having discharged his duties in Albany, he felt bound to return to winter headquarters at Valley Forge. But as we reached the road where he would take his leave of us, Monroe didn't seem to want to go.

It was hard to credit that such a big strong soldier could be so shy, but as he prepared to leave, Monroe reddened to the tips of his ears and stammered. "D-do you think your father would find it permissible, Miss Schuyler, for me to write to you?"

Was it such an improper thing for Virginians to correspond with a lady friend without her father's permission? Or did he mean to imply the beginnings of a courtship? I wasn't sure, but I am more apt now to think it was merely an attempt at gallantry owing to the antiquated peculiarities of James Monroe. Or maybe to his southern charm. Perhaps they were one and the same.

In any case, what I said was, "Well, what if I were to say you have my permission, sir? And that's all you need."

He gawped a bit at my brashness, and the fact that I'd taken up the reins of the sleigh, as if I meant to drive it. Which I *had* intended, until I realized he might think it unladylike.

It seemed to me as if we New Yorkers were too aristocratic for the New Englanders, and too bold for the Virginians, which made me wonder how we'd all get along together if we weren't forced to it by our war with the king.

I parted with Monroe affectionately, though not nearly as affectionately as Lafayette did. The Frenchman hugged Monroe and kissed him upon both cheeks again and again, until the major finally seemed like a squirming cat eager to get away.

Then we continued westward onto Johnstown.

When the marquis first said that the world's eyes were upon him, it seemed a self-important boast, but he was already known—or at least known *of*—by the chieftains. And because he was a Frenchman, we were very well received where the Iroquois had gathered for the conference along the banks of the Mohawk River.

Hair streaked with feathers, their ears cut open, jewels dangling from their noses, their tattoos and painted designs visible beneath the beaded skins they wore, the old men smoked pipes and talked about politics. And so did the women . . .

This did not give Lafayette pause. "If you could see the salons in Paris, the women are the same! Even in my own family. Perhaps *especially* the women of my family."

With that, the Frenchman waded into the crowds and showered them with little gifts. Mirrors, rum, brandy, and shining gold coins—louis d'or. And the Iroquois took to him, just as we were beginning to take to him.

It was the same generosity he'd shown our soldiers in Albany. There, and with his own personal funds, he'd bought food, armaments, and clothing for the men. I would later learn that Lafayette spent more than twelve thousand dollars—an even more outrageous sum then than it is now. He'd been able to do for our soldiers what Congress could not. He put shirts on their backs, shoes on their feet, and beef in their bellies. And when he began drilling soldiers, they actually obeyed him, calling him *the soldier's friend*. As the daughter of Philip Schuyler, I might have resentfully said it was because he *bought* their loyalty. But, in truth, I admired the sincerity with which the Frenchman approached his dealings. No one could ever accuse the marquis of being unpretentious, but his enthusiasm and optimism were infectious.

Even amongst the Six Nations. And I might've been more sure of the success of our mission were it not for the fact that the most distinguished Mohawk had not responded to the messengers with the *wampum* belts. No Seneca. Next to no Cayuga. Only a hundred Onondaga. Disappointed and alarmed, I said to my father, "They won't even meet with us."

Papa squeezed my hand. "There are nearly eight hundred, Betsy. It'll be enough for word to get to the others."

Finally, the ceremony commenced on the common; the Indians arranged themselves in a circle by nation and clan, sitting on the ground upon blankets and furs, men on one side, women on the other, chairs left for the commissioners, and for me.

In the center, a large pot of meat broth boiled away over a fire. And as a pledge of sincerity, three elderly chiefs delivered to Papa and Lafayette a belt of *wampum* much more intricate than any I'd seen before, curiously worked with porcupine quills, and handsomely painted.

When it was my father's turn to speak, he didn't dissemble. He merely explained that the King of England was an ocean away and would abandon his Iroquois allies when the Americans won this war. That if the Six Nations didn't bury their war ax now, they'd soon find themselves facing a new American nation that would treat them as enemies.

I worried that he would press them too hard, but those who sat nearest to the fire—the Oneida and the Tuscarora—my father praised for maintaining the neutrality they'd once promised. And he pledged our friendship and protection.

That was all he was permitted to say for the time being. These tawny-skinned people of the longhouse abided by strict rules and rituals, and it was now time to dance.

An Oneida clan mother named Two Kettles Together approached me, bells in hand. "Are you not One-of-us?"

She was one of those who had adopted me into the Six Nations. And grinning that she'd remembered me after all these years, I readily fastened the bells on my ankles.

"I am so happy to see you," I said, introducing her to Lafayette as a warrior in her own right, who had fought at Oriskany. Armed with two pistols, she'd reloaded her husband's weapons when he—wounded—couldn't do it for himself.

"Like Joan de Arc!" Lafayette exclaimed, in warm greeting. "A French warrior woman. I have an ancestor who fought beside her. Perhaps one day, you should fight beside me."

"If you are lucky," Two Kettles Together said with a shrewd

little smile, before taking my hand and pulling me into the dance, where the Indians united by hands and jumped round the pot that hung over the fire, animated by the music of a small drum. One of the chiefs likewise took Lafayette by the hand and danced him round the circle, too. Another blackened Papa's face with grease from a pot. Whether this was a trick to excite a laugh, or a part of their actual national ceremony, I didn't know.

But my very dignified father did not like it.

And yet, Lafayette insisted he must *also* have his face greased!

Apparently charmed by his boisterous participation, the Iroquois adopted Lafayette, too, with a new name. *Kayewla. Fearsome horseman.*

I knew this was partly because they liked him and mostly because he was a representative of France. Too many of our fellow Americans dismissed the sons of the forest as simple savages, but we who lived so near to the Six Nations knew better. They were not to be trifled with or tricked. Other Indians lived in fear and dread of them. What the Six Nations wanted was a balance of power in the region. If they couldn't have it with the King of England, they'd seek it with the King of France, with the Marquis de Lafayette as the conduit.

And because I was hopeful that peace between our peoples could be achieved, I stayed late with the women, who danced, ate soup, and drank rum. I was quiet, listening to those who didn't realize I understood their language enough to overhear something not meant for my ears.

Two Onondaga women complained of going through the motions of this treaty convention. It was a sham, they said, meant only to raise our hopes. I pretended at fascination with the dance, softly clapping my hands. Only when it would draw no notice did I make ready to return to Papa's side and warn him.

But when Two Kettles Together rose to walk with me, I feared she knew that I understood. And for a fleeting moment, I felt in the gravest danger of my life.

A feeling that lessened only a little when she whispered, "You know now that the Onondaga cannot be trusted. Tell your company to be on its guard. I've heard talk of a spy in the neighborhood who has eyes on your father and, especially, your Frenchman."

Sweat beaded upon my nape as I remembered at least two prior occasions when the British sent agents to kidnap or assassinate my father. With damp palms, I squinted in the dim light of the fire, daring a glance at the faces around it, suspicious and mistrustful of everyone. I suppose Papa would be flattered to know he was, even stripped of command, still in their sights. But the marquis was the more valuable prize. "Do they mean to kill him?"

"I don't know the plan," she said. "Only that the British have put a target on his back, and the arrow man is near . . ."

"MADEMOISELLE, YOU ARE a most excellent patriot," Lafayette said when I returned to the safety of Johnston Hall, where I reported everything.

To my surprise, the Frenchman seemed sanguine. "It is good you learn of all this in secret while all eyes were upon your father and me. You have been an essential asset to the cause."

It was flattery—French flattery at that!—and I wanted to believe it was true.

But I was crestfallen at the certain failure of our mission, and worried, too.

"The British aren't the only ones who have spies," Papa said to reassure me. "I can say with confidence that the man they've sent to make trouble is Major Carleton, the nephew of the Canadian Governor. I suspected he was in the area incognito to suborn the Indians who are friendlier to us. Now we have better reason to think so."

I bit my lower lip, thinking it quite a risk for such a prominent British officer and gentleman to take; even if he was not an assassin or kidnapper, if he was caught in disguise he could be hanged as a spy. And perhaps that's what Lafayette had in mind when he said, "I shall offer a reward of *fifty guineas* to anyone who will bring him to me alive." Then, almost as an afterthought, he added, "And since there are Indians who *are* friendly to us, I will offer them, and only them, trading posts and protection."

"But might not attempts to divide them further provoke those who are against us, ending our hopes to get the Six Nations to remain neutral?" I dared to ask.

Lafayette nodded. "If we cannot get neutrality, perhaps we get something better."

At the next day's council, the Indians were in an uproar, all pretense of accord abandoned. For the magnificent chieftain, Grasshopper, of the Oneida, rose to address the warrior class. "By refusing to make peace, you sow the seeds of your own destruction. You have forced us all to terrible choices. Now, instead of being strong as six arrows all together that cannot be broken, we are in splinters!"

Six arrows. The Seneca, Cayuga, Onondaga, Mohawk, Oneida, and Tuscarora. Together, they'd formed a confederacy older than Great Britain.

The chief turned to my father. "The Oneida and Tuscarora will *not* remain neutral." Amidst murmurs and shouts, I nearly gasped as Grasshopper raised his voice over the fray. "We say to our brethren, the Americans, that we, too, are a free people with absolute notions of liberty. And we will *join* your cause and pledge to be buried in the same graves with you or to share in the fruits of your victories and peace."

The impact of the moment resounded in my bones.

I wasn't alone. Lafayette didn't hide his tears as he rose. "This man possesses the dignity of a Roman senator. The philosopher Rousseau speaks truly of man's nobility in his state of nature. For here, as much as any place in America, has taught me that we are, *all of us*, and of right, to be free."

That very day, the Oneida promised to send warriors to join Washington's army at Valley Forge and a clan mother with white corn to help feed the starving soldiers, and teach them how to prepare it so they wouldn't get sick from eating it dry.

We had meant to secure neutrality. Instead, we came away with allies, warriors, and food. Though Papa was wary, Lafayette thought it a triumph. Perhaps not as glorious as victory upon a battlefield, but a triumph that would redound to both Lafayette's and Washington's credit and help win the war.

As for me, I was so stunned by what had taken place that I allowed myself a sip of rum that night at the campfire when Lafayette offered it to me.

And then I coughed on it.

Which brought a guffaw from the Frenchman. "Do you dislike the taste of rum, Mademoiselle Schuyler?"

My eyes watered as I struggled to answer.

He laughed again. "You and I can speak candidly, now that we are kin. *Nous sommes une famille, comme frère et soeur.*"

"Pardon?" I asked, hoarsely.

"We are sister and brother, yes? Having been adopted by the Indians. We are both *savages*, you and me." Lafayette said this word as if it were more glorious than his noble title. But then, as if fearing I didn't understand, he added, "The Iroquois forests are peopled by my friends; to me, the despots of Europe are the true savages." He leaned in with a grin. "After we leave this place, come to Washington's headquarters at Valley Forge with me."

I blinked. "Whatever for?"

"Because you shall have a bevy of admirers. I would even count myself amongst them."

Fearing that the Frenchman, despite being married, meant to press an improper flirtation upon me, I'm afraid I was *quite* tart. "I do not think even with your encouragement that my father would consent for me to become a camp follower."

Lafayette threw up his hands. "*Mon Dieu!* I suggest nothing dishonorable. Men like me, the wilds remind us that when stripped of luxuries and titles, we are all the same but for our *honor*." With that, Lafayette's chin gestured in the direction of my father. "And weary men of honor need to be reminded of what they fight for. Come with me to Washington's camp, *ma chère* Mademoiselle Schuyler. You and your father, who may be safer in a military camp than facing spies and treachery on his own."

I was touched by Lafayette's concern for my father. And just then, across the campfire I spied Two Kettles Together, who went where she pleased, wore what she pleased, did what she pleased, and fought when she pleased. I knew that if it were my choice, I would go with Lafayette. But it was not my choice. "You forget the matter of Papa's court-martial . . ."

"Bah! The stain on your father's name will be lifted soon enough. Now that France is involved, the war will be so swiftly over, you will miss it all if you do not come."

I hoped Lafayette was right that the war would be over swiftly, and when it was finally time for us to part ways, I said, "Farewell, General. I hope to see you again soon."

"You will. I am certain of it."

But in the end, Lafayette was wrong. My father's court-martial didn't take place until autumn. I wouldn't see the eccentric young Frenchman again for another three years.

And even then, the war was far from over.

# Chapter Five

June 1778
Albany

MAMA WAS DANGEROUSLY ill, burning with fever in the confines of her curtained bed, pale and weak as a lamb. Though my father was sometimes afflicted by bilious fevers and gout, my sturdy mother's Dutch constitution had seemed a shield against every ailment.

Every ailment but one.

Childbirth. The most dangerous female ailment of all. And even though none of us spoke the words aloud as my mother tossed upon her fevered bed, we all feared it might claim Mama and her baby, too.

After a difficult delivery, Mama presented my father with a frightfully little infant son. As was the custom, we'd celebrated the birth with sweet pastries and cinnamon caudle, but Mama had been too sick to take part. And now, only weeks later, her milk had dried up.

Because none of our servants were breeding, we had no wet nurse. Nor could I coax the babe to suck cow's, sheep's, or goat's milk from a cloth. As the sickly little thing trembled in my arms, withering by the hour, I felt, for the first time in my life, an *ache* in my breasts to feed a hungry child.

"Betsy," Mama whispered to me, and I looked up from the rocking chair beside her sickbed. Sweat poured from her forehead, and her braid of long black hair had come frayed and lay wild. "If the Lord should take me, I need for you to know something."

Intent upon her every rasping word, I leaned closer, mopped the sweat from her brow with a cool cloth, and wondered if I should fetch the doctor again.

"You can marry," she said. "You needn't. But you mustn't think that you *can't.*"

For her to say such a puzzling thing, I decided that the tincture of saffron, sage, and snakeroot must not have done her any good. "Don't tire yourself with talk," I said, trying to hush her as I patted the baby's back.

But twisting against the sheets, Mama continued, "A son-in-law could be a great blessing to your poor father, who is so . . . harried."

"Just get well, Mama," I said, wondering if she remembered that she already had a son-in-law in Jack Carter, even if he was in faraway Boston with Angelica. "Don't worry about anything else but getting well."

After all, I worried enough for the both of us. Papa had been torn between staying close to my mother in her illness, collecting rents from our tenants, and rebuilding the charred ruins of our mills at Saratoga. Our wealth was in the timber we cut and the flour we milled there. And I knew Mama worried our family fortune would never entirely rebound.

But what she rasped was, "Peggy is quite pretty." My brow furrowed as I tried to follow the workings of her fevered mind. She blinked, as if struggling to scrutinize my face with the honest frankness of our shared Dutch heritage. "But you're pretty *enough,* my dear child."

"Worry not, Mama. I shan't let such praise go to my head." It was so mild a compliment that in the past, I might have taken pleasure in it, knowing it was not false flattery. But even though I'd had no letter from Monroe, our flirtation—and my adventure with the

Marquis de Lafayette—had opened my mind to possibilities for my future I hadn't previously considered. Even as I felt the weight of my responsibilities here, with my family, as never before.

And if my mother should not survive . . . no, I couldn't think of that.

"But if you do marry . . ." Her words trailed off. "You must promise not to run off with some macaroni like Jack Carter."

"Mama! I thought you'd come to like him."

"I do. But oh, to have missed my own daughter's wedding . . ."

"I won't give you such a pain," I promised, trying to soothe her. But my heart ached at the turn of her thoughts, and the fact that a breach between us remained. Moving to sit at the edge of the bed, I asked, "Can't you ever forgive me for helping Angelica to run off?"

Mama reached for my hand and clutched it with a surprising strength. "It's forgiven, my dear child. *Forgiven and forgotten.*"

Blinking back bittersweet tears, I gave a quick nod. But before I could tell her how much it meant to me, she slipped into a fitful sleep.

Then the babe gave a frightening weak cry and I hurried down the stairs, determined to do for him what my mother could not. I found Peggy on the lawn overseeing the littlest children as they played hoops and leapfrog. "Take the baby," I said. "I'm going to get help."

I needed to find a willing woman to take my infant brother to the breast, and I wasn't averse to using our status to secure assistance. Whatever my father's reputation, the Schuylers, the Livingstons, the Van Cortlandts, and the Van Rensselaers were the great families of the region. If I couldn't impress upon the people here, then I would cross the river to Fort Crailo, where my mother was born and raised.

"You're going to *leave*?" Peggy asked, a little panicked. "Mama is too ill to know her own name, the servants are gone, and someone needs to play mistress of the Pastures."

The servants were gone to celebrate Pinkster, she meant.

For Dutch settlers, the springtime holiday was a time for religious services, but for slaves it was a week free from work, a week during which they might travel to nearby plantations to visit family, or dance and sing at one of the festivals in Albany or New York City. Papa had been eager for the arrival of Pinkster, from which his servants usually returned cheerful. But now he feared some might not return at all.

For amongst our slaves that spring had passed sullen looks and dark whispers. From the kitchen, Dinah had sent up only cold dishes. Our dairy maid had the temerity to refuse Papa some trifling request with the cows, and he seemed too bewildered by the incident to have punished her.

I initially attributed the insolence of our people to fear. For *everyone* was fearful. No sooner had the leaves on the trees come to bud, than did four of the Six Nations attack nearby villages and settlements, just as Two Kettles Together had warned. Our slaves might've worried about the Indians, who also kept Negroes in bondage and were said to treat them harshly.

I think now, though, upon more mature reflection, that the people of our plantation must have been weighing their loyalty between us and the British, who offered freedom to runaways. Our slaves must've wondered at men like my father, ready to die for his own freedom, while holding others in bondage.

And they were not wrong to wonder.

In those desperate hours, though, I thought only of the sick little baby. "You'll just have to manage by yourself, Peg," I said, giving her the swaddled infant before bolting for the stable and galloping down the drive, bypassing azalea-festooned festival stalls, dancers, and drummers in town.

I went first to our Livingston relations at the Elm Tree Corner, where I pleaded with an indentured Irish girl who was breeding. But by the time we returned, my infant brother was struggling to breathe, let alone suckle. I'd barely dismounted when the sweet babe, with a head so tiny it fit in my palm, gasped and shuddered and perished in my arms.

In the days thereafter, Papa wrote the baby's name in the family Bible. A carpenter made a tiny pine coffin. My father dug a tiny grave. "*God gives and God takes away; blessed be the name of God,*" Papa said, determined to submit to the Lord's judgment, but Mama was powerfully afflicted, and I'd never felt so terrible about anything.

*God could not wish this,* I thought. Our ancestors' Dutch Reform faith held that much was predestined. But God could not wish helpless babes to die after only a few painful breaths. No *just* God could wish suffering, sickness, slavery, and savagery.

Wasn't that why we were fighting a revolution?

I'd never been a patient girl in church services. I'd read the Bible only indifferently and because my mother insisted. But now, at the grave site of my dead baby brother, hearing clods of earth fall upon the tiny coffin like the sound of knocking, I was struck by the powerful conviction that God put us here to make a better world.

And it is a conviction that has informed the rest of my life.

Though I burned for some heroic deed to accomplish, the uncomfortable realization of maturity was dawning. The grinding toil of duty might not be as glorious as adventures in the wild, but more necessary. To make this world a better place, my family needed to survive this war. And so I applied myself for the first time to the housework I'd always shirked, laundering clothes, feeding chickens, bundling herbs, pickling vegetables, bottling cider, and making soap. And to make sense of any of it occasioned countless trips up and down the stairs to disturb my poor mother's rest.

This was especially so because Dinah, our cook, had not returned from Pinkster. She'd been found in a barn, harbored by a Scotchman, and now marked time in jail as a runaway until Papa could reclaim her. Despite my father's reassurance that he wouldn't punish Dinah harshly, Jenny was beside herself with fear—or perhaps with guilt that she'd not joined her mother in running away. And even after a chastened Dinah returned to our kitchens, tensions on our plantation ran high, with Prince thin-lipped and more insistent upon protocol than ever.

Meanwhile, my father slept scarcely at all that spring and well into autumn.

He'd lost his child, his command, and his honor. For months now, despite his continued service, Congress denied him the opportunity to defend himself against charges of neglect and disloyalty. All while General Gates discounted our reports of devastating raids by the Mohawk, Cayuga, Seneca, and Onondaga.

It wasn't until October—perhaps under my father's subtle threat that he would publish a pamphlet to exonerate himself—that he was finally called upriver for his court-martial.

The verdict came in three days.

> The court having considered the charges against
> Major-general Schuyler, the evidence and his defense, are
> unanimously of opinion that he is NOT GUILTY and
> the court do therefore acquit him with the highest honor.

Sweet vindication! All the sweeter because it helped put an end to talk of replacing Washington. His trusted officers had proved trustworthy. Lafayette had avoided the trap of a disastrous misadventure in Canada and salvaged his reputation by recruiting Indian allies to the cause. My father had been acquitted by an honest court. Our generals and young officers had stood together with Washington.

*Semper Fidelis.*

And I will always believe it was loyalty to the cause over personal ambition that saved us. General Gates was forced to apologize for his role in attempting to undermine Washington and became, himself, the subject of an inquiry. Other conspirators resigned in humiliation. And since Mama was quite nearly recovered, it was a thing I meant to celebrate in high style.

Peggy and I determined to host a party, something to bring cheer and joy back to the Pastures. The little ones thought to make a pie for Papa's return, so we invited friends from our community troop of Blues on a foraging day to pick the last of the season's berries. A group of us ventured into the wilds, singing and joking, as we'd done since we were young.

It was an old Dutch tradition meant for matchmaking. All New Netherlander children were divided from the youngest ages into teams for races and games, outings and house parties. The Blues, the Reds, the Greens. Even in Papa's day, no chaperones were present, which was how, I supposed, my oldest sister had come to be born only a few months after our parents married.

Not that I'd ever dared ask my starchy mother about it.

In any case, amongst our children's troops, Angelica had been our undisputed leader. Never one who enjoyed the outdoors, Peggy had often groused her way through all of our troops' adventures, but Angelica had cheered our Blues in the winter as I skated to victory past one of the Livingston girls. And sang songs as we climbed through the brambles to explore the mist-slick caves along the river. And lolled on the green grass, nose buried in a book while the rest of us stuffed ourselves on a picnic of good bread, butter, and jam.

Every boy of the Blues had wanted to marry Angelica; every girl wanted to be her friend. But they called me Buckskin Betsy, and it was once suggested that I should make a new troop of the so-called strays I was known for collecting. But Angelica never tolerated a mean word to be said against me, and promised that if I left the Blues, she'd leave, too. That had been the end of it.

I'd never forgotten my sister's loyalty. And it made me miss her even more.

But our mood was so celebratory that morning as we set off that even Peggy seemed to enjoy herself. Laughing and teasing, we paddled canoes to get to the berry patch, gathering and eating the sweet berries until fourteen-year-old Stephen Van Rensselaer, the young patroon of Rensselaerswyck, suddenly lifted his hunting rifle with wary eyes on the shoreline. And everyone fell silent.

Except Peggy. "What is it?" she whispered.

"*Indians,*" he said, eyes wild.

My heart thumped a drumbeat as I measured the distance back

to the Pastures, where we might slam the shutters and guard the doors. Alas, they'd come upon us too stealthily. We'd never make it, I thought, when I spotted the Iroquois emerge from the foliage.

I knew them on sight. *Oneida.*

Friendly Iroquois. Not a war-painted party wielding hatchets, but a small delegation of Oneida chieftains dressed in buckskin and moccasins, carrying a haunch of venison. And a tall woman walked with them, a clay pipe between her teeth.

"Two Kettles Together!" I called, my voice shaky with relief. She gave a regal nod of her head, explaining that she was on her way to see my father. And she carried grave news. Though Lafayette's bounty had turned the tables on the spy, we'd never captured Major Carleton. Now he was leading coordinated raids against our settlements. And a separate force of three hundred Indians had skulked through Cherry Valley with two hundred British Rangers, laying waste to everything in their path— including the fortifications Lafayette had authorized to defend our friends. Forty women and children had been butchered, mangled, or scalped—some had their heads, legs, and arms cut off, or the flesh torn from their bones by dogs.

Our Oneida friends had tried to warn us, and for months after the treaty conference, Papa had tried to warn Gates, to no avail. Now that my father had been exonerated, I expected that he would take back his command and lead the army in reprisals. I'd been at his side in Johnstown when, with Lafayette, he promised to treat the Mohawk, the Cayuga, the Seneca, and the Onondaga as enemies if they persisted.

Someone would have to make good on that promise.

For more than a year now, I'd *burned* with a desire to see Papa again in his general's uniform, his honor restored.

But when my father was finally offered back his command of the Northern Army, he refused it.

"Why?" I asked, mortified.

"Because I have been appointed to Congress," he replied.

*Congress.* I supposed it to be a great deal of jabbering. Scarcely anyone paid the men who labored with paper and pen the respect due a major general of the Continental army.

I couldn't see the glory in it. And I couldn't imagine how my father would be content with it, given the abuse he'd already suffered. Not even when he said, "Too few legislators know anything about provisioning an army. They know even less about these territories and the real power of the Six Nations. If they did, they would quake in their boots. So it seems I am needed in Philadelphia."

I wanted to change his mind. How was he to finish rebuilding our fortunes from Philadelphia? How would we provide for the family without completed mills or timber? Shouldn't he be remembered as the great general that he was?

But before I could argue, my mother rested her hand atop his. "Whatever you decide, your family needs nothing but your presence to make us happy. Whether you are called *General* Schuyler or simply Philip Schuyler, *Esquire*."

The warm and grateful way he smiled at her made me bite my tongue.

I have since thought back many times to that moment. Remembering how graciously she accommodated both my father's pride and his sense of duty. The way she convinced him that his family would love and honor him just the same. That there was nothing whatsoever he needed to prove. That he was enough of a husband, a father, and a patriot, in and of himself. That he could be at peace with private honor over public laurels.

And I've wondered why I couldn't accomplish the same when it came to my own husband.

Perhaps it was because the man I married was not born to a great family. He was not secure in his heritage or in himself. It would be easy to blame the wounds that my husband carried that had nothing to do with me. But sometimes, in the dead of night, I wonder if, unlike my mother, I have always carried within *myself* some spark of ambition or expectation that my husband sensed he mustn't disappoint lest he lose my love.

Even if it meant his death . . .

# Chapter Six

February 1780
Morristown, New Jersey

I MET HIM DURING the worst winter anyone could remember, and in the darkest hour of the war, during a year that would see the literal blotting out of the sun and make us wonder if it were the end of days. No one could remember such a winter, so cold that one couldn't write a letter except by the fire or the ink would freeze. The river iced over so solidly, even at the widest part, that the British could wheel artillery across it. No ship could come in or out of any port. And the young officers in my military escort were forced to stop every so often to knock shards of ice loose from the wheels of the coach, wary of catching a glimpse of the king's soldiers.

They had good reason to be wary, for I carried a letter from my father to General Washington. There was also the matter of my traveling companion, a fair and feisty beauty by the name of Kitty Livingston, my cousin and childhood friend. Kitty was the daughter of New Jersey governor William Livingston—one of the most forceful and influential men of the revolution, perpetually on the run from the British, who desperately wanted to make an example of him. And there had recently been, at the Livingston family home, Redcoats pounding upon the door at midnight, forcing their way in at the point of bayonet, demanding that the governor's daughters betray their father's hiding place—which they steadfastly refused to do.

"I was certain they'd burn the house." Kitty's breath puffed steam into the air as she nestled closer to me beneath a quilt. "Though, God forgive me, at this moment, I'd gladly see Liberty Hall engulfed in flames if only to warm my feet near the conflagration."

If God wouldn't forgive her, I would, because the coals in our foot warmer had burned out. But I told myself to endure it because I was soon to see my sister.

It'd been nearly three years since Jack Carter spirited Angelica away to Boston. Now my brother-in-law's business dealings—which I never sufficiently understood—had brought him back into service as a commissary. Angelica had written that he'd been sent on a foraging expedition, and that, in the meantime, she was with the army in Morristown. Where I was determined to join her.

Given that British raiding parties skulked everywhere along the Hudson, throwing torches into homes, courthouses, and churches along the way, I expected my mother to balk at the idea of my journey. But the revolution was still, for us, a family affair. My aunt Gertrude, whose husband, Dr. Cochran, was George Washington's personal physician, invited me to visit, with a pointed reminder that Washington's officer corps was comprised almost entirely of well-educated bachelors from good families, in dire need of brides.

I was more interested in the knowledge that they were also in need of nurses.

And so I went.

When our coach came to a stop we heard a watchman call, "Who comes there?"

Standing upon a muster ground of muddied slush, an irritated sentry all but encased in ice demanded our papers. And when I leaned out to see him, I was greeted with the welcome sight of smoke billowing from a tavern chimney amidst a little cluster of peaked roofs. The tavern gave us hope of a warm drink, but when the sentry saw the direction of our eyes, he said, "Don't bother. They'll slam the door in your faces."

That's when I noticed the dark glances of the townsfolk trudging past. Startled, I asked, "They're Tories here in Morristown?"

"Aye. And they're just sick to death of us, miss." The sentry pointed down the lane. "Your kin are staying less than a mile that-a-way. Your sister, Mrs. Carter, is already in camp."

*Angelica*. The thought of her alone was enough to warm me. And my excitement was rewarded when, before our coach even came to a full stop in front of a neat little white house with a picket fence half-buried in snow, my older sister flung herself out the front door. We both cried at once:

"Angelica!"

"Betsy!"

Thereupon we flew into each other's arms and squeezed so tightly we could scarcely breathe for the sweet pain of it. I couldn't stop looking at her because she had become, it seemed, even more beautiful as a consequence of motherhood, her bright black eyes shining over an elegantly long nose that was pink just at the tip.

From the doorway, stout Aunt Gertrude fussed, "Let's get you girls in out of the cold before you catch your deaths!" She ushered Kitty, my sister, and me inside a small front parlor where a corner fireplace blazed with the most welcome fire I'd ever seen.

Meanwhile, Angelica kissed my cold cheeks again. "You must tell me everything straightaway. Whether Peggy has learned to discipline her tongue, or Mama bought any elegant dresses, or if Papa's gout has returned, and if our brothers are becoming little men. Or even if Jenny has learned to powder your hair without making you sneeze. I must know."

I *wanted* to tell her everything straightaway, but I could scarcely feel my fingers or toes. Thankfully Aunt Gertrude made some warmed cider to thaw us. Apologetically, she also offered some sorry-looking biscuits. "The best that can be done with mealy flour, a few raisins, and the last of the spice."

The biscuits were dry, but Kitty and I gobbled them up as if they were the finest of pastries. Then we were pleased to present some precious supplies. Flour, cheese, and salt—the latter of which, my aunt told us, was more valuable than gold. As our aunt went through the packages, Angelica put my adorable infant niece into my arms, while her little boy played peekaboo about Kitty's skirts. I cuddled the baby close, inhaling her milk scent and feeling beneath my breast a stirring. How might I feel to hold a little creature like this in my arms, knowing she'd be mine to keep forever? If I was to live as a spinster, I'd never know.

And it seemed as if my kinswomen had hatched a veritable conspiracy to keep that from coming to pass. "As soon as you've warmed yourself, my dear, we must see your gowns," Aunt Gertrude said. "There won't be much time to make necessary alterations if we don't start upon them at once. Surely you wish to be in fashion when you meet the most eligible bachelors in the Continental army."

Clearly, she was addressing me, as Kitty was never out of fashion, and I must've looked dismayed at the idea of sorting through ribbons and lace because Angelica broke in to say, "If men were not so blind, Betsy could beguile them in buckskin or burlap. But men are truly the most bumbling of creatures. To get their blood up, you must wave a bit of ribbon and lace before them, like a matador."

We had a good laugh at that, but Auntie protested, "They're not rutting bulls, they're *gentlemen*. And I'll have you know, Betsy, when I told a certain Colonel Tilghman that you were coming, he said he'd be *very* glad to see you again."

I very much doubted he meant it.

When I was seventeen, Tench Tilghman served with my father as an Indian commissioner, and the Iroquois had proposed to the mild-mannered Maryland officer that he take an Indian bride. Later, at a picnic that followed, our lady friends had teased him about this unmercifully. Hoping to divert their mean-spirited sport, I'd managed to humiliate him and myself by blurting that I'd volunteer to be a bridesmaid if Colonel Tilghman should, in fact, wish to take an Indian wife.

At the time, I believed that he took me for a simpleton. Now I was sure of it because my aunt went on to say, "He told me that you're the finest tempered girl in the world."

I groaned, my cheeks burning, for it was precisely the sort of polite thing a man might say about a simpleton. "He thinks I'm *addle-headed*."

Knowing the story, Angelica laughed. "My poor sister and her good intentions."

"Well, you *are* addled if you don't take the opportunity to re-acquaint yourself with Colonel Tilghman," Aunt Gertrude said. "He's an upright patriot from a very fine family."

"A Loyalist family, though." Kitty sighed, as if that ruled him out. "It is rather a wonder that Washington trusts him and keeps him so close. I cannot imagine the pain of being at such odds with your own relations."

I couldn't imagine it either. That night I slept with my sister and her babies in a canopied bed that took up most of the little front guest room with its corner fireplace. And as we curled round each other for warmth, I felt content as I hadn't in years. The scent of Angelica's hair, so familiar and comforting. The way she whispered stories in the dark that made me laugh—prompting our uncle to thump on the wall in the next room to hush us.

I felt a little guilty when, the next morning, Aunt Gertrude was bleary-eyed at a hurried breakfast. And I was nearly too nervous to eat, because it was time to meet George Washington.

~

THE BUSTLING HEADQUARTERS at Ford Mansion was only a quarter mile away. Unfortunately, there was so much snow that even with soldiers piling it into mountains on either side of the road, snowshoes were required. Which meant that we were disheveled and a little out of breath when we finally reached the large white house atop the hill where Washington's tall, powerful bodyguards demanded that we give the secret watchword.

Which, fortunately, we knew.

Aunt Gertrude was a little sour at being suspected, considering that she came often to visit Mrs. Washington and the guards knew her well. "I assure you that there aren't any deadly knitting needles in my basket."

But Angelica was thrilled, or at least a little flattered, by their zealotry. "Well, I think it was very handsomely done, gentlemen. After all, women can be dangerous, too, and important to the entire American enterprise. Our revolution is already remaking everyone's way of looking at the world, and you are very forward-thinking fellows."

With a blush at her compliment, the guards allowed us entrance to the house, where we tromped up the stairs to the door. We would've liked a moment to straighten our hair and our ribbons and make ourselves presentable. Which was why, I suppose, we were so startled when the icy door flung open, and a short, plump little woman with dark brown eyes appeared in the doorway.

Given her plain white cap, brown homespun gown, and bespeckled apron, I might have been forgiven for having confused her with the housekeeper. But whence from her lips fell a soft southern drawl, I knew better. "Why, come in from the cold," said Martha Washington, drawing us into the comfortable circle of chairs before the fire.

Though she was nearly fifty, and a bit snowy haired, she was still handsome, albeit very plainly dressed for such a grand lady as I considered her. One of her Negro servants fetched us a steaming pot of sassafras tea while I presented to Mrs. Washington a little gift of lace cuffs.

"Oh, these are so well made," she said. "Very fine work. I shall treasure them." But no sooner had she thanked me than did she return to knitting a pair of socks. "A clean, dry sock is a luxury for the soldiers. There's always so much to be done for them . . ."

"All the more difficult with everyone so crowded together," Aunt Gertrude said, her eyes lifting to the cadre of young officers coming in and out with papers and satchels.

Mrs. Washington nodded, her hands never stopping at their work. "The general likes to keep here in this house his little military family. His aides all bunk together. If I go a day without mending something for one of them, I'm astonished, but I can scarcely complain, given how hard they labor."

"I'd be happy to be put to work," I said, reaching for a basket of mending by her feet.

"Well, aren't you a sweet girl," Mrs. Washington replied. "But I cannot imagine you came to camp for a life of drudgery. I daresay a number of gentlemen will be glad for your company, my dear girls. Amongst them, colonels McHenry, Tilghman, Harrison, and Hamilton, who—"

She was interrupted by the sound of chairs scraping on the floorboards as my sister and aunt quickly rose to their feet. Kitty and I were slower to stand, and then we saw the tall Virginian who commanded our attention—and our armies.

At the sight of George Washington in full uniform, wearing tall black riding boots and a black cape, my fingers went nervously to straighten my tousled, half-frozen hair.

Meanwhile Kitty, who'd once requested—and received—a lock of the great man's hair as a token, clutched at the pendant that held it, her usual sophisticated demeanor all aflutter. I would never have been so bold as to ask for a lock of the man's hair, so I had nothing to clutch but my sister's hand.

Washington bowed to us and, upon a curtsy, I retrieved from my cloak and delivered into his hand a letter of introduction from my father. But he didn't open it. "You need no introduction, Miss Schuyler," Washington said, glancing at Angelica, who remained, as was her way, perfectly composed. "In the short time she's been with us, the enchanting Mrs. Carter has already painted such a good portrait of her sensible and saintly sister that there is not an officer amongst us who would not know Elizabeth Schuyler on sight."

Hearing him say my name, I flushed and went speechless. Not even Angelica's encouraging squeeze of my hand could seem to make my tongue untie itself. Finally, I managed to murmur, "We're glad to have arrived safely, Your Excellency."

If Washington noticed we were swooning from the excitement of his presence, he didn't let on. "T'was wonderful of you to have braved the journey. Can I expect the pleasure of seeing your father soon? Schuyler's perfect knowledge of the resources of the country, his good temper, and his sound military sense make me wish, above all things, that he would join us here."

To hear Washington speak so warmly of my father emboldened me. "I'm sure Papa would hasten forth at your summons, Your Excellency."

Papa had refused to take up his old command, but I wondered if Washington's public show of confidence would change his mind. And I was delighted when Washington gave a slight smile that didn't show his teeth. "I shall give some thought as to how to bring your father to my side. In the meantime, young ladies, we shall expect your company at the forthcoming dance assembly. When the officers learned that we were to have a visit from such toast-worthy belles, they pooled together the funds to host a proper winter's ball, complete with a French dance master. You must attend. I insist."

# Chapter Seven

*I was prepossessed in favor of this young lady the
moment I saw her. A brunette with the most good natured
lively dark eyes I ever saw, which threw a beam of good
temper and benevolence over her whole countenance.
She was the Finest Tempered Girl in the World.*
—JOURNAL OF TENCH TILGHMAN

I COULDN'T RESIST A direct order from the commander in chief,
and so I spent at least half a day with Kitty and Angelica in
preparation, curling hair, lacing stays, and deciding between
silk heeled shoes. And when Angelica powdered my bosom with
some rice powder sent especially to me as a gift by Mrs. Washington, I began to believe that a project had been made of me.

"Something's amiss," Kitty said, appraising me where I stood
in a Robe à la Polonaise of ivory silk brocade with sprays of autumn flowers in shades of gold and brown and rose.

It was another gift, this one from Angelica, whose husband
was capable of obtaining the most current fashions from overseas
without having to pay an unpatriotic tax on it. She held a rope
of my dark hair at my nape with one hand. "It's only that Betsy's
throat is bare, without anything shiny to draw the eye or entice
a man to *nibble*."

There was no use in pretending to be scandalized by my sister, who'd always said such things. But still, I felt obliged to remark, "That doesn't sound pleasant."

"*Au contraire*, you impossible girl," Angelica said. "Must I extol to you the pleasures of the marriage bed to keep you from becoming a spinster?" She fastened upon my neck a number of necklaces, all of which seemed too ostentatious for words, and I refused everything but a simple black ribbon. "I suppose that will have to do," she said.

Then we were off in the sleigh!

Despite the scant offerings of eatables and drinkables, it was, as General Washington promised, a proper winter ball inside a little tavern turned military storehouse on the green, its windows etched with frost. The second floor was positively transformed, illuminated by the warm glow of at least a hundred candles on crossbeams. And amidst the notes of flute, violin, and harpsichord, mingled a motley assemblage of about sixty gentlemen and officers.

Our Americans in buff and blue, Prussian adventurers like Baron von Steuben with medals glittering on their chests, and French officers in perfectly tailored coats with gold braids at the shoulders. And, to Kitty's great satisfaction, not a single lobster-back in sight.

"You forgot your fan," Angelica scolded me.

"It's too cold for a fan," I said, which made both my companions laugh.

"Oh Betsy," Kitty said, her green eyes glittering with worldly amusement. "This is what comes of socializing only with boys of the Blues in Albany. Without a fan, how are you to convey a message like *stay away* or *come hither*?"

A little vexed at her superior tone—at both of them fussing at me—I replied, "Why I suppose I would just say the words."

Angelica's eyes widened with delight. "Betsy has learned to bite!"

As there were only sixteen ladies in attendance, every male

gaze in the room turned our way, and Angelica gave the slow wave of her fan that said, *I am married.*

Not that it discouraged them.

Kitty's daring gown with bold red-and-white stripes ought to have made her the belle of the ball. But it was my sister, in pink silk and cream-fringed trim, who reigned over the dance hall, and we attended her like faithful handmaidens. Good thing, too, because her natural comfort in formal social outings allowed her to artfully plead thirst as a way to steer us away from the crowd of men who descended.

In the breathing space at the punch bowl, Angelica motioned with her chin toward her knot of admirers in tight buff breeches and decidedly smart dress uniforms, and I recognized a few of them from headquarters as Washington's closest aides. "They'll claim to be starved for female attention," she said. "But I assure you, there's been such a parade of debutantes come to camp to land a husband that they have learned to tumble from haystacks with the dairymaids straight into the arms of gentlemen's daughters."

As she took up a crystal glass of rum punch, Kitty said, "You must mean Colonel Hamilton."

My sister's lips quirked up at the corner. "Speak of the devil and he shall appear."

Moving with crisp military bearing, his reddish-brown hair pulled smartly back in a black ribbon, an officer I assumed must be Hamilton made straight for us, and Kitty pleaded, "My dear Schuyler sisters, *rescue* me."

"Is he a rake?" I asked, wondering why she should need rescue.

"Oh, he's naughty good fun and an excellent officer," Kitty replied, swiftly finishing her punch as Hamilton's heeled shoes closed the distance. "But he's been trying to seduce me since his school days when my father let him stay with us. And he's so relentless I fear I may foolishly give in."

Angelica arched a mischievous brow. "Would it really be so foolish?"

"Quite," Kitty hurriedly replied. "His soldiers call him the Little Lion, but he's more of a ginger tomcat. He wrote me that victory will remove the obstacles in the way of matrimony, but I doubt I'm the only lady to whom he has pleaded *but the war . . .*"

A moment later, Hamilton was before us with a gallant bow, his eyes twinkling with mischief. And when he spoke, it was with the slightest accent—one I couldn't place. "Ladies, unless my eyes deceive me, I find myself in the presence of unearthly creatures." With that, he reached to kiss my sister's hand, and she allowed it. "The Divine Mrs. Carter. You are a vision, as always. Will your husband join us this evening?"

My sister's dark eyes flashed with regal acknowledgment, her head tilting in just the right way to make her jewels sparkle. "I'm afraid Mr. Carter is away on some business for the army."

"I regret to hear it," Hamilton replied in a way that made it seem he did not regret it at all. "We shall do our best to compensate for his absence."

Hamilton then reached for Kitty's gloved hand, and a spark seemed to pass between them. "*Miss Livingston,* my very own Game Goddess."

"By what right do you claim me, sir?" Kitty asked.

"By right of long familiarity and friendship. You've little idea the fright I was thrown into when hearing of you and your sisters having to fend off the British at Liberty Hall with nothing but your wits."

"You make it sound as if we were unarmed." Kitty smirked with lips that formed a perfect cupid's bow. "I take offense."

He smiled, and I did, too, enjoying their banter. "I would never wish to imply such a thing, Miss Livingston. Only a fool underestimates the petticoat patriots amongst us. And who knows better than I do that your wits are extremely sharp and cutting?"

They both laughed, but I realized something was there, between them—something with an edge to it.

Finally, Hamilton turned his attention to me. "Who is this autumnal angel that completes your heavenly trio?"

Angelica made the introduction. "I present my sister, Elizabeth Schuyler."

At hearing my name, Hamilton dramatically pressed his palm to his chest. "Be still my heart. At long last, I make the acquaintance of the Finest Tempered Girl in the World."

I wilted, mortified, my throat bobbing under the black ribbon fastened round my neck, wondering if Colonel Tilghman had told everyone the embarrassing story.

"Your reputation precedes you, Miss Schuyler."

"As does yours, Colonel Hamilton," I replied.

"Oh, does it?" Hamilton leaned in, intensely curious.

There followed a painful moment of silence in which I realized that I could not very well tell him that we'd been gossiping about him. Fortunately, Kitty stepped into the breach. "Oh, you know it does, Colonel Hamilton, you vain creature. Is there anyone who doesn't know how you covered yourself in glory in the artillery?"

"Or who doesn't appreciate the eloquence of your pen?" Angelica chimed in. "*'The sacred rights of mankind are not to be rummaged for, among old parchments, or musty records. They are written, as with a sunbeam, in the whole volume of human nature and can never be erased or obscured by mortal power.'*"

I wasn't surprised Angelica could quote him; she read political pamphlets with as much eagerness as Peggy read romantic French novels. But Hamilton did seem surprised and grinned, *almost* modestly, at her recitation.

Meanwhile General Washington, clad in black velvet, was preparing to lead a minuet. And two bold French officers interrupted to ask Kitty and Angelica to dance. My sister gave an apologetic look before abandoning us. And as both of the beauties escaped his grasp at once, Hamilton hid his disappointment behind a veneer of politeness. Extending a hand to me that displayed a glimpse of a fine lace cuff beneath his officer's coat, he asked, "Shall we, Miss Schuyler?"

"Dance?" I asked, a little flustered.

"You do not dance?"

"I do, of course."

"Then please, dance with me. As Miss Livingston is perverse enough to pretend she finds that French officer more appealing tonight, I am in need of diversion."

It was not the most flattering offer to dance I'd ever received, but the young aide-de-camp scarcely waited for my assent before leading me to the floor where pairs of heeled and buckled shoes spun upon the whorled knots of the rough-hewn pine floor. And as Hamilton led me through the formal steps and bows, his fingers grasped mine just a fraction more tightly than they ought to have.

I wished that didn't intrigue me, because I had the strong notion it was intended for Kitty's notice, not mine. Hamilton was a decidedly handsome man. One who seemed to know precisely what he was about. And despite the gossip about his tumbling dairymaids, he was, with me, a proper gentleman.

As the center of attention, General Washington made an imposing presence—having executed so perfect a minuet that when it concluded the crowd felt moved to applaud.

After which, Hamilton asked, "Wherever did you learn to dance so well, Miss Schuyler?"

I told him about our New Netherland children's troops and the dances in our hall. "Angelica led the Blues—but my little brothers were sorted into the Greens. I'm afraid it remains a rivalry in our family to this day."

"You paint a picture of a happy family." A wistfulness crept into Hamilton's expression. "A happy childhood."

Glancing at my sister across the room, surrounded by a bevy of men vying for her attention, I said, "Very happy."

I didn't expect this to evoke sadness behind his eyes.

"Have you had refreshments, yet, Miss Schuyler? You must be parched." With that, he led me back to the punch table. It was the polite way of marooning a lady before going in search of better quarry, so I was surprised when he not only lingered, but also filled cups for us both and guided us to a set of chairs. "Dare I hope that you've come to Morristown for a reunion with a certain friend of mine?"

I blinked. "If you know the Marquis de Lafayette, I should like to see him again."

"Know him? I consider him as a brother." Hamilton's smile turned wry as he sat beside me. "Good thing, though, that the marquis is away on a mission to France or I would lose another charming lady to a Frenchman's allure. Is there, perhaps, some *other* friend of mine you pine to see?"

While a viola and a violin sang brightly over the din, I took a swallow of punch, not fathoming the direction of his question. "Are you matchmaking, sir?"

"Perhaps."

That was the other polite way of marooning a lady to go in search of better quarry, but I wouldn't mind if it meant a reunion with an old friend. One whose letters I'd waited upon in vain. "Well, I hoped to see Major Monroe, but I haven't spotted him."

Hamilton's auburn eyebrows raised with what appeared to be sobering surprise. "*James* Monroe? Well, no doubt my friend Monroe would blush and stammer his way through countless snowdrifts to pay court to you, but I'm afraid he's gone."

The word struck me hard, like a blow. "*Gone*?"

The previous winter in Valley Forge had been disastrous for the American army, many perishing of disease and exposure. That Monroe might have died there or upon a battlefield filled me with sorrow that I hadn't asked after him sooner.

"My dear lady, I don't mean to say that Monroe is *dead*. No. I only mean that after four years of fighting this interminable and wearying war, my circle of boon companions is scattered. Lafayette to France, Monroe to Virginia, John Laurens to Philadelphia . . ."

I exhaled with relief, and it wasn't lost upon me that Hamilton was keenly aware of the number of years he'd been at war. If it seemed to me that this war might never end, how must it have seemed to the men doing the fighting? So as Hamilton reached for a bit of bread, I asked, "Does it help with the weariness to remember what you wrote at the start? The sentiment my sister recited was beautiful."

"You are too kind," Hamilton said, with facile glibness. "But all sentiments are beautiful when spoken by a beauty."

I didn't believe that. I also had the impression that he expected me to say something witty or clever or flirtatious. But all I managed was, "I found the sentiment beautiful on its own merit. An inspiring reminder of the righteousness of our cause and the good we're trying to accomplish in this world."

Hamilton started to say something—perhaps something witty and clever and flirtatious—but for the first time in our short acquaintance, his mask of esprit slipped away. "You make me feel a pretender, Miss Schuyler, for these days I am disgusted with everything in this world and I have no other wish than to make a brilliant exit."

As the daughter of a general, I'd met some soldiers who seemed to crave such an end, if it were possible, and now I feared Hamilton was one of them. "What has shaken your resolve, sir?"

He took a breath, then stared off into the distance. "I begin to hate the country for neglecting us. Our soldiers are left to suffer. Our ideals of true equality are scorned. And men without talent or integrity are unjustly advanced. Schemers and slanderers—" He blinked, as if remembering himself. "None of which, of course, is proper conversation for a ball."

"It seems entirely proper, given that my family is well acquainted with the evils of which you speak."

He blinked again. "Of course. I've made the unpardonable error of forgetting whose daughter you are. It is a rare man who can, like your father, continue to serve his country without complaint or self-interested motive in the face of such unmerited abuse."

I smiled. "Surely it is a *little* self-interested to wish to avoid the king's hangman."

At my altogether too honest reply, Hamilton barked out a laugh that seemed to take us both by surprise. "Miss Schuyler, your candor is most unexpected. You may be the only lady present tonight with such a saintly virtue."

He said this in a way that made me think he didn't *quite* approve of saintly virtue. Perhaps it was for this reason, and not my own humility, that I replied, "I assure you, sir, I am no saint."

He glanced at me, then seemed to put a great deal of concentration into his glass of punch. "In such company as we have tonight, I would strongly advise you against making such declarations lest a gentleman demand proof."

"What proof should I offer that might suffice?"

With that, Hamilton set aside his cup, and seemed to lose some sort of struggle with himself. At length he turned to stare, and I thought perhaps the candlelight played tricks with me, because beneath his pale lashes were eyes so intensely blue as to give the impression of *violet*.

Those extraordinary eyes drifted to my bosom, which was delicately covered with my fichu, then to my neck, as if he did wish to nibble it. And I fell silent because I'd never before been given such an openly lascivious look. In fact, his open appraisal made me acutely aware that I'd never felt the sensual gaze of a man upon me before at all. Stolen glances of lustful boys, possibly. Respectful attention of gentlemen, certainly.

But there was nothing gentle, playful, or boyish in Hamilton's expression now. And I was suddenly, and thrillingly, made to feel as if every other flirtation of my life had been but child's play. "Until this moment, Miss Schuyler, I had not realized the disservice done to you by your admirer."

"My admirer?" I asked, wondering if it was the strength of the rum punch that left me so dizzied.

Hamilton smirked. "Don't look now, but he's finally mustered his courage."

Yet, I did look. And from a crowd of swaggering officers, wives, and daughters in rustling petticoats and delicate-heeled shoes, emerged a man in dress uniform. Quite a well-formed man, in truth. Broad at the shoulders with strong stocking-clad calves, wearing a dignified powdered wig. "Why Colonel Tilghman," I said, blushing unaccountably, as if I'd been caught in some manner of undress. "How good to see you after all these years."

"Years in which you've blossomed from a wildflower into a rose," Tilghman replied, with a bow. "I remember our picnic, and how easily you—a perfect nut-brown maid with the eyes of a Mohawk beauty—clambered over rocks while the other ladies needed assistance. I've often regaled my companions with the story."

"That he *has*," Hamilton said, drily, as I blushed hotter. "In detail that would be tiresome were his subject not so worthy."

I recognized a friendly rivalry when Tilghman pointedly turned to make the hilt of his dress sword poke Hamilton in the side. "As I was saying, Miss Schuyler, I recall you with great fondness and owe you a debt of kindness."

Genuinely surprised, I said, "And here I believed I'd left you with a decidedly unfavorable impression."

Tilghman's cheeks colored beneath the white of his powdered wig. "Quite the opposite. In fact, I was wondering if you would honor me with—"

"No," Hamilton said.

"No?" Tilghman was taken aback. I was, too.

"*No*," Hamilton repeated, more firmly, rising to his feet. "You're too late. Miss Schuyler owes me this dance." Hamilton touched my elbow, prompting me to rise. And with a glee nearly unbecoming, Hamilton crowed, "My dear Tilghman, let this be a lesson to you on what comes of being timid with a lady fair."

As he led me away from a sputtering Tench Tilghman, I whispered, "But I didn't promise you a dance."

"Didn't you?" Hamilton asked, mischief twinkling in his eyes. "You offered to furnish me sufficient proof that you are not a saint. And the dance master is calling an allemande."

"But I gave my last dance to you," I protested.

"I believe two consecutive dances are permitted during war."

"I don't think that's the etiquette at all, sir."

"Only a saint would give a care for etiquette," Hamilton replied with a wink. "So far, your proofs in that regard are sadly lacking, Miss Schuyler . . ."

The words were designed to ensure I gave way, which I did, and the dance became a flirtation set to music. A series of figures, handholds, and passés that had Hamilton turning beneath my arms before twirling me into his. When we interlaced hands, I felt the heat of him. And when I turned again, his hand brushed the nape of my neck—a shocking sensation.

Was it merely a slip, or had he intended it?

Then it happened again. This time, as he turned, his palm stroked the small of my back, and then a little lower. The rules of this dance precluded all touch except for linked arms and hand clasps, so it was no mistake. Perhaps I ought to have put a stop to it, but I'd foolishly agreed to prove I wasn't a saint.

And then there was the problem that I *liked* the stolen touches.

Round and round we twirled until I felt as if I were falling, falling into his arms. And in his extraordinary eyes, I sensed the Nix, a figure of Dutch legend whose sweet songs lure maidens to dangerous depths for a kiss . . .

I shall not dissemble or hide behind virtue and claim that I wasn't tempted. Hamilton was a winsome man with captivating eyes. He might have charmed me entirely if he hadn't *known* himself to be so charming. And if I hadn't known this dance meant nothing.

It was only to inspire jealousy. It was all play pretend. Except of a very grown-up variety.

THE NEXT MORNING was impossibly more frigid. But inside, I burned.

As Kitty groaned about having consumed too much rum punch

and Angelica complained that her ink was frozen, I was still dreaming of the ball. I'd finally danced with Tilghman, whose courtly manner did him great merit; with another of Washington's aides, Lieutenant Colonel McHenry, a medical doctor who made me laugh by reciting the worst poetry I'd ever heard; and with the stately Baron von Steuben, whose shiny military medal caught upon my lace sleeve, entangling us briefly to the amusement of all. I'd even sat a spell with the now married Benedict Arnold, who asked me with genuine fondness to thank my father for his help in trying to secure him a new post at West Point, now that his ruined leg left him unfit for active service.

But there was something about Hamilton that *lingered* beyond the impression of any of these men, and it was not merely those captivating eyes or the heat of his hands when he touched me during our dance. His intelligence, wit, and devotion to duty were plain for all to see, but it seemed to me that Hamilton had built around himself a sparkling *citadel* of courtly manner and playful flirtation. He'd allowed me, for just a moment, to glimpse past it. And I thought I'd seen wounds. Wounds that perhaps couldn't be healed, but I had the ridiculous notion that given the opportunity, I'd like to try.

And it *was* a ridiculous notion, because while Hamilton had made a powerful impression upon me, I didn't believe I had made any upon him. He seemed to give no thought to me beyond my acquaintance with Kitty, with whom he engaged in some manner of hot-and-cold courtship.

"Ladies," Hamilton said later that morning, doffing his cap to us where we sat with mending work. He'd come to escort us to religious services. "Seeing you seated at the fire with your spindle, thread, and scissors, I cannot help but think of the three Fates."

Angelica playfully snapped her shears. "Do you imagine that we're measuring out the length of your life and deciding where to snip it?"

Feeling at quite the disadvantage when it came to ancient

stories, I left it to Kitty to scold, "You should rather think we are the *Three Graces*."

Hamilton grinned. "Oh, but I would not hazard a guess as to which of you was Charm, Grace, or Beauty. After all, the last time a mortal man awarded a golden apple to the fairest, he caused a dreadful war."

"Is *that* how this got started?" Angelica asked.

He laughed in a way that told me he admired my sister's wit as well as her beauty. And, quite unfortunately, that made me like him all the better.

Because the churches of Morristown had been converted to hospitals, religious service was to take place in the home of the reverend. We'd attended both Dutch and Anglican services as children, but not Presbyterian. So as I fetched my coat I asked, "You're certain we'll be welcome though we aren't of the denomination?"

"The very same question His Excellency asked," Hamilton replied. "The reverend replied it was not the Presbyterian table but the Lord's table."

Thus, in our best church dresses, coats, hats, and scarves, Angelica, Kitty, and I took our communion. But Hamilton did not. *Surely he's a Christian*, I thought, but I couldn't muster the courage to ask.

On the way back, we strolled by a frozen pond, where Colonel Tilghman was most solicitous of me. Hamilton had the idea of a sledding party for the week next, which occasioned McHenry to taunt him in his Irish brogue. "He might be a silver-tongued courtier in a ballroom, ladies, but you've never seen a lad less made for winter sport."

"Allow me to put that to the lie," Hamilton said, launching a snowball at McHenry, who, like a naughty laughing leprechaun, ducked behind the taller Tilghman as cover to return the volley.

Then ensued the most delightful mayhem.

Slipping and sliding and thrashing one another as they ran, Washington's aides acted like brothers, I thought. Even in their horseplay, the strapping officers who rode into nearly every battle with our general were all athletic grace.

But when a shower of snow came our way, Angelica asked, with feigned sternness, "Must we negotiate a truce, gentlemen?"

From behind a fortress he'd made of a tree, Hamilton replied, "I'm afraid it's victory or death for me."

"Don't believe it, ladies." McHenry quipped with bawdy mischief, "He'll surrender his sword to any pretty girl who wants it. Three by my count in the last month alone."

"Have a care, Mac," Colonel Tilghman scolded, as if worried to offend my maiden ears. But everyone else laughed. And in truth, I knew not what to make of Hamilton's rakish reputation.

"Make way!" came a command from down the narrow, frozen lane where we stood watching the men's antics. Clutching hands to keep our balance, we trudged into a deeper drift of untrodden snow as a war-weary company of men paraded by. Their threadbare uniforms were familiar, of course, as were the abused muskets upon their shoulders and the malnourished gaunt upon their frostbitten faces. But one thing was strikingly different about these soldiers.

They were black.

A thing that perhaps shouldn't have so surprised me, for I'd heard Papa talk about the black troops who served at Saratoga. But a few of these men wore the gold epaulets of an *officer*, a thing that I'd never before heard about or seen.

Our escorts saluted the white colonel at the head of the column, who returned the gesture and shouted out more commands to his men.

"The First Rhode Island," Hamilton said to me as they passed, perhaps sensing my surprise. "Our first black regiment."

McHenry nodded and spoke in his thick brogue. "And we'll need 'em, too. We lose too many men to disease and desertion to refuse blacks in the army now, and those with reservations voice their concerns no longer."

"The British recruitment of slaves has convinced most Americans that we should do the same," Tilghman said, glancing amongst us ladies, as if he wished to make sure we knew his sentiments on the matter. "As if the standard of humanity did not make them deserving of freedom enough."

"And the other men don't mind serving with them?" Angelica asked, and I knew precisely why, for our father had complained that black troops disgraced our arms.

But I was glad that Angelica had asked, instead of me, because Hamilton actually frowned at her. "The contempt we've been taught to entertain for Negroes makes us fancy many things that are founded neither in reason nor experience. As my dear Laurens's project in South Carolina is sure to prove."

This was the second time I'd heard him mention John Laurens, and I'd since learned that the southerner was another of Washington's aides, now away on different business, and an officer, like Hamilton, with an unfailing ability to work his way into the gazettes. Laurens's most recent fame came as a result of suggesting we give freedom to slaves willing to fight in the army.

"Laurens seeks to raise a black regiment in *South Carolina*?" I asked. I could scarcely contemplate it. If a northern plantation owner with only a few slaves like my father hadn't approved of Laurens's scheme, I could only imagine how outlandish—and dangerous—southern planters would deem the idea.

But Hamilton seemed to admire his friend's audacity. "If Laurens has any fault, it is an intrepidity bordering upon rashness, but in that he is excited only by the purest motives."

It *was* rash. But now I found myself surrounded by men fighting for freedom—*everyone*'s freedom, it seemed—and I couldn't help but feel . . . sympathetic to the idea.

For didn't the men of that Rhode Island regiment marching past show the same fidelity, do the same duty, draw upon the same courage, and make the same sacrifices? What more could a country ask of its citizens, let alone its slaves?

# Chapter Eight

THE LONGER I spent in the company of the army, the more I felt within my breast the desire to contribute to the cause. So I went the next day with my aunt and uncle to the Presbyterian Church that had been commandeered for a hospital. As we approached the adjoining cemetery, we found two soldiers with axes breaking the frozen ground for a grave. A stiff corpse lay in the snow, arms bent at a grotesquely unnatural angle, his mouth locked, as if in a silent shriek.

"Will there be no coffin for the poor soul?" I asked.

"There's no time if it's a contagion." My uncle had been instrumental in inoculating the army against smallpox—and me and my siblings as well when we were younger—checking this most dreaded epidemic after Valley Forge. Still, the soldiers suffered typhus and flux, fevers and dysentery, measles and mumps. "When we made winter quarters here three years ago, we were forced to dig a mass grave. Sickness in the army was much worse then, and smallpox carried away a fourth of the town, too."

No wonder the people of Morristown treated us coldly. If the army brought with it pestilence and hardships, the townsfolk could scarcely be happy to have the army back again. And the words of the irritated sentinel came back to me now, haunting me with their literal meaning.

*They're just sick to death of us.*

"You're a good-hearted girl, Betsy," my uncle warned. "But what you've seen in an Albany hospital won't prepare you."

Carrying a bundle of bandages, Aunt Gertrude patted my shoulder. "Pay him no mind, dear. Dr. Cochran has mistaken you for some milk-and-water miss. He forgets you're a Schuyler."

Like my mother, Aunt Gertrude had learned rudimentary medicine at the barn my family turned into a hospital at Schuyler Flatts during the French and Indian War. She was sturdy and strong and expected me to be the same. So with that reminder ringing in my ears, I braced myself to witness with mine own eyes the horrors my uncle thought would shock me.

Inside the church, officers lay upon church pews, but the rank and file rested on naught but piles of straw. Nurses moved amongst the groaning mass of patients, emptying chamber pots, combing hair for lice, and dousing everything with vinegar as a purifier. It was too cold to remove my pelisse coat and fur-lined hood. I had no choice but to shed my calfskin gloves, however, so I left them upon the altar before fetching a bucket of vinegar water.

"May I tend you, sir?" I asked as a fevered man retched into the straw, too ill to answer. I sponged the sweat from the back of his neck and had just given him a small sip of wine posset to settle him when my aunt was called to help my uncle amputate the frozen feet of a sentry.

*Please let the sentry swoon*, I prayed as his screams soon broke past the bullet upon which he was to bite down. At the very least, I hoped he'd been given rum to ease his pain, but I feared otherwise, because he wasn't an officer and we were rationing the rum.

I turned to see his black toes and severed flesh flung into a bloody bucket, and I feared I might disappoint Aunt Gertrude's expectations because bile rose and my stomach rolled. It was only with great effort that I made myself go about my duties, as if screams were not echoing off the high ceiling of the nave.

At length, the screaming stopped. My uncle abandoned his bloody instruments, snapped off his gore-speckled apron, and uttered a curse for which he immediately begged God's pardon. Wearing a grim expression, Aunt Gertrude called for a stretcher.

"He can't have died," I said.

Soldiers could live without toes. Without fingers, feet, arms, and legs, too.

"T'was the pain," Aunt Gertrude replied.

Before that, I hadn't known someone could perish from pain alone. Since then, I have learned it to be true, but learned the opposite as well. That stubborn life can cling to a person, even when they are in such pain that they *wish* they would die.

Aunt Gertrude murmured a prayer and told me to return to my tasks. A few moments later, the church door opened and closed against a sharp winter wind and Alexander Hamilton strode past me.

"Dr. Cochran," Hamilton said from close enough that I could hear the men's conversation. "We're suffering a nearly complete depletion of medicinal supplies and His Excellency will need a much fuller accounting of your request."

My uncle stood rinsing his hands in a bucket. "As explained in our letter, at present, the patients bed down together. Pox victims next to amputees, pneumonia sufferers cough on boys with dysentery, and so on. We ought to separate them, and to do that we need more hospitals."

"That I understand, sir," Hamilton said. "But I'm still left bewildered as to why you should need *gunpowder*."

Though I didn't know it then, more than any of Washington's other aides-de-camp, Hamilton was an all-seeing eye over each munition and every last kernel of corn. And he looked aghast when my uncle explained that he wanted to burn precious gunpowder to purify putrid air.

I thought the willingness of our doctors to experiment was laudatory, but Hamilton's fingers flicked in annoyance. "The general finds the application for gunpowder unusual and doesn't think it proper to authorize it."

I was startled by the impression that Hamilton was speaking

for George Washington without asking. As if he were empowered to do so! My uncle looked as if he might argue, but was too weary. "Perhaps we might discuss this later, Colonel."

"I cannot imagine the answer will change," Hamilton said, with great officiousness. "But I don't wish to keep you from your work." With that, he turned to go, quite nearly stumbling over me where I crouched to tend a patient. "Miss Schuyler? I didn't expect to see you . . . I'm astonished to find you . . . here."

Rising to my feet with a pail of vinegar water, I said, "Surely you know Dr. Cochran is my uncle."

Hamilton's gaze traveled the length of me, as if to be sure the girl he'd last seen in a brocaded gown could be the same one now before him in a nurse's apron. "Of course. But I didn't realize . . . most belles could not withstand these sights and indelicate smells."

I was not, of course, immune to the putrid perfume of sweat, vomit, urine, and blood, but my discomfort hardly mattered. "I'm bothered more by the suffering than the smell."

Hamilton nodded. "Another statement that serves as poor proof against your sainthood."

I smiled. "Then my aunt must also be a saint. And Mrs. Washington, who tends the soldiers sometimes, too. How can I do less, if God has given me the capacity?"

He returned my smile, and his gaze lingered on my face. "Far be it from me to question God. I bid you good day, Miss Schuyler."

"To you as well," I replied, watching him go.

But he'd only marched five steps before he stopped, paused, then turned back. "I neglected to mention that another storm may be coming. If so, you won't want to be caught here after dusk. I'd be happy to escort you and save your aunt and uncle the trouble of conveying you home."

It wouldn't save them any trouble at all, but there was something about the way he'd debated making the offer that intrigued me, even though it could be nothing but a flimsy pretext to pay call upon Kitty. But I had completed the chores my aunt set for me and thought that perhaps I could use the opportunity to speak on my uncle's behalf.

And, in truth, I wanted to go with him.

So I washed, retrieved my gloves, and allowed him to hold the door for me as we left the church. "Colonel Hamilton, are you certain His Excellency would deny Dr. Cochran's request?" I asked as we stepped outside and walked together down the snowy lane.

Hamilton seemed amused that I might question him. "I know your uncle to be an excellent and learned physician. But I also studied medicine at King's College, before the war. And when I explain my reservations about the safety of burning *gunpowder* in a wooden church, and remind General Washington of the scarcity of our resources, I'm sure he'll see the absurdity of it."

"If you've studied medicine, Colonel, then you should know that smoke smudging is an old and revered medicine. I've seen it practiced by the Iroquois as a cleansing ritual, albeit not with gunpowder."

"At long last, a detail of your sojourns amongst the Indians that Tilghman neglected to mention," he said with a teasing smirk as we passed under tree boughs that sagged with the weight of new-fallen snow. "Nevertheless, I can only put to His Excellency a plan to part with supplies in the interest of *science,* not superstition."

That should have ended the matter. Normally I wouldn't have inquired further. But something about Hamilton provoked me. "Our men at Valley Forge were ignorant of the science behind cooking white corn. It was the Oneida allies my father and Lafayette recruited who taught them better." Remembering how Hamilton spoke reprovingly to Angelica about the unfair ways we'd been taught to view Negroes, I added, "Perhaps you dismiss Indian medicine as superstition with unfair prejudice."

Hamilton's mouth opened, then snapped shut again. "Certainly our Indian allies have proved invaluable to our cause. And they deserve the respect of humanity. However—"

"Then I appeal to your humanity to give the doctor what he requires."

Hamilton laughed, which was not at all the reaction I'd wished. "Had you appealed to my friendship or gallantry it would have been irresistible. I should think myself bound to attack windmills in your service. But when you appeal to the general principle of humanity, I must show you that even the eloquence of your plea cannot tempt our Fabius to do wrong."

"Fabius?"

"I mean General Washington, of course, who, like the Roman hero of old, pursues a strategy of evading and wearing down the enemy. Avoiding pitched battles and, above all, conserving supplies."

Hamilton obviously had done some cold manner of calculation, weighing sickness against the possibility of battle, deciding the gunpowder could not be spared. So I did not press him further. Instead we walked in silence, only the sound of the snow crunching underfoot between us, until I had to ask. "Are we losing the war, Colonel?"

It was an impulsive question, one that Hamilton shouldn't have answered. But he did. "Yes, we're losing the war."

I was so surprised by his candor that I slipped on the ice. He caught me by the arms and steadied me until we stood facing one another. And his blue eyes again gave the impression of violet against the bleakness of all that surrounded us.

"Is it—is it because of the desertions?" I asked.

"Miss Schuyler, I begin to worry you are utterly *destitute* of the frivolousness which is justly deemed one of the principal accomplishments of a belle."

"I shall take that as a compliment, sir."

"I'm not sure I meant it as one," he said.

I swallowed against a sudden unexpected wanting, and took a step back. "Still, you were saying about the war . . ."

He shrugged as we resumed walking. "We're losing the war for a thousand reasons, starting with the fact that you arrived here not long after a *mutiny*. We're not sure how much longer we can hold this army together. Oh, militia will fight if you pick a time and place and send a pretty invitation, but the hard slog of a disciplined army ready to strike whenever opportunity presents itself is what's necessary."

It was part of the trouble my father faced with militias and the Green Mountain Boys, so I understood. What he said next, I understood less.

"Then there is the deranged state of our currency—the value of paper money has dwindled to nothing. And the necessity of a foreign loan is now greater than ever." He glanced at me before summarizing. "Our affairs are in a bad way, but perhaps Europe will save us in spite of ourselves. If Lafayette returns with assistance from France, it could change everything."

"Fortunately, I know the marquis to be resourceful."

"So he is." Hamilton's expression softened. "I forget that even if you know nothing of old Romans, you are Schuyler's daughter, and a woman of the world."

"Is it your way to taunt and flatter in the same breath?"

"It is when I'm trying to win a lady's admiration."

I slanted him a glance. "Is *that* what you're trying to do?"

He peered down at me, the hint of a smile around too pretty of a mouth. "I sense that you disapprove of me, Miss Schuyler. Though it is assuredly my own fault, it is fast becoming a circumstance I cannot bear."

Did he really care so much what I thought of him? "I confess no such disapproval, sir."

"Only indifference?"

A little smile tugged at the corners of my mouth as we sparred. "I do not confess to that either."

He slowed, staring at me a moment. "I meant it for a compliment."

"Pardon?"

"Before. When I chastised you for earnestness." He cleared his throat. "You took it for a compliment and I meant it as one. I was too embarrassed to say so."

Too embarrassed? So he *did* care what I thought of him, a fact that delighted me more than it should. "Why would it embarrass you?"

He dug his hands into the pockets of his coat. "Because you possess a very strange charm. And you reveal to me a weakness in my fortifications against your sex. I've built a bulwark against guile, but have no weapon against sincerity."

"I didn't realize the sexes were in battle."

"Always," he replied with an arch smile. "The eternal one. Against marriage. Against the delusion that two people can make one another happy for a lifetime. It's a dog of a life when two dissonant tempers meet, and 'tis ten to one this is the case."

"Then you are a foe of love."

"Never love. Only marriage. Miss Livingston might have once laid claim to my heart. I ran a great chance of being ostracized by my fellows for dedicating so much time to so trifling and insignificant a toy as woman, but All for Love is my motto."

Kitty had hurt him somehow, I realized. Or some woman did. Which is why I decided not to cut his pompous self-regard to ribbons. "Kitty can be fickle."

He ducked his chin into the collar of his great coat. "I would not give her the blame. I'm a stranger from the West Indies. I have no property here in this country, no connections. If I have talents and integrity, these are very spurious titles in these enlightened days."

So Hamilton was a foreigner. That explained his slight accent—or rather, the way in which he suppressed one. That he wasn't from the colonies was of no consequence to me whatsoever, but I noted the bitterness. "And yet, your origins have not prevented you from a trusted place in Washington's inner circle. Does that not fill you with hope for your future?"

"I try not to think of a future. When I was a child, I wished for a war to improve my circumstance, and now war has been the whole of my life since the start of the revolution. So, I expect to mingle my fate with America's should she lose her struggle."

It was an admirable sentiment, if expressed with almost a sadness that made me wish to reassure him. "But what if we win?"

He gave me an indulgent look, as if he thought me hopelessly optimistic. "Then I will turn away from the corruption of the world and retire to a frugal life in the countryside roasting turnips, like the general Manius Curius Dentatus." Another old Roman, I guessed. He seemed fascinated by them. But when he saw the name meant nothing to me, he smirked. "I begin to think I should loan you some books."

"A musty tome will not tell me what I wish to know."

"Which is?"

"Whether you could be content planting turnips."

He dug with the toe of his boot in the snow. "It sounds like a lonely business."

Now I couldn't help but twit him. "Didn't Dentatus have a wife to help him plant his turnips?"

He grinned. "I suppose he must have."

"What was her name?"

Hamilton paused for a heartbeat. "*Aquileia*. A sweet and devoted woman—no coquette, not fickle in the slightest."

"Would it be unkind to think you invented that name?"

His eyes lit with mischief. "You would have to delve into one of those musty tomes to find out."

We had, by this point, reached the door of my uncle's lodgings. But instead of opening it for me when we climbed the steps, Hamilton leaned against it to bar my way.

And he sighed.

"Why do you sigh?" I asked.

He didn't answer. Not precisely. "I suppose you really *are* a perfect little nut-brown maid with eyes like a Mohawk beauty . . ."

"Do you mean *that* for a compliment?" I asked, fighting the blush that surely stained my cheeks.

"It does me no credit that you should have to ask." He inched closer to me, and as the bow fastening my hood had come loose, he took the liberty of unraveling it completely. "I suppose your beaus in Albany have paid you better tribute. And that, like a co-quette, you've shunned them and gloried in their broken hearts."

With the ribbons of my hood in his hands, he tugged me until we were so close I thought he might kiss me. And caught up in the spell, I wanted him to. Desperately. "Sir, I hope you will believe me when I say I wish to be a mender of hearts rather than a breaker of them."

It was so revealing a comment that I could have cursed myself. How cloying and hopeful and obvious. He must have taken me for a perfect *child*.

For in that moment, he stared. Then straightened up again, patronizingly fastening my hood tightly beneath my chin. "I can see why Tench fancies himself in love—and also why you should accept his courtship. He is the right sort of man for you, Miss Schuyler."

"I scarcely know him," I said, not liking the turn in the conversation or how the spell had broken. "I scarcely know you, for that matter. Which makes it all the more confounding that you should presume to guess what sort of man is right for me."

"You're a very earnest girl," Hamilton replied, as if this fact made him angry. "My friend Tench is a very earnest fellow. From a good family. He has money. You're well matched. He's almost as much a saint as you are."

I had the distinct impression he was making a case, as if before a jury. But he didn't like his own arguments. I didn't like them either.

Abruptly, he tipped his tricorn hat. "Good day, Miss Schuyler."

Thereafter, our every encounter was inexplicably strained and abrupt. We crossed paths at headquarters, where I went to help Mrs. Washington mend socks and hats and breeches for the soldiers, and Hamilton stood dumbly in the doorway of the anteroom. A ball of wadded paper had rolled at his feet, no doubt pitched by one of his laughing comrades from where they labored with ink and quill pens. And without acknowledging me, Hamilton stooped to pick it up, then walked away without another word.

A few days later, he even begged off taking us to the sledding party with a very curious note.

> *Colonel Hamilton's compliments to Miss Livingston and Miss Schuyler. He is sorry to inform them that his zeal for their service made him forget he is so bad a charioteer as hardly to dare to trust himself with so precious a charge; though if he were to consult his own wishes, like Phaethon, he would assemble the chariot of the sun, even if he were sure of experiencing the same fate. Colonel Tilghman offers himself a volunteer.*

"This is just the dance that takes place outside a ballroom," Angelica said when I told her what had happened. "Men advance, they withdraw, they advance . . ."

What she didn't say, but I instinctively knew, was that Alexander Hamilton was not in the category of men that ought to concern me as dance partners in or out of a ballroom. He had already blazed a brilliant career. He was a prodigy, an ambitious man. A peacock who ought to be matched with some society bird of showy plumage.

He'd been perfectly clear about his hostility toward marriage. Any flirtation between us was merely an amusement. And I hadn't come to Morristown to be amused.

THERE ARE PLACES in this world that wash you off the solid ground and, like a waterfall, send you hurtling over the precipice onto the jagged rocks of hard reality.

Jockey Hollow was, for me, such a place.

The first thing to strike me as our sleigh jingled into the forested hills of Jockey Hollow was how the pine forest suddenly fell away—only stumps of trees remained as far as the eye could see, almost as if some Goliath had reached down to strip the earth bare. The second was the eerie silence, as if every bird and woodland creature had fled—or been devoured. As a military sled piled with logs glided past, pulled through the snow by a bag-of-bones horse and a ragged little fifer boy, the scent of human waste assaulted my nostrils. And a worse scent, too. A scent that I could only name, even now, as suffering.

For we stood amidst the *real* encampment of the Continental army.

Four miles away from the orderly streets of Morristown, where Washington and his officers conducted the business of war and hosted glittering winter's balls, the ten thousand unwashed, unclothed, veteran soldiers lived in a wilderness city of log huts, made only of notched oak logs sealed with mud and straw.

Trapped by snow. And starving.

I'd seen soldiers in hard times before. In Albany, I'd seen undisciplined Yankee riflemen, untrained Negro boys sent as fodder, and soldiers with neither tents to shelter them nor hats to cover their heads. But that was three years ago.

This was a gaunt ghost of an army now made up of scarecrow men whose hollowed, haunted eyes left me to wonder how they were alive at all. They were so hungry they had resorted to boiling their old leather shoes. Shoes they needed, lest they stand upon the snow in bare feet and frostbite deaden their toes, a fate they avoided by wrapping them in rags.

I didn't know that while I'd donned heels and danced and drank rum punch with officers, ordinary soldiers were sleeping twelve to each log hut, living on half-rations, and wearing what only laughingly could be called a uniform. And now that I did know it, I wanted to retch up every morsel I'd eaten for the shame of it.

"Betsy," my uncle said, softly, trying to draw me to follow him. But his efforts were to no avail, because in the swirl of my horror, I'd noticed a man hanging by one arm on a picket, tied to one of the few remaining trees, red blood flowing from his shivering ribs, his bare back laid open in gory gashes that revealed *bone*. And it looked as if his shoulder had dislocated.

"Dear God, he needs help," I said, starting for the poor fellow, my petticoats dragging in the snow.

My uncle caught me by the arm. "It's a military matter, Betsy."

As a general's daughter, I'd known soldiers forced to run the gauntlet and slashed by their fellows. But the sorts of punishment meted out by the British army—a thousand lashes like to make a man die—I'd never seen in ours. And this man's suffering seemed an utter barbarity. So I broke away from my uncle and rushed to the bloody soldier.

What I would have done for him, I didn't know. Untie him. Bandage him. Give him my cloak?

I only knew that I must do *something* until the miserable fellow looked up at me from his bindings and croaked, "Listen to good Dr. Bones, lass." His words slurred. "There's nothing you can do. I was caught robbing the town folks."

"You've been punished for it, amply," I said. "By whose orders are you left here to—"

"I was d-deserting," explained the half-frozen miscreant, his eyes glassy and his teeth chattering against the cold and the pain. "Better than the imbecility in staying and starving for a country that cares nothing for us. They're likely to shoot or hang me c-come morning. So be an angel of mercy and pray for me to die."

A startled sob caught in my throat.

"Elizabeth!" my uncle barked. This time, he brooked no resistance, pulling me away by the arm and taking such long strides that I was forced to take two steps for his every one.

"He can't be left there in agony, Uncle."

"The officers will decide that. I thought your father would have taught you this. I'd never have brought you with me if I thought otherwise."

As a general, my father, too, must have ordered men flogged or maybe even hanged. I'd never questioned Papa's decisions, or his wisdom, or his mercy. But to torture a man—to torture *all* these men . . .

"This is no place for ladies," my uncle was saying. Yet I spotted women everywhere. Some even with children, also gaunt and starved. Camp followers, we called them, intimating they were prostitutes. Some *were,* but more were wives of the soldiers who, having been burned out of their homes by the British, had nowhere else to go. The women boiled water. They sewed. They cleaned clothes. And I was shamed at myself for not bearing up better when so many of them managed to.

"I'm sorry," I said, to my uncle. "I will better conduct myself."

But he'd thought better of my presence entirely. "What you'll do is go to the Wick House until I fetch you. General St. Claire has his headquarters there."

If he'd been the officer to order a man lashed to the bone, I didn't think I could face him.

Sensing my reluctance, my uncle said, "Don't keep me from tending the men."

Sorry for giving my uncle trouble, I nodded and grabbed up my skirts, then marched up a snowy path marked with blood from barefooted soldiers. I knocked upon the door of the little wooden farmhouse, but it wasn't St. Claire who answered.

It was Alexander Hamilton.

Somewhat dazed, I asked, "Is General St. Claire here?"

"I'm awaiting his return." Hamilton frowned. "What the *devil* are you doing here?" At the moment, I was so shaken, I wasn't sure. And when I didn't answer, Hamilton guided me into the small space before a roaring fire, herbs drying from the rafters and copper pots hanging on the wall. And though it was clear he wasn't pleased to see me, concern crept into his voice. "Miss Schuyler?"

"Is it right to torture a soldier like that?"

Realizing what I must've seen, he pinched at the bridge of his nose. "I didn't give that order."

My lower lip quivered. "I only asked if it was *right*."

"Miss Schuyler, we must hold the army together."

It was a coldhearted answer. And he must've known that I thought so. Because he couldn't meet my eyes. He stared at his boots. And I stared at him, hoping he would use his influence, if he could, to remedy the situation.

Instead, at length, he said, "This morning I had the occasion to pass a private talking to his mates over a campfire. An Irishman, I gather. Not a wealthy soldier. Nor a learned one. Nor a statesman. Neither were his fellows. Indeed, they were a motley group of Yankees, Irishmen, Negroes, Buckskins, and whatnot. And do you know what they were discussing?"

I shook my head. "I couldn't guess."

"They were debating whether it was right to kill the Hessians on Christmas Day all those years ago. The men still feel sorrow over it because, they said, those Hessians had no choice to fight us. They were sent by a king."

I just stared, wondering what point he meant to make.

"Remember. Not wealthy. Not learned. Not statesmen. And yet they came to the conclusion that they were fighting for the Hessians, too. They said they were fighting so that *no one* might ever again be sent to die as a slave instead of a free man."

At those words, I took a sharp breath, much affected.

Hamilton came closer. "If we cannot hold this army together until springtime, that's the end. We lose the war. We bow to the king. And *every* soldier who has fought and died in this war will have fought and died in vain. Our sacred rights erased from this earth."

"You wrote that our sacred rights could never be erased by mortal power."

Hamilton looked startled that I should remember the lines my sister recited, then made a dismissive sound at the back of his throat. "Well, I was an idealistic fool when I wrote that."

"No," I whispered, my eyes blurring with tears. I didn't believe it. He was brave to write those words. Even if the army fell apart and we lost this war and those ideas perished from the earth, I would always believe he was right to express them.

At the visible evidence of my distress, Hamilton reached into his coat as if to retrieve a kerchief, and finding none, took the liberty of drawing me into his embrace.

I found unexpected comfort in his strong arms, and we stood like that for a long time, awash in sadness. Eventually, he murmured into my hair, "You are going to be the ruin of me, Betsy Schuyler."

Still teary, I spoke words muffled by our closeness. "Why would you say so?"

"When last we spoke, I returned to headquarters so distracted I couldn't remember the watchword."

I could scarcely believe him or understand how it might be my fault. "And you lay that at my feet?"

"I've behaved very badly toward you," he said, his arms still around me, warm and protective. "I am sorry for it. The truth is, Miss Schuyler, by some odd contrivance, you've found the secret of interesting me in everything that concerns you."

Interesting him? "But you've been avoiding me."

"Not enough, it would seem." He stared at me so long I thought I'd beg him to go on, and then he did. "You aren't the only good-hearted young lady of gentle breeding in Morristown, but you're the only one who would *ever* come here. Which proves you deserve all I think of you and more, even if it's become extremely inconvenient for me."

"Inconvenient?" I asked, searching those blue eyes in an effort to understand the meaningful tone of his voice.

He sighed. "*Extremely.* You see, our little military family is the only family I've ever known. And because Tilghman is besotted with you, I ought never to have looked in your direction. But now I cannot stop looking."

With those words, he turned my world on its axis.

And while it was still spinning, he gave an exasperated little laugh. "Oh, banish those stars in your beautiful black eyes, Miss Schuyler. Even were it not for Tench, I fear we are playing a comedy of all in the wrong and should correct the mistake before we begin to act the tragedy. I'm no fit suitor for you."

That he'd given thought to such a thing awakened something in me. "Because you're an enemy of marriage?"

"Because I have no fortune. I have no family. And I'm a sinner."

"Three things that can all be remedied by the right woman," I said. It was, perhaps, the quickest answer I'd ever given in my life. And it seemed to take him off guard.

"I hadn't considered it that way." I wasn't sure I believed him. He was the sort of man who seemed to think about all sides of *everything*. But the next thing he said made me realize that perhaps, in matters of the heart, he didn't allow himself. Releasing me from his embrace, his face reddening with chagrin, he held me at an arm's length. "I'm afraid there remains yet one defect in my character that cannot be wiped away. I was born on the wrong side of the blanket and have no right to my name. I am a *bastard*," he said, his lips curling with contempt of the word, or himself, I could not say. "Undeserving of a lady of your pedigree."

I would never have guessed it of him. He seemed every inch the cultivated gentleman. "I—I'd heard rumor you were descended of Scots nobility."

"Oh, I have better pretensions than most in this country who plume themselves with ancestry. I am the grandson of the Laird of Grange. Unfortunately, my mother was a divorced woman when she married my father. Unluckily, her divorce was later deemed to be unlawful."

He'd said this soberly and swiftly. And there was good reason for it. Divorce was nearly unheard of. Certainly scandalous. And yet, I said what I believed to be the plain truth. "Colonel Hamilton, no matter the circumstances of your birth, anyone with eyes can see your merit. Why, the blemish upon your birth is merely a wrinkle in the law."

Hamilton's guarded expression softened. "You're kind to cast it in that light. Others are not so generous."

"Perhaps they envy you, since your story unmasks you as an aristocrat with a family coat of arms."

I thought I said this very handsomely, but was rewarded only with dark amusement. "One with only lint in his pockets and alone in the world. Nothing to envy."

"You haven't *any* family?" I asked.

His fingers wrapped around mine, tentatively, then tighter and tighter as if he feared I would pull away when he went on to explain that in the West Indies he had a brother, and an estranged half-brother, but that his father abandoned the family and that his mother died when he was only twelve.

My heart pounded in an agony of sympathy for him, wondering how he'd made his way, a veritable orphan, left to fend for himself. I couldn't fathom it. In no circumstance, either prosperity or wreck, would my own long-suffering father leave us to the vagaries of fate. And I realized anew how fortunate I was.

"You must pardon me, Miss Schuyler. I do not speak of these things often. And in such specificity, never. It dredges up . . ." He didn't finish but seemed to sense my welling pity. "I do not mean to paint a picture of me as a barefooted street urchin. Before my mother died, we had books, a silver tea set, and a covered bed." How miserable an inventory he felt compelled to make. "What you must think . . ."

"I think that I wish to know you better."

He smiled softly. "A saintly answer from a saintly girl."

For no reason I could understand, I was desperate to disabuse him of this notion. And between what I'd seen outside that camp and all that Hamilton had just revealed, I felt nearly overwhelmed with an urgent mix of emotion. Sadness, helplessness, pity, attraction, and desire. Obeying an impulse I could scarcely comprehend, I leaned forward to kiss him.

He actually startled, his hands grasping at my wrists as if he meant to push me away. As if he was the sort of man who never allowed an intimacy that he didn't initiate. But then his grip on my wrists tightened and held me fast. It was as if my boldness had thrown a spark that Hamilton ignited into an all-consuming fire, for his mouth claimed mine and demanded to be claimed in return.

It was no tender kiss we shared, happy and sweet. It was a kiss that tasted of grief and desperation. But also, unmistakably and forcefully, ardor. I forgot the cold. I forgot the soot and darkness of the cabin. I forgot the rank smell of the camp. Everything vanished except for that kiss and the stark terror of realizing that I was falling in love.

At length, we broke apart, and Hamilton traced my lower lip, a little dazed. "Not a saint, it would seem, but an angel . . ."

"Colonel Hamilton—"

"Alexander," he insisted. "I do believe we are on a footing for Christian names now . . ."

"*Alexander*," I said, enjoying the sound of it in my mouth. "You should know something about me and Colonel Tilghman."

He frowned, deeply. "Tell me."

"In all the years your friend allegedly harbored feelings for me, he never confessed them to me. And I never felt more than friendship in return. He has no prior claim to my affections."

"Then to the devil with Tench Tilghman," Hamilton said, stroking his knuckles along my cheek. "For I have serious designs upon your heart, Miss Schuyler, and I flatter myself that I am no bad marksman."

After that, Hamilton was nearly every evening in my uncle's parlor, with conversations that lasted so late into the night that my uncle groused about wishing to take his ease upon the settee and my aunt was forced to all but oust the young officer from the house.

When Aunt Gertrude had finally shooed Hamilton out the door, she'd shaken her head and said, "Oh, Betsy. Of all Washington's fine young officers, you choose the—"

"Stray," Kitty broke in. "There's no help for it. Betsy has always been too softhearted."

"Well, I like Hamilton," Angelica said, rising to my defense with my nephew in the crook of one arm, and a book in the other. "He's an ambitious and clever fellow. Should we win the war, there is no limit to his future. And if Betsy wants him, she should have him."

Kitty shrugged, as if she didn't care one way or the other. And I hoped she didn't care, because I *did* want him. Quite shamelessly, it would seem. For on a particular evening when he pressed the advantage of my family's distraction gossiping over mulled cider in the dining room, I made only the faintest protest against his fevered embrace. One in which he seemed to be trying to forget the horrors of the war.

"God," he groaned into my hair. "I am Phaethon, undone."

"Who?" I whispered, my head thrown back, too much wishing to forget the horrors of the war myself. But as much as I desired him, I didn't wish to be just one more girl with whom he could forget.

Hamilton seemed dazed, entirely intent on kissing and nibbling the flesh beneath my ear—which was very pleasant indeed. But my question seemed to pull him back to himself. "Phaethon. I mentioned him in the letter I sent when I refused to take you to the sledding party. He was a figure of legend. The bastard of the Greek sun god. He died trying to prove his parentage by driving his father's chariot, and set the world aflame. '*And though greatly he failed, more greatly he dared.*'"

It sounded as if Hamilton admired the boy's hubris.

And it made me remember that he had, at least three times in our acquaintance, alluded to easy acceptance, if not a wish, for death. He'd done so first at the ball. Then in our walk home from the hospital. Then again in his note about this fabled bastard boy who died trying to prove himself. And now he was again comparing himself to that boy.

Which was what gave me the strength that propriety didn't to withdraw from his arms. "Colonel Hamilton," I said, forcing him to look at me. "Alexander . . ."

He blew out a long breath, then appeared as if he was considering an apology.

Before he could manage one, I laced my fingers with his and hastened to say, "I am too much a general's daughter not to understand that a soldier's courage is found in overcoming his fear of death." I swallowed, mustering my own courage to broach this, for I was keenly aware that in giving my heart to a soldier during wartime, I might lose it—and him—at any moment. Especially since I'd already heard tales of how Washington's aides seemed to try to outdo one another in brash acts of battlefield bravery. Perhaps Hamilton was no different, in this respect, than Tilghman or McHenry or even their idolized, nearly mythical, John Laurens, about whom they never ceased to boast. "But—but surely you know there are other paths to glory besides death."

A little spark of surprise lit behind his eyes. And I hoped . . . what exactly? That he would stop saying such things? That he would stop feeling them? That he would promise to never *act* on them? Or maybe, instead, that he would unburden himself to me, so that he never entertained any imaginings of the glory of death ever again?

But he only seemed to retreat a little behind a facade, affecting an insouciant smile and a careless tone. "Not many other paths, it would seem, since General Washington pleads I am too indispensable to do anything but write his letters."

My sister's words returned to me then, and I said, "With the right connections, there would be no limit to your future." Fighting the blush against what I implied, I hastened to add, "You're so witty and well read, and you speak French, and you understand finance, and you're curious about seemingly every idea and philosophy. You remind me very much of . . ." I trailed off there, in embarrassment.

His eyebrow rose in question. "Major André?"

I blinked. "Pardon me?"

"John André," Hamilton said. "I suppose he was a lieutenant when you knew him. Sometimes we must treat with the enemy. And when we do, you've occasionally been the toast of the table."

It'd been some time since I'd given any thought to that British officer, but I flushed to know he remembered me kindly. And to sense that Hamilton felt some jealousy. "Oh," I said, a little flustered. "I am—I mean, I was—very fond of Major André and flattered to think he, or any of his officers, toast me. And he was—or is—a very accomplished gentleman. But, no, that's not who I was going to name."

"No?" Hamilton asked. "Some other beau then?" I shook my head in denial, but he continued on. "I shall be cross if you compare me to my good friend Monroe, who speaks French well enough, but has a much slower wit."

To see the insecurity hidden behind Hamilton's words hurt my heart, for he had all but obliterated every thought of any man before him. And so I rushed to tell him the plain truth. "I was going to say you remind me of my sister. And please trust me when I say that is one of the highest compliments I could offer. If Angelica were a man, she would—"

"You've no need to convince me of Mrs. Carter's merits," Hamilton said with a reassuring smile. "Charm and courage run in your family, from the *paterfamilias* to all his children. I am an admirer of your father, already, as you know."

"As am I, for he is both a soldier and a statesman."

"A *statesman*," Hamilton said, and I could not tell if he took me seriously or not. "You think there is glory enough in that?"

"I do," I replied.

I wish now that I'd said more.

I wish I'd said that he need not prove himself to me or to the world. I think I didn't say it because I was young and foolish and quite out of my depth when it came to the demons that haunted the man I loved. But I sometimes fear that I didn't say it because I didn't believe it.

And that he knew.

After the door closed that night, and I went up to bed, Angelica asked, "How desperately do you want him?"

I'd not given voice to the depth of my feelings for Hamilton yet, not to anyone. But if anyone would understand, my sister would, and I wished most deeply for Angelica to approve. "I think I fathom now what you said that night."

She wound her fingers with mine. "What night?"

"When you eloped," I whispered. "Love *is* a thing beyond reason."

"Oh, my sweet sister. Yes, it is." She pulled me into a hug and peppered me with a million questions about all that had happened between us, finally concluding with, "He's a hardworking man, Betsy. You know I'm fond of him. But he's also an ambitious one. Could you be satisfied with a man who is always striving for more?"

I gave careful thought to her question, but I didn't consider ambition a fault. After what Hamilton and I had discussed earlier in the evening, I took some *solace* in his ambition, for I believed that in pursuing it, he'd find the glory he so seemed to want without having to share Phaethon's fate. And everything I knew of what Alexander Hamilton had overcome and achieved, I admired. So, whatever he accomplished next, I would be proud to stand at his side, should he ever wish it. Perhaps I was a fool for thinking he would.

"I'm not sure if I could be happy with him," I admitted. But happiness seemed too flimsy a thing to reach for. I might have found happiness with a less complicated man—a polite and dutiful man like Tench Tilghman. Instead, I was drawn to Hamilton, who challenged me to be so much more than a fine-tempered girl. And the person he brought out in me—I wasn't sure I could be happy again without.

### Answer to the Inquiry Why I Sighed

*Before no mortal ever knew*
*A love like mine so tender, true,*
*Completely wretched—you away,*
*And but half blessed e'en while you stay.*
*If present love, obstacles face*
*Deny you to my fond embrace*
*No joy unmixed my bosom warms*
*But when my angel's in my arms.*

—Sonnet by Alexander Hamilton for Elizabeth Schuyler

*Plink. Plink. Plink.*

The sound of pebbles hitting glass scarcely cut through my dreamless nighttime reverie as I read a sonnet Alexander wrote me. It was all, everything, happening so fast. And I couldn't quite believe it was happening to *me*.

My sister shook me, holding a candle aloft. "Betsy, your suitor is at the window."

"But it's the middle of the night," I whispered, and though I ought to have been delighted to see him again, my breath caught with worry, remembering the expression on Alexander's face just before he'd left my uncle's house that evening, some dark cloud before his eyes. Surely it was nothing, for I had proof of his love in my hands.

Kitty groaned and covered her face with a pillow. "Oh, fasten a robe and go down to that prowling tomcat or he'll never go away!"

I said, "But Aunt Gertrude will hear—"

"For pity's sake, you're hopeless," Angelica said. "Have I let her discover you holding hands and kissing before? The baby and I will go down with you. If Aunt Gertrude hears us, I'll tell her the little one was fussing."

It sounded unforgivably duplicitous, but it was precisely the sort of mischief at which Angelica excelled. And because I could still feel the brush of Hamilton's hands upon my skin, and because my lips were still sweet with his kisses, I was powerless to resist either of them.

In slippered feet, Angelica and I both stole down the stairs. Quietly, I unlatched the back door to find Hamilton there, his eyes bright as he slipped inside the house. "Ladies—"

"The keeping room," Angelica whispered, nudging us to where the silver and valuables were kept and servants were not permitted. Then, with my baby niece in her arms, Angelica posted herself as guard, closing us in alone in the darkness with but a single candle.

"Is something the matter?" I whispered to Hamilton in the dim light.

"Yes," he said, quite gravely, a tremor in his voice. "I have something to say, and if it waits another moment, I shall lose my nerve."

I'd never seen him afraid before. Angry, dutiful, officious, charming, reckless, smug, cynical. All those things. But never afraid until now. "The story I told you before. The one about my parents. There is another version."

"Another version?" How could there be more than one?

He took my hands in his, gently stroking his thumbs over my knuckles, then bringing them to his mouth to kiss. "There is a version of the story I have entrusted to no one else but my dear friend Laurens. But I cannot bear to deceive you."

I should have given that casual admission more thought. That there was someone Hamilton trusted. Someone he had trusted more than me. A man I'd never met. A man of whom he spoke worshipfully. And Hamilton was not a man to worship. But all I knew then was that he was speaking of deception. That he was making me afraid now, too. And I'd always believed bad news should be delivered quickly. "Please tell me."

"I let you believe my illegitimacy was a mere wrinkle in the law. What I didn't say was that my mother was jailed for multiple adulteries. Suspected of worse. Held captive in a dank, dark cell, half-starved for months. And when she died, she was denied even the right to pass on property to her whore-children."

I will never forget the way in which he uttered the word *whore-children*, as if hissing from a brand pressed to his skin. And it made me grasp his hands tighter, tears in my eyes. "Oh, Alexander . . ."

He swallowed. "I don't even know if the man who I called Father *is* my father."

I swallowed, too, meeting his eyes so that he would know that I meant what I said. "I understand. And I hold you blameless. None of it is your doing."

Manfully, he squared his shoulders. "That is kind of you to say.

But in courting you, I've shot quite above my station. I can only plead love in defense of myself."

Emotion lodged a knot in my throat. He *loved* me. His sonnet had confessed as much, but to hear it from his mouth, to see it in his eyes . . .

He continued, "My feelings for you make me restless and discontent with everything that used to please me and I began to imagine the world might be different. But I'm a man of hard realities. If this must end things between us I will harbor no ill will."

So, this was why he'd looked so tortured before he left earlier tonight. He thought it might be our last night together. And now his hands actually trembled in mine.

I reached for his cheek, and touched it, tenderly. "Alexander, this makes no difference to me."

"It has made *all* the difference to my life. It's bad enough people think I am—"

"I don't care what anyone else thinks because I love you. I love your mind, the variety of your knowledge, your playful wit, and the excellence of your heart. I love you for reasons that defy any explanation at all."

Angelica had been right. Love *was* a thing beyond reason, beyond *control*. A thing almost predestined. And now that this powerful emotion had finally taken hold of me, I was entirely helpless against it.

He must have felt it, too, because his mouth closed over mine with such hunger it nearly frightened me. Or maybe the hunger that frightened me was my own. I realized my compromised state, only my nightclothes between us. But as his hands slid down my back with carnal intimacy, and his mouth went to my face, my neck, and my hair, there was no liberty I would not have allowed him.

"Betsy," he said, hoarsely, stroking my hair. "You deserve better. With me, your future rank in life would be a perfect lottery. You might move in exalted company or a very humble sphere."

"I don't care." All I heard was that he was speaking about a life with me. A future with me. "I love you." I said it like an incantation.

"Could you truly be an Aquileia and cheerfully plant turnips with me?"

"Yes," I whispered, smiling as I clutched at him.

"Even if America were lost?"

I knew how desperate the circumstances were but could not bear to think of the war being lost. Not after all the suffering and sacrifice. That was the only reason I hesitated to answer.

Alexander swallowed. "I was once determined to let my existence and American liberty end together. But you give me a reason to outlive my pride. If the war is lost, could you live as the wife of a fugitive, leaving behind your home and everything you know?"

"I'm already the proud daughter of a rebel, sir."

He smiled at that. "What think you of Geneva as a retreat? I'm told it is a charming place, favorable to human rights. Would you go with me?"

This time I didn't hesitate. Not even long enough to think. "I would go anywhere with you."

He pressed his forehead to mine. "Then, Elizabeth Schuyler, will you consent to have me for a husband?"

"Yes." *Yes* to anything. Yes to *everything*. Perhaps my parents wouldn't approve. But I wouldn't let them stop me. I felt certain that I could never be happy again without this man. I wasn't even sure I was myself—or who I'd been before. Every plan, every desire, every hope was lost to all-consuming passion. "I want to be yours this very night."

"Temptress." Hamilton groaned and pressed against me, giving me evidence of his desire. And I desired him, too. So much so that the only thing that seemed *right* was for us to come together, skin to skin. But at length, he held me away and took a steadying gulp of air before we lost our heads completely. "It must all be done right between us. I must write for your father's blessing."

"He might not give it," I admitted.

But Hamilton replied, "I am told I am very persuasive with a pen. Especially when I want something. And I want you."

My breath caught to hear it. I knew he was persuasive with a pen; his beautiful sonnet was proof of that. But with my blood afire, I wanted it all to be done now. "It will take too long to wait for permission. Papa will forgive us." After all, he'd forgiven Angelica. "Go wake the reverend."

Hamilton groaned again. This time, with more pain. "Betsy, I can't. I *can't*. What would people say if I were to run off with the daughter of General Schuyler? They would say I'm a self-seeking, fortune-hunting seducer, angling for advantage."

I realized that I would have loved Alexander Hamilton even if he were all those things. Even if he loved me only for the advantage I could bring him. "Let them say it."

"You know what I am." A *whore-child*, he meant, as if it was a crack in his soul that threatened to break *my* heart, too. "I cannot risk even a spot upon the reputation of any child we might have."

A self-seeking seducer angling for advantage would not pass up an opportunity to elope with the daughter of Philip Schuyler. Nor would he worry for the reputation of his child.

Only a man of honor would do that.

*He might not be descended of a Scottish nobleman*, I thought. But, he had something more important than a noble title. Like my father, he had nobility of character. And though I knew it was madness that two people should come to love one another so passionately in such a short space of time, I wanted nothing more than to be his wife. Even if it meant I had to wait.

# *Chapter Nine*

*December 1, 1780*
*Albany*

AM I MAKING *a mistake?*
I had been so certain of Alexander Hamilton. Ready to run away and elope with him if he had allowed it. But now Benedict Arnold was a traitor, and I wondered how anyone could be certain of anything or anyone.

*Benedict Arnold*, the Hero of Saratoga.

The man who'd lost much of the use of his leg in service to this country. A man I'd admired. A man who'd eaten at our table and flirted with my sister. A man who'd used Papa's long friendship to secure a posting at West Point, all while scheming to turn it over to the British, apparently believing my father would go along with his treachery.

Never!

But just as Papa's reputation had recovered, his friendship with Arnold now tainted him again. At the very least, it put his judgment into question. The betrayal was a blow both personal and symbolic, and Arnold's attempt to sacrifice West Point and the men inside it was a treason of the darkest dye.

Despite Lafayette having suspected a traitor long ago, Arnold's treason was discovered only by some miracle of coincidence, in the nick of time, and Alexander had been there.

*Arnold immediately fled to the enemy. I went in pursuit of him but was much too late,* my betrothed wrote from the field.

Arnold had gotten away. But they'd captured his British spy-master instead.

John André.

The injustice of it! That good, honorable officer—even if he was an enemy—would now hang for Arnold's crime. And his death would be brought about, in some part, by the man I was to marry . . .

Alexander was bitterly sorry for it; so much so that when I pleaded with him to use his influence to allow André to be shot like a gentleman, not hanged as a spy, he did as I asked. Though Washington would not hear of it.

"It isn't *just*," I'd fumed to my father.

But Papa blamed Benedict Arnold. "Very little is just in war, my child."

In his letters, Hamilton blamed Arnold, too, expressing sympathy only for the wife he'd abandoned.

*Her horror at the traitor is lost in her love of the man. But a virtuous mind cannot long esteem a base one, and time will make her despise him, if it cannot make her hate. My angelic Betsy, I would not for the world do anything that would hazard your esteem. 'Tis to me a jewel of inestimable price and I think you may rely I shall never make you blush.*

I believed him, though I shouldn't have, because in time, he did make me blush. Worse than that, he made me despair of the traitor in him, too. For though Alexander Hamilton did not betray his country, he did betray me. And now, I struggle with whether love or hate burns more intensely inside me.

But then, as a young woman contemplating marriage, the

Arnold situation was a stark reminder that to marry a man was to share his fate and be vulnerable to all his decisions and mistakes. The traitor's wife and child would forever bear the brand of his treason; and I wondered, did Mrs. Arnold have an inkling of the darkness that dwelt within her husband, or was she now bewildered at the stranger she had married?

Still, Arnold's treason wasn't the only thing to fill me with doubts.

When I agreed to marry Hamilton, I'd worried that my father would not give his consent for our marriage. Especially when Alexander insisted upon confessing his sordid origins to Papa. My parents—both of proud lineages—had objected to my brother-in-law, Jack Carter, because they knew nothing of his family. And yet, my father told Alexander, "Your eloquence and George Washington's recommendation make me glad to welcome you to our family."

That, and perhaps Papa's sense that if he did not give his permission, I would elope, too. I suspected as much because Papa also told Alexander, "It gave Betsy's mother great pain to miss her daughter's wedding, and me as well. I should not like to suffer it a second time."

"We'll see you married properly, Betsy," Mama said under her breath before she embraced Hamilton when my family came to Morristown. "Don't you dare follow in your sister's footsteps."

But we'd long since left that winter camp and six months had now passed in waiting because Alexander feared to neglect his duties in such a perilous time, and he'd therefore refused to take a leave of absence for our nuptials. He'd even considered delaying in order to pay a visit to his friend John Laurens who, having been captured and paroled by the enemy, was not permitted to leave Philadelphia until a prisoner exchange could be arranged.

Worse, the many beautiful love letters Hamilton sent while we were apart were so filled with misgivings that they'd begun to stir my own. Though he wrote that I was his charmer, his angel, and his little nut-brown maid, he also wondered whether our feelings would change while we were separated. He wrote of his friendship and his love, his affection and his desire, but also kept an accounting of who wrote more letters, fearing his greater frequency was a sign of my lesser affections.

I wrote. Of course, I did. It was only that I couldn't keep up with the pace of his correspondence!

He still asked again and again if I wanted him, and entreated me not to deceive myself if I couldn't truly be happy as the wife of a man without means. He even teased gently about a dream he'd had in which he arrived to Albany to find me asleep in the grass holding the hand of another man who had a prior claim.

If I'd asked the name of this man with a supposed prior claim, he'd have dismissed the matter artfully. Or teased that he meant Tench Tilghman. But I knew better. It was André he meant.

He feared that I blamed him for the death of a man I'd known first. A man Hamilton himself admired. A man I grieved for, in truth. But fearing it might come between us, I answered playfully,

> *Sir, your dreams malign me. For there is not now, nor ever has been, a man with prior claim.*

Even so, his letters leaped from flattery to taunts, from arrogance to insecurity, from love to despair. And in doing so, they pushed doubts into my mind such that I had to force my attention to the embroidery in my hands.

"You'll never finish in time for the wedding if you just stare at your needle," Peggy said from where she sprawled upon our shared bed.

I'd been working for days on a wedding gift. Once completed, the matting would form a decorative frame for a miniature portrait of my betrothed. And as I awaited Alexander's arrival I carefully worked the needle through linen held taut by a wooden hoop. Satin stitches. Stem stitches. French knots. Each one making me think about the fact that our lives were soon to be tied together, too.

If, indeed, he would *finally* come for our wedding.

Almost against my will, I remembered Kitty's words.

*I doubt I'm the only lady to whom he has pleaded "but the war"* . . .

I'd scarcely shaken the thought away when, at last, the clatter of hooves upon ice-covered oyster shells reached our ears. I bolted to my feet.

I wasn't the only one. "Is he here?" one of my brothers called from across the hall. The house erupted in near pandemonium.

My family liked Hamilton. In the course of our courtship, he'd managed to win over each and every one of them. He talked finances with my father, philosophy with Angelica, Dutch traditions with Mama, war stories with my brothers, and beaus with Peggy, advising her how best to catch and keep one.

And now my siblings and I raced down the stairs to greet him, even as Prince scowled in disapproval at our lack of dignity as he opened the door.

I ought to have waited for Mama, who was pregnant again, to heave herself up from where she lay abed to come down and greet our guests. But I was far too eager. In fact, I quite nearly raced past Prince out into the blustery cold and swirling snowflakes in the open doorway, where stood two men wearing ice-crusted cloaks over blue and buff.

But only one figure gladdened my heart to bursting.

*Alexander.* The smile he gave me before presenting himself with a great formal bow all but erased the trepidation I'd felt moments before.

"Miss Schuyler," he said, his satiny voice bringing back memories and making my pulse fly.

I wanted to throw my arms around the neck of my betrothed and shower him with kisses. Instead, I beamed. "Alexander." My eyes lingered on him as long as I dared before politeness forced me to slide my gaze to his companion, who I recognized at once from Morristown. "Mac!"

At my exuberant familiarity, James McHenry grinned and doffed his cap, just as my father reached the entry hall. "Ah, Colonel Hamilton!" Papa said, coming in from the back door where he'd been making preparations in the courtyard. "You've joined us at last."

"General Schuyler," Alexander said, almost standing to attention.

Papa hung up his snow-covered coat and the large feathered hat he favored, then made his way across to us. "Welcome back to the Pastures," he said, holding out his hand.

Alexander shook it. "Thank you, sir. General Washington sends his regards and regrets that he can't join the celebration." Papa's smile broadened at being mentioned by the commander in chief. "I think you must remember my friend and colleague on General Washington's staff, James McHenry. He's, uh, well—he's my guest for the wedding."

The only one.

Tench Tilghman had sweetly and sincerely sent his best wishes and a small gift. But General Washington couldn't spare him or any other aides-de-camp with Alexander and McHenry gone. And as for Alexander's family, well . . .

How I loved my father for having made no issue of Alexander's illegitimacy. And now Papa simply behaved as if all were quite normal. "Ah, McHenry, but of course. Come in. Dry off. Get warm. We're pleased to offer every comfort during your stay."

Thereafter Prince collected hats and cloaks, departing our merry circle, but not before instructing other servants to relieve our guests of their satchels. And having finally made her way down the stairs, Mama held her lower back and said she would see to supper.

Conversation turned to weather, war, and wine as McHenry followed Papa into his study. But Alexander quickly crossed back to me, his fierce blue eyes seeing right into the heart of me. "Betsy," he said softly, intimately. "I want you to know that all these months, the only thing that alleviated the pain of your absence was looking forward to the moment we shall finally become each other's forever."

Unable to express the welling feelings inside me with the eloquence with which he always wrote and spoke, I managed only, "And you were always in my thoughts." He smiled as though I'd versified a sonnet, encouraging me to go on. "But I much prefer you at my side."

"Well, then, at your side I shall endeavor to stay. After all"—his eyes twinkled—"as you will soon learn, whatever affords you pleasure will always be most agreeable to me." My face warmed despite the chill in the hall, but fortunately Papa's booming voice called my intended groom to join him. And Alexander promised, "I shall see you later, my lovely girl."

THE NIGHT BEFORE our wedding, the ball at our house was attended by all the best of Dutch Albany society. The Van Rensselaers and the Van Burens, the Ten Broecks and the Ten Eycks, the Van Schaicks and the Douws, and so many others. Neither snow nor ice nor howling wind seemed to deter our New Netherlander friends and neighbors from coming out to the Pastures for the celebrations.

Amidst boughs of holly and the light of countless candles, the salon on our second floor hosted festivities that included food and drink, dancing and music, and games and toasts. We danced minuets, cotillions, and Scottish reels until my feet ached and my heart soared. Alexander never seemed to tire, and I determined to keep up with him through every bar and set. I danced with Mac and my brother-in-law, Mr. Carter, a man eight years Angelica's senior, whose business supplying the army for once permitted him time to join in the festivities. But Alexander could never wait long before declaring himself impatient and claiming me again.

My fiancé appeared more at ease than I'd ever seen him before, and perhaps that wasn't a surprise, as these days of rest and merriment were the first break from military service he'd had in five years. Indeed, his eyes sparkled as he asked, "May I steal you away for a moment?"

"By all means." I'd been hoping for a quiet opportunity to give him my gift. He took my hand and led me around the edge of the dance floor as we were stopped again and again by well-wishers, until we finally escaped down the stairs and into the cooler air of the dimly lit sitting room, which afforded us a modicum of peace and privacy. There, Alexander asked me to wait. And while he ducked away I seized the moment to pull my gift from its hiding place in the cabinet next to the fireplace. Alexander returned before I'd barely completed the task—and held a large sack of his own.

"Whatever is that?" I asked.

He grinned and nodded at what I held in my own hands. "I could ask the same."

I smiled. "A wedding gift for my husband."

He feigned a frown and stepped closer. "Your *husband*, madam? Do I know him?"

Playing his game, I said, "Oh, you know him very well, sir. And your gift is for?"

He came closer yet. "For my wife-to-be. And before you ask, indeed, you know her well. She has a good nature, a charming vivacity, and is most *unmercifully* handsome"—he arched a brow and closed the remaining space between us—"and so perverse that she has none of those affectations which are the prerogatives of beauty."

How did he always manage to set my world a-tumble with his words? "Oh, you must be a lucky man, indeed. I hope you've shown her your appreciation."

He barked a laugh. "You saucy charmer!"

I sat in the chair closest to the fire so that I could see by the greater light there, and Alexander pulled up a chair of his own so that our knees touched. With a nervous smile, he placed the heavy sack onto my lap. I untied its string and worked the coarse cloth over the solid object inside. Impatience rolled off him so forcefully that I had to tease him further by taking great pains to slide the sack evenly off, a little on this side, and then a little on that.

"And to think someone once told me you were the Finest Tempered Girl in the World," he said with a chuckle.

I yanked the sack away then as we both laughed. Removing the wrapping revealed a fine, carved mahogany sewing box. "Oh, it's exquisite," I said. I carefully lifted the lid, only to find another treasure tucked inside. A small, round, pearl-encrusted pendant. The pendant alone would've enamored me, but combined with the inscription and personal token inside, I knew not what to say.

"General Washington mentioned that Kitty Livingston had asked for a token of his esteem," Alexander explained. "I guessed you might like one from His Excellency, too."

"You guessed right," I said, in awe as I stared at the circle of General Washington's dark blond hair under a glass covering inscribed with his name.

How had Alexander afforded such finery? I couldn't imagine, but I could barely think on it through my embarrassment that Washington may have thought me a frivolous girl to want a clipping of his locks. Still, I wasn't so embarrassed that I didn't wish to wear it straightaway!

Fastening the chain, I said, "I'll cherish it forever." I looked up to find Hamilton beaming, and I added, "But I should not like you to think that I am the sort of woman who expects expensive—"

"You are the kind of woman who *deserves* this and every last penny I have squirreled away," he interrupted. "Besides, I am not entirely impoverished, my angel. And I am fortunate in my friends. John Laurens regrets very much that he cannot be with us on our wedding day and insisted upon advancing me a tidy sum to purchase this for you."

"I shall have to thank him when we finally meet," I said of his mysterious and much-admired friend. "His generosity of spirit shall stand present for him as if he were a guest. And I shall wear this pendant near my heart on our wedding day."

"Good." My beloved's voice turned stern. "But don't think it will not irritate me a little to have another man's name so near your heart. Even *Washington's*."

I laughed. "Near to my heart, but not inside it, for there is room there for no man but you. Oh, and the box is a most perfect gift, too."

"Oh, 'and the box,' she says," Alexander grumbled playfully. "My turn, then?" When I nodded, he tore at the ribbon, and then unfolded the plain ticking I'd used to cushion the framed matting and portrait. "Oh, my angelic girl. What have you done?"

"I had your portrait rendered by Mr. Peale in Philadelphia, and then I designed and sewed a frame for it," I said, suddenly nervous. "I wanted you to see how much I've thought of you all these months."

"What fine, detailed work." He paused in his admiration of my embroidery. "Only you must think me vain to keep a portrait of myself."

"Well, I hoped you would leave it with me if ever you should have to go away again," I said, feeling a little foolish that I'd made him a gift I wanted myself.

But he intertwined our fingers and leaned to kiss me. "I love you more every hour."

I very much wanted that kiss, but unfortunately, we were interrupted.

"There you are," Peggy said, leaning into the room.

Alexander cleared his throat. "Why hello, little sister."

"Sorry to intrude on your private celebration," she said, though Peggy was never sorry for such things. "Mama beckoned me to find you to say good night. Guests are leaving."

Before long, everyone was gone, and I had the great pleasure—for one last night—of sharing a room with both Angelica and Peggy for old time's sake. Years had passed since the three of us had stayed together, and just like we used to, we talked and laughed and teased until long after we should've gone to sleep. "I can hardly believe that tomorrow, I'll be *wed*," I whispered into the darkness, for the candle had burned down some time before.

"And *bed*," Angelica said.

"Angelica!" I cried, my stomach tingling.

But she only laughed. "What's the use in having a more experienced older sister if she can't divulge the secrets of marriage?"

"Do tell!" Peggy said.

I pulled the covers over my face, which of course they tugged back down. "I'll say this," Angelica began in her world-wise way. "A man enjoys a woman to be an active participant and desires her pleasure. So don't be shy, Betsy. What you don't know, Hamilton will teach you."

My face burned, but I couldn't deny my interest in her advice or the way my body warmed at the idea of what Alexander might teach me. "I shall take that under advisement," I said with as much dignity as I could. "Now, please be quiet before I die."

My sisters burst into giggles at my expense, but I was too happy to care.

*December 14, 1780*
*Albany*

"Betsy?" Papa called from the hallway. "It's time."

With teary eyes, Angelica took my hands. "You are a vision."

"I doubt that," I said, a little discomfited by the attention. I wished to be a vision, but I would content myself to be *unmercifully handsome* in my bridegroom's eyes.

"Oh, but Angelica's right about something for a change," Peggy said, her hands clasped to her breast.

Smoothing the fine sky-blue silk of my new gown, my fingers

running over the embroidered flowers and tiny hand-stitched beads and pearls, I took a breath and reached for both of my sisters' hands. "I don't know what I'd do without you."

"Well, silly, you shall never have to find out," Peggy said, sniffing, and I caught her swiping at the corner of her eye when she turned away. Papa knocked again just as the tall case clock in the hallway struck noon. My heart thundered in time with the deep chimes, and it felt as if my knees might go soft. But, somehow, I made it to the door to find Papa dressed in his best dark gray velvet suit, the one with the high collar, silver piping, and matching waistcoat.

"My lovely child," he said as Angelica and Peggy gave me one last hug and kiss each before they rushed downstairs. "Why, it's like looking at your mother on our wedding day all over again."

"Oh, Papa," I said, the emotion in his voice making my eyes sting.

And he sighed, as if he were looking at me for the last time. "*My little Betsy*—though I suppose, as a married woman, we shall now have to call you Elizabeth or Eliza."

It was the custom to give up childhood nicknames upon marriage, but I didn't wish for Papa to ever look at me differently than he did now. "Betsy will do. I'm accustomed to it."

My father gave a rare grin and held out his elbow. "Well then, I do believe there's a very eager young officer waiting to marry his bride just downstairs. It wouldn't do to keep him waiting."

I took his arm, and down we went. Just outside the doorway to the formal blue-and-gold parlor, the members of our procession stood assembled—the minister, Mama, my sisters with the hand-painted silk fans I'd given them for the occasion.

And Alexander.

My fiancé cut a fine, dashing figure in his dress uniform. His smile beckoned me to come to him until Papa was relinquishing my hand. When the harpsichord began to play, the minister led us up the aisle of chairs filled with family and friends, the whole assembly brightly lit from the winter sunlight pouring in through the windows. The service was conducted in Dutch and English, out of respect to the groom, but I barely recalled a word because I'd never seen such unbridled joy shine from Alexander's countenance.

With love, yes, I believed that. But there was something else, too. In wedding, my family became his, too, and I sensed that gave him a sense of belonging.

I promised myself that I would always ensure that for him. My parents would be his parents, my sisters would be his sisters, and my brothers would be his brothers.

He'd never be without family again.

I wanted to be alone with him to tell him so, but after the ceremony there commenced an open house of visitors who nibbled on honey cakes, marzipan, candied almonds, and my mother's famous *olie-koecken*—sweet dough fried in hot lard until golden brown. Then a sumptuous wedding feast of roast duck with dumplings, pork with cabbage, and baked apples and raisins. For dessert, imported chocolates, cinnamon bark, and spiced *koekjes*—or cookies, in English.

Alexander and I never had time for more than an affectionate smile or a stolen kiss. Until, suddenly, we were alone in my childhood room, now turned into a bridal chamber, lit only by a warming fire.

Music and laughter reached us from below stairs, but it felt as if it came from a thousand miles away when Alexander looked at me with desire. "You're finally mine," he said, his voice tender but full of a gravity that hadn't been there before. His hand clasped mine, and his thumb rubbed over my wedding band, a ring made of two linked circles of gold that swiveled to join as one. Alexander had engraved them with our names. "And I am yours, too." He spoke as if he were trying out the premise, drafting an argument and seeing if he could make it work.

I was determined that he would. "Show me . . ."

He unwrapped me as he had my gift the night before, with eagerness and curiosity and hunger. And I found that the more ardently he touched me and kissed me, the more I shared his hunger. When he wore only his shirt and I only my shift, he guided us to the bed, under covers that his ravenous hands and body quickly made warm.

That night, Alexander's heated whispers were in French as he made love to me. I didn't know enough of the language to decipher the words, but his meaning had never been plainer.

All my life, I'd been the boyish sort of girl who preferred climbing trees and hiking through the woods, or the veritable spinster, more concerned with nursing sick soldiers than landing one for a husband. I was the general's daughter who'd inherited the fervor of his warrior's heart. But Alexander's lovemaking found the woman in me, and the more claiming his touch, the more ecstatic my escape. He was as relentless in bed as he was in everything else, craving my surrender and winning it again and again.

"Oh, lovely wife, crown me with everything that is tender and kind and passionate in you. Love me," he commanded.

And, I did. Oh, I did.

# Chapter Ten

*On the first days of your wedding I dare say you wanted*
*nothing to do with anybody's letters. But I will now become*
*bolder in interrupting your amorous occupations, as the*
*importance of the matters I have to mention deserve some*
*minutes' respite. You may therefore, my good friend, take*
*this opportunity of catching breath with decency, which will*
*be attributed to the strength of your friendship for me.*
—MARQUIS DE LAFAYETTE TO ALEXANDER HAMILTON

AN EXTREMELY WAGGISH letter interrupted our honeymoon, reminding me that I was now a soldier's wife. An *ambitious* soldier's wife.

The marquis had returned from France a few months earlier with the aid our cause so desperately needed. Supplies. Money. A fleet of ships under the command of French general Rochambeau. It could change everything. It could turn the war. If we found the right opportunity. And my new husband was looking for not only an opportunity of victory, but also a chance to rise in station.

The same man who pretended he could have been content to plant turnips enlisted Lafayette's help in a campaign to secure a promotion to adjutant general. And when that failed, Lafayette undertook to get my husband appointed as an envoy to France on a mission to obtain loans and expedite supply shipments.

"Paris?" I gasped from my seat before the fire in the sitting room. How would I fare in the social whirl of such a cosmopolitan place? But I'd scarcely had time to wish I'd better applied myself to learning the French language when we learned the appointment had gone to someone else.

"Worry not," Alexander said, bracing his hands upon the mantel and staring into the flames. "It appears I'll be shackled to a desk forever while my friends cover themselves in glory. Shall I never receive an opportunity for advancement?"

I went to him, searching for the best way to soothe my husband, as a wife should. "You're Washington's most trusted aide," I said, hoping the reminder of the vital role he played in the war would offer solace. "And as such, you daily command generals in the field even though they outrank you."

"Once, that might have been enough," he replied, unconvinced. "But then I met you." He turned and took my hand. "And now, instead of chasing a glorious death, I must somehow make a glorious life. Which is a *great* deal more trouble, wife."

"Fortunately, husband," I replied, kissing his furrowed brow, "you needn't do it alone."

He sighed. "Alas, my duty is soon to separate us. You could make me forget the whole business of war entirely, but I suppose you are so much a Portia that if you saw me inclined to quit the service of your country, you would dissuade me."

"A Portia?" I asked, then instantly wished I hadn't. "No, *please*, not another Roman . . ."

"But I pay you a compliment," he protested, telling me—at great length, with many quotations of the original Latin, plus a tangential dart into Shakespeare—of an ancient lady who, amongst other heroic things, patriotically concealed her sorrow to be separated from her husband when he went to war.

But I didn't wish to be separated. I had no children to care for, plantation to manage, or homestead to defend. I had a husband whose joys and travails I had pledged before God to share. And a war that I wished to have a part in winning.

When I told Alexander that I intended to accompany him on his return to headquarters, he kissed my forehead and assented. "I was hoping you might. My Portia. According to Plutarch, Portia's husband said of her, as I would say of you, *'though the natural weakness of her body hinders her from doing what men can perform, she has a mind as valiant and as active for the good of her country as the best of us.'*"

It was, I thought, the best compliment anyone had ever paid to me. "Why, Colonel Hamilton, I seem to learn something new whenever in your company."

Heat banked in his eyes. "Perhaps if you submit yourself to my tutelage, you shall have a real education by spring."

An answering heat rushed over my skin, and I eyed him with curious hunger. "Whatever would you teach me?"

"To start with," he began, drawing me back to our bedroom, "your classical education is in vast need of improvement . . ."

Whereupon he taught me, by way of demonstration, some choice Latin terms that would have scandalized a harlot. And I minded not at all. In truth, I counted myself the happiest of women, altogether.

Thus, after a perfect Christmas holiday with my family, I went with Hamilton from nuptial splendor and plenty, to the scarcity of the army.

General Washington's new headquarters was situated at a small Dutch farmhouse near the village of New Windsor, New York. Conditions for the ordinary soldier were dismal, the vast majority clad only in tattered uniforms, shirts, and breeches, shoes worn through, and not enough food or munitions by half. If they were lucky, they shared a single blanket between every two or three men.

It was Jockey Hollow again, with milder weather. How had nothing else improved?

It was unthinkable, but Congress claimed to have no legal power to tax and raise funds for the army they'd called into the field. Alexander argued that the power was implicit, that having declared independence and war, Congress should consider themselves vested with full power to preserve the country from harm.

He was not the only one to think it.

After the expiration of the three-year enlistments that most had signed, the soldiers were *angry*—at not being permitted to leave, at not being paid, at *everything*. Indeed, their discontent had boiled over into another mutiny only just resolved, and the tension around camp was still as thick as the frozen mud covering the ground. There was not a little fear that the troops might join Benedict Arnold, who had donned a red coat and recently captured Richmond, Virginia.

For the British.

It was within this surly atmosphere that Alexander secured for us a cramped and dreary room in a boardinghouse, but I could hardly complain when I saw what our countrymen endured. Instead, I donned practical and patriotic homespun and endeavored to make myself useful to Mrs. Washington at headquarters. There, alongside the great lady, I threw myself into writing letters to raise money, hosting dignitaries who visited camp, and helping the slaves prepare meals for Washington's little military family—repetitive suppers of bread, butter, and a spicy tripe stew, the scent of which was not altogether appetizing, but better than what the ordinary soldiers ate by far.

It was at one of these dinners that we were reunited with the Marquis de Lafayette. Having just negotiated the end of a mutiny in the Pennsylvania Line, he returned to headquarters and broke the sour mood by hugging—and even kissing—everyone.

I was startled that General Washington, a very formal man who did not like to be touched, allowed the marquis this familiarity. Then Lafayette treated me to the same exuberant greeting. "*Mademoiselle Schuyler*—or shall I say *Madame Hamilton*, now?" he asked, kissing both my cheeks.

"Marquis," I said, smiling.

But before I could decide whether I was meant to return these kisses, Lafayette withdrew and wagged his finger at me. "I'm afraid I have a quarrel with you. I invite you to camp some years ago. You refuse me. Yet, for Hamilton, here you are. I would take offense did I not so much approve of your choice."

"As do we all," said Colonel Tilghman with a polite smile.

Seemingly caught off guard by the warm sentiment of his friends, Alexander flushed.

Even as McHenry called, "Speak for yourself, Tench. If you'd seen Ham strutting at his wedding, you'd know he doesn't need a thing more to swell his head."

Before *I* could flush at what might have been Mac's innuendo—and in front of the Washingtons!—Lafayette unveiled a crate of champagne he'd acquired from somewhere and smuggled into the house. "Since we could not all see the wedding, we celebrate tonight, *oui*?"

Quietly, from his end of the table, General Washington said, "A capital idea." And that was all the approval the younger men needed to pop the cork and start pouring.

"May I propose a toast?" Colonel Tilghman asked from where he was seated beside Mrs. Washington. Tench didn't wait for an answer but rose to his full height and raised his glass. "To our Little Lion," he said to Alexander, respectfully and with genuine fondness. Then turning to me, he added, "And to the finest tempered girl in the world. A perfect match. May it endure and prosper with our country. With my blessing and unalterable friendship."

His graciousness moved me, and I hoped Tench might one day find a woman to love him as he deserved. I tipped my glass to him in return, hoping he could feel my good wishes before we drank. And then it was all laughter and merriment.

"Congratulations, my boy," Washington said to Hamilton with a fatherly tone, and my husband seemed not quite certain how to take it.

Perhaps to ease the moment, Tilghman continued, "We all knew your husband was a gone man for you, Mrs. Hamilton, the night he forgot the watchword."

At the reminder, Mac roared with laughter, recounting details Alexander never told me. "He's lucky he managed to wheedle it out of that boy who lived at headquarters or the guards would've let him sleep in the snow."

Grinning, Hamilton protested, "I was determined to keep what little dignity I had left! I had to pretend I'd just been testing the guardsman."

Even Mrs. Washington chuckled at this, shaking her head. And the toasts continued long after the Washingtons went to bed.

"Thirteen toasts," Hamilton insisted. "One for each state!"

Mac raised his glass, his Irish brogue more pronounced with every raised glass. "*Here's to the four hinges of friendship. Swearing, lying, stealing, and drinking. When you swear, swear by your country. When you lie, lie for a pretty woman. When you steal, steal away from bad company. And when you drink, drink with me.*"

"Huzzah!" we cried until all thirteen toasts were made.

I still remember the international brotherhood of that night so vividly. The French Marquis de Lafayette. The Marylanders, James McHenry, Tench Tilghman, and Robert Hanson Harrison. The Connecticut Yankee, David Humphreys. And Alexander Hamilton of the West Indies.

My husband told me they were the only real family he'd ever known, and now I saw that they *were* a family. What's more, I felt privileged to be included. At our wedding, I'd sworn that my people would be Hamilton's. But now I said another silent vow that his people would also be mine.

"MY DEAR, I must pay you a compliment," Mrs. Washington said.

We sat together, huddled by the fire as cold whistled through cracks in the weathered walls, great piles of mending at our feet in baskets. I'd been wondering how we'd ever make a dent as my fingertips stung from working the needle through the coarse cloth when her words drew me from my thoughts. "Oh? What-ever for?"

I thought she'd praise my stitchery, but instead she said, "You've made our Colonel Hamilton very happy. I wasn't sure anyone could."

Pride stilled my hands, for she'd known my husband for far longer than I had. "You do me a kindness—"

Just then, shouts erupted from outside and footsteps pounded down the staircase. General Washington *ran* past us, out the doorway, and his flight set my heart into a thunderous beat. His Excellency was so measured in all things that his alarm sent us following him out the front door into the biting afternoon.

I braced myself for any possibility—mutinous soldiers, perhaps even a British attack! And with all the general's aides, including Alexander, dispatched on errands. But I never expected to see the adjoining shed afire, hungry flames consuming the wall closest to where the enslaved laundresses worked over a campfire. Nor did I expect to see General Washington single-handedly heaving three enormously heavy washtubs of water upon the blaze before it spread to the house.

Not knowing what else to do as the bodyguards came running, I rushed to get more water, but Washington already had everything smothered—only smoke and black scorch marks remained. Then the general leaned back against the house to catch his breath.

"Good heavens," Mrs. Washington uttered, her hand on her heart while the laundresses fell into apologies before the great man, realizing their fire had sparked the ignition, and perhaps expecting punishment. But the general kindly reassured the women before coming up the steps of the porch where we stood.

"Are you unharmed, sir?" I asked, noting his weariness. His hair was much grayer than it had been when I'd first met him in Morristown. More so than the hair I wore in the pendant round my neck.

"Quite, Mrs. Hamilton, but your concern is appreciated," he said, reaching for the door to return to his work, as if nothing remarkable had just occurred.

Noting the pallor of Mrs. Washington's face, I gave her hand a reassuring squeeze.

"Thank you, dear," she whispered with an appreciative glance, then stepped inside with the general. The quick exchange made me wonder who Martha Washington, so often without female companionship while in camp, had to confide in and rely upon. Perhaps it wasn't my place, but I'd consider it a privilege to call Mrs. Washington my friend.

A moment later, Tench rode up to the house, eyes bulging at the sight of the scorch marks. When I told him what happened, he shook his head. "As if the weight of the whole war didn't already lie upon his shoulders, now he's *literally* putting out fires."

It was a sentiment that stuck with me.

One I shared with Alexander when he returned from his duties that night to our little room at the boardinghouse, his hair ice crusted and his cheeks raw from the wind. But not before I helped him remove his sodden cloak and draped it near the fireplace. "Can I get you something hot to eat or drink?"

He peered over his shoulder at me as he opened his satchel and pulled out a thick sheaf of papers. "Your very presence warms me, my love. My travels kept me from finishing today's correspondence, so I must attend that before I can sleep."

"Of course." Moving quietly about the small room, I readied for bed. The crackle of the fire and the fast scratches of Alexander's quill were the only sounds in the dim room. Kneeling at the hearth, I added two logs to the blaze, then held out my hands to soak in the heat when, on a sigh, Alexander stamped a seal against the page and then set the letter aside.

"I saw something quite remarkable today," I said, having waited impatiently for him to finish. "General Washington single-handedly put out a fire upon the shed at the headquarters."

Alexander turned in his seat. "So I heard."

"I saw him *run* to put the fire out. I didn't even know he *could* run, he's always so dignified."

"It sounds as if this made quite an impression on you," Alexander said after a long moment. Then he frowned and got up to pace, his expression suddenly stormy. "Perhaps you would hold me in such regard if I received an appointment or command befitting my talents."

My stomach dropped. "Oh, but I admire you more than any other." When he didn't answer, I asked, "Have I said something to upset you?"

Alexander shook his head, rueful. "No. I'm sorry. It's only that I've engaged in military service since the beginning of '76. I began in the line and had I continued there, I'd be in a more advanced rank than I now am."

"Of course," I said, realizing the cause of his peevish agitation. Alexander worried over his future. Over *our* future.

He threw himself back into the chair. "And yet, *here I sit*, writing letters of introduction for John Laurens while I am yet again passed over."

I felt a little nauseated for him. That an appointment he wanted went to his friend both soothed and salted the wound. "Alexander, you will receive a command—"

"When? Dammit Betsy, I have yet to *once* merit the confidence and esteem of the man you admire so much!" His raised voice echoed in the small space.

The quiet that followed was just as loud until I could no longer tolerate the space between us. Going to him, I rested my hands on his chest. I opened my mouth to tell him that of course he had the confidence and esteem of Washington. Why, the great man relied upon him more than any other. And hadn't he heard Washington's term of endearment at dinner?

But sensing Alexander didn't want to be thought of as anyone's *boy*—not even Washington's—I looked into his fiery blue eyes and simply said, "I love you. I admire you in every way a woman can admire a man. More than any other man."

I meant that sincerely. Though now, in the fullness of years, I realize that what I felt was only a fraction of all that I would feel for him. That the love I felt then was of a simple, unalloyed, untested kind. That like a captain navigating a new river, I didn't *know* Hamilton yet.

Not the breadths nor depths of him.

Nor the rocks upon which we might run aground.

He softened as he gazed at me, and then he tenderly leaned his forehead against mine. "Forgive me, my angel. You don't deserve my ire."

"I will ease you however I can," I said, realizing that this was one of the things Alexander needed from me as his wife, and something I could easily provide. Soft comforts against the hard realities of our war-torn world. An attentive ear. A warm touch. Kind, encouraging words.

Heat slipped into his eyes again, but not the heat of anger. "You always do," he said, kissing me like he did all those nights of our honeymoon. "And now I think it is time for bed . . ."

*MUTINY! MUTINY! MUTINY!*

The shout carried to us from some crier in town, and my husband came fully awake, leaping from the bed to yank on breeches and boots while I was still rubbing sleep from my eyes. A moment later McHenry was pounding on the door, and my shirtless husband threw it open, perhaps forgetting entirely that I was in bedclothes, or in the room at all.

Fortunately, Mac seemed not to realize it either. "It's the New Jersey Line," he said, grimly.

"Where?" Hamilton barked.

"Fifty miles out," Mac replied. "They broke against their officers and are marching on Trenton to demand that the state legislature redress their grievances."

Fifty miles away. *Better than here,* I thought. Marching to demand the pay, clothing, and supplies they were rightly owed by a state that recruited them to war was better than deserting or going over to the British. Maybe my husband thought so, too, because his motions to dress became less frantic.

But Mac clapped him on the back and said, "Saddle up, lad. The general thinks we made a mistake negotiating with the Pennsylvania mutineers. He means to go after them this time, before it spreads like a contagion."

Mac started to go, but my husband called after him. "Grab that crier by the ears and give him a knock-about, will you? The fewer people who know about the mutiny the better."

Mac nodded, then was gone as soon as he'd come. Meanwhile I found my husband's shirt in the bed linens and tossed it to him, at which point he colored at realizing my presence and my state. "A thousand apologies, Betsy—"

"Don't make even one," I said, understanding the urgency. "Did McHenry really mean that you're going after them?"

Hamilton nodded. "We'll stop the mutineers before they get to Trenton. And this time we'll make an example of them."

I bit my lip at the horror of American troops fighting American troops, feeling a little disloyal to my husband and to Washington, because it seemed to defy all notions of justice. These mutineers had sacrificed so much and suffered for so long. Did they not have the right, as free men, to petition their government for redress of their grievances? They wanted nothing more than what any human being seemed due—food, shelter, clothing.

Freedom.

The thought of punishing them for it unleashed a pain within my chest. A pain that worsened to know that my own husband might have some part in their punishment. And though I said nothing, he must've seen that pain in my eyes. Buttoning the collar of his shirt, Hamilton asked, "What happens when the mutiny isn't fifty miles away, but here, at headquarters? As it is, Lafayette is afraid to leave General Washington alone for fear that disloyal troops might turn their coats and hand him over to the British."

"They wouldn't," I said, only because it was treachery too black for my heart to even contemplate.

"Maybe not," my husband said. "But we lost more than a thousand soldiers in the negotiations with the Pennsylvania Line when they were released from their enlistments. We can't lose any more men. Not when Arnold is unleashing hell on Virginia."

*Benedict Arnold.* I couldn't hear the name without erupting into a fresh rage. That traitor knew everything. Our strengths. Our weaknesses. Our strategies. Maybe even our spies. He'd already burned Richmond for the British, looted it, and sold off the plunder for his own financial gain. There was seemingly no end to the depravity of which Arnold was capable nor the damage he could do. I hated him for all that, for John André's death, and for having compromised my father, too.

But now I had further reason.

Good patriots were going to hang or be shot, at least in part, because of Benedict Arnold, and my husband's hands would be stained with their blood the rest of his life. As if to steel his courage against it, Alexander eyed me beseechingly and said, "I hate Congress. The army. The world. I hate *myself.* But we must hold this army together."

"I understand," I whispered as he stooped to kiss me goodbye. And I did understand, after a fashion. I remembered that he'd said it before, at Morristown, when I asked him if it was right to torture that poor deserter. He'd defended himself then by saying that he hadn't given the order. But this time, he might. He would, in fact, ride out that very same day with Lafayette and Washington for the trials that would condemn several mutineers to execution.

But before he left, Hamilton stopped in the doorway and stared at me where I sat fighting back tears. And his own voice thickened with emotion. "When the fighting is done, I will make this a better world, Betsy. I promise you."

An audacious vow no mere mortal should make. A vow born as much of egotism as of idealism, as much self-justification as godliness. But young and hopeful as I was, I believed him. I put my faith in him.

And at least in that, I was right to.

Because whatever else he did, Alexander Hamilton *did* make this a better world.

He kept that promise.

In truth, he spent his *life* keeping that promise.

# Chapter Eleven

*February 16, 1781*
*New Windsor*

I T WAS, AT long last, time to make a stand.

After the mutinies had been put down and their leaders executed, all the men were weary and anxious for the coming—and hopefully decisive—battle with the British.

For almost a year now, the French general Rochambeau's fleet had been blockaded in Rhode Island. Now he was ready to abandon his ships and march his well-equipped and well-trained French soldiers with ours in what we all hoped might be the decisive battle for American independence.

All that remained to be decided was when and where we would fight.

In the deciding, Alexander was gone many nights until well after the fire had died and I'd fallen asleep. I'd taken a terrible cold, and so had poor Colonel Tilghman, who forged on with his work anyway.

For myself, in the most secret part of my heart, I was terrified. I believed in our soldiers and our cause and our chances, but from what I overheard at headquarters, it seemed that we were now racing week by week headlong toward a battle from which there could be no retreat or stalemate. This time would be for all the world.

Win, and nothing would ever be the same.

Lose and, well, my husband, my father, my family, my friends—we stood to lose *everything*.

Knowing what was at stake, I didn't mind my husband's late hours. What alarmed me was Alexander's arrival to our room in the middle of the afternoon. I'd never before seen him so distressed. Sitting up in bed, where I'd been endeavoring to rest away a headache and sore throat, I ran my gaze over him, trying to determine what could be wrong.

Slamming the door, he stomped inside and threw his satchel to the floor. His cloak followed in a great flourish of dark fabric, all the while he muttered and cursed to himself. Slipping out of bed, I wrapped a blanket around my shoulders, and he came straight to me, his blue eyes stormy. "You shouldn't get up. You need rest."

"But—"

"There's been an unexpected change," he said, a strangeness to his voice, a wildness to his expression. "I am no longer a member of the general's family."

I almost couldn't make sense of the words. "I don't understand."

He pulled me to sit on the edge of the bed. "General Washington and I have come to an open rupture. He accused me of treating him with disrespect." My husband's tone was equal parts anger and dismay.

I took his hand. "You? Disrespect His Excellency? I cannot imagine it. Tell me what happened."

Alexander squeezed my hand and then rose. For a moment, he stared into the fire, and then he began to pace, as he so often did when agitated. "There is very little to tell. He asked to speak to me, and I nodded, then continued down to hand Tilghman a letter. The marquis asked me a question, to which I gave the most concise of answers because I was impatient to return to the general." Hamilton heaved a breath, his hands raking at his auburn hair. "But instead of finding Washington as usual in his room, I met him at the head of the stairs. Do you know what he said? That I'd kept him waiting ten minutes and had treated him with disrespect. Can you imagine?" Alexander whirled on me. "I sincerely believe my absence didn't last two minutes."

"Of course," I said, my mind racing. "It was just a misunderstanding. Surely this can be remedied."

"No, it cannot." He shook his head. "I argued that I was not conscious of any disrespect, but since he thought it necessary to tell me such we should part. He agreed. So here I am."

Alexander had barely finished recounting the tale when a knock sounded upon our door. My husband crossed the room and opened it, the rusted hinges creaking in protest. And I heard Tilghman's voice from the other side. "General Washington has sent me. May I come in?"

"I don't think so, sir. My wife is indisposed." Alexander gave a curt nod and made to close the door.

I was aghast at his rudeness. "I am perfectly well," I called, not willing to let him use me as a rationale for not resolving this disagreement. And I was becoming accustomed, at this point, to my husband's colleagues bursting in upon us at any hour of day or night. "Invite poor Tilghman in to get warmed by the fire."

After a pause, my husband relented, and the colonel entered and gave me a bow, even as a coughing fit had him clasping his chest.

"Let me get you some raspberry leaf tea with honey," I said, pouring from the pot I'd made myself downstairs at the boarding-house's hearth.

"Thank you, Mrs. Hamilton. You're too kind." Tilghman accepted the cup.

Meanwhile, Alexander seemed impatient at all the niceties, but I paid him no mind. "I hope you bring good news from headquarters," I said, giving Tilghman a meaningful look, and I imagined I saw in his eyes a mutual understanding. *This must be fixed*. While it did sound as if His Excellency had been in ill humor, Alexander had never before responded with such stridency. They were both simply overworked. Overburdened by the weight of the war and the coming battle.

Sipping at the herb tea, Tilghman addressed my husband. "Sir, General Washington bade me to reassure you of his great confidence in your abilities, your integrity, and your usefulness to him. He wishes nothing more than to reconcile. He explained that his terseness came in a regrettable moment of passion and that he is sorry for it."

Relief flooded me. Given the circumstances, how could tempers not flare from time to time? And how gracious for a man of General Washington's stature to be the one to offer amends. But my husband remained silent and didn't seem at all relieved.

Not even when Tilghman continued, "He wants a candid conversation to settle this."

Alexander crossed his arms. "Neither of us would like what would be said in a candid conversation." He shook his head, resolution settling into his handsome features. "I won't refuse if he insists, yet I should be happier if he would permit me to decline."

I barely withheld a gasp at this outrageous reply. And Tilghman blanched, overcome with another coughing fit. "You won't even speak with him?"

My husband's voice turned to steel. "I pledge my honor to you that he will find me inflexible. He shall, for once at least, repent his ill-humor."

At hearing this, Tench set down his cup hard on the side table and abandoned every last vestige of his usual formality. "Alex, what the devil can you be thinking?" It was precisely what I wished to ask. "For pity's sake, man, you know the situation at headquarters . . ."

"I do," Hamilton replied, stiffly. "But don't worry that I'll leave it all upon your shoulders. Reassure the general that I won't distress him or the public business by quitting before Humphreys and Harrison return from their assignments. I will comport myself with the same principles and in the same manner

I always have. My behavior will be as if nothing happened. But I *am* quitting."

Poor Colonel Tilghman left wearing a stunned expression that must have mirrored my own. My mind raced for a solution. So much hung in the balance—for us personally and for the cause. Could it all be undone by my husband's pride?

"Alexander," I said, cupping his cheek in my hand as I carefully chose my words. "Of course, you didn't deserve the general's shortness. But he recognizes his error. Surely you can forgive—"

"It's more than that." As if trying to reassure me that he wasn't simply caught in a fit of temper, he pressed a kiss to my palm and grasped my hand in his. "I never wished to be an aide-de-camp. I never wished to depend entirely upon any one person for my future. I had refused to serve in this capacity to two other generals for just this reason. But I got swept up in the enthusiasm of the war and an idea of Washington's character and accepted his invitation."

I understood this. But now seemed hardly the time to change course.

Before I could say as much, Alexander rushed to add, "Washington has always professed more friendship for me than I felt for him. You've seen how he calls me 'my boy.' I need to stand upon a footing of *military* confidence rather than of private attachment. So today has been a long time in coming."

Queasiness overcame me, for *this* stand seemed utter folly. Was there any other young patriot in the country who wouldn't trip over himself to win Washington's fatherly affection? And yet my husband apparently resented it as much as if it was offered by the father who'd abandoned him. Not knowing whether to feel sympathy or exasperation, I only managed a soft, "Oh, Alexander . . ."

He shook his head again. "Worry not, dear Betsy. I will reenter into the artillery. Or perhaps a command in the infantry will offer itself. Either way, a command would leave me the winter to prosecute the study of the law in preparation for my future career in life. Either will leave me in a better position than if I stay in service in the general's family."

I still couldn't believe that my husband meant to abandon his crucial place in the war effort as Washington's most trusted aide. Not with the war at a turning point. And yet, Alexander immediately set quill to paper to inform my father and a few close confidants of his breach with Washington—the sharing of which might well embarrass our commander, making their parting irrevocable.

I tried to imagine Papa's reaction, an endeavor that made my headache worsen. What would he think of his new son-in-law who, having achieved the security of our family reputation and fortune, nearly immediately, and in a moment of pique, insulted and abandoned George Washington?

There must be some way to fix this. So, despite the sharpening soreness in my throat, and the agony of facing Martha Washington when our husbands were now at odds, I went to headquarters with Alexander the next day, working with her as I always did and sitting in quiet observation. Hoping some opportunity might arise for me to smooth over this rift.

True to his word, Alexander conducted himself that day as if nothing untoward had occurred. But Mrs. Washington knew better. Sitting beside me in the farmhouse's parlor as we wrote letters requesting funds for the soldiers, she spoke quietly, never lifting her gaze from the parchment. "Have you had the opportunity to meet the woman in camp they're calling Captain Molly?"

Mrs. Washington was referring to the wife of a cannoneer who, during the Battle of Monmouth, had been bringing pitchers of water to the soldiers when her husband fell. To avenge him, "Captain Molly" took his place at the cannon with admirable courage and service. I'd seen the stout, red-haired, freckle-faced young woman in camp. But I'd never spoken to her. "I'm afraid we're not acquainted. Should we be?"

Martha's lips pinched for a moment. "It's just that she puts me in mind of something. If our independence is to be won, our husbands must be willing to put themselves in harm's way. But achieving independence also relies on the support of our women . . . in *whatever manner* best supports the cause."

My quill paused, and I looked up at this wise lady from whom I'd already learned so much. "In whatever manner?" I asked, willing her to say more.

Her brown eyes clear, her graying hair framing her round face under the plain mobcap, she said, "Even great men require advisers, and we have our husbands' ears. Sometimes we encourage, sometimes we challenge, and sometimes we *manage . . .*"

I couldn't imagine how a man like Alexander might be managed, but perhaps she could. I returned my quill to the ink pot and sat back in my chair. "How?"

She smiled, shaking away the sand we used to dry the ink. Then she poured a circle of wax upon the page to seal it. "If I could tell you that, perhaps the war would already be done."

I suspected she had somehow *managed* General Washington into offering an apology. And now it was up to me to get Alexander to accept it. But I felt ill-equipped for the task. Martha Washington was, in my mind, the ideal of a true woman. More amiable and diplomatic than my own beloved mother. Martha had, for more than twenty years, worn around her finger a plain wedding band that symbolized her devotion to—and perhaps her influence over—her husband. Whereas I was a newlywed and still learning how to influence mine.

Foundering as if in a canoe without a paddle while I did it.

And the one person who seemed as frustrated as I felt was Lafayette.

That afternoon when taking lunch to the back room where my husband labored over the general's correspondence, I overheard the Frenchman cry, "*Mon Dieu*, the feud I started by accident! My dear Hamilton, how I wish I hadn't stopped you to talk when the general needed you. I make all the apologies."

"No one blames you, my friend," my husband replied.

"Better to blame me than His Excellency," Lafayette said

stoutly. I hesitated just outside the slightly open door, riveted by our friend's effort to talk sense into Alexander. "Your being angry with him will pass, Hamilton. But trust in someone who has tender sentiments for you—if you quit this army now, you will be angry at yourself the rest of your life."

I held my breath, because my husband had said nothing to me of quitting the army itself—only Washington's service.

Whatever Alexander replied was too muffled to hear, but the marquis's unusually soft tones were just audible. "Then make me a promise, do not resign your commission. If nothing better can be found, come fight beside me and Monroe in Virginia and command our artillery. Like old times. I will not go until you agree."

I withdrew to the kitchen, not wishing to be caught eavesdropping. How was I to make all of this better when Hamilton seemed intent on making it worse?

Some moments later, Lafayette surprised me when he walked in, nearly banging his head on the copper pots hanging from the rafters. "Madame Hamilton, you marry a most obstinate man."

"So I'm learning," I said, immediately afraid I'd been disloyal. But how was I to save my husband from behaving with recklessness, pride, and even arrogance?

Lafayette gave a rueful smile as he leaned in. "Brilliant men are often the most stubborn, but to pick a quarrel with Washington." He shook his head, and his amusement melted away. "Some would say this to be *folies de grandeurs*. But in Hamilton I know this to be a mask. And allowances must be made for his circumstances."

"His circumstances?" I asked, fearing he might raise the issue of Alexander's legitimacy.

Instead, he said, "Great pain and loss, *madame*. As I think you know."

I did know, but I was a little amazed that Lafayette did, too. And even more so at the sudden intimacy of our conversation.

"My own father was killed when I was not yet two years old," the Frenchman explained. "But still I had money and relations to look after me. Your husband had no one to look after him . . . small wonder he trusts no one but himself to care about his future. Not Washington. Not me. Not anyone, I think. Maybe not even you."

*I never wished to depend entirely upon any one person.*

That's what Hamilton had said. And I realized how well Lafayette understood his fears. Martha Washington had advised me to manage my husband's self-destructive impulses. And now I hoped Lafayette might help me do that. "Maybe you could talk to him again in a few days, when he's had time to reflect."

"Perhaps we can conspire together to make him see reason, *oui?*" Lafayette replied. "I can only write him letters because I march shortly to defend Virginia, with orders to capture Benedict Arnold and hang him dead by the neck."

With a bloodthirstiness I'd never felt before, I said, "In that endeavor I wish you *very* well, sir."

Still, Lafayette spoke of his new southern command a little glumly, for we all believed the final battle would take place somewhere in New York, and he didn't wish to miss it. "It is probable I will be in the southern wilderness until the end of the war, so if Hamilton will not return to Washington, convince him to join me. We will share our exile."

I wasn't certain that a loving wife should convince a husband who had dedicated six years of his life to war that he should endanger himself even one more day. But I was sensible to Lafayette's argument that Alexander would never forgive himself if he didn't see the war to its conclusion.

Nor was I even sure we could *win* this war without Alexander Hamilton, for these weeks at his side in camp had revealed to me the military side of the man. He was forever identifying weaknesses in enemy movements, formulating strategies about which he convinced the general before communicating them to the commanders in the field; haranguing Congress for what support the army received; negotiating with the French, and finding clever ways to stretch the army's resources—all while unburdening Washington so he could focus on the whole of the war.

So I agreed to give Lafayette's suggestion long thought. "You're a good friend," I told the Frenchman. "And I wish you the fondest *Adieu.*"

"No, no!" Lafayette cried before taking his leave. "We will say only *Au revoir*! Until we meet again. In the meantime, I wish you luck with your campaign to keep your husband from rashness. As for me, I would rather face the cannons."

# Chapter Twelve

*April 1781*
*De Peyster's Point, New York*

Two months later, I wondered if I would not have fared better against cannons myself.

Martha Washington's advice had helped me to see that my soft words and touches could moderate my husband, at least a little. By making of myself a soothing presence, I'd gently persuaded Alexander to accompany the general to Rhode Island to serve as interpreter in the strategy discussions with the French officers, for Alexander's mastery of the language exceeded that of all the other American members of Washington's staff.

I accomplished that much.

But after that, Hamilton left Washington's service, just as he said he would.

And now he appeared to be taunting our commander.

His Excellency had refused my husband a promotion partly on the grounds that he was indispensable at headquarters. Well, now we were gone from headquarters, but living in a little brick and stone house directly across the river from Washington's dwellings.

Our new home at De Peyster's Point—our first household together—was little better than a fishing shack, without so much as a dining table. It was drafty, the roof leaked, it stunk of dead fish, and the only way to get to it from headquarters was by way of a little rowboat. But it had one winning feature as far as my husband was concerned.

Namely, that George Washington couldn't look out his window without seeing us there.

Day in. Day out. Our presence—in plain sight—was to remind the general that Alexander Hamilton was available for a promotion, but until he got one, he would remain just out of reach.

For my part, I'd promised that I would live anywhere with Hamilton, and I took genuine pleasure in transforming the shack into our home. This was not, after all, a boardinghouse where we must be careful not to move anything. No, this was the first place I might decide for myself how to arrange our few sticks of furniture, where to store silver, where to hang linens, and what to store in the larder—for we had no servant with us to do it for me.

And not even Mama would swoop in and dictate how everything should be.

So, armed with bucket, a brush, and some precious lye soap acquired at far too great a price, I cheerfully scrubbed our new home from floor to ceiling. I made countless trips to the river to get wash water. And when I hung my petticoats on the line, I'd wave, quite ruefully, to Martha Washington across the way, imagining she was doing the same.

It was all a great deal more challenging than I expected. The fire needed to be tended all day if we were to have anything to eat. And having never managed a household by myself, much less attended to *all* the chores, there were a few mishaps. My first attempt at cooking fish resulted in a charred mess and a burned hand.

"This is no place for my gently bred bride." My husband said this while kissing my blistered fingers, as if to make them all better. Then his eyes fell upon the wash bucket where I'd been on my hands and knees scrubbing mud from the floor. And later that night, when I collapsed in an exhausted heap beside him in bed, he asked, "Why don't you return to your father's house in Albany before he sees what I've reduced you to?"

*Because you aren't the only one with too much pride,* I thought.

My aunt Gertrude had said I was no milk-and-water miss. Well, I wasn't about to be a milk-and-water wife, either. "Others make do with less. So can I. I don't want to leave. My place is at your side in service of the cause."

Besides, I could hardly make him see reason if I was far away.

"So you *are* a Roman wife," he said, more than a little pleased. "But I'm not entirely without hopes we'll soon have peace. Then you must submit to the mortification of enjoying mere domestic happiness. This I know you will not like, but we cannot always have things as we wish."

I laughed at his optimistic teasing, then said, "Martha Washington stays with her husband through hardship and I intend to stay with mine."

By mentioning Mrs. Washington, I also hoped to remind him of all the people who sacrificed their comfort and personal desires to remain at Washington's side. But what he seemed to take from it was a reminder that Martha Washington had servants and I did not. A thing remedied the next day in the form of a young enslaved Negro woman Alexander hired from her master. Though I was happy for the help, I didn't know if we could truly afford a servant and was surprised to feel discomfited at being entirely in charge of supervising one. I'd grown up in a house run using the labor of slaves, but they'd always been *Papa's* slaves. Certainly, they'd tended to me, but as a child living under my father's roof I'd not been given a choice in that.

Now, I had a choice. Though she'd only been temporarily hired out to us by her owner, this was the closest I'd ever come to being a slaveholder in my own right.

And I found that I did not like it.

I did not like it at all.

Not when I thought about the black soldiers at Morristown. Not when surrounded by soldiers preparing to die for the cause of liberty and independence. In any case, I didn't share my misgivings with my husband because he'd done me the kindness of giving me exactly what he'd thought I'd wanted and needed, likely against the pangs of his own conscience.

I was only just beginning to see the inherent contradiction between the ideals we said we were fighting for, and the reality of slavery in our daily lives. Hamilton had opened my eyes to it.

But I wasn't sure what to do about it.

We were, I suppose, both of us, still a ways from a full awakening.

IT MUST NOT be thought that Hamilton was idle at De Peyster's Point.

Quite the opposite. While my servant and I cooked and cleaned and caught fish in the cold brackish water, Hamilton cast about for any sort of opportunity fortune might cast up. Not only pestering Washington near *daily* to give him command of troops, but also writing other generals, too, in the hopes they had some leadership role for him in the forthcoming campaign. He even wrote to my brother-in-law, who apparently informed Angelica of his ambitions such that she became anxious to exert her own influence on his behalf.

"Good news," Alexander said one day as he came rushing in the door, tramping spring mud all over the floor. Rain had fallen for two straight days, causing the river to overflow its banks and making of our yard a quagmire. "Betsy, if you will hear—"

I held out a hand before he could cross the room. "I would love nothing more than to share in your good news, my dearest husband. After you've removed those boots."

A stack of books and papers in hand, he appeared completely confused, and he finally peered down at himself, as if he'd momentarily forgotten he had feet. With a chuckle, he juggled his load and pulled the tall boots off, and I wondered if he'd finally been given his command. But Alexander said, "Congress has acted as I hoped they would. Robert Morris has been appointed as superintendent of finance." My husband had not been much impressed, in early March, when the Articles of Confederation were finally ratified, thinking them far too weak a system. But now he was hopeful and nearly vibrating with excitement. "Finally, we shall have men of the first abilities, property, and character in charge of the departments of the executive."

I smiled and said how wonderful it was, though this was not the sort of news that excited me. And as he sat, I took in the pristine spines of books sprawled across the table to find a series of what appeared to be philosophical texts on government and economy. Price's *Observations on the Nature of Civil Liberty*, in two volumes. Hume's *Political Discourses*. Postlethwayt's *The Universal Dictionary of Trade and Commerce*. Beawes's *Lex Mercatoria Rediviva*.

Given this reading material, I was happy to leave him to it!

But when I returned a short time later, I found that he'd discarded his coat and loosened his cravat. Ink dotted his fingers and smudged his cheek, and his hair had the appearance of having been blown by the wind from the way he raked his hands through it when deep in thought.

"What *are* you working on so feverishly?"

"A letter of congratulations to Mr. Morris," he said, working with an intensity I'd never seen in another—not even my father. His focus unwavering, his quill scratched fast against the page. It was strangely enthralling to watch. Utterly appealing.

I blinked at the stack of thick leather tomes and what looked to be at least ten pages of writing. "A very long note of congratulations, I should say . . ."

"Well, I'm also sending him my thoughts on the topic of establishing our economy," Hamilton said with the same nonchalance with which another might talk about the weather or the price of tea. "Betsy, if we win this war, we turn to the great project of building a nation where none has yet existed. Rarely does mankind have such an opportunity, nor such a burden. We must get it *right*."

Clearly Hamilton believed he knew how to get it right.

And I listened as he told me all he'd learned of world finance when, at the age of fourteen, he'd worked as a clerk at an export and import company in St. Croix, trading sugar, timber, cattle, and even slaves. I hadn't realized he had such a passion for finance—or really, that anyone *could* have such a passion for it. Truthfully, it was a passion I didn't share. But I listened in rapt attention because it was one of the few times Alexander ever spoke about his childhood, and the hard lessons it impressed upon him.

Lessons he was very keen to impart to his new country.

Even then, as a starry-eyed newlywed, I feared there might be some manner of hubris in a lieutenant colonel with no expertise in finance *other* than his own experience as a fourteen-year-old clerk condescending to write the new superintendent of finance an economic manifesto. But at the time, having mostly witnessed the soldier in Hamilton, I was also much intrigued by the scholar. More importantly, his enthusiasm for the project of building a nation—for thinking ahead—helped give me much-needed courage that we *would* win this war.

And with a little hubris of my own, I asked, "Is there . . . something I can do to help?" He'd already refused a bowl of fish stew for dinner, as if he couldn't take even a moment away from his pen in exchange for a spoon. And now he was rubbing with one hand at the back of his neck, as if it pained him. When he glanced at me quizzically, I suggested, very tentatively, "I see that you're copying your notes and calculations. Maybe I could do the copying for you."

"You want to write for me," he said, arching a brow. "Like a clerk?"

"I should rather be your long-suffering and extremely loyal aide-de-camp," I replied.

He smirked at my impudence. "Your simmering disapproval of

my decision to leave the general is duly noted." I started to object, but he held up a hand. "That was not a point subtly made, my love. And I intend to thoroughly punish you for it by accepting your offer."

I felt a little thrill of excitement. When I'd thought of being his partner, I never imagined being so directly involved in his work. To be a patriot in heart and sentiment, but also in deed and ink. "Just tell me what to do."

Before long, I had a stack of pages in front of me. While Alexander wolfed down his dinner and worked out more calculations, I copied his notes for hours, concentrating on penmanship, until my eyes glazed over from recording lengthy discussions of generating revenue, paying for the military, currency depreciation, foreign credit, and instituting a national bank. But his long complicated calculations made me think of Papa's love of equations, and I smiled at the comparison.

When I had written my twelfth full page, I set down the quill but found that my hand had cramped in a curled position. I laughed as I rubbed at my palm and fingers. "How do you do it?"

Hamilton's brow furrowed. "Do what?"

"Write so much. Some days the only time you're not writing is when you're asleep. Why, I've even seen you writing while saddled upon a horse. Yet, after just a few hours at the task, my hand feels as though I've suddenly developed rheumatism."

He frowned and made as if to set aside his work. "I'm sorry, love. You don't have to continue."

"No, please," I said, smiling. "I want to help. I only mean to convey my admiration, Alexander. You are remarkable, truly."

Slowly, he settled back into his chair. "Remarkable? How?"

"Oh, Mr. Hamilton, what I'd known of you pales in comparison to what I've learned this night. Why . . . I begin to think you're a *genius*. And I say this as the daughter of a man who has always delighted in calculations and equations and theory and philosophy. I may not understand all your work, but I recognize the cleverness . . . no, the *brilliance* behind it all the same."

And it was true, because to my mind it appeared that Alexander was in the process of single-handedly laying out the foundations for everything the American union might yet become, of creating the better world he'd promised to create. That might have been the proud wife in me speaking, but I didn't think so.

His brow lifted, as if in surprise, but then wariness settled into his blue eyes. "Are you still teasing me, Betsy?"

"No, my dearest, I'm trying to tell you that in *spite* of my simmering disapproval of your decision to leave the general, I am so very proud of you."

Alexander ducked his chin and cleared his throat, as if embarrassed or overwhelmed by my compliment. Had no one ever said such a thing to him before? Or had no one made him believe it? I couldn't resist the urge to make sure he knew the truth of my feelings.

I moved to him, crouched by his knees, and peered up into his handsome face. "I am so very proud to be your wife."

He grasped my hand hard where it rested on his leg, and when he looked at me, his gaze was filled with a depth of gratitude that made me fall a little more in love with him, and it stirred a longing in my body.

Tentatively, I reached for him until I captured his mouth with mine. The soft contact was like putting a match to kindling. It unleashed something within him—in truth, within us both. He took me to our bedroom, whispering, "I need you, Betsy. How I need you." Warmth bloomed inside me at the sentiment, and then flared hotly as my husband grasped at the material of my skirts. "I just need . . ."

We came together desperately, frantically, but I'd never felt more loved and cherished.

Afterward, he turned to me, his arm cradling my neck. "I wish I'd met you earlier. That you'd been at home that first time I visited your father in Albany. I wish I knew you even when you were a girl—"

"You wouldn't have looked twice at me then," I teased, though I believed it to be true.

"You're wrong. I'd have loved you, and wished to learn everything about you. I'd have tried to be worthy of you that much sooner and been a better man for it. You ease me, Betsy. My mind races, but your touch calms me. My thoughts fly, but your presence allows me an escape. I want nothing more than to please you in return. In your eyes, I wish to be the most amiable, the most accomplished. And when I'm not, I will endeavor to make up for all I lack with love."

I pressed my lips to his. "You are the most amiable." I kissed him again. "And so very accomplished." Again. "And even more handsome."

How strange it was to reassure a man whom every other woman in the world seemed to desire. His smile grew as humor slid into his gaze. "How handsome?"

I feigned exasperation with a roll of my eyes, but couldn't hide my grin. "Are you fishing for *more* compliments?"

"From the mouth of my angel? Always." His touch turned hungry once more, and his lovemaking that night won me over again and again with the belief that Alexander Hamilton—this brilliant, complicated, flawed man—*needed* me.

And I needed him, too.

Heeding Lafayette's words, I'd done what I could to encourage him to return to Washington's service, but now I thought better of it. If my husband wished to resign his commission in the army, I would encourage him to do so. Because I had now glimpsed the statesman in him, and I knew he would blaze a trail of glory in whichever path he chose.

Besides, it was much *safer*, I thought, to be a statesman than a soldier.

How naive I was.

"WELL, YOU'VE FINALLY done it, Ham," said Tench Tilghman, with a lingering cough. With the coming of summer, I'd left the door open to a breeze, and now looked up to find the colonel's height filling the entryway of our home, an expression on his face that warred between admiration and annoyance. "You've forced the great man's hand."

"What?" Hamilton asked, rising up hastily from the table where he was composing political essays on the defects in the Articles of Confederation.

But Tilghman, perhaps vexed that he'd been forced to cross the river in a rowboat just to deliver this news, was in no hurry to satisfy my husband's curiosity. Instead, he turned his attentions to me and grinned, tipping his hat. "I shouldn't have been so long without seeing you, Mrs. Hamilton." He glanced out the window at the river he'd just rowed across. "It's only that your jealous husband put an actual *gulf* between us."

I laughed, and offered to have our servant fetch him some porridge. But Alexander thumped the table impatiently, "Out with it, man. What news?"

"Washington is not about to let you resign your commission as you've tacitly threatened to do," Tilghman replied, and I could see that was the part that annoyed him. "So you're getting your command."

My husband tensed. "Tell me."

"A New York light infantry battalion."

The glee that broke out on Alexander's face defied all description. He was, thereafter, in a celebratory mood, and invited Tench to stay for a meal. The next morning, my husband was eager to meet with the generals about the long-awaited battle and left early, finally, and at long last, crossing the river back to headquarters.

And I was absolutely nauseated over the thought of him finally going off to fight. I couldn't tolerate my breakfast, and could only nurse a cup of tea until the nausea passed. It took three days in a row of this same discomfort before I counted back to my last monthly courses and it finally dawned on me.

I was pregnant. I was going to have a baby.

I debated when to tell Alexander about my suspicions, wishing to be more certain before I raised his hopes. But my husband forced my hand, just as he'd forced Washington's.

To take command of his troops, Hamilton needed to ride south, and this time, he couldn't have me with him. We'd all assumed that the summer campaign would take place in New York, but new intelligence from Lafayette—which I later learned had come from a Negro spy the marquis had recruited—suggested that we might better gamble it all in Yorktown, Virginia.

Whichever choice was made, Hamilton would have to be ready to ride into battle in an instant. Which meant we had to say our good-byes.

*Oh, God. What if he doesn't come back? What if he never meets his child?*

As I had this thought, my husband came immediately to my side. "Betsy, dearest angel, what is it? You've gone so pale. Are you still unwell?"

"No," I said, gulping a deep, steadying breath. "Well, perhaps a little."

Alexander frowned. "I'm calling for the doctor. But let's get you to bed first."

"That's not necessary," I said, letting myself be pulled from the chair. "Alexander—"

"I'll row out and retrieve him right away," he said, a tinge of panic to his words. "It won't take long. I promise."

"I'm not ill," I said abruptly, rushing to allay his fears. "I'm pregnant."

Alexander froze. As my announcement sank in, my hands went to my belly. His gaze followed, and then he was looking at me with the purest expression of wonder I'd seen on any man's face. "You're pregnant."

"You're going to be a father," I said, heart beating hard against my breast.

Slowly, Alexander placed a hand atop my own, and when he lifted his eyes to mine, they were glassy with joy and awe. "I'm going to be a father."

Smiling, I nodded. And then we were laughing and embracing even as Alexander asked a hundred questions and insisted all over again that I needed to lie down. That night, I whispered into the darkness, "Whatever happens, you must come back to me, to us."

Alexander pulled me tight against him. "Oh, Betsy. It costs me a great deal to be absent from you, but I promise we won't be separated for long."

I tried to believe him.

The next day, as he put me in the carriage for my father's house, his expression a mask of regret, he said, "I miss you already."

"As do I miss you." Tears stung my eyes, but I wanted to be strong for him, when all his focus needed to be on the coming fight. "I love you," I said, then insisted more fiercely. "Come back to me."

"I will," he whispered, his voice strained. He closed the door and tapped on the side of the carriage, and it lurched to a start.

And I could only hope that in having unleashed the forces of war, my husband would not, like Phaethon, be struck down for hubris in his quest for glory, our dreams of the future mere ashes for me to mourn.

# *Chapter Thirteen*

*August 1781*
*Albany*

**O**UR ARMY WOULD risk everything in Yorktown.

There, in Virginia, Lafayette had somehow cornered the British general Cornwallis. And success relied upon the trustworthiness of James Armistead, the black spy who was posing as a runaway slave in the British camp and feeding Lafayette critical intelligence. Papa, who was privy to the strategy, seemed confident of victory. And I tried to be, too.

But we'd been losing for so long, and now, with a child on the way, I had more to lose than ever before. After seven years of fighting, we'd so many times seen victory slip away. Only for the flower of our youth to perish ingloriously for a cause that might never be won. And in my secret heart, hope became to me a fleeting mirage. No matter how desperately I reached for it, it felt always just beyond my grasp.

So I dared not believe my husband when he wrote to me at my father's house, where I'd taken refuge with my family, to promise, *Cheer yourself with the assurance of never more being separated after the war. My object to be happy in a quiet retreat with my better angel.*

I felt like no angel.

I had neither wisdom nor peace nor the power to protect those I held dear. To keep me safe, Alexander had sent me home, where all I could do was await news of the war.

Until the war suddenly came to us.

"Bar the doors," Papa said, his command punctuated by a clamor of silver and plates as we sprang from the table.

For years, the enemy had been trying to seize or kill my father. And now our fears were finally at hand. A stranger had come to the back gate, insisting my father come outside.

Fortunately, Papa had been forewarned by his spy network that they would use just such a ruse to lure him out of the house, and now he barked, "Upstairs!"

Racing like a much younger man, Papa took the stairs two at a time to get his weapons. Meanwhile Angelica grabbed her daughter and I grasped the first little one within my reach—my three-year-old nephew, who'd been dozing in the window seat—then hurried up the stairs behind my father.

At the landing, I stopped to pull the shutters closed. That's when we heard the shrill war cry that turned my knees to water. I caught a glance in the yard below of men in moccasins and feathers—Mohawks or Loyalists disguised as Indians, I couldn't be sure. But what I did know was that it was a *war* party, and a loud commotion at the back door told me that they'd overpowered our guards.

*They're in the house!* I fought down the panic, for my sake, and for that of the babe in my womb. Would it all end in tragedy before I met my beloved child?

Not if the Schuyler family had anything to say about it. My seventeen-year-old brother, Johnny, grabbed muskets from the cabinet in the hall. Papa threw open a window and fired a shot from his pistol as we heard the grunts of men locked in struggle below stairs.

Meanwhile, my five-year-old sister wept, clinging to my father's knees. "They've come for you, Papa. We won't let them get you!"

Just then, we heard the wail of an infant below, and a sickly terror gripped me.

"Where's the baby?" Mama cried, her usually stern voice betraying panic.

*Dear God.* In all the chaos, we'd left my new baby sister, Catherine, sleeping in her cradle by the front door. We'd *left* her. And now our enemies had breached the door.

"They won't harm her," Angelica said. If there were Iroquois with them, they might *take* her. And that I couldn't allow. I started for the stairway, but Angelica grabbed my arm. "You're pregnant."

"I must get her," I replied without a second thought. I was the best runner, a strong climber, the one who adventured like a boy while Angelica buried her nose in books and Peggy preened in front of a mirror.

And yet, Peggy said, "I'll go."

"No!" I cried after her. But Peggy dashed to the stairs—her figure a bobbing blur along the walnut banister of our elegant staircase. I crept down after her, feeling faint with fear as the shouts and scuffles of fight from the back of the house escalated. A moment later, Peggy rushed back, the baby bundled in her arms. "Hurry!" I cried from the landing, reaching down for Peggy to surrender the baby to me as a crash sounded and war whoops echoed throughout the house.

Just a few steps farther and . . .

A hulking white man with a hatchet lunged from the dining room, grabbed Peggy, and shook her. "Wench, where is your master?"

He'd mistaken her for an indentured servant. Maybe because, due to the heat, we hadn't dressed for dinner. Whatever the reason, Peggy's eyes narrowed in contempt and confusion, and I thought it would be just like her to say something she shouldn't with her very last breath on earth.

Instead, my little sister masterfully transformed her expression into servility. "General Schuyler's gone to alarm the town. He was warned you were coming. Please, sir, that's all I know."

Just then, I glanced up to the hidden top of the stairs to see Papa, pistol in hand, his expression murderous. I shook my head at him and pleaded with my eyes for him to stay where he was, out of sight, because the brute was buying Peggy's clever ruse.

"Please let me go." Peggy sniveled. "I tell you truthfully, he's gone!"

Biting out a silent curse, Papa disappeared into one of the bedrooms. And then, taking advantage of Peggy's lie, he shouted out an open window. "Come on, my brave fellows, surround the house and capture the scoundrels!"

It was enough to convince our marauders that Papa's patriot forces had arrived to rescue us. And, in frustration, the villain holding Peggy shoved her so violently that she fell at the foot of the stairs, trying to shield the wailing infant.

The man lifted his tomahawk as if to butcher them both, and I yelled, "Don't you dare, you devil!"

But perhaps he only meant it to frighten us, for when he brought the hatchet down, the blade buried itself in my father's fine wood railing with a *thunk,* sending a spray of wood chips into Peggy's hair. Then he fled through the entry hall, from whence a clang of falling silver rang out. Meanwhile Peggy called down hell and brimstone after him as he escaped with his booty.

The intruders melted away from the house as suddenly as they'd come, but they'd dragged away three of our guardsmen as prisoners. And before the attack had even subsided, I flew down to help Peggy rise. "Dear God, are you hurt?"

"We're both unharmed," she said, though there was a tremble in her voice. "Can you take her?"

I accepted my wailing infant sister into my arms, and an immediate rush of relief flooded me—for her and the baby in my womb. We were safe. All of us. We'd survived the assault. "We all have you to thank," I told Peggy. "That was incredibly brave."

She ran shaking fingers along the line where the hatchet remained buried in the wood, then peered up at me with uncharacteristic humility. "I knew it's what you would've done, Betsy, but I could hardly let you do it. So I had no choice but to be brave."

It was possibly the sweetest, most tender moment we'd ever shared as sisters, and I couldn't resist hugging her. Realizing that perhaps I had always misjudged her a little.

Mama offered comfort to my terrified siblings while Papa snapped orders to a surviving soldier to ride for help.

And I went to tend the wounded.

Without hesitation, I tore the hem of my own muslin gown to make bandages. I thought nothing of it. Nor should I have. The attack on our home stripped from me and my sisters any remaining illusions that we might go on as dainty ladies in such a fraught enterprise as a fight for freedom. And so much the better. I vowed to myself that if our attackers came back, it wouldn't only be my father and his sons who armed themselves with muskets.

I would bear one, too. Because there was no safety for the wife or child of a revolutionary but in victory.

~

*October 18, 1781*
*Albany*

How strange it is to recall that though I met my husband in the coldest winter, in the darkest hour of the war, I met Aaron Burr on a shining sunny day of thanksgiving.

"They're saying your husband is a great hero, Mrs. Hamilton," the man said when I found him waiting in the blue parlor for an interview with my father. One of Papa's guards informed me that we had a caller—a veteran who'd resigned from service due to failing health, though his unforgettable hazel eyes flashed with vigor. And he appeared every inch the urbane gentleman in a tailored suit of gray satin.

I'd come to tell him that Papa had gone to town, but the promise of news about Alexander completely diverted me. "You know of my husband, Mister—"

"Colonel Burr," he said, stepping to reach for my hand and bringing it to his lips in greeting. With a mouth set in a mischievous smirk and those shrewd eyes, the colonel was extremely handsome. "Aaron Burr. I served with your husband."

I could remember no specific anecdote or story about Burr—my husband's most colorful stories were always about Lafayette and Laurens—but I was too anxious to learn what he knew of Alexander to think of anything else. "I meant . . . you've heard news of him?"

No sooner had I asked than did my heart leap to my throat, for I became suddenly quite fearful that this man in his elegant clothes had come to tell me not that my husband was a hero but that he'd *died* as one.

Burr's features slid into an enigmatic expression that couldn't quite be called a smile. "No doubt your father will receive the dispatch, but a wife on the verge of motherhood ought to know straightaway. So I'm very honored to tell you there are whispers of a great victory at Yorktown."

"An American victory?" I asked, hands on my protruding belly, my breath quickening.

"An American victory." He nodded to reassure me. "Madam, if the reports are true, your husband personally led a bayonet charge across a shelled field, dodging fire and springing onto an enemy parapet to take the redoubt."

The blood drained from my face, leaving me clammy and cold with horror at the danger my husband—the father of my unborn child—had exposed himself to. Even in leading a charge, shouldn't Hamilton have been atop a horse, commanding his troops, rather than at the front, daring his enemy and braving a bullet? A flash of this image passed before my eyes, and for the first time in my life I fell quite literally into a swoon.

Colonel Burr was forced to steady me, a hand at the elbow and one at the small of my back, before easing me into a chair. "We've won," Burr was saying, but I could scarcely hear over the strange buzzing in my ears. "We'll have Cornwallis's surrender soon. Or perhaps it's already been accomplished."

Dragging in ragged breaths of air, I pleaded, "And Hamilton?"

He gave a slow blink. "Of course. I didn't intend to leave you in suspense; your husband secured the victory without a scrape."

Both hands flew to my cheeks with a mixture of exhilarated pride and relief. "Thank you!" I wanted to run through the house shouting the good news like a crier. But I was still in a haze of half-disbelief, dizzied and trying to remember my manners. "Oh, thank you. Bless you for taking the trouble to come here to tell me!"

"Your father has agreed to help me get established in town, so it was my pleasure to deliver this news, Mrs. Hamilton," Burr replied with silky gentility. "And the rule of my life is to make business a pleasure, and pleasure my business."

Do you know, in that moment, how much he reminded me of Hamilton? Slender, with a military bearing, a sly smile, and a clever wit. I liked Burr very much. Right from that first meeting. I laughed and said, "Still—I am not quite myself, sir."

Glancing at my swollen belly, he smiled. "There is little wonder why, given your happy condition and your family's recent travails. It would have been a great loss to our country had your father fallen into British hands."

Though I did blame all that for my momentary swoon, I also blamed the shock of joy at realizing the British were defeated and the relief of knowing my husband would come home to me after all.

But it was also, surely, that for a brief moment, Burr had made me fear that Alexander had died. And, looking back, I wonder now if the dark swirl of my nearly losing consciousness was more than a *fear* of death but perhaps even a premonition of it. Because though Burr was the herald of great joy that day, he would one day be the cause of my greatest misery.

*Huzzah! Huzzah! Huzzah!*

That's how our guardsmen stirred the household to hail my conquering hero.

In his haste to return to me and our unborn child that autumn, Alexander had ridden so hard from Yorktown to Albany that he'd exhausted four horses, and himself. I ran out the door to meet him and found him stumbling toward the house, his face slathered in sweat and grime, his clothes smelling of horse and the road. I didn't care—not one bit.

Under a canopy of yellow, orange, and red leaves, I grasped my husband and kissed him on the mouth like the most brazen harlot who ever lived.

Shocked at my conduct, Hamilton startled but didn't pull away. Instead, he threaded his hand into the hair at my nape, his teeth grazing my lower lip in gentle threat of sweet reprisal.

Behind us at the door, Mama gave a shocked gasp and Prince a disapproving *harrumph*. But I didn't care about that either. Let the whole *world* disapprove, for in that moment, the only thing that mattered was seeing my husband alive and whole. And because I had no words to express it, only the language of a passionate kiss would do.

But once spent of those kisses, and having marveled at the changes nearly six months apart had wrought on my body, Alexander was tired in a way I'd never seen him tired before. As if he'd been feverishly staving off exhaustion with his talents and superlative industry for all the years of the war, and only now, in victory, did his body succumb to its toll.

Once he was bathed and fed and put to bed, he stayed there. Not for a day, or even two. In truth, he scarcely rose from bed for two months. I began to worry he suffered from some contagion, for Cornwallis, exposing a deranged lack of character in his desperation, had infected liberated slaves from southern plantations with smallpox, forcing them to approach enemy lines in the hopes of spreading the illness to the American army. And this, from the man who'd offered them freedom!

Thankfully, my uncle, Dr. Cochran, had helped to inoculate our troops against the dread disease and Mama assured me that Hamilton had no symptoms of smallpox. Moreover, despite the breakdown in his stamina, Alexander remained in good humor. And I will confess, with some delight, that not *all* the time he spent in our bed was as an ailing convalescent. Despite my being eight months along, I was only too pleased that the comfort he required was not entirely of a medicinal nature . . .

"Is the war finally over?" I asked in the early days of his recovery as he wolfed down a breakfast of hot tea, eggs, ham, and my mother's spiced pastries. My question was put softly, in a voice that struggled not to tremble, because even though everyone seemed to think the victory decisive, there had been too many disappointments to put my faith in it.

"Perhaps a few skirmishes are left," he said, reaching for my hand and brushing his lips to my palm. "But if there should be another occasion to fight, it will not fall to me. For us, my charming wife, the war is at its end."

How blithely he said it, and I was foolish enough to believe him. Foolish because I was desperately in love and puffed with pride. "And you've won it," I said, having cut out every mention in every newspaper to keep as tokens of his glory. So many others had worked to achieve this victory. Many had died for it. But I believed—and still believe—what I said to him that day. "You *are* a hero, Alexander."

And, to think, even *Burr* had once called him that.

"A small feat in this family," Hamilton said with a smile that attempted, but failed, to be self-effacing. "Why, after seeing that tomahawk gouge in the staircase, I'm ready to recommend Peggy for a commission in the army. And yet, if you are inclined to *reward* me as befits a hero, I shall not mind."

"Oh?" I asked, delighted at the sparkle in his eye. "How shall I reward you, Colonel Hamilton?"

In answer, he trailed his fingers over my swollen belly. "Present me with *a boy*."

I laughed, kissing his face. Every inch of it. "Won't a girl answer that purpose?"

He grinned. "By no means. I protest against a daughter. I fear that with her mother's charms, she may also inherit the caprices of her father, and then our daughter will enslave, tantalize, and plague every man on earth."

"I do see your point," I replied, feeling a bit enslaved by the charismatic pull of his eyes, and tantalized as he drew me under the covers.

I knew that in the coming weeks I would be called on to exhibit a sort of heroism of my own. Though my mother had assured me that giving birth was not to be feared in a family such as ours with such hearty Dutch constitutions, I remembered how sick she'd been after the birth of the little brother who died in my arms. And lest I dismiss that as merely a function of Mama being a matron of nearly forty-seven years, my sister Angelica's most recent birth had also gone hard. Even now, after two months, Angelica had not quite recovered her health, and the little boy was sickly. So my fears for myself were eclipsed by my fears for the child inside me, whom I loved already, boy or girl.

I would love my child with every breath for as long as I lived, whether it obeyed its father's commands to be born male or no. And that gave me courage. Then, in the new year, after a whole day's labor, my child emerged from that first breath, a culmination of all his parents' wishes and desires, and a reflection of all that was best in each of us.

A son. A little boy with eyes like his father's and thick, dark, unruly hair like mine. Ten fingers, ten toes, with wondrously fat little legs. Papa affectionately called him a piglet, but in my eyes, my son was perfect in every way!

And if he *did* inherit Alexander's caprices, he would undoubtedly enslave the fairer sex, for he'd already captivated me. In truth, my baby stole my heart upon his first little cry.

While Mama oversaw the birth, my sisters had been attending me, Angelica on one side, and Peggy on the other, holding my hands through the screaming while Alexander paced the black and white floor downstairs, knocking back glasses of my father's best imported wine as if he could not be sober while my sisters forbade him from the birth room. But once the baby was cleaned and swaddled and put into my arms, my sisters finally gave up their vigil, and abandoned their posts so that my husband could meet his son.

Tears sprang to Alexander's eyes the moment I surrendered the child into his arms. I knew my husband could be tender—there was a softness in him that others might have taken for weakness. But these tears, as he stooped to kiss me and our baby, were fierce expressions of love. "We'll call him Philip," he decided, choosing to honor my father rather than his own.

Then he vowed that he would never abandon me, or our son. And I believed him.

I FELL IN love with my son that spring. In truth, I fell in love with the entire world. Because with the war nearly over, everything seemed new. And in my baby's eyes, everything seemed possible.

Philip was as sunny a child as ever lived. One who so commanded my heart that I could refuse him nothing. And I knew my indulgence was not to be remedied by the influence of a stern father. Because in those delightfully domestic months, one might be excused for thinking that—like Ben Franklin and the lightning rod—my husband had *invented* fatherhood.

Fractured by our son's every cry and transported to heaven by every gurgle and smile, Alexander doted, day and night. Staring into the cradle, he boasted, "Philip is truly a very fine young gentleman. The most agreeable baby I ever knew—intelligent and sweet of temper. Don't you agree?"

"Yes," I agreed, with a laugh. "Of course."

Sensing condescension, Alexander turned in mock outrage. "It's true! He's handsome and his eyes are sprightly and expressive.

And he has a method of waving his hand that announces a future orator."

*A future orator.* Such grand plans he had for our boy, before he was even out of swaddling.

But having been abandoned by his own father, it made sense for my husband to draw so close to his infant son. For him to feel not only the natural bonds that draw a parent to a child, but also the desire to make up for what he'd lacked. It was as if Alexander thought to somehow tip the scales of cosmic justice by giving his son all the love he hadn't received.

"How entirely domestic I'm growing," Alexander later said, bouncing our little Philip on his knee at Papa's dinner table. "I sigh for nothing but the company of my wife and my baby, and have lost all taste for the pursuits of ambition."

Kissing our father atop his head as she slipped into her seat, Angelica gave a delicate snort. "You without ambition? Betsy, call for a doctor. Hamilton must be sicker than we knew."

The whole family laughed, because she wasn't wrong to doubt him. Especially when his desk in the upstairs hall was piled with leather-bound, gilt-edged law books. Tory lawyers would no longer be permitted to practice in state courts, which left an opportunity for men like my husband to step into the vacancy, and Alexander had designed an ambitious plan to condense his study of the law and start his own practice.

Though he seemed content to live in my father's house—and Papa was very happy to have us—I knew Hamilton yearned to make his own fortune. Late one night, he returned from his duties as a tax collector, and settling into a chair next to our sleeping baby, he opened a law book and whispered, "Go on to bed, love. I will now employ myself rocking the cradle and studying the art of fleecing my neighbors."

Tax collecting by day, studying law by night, and somehow managing, in the midst of it all, to conspire with my father to build this brave new American world.

The Articles of Confederation had made less a new nation

than a loose alliance of states. Hamilton and my father dreamed of something grander. And oh, how it filled my heart to see them together each night, talking through ideas, my father's wisdom tempering my husband's more passionate arguments—I took great pride in realizing that I'd given my father more than a son and my husband more than a father; I'd given both a trustworthy friend.

We were happy. I was never happier, I think.

In addition to getting to know my own little family that spring, we also had the chance to become better acquainted with Angelica's. With the war winding down, Mr. Carter found more time to spend with us at the Pastures. He was debonair and worldly, and I could easily imagine how my brother-in-law's dashing looks had won over Angelica. But his English reserve made them an odd match. Still, watching their four-year-old Philip hold my little boy on his lap for the first time filled my heart to bursting with the idea that our children would all grow up together, running these fields and playing in the river with their own New Netherlander children's troops just as we had.

The only thing we needed now was for Peggy to add her own little brood . . .

I decided to broach the matter at the Pinkster festivities, where Albany's slaves and freedmen performed African dances to wild drumbeats and sold us oysters and herbs from brightly colored carts. Pinkster was a time for setting aside the usual order of things. Blacks, whites, and Indians mingled and played games. Slaves slyly mocked their masters with relative impunity. And sweethearts stole away without any thought to propriety. So when a gentleman admirer dropped a bouquet of azaleas in Peggy's lap and she rejected his suit out of hand, I said, "Alexander's no Barbary pirate, I suppose, but I'm married off now, so what's stopping you, Peg?"

Seated beside me on a quilt, a bucket of shucked oyster shells beside her, Peggy rolled her eyes, some sharp retort no doubt on her tongue. But before she could speak, Angelica dropped down beside us, smoothing her skirts. "What's this about Alexander being a pirate?"

I chuckled, wondering if my husband's ears were burning at the foot of the hill where he and my brothers were playing a game of ninepins. "Peggy once wished I'd marry one."

Peggy batted her eyelashes and coyly threw each of us a glance. "For all you two know, what with how busy you've been making babies, perhaps I'm *already* betrothed."

I gaped at her audacious reply. "You must tell us all the details at once."

"It best not be a certain young Van Rensselaer boy," Angelica said with a sly laugh. Stephen Van Rensselaer from our Blues troop, she meant, who was to turn eighteen in the fall. And who had spent much of the spring paying call to the Pastures. "I overheard Papa say he is far too young to marry."

"Fortunately, Mama doesn't agree," Peggy said with a self-satisfied little smirk.

I could well imagine that our mother might truly approve of the match. Mama had always hoped that her daughters might marry into one of the great families of New York. And given the unconventional choices Angelica and I had made in husbands, Peggy might be my mother's last hope until our little sisters came of age.

It *was* a bit unusual for a woman of Peggy's age to marry a younger man, but then again, Stephen was set to inherit one of the largest and oldest estates in New York, so there were great advantages to the match, too.

I gave Peggy's hand a squeeze, wanting her to find the same happiness I'd found. "Well, if you have Mama on your side, Papa will surely give his permission."

Peggy bit her lower lip, then it all came out in a rush. "He *has* given his permission. On the condition that we wait until Stephen finishes his studies and is old enough that his family should not object. Also on the condition that we don't tell anyone. Which is too cruel!"

I laughed and felt badly for laughing, because it did seem some manner of cruelty to make Peggy keep this secret. So, to distract her, Angelica and I devised all manner of dinner parties and other socials, where my sisters and I played the pianoforte and my brothers played the German flute to the amusement of all. And some of the most amusing gatherings were attended by the newly married Colonel Burr—whose dry wit was a charming accompaniment to my husband's more sparkling playfulness.

In the months after our first meeting, Burr had become a near-constant fixture at the Pastures as he and Alexander shared Papa's library in their studies of the law. At all hours, they could be found hunched over their books and papers, debating one point of law or another. I knew very well, of course, the brilliance of my own husband's mind. But it surprised me that Colonel Burr proved quite nearly to be Alexander's equal. For at every meal, party, and gathering, they insisted upon demonstrating their intellects, trying to outshine one another to the amusement and, sometimes, exasperation of all.

Indeed, Burr spent so much time at the Pastures that he had no compunction whatsoever about debating Angelica as if she were a man, good-naturedly disputing with my husband about what should come next for America, and arguing whether the principles spelled out in the Declaration of Independence really would become the basis of the enterprise.

The rest of us were all marvelously hopeful.

So it was notable when, in the midst of one of these dinner parties, my husband received a packet of letters and started for the stairs without a word.

"Where are you going?" I asked, but Alexander only mumbled something inaudible in reply.

I wished to follow him but needed first to politely disentangle myself from a surprisingly learned discussion with Angelica, Peggy, and Mrs. Theodosia Burr, a lady of daring outspokenness whose friendship and frequent companionship had further ensured my fondness for Colonel Burr. "What do you think about voting rights for women?" she asked in her typically provocative way.

"Our Livingston cousins never tire of reminding us that women have been granted the right to vote in New Jersey," Peggy said conspiratorially.

Angelica nodded and raised her glass, as if to toast. "So why not New York?"

But I was entirely too distracted by my husband's unexpected withdrawal to be drawn into even such an exciting conversation. "Please excuse me," I said, forcing a polite smile. "I'll rejoin you shortly."

I thought to find Alexander at his desk or, failing that, checking upon our child, as was his nightly habit. Instead, I found him seated on the edge of our bed, his head in his hands.

"Alexander?" When I reached for him, he actually flinched. "What's happened?"

He didn't look at me. He didn't reply. My usually loquacious husband didn't say a single word, which made me sure something was dreadfully, horrifically wrong. For answer, I was left to glance at a letter, discarded upon the pillow, that informed of the passing of John Laurens.

Quickly grasping the loss, I reached for him again. "Oh, my love . . ." This time he didn't pull away, but he also didn't soften to my touch.

Though I'd never met Laurens, I knew he was as dear a friend to my husband as any other member of Washington's little military family. Since hearing them talk about Laurens at Morristown, he'd loomed large in my imagination as a man I would admire if only because everyone else admired him.

"How tragic," I whispered, reading the rest. Colonel Laurens had led a small force to attack a British foraging party in South Carolina, one of several footholds in America to which British forces still clung, but was himself ambushed and mortally wounded in the first volley of battle. He was, I would later learn, one of the last casualties of the war.

An unspeakable, unnecessary tragedy.

And though my heart ached for his family, it also ached for my husband, who still hadn't moved or spoken. And he didn't speak the rest of that night, even after Papa had seen out all of our guests. Nor did Alexander utter a word the next day.

"You're frightening me," I finally said, when he wouldn't hold our baby boy. "Won't you speak to me?"

It was a jest between us that my husband ran hot—his temper, his blood, his skin. And yet, when I reached for his hand that sweltering summer day, it was like ice.

"I can't," Hamilton rasped, as if forcing just those two words was an agony.

"Alexander, I'm your wife. I'm—"

"You didn't know him. You can't understand."

He was right. I didn't understand. John Laurens was not, after all, the first of my husband's comrades to fall in battle. And though Hamilton always spoke of the fallen with grief and respect, their deaths had not made of him a shell of a man. Not like this. I thought perhaps it was because we believed the war to be finished, that all the sacrifices were now to be rewarded with glory, not loss. Or perhaps it was because, in the army, there hadn't been time for grief and this was the outcome of Hamilton holding himself together for so many years.

There was something else that alarmed me. Quite beside the pain at having my own attempts to comfort him rebuffed again and again, there was the bewildering realization that my husband had retreated someplace inside himself I couldn't reach. Some dark place I hadn't even known was there. And so instead of shaking him, I asked, "Who *would* understand, then?"

Alexander turned, warding me off with an upraised hand, as if willing me to be silent.

But I persisted. "Who will you talk to?"

He merely went to the window and stared.

Frightened and at a loss as to how I could help him, I again offered, "I'll bring up tea. Or coffee. Or something to—" I cut myself off, realizing that he wasn't listening.

He had his back turned to me, maybe turned to the whole world.

Perhaps what he needed was time to grieve in his own way, to make his peace with the sorrow. Perhaps Papa could make my husband see sense. I turned to the door, thinking to do just that, when I heard Alexander whisper, "Lafayette."

"What?"

"Lafayette would understand."

And then, suddenly, so did I.

My husband maintained friendships with all his fellow aides-de-camp. But none of them seemed to know the depths of his emotions as well as the Frenchman, who had warned me from the start that behind my husband's mask was *great pain and loss.*

If I could have summoned our friend to the house in that moment, I would have, but an ocean now separated us, because Lafayette had returned to France. So I went to my husband's desk, intending, I suppose, to take the liberty of writing a letter to the marquis. But there already, to my surprise, was a letter *from* Lafayette, a fact that nearly startled me with its prescience.

> *However silent you may please to be, I will nevertheless remind you of a friend who loves you tenderly and who by his attachment desires a great share in your affection.*

Though Lafayette had written before Laurens died, the marquis was, like me, faced with Hamilton's silence and waiting for a reply.

And that decided it for me. I took from the desk a blank sheet of paper, an inkwell, and a quill pen. Then I returned to the window where Alex stood and pressed the pen into his palm. "Write him."

"Betsy—"

"If you won't speak to me, speak to Lafayette," I insisted.

Then I left him.

By the light of dawn, my husband had managed to scribble only two lines.

> *Poor Laurens; he has fallen a sacrifice to his ardor in a trifling skirmish in South Carolina. You know how truly I loved him and will judge how much I regret him.*

Those two lines were enough.

Though he didn't send them to Lafayette for a few months—and even then, only as a postscript to a letter—it broke the dam open, allowing my husband to flow back to me and to our son.

But he never again spoke to me of John Laurens.

The subject remained closed for the rest of his life.

How I wish it remained closed for the rest of mine.

# Part Two

## The War for Peace

# Chapter Fourteen

*February 1783*
*Philadelphia, Pennsylvania*

I WAS NOW A congressman's wife.

In the year since the fighting ended, Alexander had been elected to serve as one of New York's five delegates to the Congress of the Confederation. We rented a little house in Philadelphia, and though I'd been there only a month, I'd already learned that it was the fate of a politician's wife to find herself unexpectedly with guests.

And sometimes even engaged in a bit of very irregular entertaining.

*Three quick raps upon the back door followed by two slow ones.*

That would be Mr. James Madison and the signal for me to answer the back door to the darkened alleyway that I'd never otherwise open past dusk. "Come in," I said to the slight-statured Virginia congressman who'd become my husband's unexpected ally within Congress.

Dressed all in black, unprepossessing and bookish, Madison's manner was somber and reserved to the point of being shy. In fact, he was my husband's opposite in seemingly every way—except, I learned, in the most important way.

Both men supported a strong union and believed that the Articles of Confederation required revision to ensure it.

I did, too. I recalled too starkly—sometimes even in nightmares from which I woke in a gasping, cold sweat—the terrible conditions of the soldiers during the war. The gaunt faces. The bare feet blackened from frostbite due to exposure. The shrieks of amputees operated upon without medicines to dull the pain. Deprivations all caused by the unwillingness of the states to adequately support the national cause . . .

Now, Alexander's and Mr. Madison's work to find a way to pay the army, fund the war debt, and bring the states together as a nation was being undermined at every turn by a faction in Congress more attached to state interests than to the federal. The only way to get anything done was to do it out of the public eye. Which was the reason for the subterfuge.

And I was rather proud of the fact that the plan had been mine.

My idea came when I'd awakened one night to discover the bed cold beside me and Alexander hunched over his desk, writing furiously in the light of a single candle. "What are you working on?" I'd asked, laying my hands upon his shoulders.

He'd eased back into my touch, pulling my hand to that sensuous mouth and pressing a kiss to my knuckles. "I've been appointed chairman of peace arrangements. I'm to provide a system for foreign affairs, Indian affairs, a peacetime army, and naval establishments."

"Oh, is that all?"

He peered up at me with a weary chuckle. "Well, and also to help pacify the army—who would like, at long last, to be paid. One can scarcely blame them for being on the verge of uprising against Congress." He shook his head, especially since he'd given up his own soldier's pay for fear of appearing self-interested in the matter. "But what has pulled you from bed at this hour?"

"In truth, thinking about all you're trying to accomplish here."

He frowned. "I don't wish my duties to disturb your peace of mind, my sweet girl."

I wanted to be more than a sweet girl to him, which was why I blurted, "Perhaps you can get more done if you conduct negotiations in private."

His brows raised over those blue eyes. "Something you learned watching your father at Indian conventions?"

I nodded, hoping he wouldn't discount those experiences. "If those who stand against you in Congress don't realize the extent of your alliance with Mr. Madison, they'll be less prepared to thwart you. If you make your strategies behind closed doors, you can take your foes unawares on the Congress floor."

His eyes narrowed with appreciation. "You *are* a general's daughter," he said approvingly, taking me back to bed.

I shook my head and helped him lift my shift. "I'm a congressman's wife."

"Yes, you are," he said as he covered my body with his. And after bringing us together, he jested, "Perhaps I should recommend you for appointment for the New York delegation. You have more passion for it than those who actually hold the posts and who worry more about their own individual welfare than the common good."

His compliment pleased me, but even more satisfying was that Alexander took my advice.

Which was how, a few days later, I came to be standing in a darkened kitchen of the house we'd rented near Independence Hall with my fussing one-year-old son on my shoulder, and a nervous Virginia congressman stomping snow off his boots by my hearth. "Colonel Hamilton will be home shortly," I said, taking Madison's snowy coat and hanging it upon a peg. "Can I offer you some hot tea?"

"Oh, no, thank you," Madison said softly, eyeing the little boy in my arms. "You have your hands quite occupied with young Master Hamilton. I couldn't trouble you to serve me." Perhaps because Madison was the owner of a vast plantation with many slaves, he seemed overly aware that we kept no servant with us—the work of caring for the baby and keeping our little household entirely mine. "It's trouble enough that I'm dropping in on you so late."

"Nonsense. You're always most welcome, Mr. Madison," I said, wanting to put the congressman at ease, and taking more than a bit of pride in the modest feast I'd managed to keep warm. Beef tongue, peas, and potatoes in an herbed butter sauce. "Some wine at least?" I offered, leading him to the dining room, where the drapes were pulled tight against prying eyes from the street.

"Yes, thank you," Madison said, but as I began to pour, my discontented son kicked his feet, nearly toppling the glasses.

"Careful little man!" Madison cried, catching Philip playfully by the toes. And when my son giggled, the congressman smiled and held out his hands. "May I?"

Surprised at Madison's change in demeanor—for though there was often kindness in his eyes, the soft-spoken congressman rarely smiled—I surrendered my babe into his arms. "You must be a father, Mr. Madison."

"Unfortunately, no," the man replied wistfully. "I'm a confirmed bachelor, as fate would have it, but children take to me." And it was true. While I poured wine, Madison whispered something into Philip's ear that made him laugh and laugh.

"Whatever did you say to him?" I asked.

"I'm afraid it's a secret," Madison replied, bouncing my son in his arms. "Between gentlemen."

Just then my husband came in the front entrance. "Betsy, I'm home," Alexander called, slamming the door shut. "Is Madison—"

"In here, charming our child," I said, and my husband appeared in the archway, blowing warm air into his hands.

I finished setting plates and silver, then took the baby as the men settled at the table and dug into their meal as if they hadn't eaten all day. And given what I knew of Alexander's schedule, there was some likelihood that was true. Even as they ate, they spread letters and ledgers out on the table between them. And afterward, I brought them a tray of tea and my mother's shortbread I'd saved in a jar, for I'd learned to always keep a supply of some baked goods on hand for just such occasions.

While I poured tea, Madison pulled a well-used notebook

from his pocket and began to write. As the two men collaborated, Alexander stabbed at a page with his fingers. "Our debt stands at forty million. The state of our finances has never been more critical. There are dangerous prejudices in particular states opposed to giving stability and prosperity to the union, thereby weakening us in our peace negotiations with Britain, which could yet fail. It is the first wish of my heart that this union may last, but feeble as the links among our states are, what prudent man would rely upon it?"

Madison listened intently as my husband then rattled off all our problems *at length,* and then nodded and said, simply, "All of this can be solved with a federal tax. Congress must have power and autonomy in financial matters."

Alexander opened his mouth as if to protest that the matter was more complicated but then seemed content with Madison's simplification. Their personal friendship and political alliance worked well because if Alexander was a born orator, able to lay siege with a barrage of impregnable arguments, Madison was skilled at quickly and quietly cutting through the weeds.

Moreover, as I was later to learn, Madison could have a dry and wicked sense of humor when it was just the three of us. Or four of us, more truly. "What is your magic formula?" I asked one night when Madison was able, with more whispering, to lure my son to sleep.

"Bawdy jokes," Madison quipped with a wink of which I would not have thought such a shy little man capable. "As I said, secrets between gentlemen."

In the weeks that followed, Madison's nighttime visits to our home became more frequent, and I found myself enjoying the company, as the bachelorhood of many of the other delegates meant that I hadn't yet found much society of my own despite the size and affluence of this city. In Albany, I'd had my sisters and our friends from our childhood troop of Blues, not to mention the Burrs, with whom we'd had the pleasure of becoming close.

But in Philadelphia, my society was all politicians—which was how I came to meet the primary author of the Declaration of Independence for the first time.

On short notice, Alexander asked if I could host a small dinner party for *a friend of Madison's*, a widower who temporarily resided with his young daughter in the same boardinghouse where Madison stayed. I thought nothing more of it until Mr. Madison's friend stood before me in my parlor. Tall with fiery ginger hair and a refined southern accent, the man gave me a soft smile and a graceful bow. "Thomas Jefferson, at your service, madam."

Oh, my husband. Some friend, indeed! It was not yet widely known that Jefferson had penned the immortal lines of our Declaration, including *all men are created equal*. But because of my father's service in the war and Congress, I did know of Jefferson's powerful contribution. I also knew that as one of our foremost statesmen, he'd been chosen to help negotiate the peace proceedings in France. And I managed a curtsy despite my shaking hands and trembling knees. "Mr. Jefferson, it's an honor to welcome you to our home."

"Thank you. May I introduce my daughter, Patsy?" the Virginian asked. "I fear she is too infrequently in the company of ladies, as I've dragged her from seaport to seaport searching for a ship that might take us to Paris despite enemy vessels still in the waters."

A tall, strapping girl of about ten stepped near her father. In a yellow calico frock with white bows, she shared her father's coloring and had his intelligent eyes. She gave a quick curtsy. "Madam."

"Hello, Patsy. You must be having quite an adventure with your father."

She smiled with an adoring gaze at Mr. Jefferson. "Oh, indeed. Papa and I have been *everywhere* searching for a ship. I have seen Baltimore, New York, and even Boston."

Her enthusiasm was charming, and her presence eased my surprise in hosting *the voice of our independence* at my little dining table. "Well, you're already much better traveled than I am," I said, extending a hand that she took when her papa gave her an approving nod. "You must tell me everything."

As they were wont to do, the men turned to politics over dinner. Alexander spoke candidly about the need for federal revenue and standing armies and permanent navies, and I didn't think I imagined the way Jefferson's lips pursed and his brow furrowed, even though his replies were always polite and measured. I sensed, in Jefferson, a fundamental disagreement about the nature of our country's government, citizens, and future. Worse, I noticed the way Madison deferred to Jefferson's thinking as the conversation progressed.

And it made me worry.

Though Madison's patient solicitude and my husband's fiery passion had always seemed to make them an odd team, the two men used their differences to attack the same problems and achieve the same ends from different directions. I thought it a great partnership. Moreover, I was learning that my husband didn't make friends easily with men outside of the army. And yet he'd taken to Madison straightaway.

Now I worried for Mr. Jefferson to come between them.

As the tulips and hyacinths bloomed all over the city, and Congress finally ratified the provisional peace treaty in mid-April, marking the end of eight years of hostilities, Alexander and Jemmy Madison—as I heard my husband sometimes call him—took to organizing a series of secret nighttime meetings with select members of Congress. The Quaker culture of Philadelphia meant that the streets, well lit by whale-oil lamps, tended to empty at night, creating a special challenge for men attempting to sneak about, yet secrecy was more urgently needed as rebellious troops threatened to march upon the city to get the pay long owed to them.

I didn't realize the seriousness of the situation until, on a rare summer night when he came home alone, Alexander said, "You must go, Betsy. You and the little one. First thing tomorrow."

At sixteen months old, our Philip was now a toddling, talking, curious boy who already promised to have his father's good looks. "Why must we go?" I asked, handing Philip over as he reached out for his papa.

Alexander showered his son's little face with loud kisses that made Philip giggle. "Because the army is coming from Lancaster, and picking up men along the way, and the government of this state refuses to do anything to stop them or protect Congress."

*Another mutiny,* I thought, for lack of a better word to describe it. But it seemed much more serious than any of the others—with our own army ready to attack our fledgling government after having so recently toppled King George. How had it come to this? "What about you?"

"I'm not afraid," he said. "I'm a friend to the army, zealous to serve them, and espousing their interests in Congress. I trust that they know this, and will listen."

But I still remembered how my father's soldiers turned on him, suspecting him of the blackest treason. "Alexander—"

He embraced me then, little Philip between us, and tangled his hand in my hair as he brought our faces close. "You must go. Both of you. I can't have you in harm's way. Worry not about me, for if Pennsylvania won't protect Congress, we'll flee, too."

After a sleepless night, I set out the next morning with little Philip in a carriage of others fleeing the oncoming threat. During the journey to Albany, I had little idea what fate had befallen Alexander, Congress, indeed the country itself. And it was then that I realized just how fragile this thing called independence really was.

*June 1783*
*Albany*

"Peggy's eloped!" Angelica said before I'd even alighted from the carriage in front of the Pastures. "After a fashion, anyway. Mama and Papa are in a state."

"Not again," I said, recalling the turmoil Angelica's elopement had caused all those years ago. "Did you speak to Peggy? What did she say?"

Angelica took little Philip from my arms and pressed a kiss to his cheek. "Peggy said that since Papa had already given his blessing, she simply tired of waiting. And it's a good match for both of them. Stephen's to be the ninth patroon of Rensselaerswyck, after all."

That much was true. Peggy's new husband stood to inherit a vast ancestral estate passed down from one of the founders of New Netherlands. I couldn't help worrying over the scandal it might cause for *two* of Philip Schuyler's daughters to have run off this way, but that wasn't my greatest concern. I put a hand on Angelica's arm. "Does she love him?"

My sister's expression softened. "She does."

That was enough for me. After all, I would've run off with Alexander if only he'd permitted it, so I had a keen sense of sympathy for Peggy's need to fly to the man she loved. And I welcomed the distraction from worrying about my husband in Congress, facing off against angry veterans.

Therefore, in the coming weeks, Angelica and I led a cautious campaign to win over our brooding parents. We exclaimed over how close Peggy would still be to the Pastures, for Van Rensselaer Manor stood just a few miles up the Hudson. And we excitedly imagined how soon it would be until Peggy began her own family, which being twenty-five already, she was ripe to do.

Unexpectedly, Mama was easily won over. In truth, she'd seemed so eager for Peggy to wed that I almost suspected, were it not for the scandal, she would have helped my sister climb out a window to run off with her betrothed, despite how angry she'd once been at Angelica for doing exactly that. And Mama was so swiftly reconciled to it that Papa behaved as if it was all done according to his wishes in the first place.

So it was that our parents welcomed Peggy home with open arms and a reception that reminded me of the one Alexander and

I had on our wedding day. This time, however, I'd helped arrange the festivities, working with Mama and Dinah to set the menu, and having Jenny pull together large vases of fresh flowers from the garden to brighten every room. Once again, all of Albany's finest families attended, as well as some of its newer arrivals, like Colonel and Mrs. Burr. And even though I delighted in catching up with Peggy, welcoming Stephen to the family, and learning the latest gossip from Theodosia, it all made me miss my husband even more, especially given all the indignities he was being made to suffer as a congressman.

Though I did not know it at the time, I'd fled Philadelphia just before our angry, unpaid soldiers seized the city arsenals and held my husband, Jemmy Madison, and the rest of Congress at bayonet point in a standoff. After that, Congress became a runaway government, fleeing from Pennsylvania, to New Jersey, then Annapolis.

All summer long, our Confederation Congress was abused, laughed at, and cursed wherever they went, and I could scarcely imagine what Alexander—who'd done as much as anyone to resolve the disputes before it led to all of this—must have been feeling. It was almost as humiliating for our fledgling country as it was frightening.

When Hamilton finally returned to me at my father's house in August, he claimed to be done with it all. Frustrated and demoralized he said, "If the army's mutiny didn't convince our countrymen to replace the Articles of Confederation with a stronger government, nothing will. So, as for you and me and our baby boy, we'll now settle into a purely domestic life."

His proclamation suited me just fine, especially when, as the crispness of fall crept into the evening air, Peggy announced after church services that she was expecting her first child.

"Oh, we're all to be mothers together," I said, hugging her.

Even our little ones joined the celebration when Angelica's son pointed at his aunt Peggy's belly and said, "Do you have a boy in there? I hope it's a boy!"

Peggy and I laughed. But Angelica didn't. Mustering a forced smile, she said, "I have exciting news, too. Carter is taking me to Paris."

I blinked. "Whatever for?"

"My husband is to be a U.S. envoy to the French government," she said, her voice overly cheery.

"When do you leave?" Peggy asked, her hand on her still-flat stomach.

"Before winter." Angelica sighed with a note of regret. "Months away! We'll have plenty of time together before I go."

But those months passed far too quickly. And when November came, I worried at the damp lace kerchief in my hands as we said our farewells. I was fearful of the dangers of Angelica's ocean journey and pained, as I always was, to be parted from my sisters. "I'm going to miss you both more than words can say."

"Poor Betsy," Angelica said. "You're taking it almost as hard as Papa."

"How else should I take it? You'll both be so far from me."

"I'll be just a short boat ride away," Peggy said, blushing pink, as if she were quite pleased to see me weepy at the thought of parting with her. But even though Van Rensselaer Manor wasn't far from the Pastures, Alexander and I were shortly destined for New York City, so that boat ride would require nearly a week to accomplish.

"And I will also be just a boat ride away . . . albeit, a longer boat ride," Angelica said, squeezing my hand.

"How long will you be in Europe?" I asked, clutching her hand in return.

"Not long enough to see everything that I'd like." Angelica sniffed. "Which is why you shouldn't envy me; I'm to have a taste of the fruit without being given the whole apple . . ."

She was teasing to distract me from my sorrow, of course, but the fear that she might believe my sadness resulted from *envy* was enough for me to force a deep breath and calm myself. My sisters had both married wealthy men who could take them to the ends of the earth, whereas my own husband's circumstances were nowhere as grand. Still, I would never wish to deny my sisters pleasures I couldn't have for myself. "You'll write me? Every day?"

"If I were to write every day, I should have even less time to see the sites," Angelica protested with a blasé expression her sniffles belied. "But I'll try to see everything as if through my darling Betsy's eyes, for that is the kindest and most enjoyable way to see everything." I smiled through my tears because like Alexander, my sister had a way of rendering me helpless to her charms. "In the meantime, you'll have an adventure setting up housekeeping for my amiable brother-in-law and your darling little one."

"I know," I said, and the idea filled me with pleasure and anxiety in equal measure. We'd be in New York City before year's end, where Alexander intended to set up his law practice and serve as the agent looking after Mr. Carter's business interests while he was away.

It was a time for building anew. A family. A home. A country.

So it was in New York City that I finally said a tearful farewell to Angelica. With her little brood of children, she climbed aboard a ship to cross the sea, leaving me with a fear for her safety and an ache even greater than when she'd slipped out that back door of Papa's house so many years before.

And she was not the only one to go.

At long last, the Treaty of Paris had been signed, granting America her independence—and having won it, we were all eager for the British soldiers to leave. Leave they finally did, and with them went almost thirty thousand Loyalist merchants and citizens, refugees from all over America, who fled that winter to start new lives elsewhere—not to mention thousands of slaves to whom the British had promised freedom, an uncomfortable reminder that our enemy had maintained its promise of liberty to the enslaved much better than had my own country.

We were there in the crowds down at the Battery on that cold but glorious evacuation day as the British boarded their ships and sailed away from New York, making way for Washington's coming procession with the American army to retake the city. I jogged little Philip in my arms, showing him the sails of our enemies receding, so proud that tears sprang to my eyes. "See what we've done?" I whispered in my son's ear. "We've chased a king back across the sea, darling."

Even the final trick of the departing British could not bring down my jubilation. The British had left their flag flying, tied high to a greased pole. And I laughed that it was a Hollander who gave his wooden cleats to be nailed as rungs to the pole so that it could be climbed and the flag torn down. The crowd's roar when that Union Jack finally fell to the mud was something I will never forget. A roar that grew to deafening volume when the retreating British fired one final defiant shot and our bold Stars and Stripes were raised before the fleet sailed out of sight.

*Huzzah! Huzzah! Huzzah!*

The war was over. It was finally over.

And I let out a breath that seemed to come from the very core of me, as if I had been holding it for years. Perhaps I had been. But even that moment couldn't compare to the crowd's eruption when our victorious commander in chief and his officers marched into the city. We waved flags and cheered and wept . . .

We were Americans, now. Every one of us.

And I think not a single person there had ever felt it more than when General Washington passed by upon his cantering gray-white horse. Amidst the revelry, still I saw the signs of the sacrifice that'd been required to bring us to this moment. Mothers who had lost sons. Widows who had lost soldier husbands. Soldiers who had lost limbs and eyes and years of their lives to the fight. I felt those losses to the core of me as well, because I knew I could have lost my husband.

I closed my eyes and offered a prayerful thanksgiving that Alexander stood at my side now, that we were together, and that the danger was behind us. Drums, cannon shots, bells, and song filled the air, and celebratory bonfires burned well into the night.

It wasn't until the morning that we were reminded of how much there was still to be done. In my childhood visits to the city, I remembered the bustling wharf, the grand buildings, and the broad tree-lined avenues. What we found in the wake of the long British occupation was a shelled city of scorched and burned-out edifices now unrecognizable. Livestock roamed freely amidst trash and weeds, fences long gone, and nary a stick in sight. In addition to the looting and the burning, the British had cut down trees and stripped manor houses of wood, burning nearly anything they could find for fuel. And the stench from the mud-choked wharfs and excrement in the streets . . . I couldn't describe it if I tried.

"It should all be torn down and replaced," Hamilton said of the hovels that remained.

Of course, Alexander saw *possibility* in all this destruction. He thought much opportunity was to be had in engineers who would make stately homes for the city's new residents. He was already making plans to rebuild the city to its former glory, but for the time being, my husband rented a three-story house on Wall Street, where the best merchants made their homes, though we could only afford to live at the eastern end, where houses with crumbling mortar, fading paint, and sagging roofs huddled amongst shops and taverns. In fact, our new home was quite near the Queen's Head Tavern, run by a West Indian tavern keeper named Samuel Fraunces. And it was that very tavern that became the epicenter of our first marital quarrel.

We quarreled not because my husband stayed there drinking all hours of the night, as so many wives were apt to complain. But instead because, when the occasion called for it, my husband simply refused to go to the tavern at all.

"General Washington is leaving the army," I said, broaching the subject for the third time in as many days. But since the invitation had arrived, Alexander's mood had turned dark. "He's saying farewell to his officers at the tavern, and were you not first and foremost amongst them?"

Though I believed right down to the marrow of my bones that my husband had been the best and brightest of Washington's officers, I still expected him to modestly protest that generals like my father, Nathanael Greene, Lafayette, or Henry Knox had been more instrumental to the victory. But modesty was never one of Alexander's virtues. Instead, he complained, "Congress has not seen fit to recognize me as such."

"Alexander—"

"I'm not going."

Something had changed in him, I thought.

Something ate at him, night and day, and I didn't think it was Congress.

I wished I understood it.

"But Washington is laying down his sword," I said. "Such a moment will surely be recorded in the annals of history, Alexander. Shouldn't your name be noted as one of those in attendance?"

It was then, for the first time, that I learned what it was like to *truly* stand in opposition to Alexander Hamilton. For what followed was not an indulgent remonstration. Nor even a small lecture on all the reasons he should not—would not—attend.

It was, instead, an *onslaught* of arguments, stinging in tone as if I were not merely a nagging wife but also an enemy to be destroyed. Raising every objection I had made or might make as a target, Alexander fired off ten, twelve, twenty points in rapid succession. Not just vanquishing my opinion, but also snapping even at the fly-wisp ideas that might have still buzzed around its corpse in my brain.

When, stunned, I finally opened my mouth to reply, he snapped his paper open. "No more, Betsy."

I cannot decide whether my rebelliousness was stoked by the lawyerly tenaciousness with which he harangued me, or the high temper with which he did it, or simply the knowledge that my own mother would never have allowed such an episode to pass in her parlor without exacting a heavy price from my father's peace of mind.

The truth was that in refusing to say farewell to Washington, I believed my husband to be doing something enormously foolish that he might one day regret. Sitting there beside him, Mrs. Washington's advice came suddenly to mind. *"Sometimes we encourage, sometimes we challenge, and sometimes we manage . . ."*

And so, instead of staying silent, I challenged him with the one thing I knew to be unutterably true. "George Washington is a great man."

My husband's intense eyes fixed on me with dark, stormy disapproval. An edge of contempt and enmity I'd never before imagined could come from the expression of a man as dear to me as life. "I told you, 'No more.' A certain indulgence must be afforded a Dutchman's daughter in matters of hearth and home, but I'll teach you the absolute necessity of implicit obedience if I must."

It was not the first time my husband warned of discipline. He had, in fact, written similar words in love letters. But those were playful threats, embellished with a courtier's wit. This time, he seemed in earnest.

Would he *dare* raise a hand to me? Though the Bible might have confirmed his right to, my fists balled with a sudden urge to turn my back, summon a carriage, and return with our baby boy to Papa's home in Albany at once.

Other fathers would refuse to step into a quarrel between a daughter and a husband, but I didn't doubt even for a *moment* that my father would shelter me and his grandson, nor that he would take my part in any quarrel. And for Alexander, a breach with my father—one of the foremost men in the state—would dash his ambitions forever. So I felt a gratifying, if discomforting, satisfaction that I held a greater power of happiness and misery over my husband than he held over me. Except for one single, solitary thing.

I loved him. I loved him so deeply and truly. Desperately.

And so I let him make this terrible mistake—toward Washington and me. That night, I said not another word. Quietly seething, I went to bed. I wouldn't abandon him, as so many others had in his life, but I was no saint. And in the days that followed, I couldn't manage more than polite conversation that felt stilted by the breach.

From a newly married Tench Tilghman, I later learned that Washington—notorious for his reserve—toasted his officers, invited them to shake his hand, and actually embraced them, weeping. I wasn't there to see it myself, of course, but after it was done, I went alone with Philip to mingle with the crowds at Whitehall Wharf, holding my darling boy so that he wouldn't miss the moment as the church bells rang and everywhere along the route people pressed noses to windows and crowded balconies to watch Washington go.

At nearly two years old, Philip was an uncommonly handsome little boy who laughed with delight and raised his little fists when the soldiers, still cheering, waved their hats as Washington boarded his ferry.

I laughed, too, at the joy in the moment, but also wept bittersweet tears.

Because I feared we might never set eyes upon the grand old man again as the river carried him away. And because, for days, I'd stifled emotion that now crested over at having uncovered another dark layer in my husband that I hadn't known was there before.

I soldiered on and tried to distract myself with an upcoming dance assembly that week—a gathering of the city's finest citizens at a grand ball that would effect a reconciliation between the patriots and any Tories still left in the city. I was eager to slip into my best gown—and the more genteel life that I imagined had preceded the war.

More importantly, amiable society so often brought out my husband's playful wit and good humor, and I hoped the occasion might restore the tenderness between us. But then the poorer patriot citizens objected to the unseemliness of "dancing on the graves" of their comrades who'd died through the machinations of these very same Tories.

The ball was canceled, and we stayed in instead. And I could barely restrain the sadness I felt at the lost opportunity to restore our happiness.

Maybe Alexander sensed it, or perhaps he even shared it, for that night he climbed into bed next to me and wept apologies into my hair for his behavior, confessing a clawing loneliness I'd never fathomed.

"But we have so many friends," I assured him, stroking his beloved face. "I couldn't make an accounting of them all even using all our fingers and toes!"

"*Your* friends," he said, hoarsely.

That much was true. Friends from my childhood. Friends of my father. Friends made only lately in the bustle of his ambitions. But I realized that the friends my husband had called *the only family he'd ever known* were his brothers-at-arms, now gone from his life, dispersed like chaff in the wind. John Laurens was dead. Lafayette had returned to France. McHenry and Tilghman to Maryland. And now George Washington to Virginia . . .

I realized the true reason my husband had not said good-bye.

Because he couldn't *bear* to say good-bye.

Alexander Hamilton, the orphan, abandoned by those he loved and left to the mercies of this world, had no gift for partings. He'd left Washington's side before Yorktown in what had seemed then to be a fit of pique and pride. But now I wondered if he'd left Washington before Washington could leave him. Before he could be abandoned by yet another father and separated again from brothers who he couldn't claim by blood or law, but whom he loved just the same. And so I resolved from that moment on that I would draw closer to us my husband's companions at war.

The soldiers here in New York. The officers he'd served with. Including Aaron Burr, who'd just moved to the city and seemed so much like Alexander to me that I hoped they might become more than law partners and friends, but maybe even confidants and kindred spirits.

Of course, I realize now how naive that hope truly was, for they were as different as night and day . . .

# Chapter Fifteen

HOW MUCH?" I asked, nauseated by the scent of the fishmonger's wares.

As part of my project to reunite my husband's military family, I was hosting a dinner for Lafayette, who'd recently
returned to the United States, and the Baron von Steuben, the
brilliant Prussian drillmaster who'd served with my husband,
most crucially at Valley Forge.

It was said that Prussians loved smoked fish, though apparently my heavily pregnant body did not. So I was grateful to
be accompanied to the fish market at Murray's Wharf by Theodosia Burr, with whom I'd spent so many delightful days when
our husbands were studying for the bar together. Separated as I
was from my sisters, I cherished Theodosia's companionship, for
her worldliness and fearlessness reminded me of Angelica, and
her brashness and willingness to say anything made me think
of Peggy. With our husbands both lawyers and frequently gone
riding circuit together from court to court, we spent much of our
time together. Luckily, the Burrs lived not far from us on Wall
Street, so it was easy to always be in one another's houses, our
children playing together.

And one of the things I appreciated about Theodosia, who was ten years my senior, was her ability to haggle. "No, that's too much," she said when the merchant barked an amount that was far more for a basket of smoked salmon than anyone ought to pay.

The merchant responded by giving a price in another currency altogether.

Truthfully, no one seemed to know what sort of money we ought to use. People tried to pay for goods with Spanish doubloons, French guineas, and Prussian carolines because the continental dollar was so worthless. To make matters worse, each of the states printed their own money, leading to such chaos that no one knew the rate of exchange.

We'd finally settled on a price in British shillings, when a man in a knitted cap and filthy homespun breeches spat at Theodosia from where he lurked behind us. "Tory *scum*."

It was, of course, no small thing to be called a Tory in the days just after the war. Though our peace treaty had called for fair treatment, Loyalists had been stripped of their rights to serve in various professions and were subjected to the utmost suspicion. Even Theodosia sometimes got caught up in it. Everyone knew she'd previously been married to a British officer, that her sons were ensigns in the king's service, and she'd once counted amongst her friends Peggy Shippen Arnold, wife of the traitor who'd fled to England within weeks of the British defeat of Yorktown. To some, it didn't seem to matter that Mrs. Burr had supported the patriot cause and married a veteran in good standing.

Whatever the reason, Theodosia gasped as another knave loomed and said, "Their bodies are in America, but their heads remain in England. And their necks ought to be stretched."

"Move on, now," the fishmonger barked at the men with a scowl and a wave of his hand. "I'll take whatever money holds value, and I'll not have trouble here."

"We'll be back if you keep taking British money!" the rascals called as they moved on.

"How dreadful!" I said, my hand on Theodosia's arm. "Please don't let such ruffians wound your feelings."

"They're *scoundrels*. It would be bad enough were they driven by a mere thirst for vengeance against the British," Theodosia said as we departed the stall. Rarely did I see her anything but entirely composed, but she shuddered now and released a shaky breath even as she was gracious enough to take the smelly basket of fish from me. She nearly kicked one of the snuffling pigs who were let loose to rove the streets and eat the garbage. "But they'll accuse anyone for a fee. For any slight at all. Neighbor has to fear neighbor turning them in for profit."

Fortunately, that night, Lafayette's return and natural ebullience buoyed all of our moods and provided an occasion for celebrating. Seeing the two old friends reunite and witnessing such happiness come over Alexander as I hadn't seen in many months made me forget the unpleasantness at the fish market altogether.

"My dear Hamilton," Lafayette said, grinning.

"My dear marquis," Alexander said, both men laughing and embracing. Lafayette greeted Baron von Steuben and his aide, then next came to me, where I stood holding Philip's tiny hand. At two and a half, he was up past his bedtime, but we couldn't pass up the opportunity for our son to meet our good friend. Lafayette bowed playfully. "Madame Hamilton, how motherhood becomes you."

Nearly eight months along, the lack of grace I was able to manage with my belly belied the compliment. But I was too happy to see him again to care. "Marquis, welcome to our home."

"Bah." Lafayette winked and gave a wave of his hand. "Please let us not stand on any ceremony of noble titles." When I nodded and smiled, he crouched down to Philip's eye level. "*Mon dieu*, he is your exact likeness, Hamilton." My husband beamed while Lafayette addressed our boy. "*Bonjour*, young man."

"*Bonjoo, Laffy*," Philip said in his version of the words Alexander had made him practice.

Lafayette laughed and clapped his hands, and everyone joined him. "Oh, *merci*! You make me feel the absence from my own little Anastasie, Georges, and Virginie even more acutely," he said of his children, the last two of whom he'd named for our commander in chief and the state where the war had finally been won.

Meanwhile, Alexander lifted Philip, gave him a proud hug, and then handed him off to be put to bed by Jenny, who Papa had recently lent to us as a servant. And I escorted everyone into the dining room.

Our experience at the fishmonger that day became a subject of conversation at the table I'd carefully laid with frosted wine glasses and festive table mats I'd woven for the occasion.

After complimenting me on the meal—the heartiness of which wouldn't have been possible without the shipments of produce my mother sent from Albany every week to "ensure the baby's health"—Lafayette asked, "Is it true that New York now has roving commissioners tasked with ferreting out secret enemies?"

The question had been addressed to Alexander, and yet it was a still-disturbed Theodosia who replied. "Oh yes. And when these so-called enemies are taken to jail, their bails are set so high as to shock the senses, and their fines even higher."

"Governor Clinton encourages these *levelers*," my husband ventured.

After they'd both served as delegates to Congress the previous year, Alexander had taken a loathing to Clinton, who was both a shameless self-seeker as well as an enemy to a strong federal government. "Like a populist demagogue he will have anarchy and bloodshed in the streets."

The baron placed heavy elbows upon the table and spoke in his thick Germanic accent. "*Ja*. This is why the Society of the Cincinnati is so vital. In bringing officers of the war to prominence, we can hold together the public *order*!"

Sipping at my wine, I thought that the baron's sentiments were exactly the kind of talk that had made some of our countrymen suspicious of the new Society of the Cincinnati. Though my husband would hear nothing against it.

And neither would the fiery baron, who added, "Wait until you see the gold eagle badges we're having made for all our members to wear. They're extraordinary." As if for confirmation, he looked to his very attentive aide sitting beside him, who profusely attested to the beauty of the pieces.

Amongst our company, only Burr seemed to have reservations. "Perhaps it's not wise to draw such attention to the Cincinnati just yet. Not when Sam Adams is calling it a creation of American nobility and some state legislatures consider denouncing us as a military aristocracy . . ."

I worried Burr might have the right of it. The controversy had already lost Hamilton a few clients. Indeed, while Alexander could rarely hold any opinion to himself, Burr seemed always reticent to make his known, even to us, his closest friends. I'd hoped the man's more reserved nature might influence my husband's.

But sensing the growing tension around the table, I changed the subject. "Dear Lafayette, tell us where your travels will take you."

"Ah, of course. By way of New Jersey, Philadelphia, and Baltimore, I am to go to Virginia, where I will be reunited with our dear Monroe and finally with our dear general at Mount Vernon. And at some point, I go into the wilds to help America negotiate a treaty with the Iroquois at Fort Stanwix. Perhaps you should come with me, *madame*. For I recall how valuable you were at my negotiations with that great people so many years ago. And I remember our sweet talk over rum."

Whereupon, to my embarrassment and delight, my husband raised a brow. "Sweet talk over rum?"

Lafayette laughed. "I would reassure you it was nothing, my friend, but I see you are jealous. And you deserve to be."

Colonel Burr smiled and winked at me, raising his glass. "To what Hamilton deserves."

Everyone laughed. Including Alexander, who then grinned

and raised his glass. "To Mrs. Hamilton," he said nodding at me, his blue eyes full of affection and amusement. "And Mrs. Burr, too. These ladies are more than either of us deserve." The others joined in the toast, and the kind attention warmed my cheeks and heart in equal measure.

Returning his glass to the table, Hamilton told Lafayette, "You must pass on our regards to Monroe and General Washington. With my very sincere esteem. And compliments to Mrs. Washington as well."

At long last, my husband seemed ready to set aside his quarrel with Washington. My heart lightened to hear it. And I believe Lafayette's did, too. We shared across the table a secret conspiratorial smile as Lafayette proposed another toast. "To Washington: Savior of His Country, Benefactor of Mankind, the Pride of America, and the Admiration of Two Hemispheres. And, of course, my bosom friend and adoptive father."

"*Ja. Gut!* To Washington," the baron said, standing and lifting his glass as he struck an ostentatious pose. Everyone joined in the toast with enthusiasm, including my husband, proving once more my suspicions that his prior aloofness about Washington's farewell had stemmed from missing the company of his brothers-at-arms.

"Will you have an opportunity to look into the matter of James Armistead while you're in Virginia?" I asked when we'd all settled again.

And I was a little delighted when Lafayette's eyes flashed with surprise at me for asking. "*Oui*, for it is an injustice, like so much about slavery, that cannot stand."

Theodosia frowned. "Who is James Armistead?"

"Only the most vital American spy in the whole Virginia campaign," the marquis replied. "An enslaved man who posed as a runaway so that the British would trust him. Without him, Cornwallis might well have reinforced Yorktown and then all would have been lost!"

The marquis recounted how Armistead, while enslaved, volunteered with his master's permission to serve as a soldier in the war and was assigned to Lafayette, who quickly recognized that the man's knowledge of Virginia could make him a valuable spy. Armistead gained the trust of both Arnold and Cornwallis, who allowed him to guide troops through the state, permitted him free access to British army headquarters, and even bade him to spy on Lafayette!

"I shall never forget the look on Cornwallis's face when he came to our camp to surrender," Lafayette continued, holding the whole company rapt with his storytelling, "and saw Armistead already there. Here Cornwallis thought the man his personal slave, never once suspecting the truth."

"The problem," Alexander explained, "is that Virginia's law emancipating those slaves who served on their masters' behalves applies only to *soldiers*, not spies."

"So Armistead remains enslaved," I told Theodosia. "It's an outrageous injustice."

"Saul Matthews faces similar difficulty," the baron said, shifting in his seat with agitation as he fed scraps off his plate to the thin pet greyhound he took with him everywhere. "Many times he supplied us with the intelligence of crucial British troop movements, yet he remains enslaved. These men deserve the applause of their country."

It was a reminder of all the different sorts of people who had taken part in our revolution. Black and white. Slaves and free. Indians and immigrants. Rich and poor.

Women, too.

But my husband's thoughts remained on the injustice of slavery and he sat forward, exchanging a glance with Burr. "There's talk of a manumission society forming here in New York. We intend to join."

I couldn't help but wonder what Papa's position would be about a society whose ultimate end was to abolish slavery, for the institution remained popular within the Dutch areas upstate, but I was proud that my husband planned to be involved. It might be controversial, but if my husband's associations must be controversial, then let them be morally right.

At length, Theodosia and I excused ourselves to the kitchen to prepare dessert—stewed pears in spiced wine and fresh cream—while Jenny cleared away the dishes.

"Are you sure you're all right?" I asked Theodosia, who had seemed pale since our encounter in the market, and unusually subdued during dinner.

She merely waved off my concern. But later, when the men had gone to the parlor to smoke, Theodosia glanced at Jenny's retreating form and admitted, "I'm so tired all the time that I don't know how you manage with just one slave."

Sometimes, I didn't know, either, but the conversation at dinner had left me even more uncomfortable to have full command of Jenny on my own. All our lives, she'd waited on me and my sisters—helping us dress, fixing our hair, tending to our room. Even assisting her mother in the kitchen. And though we'd all agreed we couldn't have managed without her, we'd never once, any of us, given the reality of Jenny's *serving* us a second thought. It was just how things were. But I remembered those black troops at Morristown and imagined Armistead and Matthews, enslaved again despite their crucial service, and it all felt . . . wrong.

"She's only *borrowed*," I said, hearing how weak the distinction was even as I uttered the words. "But she's skilled and trustworthy and a great help." And I still didn't know what I'd do without her.

Theodosia turned a warm smile to me. "Well, you're an exemplary hostess."

As Theodosia was well known for her lavish entertainments in the form of French-style salons, I managed a smile at the compliment despite the discomfiture in my breast. "You're kind to say so. I'd been uneasy that the guest list was unbalanced without unattached ladies to round out the company of the baron and his aide."

At this, Theodosia sputtered with laughter. "*Unbalanced*, indeed. I daresay our baron and his very handsome *aide* are not the sort to have any special interest in unattached ladies."

"What do you mean?" I asked.

"It isn't by happenstance that the baron is unmarried," Theodosia said, her voice hushing. "Don't you know how he came to join the revolution?"

I didn't have the slightest idea. Foreign mercenaries of all sorts had flooded to our shores to join our cause. I assumed the baron to be one of those, albeit more noble, stouthearted, and brilliant than almost all the others. Save Lafayette, of course.

Now I leaned close to hear more.

"He was ejected from the Prussian military for unsavory habits with men," Theodosia confided. "Nearly jailed in France for the same. On account of the fact the baron was a brilliant soldier, Ben Franklin smuggled him on a ship to America before he could be arrested as a sodomite."

This caused me to drop the half-emptied wineglass I held, spattering the table and my new woven mats with crimson.

It seemed apt since *crimson* was also the color of my rage that Theodosia should speak such black-hearted slander against one of my guests. About a hero of the revolution, no less. "That's *outrageous,*" I hissed, thinking less of Theodosia's character than I had before. If she could accuse a good man of the abominable vice of buggery, an accusation that could end in his hanging, I wondered at the sins in her own heart. "People have been executed for such crimes."

"And *that* is outrageous," Theodosia said, bewildering me altogether.

By the time our guests said their farewells, I was still stewing about Theodosia's gossip. I was, in truth, so bothered by it that I feared to even confide what she'd said to my husband lest he suspect that his wife was the sort of creature who dealt in such vile whispers. But that night, before we went upstairs, I asked, "The baron is a man of high character, is he not?"

Hamilton smiled. "He has his imprudencies, but upon the

whole the baron is a gentleman of real intelligence for whom I have a particular esteem. I recall that when he first came to America he could speak no English. And yet, he made himself invaluable. Upon all occasions, he conducted himself like an experienced and brave officer. Did he not impress you at dinner, my dear girl?"

The truth was, the baron *had* impressed me. I liked him—and his . . . companion. I even liked his dog. And most of all, I liked the salutary effect that he had upon Alexander's mood. So I didn't ask about the baron's imprudencies. And I promised myself that instead of spreading Theodosia's gossip, I'd instead bask in the success of our party.

"You enjoyed yourself tonight," I whispered, leaning back against my husband where we paused in the doorway to watch our boy sleep in his cradle.

"I enjoyed myself very much." Alexander's hands rested warmly upon my shoulders. "You are a better hostess even than your mother."

I doubted that. I didn't have Mama's perfect understanding of everything that must be done at the dinner table and the order in which it must be done.

But before I could express those thoughts, my husband continued, "I've found a precious jewel in you." Alexander wrapped his arms around me, and then his hands drifted down to my rounding belly. "Have I told you how pleased I am that you're giving me another child?"

"I shall never tire of hearing it," I said.

He turned me in his arms so that he could kiss me. He tasted of wine and exhilaration as he lifted me off my sore feet. I remembered how happy he'd been at the birth of Philip, and it filled my heart with hope for the future.

But when we finally had our fill of kisses and turned down the bed, the watchman passed our window crying, "Past ten o'clock and Cranston, the fishmonger, is a vile hypocrite and an enemy of freedom."

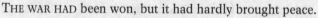

THE WAR HAD been won, but it had hardly brought peace.

Every day the clamor of the multitudes in the streets grew more menacing. While those streets were christened with new names—Crown Street became Liberty Street, Queen Street became Cedar, King became Pine—in coffeehouses, over bowls of grog, at the theater or wherever workmen struggled to clear away the debris and charred remains of war, we heard that no royalists should be suffered to live amongst patriots.

What right had men who, for eight years, had been destroying property, plundering, burning, killing, and inciting Indian massacres to expect kind and gentle treatment at the hands of a people they'd so deeply injured?

The next day, I heard a commotion outside the front window and looked out to see that the usual ebb and flow of carriages and well-dressed people on our wide avenue was now choked by an ill-clad mob, all pointing and laughing at some spectacle at their center. Heedlessly, I rushed onto the front stoop to catch the scent of pine tar, sharp in the air.

And there, to my dread, I saw Cranston the fishmonger—being forcibly stripped to the waist.

I shouted in alarm, but the ruffians ignored me completely as they slathered the warm tar over the poor fishmonger's chest and back and tore open a pillow for the feathers with which to humiliate him. This was followed by placement of a cowbell round his neck, and a sign that read "LOOK YE TORY CREW, SEE WHAT GEORGE YOUR KING CAN DO."

Fighting back nausea and defying all reason, I took hold of my skirts and waded into the crowd. "Stop this at once!"

"Get back, Mrs. Hamilton," one of the men said, daring to lay hands on me as the crack of a whip elicited a shriek of agony from its victim. "We Sons of Liberty ask you to remember all the times your husband came so near to death at Washington's side, and you'll know these traitors deserve whatever they get."

Oh, how easily any man could lay claim to the title Son of Liberty now that the war, and the danger of being hanged for it, had passed. "How do you know he's a traitor?" I asked, pulling away from the grubby self-styled patriot. "How could anyone know without giving the man a fair trial? Why the poor tailor Hercules Mulligan was thought to be a traitor until Washington himself revealed that he'd been our spy during the occupation."

"The fishmonger is no Hercules Mulligan," another man called. Perhaps he was unused to being spoken to in such a fashion by a woman, because the man stared with such contempt I thought he might strike me.

Fortunately, moments later it was Alexander who had me by both arms, forcing a retreat back to our house. I hadn't expected my husband to return from his law office so early, but oh how grateful I was to see him, even as he scolded me for being in the street. "I cannot have you risk yourself," Alexander said, his hand pressed protectively to my belly. "Especially not in your tender condition. What were you thinking?"

"I was thinking that they're going to murder him," I cried, shaking with impotent rage.

"They won't," he assured me. "They took his fish and made him bleed. That will be enough."

I prayed my husband was right, remembering that we'd both seen worse horrors. But the lawlessness unleashed in America since our victory threatened my faith. When a Tory was acquitted by a judge in Charleston, his neighbors simply laid hold of him as soon as he left the courthouse and strung him up. I feared everything we'd struggled for was all coming undone. No sooner had we driven the king from our shores than we seemed intent on proving that we were uncivilized people who couldn't live without a monarch to keep us from behaving as beasts.

"What kind of place is this in which to bring up our children?" I asked.

"I know, my angel," Alexander said, holding me. "I, too, fear the revolution's fruits will be blasted by the violence of rash or unprincipled men motivated by vindictive and selfish passions. So we must set the example and be kind to our neighbors."

I remembered a time when I hadn't set an example. When I'd failed to do the right thing. When I'd not given water to an injured Redcoat soldier for fear of what others might think of me. So I resolved to make up for that now and do just what my husband suggested.

That Sunday I put on my bonnet and marched, with great purpose, to Saint Paul's Chapel. It was all that remained of the burned-down Episcopal Trinity Church, which had been a haven for Loyalists. I made a point to seat myself for prayers near to the shunned Tory families. And it was there that I first met sixteen-year-old Elizabeth Kortright, the daughter of a Loyalist merchant who'd lost much of his wealth during the war.

We exchanged a few pleasantries as I tried to ease the girl's obvious tension, and before long she burst forth, as if the words couldn't be held inside even before a stranger. "My father took no part in the war. He stayed because he loves New York. He shouldn't be scorned because he also loved his king. And how can I help him rebuild his fortune if no man will have me for a wife?"

"You're far too pretty to worry on that score," I said reassuringly, certain that her sweet face and dignified manner would make any man overlook the sins of her father. And I invited her to tea at my house the next time I entertained ladies.

It was all I could think to do.

Fortunately, my husband did much more.

Alarmed at the violence—he set out to use the mightiest power he had at his disposal.

His pen.

And though I didn't know it then, my husband was the best writer of the founding generation. Oh, there are those who will argue that honor goes to a certain *Virginian*, but he receives enough applause from the rabble without my praise, and I despise him too much to credit his talents.

It's enough to know that it was my husband who, in this dark hour, held out so eloquently against the mob in a letter to his fellow citizens under the pseudonym Phocion, urging them to heed the principles of law and justice.

But if Alexander hoped his pen name—cleverly chosen to refer to yet another soldier from antiquity with murky parentage and noble wisdom—would shield his identity, he was wrong.

On my daily strolls with my little boy, I felt the glares of passersby. The baker was no longer content to extend me any sort of credit for bread. The delivery of fresh fruit from my father's farm arrived smashed upon my front stoop, partially wrapped in a paper that featured an anonymous poem aimed, unquestionably, at my husband, for having become a supposed lackey for the royalists.

I burned this poem straightaway in the kitchen fire, but that didn't stop Alexander from learning of it. And it wounded him gravely. Many of our friends, most especially Colonel Burr, advised him to let tempers cool and not risk his reputation, or our livelihood, to defend the Tories.

But my dear Hamilton wouldn't listen.

# Chapter Sixteen

September 25, 1784
New York City

A GIRL," I SAID, gently handing over the little bundle.

And at the sight of his daughter, Alexander murmured, "My heart is at once melted into tenderness."

"Shall we name her after your mother?" I asked, peering up at him from our bed.

He furrowed his brow and rubbed his sleeve over his joyful eyes. "Should we not name her after *your* mother?"

There were already three baby Catherines in our family, for both my mother and Angelica had used the name for their youngest daughters, and Peggy had used it for her first, too.

*Angelica.* There was not a day that passed since my sister left for Europe that I didn't think of her or wish she was nearer to me. I pined for her, treasured every gift she sent, and had even papered the walls of our children's nursery with French sheeting, all covered in pink roses and ivy. I read Angelica's letters with a selfish avarice—keeping them in a box upon my dressing table, including the one in which she shared the news of the birth of a new baby daughter, Elizabeth. She'd named her for me.

That was it. If I couldn't have my sister with me, at least I would have her namesake. "What about the name Angelica?"

"*Angelica Hamilton,*" my husband said, an affectionate smile growing upon his face. "We'll call her Ana to distinguish. I cannot think of a more perfect honor for two whom we both hold so dear." So our daughter was named. A baby with rose-pink cheeks, wide eyes, and a commanding cry. I clutched little Ana to my breast, wishing to give her all the love I couldn't give her namesake across the sea.

After I nursed her, I shifted to rise from the bed.

"The doctor says you should rest," Alexander said, moving to assist me.

"So should you," I replied, longing for his presence at my side. "You didn't come to bed last night or the night before. I can't remember the last time you slept."

"I am kept at work," he said, for contrary to his jests about how the law was a study in how to fleece one's neighbor, he'd turned the law into an instrument of justice. In court, my husband, a lion of the revolution against the British, now held himself out as a champion of unfortunate Loyalists. And he was something to behold—relentless, persuasive, almost mesmerizing. Not just a lawyer or a politician, but a *statesman* determined to change minds and build a united country at any cost.

Having heard him many nights discuss one such case based upon the Trespass Act, I'd come to the courthouse to watch him from the gallery. Every manner of onlooker packed the chamber—ruffians in homespun next to the city's finest minds and best families. Alexander was representing another Tory, and the patriotic fervor in the courtroom against his client worried me more than a little.

Finally, my husband rose before the panel of five aldermen, and a hush settled over the restless courtroom—a hush Alexander strung out until the tension was nearly unbearable. And then he unleashed a soaring campaign of words and compelling arguments about why the United States' Peace Treaty reached with Great Britain rendered invalid any attempt to persecute or prosecute the Tories under the Trespass Act. Indeed, the audience leaned forward, as if under the sway of his oratory as Alexander strode about the chamber, articulating his points one by one, as if building a wall brick by brick. And as it rose, the mood in the crowd changed. Anger turned to questions, and suspicion turned to consideration.

In the end, Alexander created a whole *new policy* of judicial review for the country when he argued, "The legislature of one state cannot repeal the law of the United States."

Alexander's client list expanded after that trial.

And no matter how many neighbors cast dark looks my way on the street, or withheld bread, or smashed up my fruit, or wrote evil poems, I couldn't have been prouder of him.

"MISTRESS," JENNY SAID from the doorway of the children's room where I was attempting to bathe a squirming Philip. "There's a gentleman caller."

"I'm afraid Mr. Hamilton is at court," I said.

She bobbed her head. "I told the man as much, but he says he'll wait."

My son squealed and splashed in the copper tub of water and I wiped my brow with a forearm, sighing with weary exasperation and the hope that he wouldn't awaken his four-month-old sister in her cradle. "Can't the gentleman leave a calling card?"

"He said to tell you he can't afford calling cards, Mistress. But he also said to tell you this *exactly*: that he's brought you a gift of coffee—real coffee—to make up for the swill he once served you in an army tent."

All at once my glum weariness passed, and with a laugh, I cheerfully surrendered my little boy—bath, towel, and all—to Jenny. I didn't even take the time to straighten my hair before bounding down the stairs. "Why, James Monroe! Is that you in my parlor?"

The six-foot strapping southerner made a strange sight in civilian clothes. Still, how glad I was to see him when he smiled widely over that familiar dimpled chin. "Well, I *declare*, it's Betsy Schuyler—or Mrs. Hamilton, now, I've heard."

"It's true," I said, gleefully. "Nevertheless, I would abandon all pretense of married propriety and give your neck a fond embrace if only I could *reach*. Dear God, what is in that southern soil that makes Virginians grow so tall?"

"The seeds of liberty," Monroe said with a quickness he'd lacked as a younger man.

"And what brings you to New York?" I asked.

He stooped to give my hand a very gentlemanly kiss. "Virginia has sentenced me to serve here in Congress."

"You poor wretch," I said with a laugh, glad that Congress was now meeting in New York City. I led him into the kitchen where we set straightaway to brewing coffee to ward off the winter's chill. I shouldn't have invited a gentleman into the house with such familiarity, but in Monroe's case, I could scarcely think my husband would mind.

"The coffee was roasted already by the grocer," the Virginian said, shaking the bag and offering to pound the beans to a powder if I could provide him with a mortar and pestle. I didn't tell him how appalled my mother would be—for she insisted that a good housekeeper always roasted her own coffee beans—but instead showed him the little coffee grinder Angelica had sent me from France.

Monroe and I fell into easy conversation as he gallantly turned the silvered handle upon the mill, and at some point, in our reminiscing, he mentioned having written me a letter before he left Valley Forge. "The letter must have miscarried," I said, embarrassed that he thought I'd neglected to reply. But letters miscarried all the time during war, as he had good cause to know. "I never received it. Why didn't you write again?"

Monroe chuckled. "Fearing I'd made a fool of myself, I couldn't work up the nerve."

I smiled fondly, remembering how shy he'd been in those

days. But he seemed far bolder now. "How is it that you're still unmarried?"

Monroe gave a good-natured shrug. "Well, for one thing, I'm a poor unpaid soldier, having inherited from my father only a small Virginia farm with barren fields turned to dust by tobacco." Then he looked up at me with those soulful gray eyes, and added, "For another thing, the girl I loved married another man."

Ordinarily, I was not so vain to have dared imagine that he meant me. Especially since Burr told me Monroe had a sweetheart in Christina Wynkoop, daughter of a Pennsylvania congressman. But the way Monroe now stared at me, blushing to the tips of his ears, made me so uncomfortable that the two of us stood there, like mute blockheads.

Fortunately, we were rescued by a knock at the back door.

It was Theodosia Burr, bundled in a fur-lined cloak. "I thought I saw James Monroe at the end of the street." As it happened, Theodosia had hosted Monroe when he was in the service of Lord Stirling, so another happy reunion took place in my kitchen. And when Monroe asked her advice on finding a wife in the city, she said, "You're a congressman, now. An important man of the people. The ladies will flock to you given your accomplishments."

Monroe gave a belly laugh. "We never *accomplish* anything in Congress. We couldn't pass Mr. Jefferson's Land Ordinance for admitting new states to the Union, because it bans slavery after the year 1800. We couldn't pass Mr. Jefferson's proposal to make the dollar a national currency. We can't agree on a site for our nation's capital—or even if we *are* a nation, or a collection of states."

"Hamilton shares your frustration," I said, readying the hot water in its pot over the stove. "It's why he's not in Congress anymore."

Monroe raised a brow. "My friend must have changed very much since the war if he is now content with drudgery at the bar while the country slides into disorder."

"Oh, Colonel Hamilton is never content about anything,"

Theodosia replied with an indulgent smile. "He's never at home. Why, it grieves my poor heart to know how often poor Betsy is left alone."

Theodosia wasn't wrong. Even when Alexander was pacing our bedroom, practicing some argument at court, he was somewhere else. But it seemed a shrewish complaint about a man who was striving to provide for me and my children, and I didn't want Monroe to think badly of him, so I rushed to his defense. "Why, I'm not alone at all. Between fine visitors such as yourselves and my beautiful children, my days are filled. And, honestly, Hamilton wouldn't be the man I married without his sense of duty."

Besides, my husband's work defending Tories had made his law practice thrive. But I didn't want to explain that to Monroe, who had little cause to know about our financial circumstances or how severely persecuted our neighbors were.

"I've heard Hamilton has helped to found a bank," Monroe said.

I nodded. Amidst all his legal cases, Alexander had written the new bank's constitution and become actively involved in its organization. "The Bank of New York, just down the street. He hopes to address the derangement of our financial situation in the city."

"Which reminds me," Theodosia said, pulling a folded broadsheet from her handbag. "You might wish to show this to Hamilton."

Inwardly I groaned, not needing to read it to know what it would say, for the New York papers vilified my husband daily for helping the persecuted Tories. He'd built his reputation on heroism but now reaped the bitter seeds of a different sort of fame. And the unfairness of it pained me.

Having seen my father accused of treason, I was acutely sensitive to public censure. And because it set my husband's temper on edge and fired his combative nature to see his name blackened in the press, it had become my regular practice to burn the papers that came to the house charging him with helping *the most abandoned scoundrels in the universe*.

I was trying to decide where to hide Theodosia's paper until I could dispose of it when she eyed the brewing coffee and said, "That's going to take forever. We should go to a coffeehouse."

Monroe, who had probably spent all he had to acquire the coffee beans, looked crestfallen. So I ventured forth with, "It's so cold that I prefer to make coffee at home. And while we're waiting, let me treat the both of you to some of my homemade waffles," I said, pulling out the Dutch waffle irons just like Mama's that she'd given me as a present. "Reuniting with old friends is worthy of celebration."

"Waffles?" Beaming, Monroe grinned. "You remembered."

"I can't promise they'll be the same as your Mammy's," I said, laughing again at the memory of how he'd blurted out his craving to me all those years ago. "But I'll slather them in butter."

Theodosia rolled her eyes but settled in at the table and assisted me as I prepared the old family recipe and heated the irons. "At least come out with us tonight. Both of you."

"Oh, I couldn't. Not without Hamilton."

"Of course you can," Theodosia said. "Your Jenny can watch over the babies and Monroe can be your escort."

At that, Monroe stared at his feet. "I—I cannot imagine that would be thought, well, at all proper."

Theodosia laughed, and the next words she spoke reminded me so much of Angelica. "Perhaps not in your country of Virginia. But you're in New York, now. A veritable vortex of folly and dissipation if the gazettes are to be believed."

I ladled the thick, golden batter into a hot iron. "Oh, be nice, Theodosia. Monroe is a very mannerly gentleman." I recounted how, upon my offering to help tend his wounded shoulder, he'd nearly tripped over my mother's sideboard table in fear my father would shoot him.

Theodosia howled with laughter while Monroe chuckled at the memory, and the impasse about our plans for the evening was solved when my husband stumbled into the house stamping snow off his boots, nearly crashing headlong into his old friend.

I could scarcely contain my amusement when Alexander murmured, with utter bewilderment, "*Monroe*?"

The two men clasped hands, appraising one another from head to toe before clapping one another on the back with glad tidings. And within hours, Alexander had sent word of the reunion and called together an impromptu gathering in our dining room of Washington's young upstarts, a heaping plate of waffles between them. Colonel Burr appeared at dusk with whiskey, and these one-time brothers-at-arms talked late into the winter's night, telling old stories and debating how, in Monroe's words, we could *cement the union*.

I can never express how much good it did my heart to see these old friends and survivors of the war all together, laughing by a fire. Nor can I find words to say how much it hurts my heart now, knowing their friendships would come to a bitter, bloody end . . .

*June 1785*
*New York City*

"British ship in the harbor!" Jenny cried, rapping excitedly on the bedroom door. And though such an utterance would have caused panic only a few years before, it was now, for me, a bringer of joy. One for which I'd been waiting for *days*. "It's a big one, mistress."

I was already dressed, my hair pinned. But I hadn't fastened my earbobs or chosen a bonnet to match my dress, and in my excitement I didn't bother with either. Instead, I flew down the stairs. "My sister's here!"

Alexander, on a rare day home from court, was holding Philip in the air and making our darling boy laugh. "You can't know if it's Angelica's ship—"

"Sisters *know*," I insisted, rushing for the door.

"I'll arrange for a coach," Alexander called after me, but I didn't wait. I didn't wait for anything. Not even a parasol to guard against the summer sun. Instead, I took to the tree-lined sidewalk and ran the five blocks to the water and Burnett's Key. As the brick streets gave way to planks and mud, I dodged horse droppings, wagons, barrels, and giant coils of rope, the unmistakable scent of the river filling my every breath.

I was sweating by the time I saw the ship moored to the dock, but I didn't care because the three tall masts and rigging of that ship were as welcome a sight as any I'd ever seen.

"Angelica!" I cried, bouncing on my feet and waving when she appeared out of the disembarking throngs wearing a fashionable French straw hat with a striped ribbon and pink flowers in her hair.

"Betsy!" We fell into each other's arms while servants scurried to collect her trunks and baggage and children. And we gazed upon each other with joy. She'd been gone nearly two years, and now I couldn't get enough of her.

Alexander finally caught up with me and had nothing but warm smiles and affection for both Angelica and her husband, whose elusive disposition brightened considerably as Alex filled him in on all the latest goings-on about the city.

That night, at a raucous impromptu supper of cold ham with thick slices of bread and butter, we all crowded around my little table, laughing and drinking wine and singing together. And when I put my baby daughter, Angelica's namesake, into my sister's arms, I fell in love with both of them all over again.

In a fit of exuberance I said, "Hamilton says there's a house for sale on Broadway. Mr. Carter, perhaps you could take it so we can all live closer together."

I blamed the wine and my overflowing heart for such an indiscreet suggestion. It wasn't proper for a woman to suggest to a man what he should buy or where he should settle his family. But we Schuyler sisters had always nudged up against the line of what was proper and been adored by our husbands for it, so I was startled at the reaction.

My brother-in-law scowled at me, and Angelica's musical laugh cut off abruptly, giving way to a gloomy expression before she stared down at my new china.

"A house on Broadway is a good investment," Alexander broke in, supporting my suggestion, as if he hadn't noticed the change in mood, or perhaps because he did. "My affection for you both made me look forward to having you as neighbors."

"We're only here for a visit," Mr. Carter explained. "We've taken a town house on Sackville Street in London where I intend to pursue a career in Parliament."

"London?" I choked out, shocked to my foundation. My sister's husband had made an outrageous profit in the war by equipping the Americans and the French, which could not have endeared him to his king. And even if that were not the case, there was the murky matter of what had caused him to flee England in the first place. "How . . . how can you expect to be welcomed there, Mr. Carter?" I asked, fighting against despair at the thought of losing Angelica again, and after I'd assumed her return to be permanent.

"Because Carter is only his nom de guerre," my sister said, finally finding her voice. "Allow me to introduce my husband, Mr. John Barker Church . . ."

My mouth fell agape as Angelica explained in an unusually flat voice that her husband was actually from a prominent family, and though he'd fled England under pecuniary, romantic, and legal embarrassments, he'd returned to Europe to learn that a man he thought he had killed in a duel was still quite alive. And he was now emboldened to return to the family fold.

Ticking off the obstacles on her long fingers, Angelica said, "Jack is now respectably married, more than able to pay his creditors, and there are whispers that he'd be welcome in the Whig party." Her words hung thick over the table, like a net dropped from a sprung trap in which we were all awkwardly caught.

Clearing his throat, Alexander tried to lighten the mood, raising a toast in honor of being able to live freely in this new world we'd created, and go by one's own name. I suspected, because of his dealings as my brother-in-law's agent, that he already knew his true identity. And though I held my tongue through the rest of the meal, I couldn't quite recover.

"Did you know?" I asked that night, undressing before bed.

Alexander's shoulders fell, answering me even before he took my hands into his. "Yes. I'm sorry I kept it from you. It was a condition of my employment as his agent."

Even as unhappy as I was, I could hardly hold duty against him. "But he's a gambler," I said, allowing myself to be drawn against my husband's chest. "Jack Carter—Church, I mean, gambled himself into debt, he gambled on the war, and now he's gambling my sister's future in returning to England."

I was being unkind, I knew. And unfeminine in expressing such an opinion upon a matter about which I knew too little. I thought my husband might scold me on both counts, but instead, he led me to bed, climbed under the covers with a book related to work he'd neglected during the day, and said only, "I know you're worried, but let's try to enjoy the time we have with your sister while she's here."

So began a frenzied, near-frantic social whirl designed to squeeze every moment of pleasure out of Angelica's very brief visit. We went with our children on long walks about the city. Attended balls and dinner parties and the theater. And we shopped. Or at least, we tried.

Peering into the shop windows disapprovingly, Angelica frowned. "Oh, my poor country. I'm afraid there's virtually nothing that can be had here in the way of dresses, shoes, or women's fripperies that can't be found better, or cheaper, in Europe."

"That's because we currently rely upon foreign nations to manufacture our resources," Alexander said, denouncing the circumstance at mind-numbing length before concluding, "We send timber, flax, hemp, cotton, wool, indigo, iron, lead, furs, hides, skin, and coal—our warehouses in the harbor are overflowing—but we will always be dependent until we can produce our own goods."

I gave him the indulgent smile I'd learned was the best response to his brilliance, if I ever hoped for his lecture to end. But Angelica seemed to actually *enjoy* these dissertations, and later gifted my husband with several books of economics as reward.

Angelica felt no compunction against going to Fraunces's on Pearl Street, where Congress had rented space to debate whether or not they had sufficient power to form commercial treaties that would bind every state. And when I wondered if her husband minded or if this wouldn't be looked at askance, she said, "The women in France do anything they like! Why, they are more avid on the subject of politics than their husbands."

Knowing Angelica was to go on to Albany to see our family and then to Philadelphia before taking her leave of America, I didn't want to share her with my friends and acquaintances. But they all clamored for her. Theodosia insisted we bring her to dinner, and it was no surprise that the equally outspoken and audacious Angelica and Theodosia got on like old friends. Likewise, Kitty Livingston's sister, Sarah, married to Mr. John Jay, pleaded with us to come to tea, where all the ladies gossiped about the prominent bachelors in town. Naturally, some of the talk was about Monroe.

"Those gray eyes—"

"That dimpled chin!"

"That *brawn*. But Monroe is no great intellect; he'd be quite a nobody without the patronage of Mr. Jefferson . . ."

"That's not true," I insisted, rising to his defense. Then I reminded them of Monroe's war heroism and service to the country until I was weary.

And I *was* weary, because I couldn't keep up with Angelica. My sister was an *indefatigable* socialite. She accepted every invitation, holding court at every party.

So the night my ten-month-old daughter was spitting up and

Angelica pouted because her husband's being out of town on business meant she ought not go without me, I said, "Alexander will take you."

And so they went, Alexander stumbling back into the house in the wee hours, complaining that my sister out-drank him, and retching over a chamber pot as he vowed that he would never imbibe champagne again.

I thought nothing of it until the next day when, while shopping with Angelica for sundries in the marketplace, we came upon James Monroe in the shade of the awning of Mr. Mulligan's tailoring shop, in less than congenial conversation with my husband.

I didn't wish to interrupt, but my sister twirled her parasol and fearlessly cried, "Hamilton! I need to arrange for a sloop up river and you're just the man to help." Angelica laced her arm into the crook of Alexander's elbow, as was her habit, but, to my surprise, my husband let his arm fall away in a most ungentlemanly fashion.

Some manner of dark look passed between him and Monroe that I couldn't comprehend. "Is my husband meddling in politics again, Congressman?" I asked with a smile to Monroe.

Monroe's jaw tightened, as if I'd asked him a very difficult question. But before he was able to offer an answer, he was nearly accosted by surly citizens who wished to complain about the latest debate in Congress.

As I departed the scene with Alexander and Angelica, she glanced over her shoulder with disgust. "What bumpkins. I don't see what you find so agreeable in Monroe. He's far too comfortable with the tobacco-chewing rabble in their knit caps crowing about liberty, while insisting anything beautiful or enjoyable must be banned lest it destroy our revolution and deliver us into the clutches of monarchy."

She wasn't entirely wrong about the rabble. But I believed her to be entirely wrong about Monroe. "He's a man of relatively modest means, but he's no *leveler*," I said.

Monroe proved it when, later that week, he joined us all at the long-awaited reopening of the John Street theater. But while our merry band of companions looked for seats in the gallery—Baron von Steuben insisting on a seat for his dog—I sensed Monroe's discomfort around our friends. "You've been so quiet, Monroe. Unusually so, even for you. What weighs upon your mind?"

At that, his gray eyes lifted and met mine. "I'm leaving New York for a time."

I was sorry to hear it. Discounting that one strange moment outside Mr. Mulligan's tailoring shop, Monroe's presence and friendship had buoyed my husband's mood and made us all very happy. And I did not wish to part with him. "For how long a time will you be gone?"

"Three or four months, I would reckon. Long enough to see all there is to see out west."

"Out west!" I exclaimed, my disappointment replaced with excitement for him. We'd shared a longing to see more of the world, and as he explained his intention to attend an Indian Treaty in Ohio, then to explore the settlements in Kentucky, I could not help but long to see them, too.

"But before I go," Monroe added, "there *are* a few things that weigh on my mind." Thereupon he stared at my sister, where she stood between her husband and mine, laughing with the grace of an angel. And I sighed with pity, counting him as one of the many men who fell so helplessly under my sister's spell.

"You need a distraction." I laced my arm through Monroe's, patting his hand with great familiarity—and he groaned as if I'd tortured him.

"Betsy." Some emotion seemed to catch in his throat and afflict his tongue. "I would never wish for you to suffer . . ." He stammered as if unable to spit it out, until he blurted, "There are still those amongst us who give a care for propriety."

I was beginning to form some vague notion that Angelica and my husband must have violated some rule of southern gentility.

The always stiff Monroe never did understand our New York ways. Much less did he understand my gregarious family and our close-knit relations. I was grateful that my orphaned husband fit in so easily. Monroe—the man who nearly toppled Mama's sideboard because I offered to nurse his wound—never would have, I thought. And realizing how badly the man needed to be set topsy-turvy, I began to laugh. "James Monroe, you need a *wife*, and I know just the introduction to make."

I'd spotted the Kortright sisters, with beautiful Elizabeth in their midst, as they made so brilliant and lovely an appearance as to depopulate all the other boxes of the genteel men therein. By the end of the evening, Monroe seemed at least a little intrigued by the young beauty I'd befriended at Trinity Church. And in making an introduction between them, I counted it a night's good work done.

I believed, perhaps foolishly, that whatever misunderstanding about my husband had worked itself into his friend's mind was wiped out in that powerful flush of infatuation with the girl who was to later become his bride.

But I hadn't understood how stubbornly James Monroe could hold on to a thing—even a thing into which he had no business prying.

No matter who it hurt.

No matter whose life it destroyed.

# Chapter Seventeen

*December 1786*
*New York City*

A BARREL OF HAM?" I asked with a long-suffering sigh, as my husband rolled his wages into the kitchen where I stirred a thin vegetable soup. With three children now— the youngest, seven-month-old Alex, upon my hip, it was becoming harder to make do, a situation resulting from the fact that my husband preferred to take on charity cases or those that established legal precedents instead of more lucrative but pedestrian disputes over trade.

"A barrel of ham is worth more than continentals," Hamilton said in defense of himself. "Besides, we can't eat a continental for dinner."

*That is true enough*, I thought as he took the baby and held him aloft. "You make a persuasive argument, Colonel Hamilton. Tomorrow, I shall cook up some ham and potatoes for us with the butter Papa sent from the Pastures, and we'll invite the Burrs for a feast before church service."

At this, he frowned. "Does your father send food to all his daughters?"

I'd seen before how prideful he could be, and how much he chafed against anything that resembled dependence. So I said,

"Well, Papa can't very well send it to Angelica over the ocean or it would spoil, but he's sent food to all his daughters before. Besides, without good butter I can't replicate Mama's cookies for the children this holiday." Alexander didn't seem appeased by this explanation, so I tried to subtly remind him that we were bickering about butter because he insisted on representing impoverished persons. "Which client paid in pork?"

"The spinster lady I mentioned."

"The one caught stealing lace doilies, painted fans, and underclothes? Did she have some innocent defense?"

"No," he replied with a hint of chagrin. "But I remember all too well what women must resort to when they're destitute and desperate."

At this declaration—at once so rare and revealing of the power his dead mother still held over him—I stopped stirring the soup and glanced over my shoulder. But the floridness of his complexion and his reluctance to meet my eyes warned me not to say any more about it. And I remembered that however spare our circumstances might have seemed to the daughter of Philip Schuyler, we lived comfortably. Far more comfortably than my husband had as an orphaned boy all alone in this world.

Our children were loved and cherished. They were fed and clothed and had a roof over their heads, thanks to Hamilton's talents. I couldn't call myself a Christian and resent him for using those talents to ease the suffering of others. Even the family in the West Indies of which he so seldom spoke. He'd made a loan to his estranged brother who was too disinterested in us to write except when desperate for money—money I was sure we'd never see again. Alexander even pleaded in vain for word from the father who abandoned him, so that he might render the old man assistance. That my husband also helped much more worthy persons, in my view, like impoverished spinsters, persecuted Tories, and downtrodden Negroes was a testament to his good heart—and I both loved and admired him for it.

In fact, I wished to be more like him.

A FEW MONTHS later, one of my husband's troubled veteran friends came to our house in the middle of the night, drunk and unable to care for his motherless baby, a two-year-old named Fanny. "I'm sorry," my husband said, when the knocking awakened me. But I wouldn't let him apologize for the tender spot in his heart reserved for the soldiers he'd fought with.

Especially not since we'd so recently learned of Tench Tilghman's death; Tench had never recovered from the cold he'd taken at the winter encampment of the army in New Windsor. It had festered into a lung ailment that killed him, leaving behind two daughters in Maryland, one of whom was orphaned before she was born. Alexander and I had wept together at the news. For if my husband would always have a tender heart for the soldiers he fought with, I did, too.

So now by candlelight and in sleeping cap, I went down with Alexander to help his army friend and the child. I took the wailing, red-faced girl to my shoulder, trying to console her. And some time later, after Alexander had seen his drunken friend to a sofa, I asked, "Will it be debtors' prison for him?"

Alexander's expression was bleak. "Worse. He's taken leave of his senses. He broke down in my arms, sobbing like a child himself. He has nightmares of the war . . ."

I peered at little Fanny where she'd fallen asleep in my arms, dark lashes spread upon porcelain cheeks. And because I still had nightmares of the war, too, I couldn't stand for her *not* to be cared for as she should. "Alexander, what if . . . we took her in?" We were too far away to render assistance to Tench Tilghman's baby daughters, but perhaps we could help this one. "We could keep her. Just until her father can put his affairs in order."

"Oh, *Betsy*." My husband pressed a kiss to my temple and whispered, "You are the best of wives, the best of women, and the best part of me. But I can't ask you to take on such a burden."

"I want to." As I stared at this man who'd once been an abandoned child, I became even more certain of my decision to take Fanny into our household. "All children need love, and we are blessed to have more than enough to spare."

~

*July 3, 1787*
*New York City*

"This is a vile *slander*," Alexander said, crumpling a newspaper in a fury.

We'd joined the Burrs on a visit to the new African Free School that my husband and his fellow members of the Manumission Society had brought into being to educate black children. And on the walk back, Alexander had purchased a gazette from a passing newsboy and become incensed by what he read.

"But no one of sense *believes* the rumor, my friend," Burr said in an attempt to pacify him.

In the hopes that our countrymen had *finally* suffered enough that they were ready to see the wisdom in forming a true government, my husband had gone to Philadelphia with James Madison in May to serve as delegate for a federal convention to revise the Articles of Confederation. What Alexander and Jemmy wanted, I knew, was more than to *revise* them. They wanted to draw up a new constitution altogether that would provide for a stronger central government. But after only two months, my husband had returned, more frustrated than before, complaining it was a waste of time and that he and Jemmy were thwarted at every turn.

And now this newspaper article accusing him of conspiring to summon the Duke of York from England to start a new American monarchy.

It was ridiculous. Burr was right that no one of any sense believed Alexander was trying to bring an English king over us again. But I already knew how much damage people with *no sense* could cause. And so did my husband.

"Ladies," Hamilton said abruptly to Theodosia and me. "Please excuse me. Burr, will you see my wife safely home?"

"Where the devil are you going?" Burr asked before I could.

"To find out who started this rumor," Hamilton grumbled, waving the crumpled newspaper as he strode away on the cobblestone street.

"*Hamilton,*" Burr called after my hot-tempered husband to no avail.

"Will you go with him?" I asked, exasperated, but hoping that Burr's measured approach to life would keep Alexander from trouble.

When Burr hesitated, Theodosia reassured him, "Oh, go, for goodness' sake. Betsy and I can find our way without a guardian."

Burr chuckled, kissed his wife's cheek, then rushed after my husband.

Watching them go, Theodosia sighed. "With rumors like that in the papers . . . sometimes I fear people are looking to start a civil war."

"I fear it, too," I replied. With Shay's rebellion, there already *was* a civil war in Massachusetts. It was spreading to other states. And it could happen here, too, especially with Congress in session in the city.

"Don't worry," Theodosia said. "Burr will look out for your husband. He has a very good nose for the prevailing winds." It's painful now to recall how reassured those words had made me feel, but they truly did, especially when she looped her arm through mine and said, "And in the meantime, we'll look out for each other."

That night, having slammed back into the house and awakened our sleeping children, Alexander was only mildly apologetic.

"And did you hunt down the source of this rumor?" I asked after putting the baby back to sleep.

Alexander surprised me by saying, "I did. And it was a no-body. Just another indebted drunkard—a ne'er-do-well named James Reynolds."

There was nothing to be gained in quarreling with a man like that. Instead, Hamilton spent the days that followed directing his anger at our antifederalist governor Clinton, accusing him in a series of essays of poisoning the people's minds against reform, and against the convention in Philadelphia to which my husband would again return.

"Are you sure that you should publish this?" I asked, reading over his shoulder. "You're drawing battle lines. Governor Clinton is a powerful man and you—"

*You're a revolutionary,* I thought, watching my husband scribble some note as if he hadn't heard me at all. He'd already gone against a king and won. He'd quarreled with George Washington and prevailed. He wouldn't be stopped by a governor.

He wouldn't stop until he'd changed the world. And I wanted to help him do it.

~

*October 1787*
*En Route to New York City*

We went to battle in the bowels of a ship.

Returning from a visit to my parents, we'd taken a cabin on a sloop bound for New York—and this narrow berth, with its single table secured to the wooden planks of the deck and one porthole, would be our war room for the week-long trip. There was just enough space for the children and their bedrolls, the gentle rocking of the single-masted boat lulling them fast to sleep.

During the day Alexander worked, and I took the little ones above deck to enjoy the passing scenery of towns on the shoreline, green pastures, and blazing red autumn foliage. As I watched the children play and laugh and even bicker, my heart was torn between joy at their innocent hopefulness and sorrow at having learned the terrible and unexpected news that Peggy's little son, Stephen, had died in his sleep. Her husband had written that she was too indisposed to travel or receive visitors, so I hadn't had the chance to see her during our visit, and I ached to offer her what comfort I could.

But by night, beneath the light of two lanterns swinging from the joists above us, I joined Alexander amidst his letters, treatises, newspapers, paper, ink, and quills. "My arms and ammunition," he quipped.

"And who are we to fight?"

"Almost everyone," he said, ruefully. "The foes of the new Constitution are many."

A few weeks earlier, my husband had returned from Philadelphia, where he affixed his signature to a blueprint for an entirely new government. He hated the plan—which he thought a hodgepodge of ideas and bitter compromises, particularly between the northern and southern states on the issue of slavery. But he'd said that "without these compromises, no union could possibly have been formed, though Washington does not think this Constitution will last twenty years."

*Twenty years.* Long enough for my sons to grow into men and get their educations. Long enough for my daughter to fall in love, marry, and have children of her own. Long enough for the new baby growing in my belly to get a good start in life. It had been only ten years since my sister climbed out a window to elope with John Church and *that* felt like a lifetime ago.

*Twenty years of peace and stability would be enough,* I thought. We could fix the rest. We could keep working to end the injustice of slavery and make the new nation live up to the ideals of the revolution. But first we needed a nation.

And nine states would have to ratify the Constitution before it would become law.

Alexander had a plan to make that happen. A *secret* plan.

"We must defend the Constitution," he said, shuffling papers. "We must *overwhelm* the opposition with evidence and arguments. The Constitution is as flawed as some of my clients, but like them, it deserves a fair trial. At least in the court of public opinion."

Resting a stack of books in my lap, I helped him clear a space upon which to write. "And how are you going to make that happen?"

"With a series of essays," he said, the scratching of his pen competing with the creaking of the boat and the sloshing of the river against the hull. "Anonymous essays. Maybe thirty in all."

"Thirty?" I wondered how he'd manage such a thing, given the other demands on his time. "So many?"

"There will be other writers, of course. Though our identities must remain secret."

Not a secret from me, I hoped. "Who will help you?"

"I don't know yet," he replied. "I intend to recruit John Jay, Gouverneur Morris, and William Duer." Jay was an experienced statesman and judge. Morris, a peg-legged bon vivant—the penman of the Constitution. And Duer, a wealthy New York legislator.

"Not Burr?" I asked.

Alexander frowned. "Not Burr. He's not a man to commit himself to paper, even secretly." I sensed, even then, there was more to it, but my husband was too caught up in his idea for me to interrupt. "The trick will be to coordinate the essays without anyone catching wind of it. How to make our writing similar enough that no outsider can deduce who wrote what, and no single man can be vilified or lionized for it."

"Ambitious," I said. But I didn't realize how ambitious until we were at home, on solid ground, and I was awakened before dawn by the faint sound of knocking downstairs. Very familiar knocking.

*Three quick raps followed by two slow ones.*

I sat up in bed to find my husband dressing in the dark. "Is that . . . ?"

"Jemmy Madison," my husband said, grinning. "He's hurried back from Philadelphia to join the project."

I was confused because I thought the project was to be *by* New Yorkers *for* New Yorkers. "But he's a Virginian."

"Exactly. And we need Virginia to ratify, too," Hamilton replied, having adjusted the scope of the work by an order of magnitude. But I understood that if he was to build a whole country, he was going to have to persuade a whole country.

By the time I'd dressed and seen the children down to the kitchen for a bleary-eyed breakfast of porridge under Jenny's watchful eye, I found the two men in the dining room, a stack of books and papers between them. It was a scene I'd witnessed a hundred times. "Does my husband have you skulking about in subterfuge at strange hours of the day and night again, Mr. Madison?"

The pale little man smiled. "I owe no small apology for waking you and your servant, Mrs. Hamilton. But I received a message last night—"

"We think we can deliver four essays a week now, instead of two," Hamilton interrupted, slapping his hand on the table to punctuate that happy fact before looking squarely at me. "With your help . . ."

They explained that they desired me to act as a sort of courier to collect the essays from the other men's wives, then deliver them to confidential intermediaries who would pass them to the publisher in secrecy. What thrill I felt to play a part in such a vast conspiracy!

But in the end, it was not so vast. Morris begged off. Duer's first essay was so disappointing my husband didn't wish for him to write more. And Jay fell terribly ill in early November after I fetched his fifth essay at a tea party with his wife, Sarah.

That left just two men to write *The Federalist*.

Alexander Hamilton and James Madison.

And most of it would be accomplished at my dining room table.

Every morning Madison would walk from his boardinghouse on Maiden Lane to take an early breakfast, bouncing my children on his knee as he compared notes with Hamilton over strong coffee to sketch out the new work for the day. Together, they wrote words that became weapons in the fight to create a real union, fired off at a dizzying and stupefying pace to meet their weekly publication deadlines. My husband hunched over a desk scribbling until his shoulders knotted and his lower back throbbed with pain. And many mornings Madison's small hands literally shook with exhaustion as he tried to revive himself with my coffee after another sleepless night. I'd never before seen men exert themselves to the point of collapse by writing alone. But in those months I witnessed just that. And in every spare moment I could find between housework, prayer, and looking after four unruly children, I read each word they wrote.

*If mankind were to agree to no institution of government until every part of it was perfect, society would become a scene of anarchy and the world a desert,* my husband wrote.

Echoed by Mr. Madison's simpler, *If men were angels, no government would be necessary.*

On and on, working late hours between courtroom trials and congressional committee meetings, and nearly killing themselves doing it, they wrote the most enduring explanation of government ever put to paper before or since.

As winter melted to spring, I witnessed their ideas grow like the child in my womb, day by day, and it made me bolder, as if I, too, were on the verge of *becoming.*

Which was why, one morning, looking over Hamilton's cramped shoulder, I ventured to say, "Does that—does that not seem . . ."

My husband turned to eye me, his brow raised. "Yes?"

Fearing I was about to make quite a fool of myself, I bit my lip.

"Well, it's only that what you've written sounds quite identifiably like *you*."

Hamilton's brow rose higher. "How?"

It was dramatic. A little dark. And altogether too complicated.

But what I said was, "Well, in the first place, you've used a great many more words to express that thought than Mr. Madison would."

For a moment, his mouth dropped open, as if he took great insult. As if he were about to say something—perhaps something extremely cross. But his mouth snapped shut again. And all at once, he crumpled what he'd been writing into a ball and threw it to the floor.

Crestfallen, I tried to retrieve it. "Oh, no! Alexander, I didn't mean for—"

"Let it not be said I cannot see through a veil of vanity," he said, grumbling as he started fresh.

Thereafter, I noticed their writing styles became much more similar, an achievement made easier by the fact that they were both so much in agreement about what remained to be written that it was no longer necessary to plan each morning. Anyway, there was no time to. As twenty-nine essays expanded into eighty-five, they burned through foolscap, parchments, quills, and slate pencils. Often one of them was still writing while the other's essay was being fit for type at the printer. There were days Hamilton didn't even have the chance to read over his own work before sending it off to press.

And I myself scarcely had time for childbirth. Two days after celebrating the delivery of a little boy we named James—after my husband's father and the man at whose side Alexander was now doing battle—my happiness was profoundly disturbed by my six-year-old coming inside from a game of hopscotch with tears of rage streaking his cheeks.

"They're calling me a quadroon," Philip cried.

I knew precisely why. Once, it was the question of whether one was Patriot or Tory that divided families, ruined friendships, and made nearly every outing confrontational. Now it was the question of whether one was a federalist or an antifederalist—for or against a strong central government.

Despite our best efforts, the authors of the *Federalist* essays had become an open secret. And even if the public didn't know *which* essays my husband wrote, they knew he was writing them. Which was why Governor Clinton sent his minions to retaliate in the papers, accusing Alexander of being a superficial, conceited, upstart coxcomb. They'd also called him Tom Shit—a reference to his illegitimate birth that implied he was a Creole bastard with Negro blood.

And now, as I tried to comfort my crying firstborn son—a child of such sunny temperament that he almost never cried—it became deeply personal. Hamilton had warned me. He'd warned me when he proposed marriage that our children might one day suffer for the ignoble circumstances of his birth. Just as I'd warned him not to pick a fight with the governor.

But now it was *war,* and I wanted nothing but the governor's complete surrender.

To that end, I decided to take the latest essay to the print shop myself instead of waiting for the printer to come to the house to pick it up. I'd never been one to lay abed for long after childbirth, and I was convinced that activity was the only way to relieve cramps. Now, I wanted my little boy to walk the streets of this city with his head held high. And I needed to show him how to do it.

So after nursing my newborn, I left him in Jenny's capable hands and took Philip for a short but painful stroll to the printer, then up Broadway past the hospital to the nearby apothecary shop. "Mrs. Hamilton," the apothecary said in a scolding tone, his bushy brows knitted behind the counter. "You're so soon out of childbed. I'd have come to you if you'd sent a servant or Colonel Hamilton to fetch me."

"I just needed some fresh air, raspberry leaves for my cramps, and a little lavender oil for my aching head."

While I kept my curious boy from reaching for one of the many fascinating corked glass jars on the counter, the apothecary rummaged through the drawers and we chatted about the various states that had ratified the Constitution—six by my count, five by his.

"You forgot Massachusetts," I said, just as the roar of angry voices reached our ears.

We both looked up toward the street to see a horde of angry men marching from the direction of the battery. A *mob*. I'd once seen a group of men like this armed with feathers and tar. This time, they had sticks and, as I was about to learn, a far more righteous rage. "Grave-robbing bastards!" someone shouted, just before a brick sailed through the glass window, sending a spray of shards at my feet. Instinctively, I grabbed my son and pulled him behind the counter. But from where I crouched, I saw the swarm move right past us on the street.

I could guess their destination.

The hospital. For the Constitution was not the only divisive thing in the newspapers that year. It had been reported that medical students, in need of cadavers to dissect, dug up bodies in the Negro Burial Ground outside the city. No one of prominence had seemed to care until the corpse of a white woman from Trinity Churchyard was also dug up and stolen.

Now the public was in an uproar.

I knew the importance of cadavers to the field of medical science, but I couldn't help but shudder at the gross indignity of having anyone I loved violated and dissected in such a way.

As we heard the crash of more windows farther down the street, the apothecary rose to wrap a sheltering arm around my shoulder. "I'll get you and the boy home," he said, rushing us out the back. Across the way, furious citizens broke the hospital door to splinters and overran the hospital, sending young medical students running in every direction. Over my shoulder, I saw a young doctor climbing from a window. And my son stared as shouting men hauled cauldrons of dismembered body parts out of the hospital, the stench of it recalling the war immediately to my mind.

We saw a bloody foot, a swollen human head in a bottle, and some poor fellow's pickled genitals hanging from a string before we fled up Broadway, only to come against *hundreds* more furious men blocking our way. The jostling crowd swept us up like a tidal wave, separating us from the apothecary and nearly tearing Philip's hand from mine. Breathless and frightened, having quite forgotten about aches and pains, I realized the mob was descending upon the original nearby buildings of the old King's College—which had been recently renamed the more republican Columbia College.

"Bring out the butchers!" someone in the mob cried, and I knew they were looking for medical students to punish.

"Keep walking," I whispered to Philip. But my son made of himself a dead weight, pointing with one hand at something I couldn't see. And then the crowd parted to reveal my husband on the college stairs, pleading with the mob to see reason.

Hamilton was a great orator, and his military voice could just be heard over the fray. "The mayor has already jailed the culprits. Allow the law—"

The mob pushed past him, breaking open the doors to the chapel, the library, and the dorms of the college he'd recently helped reopen.

Then he caught sight of us and dodged the rioters until we were all together, and he tugged us into his arms. "Dear God, Betsy, what the devil are you doing here?"

The chaos gave me no time to answer. Save to issue commands as he guided us through streets strewn with debris and damage— *stop, wait here, run!*—Alexander said no more until we'd made it into the safety of the Burrs' entry hall. Was that how my husband had led men across the battlefield at Yorktown—fearless and relentless and cunning?

Escorted by Colonel Burr, we finally made it the rest of the way home. Having no concern for our audience, Alexander took me into his arms so tightly that I could barely breathe. "When I saw the two of you, there, amongst the rioters . . ."

"God willing, it's over now," I said, returning his embrace. But by morning, the mob had swollen to five thousand—a veritable army. Double the number of men Washington had with him at the Battle of Trenton. Not that it kept Alexander nor John Jay—who'd just recovered enough to start writing *Federalist* essays again—from trying to reason with the mob. Jay got his skull cracked with a brick for his trouble. Likewise, the Baron von Steuben had been trying to persuade the militia not to fire at the rioters when he was struck by a stone and promptly changed his mind. "Fire! Fire!"

I learned all of this when the baron returned to our house bleeding through a bandage hastily fastened upon him. "*Mein Gott*. Twenty dead!" the baron roared, almost as angry about that as he seemed to be about the ruined lace of his shirt. My newborn was just as angry in his cradle, crying for the milk only I could give him while the baron's greyhound licked my baby's face. "How many more wounded no one can guess. This chaos. This *anarchy*."

This was why the Constitution *had* to be ratified.

An entire generation was growing up in a world without sure principles by which to live in peace. And I couldn't help but wonder, would my own son, after what he'd seen in the streets, come of age believing that there was no way to solve any problem but with a club or a pistol?

# Chapter Eighteen

*Summer 1788*
*Albany*

NEW HAMPSHIRE MAKES nine states!" Peggy cried, clapping her hands with glee. With Alexander in the New York Assembly arguing for the adoption of the Constitution, I'd taken the children home to the Pastures to await news. And now Peggy prodded me. "Why aren't you smiling? You said the Constitution only needed nine states to ratify it."

"Officially," I said, swallowing hard against hope, knowing how happy this news would make Alexander, and how devastated he would be if all our efforts came to naught. "But it means nothing without Virginia and New York. If the largest and wealthiest states don't join this union, there won't be one."

Our only hope was Jemmy Madison. If—half dead of exhaustion and a bilious fever—Madison could convince his state to ratify, New York would be forced to follow suit or lose influence. Which was why Hamilton's strategy in the assembly was to delay, delay, delay and hope we were saved by Virginia.

"In the meantime," Peggy said, "let's go shopping."

Which was how, a few days later, we found ourselves coming home from the dressmaker on Market Street when riders came galloping through in a cloud of dust shouting, "Virginia has ratified! Virginia has ratified!"

Peggy and I ran almost the whole way home where my brothers Johnny and Jeremiah—grown men now—popped the corks on bottles of Papa's best sparkling wine in the main hall under the chandelier. I worried it was ill luck to celebrate prematurely, but inside, some part of me began to believe. Peggy grabbed a glass and raised it. "To Virginia!"

"To Virginia," I agreed, laughing, never realizing it would be the last time I ever had reason to celebrate that accursed state.

In anticipation of our own state's ratification, the celebrations continued in New York City. Bricklayers and wig makers rallied on Broadway with colorful ribbons, banners, and flags. Bakers marched a giant *federal* loaf of bread down the street. Brewers rolled a massive cask of ale. Sailmakers carried a twenty-foot flag depicting my husband with a laurel leaf and his Constitution. And when New York finally ratified, Hamilton was so celebrated that, as fireworks lit the skyline under a bright moon, the people of Manhattan suggested the city be renamed Hamiltoniana.

At last—the honors and glory my husband craved.

The legacy he'd made for a name he wasn't deemed fit to carry. The base-born orphan from Nevis who might have toiled in poverty and obscurity if God hadn't bestowed upon him a giant intellect and ambition to match. And the honors were no more than his due.

He'd done it. He'd vanquished Governor Clinton and all our antifederalist foes. More than that, he'd battled back the forces of ignorance and anarchy with his pen and the power of his ideas. He was, at that time, perhaps more than any other, my conquering hero. Like the son of an ancient god who'd driven that chariot of the sun after all. And when we were finally reunited, I wrapped my arms around his neck and teased, "The people love you. But *remember, thou art but mortal.*"

It's what the old Romans whispered to conquering heroes

so that they might never fall victim to hubris. And Alexander laughed. "So you *did* read those books I gave you."

Not well enough. Because if I'd studied the ancient stories, I'd have known that the same people who could lift a hero and his family out of obscurity could also tear them to pieces.

～

*March 1789*
*New York City*

We had a new Constitution, a new government, and a new baby.

It was everything for which we'd worked for so long.

And then, to make my happiness complete, my sister returned home from London for what she promised, this time, would be a long visit.

*Oh, Angelica.* Her dark hair, worn in a chignon beneath her fashionably plumed bonnet, smelled of rosewater. Cinched beneath her bosoms, her muslin gown was perhaps more fitting for the boudoir than the docks of New York. I felt drab and shabby in comparison but couldn't get enough of looking at her. We embraced again and again as her servants carried her boxes into her new dwelling.

"You should stay with us," I said again, even though I knew she'd insisted Hamilton rent for her very handsome lodgings nearby, so as not to burden us. As if having my sister at my side could ever be a burden.

"Oh, my sweet, generous Betsy," Angelica said, kissing my nose, as if she still thought of me as her baby sister. "No doubt you'd give up your bed to make room for me, but where would the servants sleep?"

In London, she was accustomed to a great many servants and a great many rooms. No doubt our narrow little abode with five children underfoot and chickens in the yard would scarcely suit. "I suppose we would have trouble stowing your luggage . . ."

"I brought only eight trunks," Angelica said, laughing. "How else was I to carry gifts for your cherubs?"

At the prospect of gifts, my children danced around their aunt Angelica excitedly. I was only sorry that their cousins—safely stashed in the best European schools—hadn't made the journey with their mother. But we consoled ourselves with Angelica's undivided attention, and already my head was full of plans for her visit. What's more, my husband seemed to bask in my happiness.

Eyeing the mountain of my sister's luggage, Alexander teased, "Given how little you've carried from Europe, sister, I worry you'll have nothing to wear."

Angelica laughed. "Well, I must tell you, brother, that in some parts of Europe, it's very much the fashion to go out in *the state of nature*!" This comment made me gasp, which only encouraged her. "Mr. Jefferson told me that when we were in Paris together. He heard it from Mrs. John Adams. Oh, you have no idea the exalted and interesting people I met across the sea, but none could make up for your company. How I've missed you both! My dearest beloved sister and the *great man* she lured into our family."

Preening at her praise, my husband fiddled with what appeared to be a broken latch on one of her apartment doors and promised to have someone out to repair it in the morning. Then, with regret, he said, "Ladies, I console myself to know you can find ways to amuse yourselves while I'm gone. Alas, I must rush to an appointment . . ."

"So soon?" I asked, not wishing to lose him again to his books and papers. "You've worked so hard. Too hard . . ."

"You *both* work too hard," Angelica said, grasping my hand in her soft, manicured, bejeweled fingers, as if horrified to find mine rough, dry, and reddened from scrubbing linens, sewing clothes, and keeping house alongside Jenny. "My dear Hamilton, my servants will prepare dinner for all of us. I'm going to take care of you, my darlings. You shall have a *holiday* when home. I insist that you dine with me tonight."

"Oh, please, Alexander." I wanted nothing more than to be around the same table with the two people whose company I loved best in the world.

But my husband sighed with regret. "I'm afraid I'm to dine with some gentlemen at Fraunces Tavern."

"Invite them here," Angelica said, and a look of panic flittered over the faces of the servants who'd just emerged, half seasick, from the bowels of an oceangoing ship, and were not even settled into a new home in a new city. I couldn't think how they might be ready to entertain on a moment's notice. But that didn't stop my sister from making the offer.

Nor did it discourage Alexander. "How can I resist my two brunette charmers?" With that, he kissed me, then grabbed his coat and embraced the children, making the older ones promise to behave while he was gone.

"Invite whoever you like!" Angelica called after him when he made for the door. "The poor baron and his dog are always in need of a good meal. And what about the Burrs? They're wonderfully droll."

"Not Burr," Alexander said sharply, just before bounding out.

As we watched him disappear with the crowd on the street, I explained, "He's vexed with Colonel Burr for throwing in with the antifederalists and accepting a job from Governor Clinton." *Clinton, the man whose minions called my husband Tom Shit.*

Angelica leaned closer, keen for gossip. "And that's cause enough to prevent him from dining with the man?"

Only someone who hadn't lived through the recent hostilities could be surprised by this. "Not always. Sometimes I persuade him to turn the other cheek for the sake of my friendship with Theodosia, but I fear it a lost cause . . ."

"Well, even so, you're recompensed to have a husband so handsome and of such merit and abilities. A husband who—" Her voice caught, and she bit her lip. "A husband who plainly loves you."

Tears sprung to her eyes. *Tears.* And my heart nearly stopped in my chest because I wasn't sure I'd ever seen Angelica cry before. Not even when we were children, lest rivals for leadership over our troop of Blues think they had the advantage.

"Oh, Angelica, why are you crying?"

"Because I'm so happy for you, of course." She dabbed at her eyes with a perfumed kerchief. Then, as if she couldn't bear for me to see her this way, she retreated to the parlor. I followed, still alarmed, even though I ought to have been minding my children, whose shoes were clopping on the polished wooden floor as they ran circles around the empty dining room. And when we were alone, she confessed, "My husband doesn't love me."

I was sure I'd misheard. *Everyone* loved Angelica. "That can't be true."

"It is," she said, with a miserable shake of her head. "Church admits it."

My mouth dropped open. "Your husband could never be so cruel. He must've been drunk. Half out of his mind."

"He *was* drunk," Angelica replied softly. "But I fear that only made it easier to tell the truth. That he loved me once, but not any longer."

In numb shock, I murmured, "Is there—is there—"

"A woman?" she asked, with a bitter laugh. "Look hard enough and there's always a woman. But he's not in love with someone else. That, I could understand. That would make sense. But no. There are only three things my husband loves now. Money, gambling, and the politics of the British Parliament."

I could scarcely credit this. We hadn't approved of Church to start with, but we'd all become affectionately attached to him. Even Mama, who'd once called him a *macaroni*. "I'm sure he loves you and the children, Angelica, no matter what he says."

"Jack loves our little brood," Angelica admitted, sheepishly, as if she'd wronged him. "I shouldn't have implied otherwise. His children delight him. But I inspire him to feel nothing."

A little sob escaped her, and her red watery eyes met mine. "Have I lost my beauty? My wit? Tell me, Betsy—what has changed about me that could make me so unlovable?"

The bleeding anguish in her gaze revealed a wound as plain as I'd seen in any hospital and pity overtook me. My dazzling sister— who'd always been confident and strong and triumphant—had somehow been carved up and *diminished* by the man she married. And I was furious. Setting my jaw, I told her the plain truth. "You are more charming and beautiful than you've ever been."

Her smile was fleeting. "What a Schuyler you are. Always loyal. I don't feel beautiful. Or charming. Or even welcome in my husband's home." She said the next more emphatically. "Of course, England was never *my* home. Perhaps by pleading to return to America . . . maybe that's what did it. I've been so homesick that I let my own misery drive away my husband's love. Do you know—I—well, you'll think me terribly wicked . . ."

She wouldn't meet my eyes, as if afraid to tell me more. And I became even more distressed. "Wicked?"

"Our friends in Europe are more broad-minded about love than we are here. They taught me how to take vengeance on a neglectful husband. When I met our American ambassador to France, the widowed Mr. Jefferson, and he took a fancy to me . . . I encouraged him."

For a moment, I was so scandalized I lost all power of speech.

Seeing my expression, my sister quickly added, "Oh, it was only a flirtation. I'm not one of Mr. Jefferson's lovers. But I hoped by encouraging such a tall, stately, important gentleman that my own husband might . . . well, that Church might feel jealousy."

"Oh, Angelica." I breathed, bringing my hands to my face.

Absently, she ran her fingers through the dust on the windowsill. "Unfortunately, Church scarcely even noticed."

"You should count yourself lucky your husband doesn't think you guilty of adultery!"

"He wouldn't care if I were guilty of adultery." She sighed, as if that were the worst part. "I know this because at a card party someone jested that the Prince of Wales might choose me for a new mistress, and do you know what my husband said?" Swallowing, I hesitated to ask, for such jests caused duels. "Church quipped that it might help him, politically. And that the next time he was losing a game of cards with the prince, he'd add me to the wager."

"No!" I cried, horrified.

Obviously humiliated, a teary Angelica rushed to add, "Church was *very* drunk when he said that. He apologized. Begged a thousand pardons. I shouldn't have told you. I just—I feel so ugly and unwanted and *lonely*. Even in a crowd, I'm so alone."

Here she broke down sobbing and I could do nothing but stand by, awkwardly stroking her back. This wasn't the way things were between us. She was the older sister, always comforting me. Helping me when I skinned my knees and wiping my tears. It was a new world as I contemplated how to take care of the sister who'd taken care of me.

After a moment, she bravely swiped at her eyes. "Well, romantic trouble isn't so terrible in the scheme of things, is it? Given my good fortune in comparison to others, I've no right to feel sorry for myself." She smoothed the bodice of her gown, such that the sunlight streaming into the airy windows made her rings glitter. "Scarcely a couple I knew in London made a match based on love. They marry for land and titles and are happy enough. Church and I have respect . . . at least, we had it. That's why, if I return to him, I must return as the Angelica he used to know."

I missed a breath. "If?" The word escaped my lips, but Angelica barely seemed to notice.

*If* she returned to him. Why, there couldn't be any choice about it, could there? Divorce wasn't impossible, but it wasn't easy or desirable. Not for women like us. Not without adultery or some other provable cruelty, and even then it was a scandal. Women sometimes lived apart from their husbands if they had means. If they had somewhere to go. But even then, their children could be taken from them . . .

"I have to stay gone long enough for him to miss me," Angelica explained with a little shrug. I realized that this was a new scheme, and it settled a knot into my stomach. "Long enough to convince myself there are people who still love me. Because I feel as if no one else could possibly love me if my own husband doesn't."

That's how it was, wasn't it? A wife's purpose was to make her husband happy. To give him children and merit his love and esteem. Even though Angelica had done that, people would fault *her* for the cracks in her marriage. Especially if she let them show.

I'd never before considered the unfairness and injustice in that. And in defiance of the very idea, I threw my arms around her. "Oh, but you are loved! We're going to remind you of it every day. I promise we'll never let you feel lonely here. Not for a moment."

I stayed at her side the rest of that afternoon as weary servants scurried back and forth to the market. When I finished nursing ten-month-old James, and put the children down for a nap on Angelica's enormous canopied featherbed with its damask drapes and claw-shaped feet, I helped her rearrange furniture and spoke cheerfully, trying to raise her spirits. I asked about her children, about London, about any subject that would not tread too near her troubles. But my poor sister's spirits had been shattered to pieces.

All those years ago, she'd put her faith in love, and now . . .

When Alexander returned that night for dinner with his gentleman friends, I whispered, "Please compliment my sister's gown."

Alexander arched a brow, as if he hoped some amusing game was afoot. "Hmm?"

Clutching his arm with urgency, I leaned closer. "She's very much in need of kindness."

My husband cocked his other eyebrow only briefly before turning his charm on my sister like a cannonade, blasting her with compliments until, for just a moment, I imagined we were back in a Morristown ballroom where he'd called her the Divine Mrs. Carter.

When Angelica's servants brought expensive port and custard-filled profiteroles purchased at the nearby patisserie, he conversed with her in French.

I didn't know what he said, but whatever it was made her laugh with delight.

And I was grateful. So very grateful.

A little mesmerized, too, by the way Angelica managed to affect a mask of joy in the presence of her guests. While the baron told jokes in his harsh guttural accent, she fed his dog little tidbits, as if she didn't even mind the creature in her house. Not a trace of her misery slipped out as she poured wine and sang songs and insisted that we all play cards together despite the mixed company.

She was, I realized, an extraordinary actress. And as the exhausted servants cleared away the dishes, I wondered how much of what I'd always taken for my sister's confidence and daring was a shield for vulnerability that I never knew was there. I'd always been too busy and curious about the world to dwell on insecurities, but I'd certainly felt myself to be less beguiling—less interesting—than my sisters, so it was a revelation to learn that my bold, charming Angelica might harbor such feelings. Knowing this made me all the more affectionate and protective toward her.

From behind the white lace of her sleeve and the fan of her cards, my sister asked, "How did you let the insouciant Colonel Burr become an anitfederalist?"

"Burr is worse than an antifederalist," Alexander groused, slyly sliding his card onto the table while the baron puffed at his pipe. "He's turned out to be an opportunist. Burr only decided to oppose the Constitution in order to curry favor with Governor Clinton, from whom he has now accepted a post."

Hoping to stave off what I knew would be a lengthy diatribe, I patted my husband's hand and grinned at him. "We *won*, Alexander. Clinton tried to stop you, but you got the Constitution passed and became a hero to the city. You even crushed Clinton's candidacy for the vice presidency. Isn't that enough?"

Alexander turned on me like a lawyer at court, as if my sister were the judge. "It will be enough when Clinton holds no influence anywhere or with anyone, including Burr."

"Oh, my dear brother," Angelica interrupted, with a laugh. "You mustn't chide Betsy for elevated instincts. Unlike Machiavelli she's far too saintly to adhere to the principle that once one makes an enemy of a man, one must not leave him alive to get revenge. At least not politically alive. Betsy is too kindhearted for that, whereas I have no such scruples. If Clinton got in your way, I approve of any and all measures to be rid of him, even if it means shunning Colonel Burr. It's a matter of loyalty after all. *Semper Fidelis*."

"CHURCH," PEGGY GROUND out through clenched teeth, keeping her voice low, so as not to wake her new baby in his cradle. "And to think we called him *brother*." She had, *praise God*, come through her ordeal and given birth to a son. Another Stephen. And the little boy was so healthy that a happy Peggy joined the rest of the family in New York City for the inauguration of our first president, George Washington.

Unfortunately, I'd ruined Peggy's mood by telling her of Angelica's troubles.

I'd hesitated to tell Peggy but needed her discretion. "You mustn't say anything. For Angelica's sake. I only revealed this because you must help me to divert the family from asking questions that our sister finds too painful to answer."

Blowing dark curls out of her eyes, Peggy speared me with a side glance. "I'll try, but you know how Mama can be. She'll sniff out the trouble in a minute."

On inauguration day, all of Wall Street was a sea of straw hats, colorful parasols, and children hoisted aloft on shoulders, straining for a glimpse of the president. Banners danced in the early spring breeze, keeping time to the lively music made by minstrels on every corner.

Troops marched in blue coats with red facings and gold embroideries, cocked hats with white feathers, and black spatterdashes buttoned closed from the shoe to the knee. Scottish infantry marched in full Highland costume with bagpipes. And we Hamiltons and Schuylers crowded onto my upstairs balcony to watch the spectacle occurring just across the street at Federal Hall.

The building had been recently renovated with elegant stone archways, white neoclassical marbled columns, and a majestic glass cupola. And as we gazed in admiration, the crowd went silent. The president emerged onto the outside gallery, and now, with several attendants, stood between two pillars in a dark brown coat, waistcoat, and breeches, with white silk stockings and plain silver buckles glinting on his shoes. The secretary of the Senate held an open Bible upon a rich crimson cushion as the oath was administered.

"It's regrettable that Mr. Church could not be here to share such a celebratory moment," Mama said, her too-observant gaze upon Angelica.

"Look! Washington is raising his hand," Peggy exclaimed, stepping between them as she patted her baby's back.

"He's so distinguished," Angelica said softly, giving Peggy an appreciative glance. "Like a statue, or an old pagan god."

Alexander had persuaded George Washington that he was the only man who could hold the new government together as commander in chief, and certainly his dignified bearing inspired confidence. But I was struck by the strangest notion that Washington looked *frightened*. And I clutched at the pendant worn round my neck, as if, through the talisman of his hair clipping, I could lend strength to him. We could not, from our place, hear the words of the oath distinctly. But we did see him bow to kiss the Bible, his eyes closed as if in prayer.

And my husband and my father closed their eyes, too, in relief or thanksgiving or both. This moment had been a long time in coming. Both of them had lost friends to the cause. All of us had sacrificed for it. And my lower lip trembled when someone from the crowd below shouted, "Long live George Washington, president of the United States!"

The sentiment was punctuated by the boom of a cannon that frightened all our little ones. Mama ushered the children back into the house while the crowd roared its approval, and the deed was done. All that was left was to celebrate.

But Angelica seemed reluctant to come out with us. Infected by the thrill of the day, and my fear of leaving Mama and Angelica alone together, I insisted. "I must show you a new invention on the streets. Artwork, painted on transparent canvas, to be illuminated behind in such a way as it brings the pictures alive."

Angelica smiled sadly. "I saw such in France."

"You haven't seen the entire harbor illuminated with lamps and fireworks! Besides, Hamilton is so looking forward to your company."

Angelica flicked a fond glance at my husband. "Well, he *is* the hero of the hour . . ."

My husband didn't deny it. Instead, he said, "And the hero is entitled to the spoils. Come out with me, my beautiful brunettes, and I shall be the envy of every man in the city."

We laughed, thinking it quite a wonderful thing to be envied. In those heady, happy days, we'd not learned yet that envy is a poison to which none are immune . . .

# Chapter Nineteen

May 7, 1789
New York City

IT'S GOING TO be the most brilliant of entertainments," I said. "The inaugural ball is a celebration of *all* our hard work and sacrifice."

"Not for me. Not without my husband." Angelica strolled to the window, staring out over the street at the passing carriages on the busy thoroughfare. "You'll say that I've gone to balls without him before, but that was different. I wasn't a castoff wife to be pitied and scorned."

The post had come without a letter from her husband or her children. She'd taken it hard, and I was determined to cheer her. "No one will pity or scorn you," I said, though I suspected it to be a lie. "No one will even guess that anything is amiss."

She forced herself to smile. "Except for you, Betsy. You'll spend your evening fretting over me and I would never wish to take away from your happiness when you're soon to be such a grand lady."

Looking down at my stained apron, I said, "I'm hardly a grand lady."

Angelica also looked at my stained apron and made a face. "You'd best transform yourself into one, then, because everyone will look to you to set the style. Mrs. Washington hasn't yet arrived in New York City to take her place at the president's side. Mrs. Adams isn't here yet, either. And Mrs. Knox has grown too fleshy to delight in dancing anymore."

Still, I was scarcely in any position to replace any of those ladies. "No one will look to me. I'm just the wife of a New York assemblyman."

At this, Angelica let out a sudden howl of laughter. "You dare not let Hamilton hear you diminish his stature in such a way! His pride couldn't let the insult stand. You're the wife of the mastermind who brought this presidency into being, and everyone knows it."

That was true enough. I glowed with pride at my husband's accomplishments, but I didn't wish to indulge my own vanity.

"And who knows what he'll go on to do next," Angelica gushed.

I had an inkling that Alexander was considering a cabinet position, though he hadn't shared more than the idea that it was a possibility. Selfishly, perhaps, some part of me hoped he could be content with his private law practice. For public life came with endless outrages. There had been, only recently, a poisonous screed in the papers imputing all manner of villainy to my husband, including infidelity to our marriage bed.

*He will not be bound by even the most solemn of all obligations! Wedlock.*

I thought it an absurd accusation—for even if my husband were a sinful sort of man, where would he find time to betray me? Some days, the man barely slept nor found time to sit for a meal, let alone spend time with his children.

Angelica came to sit beside me. "You *know*, don't you? Well, tell me. What position is he being offered?"

"I *don't* know," I said, the words uncomfortable on my tongue. For why *didn't* I know? "Only that he's being considered for the cabinet."

"I'm not surprised. Washington might be president, but like a king, he'll need a . . . a prime minister! And who else would it be but Hamilton?"

Of course, she was right. But tonight, I wished to focus on the celebration, not the reality of governance and the challenges such an appointment would represent for us. "Then that's even more reason why you must join us at the inaugural ball," I managed. "And I won't take no for an answer."

Angelica squeezed my hand and winked. "Now *that* sounded like the commanding voice of a prime minister's wife."

That evening, I dressed in a dark blue gown with painted flowers I'd commissioned specially for the occasion, and we wedged ourselves into Angelica's hired gilded coach for the short ride down Broadway to the Assembly Rooms. My sister believed a man of my husband's stature needed to arrive in a grand fashion, and she was probably right. But my mind was unsettled about Alexander's intentions for our future, and the way my powdered hair, styled very tall, bumped the carriage rooftop with every jolt of the wheels didn't help.

By contrast, Angelica seemed at ease, and woefully underdressed. She insisted it was now quite in fashion on the Continent to go with natural hair, wearing the simpler gown she claimed had been popularized by the Queen of France. And everyone was very interested in all things French that summer, since the king had, at Lafayette's instigation, called together the Estates General to reform France's government in accordance with the principles of liberty.

Heaving a dreamy sigh, Angelica told us, "Mr. Jefferson believes that our revolution has unchained the mind of man, and that the whole world is now making itself over."

She spoke often, and recklessly, of her flirtation with Mr. Jefferson, boasting to all who would listen how tall he was. How learned and courtly. What a wonderful father he was to his little motherless daughters. Even confiding to us the man's secret dalliances. Exasperated, Alexander teased that she'd perhaps formed an improper attachment to the man.

I feared she might take it as a rebuke, but instead Angelica seemed delighted by the suggestion of jealousy in his voice. "Oh, but who can know what is proper anymore?"

My sister was not the only one to wonder it as three hundred well-coiffed guests all jockeyed for position in the entryway of the festooned ballroom.

With Mrs. Washington absent, ladies of rank had donned their most exquisite gowns, flashed their jewels, and flaunted their connections to contend for influence and position in this brave new society. Ordinarily, Governor Clinton's wife would have been next in line to set the tone and protocol for the event. But the formidable Mrs. Knox, wife of the new secretary of war, seemed to believe the honor was hers. Mrs. Knox had been the one to buy the brown cloth for the president's inaugural suit—all of American manufacture. Mrs. Knox was the one who hosted the party after the president was sworn in, where we watched firecrackers explode in bright, glittering display over the Hudson River. And Mrs. Knox was the one to have insisted upon commemorative gifts—ivory fans, imported from France, each depicting a medallion portrait of Washington in profile between the hinges and elegant paper covering.

So I was happy to let her have her due, especially at the expense of a Clinton.

"Oh, how marvelous," Peggy murmured as she joined us, fluttering her eyelashes behind the fan. "A keepsake to treasure."

I used mine to wave across the room. "Mr. Madison!"

As always, Madison wore black, leading me to worry that the poor bachelor owned just the one suit. His eyes kept darting to the entryway, as if he were reconsidering having come at all, ill at ease in society as he always seemed to be.

And seeing him fidget as I waved to him, Angelica's eyes widened. "Oh my. Tell me that pale little creature isn't the exalted Mr. Madison that I've heard you talk so much about!"

"Be kind," I whispered. "He's very clever but very shy."

Peggy made a face behind her fan. "He looks like some sort of incorruptible parson."

Which made my husband laugh. "A rather apt comparison. That he is uncorrupted and incorruptible I have not a doubt."

At last, the bookish congressman made his way through the press and offered a bow. Clapping Madison on the back with enough force to make him cough, Hamilton introduced his brilliant colleague to my sisters. And the mere sight of Angelica seemed to force Jemmy to retrieve a kerchief from his velvet coat with which to wipe sweat from his brow.

"Congratulations upon your recent election to Congress, Mr. Madison," I said.

"Hopefully condolences aren't in order," he quipped. "How are my favorite little Hamiltons?"

That he always remembered our brood of children so tenderly made me ever fonder of him. "Philip can hold whole conversations in French with Alexander and Angelica. I'm quite left out."

While Jemmy and I chattered, Peggy sighed impatiently. "Is there no formal order to this reception?"

Angelica's gaze searched the room. "I'm told the president's levees are very formal. Are we to be announced, or curtsy as in a royal court?"

Madison cringed. "I'm afraid we're in a wilderness without a single footstep to guide us. And here we are setting an example for the whole world."

*The whole world.* I gulped to think that might not be an exaggeration. After all, no one seemed to know what should be proper in a republic. We were all grasping for ways to behave.

When the president first arrived in the city, he'd been mobbed with well-wishers, job seekers, former soldiers, and gawkers of all classes and variety. Now people—if well dressed—were allowed into his mansion on Fridays. Out of respect for his own majesty, when the president went out, he did so in a richly appointed buff carriage, pulled by six gleaming white horses and two drivers in presidential livery. But he also made a point of taking a walk every day at two o'clock, to see and be seen on the streets— which, though cleaner since the war, still echoed with the noise of rattling carts, roaming livestock, and merchants hawking their wares.

We weren't even sure what to call the president.

Mr. Adams, in what my husband called a fit of madness, had suggested "*His Highness, the president of the United States and Protector of their Liberties.*" That had been roundly condemned as having the foul stench of monarchy about it. And perhaps because the antifederalists dared not criticize George Washington, they turned their merciless venom on Vice President Adams, addressing him as "His Rotundity" and "The Duke of Braintree."

Just then, the hall broke into applause when Washington appeared at the front of the room, Adams standing beside him. Before a backdrop of gold stars upon a blue field, the president offered the shortest of possible welcomes, as if he were embarrassed by the attention, then gave a nod that bade the musicians to play.

With the majority of revelers looking on, Washington led a minuet. Alexander turned to me, holding out his hand. "Shall we?"

Finding Angelica and Peggy in animated conversation, I readily accepted, and soon we were moving through the formations. The crowd and low-hanging crystal chandeliers quickly heated the room, and the wax was still warm when it dripped down onto our shoulders from the candles. And I became acutely aware of the envious stares of ladies, all of whom, it seemed, wished to dance with my handsome husband.

They whispered behind their fans, tittered when he came near, and one of his young female admirers was so entranced that she did not notice that one of the chandeliers had set fire to her ornate ostrich feather headdress until one of the president's aides clapped the feathers in his hands to rescue her.

"Ask Angelica to dance next," I said to my husband when our set came to an end.

He kissed my hand. "As you wish."

I'd no more than sipped at a cup of punch when President

Washington appeared beside me. "Mrs. Hamilton," he said, his tone formal as ever.

"Good evening, Your Excellency, and congratulations."

"May I have the pleasure of this dance?" Washington asked with a little nod.

A most brilliant entertainment indeed! "Oh, it would be an honor."

The president pulled me into the center of the dance floor and guided us through the figures of the minuet with his characteristic dignity and grace. And all the while I felt the weight of hundreds of gazes—congressmen, cabinet officers, foreign ministers, *and* those of their wives and daughters—and my conversation with Angelica came rushing back. Had President Washington singled me out because he intended to make my husband one of his cabinet officers? The thought caused me less anxiety than it had before—for, knowing that Washington and his lady were leaving behind their beloved home at Mount Vernon to serve this country again, I could hardly argue that Alexander and I shouldn't reconcile ourselves to a lesser sacrifice.

When the music ended, the president bowed, and I beamed. Especially as my sisters ran up to exclaim over the mark of respect he'd paid me. "Mrs. Prime Minister," Angelica whispered, probably too loudly, considering that we were suddenly encircled by ladies with whom I had only the most sparing acquaintance.

Except for my old friend Kitty Livingston.

Though we hadn't often spent time together since Morristown, I was pleased to see her now. "Kitty!" I cried, at first surprised that she'd come to town for a visit without telling me. Then altogether startled when she turned her back, as if I were a stranger. "Kitty, have we been so busy with our lives you've forgotten us?"

All at once, Kitty whirled upon me in a swirl of pink-striped satin, eyes burning with anger. "I haven't forgotten anything. Unlike your husband, who forgets who helped him get his start in this country. My family introduced him into society, but I suppose he has new friends now . . ."

"How appallingly *rude*," Peggy spat at Kitty.

Kitty turned on her. "Rude? And yet you were the one jesting loud enough for everyone to hear that Mrs. Church would like Hamilton to become a knight of her bedchamber."

Peggy's mouth dropped into an oval. "I never said any such thing!"

Meanwhile, my cheeks heated at the insult of being confronted this way in public. "Kitty, I—I don't know what you mean by any of this."

"Pay her no mind," Peggy said, linking our arms and attempting to pull me away.

"Yes, you do know what I mean," Kitty accused, placing herself in our way. Even more malevolently, she added, "Then again, you've always made it your business to remain unaware of anything you didn't wish to be aware of, Betsy. So let me explain. Your father, who is certain to get a Senate appointment, promised that your family would support my cousin for the other Senate seat. But now that Hamilton is to command the nation's treasury, he's violated the agreement and thrown his weight behind some . . . *upstart*."

With a rustle of her skirts, Angelica interposed herself between us like my guardsman. "Oh, but Kitty, you'll put a wrinkle in your forehead worrying about politics! Let the men sort it out while you tell me where you found this divine pink robe."

Never before in our whole lives had my older sister been content to leave politics to the men. In fact, Angelica was, in her own dulcet way, performing a political act by trying to divert the conversation. And as striking as that was, what most stood out to me was Kitty's certainty that Alexander was to be appointed *treasurer.* How did she know that when I did not?

Kitty was not distracted by my sister's diversionary talk of fashion. "As always, you Schuylers stick together. But remember, so do the Livingstons." With that, Kitty flounced away.

"She must have misunderstood something," I murmured, my head spinning as I turned to Peggy. "What *was* she on about anyway?"

Angelica gave a wave of her fan. "Much ado about nothing. I dropped a garter during the dance, and Alexander gallantly swept it up and returned it to me. So of course I teased that in America he can't be a Knight of the Garter." She grasped me by the shoulders. "Pay Kitty Livingston no mind. With power and influence comes jealousy, Betsy."

"Yes," Peggy said, quickly. "Don't let her upset you."

"I won't," I said. On any other night, I might've fretted about the confrontation, but I refused to do so on *this* night—not when we'd worked so hard to get here, and not when I wished to cheer Angelica, and certainly not after President Washington had done me such an honor.

Peggy sighed, and I followed her glance in the direction of Governor Clinton. "But your husband *does* have a penchant for making powerful enemies."

"He has to," Angelica replied. "It's the way of the world. You can't rise in station without something, or someone, to step on. With Papa now in the Senate, and Hamilton possibly leading the new treasury department, our family is in ascendance. The Livingstons will simply have to learn to cede to their betters."

"MRS. HAMILTON," MY HUSBAND purred against my neck. "You were tonight, as you were in Morristown all those years ago, the belle of the ball."

I peered at him in the mirror of my dressing table, where I sat removing my pearl earbobs. Despite the unpleasantness with Kitty, the ball had been thrilling, and I was both exhausted and exhilarated. The grandness of the occasion, my husband's unfailing attention, the liveliness of the society—and the dance with our country's new president. It had all been a delight. We deserved this celebration, this moment, this *joy*.

"The belle of the ball? Is that so, Colonel Hamilton?" I asked coyly.

His very warm hands moved to my embroidered stomacher. "It is."

I sighed. "And yet, when the rooster crows, the children will awaken and I shall be transformed to a simple Dutch housewife once again."

"Then I'll make good use of the hours between now and the rooster," he said, playfully pulling a pin from the fabric and carelessly letting it drop upon the mahogany table with a soft *plink*.

"Alexander." I shifted toward him, my blood heating with the feel of his breath on my nape. Fleetingly, I worried about the possibility of conceiving another babe when I already had an orphaned Fanny and four of our own little ruffians underfoot, all so close in age. And yet the erotic edge in his voice, and the scent of brandy on his breath, made it impossible to resist.

"Careful," he said, plucking another sharp pin. "Except for that first rapturous instance upon our nuptials, I would not wish our trysts to be bloodsport . . ." He dragged the point of the pin harmlessly over my bodice. I felt quite at the mercy of his sweet assault in a way that made me feel more lover than wife. One pin led to another, and before long the whole gown was in pieces at my feet and my husband's touch drove away all my worries.

Afterward, Hamilton held me in his arms in the quiet dark of our bed. "The president wishes to appoint me secretary of the treasury."

So, there it was. Finally.

I swallowed as competing reactions fought to be voiced. I was proud, of course, but also worried about how we could manage as his duties became more demanding. As it was, he was so often gone, leaving me almost always alone to bear the heavy burden of our domestic responsibilities—not just the children but also our occasionally insufficient means.

But even more, and perhaps ridiculously, I nursed a little ache that he was only now telling me something others already knew. Going back to our little shack at De Peyster's Point, he'd always brought me into his work. I'd helped him in the writing and publishing of *The Federalist*. So I suppose I'd taken the liberty of thinking that we were partners in the enterprise of his career.

"That's a great honor, husband," I managed. "Am . . . am I the last to know?"

Alexander blew out a breath and pulled my back to his chest. "I didn't wish to concern you with it until the details were confirmed, and now they are."

So it was decided, then. It was a decision that would determine my future, and the happiness of my family, but I wasn't consulted as a partner would be. I was *told*. And it made me feel childish and naive and small, not like the *prime minister's wife*, which I was to be, after all.

"I should like to have known you were considering it," I murmured, knowing Robert Livingston also wanted that job, and if it went to my husband it would create an even deeper rift between our families.

"You know why," Alexander said, frustration causing his voice to rise. "I brought this government into being and I'm now obligated to put the machine into some regular motion."

It didn't escape my notice that he hadn't actually responded to what I'd said, and that turned my hurt to resentment. "May I ask the salary?"

"I predict about thirty-five hundred dollars." It was so far below our already stretched income that I feared to take a breath. Perhaps sensing my panic, he said, "It is a financial sacrifice, I know."

"No. I don't think you do know." I'd kept the burden of that knowledge from him, well aware of how he resented dependency. So while he went about accepting payments from clients in barrels of ham and sending money to his ungrateful and dubious relations in the West Indies, I'd made certain that he didn't know about the loans from Papa or the extra shipments of food from Mama. Dinner came to his table on plates given to me by my sisters, and he never asked how it got there. Alexander didn't know how I patched clothes for one child to pass down to another, how I stretched our stores of root vegetables from season to season, or how I traded homemade preserves and table mats in exchange for wine to serve important guests.

He turned me to face him, and his eyes were an ocean storm. "Before we married, madam, I *asked* you countless times if you could be happy—"

"As a poor man's wife, yes. And have I or the children once complained? That is not my concern, Alexander," I said, my heart aching that he would question my loyalty.

"Then what is?" But he didn't allow me to answer before sitting up and charging on. "I've shed blood, Elizabeth!" Though he burned hot, he wasn't often a man to shout, but the moment I mentioned the little ones, something seemed to have snapped in him, as if he felt I'd impugned his honor as a *father.* "I've killed men in the cause of this country. And how shall I answer my children—or God for that matter—if it should all be for nothing?"

God? That he—who had only reluctantly consented to baptize our children at Trinity Church—should fling salvation at me!

*You are not the only man who shed blood in the cause of this country,* I wanted to say. And having been forced so often to listen to chatter about forms of government, I knew the point of a republic was that nothing should rest entirely upon one man. Surely the whole enterprise would not fall to pieces simply because thirty-four-year-old Alexander Hamilton did not have command of its accounting books.

But I didn't say any of this for fear he would bury me in an avalanche of arguments. Instead, I kept quiet, and what he mistook for submission seemed to ease him. Heaving a breath, he pulled me to him again. "My angel, the treasury is where I can do most good for the country. And this consideration must outweigh every consideration of a private nature."

It was a reminder that I was a general's daughter. A colonel's wife. That ours was a family that had led soldiers in the cause of the country and must see it through troubled times to safety.

Perhaps I was more saintlike than I'd wanted to admit, because I found myself softening to the one approach that had the power to cut through my anger—patriotism. Moreover, I knew what a godly woman would do. A saintlike woman. She'd resign herself to the will of her husband and master, and devote herself with resignation to his decree. Besides, if Church could stop loving Angelica, who was so charming and agreeable that she'd fascinated royalty, how easy might it be for Hamilton to stop loving me?

Suddenly, the hurt I felt that he hadn't consulted me felt petty, so I didn't give voice to it. Not when I wished to right the wrong I'd caused between us. I gave a little nod. "Of course, Alexander. I understand."

His expression softened and he fastened those irresistible eyes on me. "This position is what I've been hoping for—planning for—all along."

And all at once I knew it was true. All those treatises on economic policy. All the late-night conversations with Papa and the powerful financiers of New York. All the books on economic systems. All those times Hamilton had gone off to war or to Philadelphia and left me alone for months on end—or even when he was so absorbed in his work that he didn't look up for days.

I'd been planning our domestic life together.

But he'd been planning *this*. And it made me realize I still had so much to learn about my husband's ambitions.

# Chapter Twenty

*June 1789*
*New York City*

**W**ELCOME TO THE menagerie," I said to James Madison as a cacophony of our chickens squawked in their pen in the yard. There were advantages to living across the street from the busy Federal Building—for example, when my husband left the house to attend business there, he wasn't far—but it was also too easy for him to return home with colleagues.

One hot summer afternoon when my daughter was shrieking at the top of the stairs because one of her brothers had taken her ribbon, I was obliged to receive Mr. Madison. As I wrangled the children, he glanced out the back door—propped open to permit a cooling breeze—and asked, "Is that—"

"The neighbor's monkey," my husband answered, with more gravity than I would've expected. He led his friend into the yard for the shade of a tree. "It keeps climbing over the fence to taunt the chickens."

I watched the men settle themselves, fretting over Alexander's pensiveness. And I took them some lemonade. "Is anything the matter?"

The men exchanged a glance that made my stomach drop. "Washington has fallen ill," Alexander said, glumly. "They say it's anthrax. I worry for the man, of course, but more than that, too. What comes of the Constitution if he dies?"

Madison's expression was equally grim. "The crisis this could bring about in our public affairs may be insurmountable." It was already bad enough, he explained, that our countrymen were getting into tavern brawls over whether we should prefer to trade with the British or the French. The only thing everyone agreed on was George Washington. "If Washington dies, we're to entrust the whole enterprise of the federal government to a man lambasted as His Rotundity, the Duke of Braintree?"

John Adams, he meant. And yet, was the possibility of the president's death not the entire purpose of having a vice president? So my prayers, when I made them, were not for the Constitution. I prayed for the president and for Martha Washington. Because how would she bear it if her husband were to die?

Leaving the men to talk, I sent Jenny to fetch more water and cut lemons to fill a pitcher for more lemonade—all this before greeting Angelica at the front door and hefting fourteen-month-old James into my lap to nurse.

I told my sister the news, then shook my head. "Mrs. Washington must be frantic. I should like to visit her to offer comfort or assistance."

"I'll go with you," Angelica said.

But I wondered if a visit with the president's lady was truly possible. Because Mrs. Washington's position meant that things had changed between us. At her receptions, I always found the president's lady seated atop a dais, her round face smiling benevolently down upon us from beneath a modest powdered coiffure and lace veil. And there she regally received each lady in turn.

The first time I'd seen her that way, I realized, with a start, that Martha Washington and I might never again be easy and familiar together. She was the closest thing we had to royalty. There must be a distance now, I thought, almost sadly. And as I made my way to the dais to present myself, I'd been acutely aware that I'd never attended a royal court. I hadn't known how low to drop or how long I ought to hold the curtsy. In the end, I'd grasped my skirts and endeavored to a posture between obsequiousness and mere respect, hoping, quite sincerely, that I wouldn't somehow teeter off my embroidered silk shoes.

Much to my relief, when I rose, Mrs. Washington's smile had widened. Almost a secret message just for me, as if to reassure me that a friendship remained. But that friendship would never be the same because she was now, more than ever, a public figure. Every gesture and smile a reflection upon her husband until the day he died, which I prayed would not be soon.

"President Washington simply *must* recover," Angelica decided, making herself helpful by brushing little Fanny's curly hair. "And he will. At the inaugural ball he looked as strong and vigorous as ever. So right now I refuse to worry about anything but you." She nodded toward the babe at my breast. "I don't know how you manage all this. And you're expected to host a dinner tonight besides?"

I nodded, eyeing a gown piled atop the chair that I needed to mend before I could wear it. "Some gentlemen are coming to arrange for the care of Alexander's legal practice when he takes up his new position."

Angelica sighed. "This won't do. It's too much for you without more servants. It's too much for Jenny. It isn't seemly for the wife of such an important man to scrub floors next to her maid. It wouldn't be fitting for the president's lady to stoop to it."

In light of the current crisis, I could scarcely imagine such a position. Certainly, I didn't want to imagine it. "I am not the president's lady."

"But you might be, one day," my sister replied with a sly smile.

My mouth went dry, for the situation cast Angelica's comment in a too-calculating light that made me uneasy. And it was more proof that, though I was coming to better understand my husband's ambitions, sometimes it seemed as if my sister sympathized with those ambitions more than I did.

I didn't want to be the wife of the secretary of the treasury, much less the president's wife. And I shuddered to think I might ever find myself in Martha Washington's position. Especially given what she was facing now.

Perhaps sensing my panic at the idea, Angelica sighed and said, "Oh, Betsy. You blanch when you should blaze! If Hamilton must entertain, have him take his guests to my lodgings where servants can wait upon them as befitting the household of a great man."

Oh, the relief of that idea. I couldn't deny that the elegance of my sister's household was more in keeping with expectations—to say nothing of the absence of children, chickens, and monkeys.

Though, on this particular afternoon, with such grave news hanging over our heads, the monkey looked to be having a salutary effect on the men. For when I went out to refill their glasses, I found my husband and Mr. Madison, heads close together, laughing and teasing the creature as it swung from the tree by its tail and pelted them with leaves.

"Where did the little devil come from?" Madison wanted to know.

"Our neighbor won the monkey from a sailor in a card game," my husband explained.

"A British sailor or a French sailor?" Madison asked, archly, as if ready to come to fisticuffs about it. Whereupon they both laughed before their conversation turned to finance and Alexander's upcoming position—topics that had me retreating back into the house.

The next afternoon, Angelica and I tried to call upon Mrs. Washington, only to be denied access, as I feared. The street had been roped off so that carriages would not disturb the president's rest. I returned home early, dejected, only to find the house strangely empty and quiet.

"Jenny?" I called, but when I had no answer, I guessed she must have gone to the market.

It was too soon for Alexander to be home, and yet, from up

the narrow stairway, I heard my husband's voice, soft and tender, speaking of love.

Not stopping to remove my hat and gloves, I climbed the stairs and cautiously pushed open the door. There I found Alexander seated on the floor of our bedroom, rocking little Fanny in his arms where she slept, his lips pressed to her hair as he murmured that he would love and care for her.

"What's happened?" I asked. "Has she fallen ill, too?"

Hamilton didn't look up. Perhaps he couldn't. "Her father is dead."

Oh, poor orphaned girl! I didn't ask how. I supposed it didn't matter. What did matter was that my grief-stricken husband looked nearly as broken and vulnerable as when he'd received the news of John Laurens's death.

His voice catching, Alexander said, "Her sisters are still too young and impoverished themselves to take care of her. I know it's too much to ask . . ."

I knelt and pressed my forehead to his. "You needn't ask. We'll keep her. We'll love her as our very own. Why, with those bright black eyes of hers, Fanny could pass for my daughter."

He peered at me, tearily. "I fear it's too much of a burden on you, my love."

"A small burden when compared to the ones you shoulder," I said.

For it was in his pain for this little girl, and the obligation he felt toward her, that I finally understood his calling. Not just to help provide a future for the child of one fallen comrade, but to provide for the children of all of them. The ones who had been orphaned in a war he helped unleash, in battles he helped plan, and mutinies he put down. He was, I knew, trying to keep the promise he made to make this a better world.

And, I felt sympathy for all that my husband was trying to do.

Fortunately, by the grace of God, the skill of the doctors, and the stoic disposition of the president, George Washington survived his ordeal that summer. But the scare made us all realize how much the country needed this man.

And I embraced the fact that the country needed Alexander Hamilton, too.

*With special trust and confidence in the patriotism, integrity, and abilities of Alexander Hamilton of the City of New York in the State of New York, I have nominated, and by and with the advice and consent of the senate, do appoint him Secretary of the Treasury of the said United States.*
—George Washington

*September 13, 1789*
*New York City*

Dinner parties and balls filled our evenings, now that Alexander was a member of Washington's new cabinet, and at every one I reveled in having Angelica's tutelage in becoming the socialite wife of an important man. I studied my sister as she conversed in French, made literary allusions, shared gossip—always the gentlest kind—and carried herself with an air of dignity and charm.

And while the wit and guile of society would never come as a natural talent to me, I began to understand it as a craft that could be *practiced*. Especially when I had such a good and loving teacher as my sister.

But our celebrations were abruptly cut off by a pair of unexpected blows.

After seven months in New York, Angelica received word that her children were ill. Frantic to hold her babies in her arms—even if it meant returning to John Church—my sister made haste to sail back to England. An ocean would again separate us, and she'd be in her husband's grasp. He could keep Angelica from us forever if he wanted. That was a husband's power.

And I was devastated to think I might never see her again.

"Take heart, my angel," Alexander said, to soothe me. "Your sister wants to live here in America, near to us. And she is precisely the sort of woman who knows how to get her way."

He meant to make me laugh at the idea that it was Angelica who would make Church bend to her will, as she so easily bent everyone else to it. But I couldn't even smile. "What if her ship is lost? What if—"

A thousand calamities seemed possible. But I cut myself off from expressing any of them when my sister's carriage pulled up in front of our house. I did my best to dry my eyes, wipe my tears. But when she'd finished kissing all my children farewell, Angelica drew me aside and smoothed at my cheeks with her thumbs. "You've been crying."

"No," I said, trying to be brave for her sake.

"I really hoped I'd taught you to lie better than that," she said, a little teary herself. "Your eyes are bloodshot and your nose is red and my heart is breaking to leave you."

"I know you must go for your children's sake, but I'm going to miss you terribly. I've been so happy these months. We've all been so happy together, and now what will I do?"

"Now you will *shine,* Betsy. You'll become all you were meant to be. You and Hamilton both. And I couldn't be prouder of either of you. You're making a new country, and I'm only sorry I cannot stay to be a part of it."

Angelica was proud of me. I hadn't realized, until that moment, how much I had longed to hear it.

And my lower lip began to wobble until she said, "Oh, you really must stop looking at me that way. You're going to make me cry, too, and it will ruin my powder."

For her powder's sake—and for my own dignity—I didn't dare see her off at the pier. Instead, we said our farewells in my parlor, and then my husband, young Philip, and the baron took her to the ship. Meanwhile, I retreated to bed, felled with an ache in my heart and my head.

That night my husband was forced to finish the letter to Angelica that I'd started, sharing in my misery at her departure. As if the loss of her was as genuine a wound for him as it was for me. Which made me love him even more.

"I fear I've lost an ally, not to mention a friend," he confided one morning soon after.

Fighting my own fears that I would never see my sister again, I whispered upon our pillow, "She'll always be an ally. Always your friend. Always your sister, even if an ocean away."

With a huff, Alexander clamored from the bed. "I meant Madison. I would never have accepted this office if I didn't believe I had his firm support."

Jemmy Madison, now not just a congressman from Virginia, but *the most influential* congressman besides, had unexpectedly pulled his support from Alexander's financial plans.

On top of the loss of my sister, Madison's desertion was as depressing as it was confusing. "Did he say why?"

"He thinks it unjust that speculators might get a windfall from buying up debt from ignorant country folk, but that's just how investment works. He's letting Jefferson's ideas about the nobility of the simple yeoman farmer sway him away from financial reality."

Jefferson had only recently returned from his post as minister to France to take a new position in the president's cabinet. But already Alexander was wary of Jefferson's influence and perhaps he was right to be. Jemmy seemed to idolize his fellow Virginian, with whom he shared a friendship long before we met.

I had worried, once before, that Jefferson might come between Madison and my husband.

And it was vexing to think my fears could be coming true.

How many times had I hosted Jemmy Madison in my home? How many times had I admired his tender touch with my children? He'd become a friend to me. Worse, I realized belatedly, he'd become a *brother* to Alexander.

So the relationship simply must be salvaged. Trying to soothe my husband's temper over breakfast, I pointed out, "Madison opposes only *part* of your plan, doesn't he?"

Hamilton rattled off a list of reasons why even that disagreement was intolerable. "Debt and credit are an *entire thing*. Every part of it relies on every other part. Wound one limb and the whole tree shrinks and decays," he said, waving an impatient hand. "No, Jemmy's opposition to me is a perfidious desertion of the principles he was solidly pledged to defend."

I let him vent his spleen and, with Mrs. Washington's wise advice in mind, I tried another tactic. That my husband was a man of studied principles, I knew without question, but I also wished that he could occasionally muster a modicum of forbearance for the foibles of others. One that might preserve one of the most important friendships in our new nation. Just this once. "So, Madison has been corrupted?" I asked.

My husband slanted me a glance. "I wouldn't go so far as that."

"He's a madman, then? One day working with you side by side, then changing his mind on a lunatic whim . . ." Alexander didn't answer, which was, in itself, a concession. And when I noticed Jenny smirk knowingly as she refilled his coffee cup, I pressed the point. "Did Mr. Madison hit his head and damage his brilliant faculties?"

Hamilton grumbled. "You make too much of his faculties. Although Madison is a clever man, he is very little acquainted with the world."

"That may be true. But it is still no *personal* opposition to you. What reason would he have, other than a difference of opinion?" I let the question hang there as Hamilton finally calmed enough to resume eating the stewed apples on his plate.

"He has no personal reason to oppose me. None that he should be aware of anyway." He said the last quietly, in a nearly absent fashion, then winced, as if he'd not meant to speak it aloud. My raised eyebrow must have demanded an explanation, because he sighed. "Last year, when Madison introduced his foolish ideas about the Tariff Act, I whispered in a few ears and made some obstacles for him. Perhaps he found me out."

"Oh, Alexander." My husband was a strategist, and the legislature was his game board. He was certainly not the only one to engage in backstage dealing, and his machinations were more honorable than most. This wasn't the first time his secret schemes created mistrust amongst friends. But there was nothing to be done for it now. "What does the president say?"

"He urges me to compromise with Madison."

I smiled, as so often George Washington and I saw things in the same way.

"So then do that, Alexander. I'll host a dinner," I suggested. It would be a great deal easier if Madison had a wife—the friendship of women being a necessary lubricant to remedy social frictions—but the Virginian was too mannerly to refuse our hospitality, and I felt certain we could win him back. "I know just the occasion. A party for the new secretary of state."

LATELY ARRIVED FROM France, Thomas Jefferson appeared worldly and elegant in a fashionable dove gray satin coat and fine French lace cravat as he presented himself at my threshold. His tall frame filled the doorway, making Madison seem even shorter by comparison.

"Secretary Jefferson, what a pleasure it is to see you again," I said, welcoming the men in from the October chill. "And Mr. Madison, it's been too long."

"Your invitation was most welcome, Mrs. Hamilton," Jefferson said with a little bow. Wisps of silver shot through the Virginian's ginger hair, but otherwise he looked much the same as he had all those years before in Philadelphia.

Madison bowed, too, and spoke with even more formal reserve than normal, a thing that concerned me. "Mrs. Hamilton. Thank you, as always, for your hospitality."

"Of course," I said, showing them into the dining room, where I'd worried over every detail. Angelica had told me that Jefferson was a connoisseur of fine wine, so I had Papa come and bring his best Madeira. I knew, too, that the new secretary of state ate little meat, so I planned a menu with an abundance of peas, greens, and vegetables of every variety. I had Jenny set the table with my finest dishes, and everything was so perfect that Angelica would've been proud of me. "Mr. Jefferson, how is your lovely daughter Patsy?"

Jefferson's smile revealed great fatherly pride. "Patsy has recently married. She's Mrs. Randolph now."

"Well, then we shall add that happy occasion to our list of things to toast this evening," I said.

"A happy occasion indeed, madam," said Jefferson just as Alexander entered the room and greeted our guests. Though Jefferson accepted the seat of honor at the table when my husband made a show of offering it, he said, "Please, there's no need for formality among old friends, which I feel us all to be, given our past acquaintance and all your sister-in-law has told me of you. In fact, Mrs. Church sent as a gift to me a copy of *The Federalist* that your amiable wife inscribed for her."

Perhaps it was my own vanity in remembering my part in the publication of those essays that made me ask, "Have you had the opportunity to read them?"

"Indeed," Jefferson said with a smile. "I found it to be the best commentary on the principles of government ever written." The praise should have made Alexander smile, but neither Madison nor my husband seemed at ease.

Fortunately, Jefferson's good social graces smoothed things over quickly, and he and Alexander fell into such deep discussion and swift agreement about coins and the mint that they did indeed seem like old friends.

I was glad for that, but the true aim of the occasion was to mend fences with Jemmy Madison, who hung on Jefferson's every word. When Madison's eyes lifted to the ceiling at a particularly loud shriek from the children's nursery, I moved in to say, "My apologies. I believe that's my daughter. I'm told that little girls are soft and manageable creatures, but mine has a war cry that would make an Iroquois chief proud."

Madison chuckled at that, but no more. The man had accepted my invitation, as I knew he would. Yet, again and again, I found it difficult to draw Jemmy into conversation. How had a political disagreement about economic policy so chilled our friendship? Perhaps Alexander was right, and Madison *had* learned about my husband's machinations against his tariff.

While I worried for Madison's mood, Jefferson opined on the virtues of the French people. "I've been fortunate to see in the course of fourteen years two revolutions as the world has never seen before."

Jefferson had a way with words that excited within me the idea that we were living in extraordinary times. My husband, by contrast, seemed less inspired by France's attempts to throw off their monarchy. "As a friend to mankind and liberty, I rejoice in the efforts," Alexander said. "But I fear much for the fate of those caught up in it."

Specifically, we worried that harm would come to our friend Lafayette, who was championing the revolution in France. We knew the righteousness of his cause, but the stories of violence in Paris frightened me. I did not believe the French nobles would give up their privileges so easily. And it seemed to me as if the French revolutionaries themselves were beginning to fracture into dangerous rivalries.

But Jefferson sipped appreciatively at the Madeira and asked, "Why should you fear it, Secretary Hamilton?"

To my great vexation, my husband's eyes traveled the length of the table and settled on Madison. "Because we should all dread destructive and *petty* disagreements amongst those who once stood united . . ."

My wine lodged itself in my throat, and only with a cough, and some difficulty, did I manage to swallow. If I'd learned anything about Virginians it was that a thing must be approached with them from the side. So why did my husband insist upon a frontal assault? Hadn't my work in hosting this party been aimed at Alexander's reconciliation with Madison—if not out of regard for their friendship, then at least in consideration of the fact that he was the one man who could thwart my husband's plans?

Mr. Jefferson smiled indulgently, appearing to take no notice of the undercurrents. But there was a shrewdness in his eyes that made me think he missed nothing. "I think the present disquiet in France will end well. The nation has been awakened by our revolution, they feel their strength, they are enlightened, their lights are spreading, and they will not retrograde."

His words caused a swell of patriotism within my breast. "I have always believed our revolution would be a force of good in the world. That all our suffering and privations would mean more than a new nation for us, but also a new age for mankind." And I thought that Jefferson—a man with such vision—should be a natural ally for my husband; surely he would understand the magnitude of what Alexander was trying to do, and help in it.

"Well said, Mrs. Hamilton." Jefferson gave an extraordinarily sunny smile that filled me with pride.

I was, in fact, so swept up in Jefferson's idealism and charm, that I understood how Madison could be enthralled by the force of that man's character and charisma. Though I didn't know it then, that force, which made Jefferson so effective as the voice of our revolution, and so rousing as a politician and the father of a political party, was something, like love, quite beyond *reason*.

Like the earth's own poles, Jefferson and my husband had the power to both repel and attract, and I realize now that Madison was trapped between them, pulled to Jefferson as much, or maybe even more, by that force of charisma as by any alignment of their ideals.

But at the time, I only knew that I wanted these men to remember all they had in common, and I lifted my glass in abandonment of all etiquette. "To the revolution, to independence, and

the Constitution. And to the men at this table, all of whom
made them possible."

At that, Madison seemed to soften, giving me a private little
nod as he joined in the toast. Alexander seemed more cordial,
too. "And to the women as well," he said, generously. The good
feelings that finally surrounded us persuaded me to henceforth
adopt a policy for the dinners that took place at my table: no
man's politics should be held against him, and all were welcome.

Conversation flowed with more ease after that, and when
Hamilton saw Madison and Jefferson out, he made an invitation
of his own. "Gentlemen, let's do this again. Just the three of us. I
have some thoughts on the matter of a national capital. Perhaps
we can reach a compromise . . ."

# Chapter Twenty-One

*November 1790*
*Philadelphia*

OVER A SECOND, private dinner of just the three of them, they'd struck a bargain.

A grand compromise.

Madison yielded, agreeing to get my husband the votes he needed for his financial plan. And on the heels of his victory, Alexander brimmed with excitement, swooping little James into his arms to spin him around. But I was too much the daughter of a Dutchman to think such a victory would come without a price. "And what do the Virginians want in exchange?"

Alexander was suddenly, decidedly less giddy. "I agreed to use my influence to move the capital city from New York to the wilderness of the Potomac."

Already imagining the uproar it would cause amongst our New York friends, I tried to reconcile myself to the news. "It will take time to build a new city. Surely, in the meantime, we'll remain here?"

Hamilton shook his head, more than a little frustrated at the outcome. His enemies had whispered that the capital city was to be called Hamiltonopolis, so he'd been forced to give New York up even as a temporary home for the government, lest he appear to be self-interested. "All of us—the congressmen, the senators, the cabinet officers and their wives—are to pack up and migrate to Philadelphia."

I didn't relish upending our life on Wall Street, but there was nothing for it but to close up the house, pack up the children, and sell the chickens.

But that autumn, with the move entirely in my command, I was inconsolable.

Not to leave New York—but because our faithful Jenny fell prey to yellow fever.

It'd started as a fever and some aches, and though she insisted she felt better, I sent her back to the Pastures for a rest and a visit with her mother. She never made it there. She died on the sloop, it was reported to me, bleeding from the mouth, nose, and eyes, screaming in pain. And I grieved as much that she had died alone, without me to tend her, as I would have for a member of my family. Which made me deeply ashamed.

For I had not treated her with the love and respect someone ought to treat family. Instead, I'd told myself polite lies to disguise the fact that I'd "borrowed" Jenny. I'd taken her away from her mother at the Pastures and I'd taken her labor and kindness as if I had a right to them.

Jenny had been a servant, yes. Why say it politely, even if it was the custom? She was a slave. She'd been my children's nurse-maid, and they loved her. She'd also been my helpmate, and I considered her a friend. I should have told her that. No, I should have *treated* her like a friend. I should have treated her like a *person*, with the same God-given rights as any other.

I should have seen to her freedom. And now it was too late.

Papa had joined the New York Manumission Society; he wasn't insensible to the injustice of slavery. He meant to do away with it at the Pastures as soon as he could afford to. But even if Papa wouldn't have released Jenny from bondage, I should have paid her a wage.

In guilt and grief over her death, I wanted nothing more to do with slavery.

Now I vowed never to own, rent, or *borrow* another human being.

That wasn't enough, of course. Not enough to wipe away the stain on my soul or the everyday injustices of the institution. But I kept true to my vow.

I'd been born and raised on a plantation; my happiness had been built on the subjugation of others. My past was tainted with it, no matter what excuses I made for myself. But I could change. The country could change. So I put slavery—and New York—behind me in the hopes of bringing about a government that would help guarantee that all men, and perhaps all women, would be treated as equals before the law.

Determined to make a fresh start in our new capital, we found ourselves renting a home in Philadelphia on the corner of Walnut and Third streets, not far at all from the theater. Our neighbors were *thee-and-thou* Quakers, including Mrs. Dolley Payne Todd, who welcomed us with a warm apple pie from her kitchen. Like my husband, I admired Quaker morals and their antislavery stance, but upon hearing of our move Peggy had complained about Quakers having *humorless pretensions to gravity* and *ostentatious plainness*. I thought she'd change her mind if she ever met the vivacious young Mrs. Todd, who, even then, had such an impeccable sense of style that her dark workaday frock gave the impression of good fashion, its somber hues lightened by a smattering of whimsical Swiss dots.

In any case, I was grateful for the pie and the knowledge of a friendly face only a block away on Walnut Street where, rising up from the red-bricked streets, our snow-dusted stylish new abode was enclosed by a wrought iron gate, leading to a yard that provided more than enough elbow room for children, chickens, or even monkeys if we should want them.

"Much more in keeping with the style to which you grew accustomed as General Schuyler's daughter," my husband boasted as he showed me into the drawing room, where some expensive French chairs were already invitingly arranged by the fireplace. "And best of all, only a block from the new treasury. Such as it is."

Alexander was so very proud of himself that I couldn't help but set down my bags, straighten my bodice, and give him a very proper kiss. "Well, then, what is to prevent you from tumbling from our bed straight into the chair at your office without so much as running a comb through your hair?"

I said it only to twit him, but it wasn't far from the truth in the months that followed, where our lovely new house became little more than the place Alexander Hamilton slept—when he slept at all. My husband's mind was filled with the details of establishing American commerce. At breakfast he muttered about lighthouses, beacons, and buoys. At lunch—if he came home for lunch—it was talk of coins, candlewicks, wool, and manufactures. And before bed, it was banks and paper instruments and international trade.

Yet, despite the demands of his position, the gay social life of Philadelphia seemed poised to bring us happiness, especially when we were joined in the new capital, just in time for the holiday, by James Monroe, who now served as a senator from Virginia.

I ran into Monroe, almost quite literally, at a coffeehouse, which made us both laugh.

With the rich scent of beans making our mouths water, he gave me a flourishing bow. "Can it really be you, Miss Schuyler, still bundled up against the cold, pink-cheeked and bright-eyed as you were all those years ago when I served you swill in a military camp?"

Grinning, I nodded. "Yes, but I remind you that I'm *Mrs. Hamilton* now, as you well know, and as a mother of five I fear I am very much changed from those days."

Monroe kissed my hand in courtly and proper fashion. "Well, I do declare, you are as lovely as ever. Second only to my own Elizabeth."

A moment later, the beautiful Elizabeth Kortright Monroe emerged from a circle of ladies to join us at a table decorated with candles, holly bush, and pine. Together we watched the snow fall and shared gossip. "The fashions in Philadelphia are so *daring*," Mrs. Monroe said, a little bit scandalized and a little bit delighted. "It's all bare arms and bare bosoms—I hesitate to guess what will be bared next!"

I laughed. I liked the Monroes. I liked them very much. Together we visited Philadelphia's famed statehouse bell in the tower over Independence Hall. We shopped for baubles at the arcaded market on High Street. We admired the architecture of the new courthouse. We took our children to the circus together, where acrobats tumbled and clowns made us laugh.

And I insisted on having them to the house for dinner, even though my husband grumbled that Monroe had fallen in with the antifederalists. That was true. He'd led them in Virginia, arguing that the Constitution ought not be ratified without a bill of rights. But now we had a Constitution and a Bill of Rights, and none of it changed the fact that Monroe was our longtime friend.

Besides, I held fast to my policy that no man's politics should be held against him at our dinner table. Or I tried to. But circumstances in the months that followed made that increasingly difficult as the antifederalists coalesced into a political party intent on opposing my husband.

But Hamilton was, in those days, an unstoppable force of nature. Some said the most powerful man in the government, with Washington as a mere figurehead, just as my sister had predicted. It wasn't true, but my husband did seem invincible. He'd bargained with Madison and Jefferson to bring his financial system into being. And now there was nothing anyone could do about it, except look for vulnerabilities and petty ways to undermine him.

They found this in my father, Senator Philip Schuyler.

"The antifederalists found a way to get their revenge," Papa said quietly.

Having moved with us to Philadelphia, quite confident in his reelection to the Senate, Papa now learned of the surprise upset. In the same election that brought James Monroe back into my life as a United States senator, my father had been defeated, and by, of all people, Aaron Burr.

Between our move to Philadelphia, my husband's ascendance in the government, and the colonel's antifederalist leanings, we'd grown apart from the Burrs, but that didn't make his opportunism at Papa's expense any less cutting. And to think, my father had given Burr his start!

"Another betrayal," my husband raged, his temper as warm as my father's was cool.

And I could not soothe him because it had begun to feel, even to me, as if we were being abandoned by our friends. Monroe going over to the antifederalists. Madison's reluctant support and increasing preference for Jefferson. Burr's disloyalty.

Alexander was not wrong to think this was a strike against him, a shot aimed to remove a solid ally in the Senate and wound him personally besides. But it was my father who was the casualty. Poor Papa, who'd already suffered so much indignity in his public career, was now to be discarded by his nation in the wreath of his venerable age. I was mortified that my father should have to suffer for my husband's ambitions—and at the hands of Colonel Burr, whose wife I'd once counted as my friend and whose family I'd fed at my own table.

From the doorway, my nine-year-old son, Philip, asked, "What will you do now, Grandpapa?"

It was a question I'd dared not ask of my fifty-seven-year-old father who'd already fought enough battles—political and otherwise—for a lifetime. So I was surprised to see Papa smile as he summoned his grandson forth and ruffled his hair. "Why, I'll return to Albany and wait for an opportunity to retaliate."

That was Papa's way. He was as patient a politician as he'd been a general. Taking no time to brood over a lost battle, but slowly and steadily moving to gather allies about him and obstruct his enemies' progress until he was ready for another fight.

Unfortunately, patience was very much *not* my husband's way.

With the gratifying support of Madison in Congress, my husband had already moved to levy a tax on whiskey, much needed to fund the government's debts. And we were all relieved that the two architects of the government were once again working in good harmony. But Madison's support was no longer a thing upon which my husband could rely.

When Alexander proposed chartering a Bank of the United States, Madison wouldn't go along. Prickling with every word, my husband explained, "I think Jefferson has him convinced that by establishing a bank in Philadelphia, I mean to go back on the bargain to move the capital."

It was, of course, an affront to my husband's honor to be thought to have negotiated in bad faith. And I wondered why Mr. Jefferson, so cordial in mixed company, claiming to view us as old friends, would suspect Alexander of perfidy. Perhaps Jefferson's time in the French court had led him to look for intrigue behind every damasked curtain. But there seemed, to me, a remedy that ought to put Jefferson's mind at ease about my husband's intentions. "Why not, then, charter the bank on the Potomac?"

"We need a bank *now*," Alexander snapped. Each new loss of a friend and ally had set him ever more on edge, and made him dig in his heels until he was nearly insufferable. "Madison is a fool not to realize it."

I took a breath and cautioned, "If you express such sentiments in public, of course Madison will oppose your bank. It will be harder for southerners to invest if it's located in a northern city."

"I don't need Madison or the southerners."

It unnerved me to hear the hubris in his voice. "Remember, husband. Madison is the most important man in the Congress."

Hamilton's mouth opened as if to list a hundred ways in which I was wrong. But then, all at once, his temper broke, and he laughed, drawing me into his arms. "My angel, you are too good, and innocent, and tender-hearted for me to burden you with this business."

His kisses, which rained down upon my face, ought to have been enough to distract me, but something in the way he brushed my concerns aside made me insist, "You *need* Mr. Madison. You brought the Constitution into existence together. And now you must govern together. You need him."

Hamilton's eyes gleamed with triumph. "I don't. I have the votes. Even without your papa in the Senate." More kisses trailed down my neck. "So, you see, I don't need Madison. Or Monroe. Or Jefferson. Or Burr. I don't need any of them."

His sense of power and confidence was a heady erotic thing, and I would be lying to say I didn't feel its intoxicating pull. In truth, my husband seemed drunk on it, turning me in his arms so that I was forced to brace myself against the table.

Then he raised my skirts.

What he wanted, I knew. I wanted it, too.

It was not only out of a reluctance for more children that I stopped him. I told myself it was also a concern for decency, that he should try to make love in the middle of the day. But there was something else, too—an instinct that he was attempting to master me, and not only for mutual pleasure. I felt suddenly as if, in bending me over this table, I stood in place of all the other frustrations and obstacles in his way.

A part of me wished to give in, to be for him a relief and comfort.

Certainly, it was my duty as a wife to do so.

But I felt some inexplicable assault to my dignity to be taken this way, by him, in such a mood. *I don't need any of them.* There was a recklessness in his words that I felt in his hands, and both unleashed a foreboding in my heart that I wished I'd better heeded.

So I turned him away.

And perhaps if I hadn't, everything would have been different.

⌒

*February 1791*
*Philadelphia*

"I won't be coming to bed tonight," Alexander said, scarcely looking up from his desk.

He'd been gruff since the afternoon I rebuffed his advances—as if no woman had ever refused him anything before. Or perhaps it was simply that he assumed his wife never would.

"In truth, I doubt I'll come to bed any night this week," he added. He had an excuse in that President Washington had given him only a week to write up an argument for the necessity and constitutionality of a national bank. "The president knows perfectly well the necessity," my husband had fumed. "Yet he's allowed the Virginians to shake his resolve."

It seemed, to me, that it was my husband who was shaken.

By Mr. Jefferson, most of all.

Though our tall Virginian secretary of state spoke eloquently about the ideals of liberty, he was proving to be a stubborn opponent of any *practical* reforms. "He's a landed aristocrat who waxes poetic about the virtues of the common man," Hamilton complained. "Which might be admirable did he not do it seated in his whirligig chair, sipping the finest wine his inherited wealth can buy, toasting French rioters who shout, 'Death to the rich.'"

My husband didn't trust men who spoke of the glory of the revolution without having fought in it. Even Madison had volunteered, briefly, in the militia. But soldier or not, Mr. Jefferson was a formidable foe whose strengths were my husband's weaknesses.

Jefferson knew how to employ a wise silence and patience.

Meanwhile, my husband took too much for granted that he would have everything his way. He'd even taken for granted his own staggering capacity for hard work. For in writing *The*

*Federalist,* he'd drawn strength from the collaboration; he'd pushed through his own exhaustion and agonies because he had Madison to commiserate and suffer alongside him. He'd had Madison's intellect to challenge him and Madison's friendship to encourage him.

But now he worked alone, almost as if to punish himself for having allowed anyone to share his burdens. As if to remind himself of the stern lesson of his childhood: he ought never trust or depend upon anyone.

Which was why, I think, he refused even my help, except to say, "Bring me a pot of strong coffee." Some nights, it was the only thing he said.

At least until, in exhaustion and defeat, he confessed that he wouldn't finish before the president's deadline—a thing that had never happened to him before.

I went to where he sat with shoulders bunched in pain and gently took the pen from his palsied hand. "Betsy, what are you doing?"

"Taking you to bed. In the morning, tell the president that you need another day, and I'll help you." He thanked me with loving gratitude. And when I helped him copy it out the next night, he said all the right words to make me believe he was sincere.

He convinced the president.

He got his bank.

But I think I sensed in him, even then, resentment. Resentment that he hadn't been able to do it himself. That he *did* need someone, even if it was me. And I believed that's why he sent me and the children away from the heat and bustle of Philadelphia that summer.

He insisted, actually. And in those days, my husband was not to be denied. Not by Congress, not by the president, and certainly not by me. I'd lived with the consequences of having done it once, and I didn't want to attempt it again. So I spent the summer with my father.

That summer.

*What did Eliza know?*

That's what everyone wonders. Though no one has ever had the gall to ask. If they did, I'd say I knew nothing. And remembered nothing. That it was all, entirely, beneath my notice. But now, questions bite at me like insects in the night.

Before I left for my father's house, was I there, at the table, slicing bread for my children to take on our journey when the woman came to our door with her sad story? Perhaps I was in the kitchen, setting a kettle to boil. I may have looked up over the wrought iron garden fence to wave to our Quaker neighbor, Dolley Todd, as she passed, and I glimpsed instead an ostentatious woman with golden curls.

To explain our unexpected visitor, surely my husband said, "Just a poor unfortunate woman. Abandoned. In desperate straits."

"And you sent her away?" I would have asked. "Is there nothing to be done to help her?"

"I'll see what I can do," he would have replied, kissing our children atop their heads. "But after dinner."

That's how it started, if the story he told was true. So banal a beginning it would have escaped my memory. But sometimes I fear that I don't remember it because it never happened the way he said it did. That it never happened that way at all . . .

# Chapter Twenty-Two

September 1791
Philadelphia

AFTER A BLISSFUL summer with my family in Albany, I returned to a new house. Situated just across the street from the president's mansion in Philadelphia, it was bigger and more majestic in every way with Corinthian pilasters, dentil molding, and arched windows. My new drawing room alone was twenty-five feet square, and Lady Washington's voice echoed in its empty confines. "How lovely."

It *was* lovely. It was also more than I thought we could afford on my husband's paltry government salary. But when I expressed this worry, Alexander said he'd take a loan from Angelica's husband, and that we must keep up appearances.

Perhaps Lady Washington agreed, because she leaned in to confide, "I shall be so grateful for you to entertain here, in my place."

"I could never take your place," I said.

Though I knew she was weary and longed for the quiet solitude of Mount Vernon when she confided, "They call me the first lady in the land and think I must be extremely happy, but they might more properly call me the chief state prisoner."

I laughed. "Then I certainly would not *wish* to take your place, even if I could."

A sparkle came to her eye. "Oh, but you're too young to deny yourself the pleasure. When I was your age, I enjoyed the innocent gayeties of life. Thanks to the kindness of our numerous friends, my new and unwished-for situation is not too much a burden. That is why I am delighted we are closer neighbors. With a little bit of furnishing, this fine new house shall become the social center of the city."

Should that prove true, I would rise to the occasion. I'd learned from my mother how to set a fine table and behave with decorum. I'd learned from my sister how to dress and to flatter. I now knew how to preside over a grand salon, and Hamilton expected no less from me.

"It will need lights," I said, fretfully, hoping that my sister could send me elegant chandeliers and torchères from London. Rustic lights and lanterns would not do for the secretary of the treasury, for whom our previous abode had become suddenly unbearable. *Too small* for a growing family, my husband said. Too small for a man of his stature, he meant, a man whose portrait now hung in City Hall. A man whose department of government was growing every day, and whose power grew larger with it.

Certainly my husband's physical stature had become somewhat larger. Sedentary toil had taken its toll. But I rather liked the softer lines of Alexander's face, and the new weight of his arms around me, as if it somehow made his need for me more substantial. In truth, I liked it so well that when the winter's snow came, I wasn't surprised to discover I was again with child. And my husband startled at my suggestion for a name, should it be a boy. "*John?*"

"After your friend," I said, gently, hoping to please him. But instead of it drawing him closer to me, he stared into the distance. To prevent the complete retreat that any mention of John Laurens inevitably occasioned, I quickly added, "And after my brother-in-law. If Church brings Angelica home, I could forgive him everything. It cannot hurt to remind the man of his family bonds in America . . ."

Hamilton nodded, slowly. "Clever. I fear I have finally corrupted you and turned you into a politician."

"Never," I replied, for I was still sometimes too earnest for the insincerity and idle gossip that served as currency amongst politicians and their wives. I disliked immensely the game I called Who Is Out of Fashion, in which the ladies of the town seemed to collectively decide who must be shunned for some embarrassing faux pas, exaggerated sleight—or even for wearing the wrong gown. Lady Washington's dignity was such that she transcended the game, and my dear Hamilton teased that I was too much of an angel to know the rules. But I *did* know the rules of the game. I just didn't wish to play.

Especially not now, when my husband was a man of fraying nerves.

Darting in and out of the house for meetings at irregular hours. Short-tempered with the children—even the girls, whom he doted on. If I didn't know his urgency about the country's business—and a vengeful obsession with keeping Aaron Burr from running for governor of New York—I might have suspected something nefarious afoot.

Especially when, one afternoon in December of 1792, my husband advised me not to answer the door to strangers when he wasn't at home. "Are we in some danger?" I asked.

Snapping open a gazette, Alexander said, "It's only that I have enemies in this city who would be happy to abuse my wife's ears. And you're too far gone with child to risk any unhappiness."

I didn't doubt that he had enemies. A new partisan newspaper had been started, with, as its sole aim, the destruction of my husband and his policies. And there were whispers that the paper was funded by none other than Mr. Jefferson, though I disbelieved he'd stoop to it.

All my husband's plans, all his schemes, were *working*—the promises of stability and prosperity finally being realized by our countrymen. And yet, the antifederalists saw in him some manner of corrupt, power-hungry upstart intent upon crushing the rights of our states and enriching the North at the South's expense. They used pseudonyms, but we knew the identity of at least one of the writers because perhaps no one else in the world had better cause to know Madison's writing than we did.

And it had crushed Hamilton's spirits to see our old friend's formidable pen turned against us. Still, I didn't fear little Jemmy Madison coming to my door to berate me. I couldn't even imagine such an absurdity, and if it came to pass I should have no difficulty driving him off with a frying pan. So I couldn't fathom my husband's fears. "You're sure it's not more than that? When loyalists came to abduct Papa, we were better off for having been forewarned. If I should need to fear a tomahawk splintering our stair rail, I'd rather you tell me."

Hamilton grimaced, as if not realizing I was making a jest. "Just don't open the door to strangers."

*December 12, 1792*
*Philadelphia*

I shouldn't be able to remember the chill in my bones that wintry night. Or the little mewling cries of my newborn, who awakened me for milk. But I do remember. I remember how I climbed from our bed and took the candle into the nursery—only to find my daughter Ana already there, staring out the window that overlooked the street.

"Bad men are coming to get us, Mama," she whispered, standing at the window. With a freckled nose and dark auburn hair, she was an imaginative child who invented beautiful songs and countless ways to amuse herself. But like her father, she was easily agitated.

"Why are you awake, my darling? No one is coming. It's only your dreams." I shooed her back to bed before I saw them—

two shadowy men lingering across the way near the president's house.

They stooped in the darkness against a low brick wall, the light of a lantern between them, their breaths puffing into the air. Then a newcomer joined—a lady—though no woman of good reputation would be on the streets alone with two men at this hour. They bent their heads, motioning toward our house.

Then these plotters, these obvious ne'er-do-wells, sent her, a slender slip of a thing, to climb our icy stairs and rap at our front door.

*Don't open the door to strangers.*

Still cradling our babe, I remembered my husband's admonition. And a shudder ran through me as I realized how easily he might be lured outside by a young woman pretending at distress. Rushing to our room, I found Alexander already donning a robe.

"Don't answer," I said, hurriedly telling him what I'd seen.

"I'm sure it's nothing," he replied, retrieving a pistol—one I hadn't guessed he kept in a drawer by the bed until that very moment. "But I will be cautious."

I stood at the landing, listening as he made some low murmuring answer to the woman at the door, sending her away. But when he didn't come back up, I went down to find him seated on the bottom stair, his head in his hands.

I went to him, filled with dread. "What is it? What's happened?" I took his hand. That's when I realized he was cold, his fingers gone to ice, and given his obvious torment, I could do nothing but guess. Good news did not come in the dead of night.

Remembering how learning of John Laurens's death had so devastated Alexander, I could only imagine the news was of a similar nature now. So I feared it was Lafayette, another brother-at-arms, who last we'd heard, awaited execution in a prison. Contrary to Mr. Jefferson's sunny predictions, the French Revolution had taken a very dark turn. A political faction calling themselves Jacobins had somehow seized the reins of government, arrested the French king, and condemned Lafayette as a traitor. Our French friend had fled France but had been captured and imprisoned in neighboring Austria, last we heard.

"Is he dead?" I asked, my throat tightening with emotion as I knelt beside my husband, preparing for bitter grief. For a time, it had seemed as if we could save Lafayette. My husband supported the president's effort to formally request Lafayette's release. Our ambassadors—William Short and Gouverneur Morris—tried to negotiate his freedom. In London, Angelica recruited rescuers to break Lafayette out of prison. Even Secretary Jefferson discovered a loophole by which payment for Lafayette's war service could be sent for the upkeep of his family. Lafayette was the one thing all American factions agreed upon, but now I feared all efforts to save him had failed. "Has he been executed?"

"Who?" Alexander asked, blankly.

"The marquis," I said, as much bewildered as relieved. "Have you received news?"

"Bad news," he said. "But not of Lafayette. There is something I must tell you, my angel." I nodded, steeling myself, even as relief flooded through me that it was no bad news about our friend, and I hoped he still survived. "There's been a fraud in the Treasury Department involving stolen war pensions."

I let out a breath, for it was merely a government matter, though why such a thing would be communicated in the mid-night and by a woman at that, I couldn't imagine. "How terrible. I hope the culprits may be prosecuted to the full extent."

"They won't be," Alexander replied, his voice now as shaky as his hands. "Three of Mr. Jefferson's partisans have, as a consequence of this, begun an investigation into my conduct."

"*Your* conduct?" I asked, stunned. My husband's gaze fell away. He tried to speak, but from that notoriously eloquent mouth, came naught but silence. In the hurry to put together a Treasury Department, my husband had trusted the wrong people. His former assistant had only recently been thrown into debtors' prison for speculation schemes, setting off a financial panic. Now, some corrupt clerk had stolen government documents right under Alexander's nose. "They're going to blame you."

Hamilton glanced at me, then away again. "They'll blame me for the fraud and for anything else they can lay at my doorstep. Speculation. Corruption. These are the charges." Suddenly my husband leaped to his feet, pacing, while I tried to rub the chill from my arms. "And Jefferson's paper once called *me* a cowardly assassin who strikes in the night!"

I thought to quiet him so as not to wake the children, but it was better to see him angry than anguished. Better by far. My husband was quite possibly the most combative man I knew, and if he was ready to fight, he would win. "Have a word with Madison," I suggested. "Whatever your disagreements, he knows your character and—"

"Madison is my *personal* and political enemy now," Alexander insisted. "To think I once mistook him as being naive, but incorruptible. The sort of man who has so many slaves at his beck and call that he's seldom had to so much as wipe himself clean in the privy."

"That's hardly fair," I said. I knew he was angry with Madison; I was, too. But I didn't want to believe we were *enemies*.

"Isn't it? Madison has fallen entirely under the spell of Jefferson's utopian philosophies. Either that, or Madison has always been a facile, deceitful little man. He won't help me."

At a loss as to what else to do, I followed my husband into his study, where broken feather pens littered his desk and an untidy stack of books made me feel a neglectful housekeeper. My hands to my face, I shook my head. "Alexander, none of this makes any sense. Why would a woman come to the house in the middle of the night to tell you this?"

On a groan, he braced against the top of his desk. "They must have believed it was the only way I'd open the door."

I heard what he said, but his explanation only added to my

confusion. "But why would they use a woman to communicate the charges? Who are these investigators?"

"Monroe is one," Hamilton answered, bitterly.

Well, that was some good news. Whatever the other Virginians might do, Monroe had fought in the war beside my husband. "He'll exonerate you when he finds no evidence of wrongdoing. He might chastise you for hiring scoundrels, but he'll see you're not guilty."

*Guilty.* That word made my husband wince. Why should that be? He wasn't guilty. He couldn't be guilty. Not my honorable husband. He could never be involved in a scheme to cheat soldiers' families and defraud the treasury. And yet, he stared bleakly out the frosted window onto the now-empty street.

"Alexander, tell me you had nothing to do with these swindlers . . ."

I expected he'd fly into high dudgeon at the mere suggestion. At the very least, he should have turned to shout *Good God, woman, is that what you think of me?* But instead, to my increasing dread, the man who was almost never at a loss for words still said nothing.

The bottom of my stomach fell away. I could not—*would not*—believe that my husband would steal from the treasury, for even if he were such a knave, such a blackguard, he was a man of such brilliance and easy financial connections that he could find a thousand untraceable ways to make a fortune. Yet, in the back of my mind, a treasonous thought lingered.

*Is this why he thought we could afford a new and bigger house?*

All at once, my husband said my name with another groan. "Betsy. My God, what have I done?" With that, he sank to his knees, pressing his cheek against my belly in supplication, and I felt heartsick. What *had* he done? To see my husband—my strong, proud husband, who could face bayonets and cannon fire—on his knees before me was too much.

Not knowing what else to do, I stroked his hair.

And then, to my horror, he wept. "I'm sorry, so sorry . . ."

"Oh, no, Alexander." Tears pricking at my eyes in a panic, I insisted, "You didn't betray your country. You couldn't."

"I didn't betray my country." He made fists of my sleeping gown as he rasped, "I betrayed you."

It all came out then, in a pleading, impassioned confession. As if he were arguing before judge and jury. But I heard it as if through a tunnel, as if I'd floated away and watched us from a distance. A woman had come to our door more than a year ago with a tale of woe, abandoned by an abusive husband and left in a strange city with her little daughter. A story tailor-made to appeal to my husband's sensibilities. My husband—the bastard of just such an abandoned woman. My husband, the special patron of orphaned children.

Suddenly, the woman sent to our door made much more sense . . .

"It was a trap," he explained, his eyes imploring me. "My enemies must've known I would feel pity for her circumstances. This woman, this Maria Reynolds, she pleaded for money, just enough to return to her Livingston relations in New York."

The Livingstons. Kitty's family was somehow a part of this?

"I took her for a respectable lady," Alexander continued. "At least, until I delivered the money to her at her house, where she led me to her bedroom and—"

"Oh God," I murmured, a wave of nausea washing over me. How had it taken me this long to understand what he was confessing?

Adultery. He was confessing adultery.

Sweet, saintly, stupid Betsy.

*Look hard enough and there's always a woman,* my sister had said. And I'd dismissed it, smugly refusing to believe anything or anyone could ever come between us. Now, Hamilton looked up with tears in his eyes. "My darling, please—"

"Oh God," I said again, jerking away from the grip of his hands. Hands that I'd supposed to have touched only me since we'd wed.

*His hands, his lips, his . . .*

He clutched me like a drowning man, still explaining. "Mr. Reynolds discovered his wife's infidelity and threatened to tell you if I didn't pay him."

He kept talking and talking now. But I could scarcely hear a word because my mind whirled in a tornado of questions and confusion.

*Was Maria Reynolds beautiful? Even Angelica agreed that Alexander appreciated beautiful art, beautiful furniture, beautiful music. My husband had an eye for beauty in everything. Oh God, was that Mrs. Reynolds who'd been at our door just now?*

"Betsy, you must believe me," Hamilton pleaded. "It was done by design to tempt me."

He wanted some answer of me. Some reply. But I was too much in a daze. Too lost in a barrage of brutal imaginings.

*Did he kiss the back of her neck, the way he kissed mine? Did she smell of sweet perfume or a lustful feminine musk instead of milk and sweat and motherhood like me?*

Hamilton finally rose and pressed his forehead to mine. "You must say something, my angel. If only to condemn me for the sinner I am. You must say something."

But I said nothing at all. Because words were his weapon; silence was mine. And he couldn't win an argument if I didn't start one.

Instead, in agony, I slipped from his grasp and seemed to float up the stairs, light and insubstantial, as if I meant nothing to anyone. Not even myself. I'd been the woman Alexander Hamilton chose to love and was, therefore, of consequence in the world.

What was I now?

*Inconsequential.*

If this story was true. If it was real and not some nightmare. I couldn't shake myself awake, but perhaps if I went back to sleep . . .

And so I scooped our newborn baby into my arms, and

crawled back into bed. But then, I got back up and turned the key in the lock to keep my husband out.

~

"*BETSY*." KNOCKING FOLLOWED. "Please open the door."

The humility in my husband's voice—a voice that was never humble—told me it was no dream or nightmare. And in any case, I hadn't slept. For that matter, neither had he. He'd been calling quietly for several hours now. And I'd been pretending not to hear. I couldn't bear to see him.

The only person I wanted to see was Angelica. The only person I could tell. The only person who would understand and keep my secret. Could I go to her? Simply wander in my sleeping gown to the docks and sail across the sea to my sister's arms? I supposed that was a fantasy. Much like the life I'd been living, believing in a man who'd betrayed me. This man who'd allowed me to believe that I knew him so intimately.

He was a stranger.

It was only after nursing the baby, passing water into a chamber pot, and washing my hands and face that I finally unlocked the bedroom door to find Hamilton there, his eyes bloodshot.

"Well?" I asked, wondering what he could possibly have to say for himself.

"I must dress," he whispered, apologetically. "I have an early appointment."

Of course he did. Alexander Hamilton was a very important man. And I was just a betrayed wife. The business of the government, and his all-important administration, would go on. So, I sat at the edge of the bed, careful not to disturb our sleeping son, and watched my husband dress.

At the appearance of his strong, well-formed arms—his naked torso as he stripped off his sleeping garments—I felt a stab of renewed pain. He was still as handsome as he'd been as a young officer; perhaps more so now, with a little gray at his temples, wearing a mantle of gravitas. Any woman would want him. Every woman *did* want him. And once, at least, he'd wanted them back, an instinct I'd been naive enough to believe love and piety held at bay in the dozen years since we'd taken our vows.

Now I couldn't stand the sight of him, so my gaze fell to our son. "Was her child there when you made love to her?"

We both startled at my question, for I hadn't meant to speak. And I doubt those were the words he'd expected to hear from me. "Dear God, Betsy, it wasn't *love*. I've told you—"

"You said she had a daughter," I broke in, unwilling to allow him to make a jury argument. "Where was the child when you went to this woman's bed?"

A flush of scarlet crept up his bared chest. "The child was sleeping behind a curtain. You must understand it was a very squalid little apartment, to give the impression . . ." He trailed off, perhaps realizing that the picture he painted didn't make a better case. "It was a sin." He knew adultery was against the laws of God. I'd be lying to say that the sin against the Lord pained me more than the sin against me.

But I didn't feel worthy enough, in this moment, to think his crimes against me merited notice. For he'd made true every ugly bit of gossip I'd ever heard or read about in the papers, and they all rushed back to me now.

*"He's a ginger tomcat. I doubt I'm the only lady to which he has pleaded, but the war . . ."*

*"He'll surrender his sword to any pretty girl who wants it. Three by my count in the last month alone . . ."*

*"He will not be bound by even the most solemn of all obligations! Wedlock."*

I'd prided myself on being such a practical woman, but I suppose I must've been a dreamer to believe that ours was a marriage of true hearts. And now, as all my illusions were most cruelly stripped away, I found that I couldn't ask the questions I wanted to ask for fear of the answers.

*Is she prettier? More interesting? Do I not satisfy him? Had I* ever *satisfied him? Was it only the one time? Was it only the one woman?*

I'd be a fool to ask. And I didn't want to be a fool ever again.

"They want to ruin me with this, Betsy." He sat beside me. "They can't win an argument against me. They can't win a vote against me. So they used the only true weakness I have. *You.*"

As if I were the liability! I gave an indignant little snort. "I mean nothing to you."

He winced. "Never say it. You're my angel. My beloved—"

"I'm not *beloved*," I hissed, lurching off the bed, away from him.

"You *are*," he insisted, coming to take my chin and forcing me to look at him. "It would never have come to this if I didn't love you, after all."

I quite nearly slapped his hand away. Was he blaming me? I was struck with a memory of the time I refused him when he bent me over the table. Of nights I'd been tired, or suffered a headache, or was preoccupied with the children. A wife had a duty to satisfy her husband's needs, and this I'd apparently not done. But the only thing worse than to hear him blame me now would be to accept the blame.

I simply refused.

Faced with my quiet, defiant fury, he reached to tuck a tendril of hair behind my ear, but I flinched, and he dropped his hand. "Betsy. They could never have blackmailed me if it weren't for my love for you. Your happiness is most dear to me. How could I, but with extreme pain, wish to afflict you with this confession?"

"The confession is not what afflicts me."

He cleared his throat. "You're the only person I dread to disappoint. If Reynolds had threatened me with *death*, I'd have faced it more manfully than the specter of hurting you. To prevent that, I would have paid nearly any price."

"I don't believe you," I whispered, seething.

"Yes, you do," Hamilton said. "And you must forgive me."

"Oh, must I?" The look I gave him should've turned him to stone.

Somehow, it did not. "I surrendered to temptation, and I ask your forgiveness. Remember, Betsy, that you are a Christian . . ."

That he should dare throw that in my face!

Yes, God commanded forgiveness. Perhaps that should've been enough to soften my heart and resign me to the difficulties of this marriage that I'd undertaken in the Lord's name. But it wasn't. Wrapping my arms around myself, as if to guard from the chill in my own voice, I asked, "Would you forgive me if I surrendered to such temptation?"

He reeled back like a man kicked by a horse. It was a moment before he could even muster the composure to argue. "An unfaithful husband cannot be compared to an unfaithful wife, whose actions cast doubt on the legitimacy of their children. And what man would—"

He stopped, abruptly, before he said worse.

But I had a suspicion as to what he'd been thinking, and rounded on him. "If you think I've not had need of avoiding the affections of other men, I disabuse you of that notion now."

"No, no, of course that is not—" His color deepening, he interrupted himself to ask, "What men? Name these men who have pressed affections on my wife and I shall call them out!"

"Call them out?" I laughed, darkly. "You, prostrate with your own crimes, shall call for a duel of *honor*?"

Our voices awakened the baby, who gave a stretch and half-hearted cry before settling again.

My husband was too clever a man not to realize his blunder but was too hot-tempered to retract. Instead, he took me by the arms and gave me a little shake. "Let us reach an understanding, you and I. You would never betray me, Betsy. It isn't in you. But I would forgive you if you did. Do you understand? I'd forgive you *anything*, so long as you loved me. For love is the power that binds us. That, and our children, and the life we have together."

*I'd forgive you anything, so long as you loved me.*

He'd turned upon me the full blaze of his extraordinary blue eyes. The heat of his body. The power of his charisma and an appeal to our love, and yet, I whispered, "I don't believe you."

His grip tightened. "You do believe me. I've caused you pain, but I love you. Deep in your heart, you know it's true."

What did that matter? My heart, after all, had proved to be an untrustworthy instrument. The only thing I could rely upon was my head and cold, hard reason. And so I asked, "What price did you pay? You said you paid the man. How much?"

He swallowed hard and stared a long moment. "Just over a thousand dollars."

Nearly a third of his income in any given year. A sum so shocking that I pushed his hands away. "Please tell me, at the very least, it was your own money," I bit out.

"God. Of course. I couldn't bear for you to find out, Betsy. Would a man who did not love you pay so much?"

He meant this to be a branch for me to cling to while I drowned in humiliation. I grasped at it, only for my sanity. "Well, now I know. So, they have nothing more to hold over you."

He blanched. "They do. That's why he was at the door last night. Reynolds has been released from jail, but if I don't get him clear of the fraud charges, he'll tell a story to the investigators. I cannot do what he wishes, but I will meet with him this morning and persuade him to keep quiet anyway."

*Now we come to the real reason for this confession*, I thought. *He's been forced to it.*

For there was, indeed, something Hamilton dreaded more than my discovery of his infidelity, and that was an end to his administration. He believed that in these early years of the American experiment, faith in him was the same as faith in the government he served.

That if Hamilton was thought to be corrupted, the system he built would collapse.

Alas, I couldn't say that he was wrong.

Now, spent of his confessions, my husband eased himself back upon the bed and nestled our baby boy in his arms. Stroking

Johnny's peach-fuzz head, Hamilton whispered, "I know I've done wrong, Betsy. Even if you forgive me, I cannot forgive myself for risking that our children be thought the descendants of a thief who stole from the country he was entrusted to defend. I have only ever wished to give my sons an honorable name in which to take pride . . ."

*An honorable name.* It's all my husband ever wanted. And when his father hadn't given it to him, he made one for himself out of nothing but sweat and courage.

Now that name belonged to our children. And should our children suffer for their father's sins?

Though I should be weeping, in that moment I was too numb to fall to pieces. For a long moment, my head was a maelstrom of confusion. But then, clarity stole through. "You cannot rely on your blackmailer to keep quiet. Better to summon the investigators, tell them the truth, and throw yourself upon their mercy, as gentlemen, to keep your private failings in confidence."

"Summon them *here*?" Hamilton's eyes flew open. "With you and the children . . ."

I nodded, swallowing over fury and pain. "Invite them into our home. Let them see me and your little ones. Remind them who will pay the price for wagging tongues."

As if apprehending what I'd have to endure, he groaned. "I couldn't ask you to do this for me."

"Good thing, because I would not do it for you."

I would do it for my children.

It was, after all, the only wise, politic choice.

And Alexander Hamilton had, at long last, made me a politician.

# Chapter Twenty-Three

R EYNOLDS. REYNOLDS. REYNOLDS.

As I kneaded dough, I couldn't get the name out of my head, sure I could place it. Maria Reynolds was a harlot, my husband insisted. A woman whose husband prostituted her. A woman beneath my contempt. I imagined her as a dainty sparrow of a thing. The kind who might flutter about, as if with a broken wing in need of tending. Ought I do the same when the investigators came to my house?

I was broken in earnest. Heartbroken. And perhaps, if I showed that heartbreak, it would evoke sympathy. Or perhaps it would subject me to their laughter.

*James Monroe would never laugh at me,* I thought. In loyalty to my husband, I'd never attempted to untangle or name my feelings for Monroe or his for me—but I'd always believed our connection to be deeper and more complicated than friendship. Monroe was the first man to stir romantic feelings in my breast—a man with whom I felt a kinship in wanderlust and passion for the cause.

He would have never broken my heart. Nor would have Tench Tilghman, for that matter. If I'd made a match with either of them—good soldiers, solid gentlemen with respectable upbringings and a concern for morality—I wouldn't be suffering this now.

But I'd chosen *Alexander Hamilton.*

A fact I reminded myself of as I methodically scraped the loaf of sugar for a confection I couldn't taste, for the world had become devoid of flavor. I could scarcely see color, which made it a trial to choose what to wear. If I wore something dark and plain, would the investigators feel sorrier for me? Or perhaps I should wear my gauzy white dress, the one that left less of my body to the imagination, so they'd think my husband a fool for betraying me.

I was never a beauty. It was only that, until a few days ago, Alexander had made me feel like one. Now I felt like nothing.

That night the investigators came to my house, just as I'd suggested. Two legislators I knew by name only, a treasury official, and James Monroe. While my girls played by the fireplace with their new toys—brought by Sinterklaas in burlap sacks days before—I welcomed the men into the house with a plate of rye-flour *pepernoot* cookies, fragrant with cinnamon, anise, and clove.

"Compliments of the season," Monroe drawled, with a very formal bow that seemed somehow at odds with his brown hunting boots and the black tricorn beaver felt hat that was swiftly going out of style. Meanwhile, my boys ran about like rowdies, led by a laughing, taunting ten-year-old Philip, pelting one another with extra *pepernoot* they'd stolen from the kitchen, which was not strictly the custom. But I was too weary to take a firm hand with them, especially when I had grown men to manage.

"Coffee?" I asked Monroe, forcing a smile.

"What else?" Monroe chuckled softly, as if a little abashed to be upon this errand. And as if, perhaps, he thought I didn't know why he'd come. Clearing his throat, he said, "Mrs. Monroe sends her warm regards."

"And I return mine. I hope to see your wife and your darling little daughter at a holiday tea after church this Sunday." Monroe's smile warmed so I added, "We've come such a long way from an army campfire, haven't we, Senator Monroe?"

"Indeed we have. How young, hopeful, and idealistic we were . . ."

"I am still hopeful," I said, filling his cup to the brim just as bitterness filled me up inside.

Once I'd finished serving refreshments, Alexander stood, ready to furnish all the information they could require to acquit him of a crime—receipts of his blackmail payments, I assumed—so I retired from the room and kept the children quiet upstairs.

It was quiet downstairs, too. Maddeningly so. I didn't know what to make of it, especially when the men remained closeted together much longer than I thought necessary. Indeed, the interview seemed to go on and on until I grew weary watching the hands on our grandfather clock move.

When, at last, I heard the scrape of chair legs on wood—the sound of a meeting reaching its end—I hastened downstairs again. Alexander should have seen the men off. But I'd persuaded him that I should be the one to do it. And so I forced myself to say a kindly and proper farewell.

Given what my husband had just told them, I wasn't surprised that the investigators whom I didn't know well couldn't meet my eyes. But James Monroe's face burned scarlet at the sight of me and he lingered in the doorway long after the others departed, a sheaf of papers under his arm.

With a shake of his head, he began to stammer. "I— Mrs. Hamilton—Betsy . . ."

It'd been a long time since he used my name with that soft southern drawl. The intimacy of it seemed somehow improper. But the sound of it carried genuine sympathy. Oh, why had I feared the men's laughter instead of their pity? Pity was worse. Far worse. Especially from him.

Though I wanted to flee, I somehow made myself stand there and say, "I trust you're satisfied with my husband's innocence on the charge of corruption?"

Monroe's color deepened, if that was possible, at the word *innocence*. In fact, he cast such a bloody-minded look in the direction of the study that I feared it'd all gone badly. "Secretary Hamilton has provided me with exculpatory documentation and we will not make any report to the president at this time. I believe your husband will acknowledge that our conduct toward him has been fair and liberal—and that he could not complain of it."

Oh, Alexander *would* complain of it. But he should be grateful for Monroe, who actually cared whether or not he complained. And I could see that Monroe cared very much.

"Mrs. Hamilton, please believe that I wish you every happiness."

Monroe had flushed at the word *innocence*, but I now blanched at the word *happiness*. He noticed and all pretense fell away. Either I was no good at pretense, or he knew me well enough to realize that I was aware of my husband's infidelity.

"You are a kind, lovely, and charming woman and you deserve much better than—"

"Pray don't say another word," I whispered, wilting with humiliation. Why did I think I could do this? Why did I think I was strong enough? To my horror, tears welled before I could blink them away. "I should plead for your discretion as a gentleman on behalf of my husband, but in truth, I beg of you, for myself—"

"Dear God, to see you cry," Monroe said, setting down the papers and reaching inside his sleeve for an embroidered kerchief, which he offered me at once. "Insofar as is in keeping with my duty, the papers will remain *sealed*. As will my lips, for your sake. You have my word of honor."

His kerchief smelled faintly of tobacco and pine and I let out a tiny sob into it full of relief and sorrow. It would be better if no one knew what Hamilton had done. No one. Not my friends. Not my parents. Not even Angelica, for such things could never be entrusted to a letter across the ocean. So the only person to whom I could confide was James Monroe.

"The tears will pass," I said, trying for bravery. "It's only the lingering shame."

"Not *your* shame," Monroe said, his fists tightening, as if he meant to turn, march back into my husband's study, and beat him.

"Nevertheless, I don't know how I can bear it."

Monroe didn't have to be told how society looked upon a wife who wasn't enough to satisfy her husband.

*Not enough. Not enough. Not enough.*

As these words battered my insides, I felt undone. Quite low. Indescribably miserable.

Vulnerable in every way.

And so I was grateful when, with exquisite chivalry, Monroe drew my hand to his lips for a gentlemanly kiss. "The girl I met in Albany who could gamely drink some poison concoction without complaint, play a ruthless game of backgammon, and set off into the wilds in a sleigh—that girl could bear anything."

"That girl is long gone."

"She's still here," Monroe said, offering a tender smile and pressing my hand, for just a moment, to his heart. "Where she will always reside. My dear friend, I've held on to those memories, and I urge you to hold on to them, too."

My breath evened at the unexpected intimacy, at the strong pulse beneath my palm, at the knowledge that there were paths in my life I had not taken and the glimmer of hope that even if I couldn't see past my own sadness now, there might still be new paths to discover. "Thank you," I whispered.

Monroe nodded, gravely. "Your husband is the luckiest of men, and I hope, at long last, he realizes it." He didn't need to give me that one small bit of flattery; perhaps he shouldn't have. But it was a mercy, and it gave me the strength to dry my tears. When I was composed again, I found a plate for him, covered in a white linen napkin. "Pastries for Mrs. Monroe."

He smiled when our fingers brushed lightly as he took the plate. "Perhaps we can all share them together in more sociable circumstances."

Alas, there would never be more sociable circumstances for us. Not ever again.

*April 1793*
*Philadelphia*

*Vive la République!*

While I made my way through the crowds, church bells rang, cannons blasted, and Philadelphians sang in honor of the French, who had outlawed the monarchy, beheaded their king, and now found themselves at war with Great Britain.

In spite of our old treaty with France, President Washington had declared American neutrality in this war, but everywhere I went, my countrymen took up the cry of our old allies.

*Vive la République!*

On this day, the celebration was for the arrival of a frigate the French had taken from the British. Upon her coming into sight, thousands and thousands of the yeomanry of the city crowded the wharves and, when the British colors appeared reversed, the French flying above them, people burst into peals of exultation.

But I wasn't in this squalid part of Philadelphia to celebrate.

I'd come for a less dignified reason, one that wisdom should have cautioned me against. In the aftermath of my husband's betrayal, I'd spent a dark miserable winter on my knees in prayer. Now springtime had stolen upon me, insulting me with its showy, colorful, perfumed glory.

And I had to see her.

I had to see Maria Reynolds.

*Men stray*, my sister Angelica would've told me. I could hear her words as if she were standing beside me, warning me to leave off this nonsense. *It's in their nature. You're making too much of it. Your husband still loves you, and you're lucky to have him!*

Certainly, since Hamilton's midnight confession, he'd been solicitous, sharing in the care of the children, staying home at night, and sheepishly turning down meetings with colleagues in deference, he said, to his *growing and hitherto too much neglected family.*

But in recent weeks, more confessions had spilled from his lips. It was not, as he'd first intimated, just one night with this woman. For nearly a *year* he'd gone to her bed, and I, the trusting fool, had never suspected. And when I demanded to know why he'd not simply told me everything all at once, he said, "*I thought you might take easier to a thing if it was gradually broken to you, my angel.*"

Which left me to wonder what other painful revelations remained.

I knew my husband regretted this woman. I also knew most wives overlooked infidelity. Only a select few divorced. But in New York State, adultery was the only grounds upon which a woman *could* seek a divorce. And I will not say I didn't flirt with the thought at night, in our now very cold bed.

But to what end? It wouldn't undo the pain. And who would I be if I wasn't Alexander Hamilton's wife? Weeping into the kerchief Monroe had pressed into my hand while offering comfort and strength, I felt as much a stranger to myself as Hamilton was now to me. I scarcely spoke to my husband, beyond that which was necessary for the children's sake. And I felt too exhausted to care for my own dignity. The need to see Maria Reynolds became a compulsion—perhaps as powerful as the one that led my husband to her in the first place.

Which was how, after a few discreet inquiries, I found myself at the corner, near the public square, staring up at Maria's window in the house she shared with men it would be too kind to characterize as genteel boarders. Her curtains had been thrown back, allowing me to watch her brush her long hair. *Fair* hair. Would it have been better if she'd been a brunette?

Maria was beautiful. Young. And, overtaken with some sort of madness, I meant to confront her. I would shame her—make her feel the shame I felt. I would demand to know why she'd hurt my family and wrecked my happiness. Pushing through the crowds, I marched up the stairs to her weathered, red-painted door.

But as I reached for the knocker, the dark spell was broken by the laughter of a little girl coming from her window. *Her daughter.* A poor innocent child with an unfeeling father, a harlot for a mother, and no future whatsoever.

Oh, the folly in coming here! It crashed over me in another wave of shame.

To stoop to converse with a prostitute. To demean myself. If I couldn't forgive this, then I must forget it. Forget her. And be gone from this place before someone wondered what the wife of the treasury secretary was doing lingering near what must have been known as a bawdy house.

Unfortunately, it wasn't easy to leave. Not with the parading crowds. I was forced to combat the press of bodies, the scent of sweat, the indifferent shuffling of so many feet, vivid memories of the Doctors' Riots making me anxious. To break free of the crowd, I'm afraid I wielded my parasol with unladylike force, but there was no fighting the rush of so many.

*Vive la République! Vive la République! Vive la République!*

I was swept along the streets of Philadelphia for half a block before I was rescued—veritably plucked from a churning sea of people—by a very tall, freckled man in an exquisite French suit with fine lace cuffs. "Why, Mrs. Hamilton," Jefferson drawled, gently pulling me to the relative calm of the corner curbside where he stood with James Madison. "What a surprise to see you here . . ."

My heart sank. I could think of no two persons I should least like to have discovered me so near to Maria Reynolds. And my mind spun with a persecuted turn, not unlike my husband's. Hamilton had said that his political enemies lured him into the scandal, and I'd dismissed it as a paranoid and egotistical excuse. But if his foes learned of the affair, they might use it.

I wanted to trust that these Virginians were gentlemen—that they'd never serve us up to the public. But if my own husband couldn't be trusted, why should I trust anything? Or anyone?

"I—I was on my way home," I said, trying to catch my breath, hating the edge of fear in my voice, and unable to think of an able lie that would avert their suspicions. If they *had* suspicions.

By God, what a misery to think like Hamilton, wondering at some poison in every person's smile! I felt guilty for it when Madison offered me an arm with genuine concern. "Are you quite all right, Mrs. Hamilton?"

"Just alarmed by the crowds," I said.

The cultured Secretary Jefferson casually pressed his back against the bricks, as if he cared little for keeping his satin coat clean. From his lofty height, he surveyed the vista with eyes he shielded from the sun and pronounced, "There is no need for alarm, madam. Why, I think I spy your boy just across the way, having hoisted himself onto a barrel for a better view."

"My boy?" I asked, sure he was mistaken.

"Young Philip," he said, pointing. "There with my youngest daughter Polly. Perhaps we may make a match of them."

It was meant in jest. And yet, I didn't laugh. "My son should be at home."

Jefferson gave a sunny smile. "Ah, but it's too marvelous a day to be inside. The spirit of '76 is in the air."

The spirit of revolution, he meant. And I was struck with the impression that Jefferson still fancied himself a revolutionary in search of a tyrant to tear down instead of a statesman charged with a new government to build. Thus, with a meaningful look at Madison, I couldn't help retorting, "I prefer the spirit of '87."

That was the year we forged a Constitution, and I doubt Madison missed my meaning. "Either way," Jemmy replied. "A marvelous, celebratory day for the revolution."

He spoke of it as if it were ongoing. As if the French Revolution was a part of our own. And I knew I should have nodded politely and made chitchat about the weather. But nearly confronting Maria had left me agitated enough to say instead, "I'm afraid I cannot celebrate violence."

"Oh?" Madison asked, because inside that owlish head was a whirling brain that missed nothing. He knew that I *had* celebrated our soldiers, our war, our victories, and he probably thought me a rank hypocrite. "Despite the follies and barbarities in Paris, the French Revolution has been wonderful in its progress, and stupendous in its consequences."

He was wrong. The French Revolution was devolving into anarchy.

I knew—certainly I knew—not to argue with these men. Especially here and now. How often had I counseled my husband to govern his tongue? And yet now, unmoored by my anger at my husband, mine flew free. "It certainly *is* stupefying that a revolution inspired by our own should turn upon those who fought heroically in the cause of our freedom. Rochambeau and Lafayette both in prison."

At the mention of Lafayette, Jefferson's voice gentled and his clear blue eyes filled with sympathy. "Mrs. Hamilton, my own affections have also been deeply wounded by some of the martyrs to this cause. But the liberty of the whole earth depends on this contest. And rather than it should fail, I would see half the earth desolated. An Adam and an Eve left in every country, and left free, it would be better than it now is."

Though the season was not cold, gooseflesh rose on my arms. What a strange man to be so courtly, so charming—and so blithely condemn half the earth in pursuit of a philosophical ideal. Chilled to the bone by this remark, I glanced, disbelieving, at Jemmy Madison, who had the grace to wince.

As the crowds celebrated a new sister republic with a cannonade, all I could think of was the French king's downfall. This same king who'd come to our aid in the cause of independence. A king who'd put his fate into the hands of his people. The people who claimed to love him.

And he'd been cruelly betrayed.

I'd read in the papers that the French thronged to watch King Louis die, and cheered when the blade fell and severed his head. They stuffed the king, head and all, into a box. And, afterward, the peasants wanted cuttings of his hair, scraps of his shirt, anything to mount upon a mantelpiece as a trinket. The public wanted to *consume* him. Like the hounds of hell, they even knelt and lapped up the king's blood.

Here in America, some called that justice. And I couldn't help but shudder, because I wore round my neck a pendant with a trinket of George Washington's hair—a man who'd just been unanimously reelected to the presidency and sworn in for his second term but was now derided as a tyrant in the making. Perhaps even by these very gentlemen standing beside me on the street corner who I wanted to trust would never serve *us* up to a slavering public.

What a high-minded thing revolution had seemed when it started; but now I wondered if, in trying to bring about liberty, we'd instead opened the gates of endless war, bloodshed, and immorality.

"THEY'RE THROWING A ball for the French ambassador, *Citizen Genêt*," Lucy Knox huffed, perusing the lemon cake on Martha Washington's table before returning to her knitting. We Federalist ladies were always knitting, though I worried how easily it could all unravel.

A country. A reputation. A marriage . . .

We were discussing the French ambassador, who was recruiting troops to fight for France in defiance of President Washington's Proclamation of Neutrality. And radical Francophiles in our country encouraged it!

"Surely you're mistaken, Mrs. General Knox," Abigail Adams replied, peering over the length of her sharp nose. "These democrats wouldn't host a ball. A *ball* is too aristocratic. It's to be an *elegant civic repast* that just happens to be held in the city's largest ballroom where they're going to hand out liberty caps and sing '*La Marseillaise*.'"

The ladies laughed, except for Lady Washington and me. Because all I could think was that if French revolutionaries could kill a king and his ministers, Americans could kill a president and his treasury secretary . . .

Shrewdly eyeing the way my hands had stopped working my knitting needles, Abigail said, "Mr. Adams tells me we have our own Robespierres, but fortunately for us, they cannot persuade the people to follow them."

Thin-lipped, Lady Washington replied, "I'd never have guessed Vice President Adams to be such an optimist."

This *did* make me sputter with a laugh. A bitter one. Because the people seemed entirely persuadable, especially as so-called Democratic Clubs sprang up around Philadelphia based on the French Jacobin model. And I began to think nearly treasonous thoughts about this experiment with self-government. My husband couldn't even govern himself. Not when passion took him. What hope did the common citizenry have of making wise decisions for themselves?

My fears seemed justified when, a few weeks later, ten thousand people were in the streets of Philadelphia threatening to drag Washington from his house and force us to join France's war against England. Outside our door men shouted, "Down with Washington!"

They seemed to believe that by keeping America out of a costly foreign war, we were betraying our sister republic in France; that President Washington had turned his back on the values of the revolution. And I dared not go out, not even for church. Not when, clutching broadsheets depicting our president being sent to the guillotine, the mob screamed, "Enemies of equality: Reform or Tremble!"

Instead, I kept the curtains closed and read the Bible to the children upstairs where we'd gathered them, afraid and trembling, into our bed. Nearly nine years old, our daughter Ana was close to hysterical. Fanny, only a few months younger, sucked her thumb, as was her wont when she'd been a babe. While I rocked the littlest ones in my arms amongst a mountain of blankets Alexander had made for the boys, Ana cried, "Will they behead the president?"

"I will never let such a thing happen," Alexander reassured us, very gravely. "Not while I draw breath."

I knew that was true. But so, too, did anyone who wished to drag George Washington to the scaffold.

Which was why they would come for my husband first.

Having finally coaxed the children to sleep in our bed with their favorite Dutch stories of elves and river Nixie, Alexander and I retreated to the divan in the back parlor, where a few candles still sputtered in the braziers on the wall. The protesters would return at dawn, but now, in the blessed quiet, I asked, "Are you not weary of all this?"

"More than you can know. Truly this trade of a statesman is a sorry thing. But I cannot quit it. Otherwise, what's to become of our fame and glory?" He gave a wry grin, one of his most appealing. "How will the world go on without me? I am sometimes told very gravely that it could not."

He wanted me to laugh with him. But I didn't. It'd been his habit for months now to crawl into bed with one of the boys at night, claiming that their sleep was troubled or that he didn't want to wake me. This was the fiction—the polite lie—that allowed us to go on as if all was well. There was no intimacy between us now, and so I wanted no more lies, either.

"All you do is fight," I whispered. "You fight Jefferson, you fight Madison, and Burr. You fight the Jacobins, the Clintons, the Livingstons, the newspapers, the Congress, the French ambassador—"

"And I *beat* them," Alexander replied. "You mustn't fear, my love. I will defend you and the children to my last breath."

He said this with fierce devotion, leaning over to kiss me. And I could hear my sister say, *Ah, Betsy! How lucky you were to get so clever and so good a companion.*

But I whispered, "I could leave you."

I startled as if the words had come from someone else's mouth.

Hamilton startled, too, his eyes ablaze. "What?"

I straightened up, and this time I spoke clearly. "I could leave you." I'd scarcely allowed myself to acknowledge these thoughts much less speak them aloud, but now the words mutinied upon my tongue, beyond my command. "A divorce would be a scandal, but some society ladies quietly abandon their husbands if they have the means and inclination."

Perhaps Alexander hadn't believed his sweet, docile wife could contemplate such a thing because he paled. "Betsy, of all times to even muse—"

"Papa would take me back at the Pastures," I said, idly twisting the interlocked gold bands of my wedding ring as my voice gained strength. "And his grandchildren, too. I am not without options. There's only one thing that compels me to live with you, to cook your meals, to tend your house, to warm your bed. To admire your brilliance. To stay with you, at your side, even against a *mob*. And that one thing is a love you have sorely abused."

In a flash of temper, he snapped, "There is also the matter of marriage vows."

"Vows you failed to honor," I shot back.

My shot must have hit its mark, because he buried his guilty face in his hands. Still I gave him no quarter; he was, after all, the one who taught me that if blood must be drawn, you must strike at the most vulnerable place.

"You say you were lured to that woman's bed. Maybe you believe it. But I know better." His shoulders tensed, as if he would argue, but I stopped him with one word. "*Reynolds.*" I spit the name, dragging in a few ragged breaths. "I couldn't place it at first. It buzzed about like a gadfly, stinging me until at last I remembered, all those years ago, how you went to taverns seeking out the man who'd passed a slander about you . . ."

I stood up from the sofa, arms crossed over myself as I paced.

"*A nobody*, you said at the time. *A ne'er-do-well named James Reynolds*, from whom you could have no satisfaction. And yet, you wish me to believe it's only by happenstance that, years later, you fell into bed with that man's wife?"

Alexander colored. "How can you believe otherwise?"

"Because there's one thing I know about you." I whirled on him. "You never forget an offense. Maria Reynolds was the wife of a man upon whom you wished revenge. And a relation to the Livingstons, too. She was an opportunity to strike a blow against several enemies at once, so you took it. Never mind the blow you dealt me. As long as *you* had satisfaction."

A long silence followed. One so long that I didn't know whether to fear the chasm between us or welcome it. In the end, he denied nothing. "Betsy, I can never cease to condemn myself for this folly and can never recollect it without disgust, but you cannot wish to subject our children to a childhood of separation and insecurity."

His childhood, he meant. The one that had left him with these dangerous vulnerabilities and destructive compulsions.

But I wasn't the one to subject them to such a possibility, so I said, "I wouldn't wish that. Yet, in trying to cure you of your fear of abandonment, I've somehow convinced you that you may do and say *anything*, and your Betsy will stay loyally at your side. I convinced myself, too. But I think it better, in times like these, for us to acknowledge that marriage is a choice, one made, every day, anew. And trust me when I say I don't know which choice I shall make come morning."

# Chapter Twenty-Four

August 1793
Philadelphia

"BRING OUT YOUR dead!"

In the high stink of summer, when Philadelphia's out-houses overflowed gutters and dammed up alleys filled with trash, an outbreak of illness emptied the streets of rioters. An illness that may well have prevented the overthrow of the government. For now, instead of mobs shouting in front of our house, we heard only clacking carts carrying fly-bedeviled corpses.

Yellow fever.

The same horrible illness that had killed Jenny.

The fever started, they said, amongst the dock workers. They suffered chills and tremors that eventually gave way to black-ened, bloody vomit. The illness spread swiftly, with fatal effect and without known cure. People in good health one morning would drop dead the next day. In the hurry to stop the spread of the contagion by getting the victims into a grave, some were likely buried alive. And when vinegar-soaked handkerchiefs and garlic offered little safeguard against the disease, everyone who could flee the city did so.

Everyone, it seemed, but us.

As late summer turned to early autumn, Hamilton believed that the business of keeping the government going in the face of anarchy was more vital than ever. "Jefferson will make much of my supposed cowardice if I leave now. I have to set an example. If I flee, it will only increase the panic, which is depopulating the city and suspending business. But you and the children should go."

He looked away when he said this, his profile a study in agony. And I realized that he was giving me permission. Acknowledging my power to abandon him, as I had so recently threatened to do. All of it under the face-saving cover of exigency.

No one would blame me for leaving the capital at a time like this. And after the crisis had passed, we could say *Mrs. Hamilton simply can't abide Philadelphia, but the secretary visits his children at the Schuyler home from time to time . . .*

That's how it was done in high circles. Perhaps I could make that choice. Perhaps I *would* make that choice. But I was not ready to make it today. "We can rent a summer house a few miles outside the city," I suggested. "Close enough that you can return for work if need be." Encouraged by his nod of agreement, I added, "And I could ride with you, some days. Except for the few free blacks in the city who volunteered, nurses in Philadelphia cannot be had for any price. I'll help tend the sick."

"I cannot allow that. You're a mother with small children, and there's no known immunity to the disease."

Alas, he had no immunity to it either.

The next day, returning from his office at the treasury, he made it only two steps into the front door before falling to his knees and retching into a brass urn that normally held umbrellas. And at the head of the stairs, I nearly stumbled in an effort to get to him. "Alexander!"

We left that night by carriage, the children piled atop one another like cordwood. Hamilton followed on horseback at a distance, fevered and sick, his back throbbing with pain. We made it only as far as our rented summer house two and a half miles from town before he was in a near delirium.

*Please God don't let him die,* I prayed, a panic seizing me. Whatever our troubles, I couldn't bear for him to die. Perhaps *especially* because of our troubles, and all that remained unresolved between us. I sent straightaway for a physician who was, by happenstance, an old friend of my husband's from the West Indies.

"Am I done for, Neddy?" Hamilton asked Dr. Stevens. Glowing with fever, my husband complained of aches in his swollen kidneys.

"It's yellow fever," the doctor said. "Which means you may seem to get better, but that is the crucial time."

He didn't have to explain why. It was only after sufferers of this ailment seemed to recover that they would suddenly jaundice, spew blood and black vomit, and die. And so the doctor said to me, "Send the children far away. All of them. Even the baby."

I'd already sequestered the children in an adjoining house, bringing meals to the door and waving at the window, never letting them get close enough to spread the contagion. The mother in me refused the idea of sending my frightened children away in such perilous times—especially little Johnny, so recently weaned.

Sending them away felt like asking me to amputate a limb. But I'd learned during the war that sometimes amputation was necessary. Alexander was in no condition to make the choice, so it fell to me to speak very frankly with my eleven-year-old son, who would have to manage his siblings all on his own. "Philip, I need you to take your brothers and sisters to the Pastures."

My son's eyes went wide. "By myself?"

The fear on his face nearly broke my heart, but I couldn't let him see that I shared it. "If you can drive the carriage as far as Germantown, you can stay with friends there. It's only a few miles and your grandpapa will send a servant to fetch you the rest of the way. You can watch over the little ones and manage the horses just that far, can't you?"

"Why can't you and Papa come with us?" he asked from the window.

"Because your father is too ill and I must care for him."

"Father has a doctor to care for him." Because Philip had always been a boy who laughed more easily than he cried, it wounded me to see his eyes fill with tears. "If you stay, won't you get sick, too?"

"The doctor has many other patients to tend to," I said. "And you mustn't worry about me. You're a young man now. You must be the man of the family while your father is ill." If his father died, he'd become the man of the family in fact, before the age of twelve. And it would be the worst calamity of his life.

Better a mother die than a father; it was a father who could provide for the children.

Saving Hamilton was the best thing I could do for my babies.

In Philadelphia, bodies had rotted in the streets, husbands had abandoned wives in their sickbeds, mothers abandoned sick children, and children forsook their doomed parents. That seemed to me a greater evil than death. And though I'd taught my eldest son many lessons at my knee, now was the time to teach him the most important of all.

*Semper Fidelis.* Always loyal. Always faithful.

"I'm not going to leave your father alone when he needs me. Get ready to go, now. See your siblings to safety. Can we depend on you, Philip?"

Manfully, our boy swiftly wiped tears away and nodded with determination. "Yes, Mother. I can do it. But you must come as soon as you can."

"We will," I promised, watching gratefully, from a distance, as he coaxed the children into the carriage that would take them away. My heart ached that I couldn't hug or kiss them in farewell, that I couldn't inhale the baby scent of their hair. And as the carriage rolled away, I wept bitter tears, fearing that our separation might be of the eternal kind.

For what I'd not told Philip, nor even wished to admit to myself, was that I, too, now felt aches and chills . . .

Inside the house, I found Hamilton submerged in a bath of

cold water, his teeth chattering. It wasn't the treatment recommended by the city's foremost physicians, like Dr. Rush. But
Dr. Stevens refused to induce vomiting or bleed my husband with
leeches. No, he said that he'd successfully treated this fever with
baths and bark tonics. And so that's what he did.

He cared for both of us, though I was barely aware of him
because my head now throbbed intolerably and my eyes burned.
Scorching heat stole my ability to think, as if I stood on the precipice of hell's fires. Then I was cold. So frightfully cold, that not
even the warmed Madeira wine the Washingtons sent us chased
away the chill.

My husband and I were put into bed together as, at this point,
it could do no harm. "My poor Betsy," Alexander whispered beneath the blankets, trying to warm me within the embrace of
his own trembling arms. He was trying to give me the last of his
warmth, though he couldn't spare it. "Now I've done this to you,
in addition to everything else . . ."

It was this embrace, I think, that cracked the wall of anger
I'd erected between us. It was our first truly intimate embrace in
months, and I knew it might be the last. Together we tossed and
turned in sweat-soaked misery upon pillows that Dr. Stevens had
stuffed with lavender, chamomile, and peppermint. Until—to
our terror—we both awakened feeling better.

No fever. No chills. No aches. Not a trace of them.

I'd gone to sleep so weak I couldn't *walk*, much less dress
for breakfast. But now I had the appetite for a hearty meal and
the energetic desire to cook it. Doctor Stevens forbade that we
should exert ourselves in such a way—but he said that no harm
could come of a gentle stroll, to stretch our limbs. So I gingerly
donned a muslin chemise and Alexander pulled on only a shirt
and breeches. And together, warily, we emerged blinking into
the bright yellow sun, walking together to a quiet field where lingering wildflowers dotted the dried stalks, and where yellowing
leaves rained gently down upon us from the trees.

I couldn't remember a time walking anywhere with my husband when the world was so quiet and peaceful and beautiful. A portrait of nature painted by a divine hand. Perhaps we'd already died. Perhaps this was the quiet and peace of heaven. But then, where was God?

Matching my husband's stride, I asked, "How do you feel?"

"Much recovered," he said. "And you?"

"Much recovered, too." And though I feared to speak the words aloud, I thought it best to face it bravely. "Which means we are soon to die."

"*Betsy*," Alexander scolded with enough sternness to tell me that he had his wits about him and knew the strange progress of the disease as well as I did.

"Aren't you afraid?" I asked, knowing he hadn't made his peace with God.

And yet my husband, who'd once seemed to *crave* oblivion, asked, "What have I to fear? A pleasing calm suspense. Let the Earth rend. Let the planets forsake their course. Let the Sun be extinguished and the Heavens burst asunder, were it not for the dread of our children to be left alone."

I crossed my arms at an answer that could only be made by a man who had given the matter some thought. "So, you fear that we're dying, too."

"But I wouldn't have said it."

This hardly seemed the time for him to finally learn to govern his tongue. "I'd rather not waste time pretending all is well."

His eyes squinted in vague amusement. "Do you know that is the first thing I loved about you? You're entirely without guile."

Now I felt vague amusement. "Such flattery."

His shoulders rounded defensively. "It's true. I didn't want to love you, Betsy. In truth, I *tried* not to love you. But your sincerity allowed me to trust you. And I've never completely trusted in anyone else."

"Surely that is to overstate it."

In answer, he stared far away down the dusty road. "I was too often the victim of bad characters in my childhood. Unscrupulous persons happy to make a dirty, hungry, begging, bastard boy imperil his soul for a bit of supper."

He never told stories about that childhood. Never explained how he'd been made a victim of unscrupulous persons. Certainly, he'd never revealed anything he'd done to imperil his soul for a bit of supper. "Will you tell me how?"

Hamilton's jaw tightened, released, then tightened again. "Only if you insist, because it's deeply humiliating. It will also likely vanquish anything that remains of your love and make me hate myself as an inveterate sinner besides."

I didn't insist. I only walked beside him in silence.

Finally, he cleared his throat. "Poverty leaves a tarnish on a boy with no parent to guide him. An indelible stain. But when I met you, a pure angel without pretense, I was vain enough to hope that loving you would cleanse *me* instead of spatter *you* with the muck of my past. And I am sorry, Elizabeth. I am unworthy of you. I am a creature of a mud pit that I never can seem to climb out of, no matter how hard I try."

Yet, he *did* try. Everything he'd done had been a mad scramble to escape. To persuade the world that he was not that dirty, hungry, begging bastard boy, but a man of true stature.

To persuade *me* of it.

I'd watched him climb and claw his way back again when he slipped. And I loved him best when, in cold adversity, he'd find within himself the spark of his genius and stoke it to an inferno. But I didn't need him to blaze with glory. I only needed his love.

*Anger, after all, does not obliterate love*, I thought.

And I still loved him as strongly as the day I first consented to be his wife, perhaps stronger now that I knew him better. In these moments, which might be my last, I had to honor that love or die bitter and alone. "You were never unworthy of me, Alexander. If anything, I've been unworthy of you. I've not been the wife that you've needed. I hope you'll forgive it."

"You have been the best of wives and best of women, beyond what I deserve—"

"Alexander," I broke in, belatedly realizing that though he'd failed me, I'd failed him, too. I'd known how to be a soldier's wife. I'd grown up knowing. *Be strong, be brave, be like my mother.* But I'd had no inkling of how to be Alexander Hamilton's wife.

And how could I? How could any woman know how to be the wife of a lightning rod? A man who electrified his enemies as well as his friends. He was not merely a soldier nor a states-man. He was a man who was, almost single-handedly, forging an economy, a government, and a nation. He didn't need the Finest Tempered Girl in the World.

He was a lion who had needed a lioness. And I had been a lamb.

I'd been too attached to our friendship with the Burrs to have foreseen or prevented that betrayal. Too awed by Jefferson's repu-tation and eloquence to suspect him for the cold-blooded Jacobin that he was. And too fond of James Madison to suspect he might be an enemy in truth.

And now, when we were so soon to meet our maker, I wished that I'd never threatened to abandon my husband. It had made me feel stronger to threaten it, it made me feel more valuable to put him in fear. But now I wanted our marriage to be a fortress against all fear in this world and the next. "Please forgive me, Alexander, as I forgive you."

In the midst of that peaceful, country field, he stopped me with a hand upon my elbow. "You forgive me?"

"For everything. With all my heart." I reached for his hand, which he took and squeezed like a drowning man.

And yet he didn't look convinced. "You say this only because you want to die at peace with me. But what if we live? Can you live with—" He shook his head and swallowed, as if remember-ing our last quarrel. "Can you *choose* each morning to live with me in forgiveness, despite what I've done?"

What had he done, after all? He'd put his hands on another woman. He'd taken momentary pleasure in guttural breaths and animal spasms. Yes, Alexander had done violence to my feelings and to my pride and to our wedding vows. But it all seemed so transient, so temporal now. For whatever wrongs he'd done me, he'd also given me a happier life than I'd believed myself destined for. He'd opened my heart and my mind; he'd taught me to *think* and to see injustice where I'd not seen it before. He'd taught me to stand for righteous causes. I could do more.

And if I lived, I *would* do more.

But first, I forgave my husband. Because I was a Christian, because I loved him, and because I must never allow *Maria Reynolds* to define us. "I do so choose to live with you, Alexander Hamilton," I said, as if it were a wedding vow. "In forgiveness and grace and love, so long as we draw breath."

I expected he would kiss me.

But either the illness or the weight of my words forced his knees to go soft. He lowered himself onto the grass of that isolated field, where insects buzzed amongst wildflowers, and the coming harvest stood in a golden line in the distance. And I sat beside him in the waning sun as we leaned, shoulder to shoulder.

"You mustn't think that what I did stems from some deficiency in you," he said. "The fault was mine. And I'll make of myself a better husband, Betsy. I promise you."

"And I will be a different wife," I vowed. I wasn't entirely sure how yet, but I felt more like a woman and less of a girl than I'd ever before been. "I think . . . I should prefer henceforth to be called Eliza. Or Elizabeth. Not Betsy."

He nodded, clearly moved, his eyes blazing from blue to violet in the late-day sun. "So be it, *my Eliza*."

Of course, starting anew depended on our surviving. But, for now, we had this moment. "Perhaps . . . should we write our last wishes while we're still capable?"

After a moment's thought, he said, "Just letters for the children. After all, we own nothing outright but some furniture, clothing, and paintings." He gave an exceptionally wry grin. "At last, an advantage to marrying a man without means."

We laughed. We actually laughed.

It all seemed so trivial now. The trouble we went to in getting lights and upholstered divans and imported wallpaper with trellises and vines to impress our Federalist friends. We could take none of it with us to the grave, and little good it should do our children.

When yellow fever took us, we knew it would be gruesome. We would, by tomorrow or the next day, bleed from every orifice and pore. Which made me grateful that I'd sent the children away, so they might never witness the ghastly spectacle. But Alexander and I would not look away. I knew we'd hold one another through every agony, until the last drop of blood.

Fortunately, God had given us this one last beautiful day. And so we found each other's lips, until we found each other, skin to skin, as if for the first time, and there we made love beneath His blue sky, revealing ourselves in all our weaknesses to each other, and to the Lord.

# Part Three

## The War of Words

# Chapter Twenty-Five

*Autumn 1793*
*Albany*

**W**E WERE SAVED.

Alexander was certain Dr. Stevens's remedies had cured us and recommended it to others. But even medicine had become a political battleground. My husband's enemies had allegedly wished him dead, toasting to his speedy demise, and now that he'd survived they refused to believe in the cure that had saved his life.

I wasn't sure I believed it either.

*It wasn't the baths and the wine and the cinnamon and the Peruvian bark that saved our lives,* I thought. It was a miracle. A miracle of grace and love and forgiveness.

And we were both changed by it.

Our bodies were weaker—Alexander would suffer from kidney pain ever after, and it would be years before I regained my vigor—but our spirits were replenished. Having fallen in love anew, we found within ourselves a new sense of what we valued most.

"Mama! Papa!" the children cried as we climbed the hill of the Pastures with nothing but the clothes on our backs. *Oh, my babies!* We hugged and kissed every one of them until we were all laughing and crying at the sweetness of the reunion. And we were inexpressibly proud of our brave Philip, who had seen his siblings to safety.

As we recovered at my father's house, Alexander decided to resign his position in the government. "Six months and the new government would be on stable footing. Maybe less." Having come so close to leaving our children penniless, he intended to return to his law practice and rebuild his fortune. Swinging in a hammock overlooking the Hudson River, he said, "I want to leave my family with more than a memory of me sitting up all night at a desk while mobs shout outside our house. I want to sing duets with the girls at the piano and take the boys duck hunting and—"

"Plant turnips with me?" I mused, nestled against him.

Alexander laughed. "What if I were to confess that having lived nearly all my life in a city, I haven't the faintest idea how to grow turnips or any other sort of crop?"

Delighting in the way the dappled autumn sunlight illuminated pale freckles upon his face, I kissed him. "I would say you were fortunate to have married a woman who came of age on a farm . . ."

He smiled, closing his eyes to the music of our children playing hoops on Papa's lawn. "In this, and all things, I must now content myself to be guided by the wisdom of my wife."

I was myself content. But our respite was short.

A missionary friend of Papa's wishing to establish a school to help the Oneida wrote seeking my husband's endorsement and support. Not to mention the use of his name. "They wish for me to become a trustee," Alexander said. "And to call it the Hamilton-Oneida Academy."

This was an honor, I thought. But also a risk to have his name, so often slandered, associated with yet another controversial cause. Yet my husband had championed an enlightened policy toward the Indians, even after the war, when so many others hadn't.

"We've done too little to protect them from lawless frontiersmen," he said, as if to convince me. "But perhaps we can provide their children the means for a better life."

"Which is why I hope you will accept."

He beamed to find us in accord. "Then I will afford it all the aid in my power."

I swelled with pride in him. With love for him. And renewed purpose.

We returned to Philadelphia after winter's frost to find a city that had been entirely savaged by yellow fever. More than five thousand victims—amongst them doctors, clergymen, black freedmen, a former mayor, and members of my Quaker friend's family. Dolley Todd was now left widowed with a small son, forced to rent her stately three-story brick home on Walnut Street and take up work as a hostess at a boardinghouse to make ends meet.

Despite the slight whiff of scandal that attended Dolley's new situation, I saw to it that she was welcomed at Lady Washington's levees, and took food to her whenever I could. Seven months after her husband's death, when the weather was hot again, I took some freshly made *olie koeken* to the garden entrance of her boardinghouse and asked, "How are you getting on?"

"I trust in heaven that all will be right," Dolley said, ignoring the racket her son was making behind her with a copper pot with a wooden spoon. "Thou art kind to think of me when others are less fortunate."

"You're my first stop," I said, motioning to a basket of parcels I intended to deliver to the needy. For in the wake of yellow fever, I'd become convinced that God had spared me for a purpose. Not only to remake my marriage, but also to fulfill a calling.

Long before I met Alexander Hamilton, standing by the grave of my dead baby brother, I'd felt driven to a vocation, if a woman could have such a thing. And so, just as my husband was seeking to disentangle himself from his public calling, I remembered my own and felt the pull of it, stronger than ever.

"I should like to help thee," Dolley said, inviting me in and pouring us each a cup of coffee while I told her of my charitable plans.

"I'd welcome your help, Dolley. Though I'm sensible that you're still in mourning."

Glancing over her shoulder, as if for fear her mother might overhear, Dolley leaned in to confide, "In truth, I've an ardent suitor already. 'Tis the custom for a widow to wait, but keen to be wed again, I crave the advice of a woman as sensible as thee."

Remembering the trial of my own delayed marriage, I knew it was a difficult thing to wait. But still I advised, "You'll do yourself a great service in the eyes of society to observe the custom."

"If I was to observe *custom*, the wait would be eternal," she said, forlornly. "For my suitor is not of my faith and I shall be shunned if I marry the fellow."

"Oh, dear." The churches of my childhood had been Anglican and Dutch Reform. I'd baptized my children at the Episcopal Trinity Church. And having shared services with persons of different faiths, I did not trouble myself with differences of denomination. But the Quakers were much stricter about such things. I sipped at the strong brew as I debated how best to advise her. "Marriage already demands heavy sacrifice. Are you certain your suitor is worthy of it?"

"Oh, he *is* worthy," Dolley said a little breathlessly. "I admire him above all other men. He says he dreams of me and burns with such passion for me he that he yearns to relieve his flame!"

"My goodness," I said, half-convinced she would, in her excitement, run off with this honey-tongued lover by night's end. Fanning myself against the heat of summer—or perhaps the heat of Dolley's words, I asked, "Just who is this charming young Romeo?"

Dolley bit her pink lip. "An older gentleman. Decidedly good-looking."

Several dispossessed but distinguished nobles had recently fled to our shores, so I guessed, "A Frenchman?"

"A Virginian," Dolley whispered. "Mr. Madison."

I nearly choked on my coffee. She couldn't have surprised me more if she'd named a Barbary pirate. "*James* Madison?"

She nodded in answer, her smile incandescent.

"James Madison, the congressman?"

"The very same," she chirped.

And truly, in that moment, I knew that love was no respecter of persons or explainable passions whatsoever. For I would scarcely have described little Jemmy Madison, professorial and pale as a parson, as *decidedly good-looking*, nor imagined him yearning for *relief for his flame*. And though I was wicked enough to take private amusement in this revelation, I knew I must never tell my husband this gossip or he'd wield it in such merciless mockery that the whole city would be laughing.

"Well," I said, trying to smother my merriment. "Will you deprive Philadelphia of its last confirmed bachelor, then?"

Dolley weighed the question, staring down at her noisy boy. "In Mr. Madison my little child will have a generous and tender protector. But what a price, to give up one's faith."

It was a high price. But in the wake of yellow fever, I loved Alexander with such a terrifyingly renewed passion that I believed I might choose him even at the expense of my own soul. And I told her this.

Whereupon she embraced me with gratitude and a tearful little laugh. "Perhaps I will agree to marry him. I fear I never had the soul of a Quaker anyway. Or so Senator Burr tells me."

*Burr.*

I'd forgotten that he was boarding here. I was too much a Schuyler to have forgiven Burr for ousting my father from the Senate. But because word had recently reached us that Theodosia had died, the victim of a lingering cancer, I softened. "How is he bearing up?"

Dolley shook her head. "He's in a terrible grief . . . it would do the sorrowful man some good to hear kind words before he goes off to New York for her funeral."

My friendship with Theodosia had once been close, so I mourned her loss. How much worse for her husband, now facing alone the care of their eleven-year-old daughter. I couldn't think it disloyal to offer condolences. Politics be damned. "I shall call on Senator Burr, if he's in."

Pointing the way, Dolley said, "He sits on the balcony overlooking the street while reading. All day, sometimes."

I mounted the stairs and found Burr, his boots propped up on a chair, his eyes shadowed by the brim of a hat. Always of a languid air, he looked up from his book with obvious reluctance, and blinked. "Do my eyes deceive me, or do I see the wife of the secretary of the treasury?"

Despite the playful words, Burr's tone was lifeless.

"Your eyes do not deceive you, Senator Burr. I wanted to tell you how much I regret to hear of the passing of your wife. I remember Theodosia so fondly." When he didn't respond, I went on. "In those early days when I was a new mother, she offered me friendship, companionship, and advice. I remember how she watched over my children, and helped at dinner parties, and . . ."

Burr said nothing to this litany but instead stared down at the street, as if he couldn't look at me. And perhaps he couldn't. At the time, I thought that perhaps my condolences weren't welcome because he couldn't see me as anything other than the wife of a rival. But now, I know that Burr was already becoming an empty vessel, more able to separate politics from the personal than any man I'd ever known.

Into the awkward silence, I added, "Theodosia was a very interesting conversationalist and had a very great spirit." Still, he said nothing, and I wished I hadn't come on this errand. "Please take comfort in knowing that Theodosia loved you."

Hoping that was enough to extricate myself, I turned to go.

He stopped me with a chuckle. "And do you consider yourself an expert in love?" For a moment, I knew not what to say. What an odd creature Burr was. I attributed it to his grief, but then he said, "Mrs. Hamilton, I know."

Confused, I peered back at him, and the shrewd cast of his eyes turned my blood to ice.

He wasn't responding to what I said. He *knew*. Somehow, Burr had learned of my husband's infidelity. And he was laughing. For a moment, I dared not move a muscle lest I betray my horror.

Steadying myself, I looked to the street below. Horses cantered. Wagon wheels clacked. Men called to one another. But I heard not a sound but the beating of my own heart.

Then Burr's cough. "That was ill-done of me," he said, with what might have passed for chagrin in any other man; I realize now that he wasn't entirely capable of it. "My wife's death has apparently stolen my capacity for subtlety. I assumed you were aware of your husband's indiscretion, and because you're not an actress of any talent, I see that you *are* aware."

For a moment, I considered whether I could throw him from that balcony. Responses flashed through my mind, one more horrible than the next until he forestalled any reply with his next revelation.

"Mrs. Reynolds has retained me as a lawyer in filing for divorce."

It was all I could do to blank my expression. To think that we'd convinced Monroe and the other investigators to keep quiet, only for my husband's harlot to tell tales. And because I was, more and more, learning to think like my husband, I worried it might become a matter of court record in a divorce proceeding.

Burr seemed to read my mind. "I've advised Mrs. Reynolds to mention nothing of her connection to Hamilton. She will, instead, accuse her own husband of adultery, and the scoundrel doesn't dare contest it. So I think the matter that concerns you has a good chance to remain a private one and I will do my best to keep it that way. I hope that gives you some peace of mind."

That was . . . unexpected. Burr didn't have to advise Maria Reynolds to keep quiet. Indeed, he had no motive to do so, so I was immediately suspicious. "Why would you . . ."

"*Friendship,* my dear lady," Burr said, as if it should be obvious.

"I've never seen a reason why a mere difference in politics should be a reason for personal discord."

His words brought to mind the dinner table policy I'd once naively embraced. "Perhaps this reassuring message is better delivered to my husband."

"By my reckoning, Hamilton has less of a right to reassurance than you do," Burr said, eyeing me levelly. "You're the one I wish to comfort."

My throat tightened. "And yet, I came to offer *you* comfort."

"I cannot be comforted." That's when the impenetrable armor of Burr's character, which made it so easy for him to slip from one political faction to another—amiable to all, sincere to none—fell away. "My wife was the best woman and finest lady I ever knew, and now I go to attend her funeral knowing I never made enough time to attend her in life." He said this bitterly. "Do you know I offered to give up my ambitions and leave government for her? Theodosia wouldn't have it. Now she's gone and ambition is all that's left."

I should've heard the threat in those words. But at the time, my heart filled with such pity for his agony that I took the liberty of squeezing his hand—never dreaming that same hand would one day inflict that same agony upon me.

———

*September 1794*
*Philadelphia*

It was a time for terror.

For two years, the French Revolution had depended upon it. Now, a flood of refugees washed into our American capital, so many that the French language rang out on every street corner. Even the newspapers featured advertisements in that language for everything from wines and perfumes to fencing lessons and theater performances. And the refugees brought with them chilling tales of abuse and deprivation, horrifying stories of victims shortened by *the national razor,* their silently screaming heads held up for the jeers of the crowd, still dripping bloody red gore.

"*Quelle horreur,*" said Mr. Moreau, the owner of the bookstore on the corner of Walnut Street.

I'd come to replenish my husband's ever dwindling supply of paper and ink, as well as to purchase a book of French for Ana, who was learning the language from a tutor. The store was also a meeting place for some of the most prominent French exiles, and Mr. Moreau knew them all.

"Poor Vicomte de Noailles," he said, rummaging amongst the clutter of maps, engravings, and scientific instruments for sale. "He hasn't come out of his house for days."

Noailles was Lafayette's brother-in-law, and he, too, had fought heroically for us at Yorktown. Now Noailles found himself persecuted, forced into flight, and grieving the murders of those he'd left behind in France—women of Lafayette's family, too.

"Last I saw the vicomte," Moreau continued, "he kept murmuring that his wife must have been spattered by her own mother's blood going up the stairs to the guillotine. That he should've divorced her when he fled so as to spare her this fate."

Clutching Ana's book in my gloved hands, I said a silent prayer. "He couldn't have known that the monsters would come for women and children . . ."

"No," Moreau agreed. "But maybe his wife could have renounced him. Maybe it would have saved her."

*Stand by him and die, renounce him and live.*

I wondered, in her place, what I would've done.

My husband was determined that I should never find out. "I must leave you," Alexander whispered softly the next morning, regretfully rising from my pillow as dawn glowed rosy in our window.

There was an uprising in western Pennsylvania against the whiskey tax my husband had levied to pay the country's war debt.

Tax collectors had been tarred and feathered. Whiskey rebels had blown up the stills of their neighbors who paid the tax. They'd kidnapped a federal marshal. They'd even threatened to build a guillotine. Here. In America.

President Washington had been forced to muster an army. He would lead it, personally, against these rebels to establish, once and for all, that the laws of this new nation must be obeyed. That terror *here* would not be countenanced.

And Alexander meant to ride out at the president's side.

My husband reassured our children that there'd be no real fighting, that a show of force would be enough. But I also heard him tell a friend that the game afoot was for no less than true liberty, property, order, and *heads*.

I was no young bride anymore, confronted for the first time with the terror of her union being torn asunder, of losing a man who'd become a part of her to the vagaries of war. I was older and wiser. Wise enough to say, "But you're the secretary of the treasury, not the secretary of war."

"Regardless, Jefferson is calling this Hamilton's Insurrection. And in a government like ours, the proposer of a measure which involves danger to his fellow citizens should partake in that danger."

"So now you admit, there *will* be danger?" I wanted to know the truth of what we faced. All of it. "Is Jefferson our Robespierre?" I asked, searching my husband's eyes, wondering how scared I should be. "Would he cheerfully condemn us to the guillotine and lap up our blood?"

"No," Alexander said, stroking my cheek. But lest I think he said it only to comfort me, he added, "That philosophical fool would be forced to mount the scaffold behind us. A victim of the same mob he's emboldened."

Alexander wouldn't allow a repeat of the Citizen Genêt affair, with mobs threatening us on our doorstep. He meant to take the fight to the rebels this time.

*But what if he doesn't return?*

I shook the thought away. If I was sick with worry it was because I was with child again. Proof of our love and mutual desire. Proof of forgiveness and grace. This baby represented something new and hopeful between Alexander and me, and it pained me to think that after such a long struggle, everything remained so fragile.

But I was determined to be his lioness now, so I asked no more questions and said nothing more about my fears. Instead, I drew him back to our warm bed, and climbing astride, reminded him of that intimate day in a faraway field when we made love like a sacrament.

At my boldness, Alexander's hands gripped my hips, his heated interest making me wish I'd been bolder in love before. "A new start indeed, Eliza . . ."

Later that day, I saw him off on Market Street where he prepared to ride out to war with the aging president. I didn't care what anyone else said, the sight of even an aging George Washington still inspired me and stiffened my spine. And so I teased my husband, "At long last it seems I have persuaded you to return to the side of your general."

We'd come far enough that Hamilton smiled. "It seems you shall always have your way."

"Then come back to me," I said, fighting my own battle against foreboding and kissing him farewell.

Martha Washington and I clasped hands as we watched them go. Then I spent the next two months trying to keep the children from missing their father as much as I did. The boys had their schooling, but as my daughter was ten years of age and Fanny only a few months younger, I took them for lessons from the French dance master. And while they danced, I collected donations and delivered them to the needy.

"*Voici le chapeau idéal pour Monsieur le secrétaire, Madame,*" said Madame le Grand from behind the hatter's stall in the market. She held up a black felt riding hat with a black cockade.

"Yes, I'll take the hat. *Merci,*" I replied, fishing money from my purse as Madame le Grand's two barefooted children wrestled in the cold street over a loaf of bread.

Not old enough to help their mother look after their hatter's stall in the market, they were lean as wild dogs and dressed in rags that offered them no defense against the weather. And though I knew it shamed Madame le Grand, and the other refugees, to rely upon charity, they had little choice unless they would starve.

"Take this as well," I said, pressing into her hand a pouch of donations I'd collected for her. "And if you come by the house on Sunday morning before church service, I'll have some warm clothes that my children have outgrown."

"*Merci,*" Madame le Grand said, clutching the pouch against her faded linen dress, worn without stays, her eyes lowered. She'd had a little cottage outside Paris. With a flower garden. A fine tea service.

Now, without a husband, she had nothing. Alone and desperate. And I had cause to imagine myself in her miserable condition as Madame le Grand thanked me again and again, boxing up a hat for my husband that he might never wear.

"Mrs. Hamilton!" I turned to see Dolley in a swish of red cloak, a veritable rainbow of ribbons flowing from her fancy bonnet. Freed from Quaker restraint, she was never plain now. "Is that a surprise for the secretary?"

"Oh, yes," I answered. "When my husband returns home, I should like to present him with a little gift."

A basket of apples looped over one arm, Dolley glanced at my pregnant belly and chirped, "I should think a baby the very best gift of all! Or so Mr. Madison tells me."

She'd married him, even though it meant expulsion from her faith. Even though it put a little distance between us because of the estrangement of our husbands. But I didn't blame her. In marrying Madison, she'd lifted her child from poverty to wealth in one stroke. And, despite the strangeness of the pairing, the Madisons were a love match. "Well then, do you mean to give Mr. Madison the gift he most desires?"

"As soon as I can," Dolley replied, and then, with a twinkle that proved she really never did have the soul of a Quaker, she added, "I'm certainly making every effort to procure it, all hours of the night."

Halfway between scandalized and horrified by the image that conjured, I laughed too hard, and a sharp pain knifed through my abdomen. Doubling over, I gasped as the market suddenly spun, assaulting me with the sound of horse hooves on cobblestones, passing wagons, brooms being whacked free of dust in doorways.

The *roar* of grocers in the market shouting the price of mustard, apples, and sugar . . .

I dropped my purse.

And Dolley Madison was at my elbow. "Let's get her home," she was saying to a black man who steadied me. One of her husband's slaves, I suspected, and in a swirl of half-formed, absurd thoughts, I couldn't help but wonder, given the Quakers' strict antislavery position, what she thought of now owning slaves herself.

Next I knew, I was jostling in the carriage beside her, shivering with cold. Then I was being put into bed. "Here, drink this," Dolley said, bringing hot chocolate that she'd stirred together in my kitchen.

I nodded, starting to come back to myself, the pain easing. "Thank you, Dolley."

"You poor thing. You must be worried for your husband."

I blew out a breath, torn, perhaps ridiculously, between worry over my unborn child, and worry over admitting to the wife of a political rival that I was concerned about my husband's expedition against the whiskey rebels.

"I'm sure everything's all right," I said, trying to convince myself on both accounts. For I had now only the slightest of cramps.

I wanted to say more. I wanted to confide my worries to her. And I nearly convinced myself that I should. After all, Dolley and I had been friends before she met Madison. And I *did* hold a glimmer of hope that she might be a good influence on him politically.

Especially now that Mr. Jefferson had retired into private life. Hamilton feared that this retirement from President Washington's cabinet was just a ruse, that Jefferson was biding his time until he could run for the presidency himself.

But to me, the important thing was that Jefferson was gone.

In Jefferson's absence, Madison had supported my husband's whiskey tax. Jemmy also denounced the insurrection as odious. So maybe there was reason for optimism that fences could be mended with our old friend.

Still, I knew better than to confess anything that might be used against Alexander—even my own fears for his survival. "I think I've simply taken a chill," I added, cautiously.

"Well, then, I shall let you get your rest," Dolley replied, tucking a shawl around my shoulders. She seemed to sense my caution, and perhaps was as saddened by it as I was. Before she left, she pledged ten dollars to help French distressed persons, but I feared even charity was too feeble a bridge between us.

In the days that followed, I was apt to burst into tears without warning or explanation, at the slightest provocation. Or no provocation at all.

*What's wrong with me?*

I worried that like one of those pendulums with which Papa was so fascinated, swinging back and forth, there was a divine balance of happiness afforded to any one person. God had spared us. He had spared Alexander and me from death, divorce, and bitter acrimony.

*Will the price for that mercy now be the life of the baby inside me, or the life of my husband at war?*

If Angelica had been with me, she would've said I was ascribing altogether too much importance to myself in the plans of the deity. And I dared not confess my fears to anyone else lest they think me mad. Certainly, I couldn't confess them to Lady

Washington, or Abigail Adams, or Lucy Knox—all of whom, in warm shawls and dowdy bonnets, mounted an assault upon my household in near military formation even though I protested I was too sick to receive them.

Determined to combat my malaise, Mrs. Knox hovered above my bed and huffed, "Parsley is just the thing."

"Strong tea is better," insisted Mrs. Adams, elbowing her way forward.

"Dried figs," Lady Washington serenely stated, setting a basket of them at my bedside. "Figs ease everything for a pregnant woman." And though I could see they did not agree, the other Federalist ladies were forced, out of deference, to bend to the president's lady. "Don't trouble yourself about the children, my dear," Martha Washington insisted, patting my hand. "I will take little Fanny and Ana in my carriage to dancing school so you can get your rest. All will be well."

But by the time Alexander returned, victorious over the rebels, having restored order to the country and banished the specter of the guillotine, I had delivered a tiny, misshapen, dead babe.

It would have been a girl. *A little girl.* I'd hoped for another daughter. A third sister for Ana and Fanny to love. The two of them were already inseparable, but I'd imagined them, the *three* of them, piling into a bed together and laughing like Angelica, Peggy, and I used to do.

And now I couldn't be consoled of the loss.

Not even when Alexander burst in the door, clasping me in his strong arms.

"I'm sorry, so sorry." I wept violently against my husband's chest. "I lost her. I wasn't strong enough to keep her."

Alexander rocked me, tears in his own eyes. "Blame your heartless husband for leaving you. My absence was the cause. It's my fault, my beloved, my angel, my Eliza . . ."

He was not heartless; he was a hero. He'd saved the country, yet again. The rebellion was smashed. The primacy of federal laws firmly established. The government had passed its first test. And yet, when we put quietly into an unmarked grave my dead child who couldn't be baptized nor named, I couldn't find enough patriotism within myself to feel anything but grief.

"She's cold," I whispered, awakened by the ghostly cry of an infant echoing in my ears. "In the ground. She must be so cold."

I started to rise, as if to go to her, but Alexander pulled me back into his arms. "No, my love. She's with her creator now."

Icy tears trailed upon my face. "She never felt me hold her. She must've been frightened . . . and alone . . ."

"You held her," he whispered. "You held her inside your body. She wasn't frightened, my angel. Not while she felt the strength of your love. And you must believe me, for who knows the strength of that love better than I do?"

Having never lost a child before, I couldn't fathom the grief. Or that I would feel anything other than grief ever again. "I feel shattered. Broken in pieces."

"I'll hold you together," he said, making a bed for me of his whole body. "For once, let me hold you together."

I let him rock me as I whispered my most secret fears. "I took this child for an embodiment of grace and love and forgiveness, and now she's gone. What if this is the end of us?"

"This is not the end of us," Alexander said, taking my face in his hands. "I have tendered my resignation to the president. I am yours forever, Eliza. And I will never leave you alone or desperate again. I will not let this be the end of us. This is the beginning."

# Chapter Twenty-Six

*You may judge how much Hamilton must be
mortified at his loss of influence such that he would
descend to the language of a street bully.*
—EDWARD LIVINGSTON TO HIS MOTHER

*Summer 1795*
*New York City*

F LOWERS. IN THE five months since he'd left the government,
my husband filled my world with flowers. Cut hot house
hyacinths in winter. Sunny daffodils from Mama's garden
during our visits to the Pastures. Azaleas at the Pinkster festival.
And now the riot of purple aster, red roses, and orange lilies of
New York's Vauxhall Gardens where we strolled with our children.

"Buy your sisters ice cream," Alexander called after Philip
while balancing three-year-old Johnny on his shoulders.

Running wild amongst the gravel paths between the flowers
and sculpted shrubbery, our children were happy to have returned to New York. And I was, too. Some part of me would
always long for the countryside, but my husband's legal trade was
a city occupation, and there could be no better city than this one.

To me, New York City was a more hopeful, energetic place
than Philadelphia. Certainly, I felt better here—the riverside

walks and musical concerts and frenetic pace had been a balm for and a distraction from my grief over our lost child.

I was not, of course, the first woman to lose a baby. My mother and my sisters had endured the same. But I'd lived so blessed an existence that it was, to that point, the worst pain of my life, and through it, Alexander had held me together, just as he promised. He'd let me rage. He'd let me cry. He'd let me question, even, the mercy of God. And it was through my husband's unfailing strength that I forgave myself for having ever worried that another child would be too much burden.

*When I save enough money, I'll build you a country house, with a flower garden all your own,* he promised. *With room for all the children and more besides, if God should see fit to bless us with more.*

Meanwhile I found contentment with what we had. And now, watching my husband spread a picnic blanket beneath the shade of a statue near the orchestra pit, I felt like a cat purring in a warm patch of sun. I unpacked our basket as the musicians tuned their instruments with "Yankee Doodle," and I marveled at how well Alexander carried his forty years. Though his auburn hair had gone silver at the temples and his nose seemed a bit sharper, my husband was still handsome and distinguished, and *mine* in a way he'd never been before.

"Is there something wrong, my angel?"

"Nothing at all," I answered, tearing off a chunk of bread for Johnny. "In this moment, I feel as if there is nothing whatsoever wrong in the world . . ."

"Then I'm doubly sorry to tell you that your boy is about to topple that wax figure of a Roman general," said a familiar voice, and we looked up to see the wryly amused visage of Aaron Burr.

Sipping at a lemon ice, Burr accompanied his polite twelve-year-old daughter, Theodosia, who took so much after her mother that it allayed some of the wariness her father's presence unleashed in me.

"James!" my husband shouted after our eight-year-old troublemaker, while Burr and his daughter settled onto a blanket beside us to wait for the sun to set and the fireworks to begin.

"Welcome home, Senator," I said, determined to keep the conversation friendly.

Burr nodded in polite acknowledgment, having returned recently from a special session of Congress in Philadelphia, where he'd done his utmost to undermine President Washington and everything my husband had put into motion.

At least Washington remained to defend the Federalist cause. When we'd said our farewells to the Washingtons, my husband with true respect and affectionate attachment, me with a teary and grateful embrace for Martha and one of awe for the great man, I knew the president's continuance in office was the one thing that allowed Alexander to retire. The reason he could be here with us now.

We remained on cordial terms with Burr if only because he still worked with the Manumission Society to help free blacks from being snatched up on the streets and sold back into slavery in the southern states. Still, I couldn't keep myself from twitting him. "I'm afraid we missed you at the dinner in honor of my husband hosted by the Chamber of Commerce."

"Ah, well, yes. I was sorry to miss it," Burr managed, clearly attempting to play nice as well, though we all knew he'd have been pilloried by his own political party if he'd attended. The merchants of the city had given Alexander a hero's welcome, celebrating us with champagne, a feast, and a ball. Well-wishers pressed into the overcrowded ballroom to listen to my husband's *mercifully* short remarks on the virtues of the city's businessmen. And they'd cheered, three times for Washington, three times for Adams, and nine times for Alexander Hamilton.

However vilified my husband might've been in Philadelphia, he was still New York's favorite son. And I was quite sure Burr took my meaning.

Clearing his throat, he changed the subject, "I hear your law practice is thriving, Hamilton."

"I'm kept quite busy, thank you," Alexander replied, and he wasn't boasting.

After a few months of riding and fishing and hunting with my father and our sons upstate, Alexander had decided that *vacations* disagreed with him entirely. In fact, he blamed this leisurely sojourn for the loss of his bank account book, which mortified him, since he'd created the bank that issued it. He'd since become convinced that he might lose his faculties altogether if he let them rest, so he'd thrown himself into the enterprise of paying off our debts and rebuilding our fortune.

"It's a good strategy," Burr said, sipping the last of his lemon ice.

"What is?" Alexander asked.

Burr stretched upon his checkered blanket. "Temporary retreat from the political arena. Retirement is very fashionable these days amongst men who wish to be president . . ."

How relieved I was to hear Alexander laugh. "That's Jefferson's game. As for me, I'm about the care of my family now. Congratulate me, friend, for I am no longer a public man."

"Exactly what a man would say if he wanted to be president," Burr replied. "You're wise to let John Jay take the blame for this treaty of amity, commerce, and navigation he's forged with the British. Then sweep in after it passes in Congress and reap the benefits."

Almost in spite of himself, Alexander asked, "You think the treaty will pass?"

"Perhaps," Burr said. "But I can't vote for it. Not if I want to remain a senator. It's too unpopular."

Sensing a coming debate, I said, "*Gentlemen*, I beg you not to spoil the evening."

Reluctantly, they obliged me, and a lovely time was had by all. Philip, Ana, Fanny, and Theodosia—all four of them close in age—shared ice cream upon a blanket and stared up in marvel at the fireworks overhead. And nestled against Alexander's side, I felt happy as I hadn't felt in years.

Which was why, I think, I was so vexed the next evening to find Alexander pacing in the airy entryway of our rented town house on Broadway. "There's a French flag flying atop the Tontine Coffeehouse."

"A French flag over the Tontine?" I asked, in mock outrage. "Well then. Henceforth, we shall take our coffee elsewhere . . ." Which *would* be a trial, since I loved the Tontine.

Alexander, however, was not to be mollified. "A French flag hoisted blocks from my door! Next, I suppose, it will fly over the city instead of our Stars and Stripes."

"I'm sure it is only a protest against Great Britain. If we must choose a side in the European war, the people would choose our first ally. France."

"We mustn't choose any side," Alexander said, wearing a hole in the floor by the window. "It's not our war. Even if it was, we can't win another war. We can't afford it. And war would prevent the Tontine from *selling* their coffee, the fools."

Giving him a peck upon the cheek, I said, "Fortunately, it's no longer your worry."

We had plans for the theater, after all, and it was time to dress. Now that he'd returned to private practice, we could afford new clothes, and I was eager to see him in his new double-breasted white waistcoat and dark breeches, worn loosely as was now the fashion. But he continued to pace like an angry lion. "To see the character of our government sported with tortures my heart."

"I know, my love," I said, patiently guiding him toward the stairs.

He took two steps before stopping again. "Am I more of an American than those who drew their first breath on American ground? How can everyone else view this so calmly?"

As someone who drew first breath upon American ground, I defended myself. "I don't view it *calmly,* but you cannot keep writing treatises for the president as if you were still in the cabinet." He scowled, but since our marriage was now on a more equal footing, I dared to scowl back. "Oh, did you think you fooled me into believing the scribbling you've been doing late at night was for some legal case?"

For a moment, his eyes blazed with indignation, as if he meant to deny it. Then his bravado gave out. "You think I'm a fool—a romantic Don Quixote tilting at windmills."

"I think you've already accomplished everything you set out to do." It was not flattery. He'd fought and won a war and built a federal government. He'd created a coast guard, a national bank, and invented a scheme of taxation that held the states together. He'd founded a political party, smashed a rebellion, and put in motion a financial system that was providing prosperity for nearly everyone. In short, Alexander Hamilton was a greater man than the country deserved, and I wasn't enough of a patriot to willingly give him back.

Especially not when I saw what my countrymen were doing to poor John Jay.

There was not a street corner one could pass without hearing some raving Jacobin denouncing the man for his controversial treaty, which antifederalists feared prioritized closer economic and political ties with the British monarchy over support for French republicanism and therefore repudiated American values. *Damn John Jay. Damn everyone that won't damn John Jay. Damn everyone that won't put up lights in the windows and sit up all night damning John Jay.*

After the treaty was signed, Jay was—as he told us himself—burned in effigy in so many cities that he could've traveled the country at night with nothing to guide him but the light of his own flaming form. My poor cousin Sarah Livingston Jay had reason to fear leaving the house. And this could've been our fate, I knew. My husband had narrowly missed being sent to negotiate in Jay's place, had already resisted an attempt to make him a chief justice, and was daily forced to dismiss rumors that he should throw in to be the next president of the United States.

So, I was unspeakably grateful that my husband no longer

held any office. And yet, he was still giving speeches. Which was how, while I sat trying to mend a pair of Philip's shoes he'd outgrown, my now nearly fourteen-year-old son came to ask, "Can I go watch Father speak in favor of the Jay Treaty?"

Quite against the idea, I said, "Your father isn't likely to say anything that you haven't already heard at the supper table. And I dislike for you to be by yourself in a crowd."

Philip made a sound of exasperation. "At my age, my father was his own man, in command of a trading firm."

*Your father was an abandoned boy trying to make his way in the world with any job he could get.* This is what I wanted to say. But Alexander never wanted his children to know the scars of his youth; he only ever wanted them to see him as heroic. And I wanted them to see him that way too. Especially Philip.

So, if my son wanted to see his father give a speech, I could scarcely deny him. Besides, it was only a five-minute walk to Federal Hall from our new lodgings. "We'll go together. There's a new shoemaker near Wall Street," I said, giving up on mending the old leather. "If we leave now, we'll be in time to see your father's speech on the way back." When Philip grinned beneath the down of a burgeoning mustache upon his lip, I added, "Now change clothes so you look like the fine young gentleman you're becoming instead of an urchin."

While my eldest donned his best shirt, I found my straw bonnet with its white ribbon, and, leaving the younger children with our newly hired governess, we were off.

It was a fine, clear, summer day and I was astonished at the size of the crowd. *Thousands* packed into the square. Not just dockworkers in knit caps and young toughs in homespun jackets, but the better sort of people, too, including ladies with colorful lace parasols and gentlemen in top hats from the finest families. There, too, upon a stoop near our old house, stood my husband, surrounded by half-a-dozen impeccably dressed Federalist lawyers like Robert Troup and Nicholas Fish.

It was nearly impossible to push closer, given the throng. But at the toll of the clock bell, my husband's voice boomed out to ask who had convened the assembly. And that's when I first realized that Alexander hadn't so much as come to *give* a speech as to *stop* one. The gathering was for the apparent purpose of *condemning* the Jay Treaty, and my husband wasn't about to let it happen. "By what right does Livingston speak before me?"

Almost as a rebuke, a quick, spontaneous vote determined that Livingston should speak first. But I stood agape as the rest of the crowd began to *heckle*. There, on the same hallowed ground where we'd once gathered to watch George Washington take his solemn oath of office, erstwhile respectable members of the business community shouted down the hapless Mr. Livingston, who, now red-faced, suggested a new meeting place where he could be heard. "Come then, all foes of this cowardly treaty, away to Trinity Church."

It seemed to me a very wise idea to break up what was swiftly becoming a mob, and I myself searched for some avenue of retreat, prodding my boy up onto the sidewalk in the shade of a buttonwood tree. All the while, my husband was shouting, "There is the necessity of a *full discussion* before citizens should make up their minds about this treaty!"

As the former secretary of the treasury, he was used to being obeyed. But this time, he was treated to a chorus of hoots and hisses. My husband's Federalists had shouted down Livingston, but now the Republicans, slowly but surely coalescing into a party of their own thanks to this treaty, returned the favor, insensible to my husband's demand to be heard.

My son was appalled. "The *rascals*!"

A gentleman in riding boots clapped Philip on the back, perhaps recognizing him as his father's son. Meanwhile, to my right, a bearded man in a beaver cap stooped to pull a loose cobble from the street.

*Not again*, I thought, prodding Philip toward the fence encircling the nearest yard. I'd been witness to too much disorder in my life not to recognize the danger. "We're going."

I'd learned, after hard experience, to head for the edges, moving diagonally against the crowd. But I didn't get very far before the man with the cobblestone pulled his arm back and launched it. After that was pandemonium.

"Angloman! Corrupt Tory!" they shouted at my husband.

Alexander shouted back, with pugnacious bombast, calling them wicked Jacobins. "*Liberté, égalité, fraternité* say the French you admire. But what *patriot* could ally with those who executed the kinswomen of our own imprisoned General Lafayette?"

To those words he was greeted with a hailstorm of bricks and stones, and I watched, in horror, as my husband staggered, fell, and disappeared into the crowd. I couldn't see him. I couldn't see anything over the blur of heads and shoulders.

Philip broke away from me, rushing to his father's defense, elbowing his way into a knot of red-faced, meat-fisted men.

"Philip!" I cried, trying to stop him, pushing forward past a brine-scented sailor and shoving a carpenter with sawdust on his apron. "Philip!"

I couldn't have been more than twenty feet from the furious men. Close enough to see Alexander pop up out of the sea of people, holding his head with one hand even as he spat contemptuous laughter. "Well, if you use such knock-about arguments, I must retire!"

Almost comically, my husband bowed and ducked away while the crowd broke apart. Some following the Livingstons to Trinity Church. Some marching to the battery, where they promised to burn the treaty and, presumably, another effigy of Jay.

"Dear God," I said, reaching my husband's side, not knowing whether I should tend his head or give it another thump. "What, in the name of prudence, could you—"

"It only grazed me," my husband said, wiping blood away with his now-torn sleeve.

Meanwhile, my son shouted after the retreating assailants, "No doubt you want to knock out my father's brains! It's the only way you blockheads could ever win an argument with him."

"*Philip.*" Having barked his name in a fashion so like my mother that I was secretly appalled, I then rounded on my husband, hissing, "Fine things you teach your son."

Hamilton had no reply to that. Fetching his now dusty black hat from the ground and straightening his coat, he made ready to walk us home, a number of his friends following us down the block, making me feel less that he was the head of a political party and more that he led a street gang.

More and more, I wondered if there was much difference between the two.

We'd only gone a little way before coming upon some lawyers in an altercation on Wall Street. "Gentlemen," Alexander said, stepping between them. "Why don't we resolve this matter between us at Fraunces over some glasses of brandy?" Now this suggestion was more in keeping with the conduct I expected, but Alexander said, "Philip, I bid you escort your mother home."

As I was in high dudgeon with the both of them, I exclaimed, "By no means! Stay with your father and make no more mischief." *Either of you,* my eyes said.

And with that, I returned home, grateful that my husband had escaped his latest brush with the mob with no more than a scrape on the head. That evening, he said he counted it a price worth paying for having disrupted the protest, but four days later, I was to learn just how high a price he'd been willing to pay . . .

"*Kitty,*" I said, startled to find my one-time companion upon my doorstep wearing a broad-brimmed black hat and clutching a black lace parasol. We'd not spoken a word in the six years since the inaugural ball, and the feud between the Livingston family and mine had only worsened since then. Still, I found myself glad to see her, especially since I knew she'd recently been widowed. "Please, come in."

She gave a delicate shake of her head. "I should rather—well, I would prefer if we spoke in your garden."

This was becoming curiouser by the moment. Nodding, I led

her to my herb garden. "I was so sorry to learn of your husband's passing."

She self-consciously smoothed the bodice of her widow's weeds. "Thank you. Amongst many other sorrows, I'm afraid widowhood has deprived me of fashion. Do you find me much changed?"

"You look just the same," I said, though black did not flatter her and her skin no longer glowed. "I didn't realize you'd returned to New York. Are you visiting?"

"I'm here to stay. I'm to be married again in the coming year to my cousin, John Livingston."

Another Livingston, of course. "I congratulate you."

"Thank you," she said brusquely. "But I've come on a matter of more interest to you. Namely, to speak about the man *you* married. You see, I'm of the opinion that Hamilton is trying to get himself killed."

I'd stooped to pluck some flowers for the dinner table, but now stood up abruptly. "Kitty, just because a man expresses an opinion—even an unpopular one—doesn't justify your family's faction stoning him in the street."

Kitty's lips thinned. "I'm not speaking of the mayhem at Federal Hall. It's what happened afterward that has forced me to deliver a warning. Your husband is embroiled in an affair of honor. Two, actually."

*Affairs of honor.* That meant my husband had either challenged or been challenged to a duel. Two of them, if Kitty was to be believed. But I stiffened because experience had taught me not to believe anything from the unholy Jefferson-Livingston-Clinton alliance. "With who?"

"With my cousin, for one. I know you may not be disposed to believe me but I heard it from your own husband's mouth when we crossed paths outside his law office."

Now I definitely didn't believe her. "My husband told you he was going to duel with a Livingston?" I asked, dubiously. Men didn't tell women such things. It wasn't gentlemanly. It would cause alarm in a man's family. And that family might persuade a man to forgo pistols, thereby risking his honor.

"Hamilton pretended to let it slip," Kitty said with a fleeting smirk. "I still remember perfectly well what he's like when he wants something. And in this case, he wanted me to warn my cousin's wife that he'd shoot her husband dead unless she put a stop to it." Kitty's smirk now became more than fleeting. "So I thought to myself, turnabout is fair play. Which is why I'm warning you."

I sobered as my doubts were swiftly replaced with the cool chill of dread. "Fair play? Dueling is not a game, Kitty."

"Tell that to your husband," Kitty replied. "Because after leaving Federal Hall on Saturday, he not only embroiled himself in two affairs of honor in the space of an hour. He'd also thrown up his arms and declared himself ready to fight my family's whole '*detestable faction*' one by one."

The heat of shame it brought to my cheeks to imagine my husband stooping to the level of a street brawler! He, who'd been George Washington's secretary of the treasury!

But, of course, now he was not.

And maybe he didn't know what he was anymore if not that.

"Are you mad?" I asked Alexander. I had accosted him in the carriage house, where the heat gave rise to the scent of horse. And though my husband preferred that we have the conversation inside, I didn't want to give him time to formulate a jury argument. "Aren't you the same man who toiled to make this country a nation of laws? Yet, you resort to threats of duels and fisticuffs? And in front of Philip? It's barbarism."

He gave a little sigh. "It won't come to a duel."

Remembering that Angelica's husband had been all but exiled from England for having nearly killed a man in a duel, I asked, "How can you be certain?"

"Because I've been involved in affairs of honor several times before without a shot ever being fired." This staggering bit of news I'd scarcely digested before he continued, "I manage them to my satisfaction, and my opponents withdraw, which is why I tipped my hand to Kitty."

"So you *did* tell her." Given the color that darkened his cheeks, this embarrassed him, but not enough. What an incurable schemer!

"I expected Kitty to warn the womenfolk of her family, who would, in turn, exert pressure upon Livingston to come to terms with me. I never predicted she'd take license to alarm *you*."

"Well, as always, you are too clever by half."

"Eliza, this is the way of honor with gentlemen."

"If it's *honor* that you value, then perhaps you ought to guard the esteem your country still has for you by not offering to brawl in the streets like a madman."

"I am not mad."

"No?" I asked, thinking his behavior erratic. To prove it, I held up three different scribblings I'd found on his desk. "What do I see here? An essay in defense of the Jay Treaty that you wrote for the papers under one pen name. A second, written under a *different* name in which you anonymously praise yourself for writing the first. And then a raving third, pretending to add to the imaginary choir! It's madness."

"I am not *mad*," he repeated, kicking at a bit of straw on the floor.

"Then what in blazes is wrong with you? Because issuing the challenges, threatening fistfights, breaking up protests, and throwing yourself into gazette debates with such duplicity . . . all of this seems as if you're half out of your mind!"

"I *am* out of my mind!" he suddenly shouted, and then he pressed his fist to his mouth, his eyes going shockingly glassy. "I . . . I lost a child, Eliza," he choked out. "I lost a child, too." He threw down the leather satchel he carried with him nearly everywhere, and sank down onto a bale of hay. He stayed there, silent, as I nearly quaked at the revelation. He'd lost a child. Of course he had. But consumed in a mother's grief, I'd thought only of the fact that *I* had lost a child.

*I will hold you together,* he'd promised in the darkest hour. He'd done that with tenderness, patience, and devotion. But he'd suppressed his own grief so long that now he was the one flying to pieces, and I'd neither seen the cracks forming, nor done anything to heal them.

"Oh, Alexander," I said, going to his side and realizing he always kept something of himself hidden from everyone. Even in the grips of yellow fever, thinking he was soon to die, he'd been unable to reveal himself completely.

He was not the sort of man to accept pity, not the sort of man to give himself over to a woman, but I wrapped my arms around him anyway. "Let me hold you together, now. Let us *both* hold each other together from now on."

Alexander took a great shuddering breath. "What would you have me do? I should let them call me a coward, let them accuse me, there in the street, of treason, of stealing from the treasury with the connivance of Britain. Is that what you want me to do?"

"I want you to remember that you're a father, and that you promised never to leave me alone or desperate again."

He was quiet a long time, but then he nodded. "And a promise must never be broken."

In the end, one man was persuaded to deny casting aspersions on my husband's manhood. The other was persuaded to issue a lukewarm apology. My husband was persuaded to say that he was satisfied.

And I was persuaded I would never again hear another word about duels.

# Chapter Twenty-Seven

*October 1795*
*New York City*

THE SCRAP OF paper in my husband's coat pocket smelled of French lavender. And upon it, in a very fine feminine hand, was written a street address. Just days ago, Alexander warned that Maria Reynolds had returned to New York. He didn't want me to be dismayed if our paths should cross. But now I was left to wonder how he knew of her return, and if this was her address.

*I should ask him,* I thought. Or perhaps I should throw this scrap of paper in the fire. To investigate would be beneath my dignity. I shouldn't elevate my suspicions by crossing town to learn who resided at this address.

But in the end, that's just what I did, because I couldn't live with myself if I was, again, a trusting fool. Dressed in my finest gown, I climbed the crumbling steps, took hold of the knocker, and rapped firmly on the door, bracing for the pain. If this was the residence of my husband's mistress, I didn't know what I'd say or do. I only knew that I must know.

The door opened. And the sight of him—the shock of it—nearly stopped my heart.

It wasn't my husband but a stranger. And yet, I knew that face.

The length of it. The nobility of his form. That ridiculous martial pose. "*Bonjour*," he said as ruddy autumn leaves swirled at my feet. "You're here to see Monsieur La Colombe?"

Under no circumstances would I pay call to a gentleman's home by myself, in the middle of the day, as if in assignation. So I ignored his question in favor of my own. "Who might you be?"

Perhaps it was the directness of my scrutiny that made the youth's eyes dart away. I could see now that he was a boy. Perhaps sixteen. Seventeen. No more than that.

"A servant," he said.

What a dreadful liar. Because his voice convinced me that my eyes were not playing me false—that I knew who this was. "I am Mrs. Alexander Hamilton," I said at once.

Upon hearing my name, the panicked boy motioned me swiftly into the house. "*Venez vite.* Come in, *s'il vous plaît*!" Only when the door closed did he give a courtly bow, with a flourish that again reminded me of his father. "Pardon, *madame*. Forgive the ruse. My name is Georges Washington Louis Gilbert du—"

"*Motier*," I finished for him, sudden affection gripping me. "Yes. I knew your father. And you will have trouble convincing anyone that you're a servant, for you are every inch Lafayette's son."

His smile filled with pride, but also confusion. "Colonel Hamilton sent you?"

"No, I'm afraid our meeting is quite a surprise to me." And a relief, as well. For the secret my husband was keeping, I realized now, had nothing to do with that woman. "How have you come to be in New York?"

"My mother sent me. She was spared from the guillotine, thanks to Ambassador Monroe."

President Washington had sent Monroe to be our minister to France, and my husband insisted he was bungling the job. But James Monroe had accomplished *this*, for which I was deeply grateful. "Is she here? Is your mother free?"

The boy shook his head. "*Maman* insisted upon joining my father in his prison cell, to shame his captors or share his fate. But she made me go," Georges said, eyes welling with guilt-ridden tears. "I did not want to leave them behind, but she said I could save their lives. I am to go for help. To the American president himself."

I nodded, quickly. "We must get you to Philadelphia."

"Colonel Hamilton says it is not yet possible."

Not yet possible? I couldn't imagine what intrigue my husband was about. Or why Lafayette's son was posing as a servant. But my heart broke at the boy's obvious terror. "Then you must come home with me."

Young Georges shook his head. "It is not safe."

I didn't care. I'd protested my husband threatening to brawl in the streets over a matter of a treaty. But if risks must be taken, then they must be taken for the son of a man we both loved. "I insist," I said, pained to see how thin Georges was, and appalled at the shabby brown coat in which he'd been clothed. I'd have to find him new breeches and an embroidered coat. Something fitting. "I'll make you a fine meal."

Though hunger lurked in his eyes, he fretted, "But my tutor and our host—"

"They're both welcome," I said. With that I took Georges home straightaway in my carriage, though the boy insisted upon using the servants' door in the back.

He feared he was being hunted. That there were spies in the city. That the Jacobins—and their supporters—were here, in New York. *Would such men kidnap young Lafayette and return him to bloody France?*

"Almost assuredly," my husband said when he returned home to find Georges already fast friends with our Philip. The two youths ate heaps of cold mutton and buttered bread while falling into easy conversation at the table. They made a handsome pair, Lafayette's redheaded son and Hamilton's brown-haired boy.

After supper, Georges complimented Ana on her songs, saying she might one day sing at the opera house in Paris. And my delighted girl blushed with pleasure from head to toe.

"Why can't young Lafayette see the president?" I whispered as we watched from across the hall.

My husband grimaced. "Because the French ambassador is refusing to attend Washington's levees on account of the presence of exiles like Noailles. Jefferson tried to argue that these are public functions and anyone is welcome, but the new French government won't listen even to him . . . if the ambassador sees Lafayette's son in Washington's presence, they might demand we return the boy to France."

"Those murderous animals can't have him," I hissed.

That was something over which *I* would be prepared to stand and fight. And Alexander rubbed at the small of my back to calm me. "They may argue the president is violating our neutrality by harboring the son of a French traitor—"

"Lafayette is no traitor!"

Alexander hushed me. "Believe me, my love, it afflicts me with as much indignation as you, which is why I've been acting the part of a secret go-between. The president wants to embrace young Lafayette, but cannot take the lad in. Not yet."

"Then we must."

Unexpectedly, my husband wandered away from me, down into the kitchen. I found him with both hands upon the butcher block, his head hung low.

"Alexander, if the president cannot shelter Lafayette's son for fear of offending the French, we can. We should. We *must*. And when I think of how you must have felt when you were his age, coming to this city alone . . ."

Alexander sighed, staring up at me. "Here you are, ready to open your arms to another desperate child for my sake—and this after I've done so much injury to your faith in me that you'd cross town with a scrap of paper to verify my fidelity . . ."

So he knew what I'd done. Why I'd gone to an unknown address. And I was filled with shame, wondering what sort of weapon infidelity was that it should repeatedly cut both its perpetrator and its victim long after they'd forgiven one another. "I am sorry."

With generosity, he waved away my apology. "You're merely testing the ground with your foot, to make sure it's solid." He left unspoken the question, *but will you ever be sure of me?*

No wonder marriage required a vow before God and witnesses. It was no easy thing. And yet, the struggles somehow made me cherish it more. Made me cherish *him* more. Made me cherish, too, that we could offer a home to Lafayette's son.

And not only for my husband's sake.

If the worst should ever come to pass in our country, I might be forced to send my own children across the sea to safety. I saw in Georges both the untrusting boy my husband had been, and my own son, if the Jacobins had their way. And it made me *feel* like the protective lioness I'd vowed to be.

I didn't know Lafayette's wife, but we were both married to revolutionaries. And we were both mothers. So I was determined to take care of her hunted son, no matter what.

"THE PRESIDENT WILL not stand for reelection," Alexander announced as he guided me into his law office. We were supposed to be on the way to a dinner party to be held in the home of his new law partner, Nathaniel Pendleton, and we were both dressed very grandly for the occasion, but he'd insisted we needed to stop to retrieve some papers.

My stomach dropped. Not at the news, for I think I remain one of two people in the entire nation who was not surprised—the other being Martha Washington. No, my foreboding stemmed from knowing that Washington's presence at the helm of the government was what allowed Alexander to retire. After six long months, we'd finally sent Georges off with our love and best wishes to be received by President Washington. The boy was so studious, helpful, and sensible that it left us both a little bereft to part with him, but I'd also been hopeful that it was the last political crisis in which we'd be embroiled.

Now I feared to be embroiled in another. Absentmindedly shoving teetering stacks of books and papers out of his way, Alexander was despondent. "President Washington says he can no longer endure to be devoured in the prints by a set of infamous scribblers."

"Who can blame him?" I asked, taking note that one whole shelf of the wall-length bookcase behind Alexander had been devoted to storing the latest gazettes. No one wanted to serve anymore. Not when, under our new government, any man, whether a gentleman or a scoundrel, could say whatever he pleased and print whatever libels he wished without consequence. And the ignorant populists, spewing tobacco juice as they ranted, took full advantage. As if the notion that all men were *created* equal somehow meant that one need not aspire to knowledge and ability—all distinctions of class, breeding, or merit discarded, all notions of civility deserted.

Months ago, the president had persuaded James McHenry, Hamilton's old friend and fellow aide-de-camp, to serve as secretary of war. And Mac couldn't find it within himself to disappoint his old general. But *six* of the most talented men in America had turned down the post of secretary of state simply because the irrational calumny heaped upon the heads of public officials was so calculated and unrelenting as to put a man and his family in fear for their lives.

The distrust and hatred of anyone who attempted to govern for the benefit of society could drive lesser men than my husband to their knees. And it had once driven my husband there, too.

"Who will replace President Washington?" I asked as I took one of the facing seats, more than a little wary that my husband might feel compelled to put himself forward.

I'd sipped from the cup of glory and found the taste bitter. So I was grateful when he answered, "By seniority, John Adams is the heir apparent. But lacking Washington's majesty, popularity, and wartime experience, Adams is no fit replacement. Personally, I have always thought his temper too high and . . . unhinged. Still, all reservations must give way to the great object of keeping *Jefferson* from the presidency."

The Virginian had bided his time in retirement and become the leader of a genuine political party. They called themselves *Republicans*, a name that offensively implied the present government was comprised of monarchists. But we still called them Jacobins, since they seemed to have so much in common with the terrorists who controlled France.

They could not be allowed to come to power here. Still, I nearly shook with relief that my husband wouldn't be the man to oppose them. "Let it be John Adams then," I said. Alexander puffed out a snort of disgust, so I continued, "Washington's retirement is the most eloquent answer any man could ever give to those who paint him a monarchist. Someone else must now take the helm. Alexander, if you have faith in a republic where no man is king, then let it be *tried*."

Alexander took very little on faith. Certainly not this republic.

He'd never liked the ugly misshapen compromise that had come out of the Constitutional Convention, but no man had fought harder to bring forth a government from that parchment. And perhaps no man knew better how difficult it was to bring such a government into being, or how easily it could all collapse.

Sullenly, he said, "In any case, there is no persuading Washington against it. He's always been slow to take his ground, but once decided, he cannot be shaken. And he's *determined* to leave the presidency."

I reached across his desk to him. "Then you mustn't make it any more difficult for him by standing as an obstacle. Besides, John Adams was instrumental in bringing about our independence and has been the vice president all these years. That's experience no one else has. He isn't Washington, but no one is. And that doesn't mean he can't succeed."

Alexander sighed and wound his fingers with mine. "Were you always such a wise woman?"

I sputtered. "Certainly not. I've had to become wiser to better fulfill the peculiar duties associated with being the wife of Alexander Hamilton."

A spark of familiar mischief worked its way into his visage. "Very well, *wife of Alexander Hamilton*." He tugged me around to him. "I shall now call upon you to perform one of those peculiar duties."

Scandalized, I gasped. "Not in your office!"

"Oh, but I insist." He stood and put me into his chair. I burned with curiosity, having no earthly idea what he might intend. Then my cheeks burned hotter when he withdrew some papers from the secret compartment of his desk and confided an entirely innocent purpose. "The president has asked me to help draft a Farewell Address."

"Is there no one else capable?" I asked, wondering if Alexander might ever be left to enjoy retirement.

"Madison made an attempt," he replied, unable to utter the name of his old friend without scorn. "He is, after all, the one who drafted Washington's inaugural. But, as this is Washington's last address, the president won't allow the Republicans to put their stamp on it." And Madison was a founding member of the new party that stood opposed to the Federalists in all things. Our one-time friend Monroe, too. Both of them Jefferson's protegés. All of them now aligned in favor of a weak federal government and stronger states' rights, the very things against which we'd fought for the past fifteen years.

So I understood then. The president's very last address was a sacred duty.

My husband explained, "The president has asked me to take his own sentiments and ideas, and remove any egotism or partisan sentiments liable to bring criticism. To put all in a plain, simple style." Alexander threw the papers onto the desk. "You see my difficulty."

I chuckled because I did. I could think of no man less suited than my husband to write in a *plain simple style,* without partisan warmth or egotism. Alexander brought the thunder of rhetorical cannons, not the soft refrains of conciliatory prose.

But since he couldn't refuse, I tried to bolster his spirits. "You wrote for Washington as his aide-de-camp. Surely you remember how. And if you don't, consider it a stretch of your talents . . . You say Jemmy Madison drafted the inaugural. Well, if he had the first words, I know you'll want to have the last."

He laughed. "You saucy wench. This brings me to your part." Alexander leaned forward so that his hands were on both arms of the chair, seductively caging me in. "My dear Eliza, you must be what Molière's nurse was to him."

"Who?" I asked, a little wary that this might turn into another story of some ancient.

Instead, he said, "Never mind. The point is that I must test my words against your good sense."

My mouth went dry, for I didn't know whether to be flattered or terrified. *Both,* I decided, given what he was asking. "You cannot mean this seriously."

"I trust no one else. I trust your understanding of people. Your goodness and impartial heart."

"My heart is not even slightly impartial," I said.

That made him smile. "But you're fair-minded. How often have you argued with me over the malice I've ascribed to others when simpler explanations would do? I need you to argue with me now."

He *was* serious. "Have you forgotten we are on our way to Pendleton's dinner party?"

"I've forgotten it entirely," he said, rising up again to find a pen. "I'll send a clerk to Fraunces Tavern for victuals to sustain us and we'll stay here until the candles burn out."

There was a hint of familiar conspiratorial excitement in his voice now, but I reminded him, with a great deal of hauteur, "As delightful as that sounds, I am in a rare state." My gauzy evening gown might have been thought scandalous in any other era, but it was the Age of Undress. The fashion was now all empire waistlines and sheer fabrics *à la Grec*, which would have left me feeling naked without gloves and shawl. "I am dressed to be seen in society, sir!"

With the tip of his quill pen, he flicked my flimsy shawl to the floor. "And now you are not." He gave his most irresistible smile. "Your country needs you. *I* need you. You are my good genius of that kind which the ancient philosophers called a familiar." His eyebrows nearly waggled. "And you know that I am glad to be, in *every* way, as *familiar* as possible with you."

Smitten by his flirtation, I gave a helpless shrug. "Oh well, for the country then . . ."

I forgot about the dinner party. I forgot everything but the familiar thrill of matching minds with the man I married. "Not that line," I remember telling him. "That business about *the ignorance of facts and malicious falsehoods* will be taken harshly."

"That's the president's line, not mine," Alexander protested.

"Nevertheless, it portrays him as a partisan in the mud," I argued, and our debate went well into the night. In truth, it went on for days as Alexander worked on the address, scribbling words and crossing them out.

Eventually, he removed the line to which I objected. That and many others, taking into consideration my suggestions, leaving me awed with the magnitude of the masterpiece. I knew, even then, that the Farewell Address was a moving and worthy tribute to the United States and its people. A plea for unity. A statement of purpose and guidance for the nation George Washington helped bring into being.

And because of Alexander Hamilton, I had the great and everlasting fortune to be a part of its shaping.

# Chapter Twenty-Eight

> *May the present coolness between France and America*
> *produce, like the quarrels of lovers, a renewal of love.*
> —CHANCELLOR LIVINGSTON

*May 1797*
*New York City*

I WAS HAPPY.

I somehow forgot that. In the blazing trail of my husband's wake, it has been easier to remember the hard times. The wars and the riots. The illnesses and exhaustion. The arguments and betrayals. The things people call history.

But happiness grew in the cracks between great events. I was happy in the little things. In falling asleep beside my husband each night, and waking up in his arms every morning. In walking my boys to the ferry to attend their school on Staten Island. In listening to Alexander and Ana sing duets at the piano. In the sermons at Trinity Church, where we rented a pew. And in the company of my sister Angelica, returned after more than seven and a half years of separation.

Finally, it seemed, I had everything I wanted.

"Angelica!" I called, tearful with joy, waving over the workaday crowd bustling along Broadway in front of her new town house. Upon seeing me, my sister abandoned her baggage, retinue, and children to rush into my arms.

Such was the force of our embrace that her dazzling diamond earrings caught in my dark hair and we were briefly entangled, laughing and crying at the same time. "Just look at you!" Angelica exclaimed, laying both hands atop my pregnant belly. "Have you grown fat with too fond a taste for marzipan or has my brute of a brother begotten another baby upon you?"

"Brute, am I?" Alexander asked, archly, swooping forward in elegant top hat.

Angelica nearly wilted at the sight of him. "Oh, my *amiable*!" she cried, throwing her perfumed arms around my husband's neck. "You know I jest. But oh, how naughty you two have been."

"Very naughty," I replied, for my sister always brought out my saucy side. "We *do* love to overindulge . . . in marzipan."

We were caught up in a gale of laughter when my sister's brood gathered around us and I gasped at the sight of her eldest son. How in the world had the little boy who spent that frigid winter with us in Morristown grown up to be an outrageously handsome young Englishman?

"Aunt Eliza, I presume," he said, with a charming, Eton-educated accent.

"Oh, my darling nephew," I said, tugging my own boy close. "Meet your cousin, Philip Hamilton."

Both Philips grinned, mischief in their eyes, as if already wondering which one might best the other in charming the young ladies of New York.

"My friends call me Flip," my nephew said. "So, it shan't be difficult to distinguish."

Our reunion was so deliriously pleasurable that, as we stepped inside Church's grand new house, I couldn't seem to stop weeping—a thing I blamed upon pregnancy, but it had more to do, I think, with my most cherished dream to have my sister near. And for that, I had Mr. Church to thank. To please his wife, he'd retired from public service in London and moved their entire family to New York, where they planned to stay.

"Church has changed," my sister confided later, while our combined family of hooligans ran through the wide halls of her nearly empty house and her new lady's maid, a slave named Sarah, unpacked her trunks. "For the better."

"Truly?"

Angelica sighed with apparent contentment as we toured her new home. "By some miracle, we've found our way back to love. Isn't marriage funny that way?" Then she laughed. "Not that you know anything but the delight of marriage, of course! Not you and Hamilton. But for the rest of us . . ."

It made me queasy to realize that I knew of all my sister's marital troubles, and yet she knew nothing of mine. It hadn't been safe to confide it in a letter, but to keep it from her now felt almost like a betrayal of the bond we shared. On the other hand, to tell her would seem a betrayal of the man I loved.

And what did it matter, now that it was all in the past?

"A fountain!" Angelica cried as we walked out into her new garden. "You and Hamilton know me so well. You couldn't have chosen a better house for me, Bets—forgive me, Eliza," she said with a smile, observing me. I'd written her long ago about my decision to go by the new nickname, but we'd been so long separated that this was the first time she'd seen me in person since I'd made the change. "Old habits . . ."

"You may call me whatever you like as long as you are *here*," I said.

"I am here. And now that we are such close neighbors, I foresee you and I spending much time here together, presuming . . ."

When she trailed off, I prompted, "Presuming?"

She looked to the sky. "Presuming, of course, that the Jacobins don't burn it all down."

A wreath of smoky haze had enveloped the city for months, the remainder of a series of devastating fires that had been set in protest of the election of John Adams to the presidency. Not even the fact that Jefferson, having received the second most number of votes in the election, was now vice president seemed to stem the tide of discontent. The culprit had never been caught, but the stench of the ashes remained.

And like everyone else, Angelica had a definite opinion about who was to blame. "How could you let Hamilton quit the government when the spirit of Jacobinism threatens the political and moral world with a complete overthrow? He's needed there more than ever."

It had been the loss of our baby that convinced him to leave government, which she knew from my letters. Still, I felt the need to say, "He said the change was necessary and agreeable."

Angelica sighed. "The country has lost one of her best friends, and you, my dear Eliza, are the only person to whom this change can be either necessary or agreeable. Yes, I am decidedly inclined to believe that it was your influence."

*So what if it was?* Angelica had charmed all of Europe and understood more about politics and philosophy than I did, but she didn't understand all that had happened here, in our marriage and our country. I loved my sister, but I was no longer the young girl who deferred to her every opinion. Especially since she and Church still kept slaves, whilst my husband was finally free to devote more time to abolishing slavery. "No one's done more for this government than Alexander Hamilton. And he's done enough."

She blinked, then finally nodded. "Of course."

Wanting to smooth things over, I smiled. "Besides, as we now both benefit from his increased attention, you'll soon see it's *altogether* agreeable."

She laughed. "That so good a wife, so tender a mother, should be so bad a patriot is wonderful!"

*So bad a patriot.*

Her tone was teasing, but she'd somehow hit upon a guilty nerve. Was I so selfish for wanting my husband to belong more to me than to an ungrateful public? Was it wrong to enjoy the fruits of all our labor, the domestic pleasures of picnics with our children and long walks together on kissing bridges and dinner at our own table without expecting a horde of guests?

Perhaps sensing my inner turmoil, my sister sat at the edge of her fountain to say, "I suppose it's for the better. Now that Papa is back in the Senate, he wouldn't like to be outshone by his son-in-law."

We both smiled, knowing how much pleasure it gave Papa to have been reelected, nearly unanimously. He'd bided his time and Burr, sensing the change of political fortune on the wind, had resigned his seat rather than lose it. My family counted that a good thing, but I remembered what Burr had said at Vauxhall Gardens.

*Retirement is very fashionable these days amongst men who wish to be president . . .*

Angelica went on, "Besides, it's better that you have Hamilton to look over you in your condition." I half-wished to remind her that our own mother had children well into her forties, and I was only thirty-nine. But my sister had centered directly on another of my most keen anxieties, as was her way.

I feared miscarrying another child and I said so.

"This time you'll have me here with you, my dearest," she promised. "I shall watch over you with such overbearing insistence, you'll think I've turned into Mama!"

LIKE A SENTINEL who'd forgotten his duty, I startled awake. Round with a child that often awakened me in the night by kicking in eagerness to be out into the world, I was now prone to nap in the heat of the day. This time in a rocking chair on my porch while shucking peas, lulled to sleep by the sound of Ana practicing at the piano while Fanny sketched with charcoal beside me.

But now everything was silent but for the buzzing of a few lazy bees, and Fanny was nowhere to be seen. Only my husband, who stood, staring, not three feet away, his brow furrowed, his hands deep in his pockets.

Disoriented, I squinted against the blazing sun, then pushed myself up, but Alexander stopped me. "No, my darling, don't get up. I didn't mean to wake you."

Still, a mother can never be comforted by quiet; noisy little ones were much less likely to be up to mischief. "But the children—"

"They're at your sister's house for the night. I had Philip take them." The flatness of his voice told me something was amiss. My husband could, in a courtroom, exhibit a hundred different expressions from anger to sympathy to joy. His blank, haggard expression made me go hollow inside, even before he said, "There is something I must tell you, my angel."

My mouth went instantly dry.

For I remembered the last time he said, *There is something I must tell you, my angel.*

And I was sure that he remembered it, too. "I am usually a man who knows the right thing to do. But today . . ." He sighed. "I'm at a loss. I thought to shield you from this, but I don't wish for you to be taken unawares. Especially not in your condition."

"Tell me." I stiffened, wondering, traitorously, if he was going to confess another mistress. I hated myself for that.

"You know of the newspaperman James Callender?" I nodded, because that vile Jacobin scandalmonger had been the source of too many libels to count. "He's published a pamphlet dredging up the old accusations of my supposed corruption at the treasury."

I blew out a cautious breath. "A thing for which you've been exonerated at least thrée times over by my count."

"He is also exposing my connection to Mrs. Reynolds."

*Connection.*

The euphemism was a blow. And just like that, the fragile foundation I'd rebuilt myself upon began to fracture. I could almost hear the crack. I'd thought this all done and buried. Now, someone had resurrected it. Resurrected her. *Maria.*

I'd always worried that the secret might come out. That Aaron Burr might blurt it drunkenly at a dinner party. That the harlot herself might whisper it on the pillow of whatever man she was bedding now. But I'd imagined only whispers. Never that anyone would be depraved enough to *print* it.

"What does the newspaperman know?" What *could* he know, after all?

"Everything," Alexander replied, quietly. "Callender has copies of letters exchanged between us."

*Letters?* I'd somehow never understood that my husband had done more than go to bed with this woman. He wrote to her. Were they love letters? Letters like the ones he'd written to me when we were courting?

I didn't ask. Truthfully, in that moment, I didn't want to know the answer. What I wanted, most of all, in the face of this humiliation, was to hold on to calm dignity. "She sold her correspondence," I guessed.

Alexander shook his head. "No. These are the letters I provided to James Monroe. He's leaked them."

*Monroe?* My first thought was that I must've misheard. Of all the friends with whom we'd parted for political reasons, Monroe was the most upright and honorable. He was a *gentleman;* I could scarcely credit that he would trade in such filth. My second thought was that, years ago, he'd promised to protect *my* honor. And my third was that it wasn't even possible, because Monroe had been serving as our minister to France. "He isn't even in the country."

"The president revoked his credentials and recalled him. He's just returned to our shores. And, no doubt, straightaway conspired with Jefferson's loathsome faction. He's given the newspapers every scrap of evidence he promised to keep confidential."

I could make no sense of this. "But Monroe gave me his *word of honor* to keep quiet about this affair."

At this, my husband glanced at me, then again, plainly startled. "You discussed it with him?"

Under my husband's stunned scrutiny, I reminded him exactly how such conversation came about. "Yes. On the night the investigators came to the house."

Alexander's jaw clenched, though he knew what it had cost me, that night, bleeding with near fatal humiliation. "Well I regret to report that you prevailed upon his friendship in vain."

I still didn't want to believe this of Monroe. I *rebelled* against believing it. I was no longer naive about the sins men were capable of—even men I'd loved—but there seemed some part of the story untold.

I'd taken solace in the idea that there ought to be no reason for anyone to attack us if only Hamilton stayed out of the public eye. If he stayed out of politics.

"Why now?" I asked. Monroe had kept the secret *four years*. "With you in retirement, what possible advantage—"

"I don't know," my husband said, hanging his head, the weight of his guilt forcing the slump of his shoulders. "Revenge, maybe. It was upon my advice that the president recalled Monroe from France."

At hearing this, I was overcome with the urge to reach for the bowl of shucked peas and throw it. Into the yard, at the house, maybe even at my husband. I didn't know which. I'd never guessed, not even once, that the wreck of Monroe's diplomatic career was my husband's doing.

And as I struggled to calm myself, Alexander took my hand. "I promise you, my darling, I wasn't the only one urging the president to revoke Monroe's credentials. Our foreign policy must be spoken in one voice. Monroe in France and Jay in England were at cross-purposes overseas. I gave the president my best advice."

Reeling, I yanked my hand away.

He met my eyes, beseechingly. "Eliza, I didn't think it right to risk the good of the country, all for fear of a secret any man held over me. I didn't want to think that Monroe—who'd been a friend to me and a fellow soldier—would prove to be both a man mistaken in his political beliefs and *also* without honor as a gentleman." As I listened, his voice softened. "Would you have me done differently?"

I paused to think about it, but I was not, in the end, *so bad a patriot*. "No. You did precisely as you should have." There was a moment of grace between us that I could admit this. I think he felt it, too. "What will we do now?"

Bringing my fingertips to his lips, he said, "I fear I must confess my wrongdoing." And as panic tightened my throat, he explained why. Callender claimed that my husband *invented* an imaginary infidelity to cover up his real crime of having enriched himself at the taxpayer's expense.

As if we'd been at all enriched!

How often had I accepted gifts from my parents to put food on our table? How many years had I borrowed and bartered and scrimped to make ends meet? My husband had left the service of our country poorer than when he entered it, deeply indebted to my brother-in-law and without any real property of his own.

But as I wrestled with my anger at the injustice of this accusation, I also realized the perversity of the situation. "You can't defend yourself against charges of corruption without confessing the affair . . ." Worse, he couldn't defend himself without *convincing* the public of the affair.

"I've no choice but to expose everything."

But I saw a way out of the corner he'd been backed into. "If Monroe will explain to the public that he investigated the matter long ago and believed your innocence, surely that will put an end to it."

"He won't," Alexander replied.

"He *might*, if you asked him."

"Not after our quarrel this morning . . ."

I startled. "You've seen Monroe?"

There in the stifling heat, Alexander bit out a laugh. "By happenstance he's here in New York visiting his wife's relatives. I deduced his part in this conspiracy and confronted him."

"*And*?" I asked.

Alexander's gaze darkened, as if in stormy remembrance. "And some words were said that ought never be said amongst gentlemen. If it hadn't been for Church breaking us apart, we'd have come to blows then and there."

My baby kicked inside me, as if to express its own dismay at this revelation. Church had been there? My brother-in-law knew everything then. Maybe Angelica did, too. And soon, so would the whole country know about my husband's infidelity. Though I had little idea of the extent of it, I realized that my marriage was to be sported with. That I was soon to be a laughingstock, my children subject to mockery. That our enemies were going to destroy all the happiness we'd fought so hard to find—the happiness that we'd *earned*.

Unless I did something about it . . .

It wasn't a far walk to Monroe's lodgings on Wall Street, where I handed a Negro slave my calling card and was shown into a gilded parlor to wait. The hour was late for a visit, but none of the usual rules of propriety seemed to matter to anyone else, so why should they matter to me?

I hadn't told my husband of my intention for fear he might attempt to prevent me, and he wasn't entitled to. I'd taken no part in the decisions that brought us to this place, but I wanted some choice in what happened now.

I didn't ask permission. I just went.

And waited.

It'd been four years since I'd last seen James Monroe, but when, at length, the Virginian strode into the parlor, he was as tall and strapping as ever. Though he eschewed pantaloons in favor of old-fashioned knee breeches and stockings, he'd acquired a new elegance to his gait in Paris. In truth, I might've been intimidated by the personage he presented if I didn't still remember him as a blushing, stammering boy of a soldier, with a dimple on his chin just like mine . . .

Monroe cleared his throat and drawled, "I would delight in your company, Mrs. Hamilton, under other circumstances. However, as your husband has sent you, and my wife is with her family, I cannot invite you to stay."

"Hamilton didn't send me," I said, unfastening the bow of my bonnet and laying it upon the chair beside me to signal that I had no intention of leaving. "Though I've been made aware of your quarrel."

"*Quarrel*?" Monroe snorted. "Your husband launched into a lengthy diatribe, filled with accusations—"

"I'm not here to accuse you." I looked directly into the gray eyes of the southern gentleman who had, in a dark time, once been my only confidant, and felt as vulnerable to him now as I did then. "Four years ago, I didn't doubt your word when you swore you'd spare me humiliation. I don't doubt it now. Tell me that you didn't give the Reynolds letters to the newspapermen and I will believe you."

Monroe's shoulders rounded. My faith in him plainly pierced his puffed-up sense of outrage. He seemed relieved that I pledged to trust him, but his encounter with Alexander had left him still in an icy cold fury.

"Of course I didn't give the letters to the newspapers," Monroe finally said. "When I was sent to France, I entrusted my official documents to a friend in Virginia under seal. I've only just returned to the country and had no idea of their publication."

I believed him. Truly, I did. "Then the blame must go to your friend in Virginia . . ." Who could be none other than Thomas Jefferson.

But Monroe set me onto my heels by saying, "I presume John Beckley published the papers in question."

Beckley was a name I knew only slightly. A one-time indentured servant who had, through the grace of his populist political leanings, risen to be a clerk in the House of Representatives. "How should a mere clerk come to have possession of these papers?"

Monroe could no longer hold my gaze. "Because I commissioned him to copy them, never suspecting he'd make a set of his own to do mischief with." A crimson flush swept over Monroe as he admitted to me, however obliquely, that the situation was at least partly his fault.

And all at once, I felt a cold fury of my own. "Mr. Monroe, for what purpose would you have a clerk copy papers that you swore on your honor to keep confidential?"

I should not have said the word *honor*. Not to a Virginian. "It was your husband who demanded copies!"

Then—perhaps in the horror of having shouted at a lady—Monroe went silent. Perfectly silent. Meanwhile, I marveled at the folly of my husband, who had, like the lawyer he was, apparently asked for copies of the most damning evidence against him.

*Oh, Alexander.*

When Monroe finally broke his silence, he seethed. "Did Hamilton think I would stoop to set my own hand to the wretched task of copying his lengthy treasons against you?" His gray eyes caught mine again with a meaningful stare that recalled the moment, years ago, when he pressed my hand to his heart. "And if *you* think me capable, then you've never understood my attachment to you."

Once, such words might've touched me, but now my chest heaved with indignation. "Mr. Monroe, how can you claim *any* manner of attachment when I entrusted to you my fragile happiness, only to find it carelessly disregarded so as to save you a cramp in the wrist and—"

I cut myself off, remembering my purpose. It was *not* to antagonize James Monroe. It was to enlist his aid. I was becoming too much like Alexander—infected by his short temper. I struggled to regained my composure.

With a deep, calming breath, I started again. "Mr. Monroe, the scurrilous newspapermen will say what they will. The whispers I shall have to bear. But when you investigated my husband for corruption, you were convinced of his innocence, were you not?"

Monroe nodded, though I sensed reluctance. "Your husband's explanation of how he was extorted removed our suspicions of his being connected with Mr. Reynolds in speculation."

Relieved, I smiled at him. "If you will only say as much—if you will give a sworn statement for the public, then you will relieve my husband of the necessity of a defense—the extreme delicacy of which will be very disagreeable to me."

Monroe turned, strode a few paces, then returned, his voice gentler, a little warmer. "Trust that I regret the publication of these papers—but trust, too, that dragging me into it will draw more public attention to it and make it a matter of even greater consequence. It will not help."

*An easy thing for him to say,* I thought. "Still, we should like the option. And as you've been the inadvertent cause of this business, it's incumbent upon you as a man of honor and sensibility to come forward in a manner that would shield me."

I didn't hesitate to appeal to his honor now. But again, I shouldn't have, because his eyes flew wide. "*I* am the cause of this business? Oh no, madam. It was the scoundrel to whom you pledged your troth who exposed you to this. Not me."

*Scoundrel.* A word that betrayed utter contempt. The sort of word that could start a duel. The word was nearly a slap to my cheek. And perhaps I needed a good slap to bring me to my senses.

"Are you enjoying having me at your mercy, a damsel in distress?" I asked. "Do you wish for me to beg?"

Monroe pinched at the bridge of his nose. "Good God, I could never enjoy causing you distress."

"But if I'm a casualty of your partisan revenge, it doesn't trouble you?"

"That's not the way of it. In truth, I have no desire to persecute your husband, though he justly merits it."

"Does he?" I asked, bristling. The offense Alexander committed was against me. What right did Monroe have to judge him? "He's innocent of the charges that Mr. Jefferson's faction lay at his feet."

"Not according to the latest tale told by Mr. Reynolds."

A flash of rage burned through me at the implication that my husband's word should weigh no more than that of a low-bred villain who played the pimp for his own wife. That my brilliant husband stood upon the same footing as this insignificant little fraud . . .

A champion of equality might see it that way, but that wasn't why Monroe put my husband into the same category. It was because Monroe considered himself a member of a club to which a bastard-born foreigner might never truly be admitted, no matter his merits and talent. James Monroe was born on the right side of the blanket, with a speck of dirt in Virginia to call his own, and he thought that made him *better*.

"My husband is not capable of corruption."

Monroe stared as if he couldn't quite believe a woman would challenge him this way. "I presume you didn't know he was capable of adultery, either. I wish the public might behold in Hamilton that *immaculate* purity to which he pretends. But, my lady, we both know he pretends. And even if I were tempted by your friendship to say otherwise, I have other friends to whom I am obligated."

"*Other* friends? Mr. Jefferson, I presume."

He didn't answer, and he didn't have to. For partisan politics had become so strident and divisive that even someone as honorable as James Monroe refused to do what was right because it would cost him politically. He didn't want to offend Jefferson. He couldn't *afford* to offend Jefferson.

The thought of such craven calculation made me angry enough to spit. And perhaps a little petty, too. "Do you know, Mr. Monroe, that I've always dismissed the gossip that you were in Jefferson's thrall? I was foolish enough to *defend* you when Federalist ladies said that it's to Jefferson that you owe the whole of your advancement. And that you and Madison vie for his approval like royal courtiers."

Monroe stiffened. "I'm afraid the hour grows late and our interview must come to an end."

I was not finished. "I refused to believe that while my husband suffered yellow fever, you sat at a table and toasted to my husband's *speedy demise*."

"I did not join in that toast," Monroe snapped.

My heart sank, because I'd never truly believed the toast took place at all. Now, at his admission, the flame of rage scorched my cheeks, and where I would normally restrain myself, my voice boomed low like a cannon. "It seems I have been very mistaken about you, or you have changed very much. Because the James Monroe I thought I knew, the Hero of Trenton, was not the sort to sit back in *cowardice* and allow such a toast to be made in his presence."

He flinched, but I could draw no satisfaction from it.

Because I knew that accusing him of cowardice blew to bits whatever remained of our friendship, though clearly there was nothing to salvage. Monroe was a Virginian before he was an American. Maybe he was even a Jacobin before he was a Virginian. And I believed that like the rest of Jefferson's detestable faction, if it ever came to a guillotine blade above my neck, Monroe would let it fall.

What else could I think now?

Which made him an enemy.

My husband's enemy. My enemy. An enemy of the country that once called him a hero. And realizing it, I could no longer bear the sight of him or his dimpled chin.

Refusing assistance, I wordlessly snatched my bonnet and pushed myself up to go. I was halfway to the door when he said, "*Betsy,* please. Stop."

I did not stop. I did not even look back. "I am *Mrs. Hamilton*. I leave you to your conscience, sir . . . if you can find it."

# Chapter Twenty-Nine

*The public has long known you as an eminent and
able statesman. They will be highly gratified in seeing
you exhibited in the novel character of a lover.*
—JAMES CALLENDER IN AN OPEN LETTER TO HAMILTON

*July 1797*
*New York City*

ANGER HAD SOMEHOW given me a vim and vigor no pregnant woman in her ninth month ought to feel.

"Church," I said with a nod as I came upon him sitting
at his breakfast table when I arrived to collect my children.

My brother-in-law pinched the bridge of his nose, as if staving
off a hangover from a late-night card game. He jolted at the sight
of me, and though he was never a man for endearments, he cried
with cheer that rang falsely in my ears, "Eliza, my dear! I hope
you're feeling well."

I gave what I'm sure was a brittle smile. "I'm feeling as well as
can be expected."

"Good, good," Church said, his gaze falling almost involun-
tarily to where, amidst polished silver trays, a bowl of sugar, and
discarded floral teacups, a newspaper lay open. "You mustn't let
the opposition distress you. Not in your condition."

I suppose he meant well.

After all, men could work themselves up into killing rages, but women must never be *distressed*. But if he thought our political parties were merely in opposition, trading places like the Tories and the Whigs in England, he was blind. "The men opposed to my husband are nothing but a knot of scoundrels. Their words make not the slightest impression upon me." I snatched up the paper and pressed it into his hand. "And this is fit for nothing but use in the privy."

Church barked with laughter as I went in search of my sister, bracing myself against her pity, or some inevitable story about licentious Englishmen or permissive French marriages that she might offer to comfort me.

Like her husband, Angelica was not an early riser. She was still in some elegant state of undress—a white gossamer chemise, a dark braid of hair over one shoulder—when I found her in the carefully sculpted English garden snipping roses so viciously that leaves dropped like rain.

"Were you never going to confide in me about Hamilton's harlot?" she asked.

I'd braced myself against her pity. I had not anticipated wounded feelings. I suppose I should have. Not only because Angelica tended to put herself at the center of things, but also because I *had* wronged her, after a fashion. "I didn't dare confide it in a letter," I said, and that was true. For letters could be intercepted.

I'd been desperate for my sister's comfort four years ago, but by the time she'd returned, I hadn't any desire whatsoever to reopen the wound. And yet, there was another guilty truth. My sister had bared her soul to me about her troubled marriage, but I hadn't wanted to reveal myself. She'd trusted me with her vulnerability, but I'd kept mine hidden. Perhaps I'd taken some satisfaction in thinking that though my sister was wealthier, more formally educated, and more beautiful by far, my marriage was happier. I'd finally bested her in something. I hated to think this about myself, but I couldn't entirely deny it. Still, in the end, I'd chosen loyalty to my husband over loyalty to my sister. And *that* she would simply have to understand.

Perhaps she did, because Angelica put her hand atop mine. "My poor, sweet Eliza. *All husbands stray.*" A little dazed, I nodded as she uttered the words I'd imagined her saying all those years ago. "I know how tender your heart is, and how easily wounded you are, but—"

"I don't believe I *am* easily wounded." That was a different sister she remembered. I'd changed, and I wanted her to know it. So I told her the rest.

"Oh, to confront Monroe!" She put down her shears and the basket of roses and drew me down onto a marbled bench. "I would applaud if I didn't know this will come to no good. That half-wit fancies himself to be a useful acolyte in Vice President Jefferson's destructive ambitions."

Her habitual contempt for Monroe didn't surprise me, but her contempt for the vice president caught me by surprise. "I thought you counted Mr. Jefferson your friend."

"*Semper Fidelis*, Eliza. I am a Schuyler, too. I will always take my family's part over that of even the most charming friend. If Mr. Jefferson wished to stay in my good graces, then he ought not to have set his partisan lackeys against your husband. Now it's war."

I laughed, a little darkly, but for once, she was the one in earnest.

"My dear, it *is* war. Other women have suffered the pain of infidelity. But you're suffering the penalty of being the wife to the greatest man of his generation and perhaps the greatest of our age. You'd never have suffered this if you hadn't married so close to the sun. But then you would have missed the pride, the pleasure, the nameless satisfactions."

I knew how much my sister admired Hamilton. How the two of them shared the same interests and more traits of character than a casual observer might expect. I'd predicted she'd take his part. And I thought I might bristle when she did, but in the balance of things, she was quite right.

She took my hand. "Let the children stay with me a while longer. You should go home to Papa. Away from the heat of this city. Away from the malice of society. Trust me, you don't want to be here while tongues wag in every coffeehouse, people tittering behind the pages of their gazettes as you pass by."

As the days passed, the thought of escape became ever more tempting, especially when Hamilton rode off to Philadelphia to chase down Monroe, all to no avail. My husband felt forced now to make a public confession and therefore wished for me to have our baby in Albany.

"It's for the better," Alexander said. "As I imagine that you cannot much like the sight of me at present."

I settled beside him on a trunk he kept at the foot of the bed. "You imagine wrong." After all, it seemed as if some different man had broken my heart. And in any case, that heart was four years mended. Alexander and I had each grown, together, into new people. Better people. Though I would never reconcile myself to the cause of the change, I couldn't be sorry for it. We'd made of our marriage vows a more sacred thing than when we first spoke them. And this child in my womb, who would join us in only a few weeks, was the living proof of that. "Though, Angelica thinks it would be easier for me to explain to Papa."

At the mention of my father, Alexander actually shuddered. "How glad General Schuyler will be for setting aside his reservations in giving his daughter in marriage to a man of low birth . . ."

I wanted to reassure him that my father would forgive him, but I couldn't be sure of that. What I said instead was, "Perhaps we mustn't explain anything to Papa. Or to anyone. Your accusers are not entitled to a reply."

Hamilton nodded, folding his hands together. "And yet, the country deserves to know its system is not a corrupt scheme to line my pockets, otherwise these Jacobins will dismantle it and the American experiment will fail."

He'd convinced himself this was one more sacrifice he must make for his country. But I thought, *Give the mob this drop of blood and it will only whet their appetite.*

Before I could say as much, he added, "If I don't answer these charges of corruption, they'll take my name. I cannot save my private reputation, and perhaps I don't deserve to, but at least my public honor may be preserved. Which is all I have to give our children. Our children ought to always be able to hold their heads high with pride."

"And they shall," I said, though I fretted at the chime of the clock that announced Philip was quite late in coming home from an outing with his friends. "Whether or not you dignify this with a response."

My husband rubbed at his cheek, which was darkened by a shadow of stubble. Circles darkened his eyes, too. "I would like to believe that, but I remember what happened when my mother was accused in court of whoring and she did not see fit to dignify it with a response . . ."

All at once the specter of a woman long dead rose between us again. His mother had condemned her children to a life of illegitimacy by letting the accusation pass. Perhaps that is why Hamilton never, *ever,* let anything pass . . .

And knowing this, I would not ask him to.

He caught my fingers between his and sighed. "The rest of the children can stay here with their governess, but let Philip take you to the Pastures. For your sake and his. He's almost a man grown, now. His friends will have heard the gossip. I do not wish for him to feel compelled to defend me. Or maybe, I cannot bear to face his disappointment . . ."

Downstairs, we heard the door open and close, then footsteps trudging up the stairs that could only belong to a troubled boy. Perhaps my husband was right. "But I worry to leave you now, Alexander. *Especially* now."

My husband took a breath. Then another. "Eliza, if you stand beside me the public will eviscerate you. With such men as those hounding me, nothing is sacred. Even the peace of an unoffending and amiable wife. They will hurt you because of their fury against me." He took my face in his hands and stroked my cheeks tenderly. "No man who loves his wife could wish this upon her. No loving father could wish his child born into such circumstances. I realize that I have forfeited my *right* to command you as a husband, but I command you in *love* to go. To take care of yourself, to keep up your spirits, and to remember always that my happiness is inseparable from yours."

*Stand by him and die, renounce him and live.*

Once, I wondered what I would have done if I'd been caught in such a conundrum. I did not face death, of course, but the choice before me seemed strangely similar, and the answer no clearer or easier now.

~~~

*August 1797*
*Albany*

The river washed over my bare feet with a pleasant coolness, my petticoats bunched up at my knees. Seated on the dock next to Papa, who held a fishing pole in his hand and wore a broad straw hat upon his head, I squinted into the bright sun and imagined I was a girl again. Perhaps my father was imagining it, too, because, puffing his pipe, he put a worm onto the hook for me, as if I didn't remember how to do it.

A week before, Hamilton had seen me and Philip off at the sloop, simultaneously solicitous and morose. And Angelica dashed off a note that same night to tell me that my dejected husband had gone to her house thereafter and stayed well into the night, unable to speak of anything but me.

Meanwhile, we all tried to speak of anything but him.

On the deck of the sloop, my fifteen-year-old son treated me as if I were made of glass. Philip had become a man already, I'd realized with a motherly pang. He took his quick wit and devilish smile from his father, but the rest of him was all Schuyler. Tall, dark, and loyal. Having been commanded by his father to watch over me in my delicate condition, my son carried my bags, fetched lemonade, and played games of backgammon with me in our berth at night.

My family was even more solicitous in Albany. Mama had everything ready for me—sweet herbs for my pains, pastries for my cravings, and the Bible from which she read to me. Peggy came to help me birth the babe and told my son what great things were expected of him at Columbia College, where he was soon to enroll. Papa tried to distract me with talk of canal projects and the Indians.

Even Prince, now a bit bent with age, said to my son, in a whisper meant for me to hear, "Master Philip, of all these Schuyler daughters I helped bring up in this house, your mama was the one who gave me the fewest white hairs."

Philip always cringed to be called *Master*, as it did not rest easy with him that his otherwise heroic grandfather still kept a few plantation slaves in his service. And so he took the extra pillows from Prince's arms and said, "Well, my mother wouldn't want to give you any more white hairs climbing those stairs, so let me get her settled."

On the night that my labor pains began, my father finally raised the subject. Bending to kiss me, he whispered into my hair, "My dear beloved child . . . rest easy in knowing that no one of merit believes this filth in the newspapers."

I dreaded to tell him the truth, and weeks after birthing a wondrously healthy little boy named William, I still did not know how. Finally, sitting beside Papa on the ferry dock with fishing poles, I blurted, "I've forgiven Hamilton."

My father bit the clay pipe between his teeth, his lips thinning as understanding dawned that Alexander was guilty. At the prospect of my father learning the truth, my husband had shuddered. The censure of the country, he believed he could withstand. My father's judgment was another matter altogether. And I began to fear it, too, because for a few moments, the only sounds were the rush of the water. The cry of a peregrine falcon hunting overhead.

"Elizabeth," Papa finally said. "When you were born, I was an officer in the king's army—a young soldier of three and twenty. I knew next to nothing about little girls. Less of nursing, or lullabies, or medicines. That was your mama's domain."

I smiled a little to think he'd ever felt ill-equipped.

But my father didn't smile. Instead, he shook his head. "I knew only that as a father, it was my duty to *protect* you. With sword or musket or my own life if it should come to it. And this I have tried to do. When I gave you to Hamilton, I thought I had secured for you a life of security, love, and happiness. I chose a man I believed would defend you, and your heart, as I have always tried to do." His mouth tightened, ruefully. "I did not choose your sisters' husbands. But I chose Hamilton."

And he blamed himself for it. "You didn't choose him, Papa," I said, quite firmly. "You only *approved* him. The choice was mine. A choice I make anew every day. A choice I do not regret, no matter how unpleasant our enemies intend to make it for me."

My father, whose hair had gone white and wiry, whose strong arms had withered, and whose health had never been good, suffered from painful gout in his legs. I knew he was suffering now, as he took off his boots, lowered his feet into the water next to mine, and stared at the churning river. "Do you know what you're facing with that choice?"

After years in public life, I had some idea. "Yes, Papa. I'm not a child anymore."

"You are *my* child," he said quietly. "Always."

The sentiment set off an ache in my chest, for as a mother myself, I understood the depth of his meaning. I felt it for my own children. No matter how tall Philip grew, I would always see him in my mind's eye as the laughing little piglet with chubby legs.

It took Papa a few moments, but when he looked up again, he said, "Do you recall that when you, Angelica, and Peggy were small, toddling about in pink ribbons, I went to London for a year on business?"

"I recall something of it," I said, for, at five years old, dolls from England seemed almost as marvelous as welcoming home the tall and fierce warrior of a red-coated father I scarcely knew.

"While I was gone," my father continued, "I asked my commander—Colonel Bradstreet—to watch over my family. At my request, he helped your mother build our new mansion here. And I returned home to find all of you living together here with Colonel Bradstreet . . . with whom your mother had formed an uncommon friendship in my absence."

*An uncommon friendship.*

I remembered. Colonel Bradstreet was so fond of Mama that when he died, he left property to her. And all my life, I'd thought nothing of it until this excruciating moment. In shock, I whispered, "Surely you're not intimating—"

"I am intimating nothing but that the friendship was a subject of speculation."

My father's jaw hitched and my belly roiled at the thought that he might have known the pain of adultery. Yet, everything I knew of my parents forced my mind to rebel. "Mama would never!"

With more calmness than he perhaps felt, Papa puffed at his pipe. "There was gossip."

That I did not remember. That I'd never known. I was too young to have realized it. And I wondered if Angelica, who was older, had been more aware and if it accounted for her sometimes troubled relationship with our mother. "Surely Mama denied any impropriety."

A small, bittersweet smile tugged at his lips. "I did not ask her."

Indignation positively *burned* in my breast. "Why ever not?"

Papa's fingers drummed lightly upon his knee, as if he were

counting. "If she were guilty, she might confess. And how should a gentleman respond? If I ran Bradstreet through with my sword, it would have gained me nothing but a momentary pang of satisfaction and a dead friend. It would not forestall the gossip of cuckoldry, nor the destruction of your mother's fine name. It would have followed you, my dear children, and made you unhappy all your lives."

As the gossip about Hamilton would now follow my children all their lives.

To his litany of horrific consequences, my father added, "And if your mama was innocent . . . as she surely was . . . then to insult her with an accusation would make me the vilest of knaves. I should consider myself condemned to *hell-fires* if I treated your mother with such rank suspicion—a woman who entrusted herself to me, risked her very life to bring my children into the world. A woman who defended my lands, served as wise steward over my household, and blessed my life with her wisdom, friendship, affection, and love. Such ingratitude would damn me in the eyes of myself and my god."

*So, he would not ask*, I thought. He would never ask. My father, like the mathematician he was, had added it all up—the sums of love and happiness and disappointments in a marriage—and come to the conclusion that it didn't matter. Just as Maria Reynolds did not matter, regardless of what the papers said. Regardless of what *anyone* said.

"What I decided to do," Papa explained, "was to name my first son, born after there could be any question of his parentage, John Bradstreet Schuyler."

*In defiance*, I realized. My father had mustered the strength to defend his marriage with a thumb in the eye of anyone who would question it. Just as I would have to do now. And he was asking me if I had the stomach for it.

"In the matter of Hamilton," Papa concluded, "your family's view of this unfortunate episode will be guided by your calculation, Elizabeth. And *only* yours."

I'd always admired his ability to swallow bitter injustices for the greater good. But could I follow his example? Whatever I'd told myself in coming here, I knew the real reason Hamilton had sent me to my father.

*Eliza, if you stand beside me the public will eviscerate you.*

Stand by him or renounce him. Hamilton wanted me to have that choice. But I'd already made it. And taking a deep breath, I determined to begin defending my own marriage right here in this moment. "Then forgive him, Papa. As I have done. Truly. The Bible tells us no man is without sin. No man is righteous, not even one."

My father nodded. Then not another word was said about it. My family never behaved, in word or deed, with anything but devoted affection to my husband. And because of it—and because I was my father's daughter—I found within myself the strength to face the storm.

# Chapter Thirty

*Art thou a wife? See him, whom thou has chosen for the partner of this life, lolling in the lap of a harlot!*
—THE AURORA, A JEFFERSONIAN NEWSPAPER

*August 1797*
*New York City*

HOW COULD HE confess in such *humiliating* detail?" Angelica had come to my house, clutching my husband's pamphlet with white knuckles, demanding we go out and buy up all the copies. "Fifty of the best pens in America could not have done more to put him in infamy!"

"You know why he did it," I said, not wishing to go over it even once more. Ever since I'd confronted Monroe, I'd understood with a cutting clarity that Alexander would be forced to prove the affair to clear his name of worse charges. And, like a papist penitent, he'd done just that, donning a veritable hair shirt of irrefutable evidence and frank revelations, each more torturous than the next. My only regret was in refusing my husband's offer to review his confession before he'd published it. It'd been the one time I'd had no interest in bearing witness to the inner workings of his mind, when I'd been too heartsick to persuade him to moderate his tone.

And the result? The *Reynolds Pamphlet* ran more than *ninety* pages, cataloging every possible aspect of the affair—as if he thought he could drown his opponents in words and wash himself clean.

"Hamilton's pamphlet reads like one of Peggy's tawdry novels." Angelica groaned, as if she herself were the wronged wife instead of me. "Why, the letters his harlot sent him . . . children spell better! What could he have seen in her?"

*His mother,* I thought. It always came back to her. But I dared not say it, and I dared not fall back into the trap of dissecting the affair.

"Wine?" I asked instead, taking a bottle from an exquisite silver cooler. It was unlike me to drink in the middle of the day, but I took comfort where I could. Not only in the chilled wine against the August heat, but also in that the cooler was a gift from George Washington that had recently come with a note I treasured.

*A token of my sincere regard and friendship. I pray you to present my best wishes, in which Mrs. Washington joins me, to Mrs. Hamilton and that you would be persuaded with every sentiment of the highest regard, I remain your sincere friend.*

If the Washingtons stood with us in solidarity, how could I waver?

My sister took the proffered glass of wine and gulped it. "One word from you and Hamilton is ruined forever. I hope he knows it."

She'd been his defender at first, but since reading his confession, she'd become mine. And I suppose that I needed one when the newspapers' poisoned ink against him turned on me, too. I'd never been singled out for such public opprobrium before. Never bade to loathe the man I loved or be considered complicit in his sins. The insults from jeering Republicans didn't wound me overmuch; I dismissed the lot of them as a knot of conspiring, godless scoundrels. Like my husband, I was even coming to take some perverse *pride* in being the object of their rancor and venom.

But the cruelty of our fellow Federalist friends did cut me.

It was confided to me that our new president's lady, Abigail Adams, crowed to her friends that she'd always known my husband to be a lascivious debauchee, in whose wicked eyes she saw the very devil. As if *I* should've seen it, too, and made a better choice in husband. Society ladies I'd entertained on countless occasions crossed the street to avoid brushing skirts with me, lest scandal be contagious. For I was a wife who'd failed to inspire fidelity. And yet, my fidelity to him was now also to be counted against my virtue.

I could neither *leave* my husband nor *love* him without offending somebody. As the wronged wife, there was nothing whatsoever I could now do that might be counted appropriate, except, perhaps, to lay down and die of shame.

And I was not about to give anyone that satisfaction.

"I wasn't sure you'd come back to me," Hamilton admitted that night, rocking his infant son against his shoulder, and eyeing the two empty wine bottles on our table with a furrowed brow. "Unless . . ."

"Unless?" I asked, covering a hiccup.

"Unless you've returned to hire a divorce attorney." His eyes crinkled at the corners, as if he'd said it in dark jest, but there was an edge of fear to it. He watched me carefully for an answer even as he continued, "As it happens, I'm acquainted with the best in the city if you should need a recommendation."

Though I was a little tipsy and unsteady on my feet, I stood to embrace him. "I'm *with* you, Alexander." And I was. For even though the world didn't wish for us to put our troubles behind us, we'd done it. We'd survived.

And we'd become stronger for it.

Alexander swallowed, then, with our little William between us, pressed his forehead to mine. "You are infinitely dear to me, Eliza. And I am more in debt to you than I can ever pay. Please believe that I *know* you deserve everything from me. And my future life will be devoted to your happiness. I only wish I could stay . . ."

He was obliged to argue a federal case in Connecticut—one of the many cases he took on to make a fine future for our children and build the house he promised. Still, he worried, because our oldest boy, Philip, had taken ill on the boat as we'd sailed back from Albany.

A summer cold, we thought. Nothing serious. But days after my husband went off to Connecticut, as Philip tossed and turned feverish in his bed, the physician pronounced the dread verdict. *Typhus.* Typhus could leave our boy deaf or addled. Or it could kill him.

"Mrs. Hamilton, you must prepare for the worst," the doctor said, his coat thrown over the chair by the bed where my son burned with fever. "Your husband must be sent for."

"Send a courier by express," I whispered. Then I sent the rest of the children and my servants away, lest the illness spread. Angelica insisted on staying with me, so it was me, my sister, and the doctor left to care for Philip as he slipped into a state of delirium, his pulse fading by the moment. I took Philip's face in my hands and told him a truth that mothers ought never utter—that he would always be my firstborn and first in my heart.

Because Philip was too weak to move on his own, the three of us plunged him into a hot bath of Peruvian bark and rum. When he roused, I spooned wine whey into his mouth while his aunt Angelica covered him in dry blankets. But the nightmare continued as we waited for my husband's return, listening with anxiety for every chime of the clock.

At length, my sister said, "Eliza, let me sit with him while he sleeps. You should rest so his mother can be with him when he awakens."

I started to my room, stumbling away in a delirium of my own. *Don't take him, God,* I prayed that night, and again the next morning. Not Philip, who'd brought joy to us since the day he was born. Not the boy who'd been my companion during those lonely early years when his father was seldom home.

Not my *Philip*. The best of me and Alexander combined. Our best and brightest hope.

I'd just finished uttering this morning prayer when boots thundered up the stairs, the door shaking at the noise of it. "Eliza!" I found Alexander in the hall, his hair plastered to his head in sweaty ringlets, his legs spattered in mud, eyes wild. "Is he—"

"Awake," Angelica said from the doorway. "And it's no wonder with all the racket."

We rushed into our son's room to find him revived, sensible as to where he was and who we were, and we knelt beside his bed and thanked God for his deliverance. Later, while Alexander cooled his forehead with a cloth, I thought nothing else matters but *this*.

Let the newspapers say what they would. Let every woman in the country giggle behind their hands and whisper behind my back. Our family mattered more. Our family meant everything. And so long as we were *together*, I could bear anything.

~

*Hamilton is fallen for the present, but even if he fornicates with every female in New York and Philadelphia, he will rise again.*
—DAVID COBB TO HENRY KNOX

*Winter 1797*
*New York City*

"We'll never see her again, will we?" my daughter rasped as we watched the snow-covered carriage roll away from the front of our house, a tearful Fanny pressing her hand to the frosted window in farewell.

"Of course, we will," I said, fighting back my own tears for my daughter's sake. Fanny may not have been her sister by blood, but Ana had never known another. And the loss seemed to break her. She alternated between inconsolable sobs and dazed stupors, and it was all I could do to comfort her about something that broke a piece of me, too.

Because Fanny's relations no longer saw fit to let her stay with us. Her married older sister wanted to take Fanny into her household. A *respectable* household, I was brusquely informed. Thus, we were forced to surrender the girl we'd loved as our own since the age of two.

We'd packed twelve-year-old Fanny's trunks with new petticoats and pearled combs and every sort of frippery a girl should need. Alexander had vowed to the girl that she was always welcome back. We were all heartbroken at the loss.

And to comfort my twelve-year-old daughter, I said, "It's no different than when your aunt Angelica went to live in London for a while. Fanny will come back one day and you'll have each other's company again."

But Ana couldn't be comforted. She'd always been a sensitive child, but lively and clever—eager to show off her accomplishments in dancing, music, and French. Now she withdrew to her room, complaining of illness. And I wondered if the danger to my children was never to end. The physicians could find nothing whatsoever wrong with her, but she would eat next to nothing but little bits of bread. Sometimes even then, she left the crumbs upon her windowsill for the birds.

Like her father, she took loss hard. And my heart ached for her. I knew what it was to love a sister, how tight that bond could be. How difficult it was to understand one's place in the world without it.

In Ana's tenderness—the way only feeding these little birds could lift her spirits—I thought I recognized in her my own calling. Thus, one Sunday morning, I said, "Get dressed for church services, darling. Afterward, we're going to help some children as needy as our dear Fanny once was . . ."

Thereupon we threw ourselves into a cause to which I was happy to lend my name—tainted though it was. The Society for the Relief of Poor Widows with Small Children, founded by the devout Scotswoman Widow Graham, supported at least a hundred destitute widows in the city. Together with Ana, I spent afternoons assembling baskets of food and clothing for the needy in the hopes of saving them from the poorhouse.

I'd always felt best when I was busy. Besides, the unfortunate situations of these widowed women reminded me that my troubles were comparatively few. How fortunate I was. How the Lord had made me rich in every way that mattered. I imagined that it made the same impression on Ana because, by summer, she was playing her piano again for our old friend James McHenry, the secretary of war. He came to visit in a show of loyalty and support, reciting poetry and recalling old war stories well into the evening.

"To Lafayette," McHenry said, raising his glass. "The luckiest Frog alive."

"To Lafayette," we said, because the marquis *was* lucky, alive, and—after five years of imprisonment—*free*. Napoleon Bonaparte saw to Lafayette's release from prison, the only thing of merit, by my estimation, that tyrant ever did. And when we learned of Lafayette's release, Alexander wrote:

> *My friendship for you will survive all revolutions and all vicissitudes. The only thing in which our parties agree is to love you.*

After we drank, McHenry sat back and put his knife on the edge of his plate. "This veal is delicious, Mrs. Hamilton—melts in the mouth like butter, it does. You serve as fine a meal as I remember from the old days."

"You must be forgetting that dreadful wartime tripe stew . . ."

Mac patted a somewhat rounder belly than he'd had in those far-off days in winter quarters. "I was so hungry during the war, you could've baked me a sawdust cake and I'd have savored it. But *this* meal is exquisite. Have you a chef?"

"Oh, no," I replied. "We've an Irish girl who scrubs the pots, but I do the cooking."

McHenry seemed impressed. "Hamilton, my lucky friend, your wife is still as frugal and good a treasurer of your household as you were a treasurer for the country."

"Better," Hamilton said, smiling at me with warm affection. "After all, no one has ever demanded an investigation into her account books."

We laughed, then Mac shook his head. "I worried, you know, all those years ago in Morristown. How the devil did a man like Hamilton see fit to marry such a saintly girl? Now I see, Mrs. Hamilton, that you were the *only* woman tireless enough to match him."

*Dear Mac.* It was the sixth or seventh compliment he'd paid me that evening. And I was sure he did it out of a solicitousness of my feelings, to try to soothe the blows dealt by the newspapers. But he was also trying to soften the ground, because between the second and third courses, Mac revealed the true purpose of his visit—to recruit my husband back into the army. "The French have gone too far this time and it's likely to be war."

Offended by America's proclamation of neutrality in the European war, the new French government had been attacking our ships and refused to speak to an American diplomatic delegation without a bribe. To make matters worse, a French ship plucked an American vessel right out of New York Harbor.

"The gall of it. Nay, the *Gaul* of it." Mac guffawed, finishing his fourth glass of Madeira. "Not even Jefferson dares to defend the French for this. And we need you back in uniform, lad."

How relieved I was when Alexander put his hand atop mine and said, without hesitation, "I'm a private man now. And considering the circumstances of—"

"Oh, damn the scandal sheets!" Mac cried.

I'd been certain that my husband was going to talk about the circumstances of our finances and growing family. But realizing that even our friends and champions were still thinking about our scandal made me rise abruptly. *"Dessert?"*

By the time I returned with chocolate creams in fluted crystal glasses and a silver tray of caraway comfits, McHenry was still talking about the military. "As you say, General Schuyler has not been well. Gates is a bitter old woman. Knox is too stout to ride a horse. And if you didn't know it already, let me be the first to tell you that the great man won't come out of retirement unless you do, Ham."

Washington. Always, George Washington was needed at the head of our armies. But even with my husband at his side, could the old, venerable soldier truly mount up for war yet again?

Mac eyed me frankly and turned the screws. "I appeal to the inextinguishable love you bear your country. That you *both* bear your country."

I dropped into a chair with a sigh, stabbing a long spoon into my chocolate cream, and digging out a giant bite, because I knew where this would end. Hamilton could never refuse military glory or a genuine call to patriotism, and this was both.

Darkly amused but wanting to break things, I said, "To think I once harbored such a fondness for you, McHenry . . ."

Both men slanted apologetic glances my way, then Alexander squinted. "What rank would I be offered?"

"Major general." McHenry reached for a few caraway comfits.

But I snatched the tray away. "Yes, I was *quite* fond of you, Mac . . . now I shall go get that sawdust cake for you after all."

Mac laughed, merriment in his eyes. "But you were born to be a general's wife, my dear." Then to my husband he added, "And you might wish to send a note of appreciation to President Adams. T'would be a good deal easier to make you inspector of the whole army, if he didn't hate you quite so much."

Adams was an honest but irascible man who paled in stature beside George Washington. Which was why my husband had supported another candidate in the presidential election instead of John Adams. But Adams had a long memory and in backing the wrong horse, Alexander had made another enemy.

An enemy who'd now be his commander in chief.

~

*March 1799*
*New York City*

"You're a shameless woman, Eliza Hamilton."

Standing beneath an umbrella in a drizzle of rain, Kitty Livingston tried to fend me off. After she'd come to warn me about Alexander that time, we'd come to a sort of a rapprochement, and since then, Kitty had been amongst the first New York ladies to receive me back into polite society, despite her family's political feud with mine. But now, caught in a spring shower that was getting her shoes wet outside the Tontine, she wanted nothing more than to escape.

I stood stubbornly in her path. "Surely you can spare more for a worthy cause, Kitty. Not so long ago, you were a widow with a small child yourself . . ."

"I've already given you every coin in my handbag!"

I smiled sweetly. "And I promise to record that in the charity's membership roll, which we'll publish, as thanks and recognition."

"As *extortion*," Kitty protested. "I'll be made to look like a miser compared to your sister."

Kitty had the right of it. I'd learned from Hamilton, after all. Long ago, he'd arranged the order of the states in voting for the ratification of the Constitution, playing one against the other. Well, the same principle applied to raising funds for the Society for the Relief of Poor Widows with Small Children.

And Angelica was my Delaware, always first to ratify.

Knowing just how large my sister's donation had been, Kitty's hands tightened on her purse strings. "You're a *brigand*."

"I think of myself as a foot soldier for the Lord."

She pursed her lips. "Well, I suppose that if General Hamilton gets the war against France he wants, we'll all have to adopt the martial spirit."

*General Hamilton.* After four months, I was still adjusting to the idea, much less the unspoken, but very real, responsibilities of being a general's wife. My mother. Lucy Knox. Martha Washington. These were my examples. And with those excellent ladies in mind, I said, "We're already at war with France. An undeclared war, but a war nonetheless."

Lacking any military experience of his own to draw upon, President Adams had called George Washington out of retirement. The old soldier, tired to his very bones, agreed to serve as a figurehead if Alexander was named his second in command, his *inspector general.*

And no one could deny Washington.

The Republican newspapers screeched against *"Hamilton, the man who published a book to prove he was an adulterer."* But such objections seemed stale, if not quaint, when weighed against the threat of Napoleon Bonaparte. Matrons might clutch their pearls, and the Jeffersonians might spit, but in the end, the country still needed Alexander Hamilton.

Which meant that we were, again, ascendant.

Even the Livingstons knew it, which was why Kitty sighed with surrender, promising a large bank note for the charity. With that, she took her leave but not before muttering, "I still say you're a *brigand.*"

"Brigands resort to pistols." Aaron Burr doffed his cap as he splashed across the street to us. "Whereas you, Mrs. Hamilton, have somehow managed to loot the pockets of every New York notable with only the force of your will."

New York was a much smaller place in those days, and we were always running into old friends and enemies on the street. Burr, in particular, was always out and about. He had never remarried after Theodosia's death, and more often than not he had a trollop on his arm—two, if the mood struck him. He'd earned a reputation as a great seducer of women, and it was no wonder, since Burr still retained roguish good looks.

So much so that even I could scarcely deny him a smile. Nor did I want to when he took money from his pocket and pressed it into my hand. "For your widows and small children . . ."

"How generous," I said, surprised.

"On the condition that you *don't* record my name in your ledger."

"It's a respectable charity, sir, and entirely without partisan bent."

"Yes, I've heard all about your widows." By way of explanation, he added, "I spend a great deal of time lately on Slaughterhouse Street, raising mugs in the Bull's Head Tavern with the immigrants your husband's party is trying to chase out of the country."

He was referring to the Alien and Sedition Acts, which authorized President Adams to deport any foreign-born resident deemed a danger to the peace. These were wartime measures. And given what I'd seen—riots, uprisings, and American cities nearly burned to the ground—regrettably necessary, I thought. Even though I worried it set a dangerous precedent.

But I said none of this to Aaron Burr. I merely adjusted my bonnet, upon which I proudly wore a black cockade that signaled my support of this Federalist administration.

Burr must've seen that I was suppressing an argument, because he gave a wicked grin. "I intend to make Hamilton regret these unconstitutional laws."

It was Congress who passed these laws and the president who signed them; my husband was merely the general who would defend the nation. But affecting amusement, I said, "*Unconstitutional*? I don't remember your having championed that document when my husband was helping to write it . . ."

Burr laughed. "Touché. It's a miserable paper machine. I told your husband that as the commander of an army, he owes it to the country to demolish it."

I withheld my gasp because his expression was so droll I couldn't decide if he was toying with me or suggesting the overthrow of the government. Exasperated, I shook my head. "I won't allow you to bait me further, sir. And I shall happily take your donation. But why should you desire to keep it a secret?"

"Because I mean it for charity and not social advancement."

Did Burr suspect me of using good works to erase the taint of scandal? It was perfectly in keeping with the way his mind worked, so I supposed I couldn't be angry about it. The truth was, despite Burr's capacity to scandalize, needle, or otherwise irritate me, I couldn't hate him. In truth, I even liked him. A little. As much as anyone could like a man whose sole fixed characteristic was that he had none. Perhaps it was because he'd kept his silence about my husband's adultery. "Even if you insult me, I'm not too proud to take your money on behalf of children who are grateful for every scrap of bread."

"I mean no insult whatsoever. Though, if I did, I suppose I should fear being clasped in irons or sued into penury, under the new Federalist Reign of Terror."

At that, my jaw dropped. "It's your Republicans who aspire to guillotines. You might be glad of the new laws if *you'd* been persecuted so relentlessly by the newspaper as I—"

"Say no more," Burr replied wryly, holding up a hand in surrender. "I've taken endless amusement watching the way you've spent the past year and a half hectoring the buttoned-up society ladies who had the temerity to shun you. I admire it. Hamilton has, in you, a very well-matched wife. As I intend to tell him at this evening's meeting of the Manumission Society."

I softened to hear this reminder of his antislavery work. Especially as our political parties seemed often now on the verge of civil war; just last year, two congressmen had come to blows with cane and fire-iron tongs on the floor of the House of Representatives. It was heartening to remember that there were men like Burr in the opposing camp who could still find common cause on great moral issues. And it made me forgive his taunts, because it seemed he did, in fact, have *some* moral scruples. "My husband seems quite hopeful that New York will soon eliminate the practice of slavery. Do you share his optimism?"

Burr's smile was enigmatic. "I suspect it would go better to first eliminate slavery a little closer to home. At least, it would spare your husband some embarrassment."

"We keep no slaves," I said, with perhaps more pride than I ought to have, given that more than half the members of the society *did* own slaves, including my father.

"As will be discussed at tonight's meeting, your husband is the purchaser of record for a slave the Manumission Society is seeking to help gain her freedom."

I shook my head, dismissively. "I'm sure there's been some mistake. We have no slaves."

"But your sister does," Burr replied.

~~~

ENSCONCED AMONGST HER perfumes and cosmetic pots in her toilette, Angelica admired her reflection in an ivory-handled mirror. "Did Kitty wave the white flag?"

"She promised a bank note," I replied, cooing a bit over my sister's ten-month-old baby in his ornate walnut bassinet, the child being ample proof that whatever had broken between my sister and her husband had indeed been mended.

Angelica waved away a little yawn. "I'd forgotten how exhausting a baby can be, even if you give them over to a nursemaid."

As gently as one could possibly suggest such a thing, I ventured, "Perhaps if you hosted fewer parties . . ."

"But Church lives for parties. He's rich and has no place in politics, so he has little to do and time hangs heavy on his hands."

I couldn't imagine having little to do. Indolence wasn't in our Dutch blood. And I sensed Angelica was annoyed by it, too. But I hadn't come to criticize either of them. I'd come to ask, nay, to demand, "You must let Sarah go free."

My sister startled. "Sarah?"

"Your lady's maid," I replied, stiffly. "I am informed today that Alexander purchased her for you."

"Oh, yes," Angelica said, as if only vaguely recalling it. "When I knew we were returning to America, I asked Hamilton to ensure I'd have a servant when I disembarked the ship, and he did me that favor."

My husband never purchased slaves for our household. Yet his entanglement with my slave-owning family had put him in difficult positions, and pushed him to compromise his moral stance more than once. It did not sit well with me that he might have done this, for me, in order to make my sister more apt to stay in New York—which he knew would make me happy. "You must emancipate her. She's gone to the Manumission Society for help. They mean to argue her cause publicly."

A sense of indignation leaped to my sister's wounded expression at the idea she should be thought a bad mistress. "Why should Sarah wish to leave me? I've never treated her harshly for even a moment. And to beg the Manumission Society's help! This is mortifying."

"Yes," I said, because *slavery* was mortifying.

We'd grown up with Prince guarding our door, and Dinah cooking our meals, and Jenny fixing our hair. We'd told ourselves we loved Papa's servants as if they were family. And I might still argue that we did—but not with an eye to their humanity, with all the pain and possibility that entailed.

Anger does not obliterate love.

And love does not obliterate cruelty.

Slavery was cruel. A sin against God and a betrayal of the principles of our revolution besides. And if we were ever to end it, the effort would have to begin with families like ours. When I said as much, Angelica sat back in her gilded armchair and closed her eyes. "I suppose that if it were to be publicly known your husband purchased slaves, it would be another hypocrisy for the newspapers to complain about."

"More importantly, it would impede his efforts to abolish slavery in New York."

Angelica finally lifted her long lashes to slant me a glance. "I don't know how you stand it."

"How I stand what?"

"*Hamilton*," she replied. "His vanity. His outrageous zeal. He never stops."

This from the same woman who complained her husband had nothing to do. Though she still treated Alexander with affection and remained politically loyal to him, she was much more apt now to take *my* side in any disagreement.

She plainly believed that I'd been sent on another mission to protect my husband's reputation and resented him for it. But Alexander hadn't sent me. My responsibility as the general's wife was not, I knew, just to the general. It was also to set a moral example for the country he meant to defend. And even if I had no standing to do that in the matter of adultery, slavery was a more guilty sin by far. "I'm not asking you to emancipate Sarah for my husband. Nor for me. I ask you to free her—and all your slaves— because slavery violates the rights endowed to us by our creator."

I used Mr. Jefferson's words to make an impression. And at this little bit of manipulation, she apprehended me, almost as if for the first time, giving me the strangest feeling of a shift in our relationship, in which she'd always been, hitherto, of superior rank. I was sure that she would do as I asked. But she wasn't happy about it. "Why, Mrs. General Hamilton, they say two people married long enough to one another might slowly become more alike, but I never did predict it. You are becoming *him*."

# Chapter Thirty-One

Autumn 1799
Harlem, New York

T HERE WAS SOMETHING mesmerizing about the dueling pistols, with their gleaming dark walnut stocks, and the glint of the brass barrels, and the hair trigger that an expert duelist could use to gain an advantage over his opponent. Perhaps the allure was in the fact that something so beautiful could be so deadly . . .

"See how the hair trigger is disguised?" my brother-in-law asked as he showed them to my admiring sons, who all strained to get a closer look. "Try for yourself."

Grinning, seventeen-year-old Philip took the weapon into his hands, clearly fascinated despite having handled his father's own weapons many times before. "Did you have the hair trigger set in your duel, Uncle Church?"

Church settled back onto a divan beside my sister in the cottage we'd all rented together in the wilds of Harlem so that Peggy, Angelica, and I could share the season. Now our children and husbands crowded the place, making the perfect audience for Church to brag about his exploits. "I wanted Aaron Burr to know that I could kill him without any advantage if I so chose," he said, coolly straightening his white lace cravat. "And perhaps I should have."

Alexander cut in with a reproachful glance at his brother-in-law. My husband was, after all, no longer the same man who became embroiled in two affairs of honor in a single day. As a general, he'd been working to eradicate the antiquated practice from the ranks of the army. "I've been persuaded that dueling is a horrid custom, one the legislature must see fit to curb."

I wish, now, he'd said so much more. For the memory of our son Philip holding that pistol even all these decades later retains the power to make me want to retch.

Alexander held out his hand for the pistol and returned the pair to their portmanteau, though that didn't effect a change of subject because the men in my family were in a belligerent humor about Burr.

When it looked certain that we'd go to war with France, Burr had volunteered to help defend the harbor, despite his earlier support of the French Revolution. Burr had also abandoned his fellow Republicans to support the antislavery measure in New York's legislature. He'd even proposed a new project to bring clean water to the city so as to prevent yellow fever. Alexander had been thrilled to see Burr's political changes, and he'd championed them.

But it'd been a scheme. My harried husband, busy arranging for military supplies and organizing the army, had missed a few legal clauses belatedly added to the paperwork for the water utility—clauses that enabled Burr to transform the supposedly charitable corporation he started with my husband's help into a bank.

A *Republican* bank.

Burr had used him.

It'd been a masterful and malevolent joke, sly and well executed at the very time my husband was occupied in everything from designing military uniforms from sash to buttonhole, to recommending a military academy at West Point. Otherwise,

Hamilton would never have been distracted enough to let Burr slip something past him.

Seldom did anyone outsmart Alexander Hamilton.

But Burr had done just that, in a most public and humiliating way.

Alexander had privately fumed, but Church accused Burr of corruption, which brought about a duel between the men, where my brother-in-law proved himself such an expert marksman that he shot a button off Burr's coat—a feat that much impressed my sons, but not my sister.

Hearing Church boast now about how he could have killed a man, Angelica set her cup down so hard that I feared it would crack, and strong black tea sloshed over both sides. For she, like the rest of us, had learned of her husband's duel only after the fact. And the fright of having so nearly been made a widow, in complete ignorance, still set her nerves on edge.

"What if you *had* killed him, Jack?" Angelica asked.

No one in our family seemed poised to answer that question—least of all my unrepentant brother-in-law. And over our teacups, Peggy and I exchanged a look, both of us knowing from childhood experience not to tangle with Angelica when she was in this mood. But as my newborn daughter mewled like a kitten in her cradle, I was emboldened to remind everyone of our blessings. "Let's just give thanks to God that no one was hurt. Not to mention that we're all together to enjoy a respite in this beautiful countryside."

"A respite that would've been even more enjoyable if you'd named your new daughter Margaret," Peggy piped up, both changing the subject and professing jealousy that we'd named our first daughter after Angelica but none after her.

"I'm afraid I favor the name *Elizabeth*," Alexander replied with a wink. "But perhaps the next one . . ."

"The next one! And to think I once feared Betsy would be a spinster. You're like *rabbits*, you two," Peggy accused, quite heedless of the agonized cringes this elicited from my sons and the chorus of snickers from their cousins. Especially Angelica's twenty-one-year-old Flip and Peggy's eleven-year-old Steven— where they stood, still admiring Church's pistols in the open portmanteau.

Reaching to pat my husband's knee, I said, "Since the gentlemen of the family have been so fixated on guns, perhaps you might take the boys into the woods and bring us some ducks for supper."

Alexander looked as if he wished to protest but called for his new hunting dog, an overeager spaniel that answered to the name Old Peggy. That's when my Philip joked to his aunt, "You have a Hamiltonian namesake after all."

Peggy gave an indignant sputter that sounded quite like the curly-haired mongrel—eliciting howls of laughter from all of us. "My nephew is a rogue," Peggy said, affectionately ruffling Philip's dark hair. "Be gone with you to fetch our supper."

Then Alexander marched off into the forests of Harlem with a fowling piece in hand, my brothers-in-law and our boys all trooping behind.

"Do you see how Church swaggers about like a daring boy of eighteen?" Angelica hissed when they'd gone.

To soothe her, I said, "You were once charmed by Church's daring."

"That was before I loved him," Angelica replied, taking me quite by surprise. "When we eloped, that was just the seedling of love. It's taken years of careful tending, pruning, and cultivation to come to full flower. Though, if Church had gotten himself killed in a childish duel, I should doubt the whole enterprise of love altogether!"

Peggy dramatically rolled her eyes. "Oh, how would it have looked if he'd refused Burr's challenge? It's the way men defend their personal honor."

Angelica seethed. "It's never *personal* with Burr. Tell her, Eliza."

"It's true," I said, in the familiar role of mediator between them. As improbable as it sounded, Burr was, and had always been, wryly amused with life, taking it all for a game.

"Burr only cares about his political reputation," Angelica said. "Now, thanks to my husband, that sly self-seeker can boast that he didn't flinch when a bullet came close enough to wing a button off his coat. He'll tell that story every chance he gets while campaigning for Jefferson in the upcoming presidential election. And mark me a fool if Burr doesn't win the vice presidency for himself."

"Heaven forfend," I said, glad Alexander wasn't present to hear this prediction, for it would have sent him spiraling into a rage.

What I wanted was to celebrate with my sisters that we were all together. The three of us. Our children playing together outside. Our husbands good friends. Just as I'd once dreamed we'd be.

So I did my best to soften Angelica's temper until the three of us were laughing together as we did when we were girls. "I'll call her Lysbet for short," I said to Peggy of the new daughter in my arms. "And I *am* sorry, Peggy. I wanted to call her Margaret but my husband is still persuasive when he desires something."

She snorted. "Oh, and I'll bet he knows just how to persuade you, too. No doubt it involves his—"

"Say no more!" I said, laughing despite myself. "There's an innocent babe here."

Chuckling, Peggy smoothed her hand over Lysbet's downy hair. "Call her what you like. It's just good to see you happy again."

I *was* happy, I realized.

The advantage of the Reynolds scandal was that I no longer had anything to hide. I found satisfaction in my work—and in Alexander's. For on the Fourth of July, we'd toasted the state legislature's passage of a law establishing the gradual abolition of slavery. And shortly thereafter, Alexander had taken me to scout a property he meant to buy for our home—a high, wooded place not far from the river.

The country still feared an American war with France—with that tyrant, Napoleon Bonaparte. But with Washington and Hamilton at the head of our armies, we could be in no safer hands.

———

*Doctor, I die hard. But I am not afraid to go.*
—GEORGE WASHINGTON

*December 1799*
*New York City*

George Washington's passing shook the very foundations of the country. Few men on earth had done more to earn eternal rest than the former president, but we were left like children frightened to face a world without him. Even Alexander, though he was loath to admit it.

Nevertheless, like a grieving son, my husband went to Philadelphia to march in a somber funereal procession in honor of his fallen chief, wearing a black sash of mourning, leading a white riderless horse from Congress Hall, accompanied by a solitary drumbeat.

But where were the rest of the country's supposedly great men?

One would have searched the assembled crowd in vain for Jefferson, Madison, or Monroe. Though I could well imagine the three Republicans clustered around a dinner table, wickedly toasting Washington's demise and the opportunity it now gave their party to rise to power.

For my part, I was forced to steal away to the privacy of my room so that the children would not see my tears fall as I remembered the first time that godlike man spoke my name in welcoming me to his military encampment.

My heart bled for Martha.

*She must feel so alone now,* I thought. Inconsolable. She'd had children from her first marriage, but none with Washington. And she'd had only two years with her husband after a lifetime of public service. Only two years to sit together upon their piazza overlooking the Potomac and dine together in the privacy of their rooms. And yet, even then, I knew Mount Vernon resembled a well-resorted tavern, with people stopping by for a glimpse of the former president and in expectation of southern hospitality. A meal, a room for the night, a stable with feed for their horses—all at Washington's expense, of course.

*We consumed him,* I thought, clutching the pendant I wore containing his hair.

We might not have chopped off Washington's head and lapped up his blood from the paving stones as the French mobs did with their king. But we'd taken the best years of his life—his sweat, his toil, his wisdom, his vigor and energies. And what did we give him in return? For eight years we called him president. Now we called him the Father of the Country.

Who then, was the heir?

All eyes, it seemed, turned to an increasingly erratic President John Adams. But finding him wanting, some looked to Alexander Hamilton. And for the first time, I found myself almost *grateful* for the exposure of my husband's infidelity. Because it meant that he hadn't the stature to run for the presidency. Not now, at least.

We were stuck with President Adams. The alternative was unthinkable.

The alternative was Jefferson.

"Did you remember to deliver the parcel to Widow Rhinelander?" I asked Philip when he absconded with a piece of bread, trying to slip out the back door.

"I could scarcely forget, with all your reminders." My tall son leaned against the butcher block table in the basement kitchen of our rented town house, affecting a manly devil-may-care pose. He was still dutiful about helping to deliver baskets to the needy, but having graduated from Columbia College, he would not be at my beck and call for long. He was grown now—and keen to prove it. "Fortunately, Mrs. Rhinelander has a very pretty girl living next door to her . . ."

"Naughty young man," I scolded, for he was entirely too much like his father had once been—irresistibly brilliant, shamelessly flirtatious, and outrageously handsome. I'd already had to warn him against making eyes at our pot-scrubbing girl. Now I snatched the butter before he absconded with it, too. "Don't make me fear to send you on errands for the charity lest you flirt with the ladies."

"I wouldn't flirt with Widow Rhinelander." Philip's mouth twisted into a feigned expression of horror and he shuddered. "She reminds me of the Baron von Steuben, may he rest in peace. Besides, she says all her German gentlemen friends are voting Republican . . ."

Of course they were.

Which was why, for the coming elections, I found myself undertaking the most energetic role in the political wrangling that I could without forfeiting my dignity as a lady. While going door to door and church to church raising charitable donations, I'd made careful note of those with Federalist sympathies who might be approached for support. Every day that my husband—who should've been about the business of the military—rode hither and yon, haranguing passing crowds on street corners, attending committee meetings in various wards, and even enlisting our sons to stand watch at polling stations where we suspected election trickery, I pinned my black Federalist cockade to my hat and went out to praise the virtues of courage and perseverance in the Federalist cause.

It was an unseemly business to electioneer in support of President Adams, but we'd been forced to it by Aaron Burr, who opened his house to offer refreshments and a mattress upon the floor to any grubby miscreant willing to campaign for a populist sweep of Jeffersonians into the government.

And now Philip complained, "It seems Colonel Burr sent some-one to the neighborhood who spoke German. And he's drawing up lists of voters in all the immigrant precincts."

"For all the good it will do him," I said, smugly. "To vote, immi-grants must have resided here fourteen years, and own substantial property."

But, having embarked upon the study of the law in his father's footsteps, Philip explained, "Burr's found a legal loophole. He's going to have them pool the value of their property so they can qualify to vote."

Damn Aaron Burr! Was there no end to his schemes?

Of course, it was just what Alexander would've done if he'd thought of it. My husband had, after all, filled the Federalist slate with booksellers, a grocer, a mason—precisely the sort of working people who ought to appeal to populists. And, as if in diabolical mockery, Burr filled the Republican slate with rich and venerable old Clintonites and Livingstons for the cachet of their family names.

Despite what he'd said to me on the street that day, however, I didn't think Burr's tireless campaigning came from any prin-cipled stance; he simply wanted to be vice president. And per-haps that wouldn't be so terrible an ambition if he didn't want to serve under Jefferson, who would assuredly plunge us back into a world of chaos, starvation, and riots.

"We'd better warn your father," I said, grabbing up the lunch basket I'd filled with fruit and pastries. I wouldn't open my home with mattresses on the floor for every mercenary willing to cam-paign under my husband's generalship, but I was determined to feed and encourage the troops.

As I searched for Alexander and passed out my baked goods to my husband's loyalists on the streets, I heard the most outrageous talk amongst the milling crowds. Hollow, ignorant Republican slogans. Curses and taunts at our party's volunteers. Libelous ru-mors about President Adams. I felt a growing dread that if we lost this election, my future and that of my children would be thrown into a world characterized by such vitriol—all at the hands of Jefferson—an atheist in religion and a fanatic in politics.

*I would see half the earth desolated,* Jefferson once said to me. That must not be allowed to happen.

I finally found my husband outside a notorious boardinghouse on Greenwich Street warning a discontented crowd of ruffians against a Jefferson presidency.

"Alexander," I called, attempting to push through them with my basket.

But he didn't hear me, and they refused to hear him. Instead, the men shouted him down. *"Thief! Rascal! Villain!"*

They cursed my husband, their general, a man still in uniform with a sword on his hip. Stunned, I took a step back and quite nearly bumped into the Quaker proprietress of the board-inghouse waving her arms at my husband, and shrieking, "If thee dies a natural death, Hamilton, I shall think there is no justice in heaven! I'll never support anything you're about. I tell all my boarders to vote with Burr!"

It wasn't the first time that proprietress had accosted him. She'd done it months before in a courtroom where Alexander had defended the man accused of murdering her cousin. The trial had created a sensation, especially when Alexander exposed the pro-prietress as running a bit of a bawdy house. So it didn't surprise me to hear the woman shriek and rave.

Outraged, my husband tugged his military coat straight. "Hear now—"

The growing crowd drowned him out with a raucous cheer of support for the proprietress, one that made me anxious. "Alexander," I said, finally forcing my way through to him.

"Oh, dear Eliza, it's too rowdy out here today for you." He took my basket and sheltered me away from the unruly mob with an arm around my shoulders. But frustration rolled off him. "Why does that lady not recall that Aaron Burr was the *other* defense attorney in that case? Why doesn't she blame him, too?"

"Because Burr is slippery," I replied when we finally found a bit of privacy in the doorway to a millinery shop. "The sort of fellow off the surface of whom can slide almost any resentment." Whereas, when it came to Alexander, everything stuck.

Perhaps that was because Burr's ancestry stretched back to Jonathan Edwards, one of the great New England theologians, whereas Hamilton was said to be a Creole bastard. Or perhaps it was because Burr never proclaimed any position on anything until he knew which way the wind was blowing, whereas Hamilton could never keep an opinion to himself.

Late that night, sinking in exhausted despondency beside his father in the parlor, Philip groaned. "Our state election is over. They've swept the slate. It's all Republicans."

New York would give twelve electoral college votes to Jefferson. Enough, quite possibly, to tip the balance of the presidency. And it was all accomplished by the wily Aaron Burr who had, in the late hours of the election, gotten every man who couldn't vote to bring out wagonloads of those who could, even carrying the infirm and sitting them down on chairs in the middle of the cobblestone street to wait their turn.

*We'd lost New York!*

My general had been out-generaled. I suppose it had always seemed impossible to me that Alexander could fail at anything he set his mind to, and so I sank down, too, numbly.

But at the stroke of midnight, Alexander was already at his desk, drawing up new battle plans. Feverishly, he scratched out a letter to the governor, audaciously suggesting that presidential electors should be chosen by popular vote rather than by the incoming legislature.

"Such a measure would be seen as overturning the election," I warned, hoping to dissuade him from sending it. "And would surely cause a civil war."

"A civil war would be preferable to Jefferson," Philip said, perhaps remembering the sermon we'd heard at church telling us that if Jefferson became president, we'd have to hide our Bibles.

"In times like these, it will not do to be overscrupulous," Alexander said, still writing. "It's easy to sacrifice the substantial interests of society by a strict adherence to ordinary rules. This is a matter of *public safety*."

Remembering Jefferson's admiration for, and encouragement of, the Francophile mobs in Philadelphia, I agreed with him. That our fright drove us to consider radical and unsavory ideas in the few terrifying days after the election—what some were already calling the *revolution of 1800*—I don't deny. But our fever-induced proposals were never adopted, whereas the worst, panic-struck ideas of President Adams were immediately put into action.

Realizing he was likely to lose the election, the first thing Adams did was fire his entire cabinet—including the secretary of war.

"But the president blames you, more than anyone, for his probable defeat, Ham," McHenry said, having come straight from Philadelphia to report the news. He glanced at me, apologetically, as he pushed away his dinner plate, having apparently lost his appetite. "Adams thinks you brought about the loss of the election in New York *intentionally*."

The indignity of it, after all we'd done! My own appetite wavered.

Mac added, "Adams shouted that you've been trying to control the government while posing as a private man. That you're a man devoid of every moral principle—a bastard and a foreigner besides."

I flinched, because it was an insult designed to strike at my husband's weakest points, and an unworthy and unbecoming thing for the president of the United States to stoop to say besides. But, worse, few men were *more American* than Alexander Hamilton, and yet the president proclaimed him a foreigner. The same president who had the power to deport foreigners he deemed dangerous to the peace . . .

Alexander flung his napkin onto the table in disgust. "Not only the worst constructions are put upon my conduct as a public man, but it seems my birth must still be the subject of the most humiliating criticism!"

I put a hand on my husband's knee in comfort. His birth wasn't his fault, and yet, no conduct of his could ever seem to change it. And even McHenry seemed sensible of the wound he'd opened. "My dear Hamilton, with respect to the legitimacy of your birth, not one of your friends would respect you less even if *everything* your enemies say on this head were true."

"Well, that is kind, Mac," Hamilton allowed. "But my friends are precious few."

*That was only partially true,* I thought. Because even then, my husband still wore the aura of a victor. His star had dimmed but still blazed. And I confused followers for friends.

I know better now.

But at the time, I merely smiled at McHenry in gratitude.

Mac gave a long sigh. "While I'm at it, you might as well know this, too. During his tirade against me, the president declared Mr. Jefferson an infinitely better man than you; one who, if president, would act wisely. He said he'd rather be vice president under Jefferson than indebted to you, a man who ruled George Washington, and would rule still if he could."

I understood what this meant, and chills raised gooseflesh on my arms. "John Adams is changing sides. He's going to abandon the Federalists."

McHenry nodded. "You're not the only one to think the president has cut a deal with Jefferson to save his own neck."

At that, Alexander abruptly rose from the table to pace behind the chairs and looked as if he wished to throw one of them out of our bow window into the street below. "The man is more mad than I ever thought him, which he just might force me to say."

I was inclined to agree. Adams was going to abandon us to the bloodthirsty clutches of the Republican mob, who blamed my husband for every unpopular act of his own administration. And, for the first time since the days of the revolution—the revolution of '76—I began to consider that we might need to flee.

McHenry did nothing to change my mind. "Certainly, the president spoke in ways to persuade me he's actually insane."

"Very well, then." Alexander drained his wineglass, as if for courage. "Then Federalist electors must withdraw their support of Adams for president. If we must have an enemy at the head of the government, let it be one we can oppose and for whom we are not responsible, who will not involve our party in the disgrace of foolish and bad measures."

I dismissed this as merely hot talk. No one could prefer that Jacobin, Thomas Jefferson, even to an insane John Adams. And I said as much to my husband later that night, in the darkness of our bed.

His exhausted sigh crossed the space between us. "Mayhaps it makes no matter who becomes president, because four years from now I don't expect to have a head still upon my shoulders. Unless it is *at* the head of a victorious army."

~

*December 1800*
*New York City*

President Adams declared peace with France and dissolved the army. Too late to stave off his ignominious defeat at the polls.

Nationwide, the presidential election was a tie.

Not between Jefferson and Adams, whose erratic actions sealed his own fate. But a tie between Jefferson and *Burr*.

The presidential candidate and the vice presidential candidate had, through a quirk of our system, received the same number of electoral votes. But the people plainly meant for Jefferson to be president and wished that Burr would simply accept the vice presidency as intended.

I hoped for something else altogether. Because popular reason doesn't always know how to act right, nor does it always act right when it knows. Fortunately, the choice would be thrown to the House of Representatives, where my husband's Federalists reigned.

*Alexander* would choose our new president. And in this, I sensed our salvation.

Nearly laughing at the absurdity of Burr as president, I nevertheless felt a glorious relief. Burr was a trickster and a maker of chaos to be sure, but he was also a man we knew well. Burr might be a libertine, but he wasn't a chilly zealot like Jefferson, musing about the desolation of the earth in the pursuit of liberty.

In Burr, I felt certain we were to be delivered from our worst Jacobin nightmare of Jefferson unleashing the French Revolution on our shores.

So I was both stunned and dismayed to find myself in a heated argument about it when I passed by Alexander's study and overheard him telling our eldest son, "Upon every virtuous and prudent calculation, Jefferson is to be preferred over Burr."

Philip and I both gasped at the same time. "*Jefferson?*"

Alexander scarcely looked up from his writing table. Perhaps he *dared* not look at us for fear he'd lose his nerve or his lunch. Rubbing at his kidney, which had troubled him recently with spasms, he said, "There is no fair reason to suppose Jefferson capable of being corrupted, whereas Burr is bankrupt beyond redemption. His private character is not defended even by his most partial friends."

That Burr was corruptible, I had no doubt. Everyone knew he was in debt. "That only means he can be bought," I said. "And a man who can be bought can be bargained with."

Now my husband did look at me, his eyes widening, as if I'd sprouted two heads. I suppose he'd looked to me for moral direction only to find that I, too, had been compromised by this wicked world. "This is no time for saints, Alexander."

He shook his head and gathered his papers. "Nevertheless, Burr *cannot* be bargained with. Because no agreement with him could ever be relied upon."

Shamelessly, I blocked his exit. "Even so, you cannot prefer a radical theorist like Jefferson to Burr, a—a mere *opportunist*."

"Is it a recommendation to have no theory?" Alexander asked. "Can a man be an able statesman who has none? I believe not. Burr is far more cunning than wise, far more dexterous than able. In my opinion, he is inferior in real ability to Jefferson."

"As if *ability* matters," I argued, in frank disbelief. "As if these were ordinary times and not ones in which you tell me you stand to lose your head!"

It was exactly the wrong thing to say, and I realized it even before my husband stiffened. I shouldn't have appealed to his sense of self-preservation over the good of the nation. I was speaking, after all, to a man who'd been willing to fight and die for it. And I'd just questioned his willingness to do just that in the presence of our proud, patriotic son.

Fortunately, and to my surprise, Philip was on my side. "Father, the country won't survive Mr. Jefferson."

Alexander held up his hands to fend us both off. "I'm not an apologist for Jefferson. His politics are tinctured with fanaticism and he's a contemptible hypocrite. But he's *vain*. He isn't zealot enough to do anything that will destroy his popularity or our union. By contrast, Burr will disturb our institutions to secure permanent power and wealth. He's an American Cataline."

*Cataline.* Another accursed old Roman who'd plotted to overthrow the republic. I remembered perfectly well a time when Burr jested that the Constitution was nothing but *a miserable paper machine,* but I said, "You're allowing your resentments to get the better of your reason."

After all, though Jefferson always seemed to loom large, he'd been gone from our daily lives a long time, whereas Alexander had more recently tangled with Burr, been embarrassed by Burr, and been bested by Burr. My husband was too proud now to let Burr win. But I was not that proud. "Give Burr what he wants and you might win him to the Federalist point of view."

"A groundless hope," said my husband. "No, Burr is one of the worst men in the community. Sanguine enough to hope everything, daring enough to try everything, and wicked enough to scruple nothing. From the elevation of this man, may heaven preserve us!"

Philip and I remained in mutinous disagreement. In fact, the argument in our household went on almost as long as it did in Congress, through thirty-five rounds of ballots. And while Congress debated, so did we. Upon waking and sleeping. At breakfast and dinner. Before church and after church. And never in my life did I see anyone hector Alexander more relentlessly, or effectively, than my son did that winter.

While I sliced bread for the younger boys one morning after prayers, Philip argued, "By denying Jefferson the presidency and throwing support to Burr, we could split the Republican vote in the next election. The Federalists *must* support Burr."

Alexander might have made it out the door if he could have resisted an argument. But of course, he couldn't. Another father—perhaps any other father—might've resented Philip's arguments as the insolent yappings of a young pup. But Alexander was proud of our son's political passion and afforded him the same respect he'd give any other man in a political argument.

That is to say, he went on at length, ruthlessly smashing every argument Philip made, as if they were no more than a swarm of buzzing gnats.

"There is no circumstance," Alexander concluded, "not in the entire course of our political affairs, that has given me so much pain as the mere *idea* that Mr. Burr might be elevated to the presidency by the means of the Federalists. Jefferson is by far not so dangerous a man and he has, at least, *pretensions* to character. Let the people have their choice."

With this, Alexander looked to me, as if to applaud the superior merit of his argument, but I thought Philip had the right of it. That's why I said, "We *know* Burr. He isn't the sort of cold-blooded man who would murder his political enemies."

Oh, how it chills me now to remember the way Alexander replied, "He is *precisely* that cold-blooded."

# Part Four

## The War for History

# Chapter Thirty-Two

*Spring 1801*
*Harlem*

I N A LITTLE rowboat upon the Hudson, the rising tide pushed us away from our old life toward the site of our new home, our place of respite, and of our exile . . .

For Jefferson was the president. And there was nothing to do but survive the outcome.

Alexander was never able to convince me, Philip, or his Federalist Party that Jefferson was for the best—but he'd managed to convince a single elector from Delaware to switch his vote, and that had been enough.

I could only hope his gamble paid off—especially since Martha Washington called Jefferson's election "the greatest misfortune our nation has ever experienced."

But since my husband had helped him win the election, we were cautiously optimistic that Jefferson would not seek reprisals against us for my husband's long and vociferous political opposition.

"There it is," Alexander said as he rowed us to shore, his eyes shielded from the sun by a straw hat that looked nearly comical atop his general's head. He nodded at a bucolic spot on a forested hilltop. I looked up, a glint of sunlight off the dark green water momentarily blinding me, then I saw it.

Our new home upon this river along which I'd lived so much of my life. But unlike the Pastures or the little house at De Peyster's Point or our rented town houses, this home was *ours*.

Thirty-five acres. Barns, sheds, stables, gardens, orchards, chicken houses, duck ponds, and all.

The existing little farmhouse was to be replaced by a much grander mansion that my husband wished to call the Grange, after the lands of his supposed noble ancestor in Scotland. And Alexander was trying to turn a mind long attuned to the architecture of government to the simpler architecture of a house. "What say you about black marble for our fireplaces?"

As we floated pleasantly along the muddy shoreline, alone together for the first time in a while, I smiled. "I say marble will be beautiful, but expensive."

"I'll take on new clients," he replied. "Besides, your father is giving me timber. And what price is too great to pay for pure and unalloyed happiness with my excellent wife and sweet children?"

I wasn't sure my husband could be happy away from the bustle of the city, where all the most important decisions were made. But now that Jefferson's Jacobins had come to power—and my husband had decided to start a newspaper to point out their follies—it behooved us to get some small distance away from the inevitable riots and enraged mobs.

"I think I prefer white," I decided. "Italian marble. *Roman*, if you will."

"Then you will have it." He laughed, leaning forward so that our knees touched inside the little dinghy. "For it has always been my creed that a lady's pleasure is of more importance than a gentleman's."

And thereupon we lost an hour to conduct that surely scandalized the fishes.

Having run our little boat aground, Alexander laced up his breeches. Where his hat went, we didn't know or care. "If this is how we're to spend our days in the country," he said, "I believe I shall quite enjoy the leisurely life of a gentleman farmer . . ."

Rearranging my petticoats, all soaked with river water at the hem, I blushed like a girl half my age. "You won't think it's so leisurely when you must plow a field or feed the animals and slaughter pigs for dinner. There are no patisseries or coffeehouses for miles."

"Ah, my belle of the frontier," he teased. "I shall have to take instruction from you. For I am as unfit for my new role as country farmer as Jefferson is to guide the helm of the United States."

*Then perhaps you shouldn't have handed him the presidency,* I wanted to say, but I was in far too good a humor to spoil the moment. So instead I said, "It's peaceful here. It will be good for the children. Especially Ana." Our daughter never fully recovered from the loss of Fanny from our household. She'd seem better for a time but lapse again into strange tempers. My husband tried to assure me this was quite normal for a girl of sixteen, and having *been* a girl of sixteen, I saw his point. "Perhaps here, in the country, she can have a pet."

"What's wrong with our hunting dog?" Hamilton asked.

"She's *your* dog. Ana needs something pretty to cuddle. Perhaps a ginger tomcat," I said, playfully ruffling his hair, which was much less ginger now. "Mine did wonders for me . . ."

He gaped, as if both simultaneously offended that I should liken him to a pet, and also marveling that I could jest about such a thing.

But we'd come far enough that I could.

"I worry more for Philip," my husband said.

"Philip?" Our eldest was the only one of our children I *didn't* worry about. He'd grown from a sunny child into a charming young man of nineteen who could talk his way out of nearly anything. Just like his father.

"If he wants a career in the law, he needs to more seriously apply himself to his studies," Alexander grumbled, like a curmudgeon. "Without the distractions of the city." *Without the young ladies of the city,* I thought, and nearly laughed. But my husband added, "I don't entirely approve of his friends. I think they're gamblers and hooligans and mischief makers."

"At least they're not Republicans," I said.

That broke the clouds over my husband's brow as he chuckled.

In the days and weeks that followed Jefferson's inauguration, we settled into the farmhouse at the Grange. And Alexander *did* take more clients. Which meant traveling, during the week, at least three hours a day to his office in lower Manhattan. Then there were the trips to court in Poughkeepsie. And I was reminded of our early marriage, when he was so often gone with the city's gaggle of young lawyers riding in stagecoaches with circuit judges.

While packing his satchel for a journey upstate, he said, "Don't overtax yourself with the garden or with getting cedar shingles upon the ice house." Grabbing up his hat, then remembering his coat, he added, "Leave to Philip what you cannot accomplish yourself."

Poor Philip. More comfortable in velvet coat, tailored trousers, and starched shirt collar turned up fashionably around his cravat than he was in a hunter's shirt and breeches, he preferred life in the city, studying his law books, and debating politics with his friends in the taverns. But Philip understood how important it was that we embrace our new situation with good cheer, so he didn't balk at working on the farm with his younger brothers.

I wished I could've said the same for Ana, who complained that the farmhouse was too dark. Too crowded. And the night she heard the howl of a wolf, she whimpered with fright as if she were a much younger child. For a wolf to cause such fright! At her age, I was more terrified of Mohawk scalping parties. Her fears kept her inside, laboring beside me in the sooty old kitchen. At least until her father came into the kitchen, satchel in hand, making ready to kiss us good-bye.

"Why must you *always* go away?" she cried, storming out of the room and up the stairs. The slam of her door shook the whole house.

Kissing my cheek, Alexander sighed and spoke as if he'd read my mind. "Don't worry. She'll adapt to the circumstances."

I wasn't so certain, but just then, the welfare of another member of my family weighed on my mind. "Are you sure it isn't too much trouble to visit Peggy?" Though my younger sister insisted she was just tired, she'd been feeling poorly for months, so Alexander made a point of frequently dropping in at her manor north of Albany while he attended to his cases at the court.

He shook his head. "Of course, not. It's on the way. And I'll take her the basket of crabs the boys hauled out of the river."

I walked with my husband out onto the porch, where our eldest son had the little phaeton hitched to a horse. "Seeing you will cheer Peggy, I'm sure."

"Perhaps, then, I'll even roast the crabs for her. Though, as a *Creole*, I've some sympathy for them." Alexander hefted the crustaceans onto the bench seat just as little William bolted out the door and leaped off the porch, shoeless and shirtless.

As my husband swung our four-year-old ruffian into his arms, I couldn't help but muse that Alexander being able to refer to himself as a *Creole*—the word for the mixed-race people who sometimes subsisted upon shellfish on the islands where he'd been raised—was what had persuaded me that my husband had somehow, finally, made peace with his dubious origins. And with our whole life now. For Alexander would never before have made such a jest.

We'd both come quite a long way together indeed.

"Can I go with you, Papa?" William asked.

"Not this time, little man," Alexander said, pressing a big wet kiss to the boy's neck that made him giggle. "But what if I bring something back for you?"

"A bow and arrows?" William asked, clambering down with a little war whoop.

I shook my head in exasperation, for our youngest son was endlessly fascinated by stories of the Indians and the frontier. I supposed it was the Schuyler in him. Chuckling, Alexander

454 Stephanie Dray & Laura Kamoie

climbed into the phaeton and grasped the reins. "How about I surprise you?"

Grinning at our son's excitement, I hugged him to me and waved in fond farewell. "Give my love to Peg. And tell her to write."

Alas, I never received another letter from Peggy again.

*My dear Eliza, your sister took leave of her sufferings and friends, I trust, to find repose and happiness in a better country. I long to come home to console and comfort you.*
—ALEXANDER HAMILTON

The blow fell upon me like a hammer to an ox.

How could Peggy, who lived so bold a life, have succumbed so suddenly to some ignominious and unnamed disease? Though I had four sisters, I'd come of age with only two—Angelica and Peggy. From my earliest memory, I was the one in the middle. My older sister on one side, my younger sister on the other. Now, Peggy was gone at just forty-two, and Angelica and I came all unmoored.

On our knees in Trinity Church, we were bid by Bishop Moore to leave off our tears and remember the duty of Christian resignation. God had seen fit to take Peggy from us, calling her to a realm of bliss, and we must be happy for her.

But Angelica and I indulged in our tears anyway.

And we clung to each other even tighter when, not long after, Papa wrote that Mama, just a few months shy of her seventieth birthday, had passed peacefully in her sleep. The woman who'd taught me about medicine and housekeeping and Dutch traditions, who'd helped birth my children. Gone. Poor Mama!

It was almost more than Angelica and I could bear, losing them both in such quick succession, but the fire of it forged us even closer. And, in the months that followed, Angelica and I became constant companions. She made the three-hour-long round-trip through woods and farmland to see me at the Grange, complaining only a little that I'd fled the city. And I returned her visits with bumpy carriage rides to her house downtown.

On one such visit to lower Manhattan, we were treated to a noisy Fourth of July celebration during which an insolent young pup named Captain George Eacker told the crowd that President Jefferson had rescued the Constitution from my husband, who would have used his army to overthrow it.

Much accustomed to such rabble-rousing abuse, Alexander and I merely continued on to our own celebrations amongst the Society of the Cincinnati, of which my husband had become president.

But Philip could scarcely contain himself. That night, after playing billiards on his uncle Church's new game table, he exploded. "Do those mongrels realize my father *gave* Jefferson the presidency? They should be tarred and feathered for spreading such lies."

"Our son is apt to be a little intemperate," Alexander later complained.

A complaint I took for the richest irony. "There's no help for it, I'm afraid."

From behind his new spectacles, my husband arched a brow. "Because I'm his father?"

"And because I'm his mother. His Schuyler blood will out." I remembered, after all, a time when I was just as angry on my own father's behalf, wishing to defend him against malicious lies and conspiracies.

So, the next morning, I reassured Philip that patience was the best thing. "Just as your grandpapa was eventually seen for the patriot he is, so will your father be appreciated and vindicated in the fullness of time."

Then I forgot the matter entirely, because abuses and slanders had been too numerous in our lives to hold on to each one.

Before the weather turned to winter, Angelica and I accepted an invitation to play a game of pall-mall with Kitty Livingston upon her new husband's lawn. After vanquishing the other ladies with mallet and ball, not to mention haranguing them for donations, I retreated to a red velvet-covered divan in a corner where my sister and I could enjoy our tea with a little privacy.

Perhaps because the loss of Peggy and Mama still felt so recent to us, we commiserated over the trouble we'd given Mama, something we understood with greater clarity now that we both had grown children of our own. And we reminisced about how Peggy had somehow convinced General Burgoyne to make a present to her of his shiny shoe buckles, how she'd fended off a hatchet-wielding Tory, and how she'd run off to marry the man of her heart.

Of course, that was no mark of distinction in our family. In fact, elopement was an epidemic in Papa's household. Our little sister Cornelia ran off with a beau a few years prior, and now our little Caty—the very baby sister Peggy had rescued from the tomahawk-wielding loyalists—was threatening to do the same.

"I've always set the trends," Angelica said, sniffling into her kerchief. "My dear Eliza, you were the only one unfashionable enough to do everything properly."

"Poor Papa," I replied. "He has only one unmarried daughter left, and I predict she'll run off with her beau the first chance she gets."

Balancing her teacup, Angelica whispered, "Poor *us* if it's in Schuyler blood. Given her gaggle of suitors, Church is forced to keep his eye on our eldest daughter every moment. Meanwhile, I scowl disapprovingly at every penniless Jacobin who looks her way."

"Are there any Federalist boys left?" I asked, for my husband's political party had crumbled in the wake of the election, and what they considered to be Alexander's unpardonable role in helping Jefferson win. "Or are only yours and mine still standing?"

"Well, I dare say there will soon be more little Federalists. Given the scandalous behavior of the girls at the last dance I attended, there's not a young lady in New York who wouldn't run away with your Philip or mine."

The realization that my son was old enough to marry—and to

sire children—was still somehow astonishing. Almost as astonishing as hearing Angelica speak about anyone else's scandalous behavior. "How did we become the disapproving matrons, clucking our tongues at the edges of a dance hall?"

"Advancing age." Angelica scowled. "It's an *appalling* condition."

I smiled over the rim of my teacup. "I don't feel so very advanced in age."

"Because you won a vicious game of *pall-mall*? Well, you've always had remarkable stamina, but—"

"I'm soon to add another little one to the family," I said, splaying my fingers lightly over my bodice with excitement.

"*Another!*" Angelica cried in equal parts delight and dismay. "It's the turn of the century. Have neither you nor Hamilton discovered French letters?"

I smirked. "Well, you know how Hamilton distrusts all things French . . ."

My sister quite nearly howled. "You *Jezebel*."

"Oh, hush," I said because I didn't want her lady friends to overhear. So I leaned forward to confide, "If it's a girl, we'll name her after Peggy . . ."

"*Peggy*," Angelica said, her eyes misting with emotion. "How lovely." Together we melted over that sweet notion, only to be interrupted by a commotion at the door.

The wife of my husband's law partner, Mrs. Pendleton, had arrived, apparently uninvited, without a coat or hat. She appeared in some disarray, insisting that she must see Angelica straightaway. As we rose to greet her, Mrs. Pendleton literally trembled. "Mrs. Church, there is some manner of pandemonium at your house. You had better come quick. A young man has been shot and carried there and a doctor called for. I fear—I fear . . ."

My heart leaped to my throat, because I knew just what she feared—that my sister's boy had been shot. Angelica obviously feared it, too, clutching at my hand and trying to remain upright. As Kitty swiftly gathered up our hats and handbags for us, I urged my sister to calm.

I had, after all, treated many men in the war who survived gunshot wounds. Then I hurried my very pale and shaking sister to her house, where carriages blocked the drive. It seemed as if half the city's doctors crowded the entryway—with, to my surprise, my nephew, apparently unharmed.

Angelica flew to him. "Oh, you infernal boy. I feared you'd taken part in an affair of honor!"

"No," Flip said, ashen as he looked my way. "It's my cousin."

In that moment, someone steadied me; I think it was my brother-in-law, murmuring some explanation. But the only thing I understood was that it wasn't my sister's boy who'd been shot.

It was mine.

How did I make my way to the gilded guest room in which my eldest son writhed? I don't recall. My only fixed memory is crashing through the door to find Philip, his pale neck spattered in a veil of his own vivid red blood.

Alexander was there already, holding our son's shoulders as Philip convulsed with pain. Though my husband tried to warn me away with a shake of his head, I cried my son's name as I rushed to tend him, pressing frantic kisses upon his hand.

"Don't worry, Mother," Philip said, trying to muster a smile. "It just hurts like the devil . . ."

That attempt at levity cost him—his pulse raced then ebbed beneath my lips. I hushed him, as the war nurse in me frantically searched for the wound. I pulled back bedcovers to find the spot on his side where the doctors had already cut the clothing away.

What I found nearly drove me to my knees.

*Dark blood*, not bright red like the spatter on his face.

*Dark blood*, not red.

*Dark blood*, an inky Madeira.

The bullet had passed through his side and lodged itself in his opposite arm. It was the arm that bled red. But from the torso oozed the dark blood. Which meant the bullet had passed through some vital organ. There was no help for it. I'd seen soldiers suffer such wounds, and I knew, with horrifying clarity, that my son was dying.

Philip must have known it, too, because he whispered, "I need you to know I tried to escape the duel." He followed this with a gasping breath. "And when I c-couldn't, I determined to take no man's life, but merely offer my own in preservation of honor."

He grimaced again, writhing in pain, and Alexander shushed him with strained, halting words. "Oh, my dear boy. Save your strength. We could never doubt your honor."

I'd only heard that tone in my husband's voice one time before, when we lost our little baby, dead before she was born. Which meant he, too, knew it was happening again. Now.

Meanwhile, Philip was determined that we know he behaved bravely. "I reserved my fire . . . to throw in the air."

A duel. He'd fought a duel. And he'd thrown away his shot. It was all sinking in, and I didn't care. *Dear God,* I didn't care for anything but keeping him alive and I hadn't the faintest notion how to do it.

"Doctor," I cried. "He must have laudanum."

Alexander reached to still me and our fingers tangled, sticky with our son's warm blood, as he drew my attention to the bottle at the side of the bed. Philip had been dosed with it already. Any more, and perhaps we would hasten the end.

I recoiled from the thought, though my desperate mind would later fasten upon the notion as some manner of mercy when our poor boy lay hour after hour, pale and languid, his rolling eyes darting forth through flashes of delirium.

Caring naught for the blood, we climbed into bed with him, Alexander on one side, me on the other, and whispered tearful words of love and comfort as the darkness fell. "My sweet son," I said in a voice I normally reserved for the littlest children. "You cannot remember the happiness you gave us when you were a baby, but oh, the joy we felt, just to hold you between us in bed, just like this."

Philip pressed his head against mine, and in my mind's eye, he was still the little jester who'd made us laugh. The brave eleven-year-old who'd saved all my other children. The fiery thirteen-year-old who'd defended his father in the streets. And I wanted to know who did this to him. What fiendish murderer could have pointed a pistol at my beautiful, sweet boy?

I had so many questions. But they would have to wait.

For as Philip groaned in desperate pain, I realized my duty to him. I was his mother. I'd nourished him, baptized him, taught him, clothed him, and watched him grow into a man. And yet, he needed me still. Now, the most important, the most sacred thing that I could do for my son was deliver him from this world just as I'd delivered him into it.

"You mustn't be afraid," I whispered. "These pains will soon pass. They will pass, and you will find your rest with God." Alexander tried to swallow a moan but couldn't hold it back.

But Philip nodded, his blue-tinged lips trembling. "I have f-faith in the Lord and my conscience is c-clean."

He closed his eyes, already more gone from the world than still in it. So I met my husband's gaze across the expiring body of our son, and met eyes so full of agony that I had to look away.

Before dawn, Philip roused himself. "What s-shall I tell Aunt Peggy when I see her in heaven? I—I think she'll be angry t-to see me so soon." Philip said this last part with a little laugh that brought a fresh cycle of convulsions.

"Don't laugh, my sweet," I told him, choking back a sob as I pressed my nose into his hair and inhaled the scent of him. "Don't laugh if it hurts you."

Alexander echoed me, his voice cracking. "You always laughed too much. Your only fault, my dear boy."

Philip tried to turn his grimace into a grin. "Father, I shall debate you that laughter can be a f-fault."

"And I shall let you win," Alexander said, his voice a raw scrape.

"A first," my son whispered, closing his eyes with apparent relish. His breath rattled.

Then fell silent.

Frightful, heartbreaking silence.

That silence echoed through the room.

I reeled from the bed, shaking my head, vehemently, backing away in denial, nearly crashing into my sister's gilded chairs and mahogany tables. Half-hysterical, half-furious, I wanted to tear at my hair and beat my breasts and awaken myself from this cruel nightmare.

But while I retreated, Alexander clutched our dead son, choking out, "Go, my boy. Go out of the reach of the seductions and calamities of a world full of folly, full of vice, full of danger . . ."

All my life I'd taken comfort from religion, but these words offered me no solace, and from my mouth came the keening of a wounded animal, a ghastly howl of despair. My cheeks streaked with salty tears, the skirt of my delicate pink dress stained with acrid sweat and dried blood, I was overcome with a desire to smash everything in my path—silver mirrors, blue china, crystal wineglasses. To sweep off the elegant tables all my sister's goblets, candlesticks, and trinkets that held no worth in a world without Philip.

But I was stopped by the sight of Alexander hovering, shattered, over the deathbed of our boy, and the absurd thought that I couldn't endure to see one more thing *broken* . . .

And because my husband was shattered, I couldn't endure to see him.

Angelica tended me that night. She took the pins from my hair. She undid the fastenings of my pelisse coat, sliding the blood-stained embroidered cuffs off my arms. She stripped from me my stained pink dress. She bent down and removed my shoes and dosed me with the laudanum that was left. Where Hamilton slept that night I did not know, but my sister put me into her own bed where the sweet, merciful oblivion of sleep overtook me. And from that dream state, where my son was still alive, I did not ever wish to wake.

# Chapter Thirty-Three

I T WAS THE *will of heaven*," said my well-meaning Christian lady friends. "Remember the duty of Christian resignation."

*It was God,* they said, who took my child from me.

But upon my aching knees in the pew in Trinity Church, clutching my Bible, I knew better.

It was not *God* who took my son from me.

It was a Jeffersonian.

Captain George Eacker, the violent Jacobin we saw ranting against my husband on the Fourth of July. Having come across the man at a playhouse, my son and a friend had confronted him. Captain Eacker had grabbed my son by the collar and called him a rascal. *Rascal.* A word which, when spoken by one gentleman to another, demanded bloodshed.

*"Eliza,"* Alexander now whispered, his hand upon my elbow, offering to help me rise.

I startled to realize that we were alone in the church. How long I'd knelt in desperate prayer amidst wooden benches and the scent of incense, I didn't know. How long my husband had prayed beside me, I didn't know either.

It seemed I didn't know anything. I'd been at the Grange while my son negotiated his affair of honor. Blissfully unaware. But Alexander had been at his law office in the city.

Still on my knees, I peered at him. "Did you know?"

Hamilton swallowed and shook his head. He didn't need to be told what I was asking. "Philip went to his uncle for advice."

*And for those pistols*, I thought, bitterly. Philip should have come to us. I'd made plain my Christian opposition to dueling. Every parson and priest in the country decried duels. Even Alexander had issued a memo to curb the practice when he was general of the army.

But my son hadn't come to us. He'd gone to his rich, swaggering uncle with his shining dueling pistols and a reputation for deadly aim.

*No, no, no*, I screamed inside my head. Bad enough that my son had involved himself in a duel that took his life. So much worse that he'd been the one to make the unholy challenge. I didn't have to ask why. Church—our family expert on dueling—would have told my son that he couldn't let an insult stand. Church would have told him he hadn't any choice when it came to honor.

*But what the devil did John Barker Church know about honor?* He'd been born with it. He had the luxury as a young man to cast off a name and put it back on again as the circumstances suited him. He'd never had to scrape and claw to prove his worth.

Not like my husband, who took my hand in his trembling one, and tearfully said, "I learned of it only after Philip had issued the challenge."

I gasped. Then he *had* known. He'd known before the deed had been done.

With desolate eyes, Alexander continued. "You must believe I tried to set him right. I told Philip it was ill-mannered to accost a man in the middle of a play and that he must apologize. I told him he wouldn't want this man's blood on his hands. I thought that would end the matter. I thought . . ." My husband's head dropped. "Next I heard, the apology hadn't been accepted and Philip was already rowing across the river to the dueling place. There was no time to do anything but race to find a doctor . . ." His voice broke off then, as if he could say no more. And yet, he did. "Why couldn't I stop this from happening? I've stopped *armies* but I couldn't stop a duel."

My anger ebbed at the sight of his anguish. In its place, regret and pity rushed in for a father unable to save his son. My husband had led troops, advised a president, and built a nation, but he'd been powerless in that moment when it mattered most.

And now, from that prodigious mind, always spinning with plans and schemes, came an eerie vacancy. From that eloquent mouth, always arguing, proposing, and teasing, came a humbled silence. From those tireless hands, constantly scribbling out letters and essays and proposals, came only stillness.

And so, together, we were both vacant, silent, and still.

Our boy was dead. Dead for his own hubris, having initiated both a confrontation and a duel. I thought we'd taught him better. And it poured more sorrow into the bitter cup from which I was now forced to drink. All I had for consolation was the knowledge that he'd stood brave on that field, and that he hadn't taken a life. Instead, he'd let a villain shoot him so he could keep his honor.

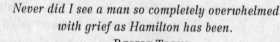

> *Never did I see a man so completely overwhelmed*
> *with grief as Hamilton has been.*
> —ROBERT TROUP

Winter 1801
Albany

"When is Philip coming home?"

The question came in the middle of the night, spoken by my seventeen-year-old daughter with a lantern in her hand. Disoriented and blinking against sleep, I was actually convinced for a moment that we'd come to the Pastures ahead of my eldest son.

That he'd caught the next sloop, and would be with us by dawn. Then the crushing reality overtook me with all its accompanying heartbreak.

We'd buried Philip in the yard of Trinity Church, where, in dropping a handful of dirt onto our son's casket in farewell, Hamilton faltered and was kept upright only by our friends. That was weeks ago. Since then, Papa had sent a coach to fetch us to Albany where he might care for us himself. In truth, I think it eased his own grief in the loss of Mama to tend us in our grief for Philip, a grief which Papa of course shared and, as a father who himself had survived several of his children, one which he understood.

But even as Alexander and I struggled to pull ourselves from bed and force small morsels of food down our throats, Ana now seemed to be caught in some blissful waking dream in which she believed Philip was still very much alive.

Throwing the blankets aside, Alexander rose from the bed to embrace her. "Philip has gone to heaven, my darling girl. A haven of eternal repose and felicity."

Ana's expression crumpled. "No. He's only gone riding just this morning. I made a pie for his breakfast. Remember?"

She didn't know where we were. She didn't know *when* we were. She didn't remember that Philip was dead. Truly, she didn't. So for the next hour, she sat on our bed and asked question after question about how Philip died, her grief as fresh and raw as if she was reliving the nightmare.

And we lived it all again with her.

Worrying for my health and that of our unborn baby, Alexander insisted I go back to sleep and led Ana out of the room. But I awakened to the sound of splashing water in the upstairs hall, my daughter singing with her aunt Angelica. In coming with us to the Pastures, my sister had left her own husband and children behind to offer comfort to mine; now I found that Angelica had Ana in a copper tub and was brushing her hair as if she were still a very little girl. "You'll feel better soon, my darling. Especially after a fresh, clean bath."

"But when is Philip coming home?" Ana asked, and I put a hand to my mouth, grateful for my sister's help and wondering how many times I would have to remind my daughter that Philip was dead.

Standing beside me, his face strongly stamped with grief, eyes downcast, as if staring into a bottomless pit of despair, my husband put a hand on my shoulder. "Let her believe whatever she must. Her mind has become disordered by the wound. We must let it heal."

The disordering wasn't entirely new or caused only by *this* wound. Now I saw Ana's distress when Fanny had been taken from us in a new light. The depth and intensity of my daughter's confusion was so much worse now than it was then, and in my grief and despair, it was terrifying. But because I felt as if my *own* mind had become disordered by the wound of Philip's loss, I could scarcely gainsay my husband. None of us would.

My father—my beloved, devoted, kind father—tread as if upon the shells of eggs trying to comfort us. And my siblings followed his example.

Only Angelica, over a melancholy Christmas breakfast, was brave enough to venture, "Do you not think we should summon a physician for Ana—?"

"I'll not have my daughter locked up in an asylum," Alexander interrupted.

He said this quietly, but with such resounding authority, it stunned us all into silence. Plainly stung by his tone, if not the injustice of the accusation, Angelica sat up straighter. "Why, my dear brother, I'm only suggesting that a doctor examine her."

Alexander didn't answer, and his silence on the matter scared me more. For he was rarely silent on *anything,* and it meant he was scared, too. Instead, he cared for Ana with saintly fortitude—singing with her at the piano and taking her for walks to watch for the birds she loved so well—but she got no better. And I feared my husband took too much pleasure sharing that fantasy in which she dwelt, where Philip was alive, rather than the reality we faced together without him.

At the turn of the new year, I found Alexander in my father's blue parlor. The very place we married, with the same snowy view of the river. That day, I'd been so hopeful, but it all seemed hopeless now. "Are you certain we shouldn't send for the doctor—"

"They'll lock her away." Hamilton folded his arms as he stared out at the frozen river. He seemed so very far from me, and his hair had turned snowy as if overnight.

"We won't permit it," I reassured him, confused by what seemed an irrational response from an otherwise rational man. "We could choose a trusted doctor. Any you prefer; we could write Dr. Stevens, or Dr. Rush, or—"

"They locked up my mother. I will never let it happen to Ana."

*They jailed your mother for adultery,* I thought. Not a disordered mind. Why should he be so fearful? No one would do anything to Alexander Hamilton's daughter without his consent. He was no longer a helpless, penniless boy in the West Indies. He'd commanded armies. A nation.

He could protect his daughter. But perhaps he didn't believe it, because he hadn't been able to protect our son. And I didn't broach it again, because I felt as if suspended on the thinnest ice, afraid to make the smallest misstep.

Lest we all should fall.

~

*May the loss of one be compensated by another Philip.*
*May his virtues emulate those which graced his brother,*
*and may he be a comfort to his tender parents.*
—General Philip Schuyler to his daughter Elizabeth Hamilton

*June 1802*
*Harlem*

Flowers again. Yellow daffodils. Purple hyacinths. Red tulips. Then Pinkster azaleas when the weather turned warmer.

In the days before and after Little Phil's birth, my husband filled my room with a rainbow of blossoms—my new room, in the house he built for me at the Grange, with its delicate fanlight in the entryway, the extravagance of eight fireplaces, and the mirrored doors of our octagonal dining room that could be thrown open to the parlor to form a rather grand ballroom.

Though I couldn't imagine we might ever host a ball.

"We will, my angel," Alexander vowed, laying a bouquet of fiery lilies across the bed. "That I promise. And a promise must never be broken . . ."

He treated me now as if I were quite a fragile thing. As fragile as our newborn babe. As fragile as our poor unfortunate daughter, whose mind remained disordered.

And, *oh*, the money he spent trying to make us all happy again.

He spared no expense in the marble Doric columns, verandas, and bay windows. Walnut side-chairs, silver oil lamps, and gilded mirrors. Wages for Mr. and Mrs. Genti, the couple he hired to serve as our cook and housekeeper. Then there were books and smart suits for our boys—especially our auburn-haired Alex, who found himself now, at sixteen, in the position of the eldest son with all its expectations. And there were little parakeets for Ana, who seemed to grow *younger* every day.

"She only needs tenderness and attention," Alexander reassured me as we took a summer stroll together on the sylvan grounds. "She will recover in time."

"And if she does not?" I asked, quietly.

For a long moment, he didn't respond. So long that I feared he might not at all. "Then we will care for her here at the Grange where she cannot be exposed to the cruelty of onlookers."

I nodded, for it was the thing I loved best about the Grange. It was far from prying eyes. It was a refuge. If ever we might be healed of our loss, it would be here. And yet, our boys must have their schooling. "But how will Alex and James and—"

"I'll take them with me into the city during the week," Alexander said. "I'll stay with them while you and Ana and the littlest ones remain here so that none of them will ever be without one parent or another."

It would be a terrible sacrifice to be apart from my husband half the week. But I, too, feared for any of them to be alone.

Alexander was with the children every day, sometimes even leading them in prayer. He'd never expressed any liturgical curiosity, but now he sought out the friendship of Reverend Mason, the Federalist pastor of the Scotch Presbyterian Church near our rented house on Cedar Street. And my husband prayed, before sleep and upon rising, scribbling notes into the margins of the Bible. So I was not surprised to hear him say, "Someday, I will build a chapel for the children. Right here, in our very own grove."

For him to come more fully to God had always been my hope. But there seemed to me something sinister in it now, as if, despairing of this world, he pined for another. And I remembered another time when my husband had cared for me while hiding that he himself was falling to pieces.

What I wanted now was for us to take care of one another.

I didn't feel as if I could ever be compensated for the loss of my son, but with another babe at the breast, I felt powerfully reminded of the sacred obligations Alexander and I had undertaken in starting a family. Our children deserved from us a celebration of life. And so I said simply, "You must forgive yourself."

My husband took a breath, as if my words had cut him, then glanced off at some fixed spot on the horizon. "Philip needed me. And yet, I failed him as surely as my own father failed me."

"No. You were his hero."

"A hero?" Alexander laughed bitterly, pressing his back against the trunk of a tree, lost in a hell of self-recrimination. "I once fancied myself powerful. What has become of my arrogance now? How humble, how helpless, how contemptible I am. A vile worm. A presumptuous *fool* to offend God, whose nod alone was sufficient to crush us into pieces."

So he believed Philip's death to be some manner of divine punishment. "No man or woman is righteous, Alexander. Not even one. A merciful God forgives. He doesn't visit the sins of the father upon the son."

Alexander straightened up from the tree and walked for the fence, as if he meant to escape me, his torment, or both. "Our boy died defending my name."

Yes, he did. And I knew that at Philip's age, if I could have, I'd have done the same. I'd have dueled for my father's honor, too. *Semper Fidelis.* It was in our Schuyler blood. And it was the first, most important lesson I ever taught him. "You gave him a name worth defending. A name in which to take pride and solace and the shape of his character," I said, reaching for my husband. "You gave him that. You gave him what you never had. And you gave *me* your name, too. If Philip died for a name, it was for *our* name—"

"*Eliza,*" Alexander interrupted, as if to fend me off, one hand to his eyes to shield me from seeing the tears gathering there.

But I would not be fended off. "You were alone as a child, but Philip never was. Not a moment of his entire life did he feel abandoned or unloved. That's why he loved to laugh—"

"He *died* because of me."

"He died because a Jacobin murdered him," I replied, with complete conviction. My son hadn't been the only one to quarrel with George Eacker, after all. One of Philip's friends had also been caught up in the same incident. Captain Eacker let that other boy—the son of nobody in particular—go unharmed.

But he shot the son of Alexander Hamilton. He shot Philip dead.

He would never face justice for it. In Jefferson's America, he'd be applauded. We had long feared the blade of a guillotine, but a bullet had done the job just as well.

"I need you," I said, and Alexander came at once to my embrace.

"Then you shall have me. Wife, children, and hobby are the only things upon which I permit my thoughts to run. Because I need you as well, my dear Eliza. More than you shall *ever* understand."

We stood there, holding one another in love and mutual comfort until our hearts beat in time. And I wish I could say that was the end of it. That, with those words, with that embrace, with that understanding, we healed each other's wounds.

But any parent who has lost a child will tell you that grief is a monster less vanquished than held at bay. That, like love, survival is a choice to be made anew every morning, and sometimes one must *pretend* at being healed just to get through the day.

Alas, my husband was not a man who could comfortably pretend at anything . . .

# Chapter Thirty-Four

*The African Venus is said to officiate as*
*housekeeper at Monticello.*
—James Callender

September 1802
Harlem

**H**AVE YOU SEEN this?" Angelica cried, bursting into our house with a stack of newspapers. I knew it must be important for her to have made the trip from the city, especially when she didn't bother to remove her coat or hat before racing into the parlor. My stomach knotted the moment she lay the papers before me because they were copies of the *Richmond Recorder*, where that despicable scandalmonger, James Callender, plied his vicious trade.

How many years had he hounded us? How cruelly he'd aimed his poison pen at my family in exposing the Reynolds Affair. And even though Angelica's expression was peculiar—something between fury and glee—I told myself that I mustn't be surprised by the depths to which the papers might sink to hurt us now.

But I *was* surprised.

For the article was not aimed at us, but at Thomas Jefferson, the president of the United States, who, it breathlessly revealed to the world, had for many years kept an enslaved woman for his mistress.

We'd known this, of course. Given my sister's intimacy with Jefferson, she was privy to a number of his secret liaisons, including one with this enslaved mulatto, Sally Hemings—and whispers said she was the half-sister of his dead wife, besides.

I took some petty satisfaction that Jefferson might suffer for this, but it was all very unseemly and uncomfortable to see anyone's intimate life splashed across the papers again. When I said as much, Angelica shook her head. "Keep reading. Where is Hamilton?" She went to the tall windows overlooking the veranda and squinted. "What the devil is he doing out there in the dirt?"

"He was planting thirteen sweet gum trees this morning—one for each of the original colonies. I'm not sure what he's doing now."

"A garden is a very usual refuge of a disappointed politician," he explained a few minutes later when we went outside to show him the news.

For Angelica had been right. There *was* something we didn't already know.

That indecent creature, that *reptile* Callender, had been *paid* to destroy us.

"Thirteen years ago, Jefferson hired him to print seditious libels," I said, indignantly shaking the page before Alexander's eyes. I wasn't sure if we should frame it, set it afire, or bury it as fertilizer in the garden. But what I was sure of was that we'd been *vindicated*. "All those years ago, Jefferson paid Callender to write that Washington was a traitor, a robber, and a perjurer. Paid him to print foul slanders against President Adams and against you."

Dark eyes flashing, Angelica added, "And now that Jefferson is president, and won't pay anymore, the serpent turns and bites the hand that fed him."

Alexander had always suspected as much but now seemed taken aback by our vehemence and heaved a great sigh. "We live in a world full of evil."

I blinked. That was all he had to say about it? The man who'd once designed governments had set his mind on our farm, deciding the ground of our orchard was too wet, that we must have grass, that we must plant watermelons, and that our cows must not be allowed to range.

We'd kept our heads ducked since Jefferson took the presidency, and what had our reward been? A dead son. Our fears of guillotines in the streets were not realized—my husband had, perhaps, been right to believe Jefferson a more cautious man than I had supposed—but if we were going to live in this country, if we were going to remain vulnerable to his rabid followers, then I did not think we should passively endure it.

And, truthfully, anger felt so much better than grief. "Alexander, you gave Jefferson the presidency. You and that horrific clause in the Constitution that allows slaves to be counted as three-fifths of a person for purposes of representation. Jefferson would have never been elected otherwise, and now he disgraces the place he unjustly fills and produces immorality by his example. If this bit about the scandalmonger is true, Jefferson must be abominably wicked and weak. I think you have a duty to the Constitution—"

"Perhaps no man has sacrificed or done more for the present Constitution than myself," Alexander said, bracing his hands upon the shovel's pole. "I've labored to prop the frail and worthless fabric in spite of all my predictions that it will fail. Yet I have the murmurs of its friends no less than the curses of its foes for reward. Every day proves to me more and more that this American world was not made for me. What can I do better than withdraw?"

I hated to see him in surrender. I'd married, after all, a soldier. A hero. Not a sad, fatalistic man, but a fractious firebrand. And I wanted him back.

I wanted the Alexander I'd always known and loved.

Later, when my sister went inside to fetch us cider, I told him, "You must engage the world again."

"I never stopped," he protested, reminding me of the near-daily eighteen-mile round-trips he made to his new office on Garden Street in town. "My practice of law remains a vigorous undertaking."

But the cases he handled now were only of the mundane variety and of no great import. The kind that didn't tax his talents or set precedents. He had, of course, almost as if in a compulsion, never stopped writing essays. Amongst them, the *Examination*, which tore apart all President Jefferson's policies. And he had, at my repeated urging, finally assisted with the publication of a newly bound collection of *The Federalist*. But when our peg-legged friend, Mr. Morris, pleaded with Alexander to take a more active role—perhaps even to run for political office—my husband refused. And I'd been glad.

But now I thought I'd been wrong. For all the years I'd complained of it, the squalid brawling of the public arena was part of Hamilton's makeup, like hair, teeth, or bones. So I said, "I think you should defend the Federalist newspaperman Jefferson is now trying to imprison under the sedition laws he claimed to hate. And Papa agrees." Out of a desire to shield my husband's vulnerabilities from other eyes—any other eyes—I'd waited for Angelica's departure to lobby for this idea, but I'd set my sister on him, too, if need be.

Alexander laughed. "You want me to battle President Jefferson. In a *courtroom*."

I glared at him for laughing. "Someone has to." When I was younger, I often asked why it couldn't be someone else. Why did it always have to be Alexander Hamilton to jump into the fray? And I'd complained, on more than one occasion, of his obsessive need to be at the center of history in the making.

I resolved now to never complain of it again.

At my insistence, Alexander relented and took the case against the newspaperman who'd been brave enough to reveal that Jefferson had paid James Callender to print slanders against all manner of public and private men. The case hinged on two constitutional issues: freedom of the press and trial by jury.

Alexander also, to my chagrin, waived the fee.

But I didn't mind so much when I saw our older boys gathered around their father as he explained his plan to establish a constitutional principle that *truth* must always be a defense against charges of slander and libel. And I could see that our boys all adored their father and wished to follow in his footsteps. Especially when he confided in them his intention to subpoena President Jefferson himself and confront him with testimony by the infamous James Callender . . .

But on the morning I lined up our boys outside the courtroom in their Sunday best to listen to their father argue the case, Alexander whispered with a colleague, then sat down hard on the steps where I knelt, tying Johnny's cravat, which he'd pulled loose again. "He's dead," Hamilton said, removing his top hat and holding it as if he'd never seen it before.

"Who?" I asked, alarmed by my husband's sudden gray pallor.

"Callender," he said. "Drowned, they say."

Before Alexander could transport Callender to the courtroom to give testimony that would have harmed the president, the scoundrel was found dead, floating in the James River near Richmond. Some said a victim of his own drunken excesses. Others said he'd been murdered to keep him quiet.

And it was as sobering a reminder of how *deadly* politics could be.

Alexander wasn't permitted to subpoena the president. And he lost the trial. Regardless, my husband made an argument that moved men to tears—his voice thundering in the courtroom while he paced like the revolutionary lion he had once been, the spark of a young firebrand still flashing in his eyes and setting my heart aflame.

Later, all the city's leaders praised it as one of his greatest speeches. Perhaps his greatest. And I was so glad my boys were in attendance when Hamilton concluded his remarks by saying, "I never did think the truth was a crime. I'm glad the day has come in which it is to be decided. For my soul has ever abhorred the thought that a free man dare not speak the truth."

*And that,* I thought with inordinate pride, *is Alexander Hamilton.*

That was who the history books should remember.

Yet, now I think, in the end, it wasn't my pride in him, or the trial, or his opposition to Jefferson's presidency that brought him back to himself.

It was Aaron Burr.

*You have attributed to Burr the most atrocious and unprincipled of crimes. If he has not called upon you, he is either guilty, or the most despicable bastard in the universe, so degraded as to permit even General Hamilton to slander him with impunity.*
—JAMES CHEETHAM, EDITOR OF THE *AMERICAN CITIZEN*

Burr was a man without a party.

By contesting the tie election in 1800, he'd gambled and lost. Jefferson despised him. He was vice president in name only. So, naturally, he was now running for governor of New York. And he was doing it against his fellow Republican—Morgan Lewis, the trial judge Alexander had argued before in the libel case—in a move that split that party in two.

"Burr can't win," I said, nearly laughing at the preposterousness of it. Burr was universally detested as a lecher and an immoral cheat, even by those who'd voted for him.

"*Eliza,*" my husband said, with an impatient tone he used only when a law clerk was slow to understand him. "Not a single Federalist has come forward to run against either of them."

That was the state of our party's demoralization, given the mud that would *inevitably* be slung at anyone who dared to serve an ungrateful public. Perhaps democracy would always naturally devolve to a state when only a man like Burr—a greedy libertine without any care for what the world might say about him—would stand for election. For what gentleman could ever wish to expose his wife and children to the calumnies that had been visited upon us?

"Do *you* mean to run for the governorship?" I asked, upon a hard swallow, bracing myself to support him wholeheartedly if he were to say yes.

But Alexander barked a laugh. "And damn the state, if not the whole country, when I lose? No. You've seen how people greet me at polling stations."

Reluctantly, I admitted, "You have, perhaps, a character too frank and independent for a democratic people. At least in the present climate."

"Unfortunately, my angel, you have the right of it. But something must be done." He shook his head and thumped his hand on the table.

In the days that followed, it became increasingly clear that Alexander was right. *Something* must be done. Because Burr wasn't merely running for governor, he was also encouraging a new movement in northern states angered by Jefferson's purchase of the Louisiana Territory. Northerners feared that the new lands would favor slavery. And their solution was secession.

"Burr won't be satisfied until he *breaks* this union." Alexander raged inside the little room by the front door that he'd commandeered as his office and painted an incongruously cheerful shade of green. "How quickly people forget all that for which we fought!"

Even though I feared he'd disturb Ana where she sat peacefully stitching a pillow, or awaken the baby upstairs in the nursery, I was pleased to see that leonine spark return to his eye. It was as if he believed himself, again, a winter soldier, fighting frightening odds in a war for the country itself. "Which is why *you* must remind them by recruiting a Federalist to run against Burr."

So we hosted a dinner party. A lavish one, where, having banished the children upstairs, we threw open the doors and hired musicians to play on the grounds. We accepted the compliments of everyone as they entered the front hall and saw the elegant painting of Washington and the bust of Alexander when he was secretary of the treasury, carved in the style of a Roman senator.

I worked the men's wives, trying to detect if any of their husbands should be willing to stand as a candidate for governor. And Angelica, still beguiling in a gown of blue satin with a golden belt, embroidered in the pattern of a Greek key, tried to recruit promising men to the cause.

Amidst the clink of glasses and forks upon my pink and yellow floral china plates, I overheard my husband say to his old faithful Federalist lieutenants, "For *God's* sake, cease these threats about a separation in the Union. It must hang together as long as it can be made to!"

If Burr got in, there'd be no more United States, he believed. Just North and South. But still no Federalist would run, leaving Alexander with an unthinkable alternative. Once again, he'd have to champion a Republican. First Jefferson. Now Morgan Lewis.

Finally, he set his mind to do just that, and the campaign against Aaron Burr began in deadly earnest. Alexander made speeches against Burr, held forth at dinner parties, and used whatever sway he still possessed to argue against Burr's candidacy. As if, unable to save our son, Alexander became *determined* to at least save the union.

The newspapers joined in, accusing Burr of all manner of disgraceful debauchery—consorting with prostitutes and other men's wives, seducing fine ladies and enslaved women alike, fathering bastards, and even hosting a *Negro ball* to court the free black vote. Alexander was not responsible for the calumny thrown Burr's way, but many suspected him of it—and they were entertained.

But the newspapers were in earnest with their blood sport.

Our son Alex had seldom shown interest in politics—that had been his older brother's fiefdom. Alex was now nearing college graduation, and because he had a head for numbers like his grandfather, we wished to place him in a countinghouse to be a merchant. He already had an offer to work in Boston after his graduation, which pleased my mother's pride. But now his brow furrowed. "The papers are trying to goad Father and Colonel Burr to fight."

I took the papers from him. "Worry not. Your father is too wise now to be lured into such a trap."

~

*May 1804*
*Harlem*

Burr lost the governorship by a great majority, which gave my husband satisfaction. He'd worried that he was washed up, helpless, and without any influence in the country he helped found. This victory proved otherwise, for Hamilton's campaigning had ensured Burr's defeat.

To celebrate, we took our children to the now raucous Pinkster festival in the city, where we mingled amongst our black citizens with a measure of gratification that though more must be done to achieve the freedom of all, every child born in New York was now born free.

We also hosted a dinner party for Jérôme Bonaparte, a nineteen-year-old naval officer of middling rank who currently stood in defiance of his conquering brother, Napoleon.

Against the wishes of the French dictator, Jérôme had married an American girl, Elizabeth Patterson, the Belle of Baltimore as some called her. And presented with the opportunity to make mischief for the French tyrant by befriending his willful younger brother, Alexander was delighted, laughing and conversing in

French, and telling stories of the Marquis de Lafayette that kept young Bonaparte rapt. Hamilton toasted old friends and new with a case of Papa's fine Madeira we'd had shipped from Albany for the occasion. And being the gracious and solicitous host who greeted every guest by name, he recalled with each one a fond memory of how they'd met or some battle they'd fought.

Watching Alexander entertain, I took my first deep, easy breath in as long as I could remember. Was that happiness that had finally crept back after the losses of recent years?

As the season turned and the weather warmed, I was struck by a new mildness in my dear Hamilton and was sure that he felt it, too. A peacefulness, even. Our victory over Burr had imparted to Alexander an eased mind and a lightened heart. Why, at the annual Fourth of July celebration of the Society of the Cincinnati, my nearly fifty-year-old husband led the men in singing old songs while standing atop a table!

But spending time with other sons of the revolution, recalling all that they'd sacrificed and all that we'd *won,* had always had a salutary effect upon him. Which was why, when he proposed that we host a lavish ball at the Grange and produced a guest list of over seventy people, I could only find myself delighted.

"I promised you a ball, my darling girl," he said. "And a promise must never be broken."

Excited by the prospect of such a grand affair—much grander than any entertainment we'd hosted before—I didn't mind the work involved, even with two-year-old Phil, four-year-old Lysbet, and six-year-old William underfoot. Happily, in that, Ana was a help, directing them in making garlands of silk ribbon, rosebuds, marigolds, and day lilies snipped fresh from our gardens. Ana might not remember what year it was or which of her relations dwelt in this world or the next, but she was still my beloved daughter, and she had a sweet, attentive way with the little ones. Meanwhile, having taken their height from their grandfather, our tall Alex, James, and Johnny strung the garlands between the house and the trees, and carried chairs out of doors because their father wished this ball to be *alfresco* in the French *fête champêtre* style.

The help of my darlings, and a French servant Angelica sent for the occasion, freed me to see to the menu with the assistance of our inestimable Mr. Genti, whose cooking using the produce of our garden always brought the highest praise. I anticipated raspberry tarts and fresh strawberry jam shortbread cookies, and the children wished to make their father a cherry pie, so I made sure Mr. Genti included it on the menu.

My gown for the occasion was an oyster-colored silk satin, with an embroidered bodice and hem in a leaf design and a beaded overskirt, an extravagant purchase Alexander insisted upon.

How many years had passed since I last dressed in such finery? I couldn't recall. And examining myself in the mirror of my toilette, I found myself pleased. Bearing eight children had not spoiled my figure *entirely*. At the age of forty-six, and having nursed eight children, my breasts had lost their shape and my hips were wider than I would have liked. But my waist was still slender and my hair was only a little silvered. If I were to have met the woman in the mirror as a stranger, I might think her dignified and handsome.

As I gazed at my image, Alexander stole upon me to fasten my necklace. "Best of wives and best of women," he whispered, kissing my nape below the graying-brown curls of my upswept hair. "As beautiful as the day we met. At a *different* ball, as I recall it . . ."

I turned in his arms and smoothed my hands over the lapels of his pinstriped silk taffeta dress coat. "And you, even more charming now. You were, after all, a little insufferable in those days."

He laughed, leaning his forehead against mine. "How I love you and our precious children." Oh, to still have this tender affection between us after all these years. There was a serenity about him as he held out his arm. "Come, let us join the revelry."

And what a gay revelry it was!

The late-day air was perfect—warm without being hot, breezy

and refreshing for strolls through our gardens. Wandering musicians delighted our guests, a special touch upon which Alexander had insisted. When the sun set, lanterns and flowers hung from the trees, creating a colorful, fragrant ballroom under the purple heavens.

All New York's best society attended. John Trumbull, the silver-haired artist of the revolution, who'd once painted a life-size portrait of Alexander that now hung in our hall. Nicholas Fish and Robert Troup, fellow Federalists with whom Alexander had served in the New York Militia at the very beginnings of their careers. Nabby Adams Smith, daughter of President Adams, and her husband. And even William Short, one-time secretary to Thomas Jefferson when he'd been the American minister to France, who had himself become a diplomat.

We danced and imbibed until midnight, until Alexander and I were the only ones still dancing and the children had fallen asleep on a blanket at the edge of the lantern's light. And the next morning we rode into town and attended services at Trinity Church where we gave thanks for it all—our lives, our friends, our family, and the Union itself. That evening found us out of doors again, having a family picnic under the trees in the grove. Lying in the grass surrounded by our children, my head against my husband's side, our fingers interlocked, we stared up at the heavens until the stars shone.

I smiled at Alexander and thought *this is what peace truly feels like*. To be at ease with the ones I loved. For once. *We've earned this. We've fought and clawed and survived to have this.*

Drowsiness overtook me as Alexander told stories to our sons, who hung on their father's every word, about how the gods placed constellations amongst the stars to honor the service of legendary mortals.

"What kind of honor is that?" Johnny asked, rapt despite the question.

"Oh, a very great honor," Alexander said, ruffling the boy's hair. "For they are memorialized for all time so that even here and now, I can tell you their stories."

And then he pressed a kiss to my temple and spoke of the heavens just for me.

"*Doubt thou the stars are fire,*'" Alexander whispered Shakespeare against my hair. "*Doubt that the sun doth move; Doubt truth to be a liar; But never doubt I love.*'"

# Chapter Thirty-Five

*July 11, 1804*
*Harlem*

**M**AMA, SOMEONE'S AT the door!" Lysbet said, dancing in front of it while William sat on the floor, playing with a set of marbles.

"Yes, yes, I'm coming," I said, giving my youngest daughter a smile. She looked so much like I imagined I must have at her age. Dark hair, dark eyes, and a smile that came to life anytime we ventured outside into the gardens or the grove of trees. I pulled open the door to find a man standing hat in hand, his head bent. "Yes? May I help you?"

"Mrs. Hamilton?" he asked, just barely meeting my eye. "Ma'am, I've . . . I've been asked to send for you. There's been . . . well, you see . . . General Hamilton has need of you." He gestured to the horses behind him. "I've brought a carriage."

Despite the growing warmth of the day, ice tingled down my spine. "What's happened?" I asked, keeping my voice even for the children.

The man couldn't seem to meet my eyes. "The general isn't well. He . . . has spasms."

"His kidneys again?" Just when I thought Alexander was over his old ailment.

"I'll wait in the carriage," he said, hurrying down the steps.

In a matter of minutes, the four children and I were on our way. I took solace in knowing that the older boys had gone into the city with Alexander two mornings before when he'd departed on his weekly trip to his office. At eighteen and sixteen, Alex and James could look after him until I arrived.

The trip was faster than I expected, given that it was the middle of a fine Wednesday. That is, until we began to encounter small crowds of people on every street corner, abuzz over some news I couldn't make out. And then I was distracted from that oddity when the driver turned the wrong way. "Sir! Driver! Where are you taking us?"

"Mr. Bayard's house," the man called in reply.

I didn't have time to process that before I heard my name. From the *crowd*. Again and again. "Look, it's Mrs. General Hamilton! His poor wife!"

A dark, hazy memory assaulted me. The crowds. The crowds in front of Angelica's house when my son was shot dead. And my heart began to hammer. Then it all but stopped when the carriage slowed in the drive before Mr. Bayard's grand mansion on the river, where another crowd parted like the Red Sea as the driver guided us through.

*Wailing.* The women were wailing. And gloom hung on every man's face.

We'd barely come to a halt when I sprung from the carriage unassisted, my voice shaking with certain knowing dread. "*Not well*," I said to the driver when he offered his hand. "You said the general was *not well*."

I saw the truth in his eyes before he spoke. "He . . . he asked me to give you hope."

Bile crawled up my throat as I remembered what Alexander once said to me.

*I thought you might take easier to a thing if it was gradually broken to you, my angel.*

He was wrong then, and he was wrong now. Already moving toward the house, I rasped to Ana, "Stay here. All of you."

Oh, merciful God, why?

"Alexander!" I cried, finding him amidst onlookers gathered round Mr. Bayard's grand bed. And when my husband's head turned to me, it nearly took me to my knees.

I'd seen that look before—the gray pallor of blood loss, the waxy sheen of fever, the cloudy eyes of laudanum. The look of death.

"Eliza," Alexander wheezed. "My angel."

Taking his hand, I nearly collapsed onto the edge of the bed. And that's when I saw the bloodied bandages around his waist. I knew the truth before it was even explained to me. He'd been shot. He'd been shot in *a duel*.

Voices I could barely hear recounted how he'd met Aaron Burr across the Hudson upon the cliffs of Weehawken, New Jersey. How, like my son, Alexander had thrown away his fire. How his opponent had taken lethal aim anyway.

"*Will he live?*" I asked the doctors, panic squeezing my throat and making it hard to choke out the words.

*Four* doctors huddled in the room—two Americans, and two French surgeons I later learned were stationed on a frigate in the harbor who were much experienced with gunshot wounds. The French had been our saviors in the revolution; maybe their expertise could save us now. "Can you save him? *Please save him!*"

"Mrs. General Hamilton." One of the doctors finally stepped forward, wearing an expression of brutal sympathy, an expression mirrored on the other men's faces. "I'm afraid the bullet has fractured a rib and, I suspect, ruptured the general's liver. The bullet remains lodged in his spine . . ."

I could hear no more. I couldn't see, couldn't think, couldn't speak. This couldn't be happening again. How could it possibly be happening again? Was I, like my eldest daughter, caught in some delusion, except in my waking dream everyone I loved was to be taken from me?

Frantic with grief, I sobbed a desperate prayer to a God who had already required so many sacrifices from me.

*Not Alexander, too. Not my dear Hamilton.*

Though his weak pulse yet gave proof of life, I already sensed his withdrawal from me. And I felt his loss in my bones, in my flesh, as if the very heart of me was being violently rent asunder. It was an unbearable agony of spirit. One loss too many, and far too soon.

As I wept and bargained and prayed and raged, Alexander murmured, "Remember, my Eliza, you are a Christian."

The first time he said it, pale and aware of his impending death, I believed he was offering me consolation, beseeching me to find comfort in my religion. Delirious with pain, he murmured it again as Angelica arrived, weeping her heart out as if joy no longer existed in the world and never could.

And I couldn't decide if my sister's anguish halved or doubled mine. I fanned Alexander's feverish face and mopped his brow and when his precious blood soaked through the bandages and the mattress to pool upon the floor beneath the bed, I begged Bishop Moore to consent to give my husband communion, despite the sin of the duel. When the bishop finally relented, Alexander declared, "I have no ill will against Colonel Burr. I forgive all that happened."

I couldn't. I wouldn't. Not ever.

But Alexander said again to me, "Remember, my Eliza, you are a Christian."

I knew then that it was a plea not for my comfort, but for my forgiveness. And I nodded my head, eager to give him what he wanted and needed before the Lord took him and I could give him nothing else. But in that crucial moment, I also turned and fled the room, because I knew I'd told my dying husband a lie. After all, how can one forgive what one doesn't understand?

How had I not known? How had I let this happen? Why hadn't I predicted that the long rivalry between my husband and Aaron Burr would come to this?

After I composed myself, I returned to my husband's side. Then, all we could do was wait and wonder if each labored breath would be the last. In the morning, though those blue eyes appeared clearer and tinged with violet in the light of dawn, my beloved lay nearly motionless. And so I did perhaps the hardest thing I'd ever before had to do as a mother—I gathered my darling babies around me and somehow uttered the words, "Your father is dying, my little loves. And we must now say farewell."

It was a scene of shattered innocence and grief that I still cannot allow myself to recall too closely. The way those little faces crumpled. The disbelieving despair. The younger ones who cried because the older ones did, not because they understood what was happening, or ever really would.

I'd lived forty-six years and I would never understand, either.

I led the children into the room and lined them up at the foot of the bed so that Alexander might be able to see them all. The fruit of our love. I lifted Little Phil, too short to be seen, to give his father a kiss, and then we waited as Alexander gave each child a final look, as if committing them to memory. Suddenly, seeing them became too much, and my husband clenched his eyes shut and pressed his lips into a tight, trembling line. Over the protests of my oldest sons, my sister took them from the room. And I was grateful for it.

I wanted to *do* something, but there was nothing to be done but wait as a man who had always burned so hot grew ever colder. So I simply held Alexander's hand—determined to hold him through every agony until the last drop of blood. *I held on to him* with the full knowledge that, after this day, I'd never get to do it again.

The clock over the mantel ticked out a mournful cadence as the last of Alexander Hamilton's life bled away. Though he couldn't move, and had trouble breathing, he retained his beautiful mind and his warrior's spirit until the very end.

"If they break this Union, they will break my heart," he said, eyes unfocused.

Finally, the chimes on the clock struck twice. Alexander breathed no more. And the silence of his passing stole what was left of mine.

For I knew that no breath I ever took again would be the same.

# Chapter Thirty-Six

*If it had been possible for me to have avoided the interview, my love for you and my precious children would have been alone a decisive motive. But it was not possible, without sacrifices which would have rendered me unworthy of your esteem.*
—ALEXANDER HAMILTON TO ELIZA HAMILTON

July 14, 1804
New York City

THEY'D MURDERED HIM.

First my son, then my husband.

Because they thought they could get away with it.

And I was sick to the depths of my soul. Sick and *enraged.* These furious thoughts echoed as church bells rang and flags lowered to half-mast and somber crowds gathered all along New York's streets. And then a military procession wearing black arm-bands arrived to accompany my husband's body to the church. To take him away.

*Come back to me,* I silently pleaded, as I'd done all those times he'd ridden off to battle.

But this time he would not return.

It was not the custom for women to attend graveside services, and I couldn't have borne so many witnesses to my grief. So with my youngest children at my knees, and my sister Angelica's hand clasped tight in mine, all serving to hold me up, the pallbearers lifted the mahogany casket topped with my husband's hat and sword.

Two black servants in turbans followed with a dappled gray horse bearing my husband's empty boots and spurs in the stirrups.

*Empty boots, empty saddle, empty hat, empty world.*

The sad staccato of drums brought a keening sound from my poor children, all of whom lurched for the casket, as if to tear it open and lay eyes upon their father one last time. But I had the absurd thought that the casket, too, was empty.

That Alexander Hamilton wasn't there.

Not in the mahogany coffin I chose for him. Not in the empty hat and boots and bed he left behind. Not in the city he loved. There was no part of him still here in this world. And I couldn't be where any part of him was now.

Clutching the letter he left—which purported to explain everything, but explained nothing—I could not shake from my mind his conviction that he must die this way or be rendered *unworthy* of my esteem.

*My God, had I driven him to this?*

He'd been content to putter about our flower garden. To learn about the fattening of our chickens. To go duck hunting with our boys.

But I had not, like my mother before me, told him that all I needed for my happiness was his presence. Instead, I insisted he take up that court case, making himself a greater thorn in President Jefferson's side. And I'd gloried in seeing the leonine spark return to his eye as he battled to keep Burr from the governorship.

*My God, my God, I* did *drive him to it.*

Before we married, Alexander asked again and again if I could happily live with him were he to lay down his sword to plant turnips. I'd promised that I could. But when it came to it, I'd wanted my soldier. I wanted the glory of Alexander Hamilton. I'd encouraged him to fight.

And now he was dead . . .

How long had he known about the duel, and how many times must he have wished to broach it with me? Was he thinking it even as he planned the ball he promised—had that been his final parting gift to me? Had he believed he'd return, or had he longed to go to Philip? I'd thought he'd been happy, that *we'd* been happy, but again, I'd missed all the signs. And I let him face it alone.

But I was not the only one to blame.

Four years earlier, Alexander had said he didn't expect to have a head still on his shoulders unless he was at the head of a victorious army. And in a way, he'd been right. Later—*much later*—I would succumb to anger at Alexander for taking part in an immoral ritual that had already robbed me of a son and now condemned the rest of our children to a life without their father's love. But *then*? Consumed in grief, the only respite I allowed myself in self-recrimination was in blaming Aaron Burr.

Our family now lay shattered by the man my husband always warned me was dangerous. Dangerous and *despicable*.

While the papers speculated about which insult or offense had precipitated this final, fatal confrontation, I knew the duel was merely the fruition of the conspiracy Alexander had long suspected. The same conspiracy that had dogged my husband's heels from the moment he rose to prominence in opposition to *the Virginians*. I knew, as deeply as I knew anything, that Burr would not, without encouragement or inducement from the Jacobins, have murdered my husband in cold blood.

After all, Burr did nothing unless there was something in it for him.

No. I was certain that he'd made me a widow to win back the good graces of Jefferson—a man who may not have brought the guillotine to our shores, but who had the uncanny good luck to have his most formidable enemies meet strange fatalities. It had been many years since I'd seen Jefferson last, but I could never recount him without a chill. Never forget the way he'd haunted my life, like a patient thief in the night, waiting to steal my happiness away. And now he and his minions had done it.

The bullet that obliterated my world was an *assassin's* shot. Alexander had thrown away his fire, then stood there vulnerable and without defense. Burr had shot him anyway. And now that Alexander's lifeblood was drained away, spent in the service of an ungrateful nation, would that be enough for these hounds of hell?

*They won't be satisfied until there is nothing left of him,* I thought. Until his memory is obliterated and they have filled the giant empty void of his life, and our nation, with lies.

But I wouldn't let them.

That night I received mourners at the Church home, where ambitious young Federalist politicians strode about with smartly upturned collars, businessmen with pipes sent up a dizzying wreath of smoke, and ladies crowned in masses of coiffed curls bit their quivering lips while offering me words of comfort.

All the while, I nodded, forcing bland niceties. *How kind of you to say. I appreciate hearing it. What a consolation it is to know he was so esteemed.*

"Gracious God, my dear sister," Angelica said, weeping into her kerchief. "Here I am, coming all apart, while you bear this affliction with saintlike fortitude."

*Soldierly fortitude,* I thought. Because there wasn't time for tears. I would shed them later. Right now, I didn't want to mourn my husband.

I was no saint. I was Alexander's angel. And I wanted to *avenge* him.

I remembered "Captain Molly" and Two Kettles Together, two women forced to *fight* when their husbands could not. And I wanted to do the same.

At some point, I looked up from a glass of lemonade that my sister had pressed into my hand to find Reverend Mason hovering over my chair. "Hamilton was the greatest statesman in the western world, perhaps the greatest man of the age. He has left none like him—no second, no third." And I was nodding, quietly *simmering*, when he added, "To shoot such a man in cold blood, the vice president's heart must be filled with cinders raked from the fires of hell."

"But is he to be prosecuted for it?" I asked.

Then I stood, abruptly, raising my voice to repeat the question. "Is Burr to be prosecuted for it?"

The din of mournful conversation fell utterly silent. The whole of New York society turned to stare. And I met their gazes, each and every one. Then, in a clatter of coffee cups, the gentlemen at a table beside me traded glances and made to rise.

But I stopped them. "Please don't stand for me unless you will stand by General Hamilton in bringing his *assassin* to justice."

A coroner's jury had been empaneled on the night of Alexander's death, but they were likely to dismiss it, as they did all affairs of honor.

Unless I did something about it.

My sister's eyes flew wide at my impulsive declaration, but the blood in my veins flowed with pure rage, and I wasn't finished. "I've heard the country is covered in mourning. I can see for myself the city is awash in black armbands. And at the dock, there was talk of burning down Burr's house." A hint of an approving murmur rumbled through the room at the threat of arson and mayhem, but that wasn't what I wanted. "My husband helped make this a country of laws. Will we permit the vice president of the United States to stand above them?"

"By God, the vice president ought *not* be above the law," said the editor of my husband's newspaper. "Witnesses must be summoned and examined."

Someone added, "Can we learn if it's true that Colonel Burr has been practicing with pistols for three months past?"

I winced, having not heard the rumor of Burr's practicing to kill my husband.

Burr had shown no remorse, no regrets, no mercy, and no fear.

But I'd seen enough moments of popular emotion in my time

to know there would never be a better opportunity to clasp my husband's killer in irons than now.

And I meant to see justice done.

~~~

IN THE BLUR of days following my husband's burial, I donned a widow's armor of black taffeta and lace, startling the owners of every prominent household with a visit, descending upon them with my orphaned children in tow, their eyes still red from crying.

It made me ashamed to exploit my children's grief, to expose Ana's derangement to outsiders, but we needed everyone to see the hapless state in which Burr left my family.

For, now that the Goliath of Federalism was slain, even Republicans found the decency to denounce Burr.

And because I'd learned the importance, in politics, of reinforcing the beliefs of the voter, I confirmed suspicions. "It was murder," I told anyone who would listen, stopping just short of suggesting that President Jefferson had ordered it. "Did you hear how Colonel Burr enjoyed such a hearty and cheerful breakfast that his dining companion couldn't believe he'd just shot a man?"

This bit of callousness never failed to elicit a gasp. Nor did the revelation that just a month before the evil deed, Burr had shown up at our door at an obscenely early hour and begged my husband for financial assistance to cover his debts. Alexander provided it and more, raising ten thousand dollars in cash for the man who met him at Weehawken bearing murderous intent.

In days of old, Burr was the master electioneer, but now I could almost *feel* the tide turning when I carried my campaign against him to the lawyers, the judges, the bankers, and the captains of industry. No less the candlemaker who lived but a few doors down from us, the baker at the corner, the carpenter, and the newspapermen. Burr would never shame or silence me while a breath remained in my body.

I wanted his scalp, and perhaps he knew it. Because less than a week after Alexander was buried, the vice president of the United States *fled* the city under cover of darkness, like a criminal, like the base assassin he was.

And I took some solace in having routed him. I'd forced him to retreat, but it wasn't enough. Oh, not nearly enough. I wouldn't be satisfied until I forced him off the continent, if not this plane of existence.

Then came the verdict of the coroner's jury.

**Aaron Burr Esq. Vice-president of the United States, is GUILTY of the murder of Alexander Hamilton.**

There it was, in black and white.

And when I showed my sister the verdict printed in the paper, I said, "If ever he dares step foot in New York again, he'll be brought to formal trial."

Angelica warned, "Please don't set your heart on this. Burr is a clever devil. He'll argue that New York doesn't have jurisdiction because the duel was fought in New Jersey."

"Well, then I must see that he's indicted in New Jersey, too."

*The first step is to gather the evidence.*

That's what I imagined Hamilton saying. I could still hear the echo of his voice, instructing Philip on the finer points of the law. How I wished I'd listened more carefully . . .

Burr was already trying to defend himself with the lie that my husband had fired at him and that he'd merely fired back in self-defense. But Mr. Pendleton had acted as my husband's second in the duel, and said otherwise. Moreover, Alexander left a letter for me expressing his intention to throw away his shot; there were likely other letters expressing the same, and I wanted them as proof.

Which was why I went, with my sister, to Alexander's law office the next morning. Upon entering the chamber, I braced myself for the familiarity of it. The sight of his leather-bound law books kept in neat rows upon the shelf from floor to ceiling. The burgundy carpet, a little worn in the path he used to pace while working out his arguments. The sunlight falling upon a desk where his quill pen would never scratch again.

Instead, I came upon clerks packing his things into boxes. And the esteemed executors of Alexander's will—Mr. Church, Mr. Pendleton, and Mr. Fish—hovering over his belongings like vultures over carrion, thumbing through his papers, bundles opened upon every surface . . .

For a moment, it felt as if I couldn't get enough air. "What are you doing?" I finally demanded, my voice trembling with anger. Someone tried to greet me in polite acknowledgment, but I was too blinded with rage to see who.

All I wanted to do was scream, *Get your hands off his things. Get out, get out!*

Alexander's leather chair was askew. Someone had been sitting where my husband used to sit. They'd even *smoked* here, for a faint trace of tobacco hung in the air. Yet, the greatest indignity was to see that the compartments in my husband's carved desk had been unlocked. And my nostrils flared as I demanded to know, "Has someone taken papers from here?"

The men stopped what they were doing but didn't answer, only stared uncomfortably. And I might have shouted at them if Angelica hadn't stepped forward. "Will you gentlemen please excuse us? *Mrs. General Hamilton* should like some privacy."

The men withdrew and closed the door behind them—all but for my brother-in-law, who'd been packing one of the boxes and now seemed puzzled by my reaction. As soon as we were alone, I rounded on him. "Where are the papers from Alexander's desk?"

"Here, somewhere, I'm quite certain." Church motioned to the crates and poured himself a glass of port, though it was mid-morning. As an executor of my husband's will, he now held trust over my inheritance, whatever it might be. And he said, "I'm sure it's all in these boxes excepting a few documents pertaining to existing legal matters and party business."

My husband's law partner would need to take on Alexander's clients. And, perhaps, matters of import to the Federalist Party. But none of this changed what felt to me a shocking violation. "How dare any of you take Alexander's words from me without so much as a *by your leave*?"

Church leaned against the desk, "Well, legally—"

"*Jack*," my sister snapped, gripping his arm to keep him from saying more.

I knew he was going to explain that executors had the right to take and sell anything valuable for the payment of debts—my husband's words being the most valuable things of all.

I knew and didn't care. Struggling for a calming breath, I said, "Sell the chair, the desk, the lamps, the carpets, even the books. But you must promise me that no one shall ever touch my husband's papers but me. Never again without my permission. I should like this *expressly* understood."

I'd never been the sort of woman to issue commands, not even with my children. And Church looked as taken aback as an Englishman would ever allow himself to be. "Now, Eliza, please be reasonable."

"I'm being perfectly reasonable. Alexander's last will says that his things are to be disposed of *at such time and in such manner as his survivor sees fit*. And I am the survivor and heir."

"No one disputes that," Church replied with a long-suffering sigh.

"Then please tell Mr. Pendleton that I must have an inventory of every scrap of paper that was taken. *Every scrap*."

"If you insist," Church said.

"I do." With that, I sat in the leather chair, put my trembling hands atop the desk, and took a moment to compose myself.

My sister pulled up a seat beside me and slipped her hand into mine. "It's only that such things must be broached softly with Mr. Pendleton. He is a man it wouldn't do to alienate at this moment."

I knew she was right. Not because Pendleton was an executor, but because he was our only friendly witness to the duel. The only man who could establish that my husband was murdered in cold blood. Because Burr's witness, William Van Ness, was telling a different story—that Alexander had fiddled with his glasses, sighted the pistol, and fired first *at* Burr, not in the air as he truly had. I hated hearing these details, *dreaming* of them, fearing that our children would hear them one day, too. But they were important to know, and to refute, in order to protect my husband's reputation.

"Then please broach it softly with him. In the meantime, I'll take Hamilton's papers with me to the Grange."

Church scowled. "Surely you realize you cannot return to the Grange."

I realized no such thing. "Why not?"

"You have limited means without Hamilton's income. It's impossible for you to be at the Grange without horses, which you can ill afford. Besides, their expense would pay for your house rent here in town. In fact, the Grange might be let . . ."

I blinked, having never considered the possibility of renting the house my husband had been so proud to build for us. Imagining strangers there was too much, on top of everything else . . .

But now I realized that the decision wasn't mine—it was yet another thing the executors might decide for me. Women had never been granted the right to vote in New York. We couldn't hold office and were barred from certain occupations. Our ability to manage property and legal matters was circumscribed. So I should have expected that my fate might be entrusted to my brother-in-law.

Certainly John Barker Church had always been indulgent with Angelica; she was as free as any woman I knew under laws that still made a husband his wife's master. But I hadn't married him and chafed at the idea Alexander should've left me even remotely under his power.

Church, the man whose accursed pistols had killed both my son and my husband.

My sister must have sensed my fury and resentment, because she gave her husband a sharp glance. "We didn't think you'd wish to take the boys out of school in the city, Eliza. You can, of course, leave them with us if you prefer to live at the Grange."

It was a generous offer, but Alexander and I had determined that our children should never be without at least one parent's care. And did I not owe it to the memory of my beloved husband to keep his children together?

Church cleared his throat. "You might as well know, Hamilton painted a rather more rosy picture of the value of his assets than warranted."

I flinched, half in disbelief. "My husband was the architect of this nation's economy. You cannot expect me to believe—"

"He was careful with the nation's money, but not his own," Angelica replied, and given her expression, I realized that my sister wished to tell me this even less than I wanted to hear it.

"I don't understand," I said, wanting to see the proof for myself.

Church cleared his throat again. "I estimate the debt to be somewhere in the nature of fifty thousand dollars."

It was so staggering a sum, I lost all power of speech. Even if Hamilton had lived, it would have taken years of hard work and frugality to ever repay it.

"You needn't be frightened," Church quickly added, affecting a smile that attempted reassurance and warmth. "Your father and I will see to your day-to-day needs, of course. And, if need be, the Grange can eventually be sold." Now it felt as if the world fell out beneath me completely. A cry of anguish escaped me before Church hastened to say, "But you won't lose it. After the auction, you'll be able to buy the Grange back at half its price."

I took in a ragged breath torn between gratitude and confusion about the house. "You're suggesting some financial trick." Perhaps something that might lose me every last penny.

"It's a political trick," my sister explained. "It seems there are people for whom your husband's indebtedness is more embarrassing than it could ever be for you."

It took me a moment to guess her meaning. Then I understood. *Federalists*. It would hurt the party at the ballot box if it were to be publicly known that Alexander Hamilton, their founder—the man of American financial wizardry—had died in debt.

We'd already lost one presidential election to Thomas Jefferson. The party couldn't risk losing another, so the Federalists would pay a great deal to keep Alexander Hamilton's children from being turned out of house and home. And I found that more reassuring than I ought to have. "They intend to make me a loan?"

"A gift, actually," Church explained. "A number of prominent men will establish a trust fund on condition of secrecy. It's to be kept even from the children."

I didn't like secrets. I'd been *hurt* by secrets. But I had no interest whatsoever in giving the public another excuse to dishonor my husband's memory. So Alexander's indebtedness was a secret I could easily keep. My uneasiness came in the realization of how dependent I was now upon the mercies of others. My brother-in-law. The executors. The Federalists.

And even my sons . . .

~

"YOU LOOK DASHING," I said, helping my eighteen-year-old Alex tie his cravat and turn up the corners of his starched white collar. "Your father would be so proud of you today."

Alex forced a smile past the grief for his father that cast its shadow over this occasion. "Dashing, but not a dandy?" he asked, buttoning his neatly tailored blue coat, but eyeing the plainer black one hanging on his wardrobe.

"No, my sweet boy, not a dandy." Like me, Alex was born unburdened with the expectations of an eldest but never pampered like the youngest. Whereas our Philip had been darkly handsome and rakish, young Alex was fair and freckled and gallant. And because he didn't have his father here to take pride in him on this day, I must lavish praise upon him for the both of us. "To *think*, Alexander Hamilton's namesake is graduating from Columbia College. Despite all your father's many accomplishments, even he didn't do that . . ."

"Only because of the revolution," Alex replied, then took a deep breath, as if he needed to steel himself against the world as bravely as his father had done before him. "And he was given an honorary degree later, wasn't he?"

I smiled softly, realizing how aware Alex was of the shoes he'd have to fill. He was now responsible for the support and care of six siblings and a broken-hearted mother. His father's will had bade him to consider it his responsibility. Worse, I now had the unhappy duty of adding to his burdens. "Alex, I cannot allow you to go to Boston to take a position in the countinghouse as we'd planned."

My son blanched. "But I've already agreed. Uncle Church and Mr. Pendleton say that I cannot now decline."

"I know," I replied, trying not to show how it vexed me that gentlemen all seemed to view me as an enfeebled creature, too broken by grief to know what was best for my own children. "But my wish is for you to stay in New York."

Alex furrowed his ginger brow. "You worry I'll fritter away my evenings." A faint note of hurt underscored his words, as if he thought himself accused of gambling, drinking, or carousing. "Or that I might neglect church and not know right from wrong—"

"No," I reassured him. "You're a good boy."

But Philip had been a good boy, too.

I wasn't worried about the evil that my son might get himself into in Boston. I worried about the evil lying in wait for a son of Alexander Hamilton. Especially one who shared his name. Every day Alex was out of my sight, I'd live in fear of him being lured into a duel or simply murdered somewhere far from his relations or anyone who could help him.

Perhaps he, too, would be found floating facedown in a river like James Callender . . .

Of course, I could say none of this to my son without provoking some show of Hamiltonian bravado. So I only said, "I'm a sorrowing mother overwhelmed with the responsibility of caring for all your brothers and sisters. I can't manage without you."

It wasn't fair what I was asking him, a young man on the cusp of making his own future. Hadn't we fought to ensure that young men like Alex could choose for themselves how and where they lived, worked, and made a name? And yet, he swallowed down his objections even if with trepidation. "Am I to . . . to farm at the Grange?"

I smiled softly, knowing that none of Hamilton's bookish boys were suited to working the soil. Nor were there resources at the Grange that might make us a profit. "We'll take a house in the city so you can study the law," I said. "A house big enough for all your brothers and sisters, and for Ana to have her privacy. And large enough to store all your father's papers—perhaps with a library that a writer might visit."

Alex squinted. "*A writer?*"

"I want to hire a biographer," I explained.

They'd murdered my husband. They'd taken him from me. But I still had his words, and they were my solace. Hamilton could still speak to me through those pages. His love letters. His ideas. His essays. Thousands of pages.

They could kill him, but they couldn't *silence* him. Not if his story was told. Not if his work was preserved. And I resolved to collect the pieces of the legacy Alexander left behind.

For, just as "Captain Molly" had taken her fallen husband's place at his cannon, I would take my husband's place fighting for his country. And this—Alexander's life, his death, and everything he stood for—had now become my battle.

# Chapter Thirty-Seven

*I pray God that something may remain for the maintenance of my dear wife and children. But should it be on the contrary, probably her own patrimonial resources will preserve her from indigence.*

—ALEXANDER HAMILTON IN HIS LAST WILL

*August 1804*
*Albany*

L ET ME TAKE you home," Angelica had urged when New York indicted Burr for murder. "Papa has been frantic to embrace and comfort you. He's too old and sick to leave the house now, but I fear he'll attempt it anyway if you don't fly to his arms. And it may kill him."

I'd won the first battle in my war against Burr, so I went. Because I was a dutiful daughter. Because I needed my father as much as he needed me. And because my sister convinced me it might do Ana some good.

Together, the three of us arrived at the Pastures, and my heart beat faster. And only belatedly did I realize why. Alexander and I married in this house. Philip had been born here. We'd started our life and our family here. And perhaps some part of me hoped to be reunited with him here, too. I longed to hear his laugh float down from the upstairs salon where he'd studied for the law and planned our future. But of course now our dreams and plans were nothing more than the dust that had collected on every surface.

*Prince would never have allowed the dust in his day,* I thought, running a finger over the sideboard beneath Mama's portrait, who would have thrown a fit to find dirt in her house. Prince had died the previous summer and been buried on the plot of Schuyler land where slaves were laid to rest. Next to Jenny, and Dinah, who had perished without having experienced the freedom she had once tried to seize for herself.

*Jenny, Dinah, Prince, Mama, Peggy, Philip, Alexander . . .*

All ghosts, and the house was like a tomb. A lonely clock ticked in the deserted blue parlor. A faded green velvet chair propped open the door to Papa's vacant study—a study we'd once made available to Aaron Burr.

And it made me remember that right from that first moment, Burr had *wanted* something from my family. He'd borrowed my father's books for his own advancement. In repayment, he'd told me of my husband's victory of Yorktown, and *oh,* I think he was jealous even then.

Burr was always clever. But what did he accomplish? He never penned any great treatises. Never signed his name to our founding documents. Never wrote a book that I knew of. Even the bank he created was birthed of trickery. He was never more than a crooked gun.

But Jefferson had aimed him against us and he struck true.

Bitterly I climbed the stairs as the memories washed over me, my fingers tracing the hatchet mark in the banister. Then I found myself standing outside the room where Alexander and I first made love.

*Empty study. Empty parlor. Empty bed.*

It took me a moment to compose myself.

Then I knocked upon my father's bedroom door, where he was confined by his illness. "Is that you, my pretty pet?" Papa called.

My youngest sister, Caty, was the pet. Which had not stopped her from running off, in what was now fine Schuyler tradition, to marry her forbidden beau. So I replied, "No, Papa. It's your *obedient* daughter."

At the sight of me, my father's eyes teared over, and then so did mine. He reached out his hands, and I went to him, where his badly damaged legs, cut and drained of gouty matter, were propped upon pillows.

Age had rendered my father smaller than I remembered. He'd let himself grow frail, stubbornly resisting the doctor's orders and taking little in the way of food. Fortunately, as we exchanged greetings, it was clear his heart was unchanged.

"I don't know, my dearly beloved child, in what condition Hamilton left you as to pecuniary resources, but I still have the power, attention, and determination to render you and my dear grandchildren perfectly comfortable."

I kissed him tearfully. "Thank you, Papa."

He pressed the point. "My fixed determination is to pass the rest of the days my creator has allotted me in promoting your happiness. So name a wish to me."

Perhaps he thought I'd ask for money or land. But I knew my wish. "I must have Alexander's letters."

Papa nodded. "When your mother passed, I found comfort in her letters. But I promised her that I'd burn them to preserve her privacy and so I did."

I was glad Alexander had never asked such a thing of me because I could still hear his voice when I read his letters. Every word was both a balm and a wound that bled anew. But that wasn't why I wanted them. When I explained myself, Papa's puzzled expression melted to concern. "Eliza, remember that we owe duties to the living, and a humble resignation to the divine. A mind so pious as yours, so deeply impressed with the duties of a mother, will feel the force of my remarks."

I did feel the force of his remarks. But I was in no way *resigned*. It couldn't be God's will that my husband's life, and his life's work, came to nothing.

I wouldn't let it.

And so, the rest of that summer, while Vice President Burr fled from city to city like the villain he was, I tended to my father—who had to be carried to the dining table in the morning and back up to bed at night. Then each evening, I sat in his study sorting through sheaves of papers.

When the leaves turned, Papa was feeling stronger and able to walk about the house, so it was time to return to Manhattan. Burr had been indicted in New Jersey, as well as New York, each jurisdiction vying for the honor of hanging him. His property had been seized and was to be auctioned, and this I wanted to see with my own eyes.

On the day we were to depart, Papa said, "In your new house, you must render yourself perfectly comfortable, and call on me, my beloved child, without hesitation. I will send you butter and pigs' feet sauce and truffles. Whatever you desire."

He'd scarcely finished speaking when my eldest daughter burst into the dining room. "Philip is gone," Ana cried.

My heart leaped to my throat at seeing her in such distress, tears in her eyes, her hair wild. I folded her into my embrace, wondering if we were to go again through her fresh grief or if she'd finally come back to herself. Wrapping my arms around her sturdy shoulders, I said, "My dear child, you know Philip—"

Ana pushed me violently away. "You always take his side."

"Ana!" my father barked.

Her grandfather's authority broke through to her, forcing her to hang her head as she wept. "But Philip promised we'd go swimming before we left on the sloop. Now he's gone ahead of us. He broke his promise, and Papa says a promise must never be broken!"

It was all too much. For a moment, I felt myself spiraling down into weariness and despair. How long would my poor daughter live in a state of madness? And would she drag me there with her?

Bringing my hands to my face as I considered what to say, my sister swept in with her satchel. "It isn't Philip's fault," Angelica snapped. Since learning of my daughter's troubles, Angelica had made it her business to study every book she could find on derangements of the mind. And there were not many, for in those days, they were obscure and could only be had from Europe. She'd never approved of Alexander's notion that we should go along with Ana's delusions. But now she did just that. "It's much too cold to swim and I told him to get the horses and go ahead of us so we can get an early start on our day." I nodded gratefully as she insisted my daughter wipe her tears. "If you want to be angry with someone, be angry with me. Now kiss your grandpapa farewell."

My daughter obeyed and let her aunt usher her out. Then, wearily, I stood at the window, staring out at a world in autumn decay. "Papa, I don't know how to be both mother and father to my orphaned children."

"You will not do it alone," Papa said. "Your sister is devoted to you. And our children will have me, too. Yes, my beloved, I say *our* children, for may it please the Almighty to let me remain in life, you and they will have my constant love and tenderness."

Deeply touched, I blinked away tears. "Oh, Papa . . ."

"You must promise to let your family be of aid and comfort to you now, Elizabeth."

I nodded, pressing away the tears with my fingertips. "And you must promise to do as the doctor bids you."

"I am much recovered!" Papa said, rising from the table on his own efforts to prove it. "Indeed, I am not without hopes of being able to visit you in the winter, if there should be sledding."

I planted a kiss upon my father's cheek, by his hairline, right where I used to kiss him when I was a small child returning from the wilds before he would haul me up into his arms. "Well, if you cannot come to us, we'll return for the holiday."

But my father didn't live to see another Christmas.

*January 1805*
*New York City*

"I'm giving you part of my inheritance," Angelica was saying while I pored over bills for meat, flour, and candles. "And I don't want an argument."

Papa's death had been a cruel blow for both of us. But for me, one more catastrophe in a parade of them. All my life, I'd taken strength from knowing I might always seek refuge in my father's strong and loving arms. In Philip Schuyler's home, power, name, and wealth.

Now my father—my first hero, the first man I ever loved—was gone from this world. And there seemed no refuge for me anywhere. Except, perhaps, in my older sister, upon whose generosity I'd unquestionably presumed too much.

She'd already made it her habit to stop by each week with parcels of clothes, food, and other necessities—much as I'd once done for impoverished widows. And I felt humbled. "I cannot accept your offer, Angelica. You're entitled to your share of Papa's—"

"What am I going to do with little patches of dirt in the wilderness?" she asked, for our father's wealth had been tied up in land that he'd divided amongst all his children—and little else, in the end. We knew Papa's wish was to emulate George Washington, who had ordered the emancipation of his slaves upon Martha's death. And so, though my father had not provided for it specifically in his will, we had directed the executors to release Papa's few remaining slaves from bondage. And seeing that finally accomplished was more valuable to me than any inheritance.

As I swallowed with bittersweet emotion at the thought, Angelica coughed on the smoky haze of my parlor. The town house young Alex had procured for us was a bargain, but every sort of thing was wrong with it, from leaky roof to a neglected chimney flue.

"Take what I'm offering, my dear Eliza. If only to rent a better house. Besides, I want you to have something you own outright—

something Hamilton's creditors can have no claim upon. Even if you only sell it off, parcel by parcel, to pay a biographer."

She knew the trouble I'd had in engaging a writer. And not only because of the disapproval of the executors, who didn't seem to realize that no greater investment could be made than in memorializing Hamilton.

My husband's name and reputation were the *only* patrimony he'd left my children, and it would determine their future prospects. Even if a biography hadn't been a mission of love, it was a mission of survival. The work could be sold for a profit if written seriously by a man of letters. But the first writer I tried to engage had—upon one glance at the thousands of pages Alexander left behind—virtually fled, quitting the project before it was begun. "You know, the writer said the strangest thing to me. He actually mused out loud that there was more money to be had in *refusing* to write a biography of Hamilton."

It'd seemed too odd a thing to mention before; I thought perhaps he meant only that he could find better-paying work. But it nagged at me.

Angelica narrowed her eyes. "You think someone is trying to thwart you?"

"I should like to think it sounds preposterous," I replied, but having been the wife of a man so often conspired against, how could I dismiss it? "It's been half a year since Alexander's death, and what has Jefferson said about it? Nothing. Silence. Which is just what he wants. An *eternal* silence from Alexander Hamilton . . ."

Even knowing all we now knew of Jefferson's duplicitous nature, Angelica didn't seem quite convinced that the president of the United States would stoop to conspire against the widow of his dead nemesis, but she allowed, "There are plenty of others who have cause to worry about what might be revealed in your husband's papers."

That much was true. Alexander had tangled with nearly every powerful man in the country. What my overly frank husband might have written about any of them—or what they might have confided to him in a letter—meant that his entire record of correspondence had the potential to ruin political careers.

Not that this would stop me. "Then the writer must not only be a man of letters," I began. "But an incorruptible—"

A scream cut off my words. In a household of children, I expected a degree of disorder. But what we heard was a shriek of pure terror.

And then it went chillingly silent.

I bolted from the parlor, Angelica close on my heels. We raced upstairs, cries and pleadings reaching us before we'd made it to the nursery. But inside, I found myself momentarily confused.

My five-year-old Lysbet sat in a ball on the floor, her head buried in her knees, sobs making her little shoulders heave. Meanwhile, my eldest daughter knelt on a tiny bed, tightly holding a pillow flat to the coverlet. And trying to make sense of the commotion, I planted my hands on my hips. "What in heaven's name—"

A child's desperate, choking gasp stole my words, my breath, what was left of my heart as I realized what was happening. Tiny feet kicked out from under the sprawl of Ana's skirt. A terrifying understanding dawned, and I lunged for her.

It was all I could do to wrestle Ana off the bed, off my three-year-old boy whose raw, desperate gasp for air sounded like sandpaper rasping across a rough plank of wood. I had Ana by the arms, but at twenty years old she was strong and in a state of raving frenzy, screaming and fighting. It was left to my sister to comfort my poor red-faced Little Phil.

Meanwhile, Ana flailed at me, so strong in her fury, it was as if a demon possessed her. I struggled to reason with her, much less defend myself from her blows as she dragged me to the floor. "Ana, please. You'll hurt yourself, my love. *Please.*"

*"Je ne vous connais pas!"* Ana spat at me.

My sister helped me pin her namesake's shoulders to the floor while I held her wrists down. Sympathy carved a frown into Angelica's reddening face as Ana struggled. "She said she doesn't know you."

And in that devastating moment, I finally faced the reality that my beautiful daughter was lost—to me, to herself, to time itself.

The loss had been a steady one, like a tree losing its fall foliage one fiery leaf at a time, so that you didn't notice the falling away until the tree was nearly, and suddenly, bare.

When the fight bled out of Ana and her muscles went lax, she curled against my sister's knees and sobbed. "He's an imposter, Aunt Angelica," Ana wailed between hitching breaths. "If he goes away, the real Philip can come home."

"If who goes away?" Angelica asked, rubbing my daughter's back.

"Little Phil!" Ana cried. "He stole my brother's name and his place in our family. And the real Philip wants to come home to us."

I cupped my hand to my mouth, believing it entirely possible that I might be ill. I hadn't ever thought Ana could be a danger to the other children. I'd even relied upon her to look after them. But now my beautiful, talented daughter had tried to suffocate her youngest brother . . . to bring back her oldest.

*Dear God. Dear God, no more.*

It was true that I'd had a double share of good fortune and blessings in my life, but had that happiness not yet been repaid many times over in grief? When I recounted all the losses—my sister, my son, my mother, my husband, my father—I wanted to scream at God that my ledger must now be balanced.

Seeing me near to breaking, Angelica nodded to the door. "Go. Take the little ones."

Dragging myself off the floor, I was a disheveled wreck—bruised, tendrils of hair askew, a tear in my sleeve. I righted myself and ushered Little Phil and Lysbet into the hall, grateful beyond measure that the rest of the boys were at school. "Are you hurt?" I asked my little boy.

"No, Mama," he said, being brave despite his quivering lower lip. I pulled him into my arms and held him tight against me in gratitude. Then reached for Lysbet and cuddled her, too.

"This can't go on," Angelica said, later. After she'd finally calmed Ana, who'd fallen into a troubled sleep, my sister had locked the door to her room. But when she put the door key beside me where I stood, staring out at a bleak winter world, I shuddered, hearing my husband's voice.

*They will lock her away.*

Angelica's hand rested upon my shoulder. "You've done all you could for as long as you could, Eliza. My niece needs more care than any one person is capable of giving."

But years of charitable visits to hospitals and almshouses had left me with a horrifying knowledge of the conditions. "I cannot tolerate the thought of Ana . . ." I shook my head and searched for another answer, another way. What kind of mother cast out her own daughter?

*They locked my mother up. I will never let it happen to Ana.*

"I know what you're thinking," my sister said, taking my hand.

But I didn't think she did. Alexander's voice didn't echo for her, as it did now for me.

*But you aren't here, Alexander,* I thought. *You aren't here to take care of her or of any of us. You aren't here or anywhere I can find you.*

Angelica cleared her throat. "Private asylums can provide the appropriate environment. She'll be offered exercise, work, education, religious instruction."

I nodded, having read the work of Dr. Rush and others emphasizing humane treatment to those with disordered minds instead of restraint, exorcism, and punishment.

*How had it come to this?* With a shiver, I admitted, "She could have killed Little Phil today."

"Yes. And she might succeed next time."

*Next time.* As much as I wanted to deny it, I knew there would be a next time. "But . . . she wasn't aware, she didn't know. It's not her fault," I managed, a knot in my throat. "She was always such a sweet girl before. You remember, don't you? She was—"

"I remember," Angelica said. "And of course it's not her fault. It's not yours, either. Even if you kept watch over her every moment of every day, you couldn't make her better. And your other children would suffer from your inattention. To say nothing of the burden on young Alex."

My eldest surviving son had taken up the practice of law to help support the family and felt the burden keenly. To add another worry upon his still slender shoulders . . .

"You must make the only choice a loving mother can," my sister concluded.

I swallowed hard. "How do I . . . ?"

Angelica pulled me into her embrace before I could sob. "Let me make the arrangements."

And she did.

It was snowing when the doctor arrived a few mornings later to take my daughter to what Angelica assured me was a reputable private asylum about ten miles away, with bucolic views of forests, fields, and the East River. My sister had even arranged for Ana to have a new piano there—for Ana still played, singing the same songs—and only the songs—she'd sung before Philip died.

To my surprise, Ana was amenable to going, assuming the doctor was a coachman meant to take her to visit her grandfather, as she'd done so many times before. I gathered my coat to join them, but the doctor held up his hand. "Madam. We find it is less disturbing to the patients to avoid upsetting parting scenes with family."

I froze at the threshold and gazed out at the carriage where my daughter already waited. "Oh," I said, hollowly.

"You can visit," he reassured me. "When she's settled. Certainly, you'll want to visit."

"Yes," I said. "As soon as possible."

The doctor smiled and doffed his cap.

Meanwhile, I looked past him to my beautiful Ana, who would

continue to age, but never grow old. My eyes saw her alive, but my heart felt like I was losing another child. I *was* losing another child. And heartbroken against relentless losses, I just stood there, numb against the cold, watching until I could no longer see my daughter's retreating carriage.

~

*March 1805*
*New York City*

They wept for Aaron Burr.

The story made all the papers. Far from shunning a man indicted for murder in two states, Jefferson invited Burr to dine at the president's mansion. But then perhaps sensing that Burr could be of no further use to him in his second term, Jefferson replaced him as vice president. Thus, in Burr's farewell address on the floor of the Senate chamber, he stood in front of God and country and dared to speak of law and order and liberty, and the need of the Senate to protect the Constitution from the silent arts of corruption and the sacrilegious hands of the demagogue.

And, on their feet and applauding, the members of that body *wept* for the man who murdered my husband.

Of course, afterward Burr suffered almost instantaneous political exile. I have ever thought that was too kind a fate by far. But he was now on the run, and that would have to satisfy me.

For I had more pressing matters to attend. Namely, my conscience. Since giving over my eldest daughter to a doctor's care, I couldn't shake the guilt. Which was why—in what I think now was partly a desperate act of penance for having sent Ana away—I turned my attention back to the Society for the Protection of Poor Widows with Small Children.

Still working with Widow Graham, her daughter, Mrs. Joanna Bethune, and several other pious ladies, I rededicated myself to raising funds, reviewing eligibility requirements, and visiting the homes of candidates for our assistance to determine whether they met the criteria. Which sometimes meant taking the ferry across the East River to Blackwell's Island, location of one of the city's most notorious almshouses.

From the outside, the almshouse was a series of sagging, decrepit, gray blocks surrounded by mud, filth, and excrement. Despite its location on an island, the air was stagnant and thick, unhealthful and miasmic. Inside was worse. The halls reeked of every manner of bodily function, and the few little ones with energy enough to spy on me around doorframes were so malnourished as to be frightening in their appearance.

"Pardon me," I said to the clerk sitting with boots propped upon the desk and a hat resting over his eyes.

Lazily, he moved the hat, and his dark gaze cut up to the basket of victuals I carried. A sneer settled upon his bearded face. "God save me from do-gooders," he murmured.

I paid him no mind. "I'm here to see Widow Donohue." He made no move to render assistance, but I was not easily put off. "Would you be so kind as to let her know that Mrs. General Hamilton is here to see her?"

Suddenly, the man righted his chair and stood. "Mrs. . . . General Hamilton." He nodded. "Yes, ma'am. Right away. And please use the administrator's office. He's out just now."

"Thank you, good sir." I smiled, for it was easier to forgive the man's rudeness when his respect for my husband was so apparent.

The Hamilton name still held power in New York, and I wasn't afraid to use it in the service of protecting children—mine *and* those of the city Alexander helped build.

"Mrs. Hamilton?" came a woman's voice from the doorway, a babe on her hip, and a wisp of a girl clinging to her dirty, threadbare skirts. For a moment, I saw not the orphaned girls but my own Little Phil and Lysbet, who were not much older, and I yearned to set them all at ease.

"Thank you for meeting with me. Please sit." Smiling, I opened my basket and laid out a few pastries I'd baked. Hunger etched the faces of the precious little girls. I gave them a nod and watched in satisfaction as they ate their fill.

"Now, Mrs. Donohue, if we might begin our interview . . . may I ask how old you are?"

"Twenty," she answered.

*Twenty. Just Ana's age. Ana could have been married. Ana could have had children of her own . . .*

It didn't take long to determine that Mrs. Donahue met the society's criteria. She had a home, such as it was. She was mother of children under the age of ten. She had no income, didn't beg or sell liquor, and appeared to be of good moral character.

The assistance we could offer would help in her daily struggle for survival, exposed to the contaminating influence of the impious, immoral, indolent, and criminal. And she was grateful. But still, she asked, "What—what will happen to my children, Mrs. Hamilton, if *I* should die?"

I had no good answer. Our charity was founded to benefit *widows*. Nothing in our charter allowed for us to help *orphans*. And it seemed to me quite an oversight.

Upon taking my leave of the almshouse, I glanced at the clerk's open ledger, listing children that had been admitted to this place—and copied it into my notebook.

*Brigit Fogarty, age 2 weeks, died of congestion of the brain*
*Catherine Connor, age 6 months, died of marasmus*
*Albert Smith, age 3 weeks, died of diarrhea*
*Charles May, age 6 weeks, died of syphilis*

On and on it went.

Children dead of overcrowding and disease and sheer misery.

Were my own children so different from these little lost souls? What should happen to them if I should fall ill and die? Though Angelica promised she'd always care for my children as if they were her own, and I believed her, I feared for my little ones to be left alone in this world to fend for themselves as their father had been forced to do.

No child should have to suffer what he did. Certainly not his own children. Left to the influence of unscrupulous persons. Left with scars and taint, and viewing themselves as having to claw up from a pit of mud. No one—not my children or anyone's children—ought to suffer this, not in a country like ours with so many resources. In a civilized world, there should be some . . . some *system* to prevent it.

And though I'd never had my husband's genius for organizing military, financial, and political matters, I had ambitions for my own civic creations. Which was why, at the society's annual meeting the following spring, I insisted, "We must do more."

I'd come to value my friendship with the serious-minded and zealously devout Mrs. Bethune. So I was delighted when she agreed. "What these children need is shelter, a refuge, an asylum of their own."

"I've long believed it," Widow Graham said, wearing a plain black frock and white cap upon her thinning gray hair. "A place where they can receive religious instruction, moral example, and be trained up to be useful and productive."

As second directress of the society, I sat at the head of the table next to our venerable founder and her daughter. Placing my hand upon the table as if a Bible sat thereon, I added my voice to the cause.

So the Orphan Asylum Society was born. Because some life must grow up from amongst all this death and sacrifice. And I was done with *losing* things.

# Chapter Thirty-Eight

*August 1807*
*New York City*

WONDERFUL WORK YOU ladies are doing," Pendleton said as I gave him and a small group of benefactors a tour of the new orphanage. "Just *wonderful* work. You must be quite proud of what you've accomplished."

"It's God's work, indeed," Reverend Mason added.

I beamed at their praise, for I *was* proud. We'd purchased a two-story frame house on Raisin Street in Greenwich Village for the children, and even though it had sixteen beds, we'd been flooded with applications in heartbreaking numbers—over two hundred in all.

In every story, in every name, I saw Alexander.

We would need another facility to help them all. It wasn't enough, but it was progress. And as I showed the group one of the bedrooms with its small beds all in a neat row, I said, "It's a start." But there was a cause more dear to my heart that I was even more eager to see under way.

Three years had passed since my husband's death, and not a word of his biography had yet been written. Partly due to my difficulty finding someone to write it, and partly due to the disorder in which my husband's papers were left. At least this was the excuse given by Pendleton, who still held back certain documents from me, claiming they had to do with ongoing legal matters. And now, whenever I found myself in the presence of the thin-lipped barrel-chested jurist who'd been my husband's law partner, I was plagued by conflicting emotions.

Pendleton had stood by his testimony that my husband threw away his fire. Pendleton had also loaned us money and taught my newly graduated son James the practice of law. I was certainly grateful to him.

But I felt resentment, too. For I could never see the man without wondering, *You were his second, his law partner, and his friend. Why didn't you stop him from taking part in a duel?*

It wasn't a fair question. Perhaps nothing but a bullet could have stopped Alexander Hamilton. But he ought to be *remembered*—which was the point I hoped to make when I gifted Pendleton with a ring I'd made with a clipping of Alexander's hair, set beneath glass. He still wore it in friendship, something I admired as everyone offered their congratulations at the end of the tour.

I stopped Reverend Mason and Pendleton before they, too, departed, and took the opportunity to remind them, "Every day, every hour, every moment that passes without my dear Hamilton's story being told is another memory lost to history."

Pendleton gave a regretful smile while pretending not to glance impatiently at his gold pocket watch. "Perhaps there's an advantage in waiting. For the Federalists shall soon sweep back into office. We are the party of Washington, and our success shall make the people remember that."

I bit my tongue, for if the Federalists were the party of Washington, they were even more the party of Hamilton. But it would do my cause here today no good to push the matter.

Thankfully, the reverend did it for me. "The general's biography will take some years to prepare and not a moment ought to be wasted." He smiled at the younger man. "Which is why I've agreed to write it, with Mrs. Hamilton's permission and encouragement."

"Isn't that wonderful?" I asked, smiling at the revelation of my achievement. I'd finally secured a scholar to write Hamilton's biography. He was not only a man of letters, but an incorruptible man of God. When *I* made requests to borrow or look at letters my husband sent other men in government, my requests were often ignored. But they were unlikely to ignore a man of the cloth.

And that suspicion was borne out when Pendleton cleared his throat and said, "Indeed. Well, you're welcome to anything at the office, Reverend."

"The only impediment now is resources," I said, first meeting Mason's eager gaze, then Pendleton's recalcitrant one. "For there will be expenses. We might have to travel—to Mount Vernon, certainly, to transcribe letters Alexander once sent to Washington."

To get the money, I could sell off some of the land Papa left to me, but this country owed a great debt to my husband that hadn't been paid. Other war widows received a pension, but I had none. In a fit of high-mindedness, Alexander had renounced the benefits he was due as an officer in the war. Now that the Republicans insisted upon destroying the country's commerce with their idiotic trade embargo, breaking up my husband's national bank, and emptying the treasury—they at least ought to be made to pay for it.

But I couldn't lobby for the pension while Jefferson was still president. I was told that upon a pedestal in the entryway of Monticello, Jefferson kept a bust of my husband across from a bust of himself, and quipped to guests that he and my husband were *"opposed in death as in life."*

That icy hypocrite wouldn't just thwart me but laugh in my face as he did it. In a very genteel, southern fashion, I'm sure. Just as he was likely doing to Aaron Burr, whose downfall that summer became something of a spectacle in which I must admit to taking pleasure.

For Burr had finally been arrested—though not, as one might have imagined, for the murder of my husband. Instead, Burr had been apprehended in Alabama on charges of plotting to annex, possibly by military force, Spanish territory in Louisiana and Mexico to establish an independent republic.

Treason!

I didn't find it difficult to believe that, denied acceptance, power, and influence in our country, Burr had resolved to create a new one. Just as Alexander warned, Burr was willing to dismantle the Union for which we'd *all* sacrificed. And I hoped to see him hang for it.

It had taken years to see some manner of justice brought to bear upon Aaron Burr. It might take years for Mason to complete my husband's biography or for me to ever have the opportunity to collect his pension.

But I knew how to use patience as a political weapon.

And I could bide my time.

~

*March 1810*
*Baltimore, Maryland*

"Are you certain you know what you're about?" McHenry asked, seated in the closed coach beside me as it jerked and jostled along the country roads.

Mac had long since retired from politics to his Maryland estate, which he named Fayetteville, after our old French friend. Mac had also long since gone from stout to portly, and his health was not good. He devoted his time entirely to domestic pursuits—his wife, their delightful children, and writing a novel.

Or at least he *had* been thus engaged until the former president, John Adams, published a series of letters in the paper purporting to tell the *real* history of his administration—the failure of which he laid squarely at the doorstep of my dear Hamilton, with McHenry in a conspiring role.

That put Mac in a fighting mood, so much so that he agreed to accompany me and my eldest son, Alex, to the nation's capital, where I intended to petition my government for redress.

Now that I had a biographer, I wanted my husband's pension. Finally, there would be recognition for Alexander's accomplishments.

Still, Mac couldn't seem to stop warning me against it.

Not even after Alex, serving as our driver, had taken the reins and got us under way.

Inside the carriage, I told Mac, "Washington City can't be *that* frightening a place."

He snorted. "Last I spent time there it was a swampy, malarious wilderness. And you'll find a friendly face even more rare than an honest man."

"But Jefferson is gone," I said, because that was the important thing. After eight years as commander in chief, our third president bowed to the tradition set by George Washington and withdrew to his mountaintop plantation of Monticello.

Hopefully for good.

But McHenry wasn't nearly as relieved. "You remember that the Federalists still *lost* the election?"

My husband's party did more than lose. We'd been obliterated. Still, I waved his concern away. "Nevertheless, Jefferson is gone and the new president is a different man."

"You think so? These Virginians are all the same."

"Washington was a Virginian," I reminded him. "Besides, I *know* James Madison."

Of course, I'd also known Benedict Arnold, Aaron Burr, Thomas Jefferson, and James Monroe. And at some point, I'd believed the best of each of them.

There was no reason to believe Madison was different. It was more of a feeling. Some *instinct* that I derived from the fact that Madison had, after all these years, remained publicly coy on the authorship of the individual Federalist essays, tentatively honoring the pledge we'd made decades before.

Then, too, there was the letter. I'd found it in one of the locked cupboards of my husband's desk at the Grange—the last letter Madison ever wrote to him, three years before Alexander died. Short and businesslike, about some matter of state, Madison had closed the letter with this line: *I have the honor to remain, sir, your obedient servant.*

That was not the standard closing. The word *remain* leaped out to me, as if Madison had meant it in wistful recollection of friendship lost. Alexander must've thought so, too, for him to have kept it locked away, separate from his other papers. It wasn't much to cling to, I admit. But it gave me hope.

Mac was decidedly less sanguine. "I don't think you know what you're up against, Mrs. Hamilton."

"I doubt any of us did when we joined the revolution," I countered, for sometimes it seemed as if it was one long war we were still fighting. And I couldn't help but remember when we were young and hopeful members of General Washington's military family. Alexander Hamilton. John Laurens. Tench Tilghman. Mrs. Washington. All of them gone now, only a few of us still surviving.

And I wondered if Mac was thinking of them too, because he grew wistful, adjusting himself in his seat with the use of his cane. "I know my pangs must be a wee drop in the ocean of your tears, but to this day, whenever the post comes, I somehow always think I'll find a letter from Hamilton . . ."

I smiled softly, as it consoled me to hear it somehow. "Alas, we must content ourselves with the letters he sent in life. And I feel as if it has become the whole of my existence to hunt them down."

"It must be wearying," Mac said. And I didn't think he meant only the hunt for Alexander's papers. Like my husband, James McHenry had dedicated the better part of his life to public service and been vilified for it. Maybe that's why he took my hand into his and clasped it tight. "Especially as you have suffered so many losses, Eliza."

Though my eyes misted at his sympathy, I swallowed back my grief lest it consume me. "I do not forget that others have suffered, too. I was so sorry to hear of your daughter's passing . . ."

Mac shook his head but squeezed my hand tighter. "An ailment of the lungs, it was. Nothing I could do for her . . . and your eldest daughter?" he inquired, delicately, for he was privy to Ana's troubles. "Have they found a cure for her?"

"No," I said, my heart bleeding even as I resigned myself to it. "We still visit Ana, but she no longer recognizes us. She's trapped in the past, but at least she's happy there."

"That is a consolation," he agreed, gazing at me with sympathy. And then we both managed a bittersweet smile. "Do you ever—" He broke off, then forced himself to start again. "You're still very handsome, you know. Bright and lively as ever."

I flushed to receive such a compliment in my fifty-second year.

But Mac's purpose was not to flatter. "In my younger days, I argued the equality of the sexes," he said. "But the world is more difficult for women now, I think. Have you never considered marrying again? Some quiet, lazy man of inherited wealth who knows nothing of politics or war? Or a fat funny fellow to talk nothing to you but business and bagatelles?"

I laughed. Of course I laughed. But I realized there was a serious question beneath the jest. Mac was the only person ever to dare ask. And maybe the only person who *could* ask. He'd been witness to our courtship. Attended our wedding. He knew how much I loved Alexander and only wanted happiness for me. And having contributed to the secret trust fund that had enabled the survival of my family, he understood, too, all the ways in which a new husband might secure for me an easier existence.

But I remembered what I said to Alexander when he professed jealousy that I should wear a pendant with Washington's name near my heart.

*Near to my heart, but not inside it, for there is room there for no man but you.*

That was still true. And in answer to Mac's question, I didn't hesitate. With a shake of my head, I said, "No. I could never consent to remarry. There could never be another man for me."

How could there be? I hadn't married a *man*. I'd married a mythic hero who'd driven a carriage of the sun across the sky. No other husband could ever measure up and it would be cruel to make any man try.

"I understand," Mac replied with a sympathetic sigh. "I only hoped to divert you from tilting at windmills."

*You think I'm a fool—a romantic Don Quixote tilting at windmills.*

I smiled to hear the echo of my husband's words. "Well, since Hamilton cannot tilt any longer, those of us who loved him must do it for him."

"Then this is just the place to do it," Mac said as we crossed a bridge over the Eastern Branch of the Potomac. "Welcome to Washington, Mrs. Hamilton."

OUR NATION'S CAPITAL was not yet a city. At least not to my eyes.

It was little more than a loose collection of urban landmarks laid upon a rural landscape, with wide muddy lanes—a jarringly humble place for the seat of a federal government. Nothing so grand as Philadelphia, or New York, or even Baltimore. And only two sections of the proposed congressional building were complete. There was no dome as you'd see today. And yet, I couldn't help but wonder what Alexander would have thought of this place. Would my husband have seen the potential in the half-finished buildings and the architecture that recalled the ancients he loved so well? Or would he think it a clumsy, monstrous effort built upon the backs of the Negro slaves we saw in wretched circumstances upon every street corner?

Given that Jefferson had ruled over the city for eight long years, it didn't surprise me to find no monuments, statues, or even placards honoring my husband. But I searched in vain for even the equestrian statue that was supposed to have been erected in honor of George Washington.

*Not enough funds for it,* I was told by a passerby.

And I was to hear that refrain again, at least a hundred more times as we paid call upon legislators, one by one, asking them to take up the cause of reinstating my husband's benefits. "I'm sorry, Mrs. Hamilton. *There aren't enough funds for it.*"

Perhaps that was true, since the most rabid Republicans always denied the reality that a government requires tax money to accomplish anything.

And yet they'd found the funds to refurbish and decorate the President's Mansion. I believed it wasn't the expense that prevented them from granting my husband's benefits. It was the resistance of enemies who insisted, even now, that Alexander had never truly been *American*.

"The Republicans won't give an inch," Mac admitted after having spoken to a few friends on my behalf. "They might make an exception for another hero of the revolution. They'd feel a pang of sympathy in their hearts. But not Hamilton."

Not Hamilton. Not the so-called *arch-intriguer, grand master of mischief,* and *evil genius of America* who had dared to forge a strong central government at the expense of the states.

"Thank you, Mac," I said, trying to remain serene while sipping at my tea in the quiet of the boardinghouse parlor where we sat together. "Unfortunately, I'm long accustomed to the hostility of these Jacobins. Or Democratic-Republicans. Whatever they're calling themselves now. Even New York has become *infested* with them."

And they were so afraid my husband's ideas might flourish that they were willing to deny me my widow's pension. I didn't know whether to be disgusted or pleased that even in his grave, my dear Hamilton remained, in the minds of many, a dangerous man.

So I was surprised when Mac murmured, "It's actually the Federalists that are your trouble."

Startled, I set down my teacup before I dropped it. "The *Federalists*?"

Mac rubbed his sore knee, seemingly unable to meet my eyes. "There are those who still blame Hamilton for our party's collapse. We've lost three presidential elections in a row."

"And how precisely could that be my husband's fault? Even his reach does not extend beyond the grave."

"It does," Mac explained. "They blame Hamilton for revealing that John Adams is a bit of a madman. They think he cost us the presidency. Then he gave it to Jefferson. Nearly all of the party leaders fear that so long as the Federalists are associated with your husband, we can never win another election, so they won't take up your cause. They'd rather be the party of George Washington and they fear you're going to spoil it for them."

I took up my teacup again, with disdain. "By reminding the world that Hamilton existed?"

He shook his head. "The rumor in Federalist circles is that you're trying to revive your husband's legacy at Washington's expense."

That was preposterous. And deeply offensive. "A malicious lie! How could I do such a thing even if it were my aim?"

"It's said that you intend to claim, in your husband's forthcoming biography, that Hamilton wrote Washington's Farewell Address."

"He *did* write it. With the president's notes, of course. How could that possibly put Washington in a bad light? You were an aide-de-camp, too. Did the letters you wrote for the man take away from his greatness?"

Mac raised his hands. "It's not me you have to convince."

I knew that. Mac had not only scoured his attic for Hamilton's papers but ridden—or at least rolled—into battle with me here in Washington City. And yet, we hadn't found even one congressman in either party brave enough to bring my cause to the floor.

Having listened, with seething disgust, to all McHenry reported to us, my eldest son had heard enough. "Mother," Alex said, running a hand through his reddish hair. "We are not to have satisfaction here. Let's go home."

Perhaps he had the right of it. And yet, I couldn't convince myself to surrender. The Republicans had killed Alexander Hamilton and the Federalists wanted to bury him. And now, it seemed, I'd have to fight them all, like the politician my husband had helped me become. "Well, if reviving Alexander Hamilton is bad for Federalists at the ballot box, perhaps I might find at least *one* Republican willing to help me."

When I explained my plan, Mac laughed like a leprechaun. "My dear lady, you combine the innocence of the dove with the wisdom of a serpent."

~

"You're CERTAIN?" MY son asked, as if we were to enter a lion's den instead of the whitewashed, neoclassical building with ionic pillars that was the President's Mansion.

I'd been so long in exile from public life that three inaugurations had taken place here without my having witnessed them. And the palms of my hands began to sweat.

*You're Alexander Hamilton's wife*, I reminded myself. I was the widow of the man who created this government. I wouldn't allow them to make me feel as if I didn't belong. So I girded my loins to sally forth like a vagabond knight-errant, trusting in Providence for my success. "I'm certain."

Together, Alex and I alighted the stairs amongst Republican ladies in fashionable high-waisted white gowns, and well-dressed gentlemen with gold-buttoned tailcoats, diamond-encrusted watch fobs, and ivory-tipped walking sticks.

Whereas I, the wife of the so-called High Pontiff of Federalism, wore only a simple black evening gown.

And yet, my resentments at their hypocrisy softened the moment I set eyes upon Dolley Madison—not seated upon a dais where guests might deliberate over how deeply to bow—but in the midst of the sunny, yellow-damasked parlor, mingling with the crowd.

I hadn't been intimate with Dolley in more than fifteen years, but it still amused me to recall the day she confided that her passionate and honey-tongued beau was none other than James Madison. Now, in pearl necklace, earrings, and bracelets, with feather-plumed turban, she looked more like a queen than a Quaker.

And she was almost pressed to death by people wanting a word with her. Dolley had been midconversation when our eyes met, and she broke into an astonished smile that somehow made me instantly glad I'd come. Abandoning her other guests, she rushed to me, taking both my gloved hands. "We're honored by your visit, Mrs. General Hamilton!"

At the sound of my name, all eyes swiveled to us under the brightly blazing bronze Argand lamps. And I lifted my chin. "Thank you for welcoming me to your levee, Lady Madison."

I attempted a curtsy, but Dolley held fast to my hands, refusing to allow it. "We call them *drawing rooms*, now," she corrected gently. "And *Lady* Madison? Goodness. Let there be no formality between friends."

She said this, of course, to distinguish herself from Martha Washington and Abigail Adams—the supposedly monarchical Federalist ladies who preceded her. But she'd also called me a *friend*, putting so much emphasis on the word that no one could miss it. "Just who is this handsome young man?"

Surprised at the warmth in her gaze, I nodded to Alex, who stood as stiffly at my side as a sentinel on parade. But before I could introduce my son, I caught sight of the president.

Oh, how the man had aged!

Poor Jemmy Madison had become a withered little apple-john, and cut a figure quite at odds with the supposed majesty of the presidency. But if I was startled by Madison's appearance, he seemed even more startled at my son's. Madison had, upon a single glance, abandoned all the important gentlemen in the room, to stare at my fair and freckled son, as if mesmerized by a face he hadn't seen in years.

At the president's approach, I finally did curtsy. "Mr. President, I present my son, Alexander Hamilton, the younger."

With an acknowledging nod, as if coming to his senses, Madison grabbed my son's hand and shook it vigorously. "Well met, young Hamilton. I remember when you were only as high as your mother's knee. And look how you've grown. Tell me how you make your way in this world."

"In the law, sir," Alex replied.

President Madison nodded. "Of course, it would be the law, wouldn't it?"

Impudently, Alex said, "I'm told it's my inheritance."

His *only* inheritance, he meant. But Madison seemed to miss the bitter implication. And to my surprise, the president's blue eyes crinkled as he smiled. "Indeed it *is* your inheritance, young man. I'm sure I don't need to tell you, your father possessed intellectual powers of the first order, integrity, and honor in a captivating degree."

To hear this *genuine* praise for my husband from the lips of a rival was nothing short of astonishing. And the terror that had been coiled inside me in the six long years since my husband's death slowly unwound.

*James Madison will not murder my children.*

Of that I was sure. And a rush of hope warmed my breast. I hadn't made a mistake in coming here. James Madison *was* the one Republican I needed.

"Sir," I said, drawing closer. "I've such fond memories of watching you work at my dining room table with my dear Hamilton. In Philadelphia, in New York—"

"I recall those days very well, madam," the president replied.

"And all you were obliged to put up with besides, with little children underfoot, and our comings and goings at all hours . . ."

We both smiled in remembrance, which emboldened me to mention the biography and ask if he had kept any of my husband's papers. "I realize it's a great deal of trouble—"

"It is no trouble at all," said the president, promising to deliver copies to me of my husband's notes.

I'd not expected this easy agreement—in fact I worried this would be a promise swiftly forgotten in the frenzy of business that occupied a president's mind. But I was encouraged when Madison put a hand on my son's shoulder, and whispered into his ear.

And Alex—my always earnest, twenty-three-year-old son—actually laughed for the first time in years. He blushed, too, to the tips of his freckled ears, as if the president had said something bawdy. And just like that, Jemmy Madison charmed another of my sons. "Young Hamilton, if the ladies will excuse us, I should like to introduce you to some influential gentlemen."

Both the president's wife and I quickly nodded our assent. Then Dolley looped her arm through mine as we watched the men go. "How like Hamilton he looks." I only smiled, suddenly too emotional to speak. "And how swiftly they grow up! My little Payne is eighteen now. No longer banging on copper pots but causing trouble all the same at his boarding school."

I laughed. "With five sons, and all the orphans now under my care, I'm well acquainted with such antics."

"Indeed," Dolley said with a sigh that reminded me she'd never been able to give Madison the gift of a child after all. Then, as if to shake herself free of that disappointment, she said, "Let me show you the President's Mansion."

With that, Dolley led me into the oval room, where I expected to see French furniture, an homage to the revolution the Jeffersonians so admired. Instead, I found the style very different. "*Greek*?" I guessed.

Dolley's plume bobbed with her nod. "Yes. Because the Greeks were free. Every citizen thought himself an important part of the republic." A sentiment that I would never argue against. "Do you see those curtains?"

I nodded, because I could scarcely fail to notice the vivid red velvet draperies that so dramatically gave the impression of blazing splendor. Dolley ran her fingertips over the soft fabric. "I insisted on these, over every man's objections. I've become quite the libertine. And I suppose I have you to thank for encouraging me to embrace my destiny as Mr. Madison's wife."

She seemed much happier in her role as first lady than any of her predecessors. And much happier, I knew, than I would have been in her place. So I didn't hesitate to tell her a story that was making the rounds. "Do you know what our Federalist candidate said when asked how he lost the election to your husband?" Dolley stiffened, as if expecting a partisan barb. But my story was a compliment. "He said, '*I was beaten by Mr. and Mrs. Madison. I might have had a better chance if I faced Mr. Madison alone.*'"

We laughed at that together. And we sat for quite a while reminiscing. There was once a time when Dolley was the needy widow, and I'd helped her. Now I hoped she'd help me in return. I'd prepared an argument. Partisans would accuse me of greed, assuming that Alexander had stolen so much money from the treasury that I must now be living in luxury. I couldn't admit my husband had died deeply in debt. And even if I did admit it, the most rabid Republicans might deny my request for a veteran's benefits out of spite. So I confided to Dolley only, "My farmland provides me no more than seven hundred fifty dollars a year. And though I have a roof over my children's heads and food in their bellies, we're beholden to the generosity of others. In exchange for the service my husband provided this government, does it not seem *just* that his children are recompensed?"

"Congress will take a hard line against you," Dolley said thoughtfully, as if the president had little influence with Congress.

Perhaps he did not. Madison was not, like Jefferson, a tall and handsome politician of immense if wily charm. And he seemed, already, to be having trouble steering Congress. Madison was once my husband's most fierce opponent in the establishment of a national bank, but he'd since come to realize its necessity, yet partisans in Congress were determined to let it lapse. Perhaps it was ill-advised for me to ask the president to use his influence on a private matter when he was fighting larger battles. But he wouldn't have *had* to fight them if he hadn't thrown in with Jefferson in the first place.

"I'm a widow of a war hero," I said, stoutly. "And more than that. General Hamilton might have made a fortune in private life, but he gave his best energies to his country." And because I believed that Dolley, as a political wife, would understand, I added, "We *both* spent the better part of our lives in service to this nation, and what do I have to show for it?"

The expression of the president's wife melted in unmistakable sympathy, but before she could reply, someone called to her.

A jowled woman who mimicked Dolley's fashion sense, wearing a fur-lined cape and turban, charged our way. It was Margaret Bayard Smith, the not-so-secret author of her husband's influential Washington newspaper, the *Daily National Intelligencer.*

"I shouldn't neglect her," Dolley said.

But before Dolley took her leave, I whispered, "Is my cause hopeless?"

"Not if you know the right ears to whisper into," she said. "And, fortunately, I do." Then, excusing herself, she left my side. And I didn't blame her. I could easily imagine what mischief might be sown for the Madisons—and for myself—by a report that the wife of a Republican newspaperman had been snubbed in favor of Hamilton's widow.

Relief stole over me, and hope, too—until I found myself staring across the room into the startled gray eyes of the man just recently appointed as secretary of state.

James Monroe.

Haltingly, Monroe made his way through the press of bodies to stand before me. "Mrs. General Hamilton," he said, that infuriating dimple still upon the chin of his now thinner face as he awaited acknowledgment at our unexpected reunion.

But what could I possibly have to say to this man?

A decade had passed since I'd left Monroe searching for his conscience. And as best as I could tell, he'd never found it. He'd lost it to ambition. Not hollow ambition, like Burr's—for that assassin never had a conscience to lose in the first place—but a weighty ambition, that grew heavier in the shadow of his fellow Virginians—Washington, Jefferson, and Madison. James Monroe hungered for the presidency and became even more of an embittered partisan when Jefferson promoted Madison, and not himself, as heir apparent.

*What did you expect from a man like Jefferson?* I wanted to say. You gave your friendship and loyalty to a man who didn't cherish it.

Not as I once cherished it.

A thing I remembered with clarity when, as if unsteadied by my presence, Monroe dabbed sweat upon his upper lip with an embroidered kerchief. *This* kerchief was finer than the one he'd given me all those years ago. *That* one I'd kept as a talisman against insecurity and sadness when I first learned of my husband's infidelity. And even after Alexander and I reconciled, I'd kept Monroe's kerchief as a sentimental token of friendship. In truth, I'd quite forgotten it until this moment, because after our last confrontation over his role in the exposure of the Reynolds Affair, I'd not wished to remember Monroe at all.

But now here he was, waiting for me to say something polite, such as, "*Why hello, Mr. Monroe. It's been too long. I hope your family is well.*"

I told myself it wouldn't cost me very much to say it. In fact, it might help me. If James Monroe were to take up my banner, Congress might reinstate my husband's benefits. After all, Monroe was a veteran and a favorite son amongst the rank-and-file Republicans. They might listen to him more than the president. And after having broken his word of honor to me as a gentleman, didn't Monroe owe me a debt?

*Perhaps that's what I should say to him*, I thought.

But in the end, I was a Schuyler as much as I was a Hamilton. And though words had been my husband's weapon, silence had often been mine.

So I said nothing at all to James Monroe.

Instead, I gave him the cut direct—and turned to find my son.

"Alexander?" I called, making rare use of his full name.

"Yes, Mother?" Alex asked, rushing to my side.

I glanced back at Monroe and enjoyed the flinch of recognition that settled onto the Virginian's face at seeing my boy, as if seeing a ghost.

"I think we've accomplished our purpose here," I said, letting Alex escort me away.

And I vowed that I'd burn Monroe's forgotten kerchief upon our return home.

It would take years before my husband's benefits were finally, and quietly, reinstated. But I knew, without question, who I had to thank for it. *Madison* had been our friend. Madison had been our partner. And Madison was good to his word about my husband's papers, too, sending copies for the biography.

I had tilted at a windmill and won.

# Chapter Thirty-Nine

*I would willingly risk my life, though not my character,
to exalt my station. I wish there was a war.*
—ALEXANDER HAMILTON

*October 1810*
*New York City*

MY SONS WERE all in rebellion.

I returned from Washington City triumphantly, with arms full of notes and documents for the biography, only to learn that, in defiance of my wishes, twenty-two-year-old James had decided to marry his sweetheart. I suppose it was the Schuyler in him.

It wasn't that I disapproved of his young lady. It was simply that, as a law clerk, James wasn't yet established in the legal practice he was pursuing. Fortunately, Mary was a sweet girl who claimed to relish the position of wife to an impoverished young man. And I saw the wisdom in my father's old admonition that it was sometimes best to frown, make them humble, and forgive.

Besides, it wasn't only James who was in rebellion.

At Christmas, Alex told me he would sail to Europe. "You

needn't worry about the expense. My cousin Flip and I are going together, and Uncle Church has loaned us the money."

Having denied my eldest surviving son the opportunity to make a merchant's career in Boston, I wouldn't now prevent him from exploring across the sea. For years, Alex had remained at my side, dutifully and uncomplainingly toiling in the law to support me and his siblings. No mother could ask more, and he'd earned a respite.

But what he said next chilled me to the bone. "I'm going to volunteer with the Duke of Wellington to fight Napoleon Bonaparte on the Peninsula."

Alex wanted to go to war. For England. Horrified, I said, "You're an *American*."

His spine stiffened. "I haven't forgotten. But when we were in Washington City, President Madison said I should take the opportunity to write to him. If I can report back to him on the goings-on in Europe—"

"*Alex*," I said, more upset by the moment.

He took my hand. "Mother, there's no way for a Hamilton to make his name in American politics. Business was foreclosed to me once I abandoned my position in Boston. That leaves only the battlefield. My father was a general. My grandfather was a general. Heroes, both of them, you've always told me. How can I want to be anything else?"

How could he want to be anything else, indeed? Alex had the right to determine his own fate. His father had fought for that principle, and I would uphold it. So, the following spring, I stood bravely next to Angelica at the docks as we tearfully saw our sons off to a war on foreign shores, grateful that they were, at least, together.

Just as we'd always been.

And a year later, Angelica and I were *still* together, worrying about our sons and taking coffee at the Tontine, as was our habit, while all the talk around us was of the war coming to our own shores. Because the British had never stopped visiting humiliations upon American ships—seizing them and impressing our soldiers. Behaving as if we'd never won our war of independence and were still merely a rebellious set of colonies.

This was the chatter of passersby that swirled around us while we warmed our hands against our coffee cups at the curbside table. My sister took hers with sugar and cream and always ordered a pastry that she never touched, saying she'd eaten too large a breakfast before offering it to me.

"I'm not a starving urchin," I said, though those were, indeed, lean times. "If anything, you're the one growing too thin." There was a fragility to her delicate features that had never been there before. Worry over Flip, no doubt. Our fear for our boys was always present, even when we gave it no voice. Maybe especially then.

"I don't want to grow as stout as Mama did," Angelica said, pushing the plate to me. "I intend to fight for my beauty to the bitter end."

Surrendering, I savored a sweet morsel of the pastry. "I believe your vanity is overcoming good sense."

"You're one to speak of good sense. You forget I have spies in your household."

She did. My children told their beloved Aunt Angelica everything. "And what do they report?"

"That you're considering a foolhardy trip into the wilds of western New York to visit an Indian school."

It wasn't just an Indian school, as she had good cause to know. It was the Hamilton-Oneida Academy that my husband helped to found for the advancement of our Indian allies, the plight of whom was always dear to my heart. "It's soon to be chartered as Hamilton College, and I don't see why I should not be present for its christening."

"Because it's a ghastly journey," Angelica said, with a sniff. "The only way my son could persuade me to visit western New York was to name a town after me." Before he left for England,

Flip *had* done that, to the not-so-secret delight of his mother. "Of course, your wanderlust is far less concerning than the other report I've received that you spend hours upon your knees, sorting through boxes of dusty papers like a madwoman."

I gulped at my coffee and shrugged. "I'm looking for Alexander's draft of Washington's Farewell Address. It's as important a contribution as anything else he ever wrote and if I can find his notes, I can prove it."

"Maybe he didn't keep notes," Angelica said. "Or perhaps he sent them to someone for safekeeping."

"I think someone took them," I replied. But I couldn't stay to elaborate, because a glance down at the timepiece suspended from my needlework chatelaine told me I ought to leave soon to interview a new teacher for the orphanage.

My son Johnny was to escort me, and he was seldom late. But on that day, he sauntered to our table slowly and sat beside us with a certain gravity.

At nineteen, Johnny was a gentle, bookish student of literature. Of all my sons, he was the last I might ever suspect would announce that he was to join the military. But he said, "As the son of Alexander Hamilton, I cannot shirk my duty."

So it was that I lost my eldest sons all at once to the Hamiltonian desire to rise up on the tide of war.

*March 1814*
*New York City*

It was called the War of 1812, though most of the fighting took place after that year. They also called it the second war for independence, and a new generation of Hamiltons were fighting it. My battle-hardened Alex returned from Europe to serve as a captain in the U.S. infantry. James commanded a New York militia brigade. Johnny served as aide-de-camp to Major General William Henry Harrison. And seventeen-year-old William—a wild and lanky mischief maker whose indifference to his studies, and to wearing shoes, would've snapped even his indulgent father's patience—now trained to be an officer at West Point.

Angelica's son had returned to fight for America, too. "When our boys come for a visit, we'll have a veritable army at our table," she said. We'd just left Sunday service at Trinity Church to stroll, taking our exercise in the brisk air. And I remembered a long-ago night when I'd had another veritable army around a platter of steaming waffles at my table—Alexander, Monroe . . .

And Aaron Burr.

Which brought me to my purpose in haunting the occupant of a little office on Nassau Street. It'd come to our attention that the tiny tin placard on the door reading MR. A. ARNOT, ESQUIRE was actually an assumed name for Burr, who'd returned to the city after a decade of exile.

After so many years, the criminal charges against him had been dropped, and now, it seemed the younger generation didn't remember him. Or what he'd done.

But I remembered.

Burr might have chosen any other city in America. But he'd chosen to return to mine. So whenever I passed Burr's shabby little door, and saw any person about to knock, I'd call, "Oh! Is that your solicitor? You should know that he murdered my husband."

Soon after I made a habit of this, Burr changed the placard on his door to MR. EDWARDS. And I wondered what name I'd force him to adopt next. If I could take satisfaction in nothing else, I smiled to think I'd deprived him of a name—the thing my husband died for.

"If it's your purpose to make him a miserable recluse," Angelica said as we walked. "I'm told you're succeeding . . ."

Burr's grandson had died of a childhood illness the previous year. Then his daughter was lost at sea. He was left alone. Without family. Severed from the human race. I wasn't monstrous enough to take joy in these tragedies.

Somedays I even wondered if these tragedies may have shaken loose some morsel of a soul, so that Burr now understood what he'd inflicted upon me. Other days, I had the absurd thought he might open his office door as we passed and beg my forgiveness.

But he never did. He was hiding from the world. He was hiding from *me*.

On this day, I peered at the bare snow-dusted window, in search of a glimpse of that crooked man in the shadows. But while I was looking, I felt my sister grasp my arm. "Betsy," she whispered, and I turned to see her go pale as death. Then, before I could steady her, my sister's knees buckled and she collapsed onto the icy street.

"Angelica!" I cried, dropping to my knees beside her. As she sprawled, gasping and staring at the sky, I feared that she'd knocked her head or broken a bone. I called for help—and some part of me dreaded that Burr might emerge from his office to lend assistance. But it was actually the Reverend Mason who happened by and helped me convey Angelica back to the warmth of her own house.

"All this for beauty?" I asked, furious when she confessed that she'd simply not eaten that day, hunger the probable reason for her swoon.

"Anxiety of the war leaves me no appetite," she protested weakly.

But two days later, in a state of delirium, her hair plastered with sweat to a ghostly white face, she whispered, "Don't tell Betsy."

I'd come to tend her with a basket of tonics and herbs, but my brother-in-law, in shirtsleeves and dishevelment, stood stone-faced in the entryway of her bedroom. "She's been unwell. She didn't wish for you to know."

"*Unwell*? What can you mean?"

"Cancerous tumors," Church replied stiffly.

It was several agonizing moments before I could take a breath. "Where have the tumors arisen?" I finally had the clarity to ask. Sometimes tumors could be surgically removed—a painful and gruesome procedure, but one with a chance for survival.

As if he knew what I was thinking, Church shook his head and rubbed his unshaven jaw. "They can't be cut away."

Which meant . . . Angelica was dying. My gaze flew past him to where my once vivacious sister lay withered and frail in her bed, moaning softly in pain. And I could do nothing to help her. I was again to lose someone I loved better than myself. And the crushing weight of our impending separation made me grasp at the doorframe for balance. Helplessly, I looked into the eyes of my brother-in-law. "How long has she been suffering?"

"Quite some time."

*Quite some time.* She'd been sick, and fearful, and hadn't told me. She'd told her husband, but not me, and I resented him, though I had no right. "Why didn't she tell me?"

"She didn't wish you to see her this way, with her mind lost to the laudanum and—"

"I don't care," I hissed. "You will not dare keep me away. You do not *dare.*"

He didn't. Especially since Angelica was soon out of her bed, making little of her illness, putting off my tearful enquiries with teasing. But now that my eyes were open, I saw the laudanum glitter of her eyes, the exhaustion of her thinning body. She quipped that she would be dancing at a ball in no time, but that attack of weakness in the street had been some catalyst of a terrible kind, because she was soon bedridden—and I found it both a cruelty and a mercy that my irrepressible sister was not long bound in the struggle of dying.

When she awakened one morning to find me at her bedside, she took my hand and kissed it. "My dear Eliza. It's only *right* that I die before you. I'm the oldest. I should have gone before Peggy. I should go before you. Besides . . . I am a sinner, and you are a saint."

"No, Angelica," I said, shaking my head in denial and anger at the Lord himself. My sister had been my touchstone—before and after my husband's death. In the worst days of my grief, I couldn't have remained standing without her steadfast support. And now the only pain worse than the knowledge she was to be taken from me was pity that she should suffer so much.

But closing her eyes Angelica said, "Envy me, my sweet sister, for a merciful God is taking me to see all our lost loved ones . . ."

Then her pain became too great to bear. We dosed her, and under the laudanum's spell, she spoke as if she were still a girl leading our troop of children in Albany. "*Go Blues!*" Sometimes she imagined herself a young mother again, singing lullabies to her babies. Or a high-society lady in France, confiding gossip about nobles, long since beheaded. Other times she said strange and haunting words about things that never happened at all. But mostly, as she died, it was the same torturous refrain.

*Don't tell Betsy. Don't tell Betsy.*

Then, finally, frantically, and heartbreakingly:

*Don't tell Betsy, Alexander.*

*Never confess it.*

*Not even if I am dead.*

IT WAS ONLY the laudanum, I told myself in the days after Angelica's death.

After all the other losses I'd suffered, I'd always found some way to get up, get dressed, feed the children, go to church, and work in the causes the Lord had pointed out to me as a sacred duty.

But not this time.

Even though it worried my children. My youngest daughter, fourteen-year-old Lysbet, climbed into the bed next to me. "Mama, it's past noon," she chided, trying to rouse me.

I reached for her and tucked a braid of hair behind her ear, even though the sight of her struck me with an arrow of bittersweet pain. Lysbet had my nut-brown complexion, Alexander's auburn hair, and her Aunt Angelica's features. I had the disturbing thought that she was a perfect amalgamation, as if she'd been born from the three of us . . .

*It was only the laudanum,* I told myself again.

People said strange things under its influence. Dying people said strange things even *without* laudanum. One could scarcely be held to account for murmurs halfway between this life and the next. That I should fixate upon my sister's dying words with dark suspicion was surely some madness of grief.

Yet I didn't cry for my beautiful brilliant sister. I didn't cut clippings of Angelica's hair. I couldn't think what the point of it might be. What the point of anything was.

Perhaps God knew, but I did not. All I felt was a slow, calm suffocation under the avalanche of relentless losses that started with my son and would not end until I, myself, found oblivion. Which was why I didn't wish to rise from the warm cocoon of my blankets. My heart felt in the throes of reverse metamorphosis, where the butterfly was to fold its wings and become the ugly, misshapen worm.

Was *this* Christian Resignation at last?

With her head upon my pillow, Lysbet murmured, "Aunt Angelica must be buried, but Uncle Church . . . well, he won't . . . he can't . . ."

That's what finally roused me. The shocking discovery that my brother-in-law couldn't afford—or simply refused to pay for—a fitting sepulcher for Angelica in Trinity Churchyard.

Though he'd wooed and won a patriot's daughter, made his fortune supplying an American army, and was the father of children in this country, Church intended to return to England. He said he couldn't endure the pain of living in a place where he'd be confronted with memories of his beloved wife. And I believed him.

For Church, too, had been at his wife's side when she whispered my husband's name.

*It was only the laudanum*, I insisted, wondering where I'd find the strength and money to do for my sister what Church could not or would not.

As it happened, it was Kitty Livingston, of all people, who offered to let my sister rest in the Livingston family vault, not far from where my husband and son were buried. After church services, and without looking at me, Kitty straightened her gloves and said, "Your family may be Federalists, but I have, over a lifetime, grown accustomed to having the Schuyler sisters near me, and I'm too old and set in my ways now to wish for a change."

Kitty was, as always, some strange combination of mean and magnanimous. An example of how virtue and vice could live inside a person, side by side. She was a living embodiment of how I could still be surprised by people I'd known most of my life. Or even, from the moment I was born . . .

After the funeral, my brother-in-law said, "Take what you like of her belongings." He sat on a chest at the foot of Angelica's bed, a drunk, unkempt stranger amidst her intimate things—a brush and a gilded mirror left casually upon the dressing table, bottles of perfume and pots of cosmetics, ribbons and silk stockings, and ornaments that she'd treasured.

Angelica had exquisite taste. Any item that belonged to her was likely to fetch a price, and my brother-in-law ought to have them valued. At the very least, he should save something sentimental for their children. That he seemed not to have thought of it made me wish to take it all. Everything from portraits to pearls to the silver nutmeg grater my sister had purchased in London.

I thought to keep my sister's elegant hats and dresses for Lysbet. Her leather-bound books, which spanned such a range of intellectual subjects from science to finance, knowing that my sons could benefit from them. Yet what I wanted most was a painted chest with a bronze latch where, for many years now, Angelica had kept her correspondence neatly folded, and wrapped in white silk to keep the broken wax seals from sticking.

"I would be grateful to select a few things for my children," I said to Church, though I was wary that he might find my next request a terrible intrusion. "But most of all, I'd like to look at her letters."

He only gave a bleak shrug, the light gone from his once-shining eyes. "As I said, take whatever you like."

*It was only the laudanum,* I wanted to shout at him. I wanted to *scream* it and shake him. Or reach for his hands and reassure my brother-in-law that the people we loved would never have betrayed us. That to let memories of Angelica and Alexander be stained with suspicions was an evil. A *sin*.

For almost forty years, I'd called John Barker Church my brother, but there had always been a wall separating us. At first, only a little overgrown hedge of jealousy for having won my sister's love and attention and carrying her away. Then, upon learning of his secret identity, and his marital troubles, I'd wondered about the character of such a man. But most of all, as I found him at the center of nearly every tragedy in my life, a fortification of resentment built between us, stone upon stone. And now, there was no crossing that barrier. So I didn't offer him comfort or accept any.

Instead, I opened the box.

~

WE THINK WE know the people we love.

We think that *love* gives us more than a glimpse into one another's souls. But the idea that human beings are *knowable* is one of the many lies we tell in the service of love. That's what I learned reading my sister's letters.

For I hadn't appreciated that in her correspondence with princes, philosophers, and statesmen that she commanded their respect, as well as their lustful fascination. And I hadn't known that in spite of countless letters from esteemed persons—including George Washington, Thomas Jefferson, Charles James Fox, and Lafayette—only one bundle of letters did she keep separate.

One bundle lay wrapped in a lace garter, with a memorial ring enclosing a tiny braid of auburn hair I knew so well. Alexander's hair. Alexander's letters. And as for the garter, I recognized it, for my sister had worn it to Washington's inaugural ball.

It was the garter that she said had slipped from her thigh while she was dancing, and my husband gallantly swept it from the floor to spare her embarrassment. Angelica had teased that she couldn't make him a Knight of the Garter in this new country of ours, where we didn't make such distinctions. And Kitty had confronted me in the middle of the ball, insisting that Peggy had said, "He'd be a knight of your bedchamber if he could."

Peggy denied it. But was it not precisely the sort of thing that Peggy would have blurted out?

More importantly, Angelica had kept the garter, wrapped closely round treasured letters. And what to make of the ring? I hadn't given it to her. Had she had made it herself as a memorial after his death, or as a token of remembrance during his life?

I dreaded to find the answer.

Knowing *for quite some time* of her impending death, surely she would have burned any letters that might have led to painful revelations. But perhaps the reckless girl who'd crept out of our father's house to run off with a beau—not caring whether it might cost Papa sleep, his rank, or even the war—was too selfish to burn what she treasured, no matter the pain it might cause.

*Stop this,* I told myself, thumbing through the pages. The flirtation between my sister and my husband had been a private jest among the three of us. I'd encouraged it. I'd read my husband's letters to Angelica before he sent them. I'd watched him write them! At least once, he asked me to deliver a letter to her personally so that his waggery wouldn't cause eyebrows to lift amongst those who didn't share our little joke. And when Angelica's letters arrived in the post, we read them together.

*There could be nothing secret or untoward in any of them,* I reassured myself.

But now, to my dismay, I found that I hadn't seen *all* the

letters. Once, when his hands were cramped writing *The Federalist*, Alexander somehow had found the time to write a letter to Angelica that taunted her, flirtatiously, about the misplacement of a comma.

*I seldom write to a lady without fancying the relation of lover and mistress,* he began, adding in closing that I sent my love. But never had I set eyes on this letter.

Surely I would have remembered.

*There is no proof of my affection which I would not willingly give you,* he wrote my sister a few months before he took Mrs. Reynolds to our bed.

And another, later that year, while he was still bedding that harlot. *You hurt my Republican nerves, Angelica, by your intimacy with Princes, while I can only console myself by thinking of you.*

Each letter brought new pain, and I held my breath upon opening every one.

*Your sister consents to everything, except that I should love you as well as herself and this you are too reasonable to expect,* my husband wrote.

But I hadn't consented to this.

What had Alexander been capable of, this man I'd loved and honored? He was capable of betraying our marriage bed. And I knew, from the stories Angelica told me of her time in Europe, that my sister might have been capable of betraying her husband, too.

Perhaps even with *Jefferson,* no less. And another thing I knew—had always known—was that at the heart of my husband's infidelity with Mrs. Reynolds, was the base motive of revenge. If Alexander could be jealous of my sister's intimacy with princes, I could well imagine his feelings upon knowing that Jefferson may have been smitten with her. Was my sister's favor another battleground over which the two men fought?

*It was only the laudanum,* I told myself, now desperate to believe it. But my heart was in shadow and could not see light.

Angelica herself once wrote me, *You know I love your husband very much, and if you were as generous as the Old Romans, you would lend him to me a little while.*

Could she have helped herself to him, and kept it secret? My sister was good at schemes and secrets. And, of course, my husband had kept secrets the entirety of our marriage, even, and perhaps especially, in the last days of his life. At some point or another, both of them hid from me the most vital things, as if I were a child.

And perhaps I had been.

Even *Monroe* had an inkling of something untoward between my sister and my husband early in our marriage. Was it any wonder that he could believe my husband guilty of any sort of corruption, thereafter? I remembered now that the very first time my husband was ever accused of adultery in print was that same spring that Angelica came to New York without her husband. When I'd pushed them together, insisting that Alexander squire her about the city to mend her broken heart. I'd allowed my sister to play hostess to Alexander and his gentlemen friends and been grateful for it. I'd allowed my sister to *take my place.*

Sweet, stupid, Eliza, still the fool.

Always the fool.

And now I was left to wonder, who were Alexander and Angelica? Who were they really?

# Chapter Forty

*June 1814*
*Harlem*

H OW WILL YOU get on here by yourself, Mother?" William asked while I unlatched the shutters to let fresh air into the long-neglected house at the Grange.

On leave from the academy at West Point, my nearly seventeen-year-old son had worked himself into a lather carting chairs and lamps and personal items into the house. But now, red-faced and dripping with sweat, William looked ready to pack it all back into a wagon if I should change my mind.

None of my sons approved of my decision to move to the home we once more owned, away from the city, our friends, and my work at the orphanage. Yet in the aftermath of my sister's death, I welcomed the isolation of the country where no one would see the darkness that had crept into my heart.

"I won't be alone," I reassured William. "I'll have Lysbet and Little Phil. And there's no reason to waste money paying rent in town."

That much was true. Having only the youngest two children in my care now, I could undertake their education myself and hire back Mr. and Mrs. Genti to help me keep up the place. Because at least this house was mine, even if the man who built it was not . . .

*Who was Alexander Hamilton?*

A traitor or a patriot? A visionary or a fool? A gentleman or a fraud?

That's what I wanted to know, and now it kept me awake all night reading the mountain of letters, pacing in fits and starts. Like Hamilton. Though my project was at once humbler and more ambitious than a pamphlet or a treatise or a book defending a new form of government. Mine was simply to learn the truth.

And there was more to read now than ever. Because I'd never stopped collecting my husband's writings. For the biography *and* for myself, I needed them. And in the ten years since he'd died, I'd hunted down thousands of letters, pamphlets, and reports from everyone and everywhere. Political essays and financial treatises. And, of course, account books, in which I now found that in the year Angelica came to New York without her husband, Hamilton paid her expenses. Not just those I'd known about, for which Church was to have reimbursed him—but unspecified expenses, too, as if Angelica had simply presented him with receipts for her shopping trips. He'd also rented rooms for her, in addition to her house.

What rooms? Where were they? And why had she needed *other* rooms when she'd had that luxurious town house? I couldn't fathom it.

And, then, in the very next entry in the ledger, I found that Hamilton had purchased himself a closed coach.

Ugly images rose to my mind.

I'd never been to Europe, where it was common for noblemen to keep mistresses, but I could guess how a gentleman might plan clandestine meetings. Secret rooms reached by a closed coach with curtains drawn. A beautiful woman inside whispering in French to a man hungry for her appreciation . . .

I remembered precisely how Hamilton was that year as secretary of the treasury. He'd likened himself to a veritable prime minister with all the powers and privileges. He'd believed himself in command of a whole nation, so why should he be denied the caresses of any willing woman?

*But that was before the yellow fever,* I told myself, trying desperately to salvage anything from our life together. Alexander was changed after the fever. A different husband. A better man. And Angelica, when she moved back to America, was a changed woman. The most reliable, generous, and loyal sister that any person could have.

*Because they were guilty,* the devil inside me whispered. *And they lied to you. They lied to you all your life and all of theirs. To their very last breaths.*

Blinking back acid tears, I realized these poisonous doubts could put the lie to my whole life. Yes, I had evidence, but it didn't prove the case. Where, but in death itself, might I ever confront either my husband or my sister and have an answer?

I needed to stop this mad inquiry.

Like my father before me, I needed to exert the self-discipline Hamilton lacked, the ability to let a thing alone when pursuing it could end in despair.

But in the end, and perhaps inevitably, I'd become more like Hamilton than Papa.

For I carried Angelica's box of letters, and my inquiry, up to the attic, where, assailed by a cloud of dust motes that floated in the light of my lamp, I made of the private space a makeshift office for my investigation. There, amidst crates of papers in the stifling heat, I sat hour after hour, hunched over yellowed pages, sneering at Angelica's coquettish missives, taking satisfaction that at least Hamilton hadn't bundled *her* letters in a sentimental ribbon.

Perhaps he hadn't loved her. But had he loved me? Had either of them *ever* loved me? Or had Alexander and Angelica clung to each other in the fevered sweat of lovemaking, laughing at me all the while?

When there was nothing left to read, I spied the engraved wooden strongbox with leather buckles where Alexander kept his old military uniforms and ornamental swords.

*His glory*, I thought, with a contemptuous snort. And all at once, I wondered if that was where I'd find the definitive evidence I was seeking. Perhaps my husband kept some treasured token of his love affair with Angelica just as she'd kept that garter. Perhaps I'd find a matching ring, with a clipping of her hair, and then all my doubts would vanish.

Knowing he was to duel, Alexander would have hidden anything incriminating or entrusted it to someone to destroy if he died. Hamilton was too smart for me. Too smart for everyone, except Burr.

Nevertheless, I unfastened the latch and was struck by the arresting sight of the blue-and-buff military coat Alexander wore the first day I met him. The wool, rougher than I remembered when I first touched him. When we first kissed. And the pain, oh the *pain* of remembering that with now jaded eyes, sliced into me like the bayonet beside the uniform.

Like a wounded soldier, bleeding my heart out, I searched every item in the trunk until it was empty, running my hands over the velvet lining . . . to find the false bottom I somehow expected. And that's where I found it.

A bundle of letters and a dark braid of hair . . .

MY HANDS SHOOK as I unfolded the pages, finding neither the scent of my sister's perfume nor the feminine scrawl of her hand. But instead, the shock of a firm, masculine signature.

*John Laurens.*

A man I'd never met, whose death dealt to Alexander his worst wound of the war. Here were the letters between them. Not only the ones Laurens wrote, but also copies of what my husband wrote to Laurens as well. That both sides of the correspondence were so carefully preserved spoke volumes of its importance to my husband.

And now I read them, with near incredulity.

*Cold in my professions, warm in my friendships, I wish, my dear Laurens, it might be in my power, by action rather than words to convince you that I love you.*

It was, in those days, the style for men to speak of love to one another. But it was not a style Alexander embraced in his letters. Not to any man I knew save, perhaps, Lafayette.

And yet, these were different. Ardent. Complete with a lewd suggestion that John Laurens had intimate knowledge of Alexander's body. Letters that indicated a liaison between Washington's young officers for which they might both have been shot.

And—quite beyond the capacity to be scandalized by anything now—I nearly laughed at my mind's sudden opening to things that ought to have been perfectly obvious before.

My husband had loved this man.

Clutching a lock of dark hair that was not, after all, my sister's, I remembered Alexander's unnatural grief for Laurens. My husband's attachment to the baron, whose handsome young male companions Theodosia Burr had once identified as sodomites. Perhaps my husband had been one of them, adopting the vice because it was forbidden.

Forbidden, like another man's wife.

Forbidden, like his wife's sister.

If Hamilton could commit those sins, why not this one? Why not sate his lust with another soldier while the winter was cold and the war was harsh?

Then, in a letter Alexander had written only months before we met, I found this:

*Such a wife as I want must be young, handsome (I lay most stress upon a good shape) sensible (a little learning will do), well bred, chaste and tender (I am an enthusiast in my notions of fidelity and fondness). But as to fortune, the larger stock of that the better as money is an essential ingredient to happiness in this world.*

Well, then.

Even sinners needed money, didn't they?

And hadn't he found just what he wanted in me? I met his cold list of qualifications precisely. It hollowed out my heart to know it. Made of my soul a barren land. Surrounded by the detritus of my husband's life, I didn't think there were any new ways in which his letters could hurt me.

But then they did.

*Next fall completes my doom,* Hamilton wrote to Laurens before our wedding.

> *I give up my liberty to Miss Schuyler. She is a good-hearted girl who I am sure will never play the termagant; though not a genius she has good sense enough to be agreeable, and though not a beauty, she has fine black eyes.*

A good-hearted girl. Not a genius. Not a beauty.

*Not enough . . .*

He wrote these things to John Laurens while whispering against my lips that I had bewitched him. While writing me sonnets. While buying me wedding gifts with John Laurens's money . . .

> *In spite of Schuyler's black eyes, I have still a part for the public and another for you; so your impatience to have me married is misplaced; a strange cure by the way, as if after matrimony I was to be less devoted than I am now.*

The page slipped from my hand.

Our courtship had merely been another scheme.

Lies, lies, schemes and lies!

When we danced together at that first winter's ball in Morristown, I'd been wary of Hamilton because he reminded me of the watery Nix of Dutch legend, luring maidens to dangerous depths. And now, at long last, I was drowning. Wrenching my wedding ring off my finger, I threw it into the trunk with the rest of Alexander's deceit, thinking to send all of it to the bottom of the river.

Because, my God, this was to lose him again. A second kind of widowhood. One that obliterated the first. For I could have no hope of meeting with Alexander in heaven now; he was more likely to be found in hell. And I hoped . . . I hoped he *burned* there.

For he never loved me. He was never mine. He made me vows before an altar and played the part, to the last. But Alexander Hamilton was as false a villain as his enemies claimed he was. He had cheated me of my whole life and got away with it.

Cheated. That was how I felt, surveying all that remained of my husband's legacy.

What *was* his legacy? Not the eternal bonds of love, not the earthly but enduring stone of monuments. Only paper. A worthless Constitution that the Republicans shredded with each successive administration. A few books filled with words he probably never meant in earnest. Just crates and crates of paper.

And I wanted to set fire to it all.

I AWAKENED TO the whisper of papers falling like dead leaves upon a forest floor. And as I blinked against the bleary haze of shadow and cracks of sunlight, I couldn't fathom where I was.

The attic. I'd somehow fallen asleep there, in the heat, exhausted by an agony of the soul. And now I saw my son's bare feet upon the wood planks, loose pages strewn by his toes. For one absurd moment in the delirium, I thought to scold William, as I'd done when he was a child, for walking about like a barefooted street urchin instead of a young gentleman.

But then I saw the lace garter clutched in his hand.

William was reading my sister's letters, and I didn't think the burning flush upon his cheek was exertion or summer heat. "I came up because I worried for you—but I didn't want to wake you when I found you asleep. You haven't slept much lately."

My heart jolted, and I shoved myself up. It was all I could do to resist pulling the paper and lace from his hands, but in doing so, I'd only expose myself. Expose *everything*. He couldn't possibly attach any meaning to that garter, which had slipped off my sister's thigh long before he was born, but oh, dear Lord, how much had he read?

"I'm sorry to have worried you," I managed, struggling for breath in the now hellish heat of the attic. Perspiration pooled at my nape, and my black frock clung to my back.

William quietly nodded, but his expression was bleak and his eyes were a storm. "My father wrote these letters to Aunt Angelica?"

Those were the words he spoke, but not what he truly meant to ask.

And I could almost see it. Almost see William standing at the precipice of a suspicion that would shatter everything he believed about his father, and about himself. And what mother—especially one clinging to that same edge by her fingertips—could allow her child to fall?

Forcing a smile, I said, "Oh, yes. Your father and Aunt Angelica were very good friends. It's such a comfort to me to read their letters and remember it."

My son—the one born while his father confessed adultery to the world—swallowed hard. He scrutinized my face, and then his gaze fell to my hand. "You're not wearing your ring."

As my mind raced, I thought I might be sick. Burr once said I wasn't an actress of any talent. It was my sister who could bury her misery and heartbreak beneath pleasantries and a fan of playing cards in her hand. But now I called upon whatever powers of deception I'd ever learned from her to say, "The heat has swollen my fingers." I kissed my boy's cheek. "Or perhaps I've been eating too much. Speaking of, shall we go down and fix some breakfast?"

"You haven't eaten *anything*," William said. "Not more than a nibble for days."

What a Hamilton he was—a dogged interrogator assembling proofs and challenging my testimony. But I determined then and there that he'd never find me out.

"Well, that explains why I'm so famished," I said, feigning a lightness of spirit I didn't feel, and might never feel again. "And thirsty. Will you fetch me a glass of switchel?"

He nodded, slowly relinquishing to me the letters and his aunt's garter. And I believed he was tricked by the mask I presented. I realized later that I was wrong.

But I didn't know that then, I only knew it was a mask I was determined to wear from that day forth. Because I couldn't deprive my children of their cherished memories of their father. Not after I'd nursed them all on a reverence for Alexander that neared worship.

I'd hoped that lionizing their father would compensate my children for the absence of his guidance, protection, and comfort. That it would somehow make up for the suffering he'd exposed them to. For the debts he'd left. And for the scandal he'd saddled us all with.

Was it comedy or tragedy that after all my husband had done to defend his name, there was not a corner of the country where *Hamilton* did not conjure up salacious gossip of harlots and infidelity? No place the name *Hamilton* did not rouse animosity amongst those who held political power. My sons had, each of them, felt compelled to become soldiers to prove themselves loyal, useful, and worthy of the country they'd been bequeathed. And given those circumstances, no mother who loved her children could ever wish to infect them with the contagion of doubt that now malingered inside my breast about what kind of man their father had been.

They knew him as the mythic hero who'd driven a carriage of the sun across the sky; they didn't need to know he'd crashed it into my world, leaving me in fiery ruin.

So there was no one with whom I could share my bitter cup of poison. I would simply have to swallow the injustice down and lie about the taste until it killed me.

Or until the shame of it burned me alive.

*I shall never forget the destructive majesty of the flames.*
—HARRY SMITH ON THE BURNING OF WASHINGTON

The nation was on fire, and part of me wanted to watch it burn. To bear witness to the end just as I'd borne witness to its beginnings. Everything to which I had devoted my life, in flames . . .

In our capital, British soldiers had put a torch to the naval yard, the congressional library, and burned the President's Mansion right down to Dolley Madison's bright red curtains. Our president was a fugitive in his own country, having been forced to flee his supper—his wife at least prescient enough to steal away with famous portraits and national treasures before it all went up in smoke.

"These blundering Republicans have led our country defenseless and naked into this lake of blood!" Alex shouted, thumping one fist on the window frame while his other hand gripped the sword swaying at his hip, and I was pained by how much like his father he looked in uniform.

My soldier sons had stopped at the Grange on their way to take up defense of New York Harbor, two of them seated by the open windows in the parlor. All of us sweltering in the heat, as if the flames engulfing Washington City reached us here, too, even where I sat with my embroidery upon one of the old, faded chairs.

"If President Madison loses this war, we lose the country," James said.

And I bit back a bitter laugh.

Hamilton had warned that the country needed a standing army and had been vilified for it. Even by Madison. Now the fate of the nation was left largely to a gutted navy and militias who had, under the direction of Secretary Monroe, already run from the fight.

"So they've finally done it," I said, startling my sons with my venomous tone as I stabbed my needle into the cloth. "The Republicans have finally wrecked it all."

The Federal City that Hamilton had negotiated to bring into existence was now burned to the ground. It was quite possibly the end. The end of the Republic. The end of our American experiment. The end of the United States of America.

What had been the point of any of it, I wondered.

The Revolution. *The Federalist.* The Constitution. The Farewell Address. The bank charters. The legal precedents . . . all Hamilton's accomplishments worthless and dismantled and soon to be forgotten. Perhaps I should, with diabolical glee, burn his papers to save the King of England the trouble!

Except those weren't *only* Alexander Hamilton's accomplishments. Other people had sacrificed to see those things brought about. They were *our* accomplishments, too.

Perhaps alarmed at the bleakness of my words, Alex folded his arms over his uniformed chest—a uniform his father had designed with my help—and said, "The war isn't over *yet,* Mother."

*But it is for me,* I thought. Because as everything turned to ashes in my mouth, I was too tired to fight anymore. Tired of fighting Jefferson and Burr and Monroe, fighting the Republicans *and* the Federalists, fighting grief and loneliness and bitterness and the British besides.

Fortunately, a new generation took up the call in defense of their country.

While my old friend Mac lay paralyzed upon a sickbed from which he would never again rise, the soldiers at his Fort McHenry fended off a stunning bombardment of rockets and mortar shells in Baltimore Harbor, giving the British just enough time to reconsider whether subduing America was really worth the fight.

And so, the three-year-long War of 1812 ended in a stalemate that allowed Republicans to pretend to have achieved something other than bankrupting the nation and destroying the Federalist Party.

Though perhaps it could be more properly said that my husband's Federalist Party killed itself as ingloriously as its founder had. My husband had thrown away his life, whether he'd intended to or not. A question that kept me up many nights. And his party dashed itself to pieces with a failed and potentially treasonous attempt at secession in the midst of a war.

*If they break this Union, they will break my heart,* Alexander had said upon his deathbed.

But I couldn't seem to care, because when he broke *our* union, he'd broken my heart, too. He'd promised that he was mine forever, that he'd never leave me alone or desperate. But then he'd rowed across the Hudson River at dawn to meet an empty vessel of a man who wasn't worth his spit, let alone his life. He'd gone knowing he might never return. He'd planned it. And he'd kept it from me. How could I ever forgive him?

All that mattered now was that my sons had survived the ordeal of their own honorable battles in the War of 1812. And so did the country, though I might be excused, if, in the ten years that followed, I scarcely recognized the nation as my own.

We were all Republicans now. Like it or not.

No one disagreed or dared to. Our new Virginian president, James Monroe—a recent convert to the Hamiltonian idea that we needed a strong regular army even in peacetime—declared it the Era of Good Feelings.

He'd actually run unopposed for the presidency, for there were no more political parties and we were not to have partisanship in the nation. We were to live in a perpetual state of patriotic *oneness.*

It was, after all, a decade of deceit.

Republicans pretended there was nothing whatsoever hypocritical about their newfound embrace of a national bank and federal institutions. Never mind that they'd destroyed my family for championing those very things.

A retired Thomas Jefferson was now the so-called Sage of Monticello, the prophet of democracy, while to hear people tell it, George Washington had been a mere general in the cause . . .

. . . and Alexander Hamilton had never existed at all.

A whole generation of Americans came of age without hearing my husband's name, unless it was in diminishment or a curse. And I could scarcely blame them. Hamilton was safely dead and forgotten. We survivors of the founding of the country all *let* him be forgotten.

Even me.

# Chapter Forty-One

September 1824
New York City

"MAMA, WE HAVE a visitor!" Lysbet whispered loudly from outside my office door at the orphanage. I peered up from the account books I kept as the society's First Directress, my hand cramped around a quill after hours of recording and resolving the entries.

At nearly twenty-five, Lysbet had declared herself a spinster, quite contentedly *on the shelf*, which was why she often assisted my work at the orphanage's Bank Street headquarters, where there were now beds for two hundred of the city's neediest children.

Lysbet reminded me of myself when I was about her age, convinced that I, too, would be a spinster. But more than me, she still resembled a more subtle Angelica, except for her unadorned hair and the spectacles she wore upon her nose whenever it was buried in a book—which was often. Lysbet was a serious and sensible young woman, without girlish caprice, so I couldn't fathom her excitement as she hovered in the doorway, positively vibrating with giddiness.

"What visitor?" I asked, not remembering any appointments.

"See for yourself," Lysbet said, stepping aside to reveal two distinguished-looking gentlemen. One, a middle-aged Frenchman.

The other, the last living general of the revolutionary war . . .

I rushed to my feet, and the familiar sight of him filled my eyes with tears.

Though I'd never seen the Marquis de Lafayette out of uniform before, he was instantly recognizable to me as a hero of a bygone age. And as my friend. Stouter than I remembered, and bent with age and whatever torments he'd suffered all those years he was held in a dungeon during the French Revolution, but still the slope of that forehead and that patrician nose were unmistakable.

"Madame Hamilton," Lafayette said, making a formal bow with cane and top hat in hand.

"General Lafayette," I whispered, rounding the desk. And that's when I realized the taller man at his side was his son. "*Georges*?"

Georges smiled and stepped forward swiftly to kiss my cheeks. "How it fills my heart to see you again. I've never forgotten what you did for me all those years ago, when I was in hiding." He ducked his chin, as if he couldn't say more without being unmanned.

On instinct, my hands went to his cheeks as if he were still a boy. But in truth, his hair was shot through with silver, and I couldn't help but think that my Philip would've been about his age now, if he'd lived.

Perhaps Lafayette was thinking this, too, because the general spoke to me in consolation for my losses and I returned mine for his. And finally remembering the rest of my manners, I presented my Lysbet, who tittered like such a flibbertigibbet, one might think she'd never met a general before.

But, of course, Lafayette was no mere general. The entire country was poised to give him a hero's welcome with toasts and spectacles in honor of the forthcoming fiftieth anniversary of the revolution. It was said that in all America there wasn't a heart that didn't beat with joy and gratitude at the sound of Lafayette's name.

Certainly my heart did.

Already the city of New York had greeted him with booming cannons due a conquering hero. Which was quite possibly why Lysbet nearly swooned when Lafayette kissed her hand.

"Mademoiselle Hamilton," he said to my daughter, his world-weary, haggard eyes crinkling at the corners with his smile. "You must not be shy. Your father was more than friend to me, he was a brother. We were both very young when our friendship formed in days of peril and glory, but it suffered no diminution from time. So you must think of yourself as family to me."

The enormity of this statement, if only for what it meant to Lysbet, melted my heart.

"And you, *madame*," he said, turning to me. "*You* are my sister, and were before you ever met your husband, *oui*?"

It was a touching sentiment. One that recalled to me long-ago days in Albany. And though I had brothers of my own, by blood and marriage, I couldn't help but return it. "I remember, and feel the same."

So it shamed me when he nodded and said, "I worried for your health when I did not see you at the welcoming parade. Georges told me no esteemed woman of sense would jostle with a New York crowd in this heat. *Mon Dieu, this heat.*" Lafayette dabbed at the sweat on his forehead. "But I could not be satisfied of your well-being until I set eyes upon you, myself. As I wished to learn more about your charity work, I tracked you down here."

I flushed at the shabby state of my crowded little office, with its decades-old desk and sagging bookshelves, but even more so because I hadn't been invited to the official celebrations by the Republicans who now held power in government. Given how shamelessly they claimed the mantle of patriotism all for themselves, my presence would have been an inconvenient reminder to everyone of my husband. Or perhaps they'd simply forgotten me as they'd forgotten him.

But Lafayette *hadn't* forgotten.

And I feared I'd given offense. But before I could offer words that might make up for my absence, Lafayette shook his head. "I hope you do not think to apologize. Especially since I wish to impose upon you for something," he said, a sly twinkle in his eye.

"By all means," I said, gesturing at the chair. "Shall we sit?" I was pained to see him leaning so heavily on his cane as he lowered himself into the rickety seat. "Lysbet, perhaps our guests would enjoy some lemonade?"

The men exclaimed their thanks, stirring my daughter from where she still stood, riveted at the door. "Oh, right away."

"I'll help you," Georges said, like the good, dutiful boy he'd always been.

"What can I do for you?" I asked Lafayette, aware of the flurry of people suddenly finding reason to pass my office door. The matron of the orphanage, checking the lock on the kitchen larder. Our cook, grabbing a broom from the hall closet. A little girl, not at school because she was sick, peeking down from the stairs.

Lafayette winked at the child, and she scampered away with a delighted giggle. "I am called to America by President Monroe to witness the immense improvements and the prosperity of these happy United States, so I can report back to the world that they reflect the light of a far superior political civilization."

Though almost everyone who met Monroe in his younger days had dismissed him for a lackwit, I'd been right about him in at least one respect. There was always, *always*, more to James Monroe than met the eye. And he'd proven, as president, to be more of a master of national propaganda than any of his predecessors. He'd somehow persuaded the nation that the War of 1812 had been a glorious victory instead of a humiliating stalemate. And now, to drum up support for his new doctrine of superiority in the hemisphere, he presented himself as the last founder of our country.

If he could somehow wrap himself in Lafayette's glory and portray southern slave owners as virtuous guardians of liberty, so much the better.

But our French hero still maintained an independent mind. "I wish to see more than what is on my official itinerary here in New

York. I should like *you* to reveal to me the true United States. What must I see?"

"Me?" I was most assuredly *not* part of Monroe's plans for this visit, the realization of which made me instantly intrigued.

"Indeed. For while I feel an inexpressible delight in the progress of every thing that is noble-minded, honorable, and useful throughout the United States, I will not look away from the flaws. And, in particular, the status of the Negro raises a sigh, or a blush, according to the company. The measure of a country is, for me, not to be found in prosperity, but in a virtuous resistance to oppression. Even as President Monroe's guest, I will not miss an occasion to raise the question of slavery and defend the rights of *all* men. Which is why I presume upon you."

My heart beat in sudden excitement that there remained amongst us a patriot willing to stand against Virginian hypocrisy. "I . . . I will do whatever is in my power if you should name it."

Lafayette smiled. "I wish to know more about your work here and at the Free School for Young Africans that your husband and the Manumission Society founded for poor children of former slaves. In fact, I would like to tour both with you as my guide."

My *work*.

During the War of 1812, I'd been too tired to fight for the country anymore. I'd decided that I'd fight only for my children. And for the hundreds of orphans who depended on me. For whatever I had, or had not been, to Alexander Hamilton, my maker had pointed out a duty to me and given me the ability and inclination to perform it.

My husband had a gift for government, but I had a gift for charity. A talent for it, if there be such a thing. I'd already helped to found a society to care for widows, an orphanage to shelter children, and a school to provide guidance and learning. There was not an aspect of the management for any of these endeavors with which I wasn't intimately acquainted. I laid cornerstones, raised money, rented property, made visits to the needy, nursed the sick, procured coal, food, shoes, and Bibles. I kept account books, wrote charters, and lobbied legislatures.

How gratifying that Lafayette should appreciate all that and treat me as a person of moral consequence. A warmth stole through me at the flattering notion that he felt I could guide him in seeing the true America. But for the recognition of my calling, I felt more honored than I could ever remember being. More energized, too, as if remembering myself after a long slumber.

~

"MARQUIS, MAY I present to you our instructors and students," I said, introducing him to the gathered ladies and rows of smiling public school children at the African Free School, all wearing *Lafayette* badges made of satin ribbon, each straining to catch a glimpse of the great man. Our tour of the orphanage had been short but had allowed me to send someone ahead to prepare the school administrators for this little assembly. And that someone was Mrs. Fanny Anthill Tappan—my adoptive daughter, now returned to New York all grown and happy with a husband and children of her own. For years now, it'd been a balm to have Fanny in my busy life again, and her eagerness to assist in my charitable work filled me with pride.

Bracing upon his cane, Lafayette kissed both of Fanny's cheeks in the French style, then he walked the length of the gathering, greeting every child. "What a bright, industrious group of pupils," he said.

"The original Free School for Africans was only one room, and could admit only forty students," I explained as we toured the new buildings, in which were educated more than seven hundred of the best and brightest. "The English headmaster finds these black children every bit as capable as white children."

Lafayette didn't seem surprised. "I regret that my own efforts to emancipate slaves in the French colonies was forestalled . . ."

He trailed off there, his mind seeming to retreat to a dark place, and I worried it was the darkness of his old prison cell. To draw him back, I said, "There's still more to be done, but our state legislature passed a law of gradual emancipation, and complete abolition is nearly accomplished. It cannot happen soon enough."

Though I'd long been a convert to the cause of abolition, I hadn't before spoken in public against the national cancer. And Lafayette's presence encouraged me. No longer needing to measure my words for fear of how they might affect my husband's political career, I felt a freedom to say exactly how disillusioned I was. "In the South, the vile institution of slavery spreads like a contagion. Such is inevitable when the country has been run these past twenty years by presidents and congresses elected by the counting of slaves as three-fifths of a person for the purpose of representation, while not otherwise counting them as a person at all. The South doubly reaps the benefits of slavery at the expense of fairness, morality, and liberty."

Lafayette turned an appraising smile on me. "I hear something of the passion of Hamilton in your speech, *madame.*"

Heat infused my cheeks as I struggled with the complicated emotions dredged up by the comparison, but fortunately, a gaggle of awed children swarmed the general, distracting him from my reaction to words which were, at once, the highest praise and a painful reminder.

Finally, Lafayette escorted me outside and turned to me with fondness. "You do good work here, Elizabeth. You will perhaps finish what we started."

I tilted my head. "What we started?"

"The revolution. It is unfinished. Maybe liberty must always be fought for. And you have kept fighting when others laid down their swords in defeat, or exhaustion, or corruption."

"I'm afraid you misjudge me," I said, feeling an ache of shame in my breast. "I stopped fighting long ago."

Lafayette gestured at the school behind us. "Then what is this school? What is your orphanage? These things seek to expand the promise of America. To give opportunity to all as free citizens."

Tears pricked at the corners of my eyes as my ache of shame melted into recognition. I'd not thought of my work as more than charity. But it always had been. Whatever I told myself, I never stopped trying to finish what we started when we were all so young and idealistic about what this nation *could* be.

"Would that my friend was here to help you." Lafayette sighed. "Will you take me to see him? I wish, with your blessing, to lay a wreath upon Hamilton's grave, but there is no ceremony planned for it."

Of course, no ceremony had been planned. For years now, even I had shied away from the monument in Trinity Churchyard where my husband was buried. I made any number of excuses for my reticence. The distressing reminder of my losses; the spectacle of people looking at me when I knelt beside the stone. The fact that I'd suffered for a public life and didn't wish my most private grief to be exposed. All these things were true, of course, but the real reason I didn't go was because both Angelica and Alexander were buried there.

For ten years, I'd hid the festering wounds of my suspicions from everyone, in every way I could. My greatest failing in that endeavor had been with William, who was, I'd learned, never fooled by my facade. He'd seen his father's letters to my sister and, worse, he'd seen me laid low. It'd changed something in him to have the heroic image of his father shattered. And we'd lost him over it. He'd withdrawn from West Point and gone west, as far as he could go from civilization, all because I couldn't leave a matter alone. So I didn't intend to reopen it now. "You have my blessing to go to the grave, of course, General, but I've already taken too much of your time. Your public is waiting."

"Let them wait," Lafayette said, offering me his arm. "Hamilton is more important."

Having no way to refuse him without exposing myself, I took

his arm, but anxiety seized me as we made the short carriage ride to Trinity Churchyard. "For your itinerary," I said, hoping to distract myself from the clawing dread, "there are other benevolent societies you might visit, almshouses and the great hospital, too. You might take in the Trumbull painting at the Academy of Arts, and I've no doubt the Society of the Cincinnati would host you for—"

"Dear sister, is it so strange that I wish to visit graves?"

"Oh. No, of course not," I said, swallowing down the nerves that had me rambling.

Lafayette's shrewd gaze told me he sensed something amiss, and I was relieved he didn't press the point. "As a young man, I would have thought so. But then, I did not expect to live this long."

"Considering the way you've habitually thrown yourself into danger for the cause of liberty, it *is* rather a miracle that you're still alive."

"You are not the first to say so." He chuckled, but then his smile faded. "Is it too painful for you to visit Hamilton's graveside?"

"No." I folded my gloved hands in my lap. Then, unable to withstand his scrutiny, I finally admitted, "Yes, it's painful. But a duty too long neglected."

"I understand," Lafayette said with a sympathetic nod. He couldn't possibly understand, but I smiled politely. "After all these years, I go too little to visit where my Adrienne sleeps her final sleep."

I realized, almost with a start, that he'd been a widower nearly as long as I'd been a widow. "Is your wife buried far from where you now reside?"

Lafayette nodded, his eyes going to the window. "She wanted to be buried with her family. A mass grave in Paris, where, after being guillotined for the misfortune of noble blood and a relation to me, the bodies of her loved ones were dumped. It is sometimes too difficult for me to go where I must bear the weight of it upon my shoulders. Instead, I made a shrine of Adrienne's room, still as she left it, and where it seems I am less separated from her than anywhere else."

This sentiment was familiar to me, having myself sought in vain for the essence of Alexander in this world. And I was moved by the raw pain in his voice for a loss experienced nearly twenty years before.

Unfortunately, his embarrassment at having betrayed that pain was obvious and he pleaded, "*S'il vous plaît, pardonnez-moi.* It is only that I wished many times to show my wife this country, and now, here I am without her, welcomed in a manner that exceeds the power to express what I feel. Thus I cannot resist an opportunity to confide my anguish to a friend who can understand."

I could understand. I once pored over my husband's letters every night, trying to recall the inflections of his voice. And every morning, gazed upon his portraits and bust, trying to remember the lines of his face. "General, you must never ask forgiveness for confiding in me. I know this same unhappiness well."

He let out a breath of relief. "It was worse in the beginning. Having married so young, I was so much accustomed to all that she was to me that I did not distinguish her from my own existence. I knew that I loved her and needed her. But it was only in losing her that I finally see the wreck of me that remains. Now, I am not unsatisfied with my excellent children or friends, but I recognize the impossibility of lifting the weight of this pain. This irreparable loss."

"Yes," I whispered, because emotion rose like a knot in my throat as he eloquently echoed my own feelings. My whole life had been fused with my sister and my husband, and having lost them both to death and betrayal, I also lost myself. I put my hand upon Lafayette's and whispered, "You must believe that your loving wife wouldn't wish you to carry this weight."

Though Lafayette didn't look at me, the corner of his lips hinted at a smile. "No, she would not. My sweet companion was a forgiving woman and an angel who, for thirty-four years, blessed my life."

It was the word *angel*, spoken so reverently, that triggered a memory of Alexander whispering it against my hair, my ear, my neck. And my mind threw up a now familiar defense against these memories whenever they assaulted me.

*It was all a lie. You never knew him. You never knew him at all.*

Perhaps that was why I murmured, with something akin to envy, "You may at least take consolation that after so many years of happy marriage, you achieved perfect knowledge of one another."

At this, Lafayette roared with sudden laughter. "Perfect knowledge! *Mon Dieu,* my wife kept secrets to the very end. Do not ask me to reveal them, but they confound me to this day. Just like a woman."

I blinked, thinking that it wasn't only *women* who could keep confounding secrets. And it occurred to me like a bolt from the blue that I was sitting next to the only man alive who might know the answers to any of the questions that burned through the fabric of my very soul.

*Lafayette would understand.*

That's what Alexander had said to me upon the death of John Laurens. The only words he would say, in fact. The thought that the general might've been aware of the true nature of my husband's relationship with Laurens made heat sear its way from the tips of my ears to my toes, leaving me in unbearable mortification.

"Are you unwell, *madame*?"

For a moment, I couldn't answer, for fear of what I might say. What I might ask. What accusations I might make. *None of it matters,* I told myself. There was no longer any possible reason to care. The opposite of love, I thought, was not hatred, but *indifference,* and for my own survival, I'd made my heart indifferent to Alexander Hamilton.

There was nothing but humiliation to be gained by asking questions.

Nothing to be gained by caring at all.

"It's only the heat," I said by way of excuse, schooling my features into politeness as the soaring steeple of Trinity Church came into view.

~

## ALEXANDER HAMILTON
### The patriot of incorruptible INTEGRITY.
### The soldier of approved VALOUR.
### The statesman of consummate WISDOM.
### Whose TALENTS and VIRTUES will be
ADMIRED BY GRATEFUL POSTERITY LONG AFTER
THIS MARBLE WILL HAVE MOLDERED INTO DUST.

The last line inscribed on the headstone had been comforting when we buried Alexander here, but I no longer believed it.

Lafayette, however, was deeply affected.

With a quivering lower lip, the old general gently rested his gnarled hand atop the white stone and spoke to my dead husband. "At last, here I am. It is Lafayette, your old and constant friend. It is my hope that wherever you are now, you will remind me to our brother soldiers who have not forgotten their long absent comrade—and to my ancient friends all gathered about you . . ."

As it happened, it didn't matter how firmly I had resolved to feel *nothing*. It simply wasn't possible to stand at my husband's grave and give dry-eyed witness to this sad reunion. My own lip quivered when Lafayette placed the wreath against the stone and bowed his head in silent and tearful communion.

He passed a long time like that, quiet and stooped.

And I found that my heart was not made of stone after all. For Lafayette's emotion stirred something in me that I simply couldn't contain. And when he raised up again, he noticed. "You will want a moment alone with him."

"No, it's—"

"I will wait by the gate," Lafayette said, withdrawing. "I understand."

He didn't. He couldn't. Because I didn't understand it myself.

Now left alone at my husband's graveside, I hugged myself tightly, trying to make sense of it. Aware that for the first time in a very long time, no one was watching me. The way the graveyard was situated, people passed gaily on the street just beyond the iron rail, laughing and going about their business without any sense of respect for the gravity of the place. And maybe I shouldn't respect it, either.

"*Integrity*?" I scoffed at the engraving. "Was there integrity in deceiving me, Alexander?" Because I didn't sense any part of him still in this world, it seemed silly to continue. But then it'd been so many years since I'd spoken to my husband that I couldn't resist imagining that he could hear. "*Valor*, I admit you had, in stupid quantity. But *wisdom*? I spent our whole marriage keeping you from foolhardiness. And if you'd told me . . ."

I blinked back a rush of bitter tears.

"If you'd told me what you meant to do that morning at Weehawken, I would have stopped you. You'd be alive, and I more the fool, but—"

My eyes fell upon the spot where our sweet, innocent Philip was buried in the earth, and I brought my fist to my mouth to stifle my words. For I'd protected the rest of my children from this anger I felt for their father. And now, absurdly, I worried about speaking these truths in front of Philip.

I knelt at my son's grave and pressed my hand to the cool grass.

"You're with him, aren't you?" I whispered, realizing that if Philip was united with the Lord, then none of this would be any secret to him. Even so, I couldn't bring myself to utter the venom at the tip of my tongue, especially not the two words that would've hurt Alexander the most.

*You bastard.*

That's what I wanted to say. *What you did to us. What you did to your children. What you did to yourself!*

For a moment, I felt as if I hated Hamilton as much as I'd ever loved him.

That's when I began to laugh. A sputtering, hiccup of a laugh. Because no one, nowhere, had ever been able to make themselves indifferent to Alexander Hamilton. My husband was loved and hated, but never a subject of dispassion. Not even in death.

And certainly I could never be indifferent to him, no matter how I'd deceived myself to the contrary. I'd never know if he went to Weehawken with the hope of losing his life. If he'd bedded my sister. Or a thousand harlots, for that matter, instead of just the Reynolds woman. These were mysteries for which I'd never have answers. And yet, coming here after all this time put me in a near state of self-destructive madness to know the truth.

It *must have* been madness, for I've no other explanation for the way I rose up again, suddenly, and charged after Lafayette. On the path by my sister's tomb, the old general turned, his eyes widening as I marched toward him with purpose and fury. "Did they laugh at me?"

Stopping amidst stone angels and sepulchers, Lafayette tilted his head in confusion, "*Madame*?"

"Laurens and Hamilton," I said, firing the names like bullets. "Did they laugh as Alexander drew up his list of qualifications for a wife, and then celebrate how easily simple, stupid, saintly Betsy Schuyler was wooed and won for her father's fortune?"

Lafayette seemed as startled by the question as I was to have allowed it past my lips. "The sun has addled your senses, *madame*. Let me get you from the heat."

But when he reached for me, I retreated. "I am not addled. Only insulted by the man I married."

"Insulted?" Lafayette softened his voice, as if gentling an unruly horse. "My memory for those years is very keen. I can say with conviction that never in my presence did any man disparage you, nor would I have allowed it, then or now. My dear lady, only a derangement of grief could lead you to think the husband who loved—"

"John Laurens," I said, thinking that perhaps I *was* deranged. For no woman of sound mind would admit this. "Alexander loved John Laurens."

There. I said it. And now it hovered between us like a cannonball just before impact.

I didn't know whether to be horrified or gratified to see a flicker of recognition in Lafayette's eyes. I thought he'd pretend at ignorance, or deny it, but instead, he shrugged. "I think so. But what of it?"

"*What of it?*"

I was, after all, not speaking of mere fraternity between brother soldiers. And yet I believed that Lafayette knew that perfectly well when he said, "*C'est la guerre.* That is war!"

Only a Frenchman would dismiss it with the permissiveness of a libertine, but *this* Frenchman defied kings and emperors in the pursuit of principle. He was known throughout the world as a deeply honorable man. And his words carried a tone that said such a relationship was less shameful than to question it. Which shocked me into silence.

"*Madame*," he said, more gently. "You are the mother of Hamilton's children, his wife, and his beloved companion of more than twenty years. Why should you be troubled by an attachment formed before you met?"

Did he think my resentments were petty jealousy—like a new bride enraged to discover her husband had once danced with a pretty girl at a ball? I, too, had formed attachments before I met Alexander Hamilton. But I did not feel guilty or disloyal for them, nor did I wish Lafayette to think me petty. "I'm troubled because I wasn't *beloved*. I've read the old letters, and they've poisoned everything."

*A good-hearted girl. Not a genius. Not a beauty.*

I could recite them line for line, but I told Lafayette only as much as I could bear, feeling diminished with every word I repeated. When I was finished, Lafayette rubbed at his face. "It is regrettable, what haunted people we are, you and I."

I stood, trembling, aghast at my indiscretion in matters that I feared must have seemed to him quite trivial. And now there was nothing to do but pray his pressing engagements would soon force a merciful end to our conversation. But Lafayette led me to a bench by the church doors, and settled into it, as if he meant to stay with me awhile.

He patted the bench. "Please, we are both of an age now when we must sit."

Suddenly tired and unimaginably weary, I sank beside him in silent mortification.

Meanwhile, he cast a serene gaze across the cemetery. "We are also of an age when we live in the past. We speak to old ghosts more real for us than the strangers of this new age who pass us on the street, yes? We try, in vain, to crawl into letters and memories for the comfort of those who cannot talk to us any longer."

Renewed shame washed over me. "I shouldn't have troubled you—"

"We have a saying in France," he interrupted. *"L'habit ne fait pas le moine.* The robe does not make the monk . . . do you understand?"

"No," I said, still trembling with humiliation.

"It means that the way things are clothed is not always as they are. Are you so modest, *madame,* that it has never occurred to you the letters Hamilton wrote *you* were the sincere ones?"

I took a deep breath as I digested his implication—that Alexander had deceived Laurens, not me.

Lafayette cleared his throat and rested his top hat on his knee. "If this has not occurred to you before, I can only think it is because of a delicate subject yet to be mentioned . . . *Bah.* What we do to women."

I brought my hands to my face with fear of what he might say next.

"My friend has left you haunted by some notion that he did not love you. And to see you in this state, I am now haunted by the idea I may have given my wife the same doubts. A husband at sixteen, what did I know! But there were other women even when I was old enough to appreciate what I had in a wife."

"Oh, no," I said, wanting him to stop talking. I *willed* him to stop talking.

But Lafayette was never a man easily silenced. "In America, a mistress is scandal. In France? Expected. In my mind, having nothing to do with my love for my wife. I am certain it was the same for my friend."

I gasped softly, my stomach clenching at the realization he was defending my husband. And all I could hear was my sister's words.

*All husbands stray.*

The memory made me so angry, I snapped, "I am long acquainted with these justifications."

"You mistake my purpose. I only mean to say that though a man might cause misfortune and pain to his loved ones, he can still love them. I spent five years in a dungeon, convinced I would die there, and yet, I did not actually know what it was to be unhappy until I lost my wife. That is how completely I loved her. My friend Hamilton loved you the same way."

"You cannot know that."

"How can I *not* know how he felt about you after a thousand intimate conversations?" Lafayette shifted toward me. "I am grateful to speak for a man who spoke for me when I was imprisoned and could not speak for myself. But what I say only echoes the voice inside you that already knows from a lifetime of kisses and tender proofs that Hamilton belonged to you. Hear me when I say there was never a person—not a soldier, coquette, or femme fatale—that he ever spoke of with such devotion, or besotted passion, as he spoke of you to me."

Oh, how dangerous were his words! Believing them would only lead to disappointment. No man could have been devoted to and besotted by me, and taken my sister as a mistress.

*Except perhaps for one man*, said that accursed inner voice that Lafayette had summoned. *Needy, insecure Alexander Hamilton, who could never forgo an impulse or resist the affections he'd been starved of as a child.*

And while these thoughts battered me, Lafayette took the liberty of resting his aged hand upon mine. "Maybe it is impossible to forgive. This I understand. But I beg of you remember that our dear Hamilton was not a man to govern his emotions. It was not in his nature. If ever you felt his love, it was real. Because to *pretend* at hate or friendship or love is possible for some men. But not for Hamilton. For him, impossible."

This, I couldn't deny. And Lafayette was, I realized, still a resourceful general. He'd somehow stolen inside my inner fortifications and brought them down. And now my defenses were left in smoldering ruins, leaving me only to retreat. "You are too loyal a friend."

"I take this for a compliment, *madame*."

Sniffing, and remembering a long-ago conversation with Hamilton, I shook my head. "I'm not sure that I meant it as one."

"Yet, I take it anyway," Lafayette replied. "Did I not sometimes find myself being angry with Hamilton, making within my heart a ridiculous fight between love and anger, and wishing for him to behave more sensibly? *Oui!* He was no perfect man. But he was a great one. It is only plain justice that his wife should remember him better. And his country, too."

# Chapter Forty-Two

LAFAYETTE WAS THE Guest of the Nation, and despite my repeated demurs, he was determined to win me to his side.

The general's campaign began the next morning when Georges delivered to us a handwritten invitation to attend the grand festival at the Castle Garden, along with a gift of a book by Fanny Wright, an advocate for women's rights and abolitionist school reformer who was traveling in Lafayette's entourage.

Clasping the book and the invitation with equal delight, Lysbet cried, "Can we go, Mama?"

I didn't relish the inevitable crowds, but it wouldn't do for me to be seen holding myself aloof from a celebration of Lafayette to which he'd specifically invited me. Besides, I wanted to make my daughter smile.

But when I told her we could go, her smile fell away. "Oh, but I have nothing to wear . . ."

My Lysbet, who'd never come out properly into society, possessed a wardrobe that consisted entirely of drab workaday calicos and one fancier brocaded gown for church. Her whole life, my Lysbet had patiently forborne the money spent to educate her brothers and the attention paid to her troubled sister. She wasn't the oldest, or the youngest, and therefore, had often been lost in the shuffle.

But she was the daughter I'd always wished for, and she deserved a ball gown.

It was far too late to employ a seamstress; there wasn't a tailor or sewing girl in the city not feverishly engaged in last-minute alterations for the forthcoming ball. But inside a very old and neglected trunk, I found a beguiling gown made of blue satin with a golden belt, embroidered in the pattern of a Greek key.

"It was your Aunt Angelica's," I said, unwrapping it. It was the gown my sister had worn to our dinner party at the Grange not long before Hamilton's death and it was now two decades out of style. I'd saved it—even when I'd wanted to burn every token of every person who ever hurt me—because when I'd burned Monroe's kerchief, it'd seemed almost to do him too much honor.

Nevertheless, I expected that the sight of the dress would pain me deeply, as all reminders of my sister now did. But when my daughter pulled the gown against herself and twirled, a different emotion rose in my breast. For the dress flattered Lysbet to the point of transformation, revealing the natural beauty she usually hid behind seriousness and spectacles.

Instead of pain, I felt nothing but my daughter's joy.

And that now seemed to be a wonderful gift. One my sister had made possible.

"Oh, but the beadwork and embroidery," Lysbet suddenly fretted. "It's too much for a dedicated spinster. Too much for me by far."

"It's exactly right," I said, taking up my needle. It'd been years since I'd dedicated much time to my sewing, and doing it now in the service of my daughter's happiness seemed the best cause. "We shall make it a perfect fit."

And when that was accomplished, I retrieved for Lysbet an ancient pair of blue paste earbobs to match. Earbobs that made me remember that whatever Angelica had done, or been, she'd also been my touchstone—always finding small ways to support and embolden me as I now wished to support and embolden my daughter.

As for me, my own formal attire was greatly simplified by virtue of widowhood. I owned one black gown proper for such an occasion, scented by the cedar chips with which it had been stored. Thus, donning a bonnet and the pearl-encrusted pendant in which Washington's hair was enclosed, I braced myself to return to society.

We went by carriage to the Battery from whence my husband first stole British cannons and made his reputation at the start of the revolution. The bridge to the Castle Garden was covered with rich carpets from one end to the other. In the middle of the bridge arose a pyramid sixty-five feet high, lit with colored lamps and surmounted by a brilliant star in the center which blazed the name *Lafayette*. And then we stepped into the magnificent entryway to find a vast amphitheater inside the circle of the old fort, containing at least a thousand torches and nearly six thousand persons.

An eager crowd jostled Lysbet and I beneath an arch formed of the flags of all nations, surmounted by a colossal statue of Washington. I expected always to encounter the Father of the Nation at any celebration, but I didn't expect to find a richly decorated marquee ornamented, upon a platform, with a bust of my husband and two pieces of cannon taken at Yorktown.

"It's Papa!" Lysbet cried with a breath of astonishment, as if she'd never expected or dared to hope to see her father honored outside of our intimate circle of family and friends. And my heart seized to see her hands go to her mouth, as if to contain her surprise and joy.

Had Lafayette arranged for this display? And was it meant for the crowd or for me?

*He was not a perfect man. But he was a great one. It is only plain justice that his wife should remember him better. And his country, too.*

I was still not convinced by Lafayette's argument, even as a murmur rushed through the crowd around us. *"It's Mrs. General Hamilton!"*

The whispers rose like the murmur of the sea, and Lysbet clutched my hand. "Everyone's staring."

They were. And I met their gazes. Each and every one. And what I saw reflected back at me, after so many years out of the public eye, was a pleasant surprise. Admiration. Curiosity.

And without question, respect.

In that moment, a curly-haired officer in uniform and sash bumped into us so hard that Lysbet would've fallen if he hadn't caught her by the waist. "Oh, dear. I am so very sorry," he said, looking not a bit sorry. Forgoing all protocol that might've required a gentleman should be introduced, he presented himself as one Lieutenant Sidney Holly.

We returned the introduction—forced as we were to it—and the young man's cheeks reddened. "*Hamilton*?" With wide eyes, he glanced at the bust, then back at us, seeming so discomforted that I thought he must be a rabid Republican. But then he said, "I daresay I wouldn't have employment without your father's innovations, Miss Hamilton. I work as a customs inspector."

"Is that so?" my daughter said, smiling shyly.

Awkwardness hung between them, and he finally gave a little bow. "If you'll excuse me," he said, apologizing again. And again.

"That poor man," Lysbet said once he'd gone. "There's no cause for him to be so embarrassed for an accident."

"That was no accident," I said, explaining what she'd have known if she'd attended as many balls as I had. "Bumping into a young lady is an old trick employed by young men lacking the means of obtaining a proper introduction. He's embarrassed because, upon hearing your father's name, he realized he blundered quite above his station."

"*Truly*?" Lysbet said, her eyes widening in apparent delight at his impudence. She turned to smile much less shyly in the direction of the man's retreat.

Just then, Lafayette appeared to the tune of "See the Conquering Hero Comes." We found our seats, and the cloths that surrounded and enclosed the hall rose like a curtain at the theater to reveal the pure and brilliant moon shining on the harbor, upon which steamboats were plying in every direction.

Several times that magical evening, dances were attempted, but every time Lafayette approached them, the dancers broke off and came to group themselves around him. Young ladies swooned when he kissed their hands upon introduction. And he obliged them all, except for one girl, who presented a gloved hand which he refused. "Your pretty glove is stamped with my face, *mademoiselle,* and I am not so egotistical that I can kiss myself!"

When the laughter died down, mothers presented their children and, asking his blessing, feeble old men reanimated in talking to him of the numerous battles in which they'd been engaged with him for the sake of liberty. Free black men reminded him of his philanthropic efforts to place them in the rank, which horrid prejudices still denied them. And young men whose hard and blackened hands announced their laborious occupations stopped before him and said, "We also belong to the ten millions who are indebted to you for liberty and happiness!"

Despite all the Republicans had done to ruin the country, I couldn't help but be a little stirred by the plain evidence of how many of my fellow Americans now thrived.

Before long, Georges made his way through the throngs of well-wishers sharing with him their admiration for his father to seek *us* out. "We wish to know if you and your mother will be pleased to share the berth across from our own, Miss Hamilton."

"A berth?" Lysbet asked, her nose pink from just a few sips of champagne.

"On the steamboat," Georges said, tilting his head. "We depart just after midnight."

Lysbet pulled her shawl around her in bewilderment. "Where to?"

Now Georges was equally bewildered. "My father says you're to accompany us on our journey up the river."

At this, my daughter gasped with delight. As, of course, Lafayette knew she would. What a wily man! Annoyed that the Frenchman should still be so sly as to wield my daughter's excitement against me, I said, "I fear your father has misunderstood, Georges. We cannot join you."

Lysbet had perhaps sipped more champagne than I realized because she put a hand to her hip and demanded to know, "Why not?"

Why not, indeed.

At the age of sixty-seven, I didn't go anywhere after midnight, much less on a journey up the Hudson. But before I could say as much, the old hero stole upon us and laughed. "She asks *why not*? Spoken like a Lafayette! Come with me, ladies, at least as far as West Point."

"General," I began, aware of what felt like six thousand pairs of eyes now fixed upon us. "We are honored by your invitation and generous attention. But the hour grows so late—"

"We accept," Lysbet interrupted me, with extraordinary impertinence. "Gladly."

"Lysbet!" I hissed.

Something had come over my daughter. I didn't know if it was the ball gown, the idea of further conversation with her curly haired beau, or seeing the bust of her father. Whatever the cause, Lysbet grabbed my hand. "Wouldn't my father go with Lafayette, and since he cannot, shouldn't we?"

Of course, her father would go. Alexander, the hero of Yorktown, would have every right, *in justice*, to ride in glory beside Lafayette. To deny it would be to deny his children the recognition and honor they craved all their lives. The cruelty of the world had denied them this.

How could I deny it to them, too?

"Ah, I see I have it wrong," Lafayette said with a mischievous wink. "She is a Hamilton through and through."

Outflanked by the pair of them, I threw up my hands. "But . . . we have nothing packed."

Lafayette made an elaborate, twirling gesture with his hand. "And what of it? When we were young, you climbed into a sleigh with only a satchel and drove off with me into the wilderness."

This memory was a warm and delightful one. It was also a story my daughter didn't know. As Lafayette told it, he made me remember the young and adventurous woman I used to be. And, quite unexpectedly, I yearned for her . . .

"So I beg you," Lafayette said. "Come with me tonight."

Despite his words, Lafayette was not begging. He was issuing a command. And though I had defied victorious generals before, I didn't have the heart to resist or resent him for it. Especially when Lysbet looked happier than I'd ever before seen her, and multitudes clamored for the opportunity to take my place.

Drunk on champagne and celebration, the whole city wished to climb aboard Lafayette's steamship and chug away with him. And so, quite irregularly and recklessly, that is exactly what we did.

THAT NIGHT, A great number of prominent citizens, unwilling to part with Lafayette, crowded onto the ship deck with us until the captain was forced to refuse even one more.

Then, to a setting moon, we lost sight of the Castle Garden amidst the noisy cadence of the steam machinery struggling against the waves and current of the river. The river that tied me to my past . . .

Though the steamboat contained more than eighty beds, the crowd had not been foreseen and the greater part of the men slept upon the deck. Nevertheless, I don't believe any of us slept much, because every few minutes cannons announced our passage by some village. So at sunrise, I abandoned my berth and went above deck to enjoy the view of the majestic banks of the Hudson.

I was at Lafayette's side when a group of old revolutionary soldiers gathered at the rail, sharing stories from their service. "There I wept for an enemy," Lafayette said, pointing to the spot where he'd sat in court-martial over the British spymaster Major

André, and seen him hanged. And I knew, should we keep chugging north, we'd pass Sugarloaf Mountain and the house on the shoreline from whence Benedict Arnold fled to the British Army, my husband in desperate pursuit.

I heard the word *traitor* murmured by more than one man. And I nearly murmured it myself, remembering that I was with Arnold when I met Lafayette, though I hadn't thought of that day in years. Now, those harrowing times of the war came back to me. Names of towns and soldiers and battlefields in this valley stirred memories for me, too. *Fort Ticonderoga*, the loss of which cost my father his command. *Saratoga*, where Burgoyne burned our home to the ground before being forced to surrender. *Albany*, where loyalists broke into my father's home and nearly chopped us with a hatchet. *New Windsor*, where Alexander and I first lived as newlyweds and where I learned the story of Captain Molly.

I had not, like Captain Molly, taken up arms or shed blood in the cause.

But I'd stitched up and cared for those who did. I'd traveled with Washington's army and shared some of its privations—and I imagined myself in fraternity with these brother soldiers, looking out upon the country we'd brought into being.

And to my astonishment, I felt as if I belonged with them on this journey after all . . .

As if to banish any doubt, Lafayette said, "When I first came to this valley, I found the high mountains, with their thick forests and naked rocks, all along this river, so imposing. It was difficult not to share the superstitious terror of the Indians. Unless, of course, one has a Schuyler at his side . . . as I did then, and now."

I warmed at his praise and the way it earned me the deference of our fellows. And as the sun glinted off the river that day, dazzling my eyes with its brilliance, I realized how the country had grown past the wilderness of my youth under the rule of the British crown. Everywhere I looked, new towns and modern wharves grew up, all peopled by two generations who'd come of age thinking of themselves as Americans.

And despite my anger and disappointments, my heart swelled with pride. *Pride and love of country.*

Could I truly still feel such a thing?

In seeking his oblivion, my husband had wrapped himself in his patriotism, thereby diminishing mine. Then, Jefferson, Burr, Madison, and Monroe had buried my family, captured my government, and claimed its flag. But it didn't belong to any of them more than it belonged to me. And I should never have allowed them to steal it away.

For they might be fathers of this unruly and flawed nation, but, surely, then, I'd been one of its *mothers.*

As if sensing some change in me, Lafayette leaned in and pointed to the aft railing. "Shall I stand in Hamilton's place and take up my ancient sword in defense of your daughter's virtue?"

I turned and frowned to see Lysbet in the crowd, flirting with Lieutenant Holly from the night before. "That impudent young man nearly toppled her into a tray of champagne at the ball just to secure an introduction."

Lafayette chuckled. "And yet, she is taken with him. It seems your daughter is very much like you."

"A fool for a man in uniform? Yes, I suppose so."

"I was going to say, a woman with a forgiving heart . . ." I stared at the presumption of his implication, and he actually laughed. "Forgive my friend, Hamilton," Lafayette said, as if he'd sensed the softening in me toward the man without whom I suppose I could never have become what I was. "You see how, everywhere I go, people press gifts into my hands. Weapons, jewelry, Indian artifacts, things of great value to them. So why not give me this gift of forgiving Hamilton?"

I peered around us, but no one paid any mind to our intimate exchange. "You take advantage, General."

He shrugged, incorrigible. "I cannot help myself, *madame.* After spending so many years in a prison, my mind becomes sharp to the things that truly matter in this world."

And *Hamilton* mattered.

We didn't have time to say more when another round of cannons fired as the steamboat docked for a day of ceremonies at West Point, where I would be Lafayette's honored guest.

Below, crowds shouted, *Long live liberty! Long live Lafayette! Honor to Lafayette! Honor to him who fought and shed his blood for the peace and happiness we enjoy!*

With a wave, Lafayette shouted back, "Honor to Hamilton, too!" I put a hand upon his arm to stop him, but he only patted it. "He should be honored. As should you. Travel with me, *madame*. I like seeing this country with you, and I am to go west."

*West.* Even at my age, I was still unexpectedly tantalized by the idea. As tantalized as the first time Lafayette asked me to go off with him into the wilds. And he must have sensed it, because he pressed his advantage. "I will pass through the Oneida homeland. Together we can call upon some of our old comrades. We shall visit Grasshopper and Two Kettles Together."

I was taken by surprise that he did not know—that no one had told him—that he would not find many Oneida left in the world. Grasshopper had passed away long ago. Two Kettles Together, only recently. And the Oneida nation had dwindled. Despite all they'd done for the nation during the revolution, and federal treaties recognizing their service, the state government had all but defrauded the People of the Standing Stone of their lands. So I explained, as gently as I could, "Very few Oneida still reside amongst us. Like the rest of the Iroquois, they've been forced to migrate."

Lafayette's usually sunny expression fell into such grave disappointment that I felt ashamed. Perhaps he was remembering how our time with the Oneidas changed the course of the war. Perhaps he was remembering his own role in helping to negotiate the Treaty of Fort Stanwix that secured the Oneida their lands. Whatever the thoughts in his mind, I knew he was one of the few persons present who cared about the fate of our allied Indians. And even those who'd been our enemies. "Then it is good we go west," Lafayette finally said. "Perhaps we will see the Oneida there. We may travel as far as the wilds of Illinois."

"Two Kettles Together's son is in the Illinois territory," I said, musing on the idea. "And so is my son William."

I smiled at the notion of adventure and of seeing William again. Because I realized that I was not only capable of the trip, but also *interested*—for the first time in so long.

But I'd come far enough.

Far enough, at least, to recover, as the French would say, my *joie de vivre*.

And I had Lafayette to thank for it all.

Just as at the start of the revolution, this Frenchman was the lucky talisman who opened the way to a better future. As much as I desired it, I didn't need to see the wilds of the country to find my place in it. I already knew. I had my work to think of, and a city full of orphaned children who needed me.

"*Bah*," he said, seeing that my mind was set. "While I am gone, at least agree you will think on all I've said. Hamilton's story should be remembered. It should be told, and it should be *written*."

"A biography has been tried," I admitted, remembering how I was hampered before by Federalists and Republicans alike. How Reverend Mason's efforts ultimately came to nothing. "But too many of Alexander's letters are scattered and too many people do not want his story told."

Lafayette's eyes narrowed a moment. "His foes oppose you?"

I chuckled a little bitterly. "With respect to his papers, it's his *friends* who have created the greatest obstacle."

A few years earlier, just before he died, Nathaniel Pendleton confessed to stealing my husband's drafts of the Farewell Address and conspiring with fellow Federalists to keep the papers "in trust and under seal," which was simply gracious language for keeping them from me. But I'd learned of this at the depths of my fury at Hamilton and done nothing about it.

Now, in defense of myself, I said, "I am refused even simple requests to see his papers."

"I think that *I* will not be refused. After all, you are the only person with the temerity to rebuff the Guest of the Nation."

I laughed, but also felt an ember of hope. "I don't rebuff you, General. It's only that I don't wish to give false hopes."

"I have been reproached all my life for giving in too much to my hopeful disposition, but one would never try anything extraordinary if one despaired of success."

"No, I suppose they wouldn't," I murmured, his words working their way into my heart.

"Then, my dear Mrs. Hamilton," he said, leaning close, "no longer despair."

# Chapter Forty-Three

*Spring 1825*
*Harlem*

THE WINDOWLESS ATTIC didn't make for a majestic courtroom. The only light to be had was from lanterns I hung
from the wooden rafters. The only witnesses, the spiders.
Perhaps that was best, since, pushing through the cobwebs of this
place—and my memories—I alone would play judge and jury.

And as for Hamilton, well, he would represent himself. He'd
been a magnificent lawyer in life. But in death, the words he
wrote would have to stand for him without addition or deletion
or the animation of his voice or expression.

And in seating myself before a trunk of letters—the personal
ones, the *painful* ones—I prepared to review the evidence again.
In the interest of justice, I told myself. Nothing more.

Because Lafayette was right. Alexander Hamilton deserved to
be better remembered by his country. His story deserved to be
written. But neither would happen unless I became his champion
again, and I didn't know if he deserved *that* from *me*.

Thus, I examined the first charge against him. Did my husband take my sister for his lover?

I'd so often heard him argue in court that I could well imagine
what he'd say.

*It hasn't been proven!*

What was the evidence, after all? There was no direct admission of guilt by either of them. Not in life nor in death. The most damning thing, in the end, hadn't been the letters or tokens or gossip or befuddled utterances under the influence of laudanum. The most damning thing had been my husband's accounting book, which proved he paid Angelica's expenses and rented for her a mysterious apartment.

And yet, if I took that for proof of an affair, must I not also note that, except for that one visit, nothing like it ever appeared in his books before or after? If there'd been an affair—

*If,* Hamilton's voice echoed in my mind with pointed reminder.

Yes, well, *if* my husband took my sister for a lover, the intimacy was most likely confined to that one visit when Angelica was estranged from Church. When Hamilton was drunk on power—drunk enough to fall into bed with Maria Reynolds and pay a blackmailer besides.

When he'd confessed that, I hadn't asked him if there were other women.

*And yet you said you forgave me everything,* Hamilton's voice echoed again, and I glared at a dark corner of the attic where I could almost see him pacing, formulating his arguments.

I had said that, hadn't I? It was just like him to remember a finer point.

When, thinking we were dying of yellow fever, I might have insisted that he confess *all* his sins. But I hadn't demanded an accounting of his infidelities or vices, nor a listing of the things he said he'd done to imperil his soul. I'd merely accepted him, the whole of him, and forgiven.

As if the yellow fever had burned us both clean of all our sins.

Perhaps that's what he believed. What good would it have done then to confess something that would've destroyed my relationship with my sister—the strength of which was sometimes the only thing that kept me alive?

*And what if they were innocent?*

I slammed the account book shut and put it back into the trunk as the notion sent a trickle of sweat down my spine. I remembered my father once saying how vile a knave he would've considered himself if he were to have accused my mother, and been wrong. It was entirely possible that Angelica's last words were only confused mutterings mixed with her determination in hiding her illness from me. Not an affair. Entirely possible that my sister kept tokens of a beloved brother-in-law, just as I'd kept tokens of beloved friends. What if I'd allowed my own heart to blacken against a loving sister and an innocent husband who had already been so unfairly slandered by others . . .

*I'd forgive you anything, so long as you loved me,* Hamilton had once said to me.

I did love him. For all the good it had done me. Maybe I'd even loved him enough to forgive the unforgivable. Because my sister was right to say that love was a thing beyond reason . . . even if it were a crime.

Before we met, Hamilton loved a man named John Laurens. But that was not the crime with which I charged him. Instead, I asked, *Did Hamilton love me?*

In the heat of our courtship, when I suggested eloping, Hamilton claimed to worry he'd be thought a self-seeking, fortune-hunting seducer, angling for advantage. Was that what he really was, in the end?

I remembered—with a start—that the girl I was then had decided to love him, even if he were all those things. And that it was Hamilton who insisted it must all be done right. Hamilton who risked losing the fortune he told John Laurens he was after. The fortune I represented, if that was his aim . . .

I pulled from the trunk the bundle of letters more yellowed and faded with age than the first time I had read them more than ten years earlier. Touching that dark lock of hair belonging to the South Carolinian gentleman who'd haunted my life seemed to unlatch my sanity a bit. Or perhaps it was merely the heat rising to the attic and addling my senses. Whatever the cause, the next words, I spoke aloud. "Well, Mr. Hamilton, your friend Lafayette has offered you a defense. Let us see what you have to say for yourself."

Straightening my spine and taking a deep bracing breath, I unfolded the pages. I'd committed the painful words to memory but was determined to give them a just reading.

> *Next fall completes my doom. I give up my liberty to Miss Schuyler. She is a good-hearted girl who I am sure will never play the termagant; though not a genius she has good sense enough to be agreeable, and though not a beauty, she has fine black eyes—is rather handsome and has every other requisite of the exterior to make a lover happy.*

That was as far as my heart had been able to see through my tears when I first read this letter. But now I noticed the next line.

> *And believe me, I am a lover in earnest.*

I noticed the date on this letter and the ones before it, too. How curious that Hamilton should've waited four months to tell his friend that he was to marry. As if jilting a sweetheart. One didn't, after all, praise a new lover to the one being replaced. One deprecated, made light of the new infatuation. And Laurens begged my husband not to withdraw from him the *consolation* of his letters. Perhaps he understood it was an ending.

How to balance this against all the letters Hamilton sent me? Since I didn't have a scale, I read them again. All of them. Even the one I tore to bits, ten years before, in rage and anger and grief. I'd ripped apart the sonnet he wrote me in Morristown. Hamilton's first declaration of love. I'd torn it up but—tellingly, I suppose—I'd kept the pieces.

Now, with a needle and thread, I sewed the fragile words back together. And with each stitch, I felt closer and closer to binding the wound.

My eyes swam with tears as I read the reassembled lines.

> *Before no mortal ever knew*
> *A love like mine so tender, true*

*Did you mean it, Alexander?* I asked myself as I pierced the final scrap of paper with the needle's tip. *Did you truly love?*

Dear God, the indignity of being interrogated after death. Whatever else might come of this trial, I decided that I would never leave my own letters behind to be cross-examined and vivisected. Like the corpses in the bloody Doctors' Riot so many years ago. Like Alexander's motives, investigated by several inquests and the whole country. And by me . . .

Which brought me to the third charge. The one I scarcely allowed myself to acknowledge.

Was the duel with Burr a fight for the nation? A vainglorious exercise in futility? Or something worse? One, last, suicidal chariot ride across the sky?

I'd read the witness accounts. I knew both men. I'd even seen Burr recently—two years ago when, by happenstance, he slunk onto a ferry just as I was getting off, and the anxious crowd parted so we were face-to-face, leaving me to stare into those eyes in search of the truth. But seeing only the pathetic emptiness of his soul, I'd left Burr with a withering glare and without answers.

For there was nothing Burr could say to right one single wrong between us.

So maybe I could never know what Alexander intended that day at Weehawken. Because the people we love are not entirely knowable. Even to themselves. But we love them anyway.

The only other choice is to live without love, alone.

*What then, is the verdict?* the spiders seemed to ask, as if they were weaving a web of memories around me.

Studying the patchwork sonnet now repaired in my lap and my wedding ring beside it, I didn't know what the verdict was. A judge and jury must deliberate, after all, so I adjourned the court. And the place I deliberated was in my garden, where I gathered the last blooms of purple hyacinths.

But a verdict was finally forced upon me by a calling card.

And by James Monroe.

# Chapter Forty-Four

**M**ONROE IS STANDING in my parlor at the Grange, and everything, my whole life it seems, comes full circle.

I should have expected it. Monroe is, after all, not so much a visitor as a closing argument . . .

"I find that the lapse of time brings its softening influences," Monroe is saying, in that deceptively sweet southern accent. "Now we are both nearing the grave, when past differences can be forgiven and forgotten . . ."

*Forgiven and forgotten,* he says. And my eyes drift to the dappled light of the entryway, where a bust of my husband has sat for more than twenty years. I've put Hamilton on trial. And now, here in the flesh, stands one of my husband's many enemies and accusers.

"I remember a time, Mrs. Hamilton, when we counted one another as friends," Monroe continues, wistfully, as if he is remembering. And, of course, I am remembering, too. Remembering with a bittersweet pang how we met, the friendship we shared in war, in peace, over games of backgammon and sightseeing in Philadelphia with our young families while building a new world.

But I remember also that James Monroe was a man who gave me his word of honor and broke it. A man who hurt me and exposed me to humiliation. He isn't the only person I've cared about who betrayed me. There have been so many others. But he's the only one I can face now. And so I do. Using my silence as a weapon, forcing him to continue speaking until he finds the words that might reach me. Because as I once said to Monroe, life, like backgammon, is a game of perseverance in which you're forced to choose the best move, even if it is only a choice between evils.

I face such a choice now.

"Despite our differences, I've tried to look after your sons," Monroe says.

Alex, he means. He named my son a U.S. attorney and a land commissioner—and I ought to be grateful. My sons *are* grateful. James especially has found a way to ingratiate himself with the Republicans. All James had to do was say that his father's policies were wrong, and pretend it was the Jeffersonians, instead of the Hamiltonians, who brought this government into being.

Perhaps I could pretend, too. Accepting this lie and making amends would raise the stature of our family. Perhaps I would even be considered a stateswoman for reconciling with Monroe. After all, they say that in the end, John Adams and Thomas Jefferson made friends again. And that was after having savaged one another in a presidential election.

So in truth, there is no good reason to hold myself aloof from Monroe anymore. Not when the man has come to my house, hat in hand. And I soften a little, remembering a time when Monroe offered me comfort and compassion when I desperately needed both.

I remember, too, what he said in defense of himself when I blamed him for exposing me to the Reynolds scandal.

*It was the scoundrel to whom you pledged your troth who exposed you to this. Not me.*

That is the plain truth at the bottom of it. I know this now better than I knew it then.

But when offering comfort, he also said, *You are a kind, lovely, and charming woman and you deserve much better than—*

I cut him off then, because he was going to say that I deserved better than Alexander Hamilton. Monroe was going to say that I ought to have married someone like *him*. A gentleman of honor born on the right side of the blanket. Monroe thought he was the better man.

No doubt he thinks it still. *That* is why he's standing here now in my parlor offering what might pass, to the uninitiated political novice, as an olive branch. He's still trying to prove that he's the better man.

But he's not offered an apology and he owes one. Not just to me, but to the country.

This is, after all, a man who was president of a nation he never wished to come into being. Monroe had opposed the Constitution. And he helped Jefferson oppose damned near everything else. The debt, the bank, the Jay Treaty, and a standing army that would've prevented the nation's capital from being burned to the ground. In short, James Monroe set himself against nearly every good measure bound to bring about the more perfect union of which he was now considered a founder.

That he was a true hero in the Revolutionary War, I will never deny. That he finally came round to seeing good sense in some matters, I will grant. I can even give grudging admiration for his political genius in wrapping himself in the flag in an attempt to prevent the nation's disunion.

But James Monroe is not now and never was the better man. None of them were.

Not Jefferson. Not Adams. Not Burr. Not Madison. Not Monroe.

And for him to speak of our *differences* as if, instead of taking opposite sides in great moral questions, we'd all merely quarreled about how many lumps of sugar to take in tea! Oh, no.

If Alexander had lived, he'd have never let that stand. He'd have challenged Monroe just as he challenged me, and everyone else, every day of his life. And I am a better person for it.

I live in a better *world* because of Alexander Hamilton.

And so do we all.

It's the promise he fulfilled while other men took credit for it. Men like Monroe.

I see *all* of them in Monroe's gray eyes. Jefferson. Burr. Adams. Every man who spread lies about us or tried to climb up a bloody ladder of political power, the rungs of which were made from my family's bones.

Which is why I won't surrender.

They cannot have my country. They cannot have my flag.

And they cannot have my dear Hamilton.

He *was* mine, even if he was not *only* mine. Just like the country and the flag. They don't belong to anyone else to define as they please without my say. Neither does Hamilton. I will *not* politely agree to lies about my husband's legacy and call it history.

A marriage is like a union of states, requiring countless dinner table bargains to hold it together. There may be irreconcilable differences brewing below the surface that can come to open rupture. And there is, in a marriage, as in a nation, a certain amount of storytelling we do to make it understood. Even if those stories we tell to make our marriage, or country, work don't paint the whole picture, they're still *true*. But to leave Alexander Hamilton out of the painting entirely is a lie.

I know the truth. Which is why I realize now—or perhaps I've known it all along and been too proud to admit it—that whatever secrets my husband kept were born from fear of losing me.

He loved me.

*Doubt thou the stars are fire. Doubt that the sun doth move; Doubt truth to be a liar; But never doubt I love.*

A verdict. At last. And I am, at long last, ready to deliver it.

"Mr. Monroe," I finally say, my voice clear, cold, and resolved, my spine straight as an Indian arrow. "If you've come to tell me you repent—that you're sorry, *very sorry*, for the misrepresentations and slanders you circulated against my dear husband—if you've come to say this, I understand. But otherwise, no lapse of time, no nearness to the grave, makes any difference."

Monroe blinks, plainly stunned. But I rejoice at the truth of my words.

*No lapse of time, no nearness to the grave or distance from it makes any difference.*

For I find inside myself love where I'd not expected it to be. Both for a flawed nation and a flawed man. *Love.* A thing so powerful it can overcome the divide of time and death. It's still there inside me, like an eternal flame, though the light it casts is different now.

As Monroe strides out of the room without another word, much less an apology, I realize I've been asking the wrong questions and examining the wrong evidence. I've asked myself who Alexander Hamilton was. I ought to have asked who *I* am. And now I know.

I am a Schuyler. *Semper Fidelis.*

Always faithful. Always loyal. And I will never again let my dear Hamilton be forgotten.

*Epilogue*

*March 1837*
*On the Ohio River*

HAMILTON ALWAYS DID have to have the last word. And so, it seems, do I.

For the past decade, I've fought to make sure my husband isn't written out of the history of the country he helped found. I've fought and *won*.

In the end, I filed a lawsuit to retrieve the papers Nathaniel Pendleton stole from me and the Federalists tried to keep from ever seeing the light of day—drafts of President Washington's Farewell Address in Alexander's hand that proved his authorship. And seeing those old scribblings—the notes we made together—I was overcome with emotions.

For that address defined what this nation is, has been, and what it shall ever be. It also defined *us*. Alexander and me. Sitting together, matching wits as partners and patriots and parents seeking to build a better future for our children, and their children, too.

I'm gratified now that I've finally held Alexander's biography in my own hands. The first volume anyway. Written by my son Johnny, the whole work will be long, wordy, thorough, and in multiple parts. Just as it should be. Having shouldered the great weight of it for more than three decades, I feel as though I can finally take a deep breath.

And now, like more and more of my countrymen, I am westward bound.

I may not have a long time remaining, but I resolve to see as much of this country as I can. And set one last matter to right. With both triumph and trepidation, I travel with Lysbet and her husband, Sidney Augustus Holly, the curly haired customs inspector she met at Lafayette's ball. He's not a man of great means, but their happiness together is evident, which is why I gave my blessing. And they both wish to accompany me partly out of curiosity and the desire for adventure, and partly because my children feel the need to chaperone me, at eighty years old—as if I haven't outlived nearly everyone I once knew, including my enemies.

Monroe passed away only a few years after our final reckoning—a heart ailment, they say.

Destitute and alone, Aaron Burr died with a grimace. His death mask is kept as an object of amusement in a museum that brags of *the busts, casts, and skulls, human and animal, of some of the most distinguished men that ever lived, along with those of pirates, robbers, and murderers.*

I know the category to which Burr belongs.

Yes, I have outlived them all. Even Thomas Jefferson and John Adams, the Jacobin and the madman, who saw fit to die on the very same day, and upon the fiftieth anniversary of the Declaration of Independence at that. In his eulogy for them, Daniel Webster said that no two men had given a more lasting direction to our country.

Webster was then and remains now, quite simply, wrong.

I give credit to Jefferson for the power of his Declaration. Even *I* can grant him that. And there's an argument to be made that we'd never have declared our independence at all without Adams. But otherwise, the two men who most shaped *America* did not die together on the fiftieth anniversary of that heralded declaration.

One died nearly thirty-three years ago. And the other survived until just recently.

Alexander Hamilton and James Madison.

Those two men made America.

I learned of Jemmy's recent passing with a bolt of unexpected grief. Now, remembering how warmly he and Dolley received me at the White House, I feel the keenest sympathy for her loss. I wonder if I shall ever see her again to convey such sentiments in person.

I'd like to. But there's a more important reunion I must bring about.

I must see my son.

I must have William home again from the wilds of America, where he fled in the wake of my suspicions about his father. I've made peace with Alexander. More importantly, I've made peace with myself. And I believe that all my husband's sacrifices and contributions—all *our* sacrifices and contributions—outweigh our personal, private failings.

I need William to see that, too.

Thus, at the first signs of spring, Lysbet, her husband, and I set off on a four-day stagecoach trip from New York to Pittsburgh, then down the wide Ohio. Weeks we steam along that waterway, and it seems only right that, despite how far William wandered, I'm still able to reach him by river, as if, all this time, we've been connected by the thread of life stitching through this great land.

The farther west we go, towns give way to villages, which give way to mere wharfs. And I'm struck by the spirit of the American people, by the bravery and ingenuity of those intrepid enough to build new homes and communities. I can't help but wonder what my husband, who once crossed an ocean to find a new land of opportunity, would think of *these* new lands.

He will never know this America, but I am grateful that I can.

Though my gratitude is bittersweet. Because these lands—and others like them all over our country's western frontier—are not settled without a price. And that great cost is borne by the Indians. With the support of southerners who want ever more land for cotton and slavery, our government keeps pushing the Indians father west.

Proof that the great project of securing human rights through our revolution remains unfinished . . .

Upon the steamboat, the great wheel creates a constant hum and vibration to which my body becomes accustomed as the weeks pass. We steam through Cincinnati and Louisville before finally reaching the Mississippi in late May. From there, we steam northward, until we pass the quite considerable city at St. Louis, which boasts of over ten thousand inhabitants. Finally, the Mississippi carries us to Galena, Illinois, the largest steamboat hub in the north.

And William is there waiting.

I barely recognize him. Not simply because twenty years have passed since I've seen him last, but also because he's embraced the look of a frontiersman. He wears the coarsest of trousers and a plain, threadbare shirt, clean but well used. Upon his head sits a slouched hat. Only his boots and his shave appear new, the latter of which is confirmed when a few of his fellows tease about the disappearance of his beard.

"Hello, Mother," he says, stiffly, helping me down off of the gangway.

"Oh, my dear William. You look . . ." I shake my head, overcome at the sight of him. Despite the rough edges, he's the spitting image of his father, and every bit as handsome. But I don't say any of that. "Well, it just does my heart so good to see you."

We embrace, but it ends too soon, and then he greets the Hollys, offers me his arm, and guides us to a wagon hitched with two black horses.

It's an hour's ride to William's home in the neighboring Wisconsin Territory. "I should like for my town to someday be known as Wiota," he says, casting me an appraising look, "but most insist on calling it Hamilton's Diggings."

I smile with delight. "Hamilton's Diggings? How grand! Perhaps I can now claim to have a town, too." He peers at me quizzically, and I remind him of a story he no doubt heard and forgot long ago. "When you were small, your cousin Flip named a town upon the Genesee River for your aunt Angelica." I've traveled a thousand miles to see my son, but in so easily mentioning my sister's name, I realize how far I've truly come.

Lysbet excitedly calls out, "Oh, how exciting! Do we have a river, too, then?"

Something close to a grin stirs upon William's face as he glances back at his sister. "We do. The Pecatonica."

I try these Indian words out on my tongue, liking the feel of their newness there. And in William, I can't help but see another similarity with his father—he's yet another Hamilton creating a new country. But I don't tell him that either. "How extraordinary," I say instead, surveying the lush greenery covering the mostly flat lands where blue-purple flowers dot the wild grasses as far as the eye can see.

"I wouldn't have encouraged you to come here, Mother," he says, adjusting his hold on the reins. "This isn't New York. Everything is raw. Though my mine has been in operation for nearly ten years, I only surveyed the town last year, and it is just eight buildings. We're at the frontier."

"Fortunately, I remember what it's like to live on the frontier," I say, tightly gripping the rail along the bench seat's edge. For the transporting of lead from the mines has rendered the roads nearly impassable. I fear the wheels will not withstand the harsh impacts, but William navigates the hazards with competence and obvious experience.

Then he waves a hand at the land ahead of us. "My partners and I claimed over a thousand acres out here. My furnace was the first in the eastern part of the county. Now miners come in droves to try to make their fortunes."

A few buildings come into view, rough hewn and strewn along a river strong enough to operate a gristmill and a sawmill. The village possesses a grocery and a general store, and we pass a small schoolhouse just beyond. In the distance appears the remains of an old fort surrounded by pickets and ditch.

William tells me it's called Fort Hamilton, and that gives me pleasure.

"Welcome to Hamilton's Diggings," he says, calling the team to a halt in front of two sturdy log cabins and watching me for a reaction. I make sure not to give him one, even as I wonder how he can possibly live in this place. For his cabin has no glass upon the window openings, and the door stands partly ajar.

He jumps down from the wagon, then comes round to assist me.

Entering the little hovel, I find naught but a rude bedstead with some dingy quilts and buffalo robes, an oaken table, a pair of wooden stools, and a few shelves of books. All is as tidy as can be with the wind blowing through the windows and door, which has only a string latch upon it. I step closer to the books, smiling to find the works of Voltaire, in French.

At forty, William has never married. This cabin makes it clear that he has no intention of doing so. And I worry that he's going to spend the rest of his life alone.

*Come home with me*, I want to say. *We'll make things right.*

But when I turn, I find my son observing us taking in his space, and I can't say a word. His smile is slow in coming, as if he thinks I won't approve of his living conditions, and perhaps I don't, but finally his grin is there illuminated by blue eyes so like Alexander's.

But otherwise, he's different from Alexander in every way. As if by design. And that brings me to why I've come. I give Lysbet a look that fortunately she understands. "Let's go explore the fort," she says to her husband.

And when they depart, I turn to my son. "I wish to say something, William, and I need you to hear me." There's a hesitancy in his gaze when he nods, as if he's been anticipating this. "I know what you suspect about your father disappoints you, but he wasn't a perfect man."

"Mother—"

"Please," I say, needing him to hear me. "The truth is, William, no union is perfect. We stumble. We fall. We hurt the ones we love." I think back on Lafayette's wisdom and draw strength from it. "But the measure of a man, of a *life*, of a union of man and wife or even country is not in the falling. It's in the rising back up again to repair what's broken, to put right what's wrong. Your father and I did that. We always did that. He never stopped trying until the day he died. And neither will I."

William's gaze is uncertain, and then he blinks and looks away. Swallowing hard, he says, "I'm glad you were able to find your peace with him." When he looks back at me, his blue eyes are blazing with that achingly familiar illusion of violet. "But I've been shaken in my conviction of who *I* thought he was. Or hoped he was. And there's no way to repair that, for me. No way to make it right between a father and a son. Not with him gone."

The pain in his expression threatens to break my heart, because I've felt that pain. I've worked the same equation. I've tried the same case. But unlike my son, I've been able to reach a conclusion, and I share this with him now.

"Oh, William," I say, taking his hand. "No man should be judged only for his best act or his worst. By only his greatness or his flaws." *And no woman either,* I think. For if my sister did betray me, did it obliterate all the ways in which she'd been my first and most constant friend?

No, it did not. And I swallow as the thought heals another broken piece inside me.

"It seems, to me," I continue, "that the only just way to judge a person is by the sum of their deeds, good *and* bad. And in the balance, your father did far more good than harm. That's all any of us can aim to do with our lives."

William's throat bobs. "I was so small when he died that I can't remember him well. And yet, I . . . I miss him," he says, as if both admissions pain him.

Reaching up, I take his face into my trembling hand. The same hand upon which I wear a gold wedding ring inscribed with my name and Alexander's; a ring that I will never again remove. "I miss him, too. You must know, William. He *loved* you. And love is a kind of faith. A blessing to everyone it touches. Your father earned my love a thousand times over and I earned his in return. So I ask you to find your peace with your father."

William looks at me a long moment, and finally, his expression goes soft. "My love for you allows me to do no other than accede to your wishes, Mother."

*Then come home with me,* I think. But I decide to savor this victory and put that battle off for later. When I know him a little better. Because the years have made him a stranger, I devote every moment of the time I have in getting to *know* my son.

He brims with passion as he shows me his smelting furnace and explains the process of removing impurities from the crude lead dug from the ground. As he discusses his work, I hear the echo of Alexander's zeal in discussing policy and politics. And, like his father, William has found success. Everywhere we go, the people all know William—*Wisconsin's Hamilton,* they call him—and respect what he's built and the man he's become.

And, despite my reason for coming here, I do, too.

When William mentions a place he describes as the great natural wonder of the north, the Falls of St. Anthony, I naturally insist on seeing it. Getting to the falls requires a steamboat ride and an eight-mile climb on horseback over winding trails, and I feel like the girl I once was, exploring the beauty of nature.

I hear the falls before I see them. God in heaven, the sight is majestic. Multiple falls curve and twist, the surging streams descending from forty or fifty feet onto water and rock below. Spray rises up in great clouds that tickle my face in the breeze, filling me with a newfound vigor.

William calls over the roar of the water, "The Dakota call the Mississippi *hahawakpa,* or 'river of the falls.' They believe spirits live beneath them." I can understand the belief, for seeing such miraculous evidence of God's power imbues me with the feeling of being in the presence of something sacred.

I am still moved when, later that afternoon, we return to Fort Snelling to find Colonel Campbell and his officers waiting at the entrance in full dress uniforms. For *me*, as if *I* was now the Guest of the Nation.

The colonel offers me his arm and conducts me inside the four-sided fort, where a very fine band plays and an armchair waits upon a carpet. He bids me sit, and then, when the music stops, he speaks to his assembled troops. "We have with us today Mrs. General Hamilton, wife of the hero of Yorktown!" A cheer rises up from the soldiers, and then, with weapons upon their shoulders, the troops march in formation, demonstrating a series of maneuvers. The display goes on for some time, and when it ends, I rise shakily to my feet, too moved to speak. For most of these men hadn't even been born while Alexander Hamilton still lived, yet have honored me this way.

And in front of Alexander's son, who most needed to see it.

When September brings cooler air and fields covered in lavender aster, my visit with dear William is near its end. Winter will soon choke the rivers with ice, making travel impossible.

I have to go home. I've intended, all along, to ask William to come, but now I realize that I can't. I can't ask him to come home with me . . . because William *is* home. I see that now. It would be wrong to deny him his place here, where new possibility hangs in the air. And yet, the realization is bittersweet, because I know I shall never return. I shall never see him again.

And I think he knows it, too.

"Mother," he says gravely, planting a kiss atop my head. "I shall always be at your side, even as I make my own path here." His voice is tight with emotion, and all I can do is clutch at his strong, calloused hands.

He's happy here. And how can I want anything more for my children than to have the liberty to pursue their happiness? It's what their father lived and died for.

And it *is* enough.

*This aged petitioner, now numbering nearly fourscore and ten years, the widow of Alexander Hamilton, and the daughter of Philip Schuyler, still cherishing an ardent attachment for the husband of her youth, wishes, before she, too, passes away, to see his publications spread before the American people.*

*Hamilton must be classed among the men who have best known the vital principles and the fundamental conditions of a government. There is not in the constitution of the United States an element to which Hamilton has not powerfully contributed.*

—CONGRESSIONAL REPORT OF THE COMMITTEE OF THE
LIBRARY ON ELIZABETH HAMILTON'S PETITION

*Washington City*
*July 4, 1848*

"Do you think they've patched up their quarrel?" I ask Mrs. Madison, who sits beside me in a carriage as it slowly rolls through streets lined with thousands of onlookers waving American flags.

We're riding together to the ceremony celebrating both the Fourth of July and the laying of the cornerstone to the new monument to the memory of George Washington. We're accorded positions of prominence in the celebration because we're the only remaining icons of the founding age. The only dignitaries left who personally knew the Father of His Country.

Dolley and I are both turned out as elegantly as two aged widows can be. Me in my fanciest bonnet. The former first lady in a silk taffeta gown, black like my own.

I live in Washington City now. So does Dolley. And she's still keen for gossip, leaning close enough that the white feather in her turban tickles my cheek. "Has who patched up which quarrel?"

"Why, our husbands in heaven, of course," I reply.

She laughs and grasps my hand. "Oh, my friend. I'm sure they have." Dolley pauses a moment before adding, "Mr. Madison never forgot that the Constitution owed much of its existence to yours. And he once confided in me that no one but Hamilton could match him, nor force him to work so hard to make an argument. It's my belief that our husbands had no peers even amongst the other great men of their time."

The truth of the sentiment lodges a knot of emotion in my throat. Indeed, it is their friendship that has brought us—and our country—to this day. For though the idea to build a monument to Washington was as old as the nation, and attempts to raise sufficient funds for the cause were nearly two decades old, it was not until the society behind the monument's erection invited *us* to take up the mantle of memory that those efforts finally bore fruit.

Working alongside Dolley, I organized dinners, teas, fairs, and every manner of entertainment. Adopting the same *martial spirit* that I'd once used to raise funds for widows, I'd cajoled contributions from passersby and merchants on my daily two-mile walk about the city. And at my annual New Year's Day open house—now one of the most anticipated and attended gaieties of the holiday season in Washington—I even required a donation to drink wine from the silver cooler General Washington gifted to us, raising a not insignificant sum for the honor!

I've used my newfound celebrity as a relic of the revolution to achieve a different end, too. Over teas with Washington's ladies and in salons in my parlor and even at a dinner with President and Mrs. Polk at the White House, I won support for a petition I submitted to Congress requesting that its library purchase my husband's papers and take over the task of preserving his legacy. I won from them, too, the long overdue acknowledgment that my husband was amongst this nation's fathers.

I hope this victory means Alexander will be remembered when I am gone.

And so it is that we, all of us, have arrived at this great moment. Cannon fire echoes against the bright blue sky, part of a series of salutes that has been ringing out all morning, and church bells chime from every quarter of the city.

Amidst what appear to be tens of thousands of spectators, carriages deliver to the designated site representatives of America— from the president and cabinet, to military units decorated in their proud, bright uniforms, to fire companies and civic organizations with their colorful banners, to delegations of Cherokee, Chickasaw, Choctaw, and other tribes wearing silver medals depicting Washington. So as to command a view of all the public buildings, the monument is to be built upon a hill overlooking both the Potomac River and the White House.

But all I can see, all I can hear, is the great crowd of my fellow countrymen. Singing, clapping, and chanting Washington's name as our carriage comes to a halt.

Dolley is assisted down first by some notable, and then an exceedingly tall gentleman in a top hat comes forth to escort me toward the striped awning where we are meant to sit. He holds out his hand, and I grasp it, peering into dark intelligent eyes.

"Thank you, Congressman Lincoln," I say.

"It is my honor, Mrs. General Hamilton," he replies.

We make a comical sight walking together, as I've become so bent in my old age that he's forced to stoop to speak to me. "I wished to mention, madam, that in recently rereading *The Federalist*, I am struck again, as one cannot help but be, by your late husband's devotion to the national good. Though I fear that he possessed a prescience which too few of our contemporaries share."

"Oh?" I ask, wishing to make him elaborate.

And he does, intoning Alexander's words, "*If these states should either be wholly disunited, or only united in partial confederacies, the subdivisions into which they might be thrown—*"

"*—would have frequent and violent contest with each other,*" I finish, for I know the words by heart. "Federalist Number Six."

A smile brightens Lincoln's rugged countenance. "Indeed. And *'every man who loves liberty ought to cherish in his heart a due attachment to the Union of America.'*"

"That was Mr. Madison," I say, unable to suppress a smirk. "Federalist Number Forty-One. But I'll give you another chance. What do you say of Federalist Number Nine?"

"Are you testing me, Mrs. Hamilton?" he asks with a twinkle in his eye.

"I am," I admit.

"*'A firm union will be of the utmost importance to the peace and liberty of the states,'*" he quotes, then leans in closer. "Have I passed?"

I cannot help but laugh. "You have, congressman." He helps me toward my seat, located in the shade near the podium. As I sit, he bows then turns to take his leave. "Mr. Lincoln?"

He raises a craggy eyebrow. "Yes, madam?"

Because I know Lincoln to believe that the institution of slavery is founded on both injustice and bad policy, I'm emboldened to say, "The true test is making certain that those who died in this country's service have not died in vain; in furthering the unfinished work our founders so nobly advanced."

He bows again. "I couldn't have said it better myself."

Finally, the assembly settles and the crowd hushes for the oration commemorating George Washington. Eyeing the block of marble that will one day form the base of a giant obelisk monument and grasping the pendant of his hair I still wear around my neck, I remember all we owe this great man.

But Washington isn't the only patriot to whom a debt is owed.

And some of them may never have a grand marble monument, no matter how much they deserve one. I'll make my peace with that, knowing that Alexander's accomplishments are inextricably entwined with Washington's. A monument to George Washington, I tell myself, is a monument to Alexander, too. And even to my father, in a way.

Both of them, I know, would be glad of this day.

Perhaps the speaker knows it, too, because he asks, "Which of us does not realize that unseen witnesses are around us? Think ye, that the patriot soldiers or statesmen, who stood around Washington in war and peace, are absent from a scene like this? Adams and Jefferson, by whose lives and deaths this day has been doubly hallowed; Hamilton and Madison, are present, *visibly present*, in the venerated persons of those nearest and dearest to them in life," he says, pausing to turn and point at Dolley and me, bidding us to stand.

We do, hands clasped. And the crowd's applause vibrates under my feet. I lift my eyes heavenward into the bright July sky, wondering if the orator speaks truly.

*Are you here, Alexander?*

As if in answer, at that very moment, the speaker recites a portion of the *Farewell Address,* calling out over the crowd: "'Properly estimate the immense value of your National Union to your happiness and to your political safety and prosperity, watching for its preservation with jealous anxiety; discountenancing any who suggest it can be abandoned; and indignantly frowning upon every attempt to alienate any portion of the country from the rest.'"

Washington's words. But Alexander's, too.

Even a few of mine.

From the corner of my eye, I see Congressman Lincoln lean forward, listening intently. And warmth steals over me to realize that even beyond the grave, Alexander Hamilton still speaks to his country and his countrymen. That he'll continue to speak to generation after generation of Americans. That he's speaking to *me*, even now, as the sunlight plays warm over my cheeks.

And I nearly laugh for the unexpected *joy* of our reunion.

For nearly fifty years, I've searched for my husband. At the Pastures, on the river, at his gravesite, and in the empty rooms of the house we built together. In portraits and busts and the faces of his children. In letters, pamphlets, account books, newspaper clippings, and treatises. I've searched for Alexander, despairing that there was no part of him still in this world, and that I couldn't be where any part of him is now.

But Alexander is here, as warm and alive as the day we renewed our marriage and made love in the sun. He's inside me and all around me in the country that was created in his image. For there's not one person in the crowd who would be here without him.

This city, this government, this *nation*, would not exist without his efforts.

Washington might be first in the hearts of his countrymen.

But this is Alexander Hamilton's *country*.

A stone monument can crumble—all eventually do. But Alexander built a monument for himself of ideas and ideals, weaving himself into the fabric of the nation such that not a thread can be pulled without destroying the whole.

Oh, there are those who tried. And I supposed they might keep on trying. But, as the speaker says, we've put the great American-built locomotive "Liberty" on its course, and now people the world over examine the model of this mighty engine, and copy its construction and imitate its machinery. Alexander is everywhere people are heard calling their rulers to account. Alexander is everywhere the cry is raised for the right to vote, trial by jury, freedom of the press, written constitutions, representative systems, and republican forms.

Which means I've been looking for my husband, all along, in the wrong place.

Alexander once wrote, "*The sacred rights of mankind are not to be rummaged for among old parchments or musty records. They are written, as with a sunbeam, in the whole volume of human nature, by the hand of the divinity itself; and can never be erased or obscured by mortal power.*"

And neither can Alexander Hamilton be.

So, as the Marine Corp band plays "The Star-Spangled Banner," accompanied by the voices of twenty thousand of my countrymen, I raise up my voice, too. For my perilous fight is nearly over. I believe that all we worked for and built—the benign influence of good laws under a free government—will continue on as our happy reward, forever, never perishing from this earth. Even as I marvel that our starry banner of red, white, and blue still waves.

# Note from the Authors

E  LIZABETH SCHUYLER HAMILTON'S extraordinary life
   spanned nearly a century. She strived, struggled, and survived the first turbulent years of our nation's founding as
the wronged wife at the center of America's first sex scandal. But
she was much more than that.

Coming of age in the relative frontier of upstate New York,
Eliza—who apparently went by the name Betsy, at least in her
early years—was the daughter of one of early America's most
prominent men and ablest generals. As such, she had a front-
row seat to the American Revolution. Descended from a line of
physically strong and relatively independent New Netherlander
matriarchs, Eliza was as well-equipped to entertain famous
statesmen at her father's table as she was to traverse the wilderness to attend Indian conventions at her father's side.

Eliza saw the chaos of war, the destruction of her family's
country home, her father's loss of command, and the growing
pains of a new nation. She also became the wife of Alexander
Hamilton—one of America's most brilliant soldiers and political minds. Whether as a participant in Hamilton's astonishing
career, helping him with his writings and publications, or as victim of his ambitions, and as an activist in her own right, she
demonstrated an admirable strength of character that made her a
wonderful heroine for a novel.

And yet, very little primary source material exists about her, much less in her own hand. Most of what is gleaned about her is extrapolated from what we know about the men in her life. The internal struggles she must have faced in the aftermath of betrayal and tragedy remain frustratingly out of reach for historians, who, without all the pieces to put together a portrait of her emotional life, have not tried to paint much of a portrait at all, especially for the fifty years of her life after Alexander died. In fact, at the time of this writing, we are unaware of a single biography written about Eliza Hamilton. Even Ron Chernow's definitive biography of Alexander pays Eliza relatively little attention and does not always delve enough into her life to offer, in our view, the most considered interpretations of her character, motivations, and contributions.

But, thankfully, fiction can go where historians rightly fear to tread.

And as novelists we were honored to look at the historical pieces of the puzzle and imagine the rich inner life that the historical fragments leave unspoken. We attempted to craft plausible answers to questions about Eliza's reaction to her husband's adultery. How she balanced her deep religious faith with disillusionment and worldly practicality. And how she might've come to terms with both the man—and the country—that she sacrificed for and which sometimes disappointed her.

We're now happy to explain our approach, as well as the choices we made and the creative liberties we took.

As with most works of historical fiction, the most outlandish bits are the true ones. The court martials, battles, duels, and mutinies all happened. The scandals, riots, plagues, and mental illnesses, too. During her extraordinary life, Eliza Hamilton was a belle of both Revolutionary balls and military camps. She did know the doomed British spymaster John André and Hamilton's letters indicate that Eliza may have argued on his behalf.

Washington is thought by some scholars to have been unusually tolerant, by the standards of the day, regarding the sexuality of his soldiers. And the Baron von Steuben was almost certainly homosexual. Eliza's uncle really was Washington's physician and a pioneer in the eradication of smallpox. Her mother and her aunt were known for helping at a makeshift hospital. According to the New York State Museum, Mama Schuyler did have an extraordinarily close relationship with her husband's commanding officer that might have troubled a husband less secure in the sanctity of his marriage. Meanwhile, a less secure Eliza Hamilton may well have put together the fact that Alexander Hamilton's entanglement with James Reynolds began long before he took Mrs. Reynolds to bed. Eliza did, indeed, assist her husband in his political endeavors—some of his writings, including his economic treatise to Robert Morris, are in her handwriting. The historical Eliza helped to establish *two* orphanages, was a tireless activist in the name of charity, and made an arduous trip to the wilds of Wisconsin while in her eighties. The Hamiltons did shelter Lafayette's son as well as the orphaned Fanny Antill. (Though we had to guess at the real reason behind Fanny's departure from the Hamiltons' home around the time of the Reynolds scandal, as well as whether Fanny's later charitable work would have brought her back into Eliza's life. We certainly hope it did.) Much of Alexander's dialogue comes from his letters (though we often had to shorten and modernize his famously long and complicated style for readability), and though most of Eliza's letters don't survive, we used them where we could, and the dialogue in her confrontation with Monroe comes from a family description of the event.

But in the interest of conciseness, we have omitted, condensed, glossed over, or hand-waved a thousand other historical details. Alexander Hamilton lived only half as long as other Founding Fathers, and yet, he managed to experience seemingly ten times as much. We could not enumerate his many accomplishments within the confines of this novel, and because this was Eliza's story—not his—we did not attempt to. Instead we've conflated or simplified events for maximum dramatic punch, and the astute reader might notice subtle changes in the timeline.

Where a shift in the chronology didn't fundamentally change the choices faced by the people involved, we erred on the side of brevity. For example, Catherine Van Rensselaer Schuyler and her daughter, Margarita "Peggy" Schuyler Van Rensselaer, did both die in the month of March—but two years apart. This was a dark period in Eliza's life that included the deaths of Peggy (1801), Philip (1801), Mama (1803), Alexander (1804), and Papa (1804). In consideration of Eliza and Alexander's arc during this troubled time, we moved Mama's death in order to highlight the couple's historical struggle to emerge from their grief in the period before Alexander's death.

To give the reader a front-row seat, we've sparingly placed our protagonist and other characters where they might not have been. One example is the Loyalist attack on Schuyler Mansion, and the chop of the wooden banister, for which there is a vivid and detailed account by a family member, but the veracity of its particulars is questionable. Another example is Evacuation Day where the Hamiltons' arrival in New York was close enough that we wished to portray it. (No one seems to know *why* Hamilton was not present at Washington's subsequent farewell in Fraunces Tavern, so we had to come up with a reason.)

Our focus, as biographical historical novelists, of course, is on character. And that is where we were forced to do the most speculation. For example, historical paintings give proof that Eliza Hamilton was a petite and attractive woman. In fact, Talleyrand thought Eliza's beauty was underappreciated. Eliza's admirer Tench Tilghman not only praised her as the finest tempered girl in the world, but also portrayed her athleticism in his diary. Even well into her old age, we are told, Eliza insisted on taking very long walks, traversing fields and climbing over fences. As for her personality, her contemporaries describe her as impulsive and vivacious. She herself copied out a prayer to envision herself as an instrument of God's will. And, within the realm of what was appropriate for women at the time, she was a relentless crusader, having, as one friend claimed, a "rare sense of justice."

These were all important details that we took into account in crafting Eliza's persona.

But our approach to biographical historical fiction has always been to find the character-defining *moment* in a person's life and build a story around it.

For Hamilton-centric historians, the defining moment of Eliza's life seems to be that she stood by her man and forgave her husband's infidelity. For *us*, her character-defining moment was the dramatic documented encounter she had with an aging James Monroe.

Just as in the novel, in the twilight of his life, the real President James Monroe wished to reconcile. But an uncompromising and stalwart Eliza wouldn't have it. What she wanted was an apology, which Monroe would not give. Again, what strikes Hamilton-centric historians about the much ballyhooed meeting was Eliza's loyalty to her husband.

But what struck *us* about this visit was that Monroe made it at all.

What would compel the so-called Last Founding Father to seek out Eliza Hamilton? Though Monroe made it a principle of politics to engender his Era of Good Feelings, by the time he paid call to Eliza he'd retired from the presidency and politics. Nor does Monroe appear to have been motivated by guilt because he didn't offer an apology when Eliza all but demanded one. So why go to the trouble? Especially since this inconvenient visitation almost assuredly took place at Eliza's home in New York, and not Washington, D.C., as is often posited. (Eliza didn't move to Washington until the 1840s, at least a decade after Monroe's death.)

The answer doesn't seem to have been Monroe's nostalgia for his old friendship with Alexander Hamilton. In the sparse sketch of their encounter from Allan McLane Hamilton, Monroe doesn't even mention his old friend and comrade-at-arms. Instead, the former president framed the speech he made to Eliza in terms of how long it had been since *they* met, and that their past differences could be forgiven and forgotten.

This raised tantalizing questions. Just how long *had* it been since James Monroe met Eliza Hamilton? What was the nature of their meeting? What sort of relationship did they share that might motivate such an unprecedented visit—and such a hostile reception? And what sort of power did she hold as a historical figure in her own right that he would prize a reconciliation with her?

It's most probable that Eliza met James Monroe when he came to New York City to serve in Congress in 1785. Possibly sooner, but we ruled out a family account published in a missionary pamphlet that places Eliza Schuyler at Valley Forge, because if she'd met Monroe there, she'd have met Hamilton as well. Yet, we noticed that after Monroe's heroics at Trenton, he became aide to Lord Stirling, who served in the Hudson Highlands during 1777.

In that, we saw an opportunity.

Because Lord Stirling tried to guide Lafayette successfully to Albany, where he conferred with Eliza's father, Philip Schuyler, we invented the notion that Lord Stirling sent Monroe to help, and that Monroe dined thereafter at Schuyler Mansion, where Eliza took a shine to him. Whether or not Eliza Hamilton would later have any cause to speak to Monroe either on the night he came to Hamilton's house to investigate the Reynolds matter or shortly before the publication of the *Reynolds Pamphlet* is not known. And as for any romantic feelings between them, we only know that Monroe was coy and secretive about his fondness for Dutch girls, one of whom turned him down when he asked for her hand after the war because she was already pledged. And of course, though Eliza assuredly was acquainted with Elizabeth Kortright before she married Monroe, the notion that Eliza introduced them is our fabrication.

We have no historical evidence that Eliza was present with

Lafayette at the Six Nations convention at Johnstown where the Oneida formally allied with the nascent United States. There is even some question as to whether or not Philip Schuyler personally attended that meeting. However, Eliza accompanied her father to at least one *other* Indian convention and was adopted by the Iroquois—something important enough to her that she mentioned it to an interviewer near the end of her life. Moreover, an Iroquois assembly with Schuyler took place just prior to Lafayette's visit in the woods near Eliza's family home in November of 1777, so we rolled the experiences together so the reader might get a better view of the milieu in which Eliza became an adult and so that we could demonstrate the revolution's impact on Native Americans.

We thought it was important to do this because the American Revolution is too often seen as a struggle between white marbled men in powdered wigs spouting fine sentiments about liberty; the truth was more complicated and the participants far more diverse. The Iroquois nations were drawn into both sides of the conflict.

So were black people, both free and enslaved. And because Eliza's father was a plantation-owning slaveholder, she had opportunities to witness and, ultimately, empathize with their struggles. Our readers might recall that in *America's First Daughter*, the story of Martha "Patsy" Jefferson Randolph, we had the unique opportunity to portray the enslaved families at Thomas Jefferson's Monticello because quite a bit is known about the people who lived there. Unfortunately, not as much is known about the approximately thirty enslaved human beings on Philip Schuyler's property. Consequently, in this novel, we hesitated to put too many words into their mouths or feelings in their hearts, but tried to honor them by using some of their names and vocations.

We also confronted the probability that Eliza's entanglement with slavery did not end when she left her father's household.

That Alexander Hamilton opposed slavery is absolutely true;

so did Jefferson, though to a less efficacious degree. That did not stop either man from compromising his moral beliefs in pursuit of personal or political goals. In short, despite his antislavery stance, there is historical evidence that Alexander Hamilton *did* borrow, hire out, and possibly even own enslaved persons. Which is why we decided to employ the character of Jenny to demonstrate the ambiguities surrounding this particular question, and Eliza's evolution in thinking on the matter.

Unfortunately, because little survives in Eliza's own hand, it's difficult to discern what her relationships were with enslaved persons; we know from one letter that she was distressed by one of her servants dying of yellow fever. And that she eventually spoke with contempt about the institution of slavery itself and its corrupting influence on the body politic.

ELIZA HAMILTON'S FRIENDS, relations, and acquaintances are a veritable Who's Who of American history, including many fascinating figures we didn't have room to introduce, such as Ben Franklin, the Vicomte de Noailles, the Marquis de Chastellux, Talleyrand, Martin Van Buren, James and Sarah Polk, and many more. She personally knew at least twelve of the first sixteen presidents, and was present with Congressman Abraham Lincoln at the dedication of Washington's monument.

The revolution—and the business of nation building—was, for Eliza Hamilton, a family affair. And Eliza was particularly close to her family. After the loss of Fort Ticonderoga, General Schuyler was certainly held in contempt and, according to contemporary Dr. James Thacher, accused of collecting a bribe from the British in silver bullets shot over the fort's wall. (Even Schuyler's future son-in-law, a young Lieutenant Colonel Alexander Hamilton, once suspected him of treachery.) But Schuyler's reputation in Albany was more secure than we have portrayed it; so much so that New Yorkers were trying to send him to Congress before he'd even been vindicated at court-martial.

Our choice to have Eliza overwrought about her father's reputation lent a nice echo for the constant worries she'd be faced with when it came to her husband's reputation later in the book. Eliza would not have believed her father guilty of the crimes for which he stood accused, nor would she have likely believed him guilty of wrongs he did commit, and so we have portrayed Schuyler here through the lens of a loving daughter's eyes. (Note that while Peggy probably did not elope, the fact that three, if not four, of his intelligent and headstrong daughters chose to do so—without real fear of consequence—speaks to him as a more indulgent father than his historical reputation for sternness might otherwise indicate.) Certainly, Eliza Hamilton honored and relied upon her father as a protector and benefactor, and his death likely forced her to contend with the world as a more independent woman than she would've liked to have been.

Eliza's relationship with the daughters of Governor William Livingston is documented. Though it is possible, and maybe even likely, that Kitty Livingston sided with her brother-in-law John Jay in political matters, we used her as a stand-in for the political rupture between the Schuyler and Livingston families.

We were particularly interested in the relationship she formed with the Burrs and Madisons. The Hamiltons and the Burrs socialized frequently together and so we've posited a friendship between Eliza and Theodosia. We moved some of the discrimination Theodosia experienced as the wife of a British officer during the war to after the war as a demonstration of public prejudices. And because Theodosia was forward-thinking in matters of philosophy and women's rights, we attributed other liberal ideas to her as well.

The partnership between Alexander Hamilton and James Madison was amongst the most fruitful in the history of government. That these two brilliant and hardworking founders could work together in such close harmony, so urgently, and with such success, only to become political enemies, is a great American tragedy. But we were delighted to find some grace notes there— the respect with which Madison treated Hamilton's family, the assistance he lent them in gathering Hamilton's papers, and the friendship that his wife Dolley shared with Eliza even after both of their husbands were in the grave.

Long before Dolley Payne Todd married James Madison, she and Eliza Hamilton were neighbors in Philadelphia in the early 1790s, living only a block apart on Walnut Street. Eliza most likely made the acquaintance of Dolley at one of Martha Washington's receptions, at which Eliza was a fixture and Dolley was a frequent guest. The willingness of these ladies to put aside partisanship so that they could work together raising funds for the Washington Monument, and orphans, suggested to us a long friendship, so we put one in the book.

Another long and heartwarming real friendship existed between Eliza and Lafayette, with whom she exchanged letters long after Hamilton's death. Lafayette's triumphant visit to America in 1824 began in New York City on August 16. He then returned to New York again in early September, and it was at this time he took Eliza Hamilton with him in his carriage to inspect West Point, expressing that Hamilton had been as a brother to him. It seems that she was amongst those who left the ball late and chugged off in a steamboat with him into the night. Lafayette returned again to New York at the end of September for another round of celebrations but in our story, we conflated all three visits for brevity and simplification. And we thought it extremely likely that Eliza Hamilton was amongst the escort of ladies associated with the Free School that Lafayette toured because Lafayette's secretary mentions, in the same breath, intimate details about the founding of Eliza's Orphan Asylum.

When he was in America, Lafayette spent much time laying cornerstones and visiting memorials of his fallen revolutionary comrades. And we know he visited St. Paul's, the chapel near

Trinity, because his secretary made special note of the Trinity graveyard. It's difficult to conceive of Lafayette visiting that graveyard without stopping to pay his respects to Hamilton. So we included a graveside scene and combined it with Eliza's emotional epiphanies.

(Additionally, there is some historical confusion over the burial place of Philip Hamilton, but we chose to accept the interpretation presented in the book of Trinity Church history that says he is buried in the same plot as his father and mother. It's also unclear why Angelica Schuyler Church is buried in the Livingston vault. Angelica fostered with the Livingstons as a girl, and there may have been a closer familial connection there. But the ambiguity fit well into the narrative and so we used it to our purposes.)

Another friend of Eliza's was James McHenry, who did, indeed, get pulled back into the political fray during the Madison administration, in part because of John Adams maligning him in the press, but also because his advice was sought with regard to the forthcoming War of 1812. McHenry escorting Eliza to Washington City, though plausible, is our invention so that he could serve as a stand-in for the Federalists she lobbied at this time.

Then there's the matter of Eliza's enemies.

Her first meeting with Thomas Jefferson probably took place in New York when Jefferson arrived to take up the mantle of secretary of state, not in Philadelphia, as we portrayed it, before he served as ambassador to France. But because Jefferson happened to be in Philadelphia with his daughter when the Hamiltons were there, we found it hard to resist giving the reader a glimpse of young Patsy Jefferson of *America's First Daughter.*

As for Aaron Burr, it isn't known if Eliza played a role in his exile from New York, but there is circumstantial evidence that she was lobbying New York society, with her grieving children in tow, only days after Hamilton's death. Eliza is known to have come face to face with him only once after the duel. The occurrence took place on a ferry and thereafter the rumor went round that Eliza had screamed upon seeing Burr's face, and that Burr coldly went about eating his supper. In fact, Eliza only stared ic-ily at Burr and retained her composure, but she never corrected the record, presumably because the story made him look heart-less and irredeemable.

Saintly or not, Eliza Hamilton could hold a grudge.

She could also hold her silence. For example, she left nothing behind to tell us how she felt upon learning of her husband's infi-delity with Maria Reynolds. Historians have inferred, from the way her family wrote to her about the controversy surrounding the *Reynolds Pamphlet* by placing the blame upon envy and news-papermen, that Eliza tolerated her husband's adulteries and that she was only distressed to see them exposed. But if that were the case, we think it unlikely Hamilton would have submitted to blackmail in the first place.

We think it more probable that those family letters—and Hamilton's own restrained mention of his wife's likely feelings on the matter—are simply evidence of the fact that Eliza had al-ready learned about the affair and forgiven it years before. Whilst he lived, Hamilton certainly exerted a measure of charm that al-lowed many people to forgive him many things.

But what about after he died? Eliza left no indication of her reaction upon reading her husband's letters after he was shot—letters so compromising that her son even scrawled upon one that it should not be published. And amongst those letters are a correspondence with Angelica Church that is flirtatious at best and damning at worst.

Though eighteenth-century people wrote to one another in more flowery and effusive ways than we do now, the fact remains that Hamilton's letters to and mentions of his wife's *other* sisters do not share the same flirtatious tone. To complicate matters, of course, is the fact that Hamilton's own contemporaries appear to have believed that he was sleeping with his wife's sister—a relationship that would have been considered incestuous by the standards of the time. More tellingly, this was believed not only by his enemies, but by his friends.

Hamilton's longtime friend, Robert Troup, believed it was a torrid affair, and though there is some confusion about the exact details regarding the incident with the garter, Eliza's sister once taunted Hamilton and Angelica about their flirtation in public. Although we're aware of no direct proof of a rift in the marriage of John Barker Church and Angelica Schuyler, there's circumstantial evidence that the marriage was troubled. To start with, Angelica's letters—flirting with other men, including Thomas Jefferson—imply that she didn't find her husband to be eloquent or interesting. That she was bored in Church's company and that perhaps he was bored in hers. Then there is the matter of Angelica's long visit to America without the company of her husband or children, during which Hamilton paid her expenses, some of which were to be reimbursed by her husband, others of which apparently were not.

Ron Chernow, Hamilton's most celebrated biographer, seems to take the position that Hamilton and Angelica had perhaps an emotional, if not physical affair. But like us, Chernow is befuddled by Eliza's reaction to the open flirtation of her husband and sister. Eliza, who enjoyed a very close and loving bond with her sisters, seems never to have objected to—and quite possibly even encouraged—the flirtation. Is it possible that Eliza knew her husband was having an affair with her sister and didn't mind? Or was it all just a very strange family joke?

We cannot know.

The only thing we can be sure of is that Eliza—like Hamilton's biographers—would've had to contend with these same letters after his death and make emotional sense of them. Which is a process we dramatized for the purposes of this novel, with regards to both Angelica and a speculated relationship with John Laurens, the case for which is stronger than we presented in the story. (For example, we held back a jocular letter from Hamilton to Laurens that seemed to invite his friend to watch him take his bride's virginity.)

Ultimately, we noticed a curious ten-year lull in the historical record when it came to Eliza Hamilton's otherwise tireless efforts to see her husband's legacy secured. Between the time of Angelica's death in 1814 and Lafayette's visit in 1824, there is a gap during which the family comes to learn that the Federalists are withholding Hamilton's drafts of Washington's Farewell Address from Eliza, and yet, she seems to do nothing about it. It's only after Lafayette's visit that Eliza returns to a frenzy of activity on behalf of her dead husband. We theorized that Eliza took these years to process any of the hurts and resentments she'd been suppressing as she reviewed Angelica and Hamilton's correspondence.

This also served as a convenient fictional explanation for why one of Hamilton's sons—William, the one born during the Reynolds scandal—abruptly withdrew from West Point, left his family, and wandered to the far end of what was then the country's borders and beyond.

FINALLY, THERE ARE the stories and rumors that we left out of the book.

Some believe that Hamilton first met Eliza when he visited her father in Albany during the autumn of 1777. But scholars at Schuyler Mansion think it likely that Eliza was visiting the Livingstons at the time. Then there's the more famous story—depicted in a painting—about Catherine Schuyler burning her crops in Saratoga so the British couldn't get them. The story is both suspected to be apocryphal and did not center our heroine, so we left it out (though we did draft a chapter portraying this scene—one of *many* that hit the chopping block and that readers can obtain by subscribing to our newsletter). We'd have loved to show Elizabeth Schuyler Hamilton at her husband's funeral, but Hamilton's biographer insists she was not there.

We did not belabor the confusion surrounding the duels that took her husband and son. Whether Hamilton fired first, fired at

Burr, threw away his shot, or fired as the result of an involuntary spasm or because of the hair triggers in the pistols remains an unsolved mystery. The same goes for the duel fought by Philip Hamilton. We didn't feel that the debate over these details served the emotional needs of the story and many other books have been dedicated to answering the questions already.

In summary, there is no child, or nation, that is ever born without leaving scars. We have done our best to be forthright and fair about the injustices and hypocrisies of our Founding Fathers. We hope the balance struck is one that furthers understanding and creates more interest.

For a more detailed explanation of our sources, choices, and changes, visit MyDearHamilton.com.

# *Acknowledgments*

FIRST, WE MUST thank our families and loved ones for endless patience with the whirlwind process of writing this novel. Secondly, our agent, Kevan Lyon, for her enthusiasm and advocacy. Thirdly, our team at HarperCollins, including Amanda Bergeron for inspiring and acquiring the book and Lucia Macro for editing it.

When it came to the research itself, we are indebted to the National Archives for their work to make the digitized letters of Alexander Hamilton and the Founding Fathers available to all Americans at founders.archives.gov. Additionally, we made use of the papers at the New York Public Library and New-York Historical Society. We're also enormously humbled by the generosity of the experts at the Schuyler Mansion State Historic Site in Albany, Ian Mumpton and Danielle Funiciello, who provided copies of letters and answered a thousand questions, large and small. Though any errors you may find in this manuscript are ours alone.

Thanks also go to the Daughters of the American Revolution and their magazine for providing research material of interest for subjects like Sinterklaas and Dutch culture in Eliza's time. Lars Hedbor for helping to nitpick the historical accuracy of everything from coffee to French uniforms. Alison Morton and Annalori Ferrell for help with French phrases. Lee Moore for suggesting that Hamilton's references to Aquileia were actually a reference to an old Roman hero famous for being satisfied with his turnips. Donna Thorland, for *so* many things, but advice on how to remove a period gown especially. Digital and public historian Megan Brett for her knowledge of the time period and help on all things James Madison. Dr. Sarahscott Brett Dietz for help with medical questions. Mary Dieterich and Isobel Carr for help with finding demonstrations of getting dressed in eighteenth-century garb. Joshua Miller for some French help and debates about Hamilton. Ruth Hull Chatlien for help on the Bonapartes. Jason Jorgenson for theological help. Keith Massey for help with the customs. A big thank you to Lea Nolan, Kate Quinn, and Stephanie Thornton for beta reading the manuscript—their questions and comments made the story so much richer. E. Knight, M. D. Waters, Christi Barth, and Liz Berry for reading, plotting, and all other forms of moral support.

Our complete bibliography is too expansive to list here, but we want to acknowledge especially our reliance on the letters of Hamilton, his family, friends, colleagues, contemporaries, and biographers in providing period-appropriate language, descriptions, and viewpoints. Additionally, we reference the New York State Museum's extensive collection of essays on early Albany and the Schuyler family. We cite the authoritative *Alexander Hamilton* by Ron Chernow, for most—but not all—of our characterizations and interpretations of Alexander in this novel.

Thanks to Chernow and Lin Manuel-Miranda's hit musical, the last few years have witnessed a remarkable renewal of general interest in our founding generation and Hamilton in specific. We're grateful to them and the influence of novelists such as Alice Curtis Desmond, Elizabeth Cobbs, and Juliet Waldron. We were additionally informed in our research for this novel by Allan McLane Hamilton's *The Intimate Life of Alexander Hamilton,* Georgina Schuyler's *The Schuyler Mansion at Albany,* Katharine Schuyler Baxter's *A Godchild of Washington,* Mary Gay Humphreys's *Catherine Schuyler,* Peter G. Rose's *Food, Drink and Celebrations of the Hudson Valley Dutch,* Anne Grant's

*Memoirs of an American Lady*, Warren Roberts's *A Place in History: Albany in the Age of Revolution*, Cornell University's *Bicentennial History of Albany*, Gerald Edward Kahler's *Gentlemen of the Family: General George Washington's Aides-de-Camp and Military Secretaries*, Joanne B. Freeman's *Affairs of Honor: National Politics in the New Republic*, Thomas Fleming's *Duel: Alexander Hamilton, Aaron Burr and the Future of America*, Roger G. Kennedy's *Burr, Hamilton, and Jefferson: A Study in Character*, Benson John Lossing's *The Life and Times of Philip Schuyler*, George Morgan's *The Life of James Monroe*, James Thacher's *Military Journal During the American Revolutionary War*, Joseph T. Glatthaar's *Forgotten Allies: The Oneida Indians and the American Revolution*, Harlow Giles Unger's *The Last Founding Father: James Monroe and a Nation's Call to Greatness*, Karen E. Robbins's *James McHenry: Forgotten Federalist*, Francois Furstenberg's *When the United States Spoke French*, Robert Tonsetic's *1781: The Decisive Year of the Revolutionary War*, J. H. Powell's *Bring Out Your Dead*, David Lefer's *The Founding Conservatives*, Joseph J. Ellis's *Founding Brothers*, Anthony S. Pitch's *The Burning of Washington*, Paul A. Gilje's *New York in the Age of the Constitution*, and Edward Countryman's *A People in Revolution*. For a more extensive bibliography please visit our website at DrayKamoie.com.

## About the authors

## About the book

Insights,
Interviews
& More...

# Meet Stephanie Dray

Kate Furek

STEPHANIE DRAY is a *New York Times, Wall Street Journal,* and *USA Today* bestselling author of historical women's fiction. Her award-winning work has been translated into eight languages and tops lists for the most anticipated reads of the year. Before she became a novelist, she was a lawyer and a teacher. Now she lives near the nation's capital with her husband, cats, and history books. ∽

# Meet Laura Kamoie

Renee Hollingshead

LAURA KAMOIE is a *New York Times, Wall Street Journal,* and *USA Today* bestselling author of historical fiction. She holds a doctoral degree in early American history from the College of William and Mary, has published two nonfiction books on early America, and most recently held the position of associate professor of history at the U.S. Naval Academy before transitioning to a full-time career writing fiction. Laura lives among the colonial charm of Annapolis, Maryland, with her husband and two daughters. ∾

# Discussion Questions

1. What do you think of Eliza's declaration that she was *someone* before she met Alexander Hamilton? Why do you think she feels it's important to remember that?

2. A young Eliza wonders how a daughter can make a difference in the revolution. Does she make a difference? In what ways?

3. How does Eliza view herself in the novel and how does that change over the course of her life?

4. Does seeing Alexander Hamilton through his wife's eyes make him more relatable as a Founding Father? How so or why not?

5. Martha Washington tells a newly married Eliza that achieving independence will require the support of women, and one way women can offer that support is by advising their husbands. What did you think of her advice? Does Eliza take it? How and when? How effective is Mrs. Washington's advice?

6. The Schuyler family's motto was *Semper Fidelis*. Always loyal. How does this play out in the book for Eliza?

7. Was Hamilton a good husband? Was Eliza a good wife? How did they change in those roles over the course of the novel?

8. What were the most important choices that Eliza made throughout her life and in her marriage? Do you agree with why she made them? Could or should she have chosen differently?

9. What did you think of the relationship among Eliza, Angelica, and Alexander? What do you make of the open flirtatiousness between Angelica and Alexander? How and why does Eliza's relationship with Angelica evolve over the course of their lives?

10. What did you think of Eliza's reaction to learning about Alexander's infidelity with Maria Reynolds? What did you think of the reconciliation they found after suffering from yellow fever?

11. How do Eliza's thoughts about slavery evolve? What factors influence her thinking? How do the depictions of slavery in New York differ from or meet your expectations and understanding of American slavery?

12. What did you think of Aaron Burr's characterization in the novel? How does Alexander and Eliza's relationship with him change over time?

13. How much was Alexander to blame for the challenges he faced in his political career and attacks launched by his enemies, and how much was he the victim of others' political machinations?

14. Though Thomas Jefferson is not often on the page, he looms large in the Hamiltons' minds and lives. Why was that?

15. In our portrayal, Eliza believes that "they" murdered her son, Philip, and her husband. Who are *they*? Why does she believe her loved ones were murdered? Do you agree— why or why not?

16. What did you think of Eliza's reaction to learning about Alexander's possible infidelity with her sister, Angelica, and his intimacy with John Laurens? What did you think of Lafayette's advice to Eliza about it? What does Eliza conclude in her attic trials and why? What does she conclude in her conversation with William in Wisconsin?

17. In what ways is the family story in this book relatable to modern families? To your family?

18. What did you think of the relationship between Eliza and James Monroe? How did it change over time? Why did Monroe represent such a touchstone for Eliza's feelings about Alexander? What did you think of their confrontation in 1825?

19. Eliza argues that the United States is Alexander's country, and that the country itself is the monument to him that she'd been searching for and wanting. What does she mean by this? Do you agree? Why or why not?

20. What did Eliza and her family sacrifice for the sake of the nation?

21. In what ways did Eliza shape Alexander Hamilton's legacy? In what ways did she shape that of the United States itself? ∾

# Walking in Eliza Schuyler Hamilton's Footsteps
## A Conversation with the Authors

While undertaking this project, the authors visited sites connected to the Hamilton and Schuyler families, and oh, the adventures they had!

**Stephanie:** The idea for this book started on a trip to New York City, where we had the opportunity to see Lin Manuel Miranda's *Hamilton: An American Musical* when it first came to Broadway and the buzz was only starting. As a work of historical fiction, the musical is absolutely astonishing. And as historical fiction authors, we were humbled. But we were also curious about Eliza—the woman who *first* told the story of this Founding Father. Her list of accomplishments was so impressive that we had to learn more, which we immediately set about doing in the back of a taxicab— both of us searching like mad on our smartphones and exclaiming with each new discovery. We knew, straightaway, that we wanted to tell *her* story.

**Laura:** We also knew that reading the historical letters wasn't going to be enough. Walking in the footsteps of our characters has become just as important to our process. Yes, it's important to spend time in libraries buried under microfiche, trying to decipher yellowing pieces of paper. But we like to touch what our characters might have touched, smell what they smelled, and view the world from their vantage points. It's always illuminating! That's why we took not one field trip for this project, but two.

**Stephanie:** We sort of *had* to, because our very first foray was a bit frustrating. If you're not familiar with America's revolutionary history, you might not realize just how important the Revolutionary War was to the history of New York City—and visiting the city doesn't make it much easier because most of the old landmarks have been replaced by new buildings. Most of the fabric of the eighteenth-century city is long gone. That progress stops for no man, or woman, is a rather Hamiltonian idea, but I was crestfallen to realize that we couldn't actually visit most of the places where Eliza lived. Instead, we wandered about Wall Street and Broadway trying to imagine what Eliza's view might have been of the river, and if she'd have smelled fish, or seen a forest of masts in the harbor. Fortunately, a few landmarks still exist. Trinity Church, where the Hamiltons worshipped and are buried. The Museum of American Finance building, which housed Hamilton's Bank of New York. And Fraunces Tavern, one of my favorite places to visit in the city, where Hamilton frequently socialized and George Washington said a farewell to his officers. Our favorite finds at Fraunces were in the museum above the tavern where we were able to see amazing artifacts such as Lafayette's sash, still stained with the blood he shed in our cause at Brandywine.

**Laura:** From there we made the trek out to Harlem to the one house in which we are certain Eliza Hamilton lived—the Grange. Hamilton spent a fortune building this country estate for his family and it's where he tried to reconcile himself to life in a garden instead of in the political arena. Thanks to the heroic efforts of the U.S. National Park Service, we were able to imagine all those rooms filled with Eliza's many children, and we stared at the bust of Hamilton just as she did, longing to meet him again. And yet— perhaps because the house has been moved a number of times to preserve it, and because the Hamiltons only shared that home for a few years before the infamous duel that shattered their lives— even as we appreciated the tall windows, the French-mirrored walls, and the restored woodwork, neither of us felt a strong emotional impression.

**Stephanie:** That's true. But the place that absolutely left a strong emotional impression was Trinity Church. I remember how much time we spent there and how it changed our entire idea of what Eliza's story might be. I'd expected some sort of grand monument to the architect of American government. Instead, we found Hamilton's relatively humble gravestone hilariously and horrifically positioned directly across the street from a bank and some shops, one of which had a sign that said, "We are probably the lowest priced in the city." Maybe Hamilton would have liked the way time—and the city—just marched on without him. But when Lafayette visited in 1824, his secretary complained of the indignity of this sacred graveyard being separated from the gaiety and commerce of the city by only an iron railing. And it was hard not to see that as a metaphor for Eliza's ▶

**Walking in Eliza Schuyler Hamilton's Footsteps** *(continued)*

struggle. She spent her life fighting a war against time and the indignities threatening to swallow her family's rightful place in history . . .

**Laura:** That was sobering to realize in that moment. And to wonder if it was a war that she won. I lingered a long time with my hand pressed to Eliza's gravestone. Then I remember that we both sat together a long time by the root sculpture just outside the church commemorating an old sycamore that used to be there before it was destroyed by the collapse of the Twin Towers on 9/11. It was the first time we both began to envision her life story as one so intrinsically rooted in the darkest days and greatest triumphs of the country. I think we both felt sad as we reckoned with how many losses she really faced, even before the duel that took her husband's life. That graveyard is where our original idea for a plucky historical heroine turned into something darker and deeper. Where we began to hope our words could be another sort of monument for Eliza.

**Stephanie:** Another place that affected me deeply was Morristown, New Jersey, where a local chapter of the Daughters of the American Revolution lovingly maintains the so-called Schuyler-Hamilton house where Eliza visited her Aunt Gertrude and was wooed by Alexander Hamilton. Given the beautiful little churches, the town square, and tales of winter balls, it was easy to imagine a charming winter courtship between the two of them. At least until I visited Jockey Hollow, where old military cabins still dot the forested hills. The realization that ten thousand men were freezing and starving to death—just out of sight of Washington and his officers—made a powerful impression. And given Eliza and Alexander's lifelong dedication to charity and public service, it doubtless made an impression on them, too. In fact, the visit to Jockey Hollow forced us to rewrite the original lighthearted romance between them, and we reimagined their attraction as one between two very earnest young people in a very dark hour, both of them desperate to make the world a better place.

**Laura:** Our second research trip occurred later that year, and once again began in New York City, where we undertook research at the New-York Historical Society and New York Public Library. We got to handle one of Eliza's letters, and getting to hold something she once held and seeing her signature across the page was another powerful moment. But first, we started at Weehawken, New Jersey, standing on that cliff's height, looking down into the forested slope where Alexander Hamilton dueled Aaron Burr, lost his life, and left his devoted wife impoverished and alone to raise their seven surviving children. We wanted to see the city as Hamilton might have seen it, and to experience the sights and sounds that might have filled his mind in those fateful moments. But in the end, we knew that our novel was not a novel about Alexander Hamilton. It was about his wife. We wanted to understand *her* journey. And that's what took us to upstate New York.

**Stephanie**: I was a little skeptical at first that we needed to visit the battlefields of Saratoga, because we have no evidence that Eliza was ever there. We had a great day in the museum, acquainting ourselves with the battles and trying on Revolutionary War costumes before walking the fields where Benedict Arnold was so fatefully injured in our cause. And the trip ended up being an important piece of our understanding of Eliza as a general's daughter and a girl raised at the frontier. Understanding her world and the way the war was literally on her doorstep gave us a richer understanding of who she came to be, and how she might have envisioned herself as part of the struggle of the soldiers around her. She lived all her life on the Hudson River and that river turned out to be the key to winning the war.

**Laura**: Our last stop, and in some ways, the most meaningful, was in Albany. We attended a little festival at Fort Crailo where Eliza's mother, Catherine Van Rensselaer Schuyler, came of age and acquainted ourselves with New Netherlander food, traditions, and customs. One thing that certainly stood out for us was the relative strength and independence of New Netherlander women. It was a reminder to us that the roles and rights of women in early America varied significantly amongst the colonies. Because of their cultural heritage, Eliza and her sisters had more options and autonomy than many women of the time period—certainly more than the women in Virginia we portrayed in *America's First Daughter.* The Schuyler sisters knew women in Albany who remained unmarried by choice and lived as property holders without any man to rule over them. Even without the revolutionary ideas swirling about their dinner table, they may have come to expect to have a choice in who they ▶

married and how they lived their lives. Perhaps that's why so many Schuyler daughters eloped against the wishes of their parents.

**Stephanie**: Our last stop was the Schuyler Mansion where Eliza and her family made their home. And that was only right, because Eliza spent much of her married life with Alexander there, too. In our research field trips we often get a feeling of a place. An impression or a mood. When we visited Thomas Jefferson's Monticello while writing *America's First Daughter*, we were overcome with a sense of bittersweet majesty. The Schuyler Mansion, a gorgeous Georgian mansion overlooking the Hudson River, had a feeling of quiet tranquility to it. We could easily imagine why Eliza spent so many summers there with her children. It must have been a relief to get away from the hustle and bustle of political life in the city. Nevertheless, there is no getting around the fact that it was a plantation where more than a dozen enslaved persons toiled for the happiness of the family, and though little evidence of their presence remains on the site, our guide Danielle was a wealth of information about their lives. We were fascinated by tales of Prince, whose presence was important enough to General Schuyler that he actually used his name as a code word. And we knew that even though the historical evidence was sparse, these people deserved their rightful place in our novel just as they do in the American experience as a whole.

**Laura**: Visiting the house was also useful for us in trying to sort fact from legend. Like the historians at the mansion, we suspect that the historical account of Loyalists breaking in to capture Philip Schuyler and Peggy rescuing her baby sister from tomahawk-wielding invaders may have been embroidered. However, because the source of the tale is a member of the family, and because the incident betrayed the risks revolutionary women like Eliza Schuyler faced, we included it. But first, we spent quite a long time meandering around the main hall trying to figure out from which angle a hatchet could have been thrown that would account for the gouge in the railing. Ultimately, we couldn't find one, so we opted to have the man simply chop at the banister instead!

**Stephanie:** As interesting as the house were the exhibits of family artifacts, some of which came to play a role in the book. British General Burgoyne's shoe buckles, which we used to show an interesting facet of Peggy's character. Eliza's sewing box, which helped us develop a theme about sewing that we—pardon the pun!—stitched into her character. And especially Eliza's locket necklace containing a clipping of George Washington's hair, which became a touchstone for her throughout the novel. Those were details that added real authenticity to the book, and we wouldn't have known to include them without visiting the site.

**Laura:** I agree. When you read a novel, you want it to be an immersive experience. As a writer, one of the best ways to create that experience is to have it yourself. And the best of both worlds is reading the book *and* visiting the sites, so we encourage you to go to them all! We hope you enjoy learning more about Eliza Schuyler Hamilton's life and journey in *My Dear Hamilton*.

*Learn more at DrayKamoie.com.* ∾

# Telling Her Story
## How *My Dear Hamilton* Differs from *Hamilton: An American Musical*

We're superfans of Lin-Manuel Miranda's *Hamilton: An American Musical*. And we've been known to sing along to the soundtrack on our road trips together. Repeatedly! But even if you haven't seen the show or listened to the music, you might be familiar with at least some of the most iconic lyrics. And you might know that the musical ends by asking a question: *Who tells your story?* Answer: *Eliza*.

However, the show's focus on Washington's right-hand man doesn't recount much of Eliza's own story. While we're inspired, awed, and humbled by Miranda's incredible storytelling, we made a number of different narrative choices. Here are the most noteworthy differences!

### Where the Story Starts

The musical starts brilliantly with Alexander's famous Caribbean backstory and his arrival in New York City in 1773. Eliza enters his story in a supporting role in 1780 when they're introduced by her older sister, Angelica.

Because our story is about *Eliza*, we debated what our starting point should be. Should it in fact be when she met Alexander? Ultimately, we decided against that. After all, as Eliza says in our opening chapter, she was *someone* before she met Alexander Hamilton. And she was. Eliza was the daughter of a general who was also a diplomat with the Indians and later ran a spy ring. The daughter of a Dutch mother with significant medical and estate-running skills she undoubtedly passed down. A frontier woman in her own right who attended Indian treaty negotiations, received an Indian name, and was fond of the outdoors. An eligible heiress who attracted the attention of Tench Tilghman and maybe even the British officer John André. None of Eliza's dynamic backstory makes it into a musical framed around Alexander Hamilton. And even her accomplishments as a patriot and activist in her own right are centered, in the musical, around Alexander's memory.

Though she might not have agreed, we thought she deserved a story of her own.

## Eliza's Characterization

In the musical, Eliza heartbreakingly contemplates whether she's enough to satisfy Alexander. Her sister says she's overly trusting, and she evolves into a wronged but forgiving wife.

But neither Hamilton nor Angelica lived to see Eliza's 1825 confrontation with James Monroe, which occurred long after the musical's last refrains, and was a big part of our inspiration for her characterization in *My Dear Hamilton*.

We asked ourselves what kind of woman would dress down a man who was once her husband's friend and until recently, the president of the United States, telling him that unless he was there to apologize, she had nothing to say to him? That strength, loyalty, confidence, stubbornness, and confrontationalism gave us the building blocks to portray Eliza as more than a forgiving wife. Certainly, she was also a woman who could hold an "unladylike" grudge!

This is, after all, the woman who assisted Alexander in copying and drafting some of his most famous political writings. And in her later life, she was known for being as relentless in her charitable and fundraising work as her husband was in his political work. In her eighties, she traveled halfway across the continent to visit her son in largely unsettled Wisconsin. And into her nineties, she was known to take two-mile walks around Washington, D.C. We took all of these into account in crafting our version of Eliza, a woman every bit as intrepid as the man she married.

## Angelica and Alexander

In the musical, Angelica introduces Eliza to Alexander after having fallen in love with him herself. That meeting serves wonderfully as the beginning of an emotional affair between Angelica and Alexander and calls into question whether Hamilton had true feelings for Eliza.

But we had more time in which to tell our story and decided to stick closer to the historical record; long before Hamilton entered the picture, Angelica eloped with John Barker Church. By the time of the famous winter's ball she'd been married for nearly three years and was the mother of two children. More importantly, Hamilton's frequent letters to Eliza during the period they were courting and betrothed are effusively affectionate and emotional, portraying what we believe was very likely as much of a love match as it was a consideration of what her wealth could do for him (a common ▸

**Telling Her Story** *(continued)*

consideration at the time for both men and women). If anyone appears as a potential rival for his affections during that period, it wasn't Angelica—it was John Laurens, to whom Hamilton wrote a number of quite intimate letters that have led some historians, including us, to question the nature of the men's relationship.

### Hamilton's Rift with General Washington

Like all historical fiction, the musical often plays with the true chronology, of necessity, sometimes superbly condensing and other times cleverly conflating historical events. For example, when the Broadway version of Washington catches Hamilton participating as John Laurens's second in the duel with Charles Lee, they have words and Washington sends Alex home, where he learns that Eliza is pregnant and that she wrote to the general and begged him to send her husband home.

The historical Hamilton did in fact have words with Washington that resulted in a breach in their relationship that some believe never fully healed. However, the real rift occurred in February 1781 when Eliza, who was not yet pregnant, joined Alexander at the army's winter camp at New Windsor. Washington had a momentary loss of patience, and Alexander used his terse words as an excuse to resign following months of frustration Alexander felt at not being promoted to a field command. In *My Dear Hamilton*, we imagined Eliza's reaction to the news that Alexander was no longer part of Washington's military family, and it was quite different from the one the musical's Eliza expressed.

### Eliza and the Marquis de Lafayette

The musical delightfully introduces America's Favorite Fighting Frenchman as Alexander's friend.

One of the great joys we had in writing *My Dear Hamilton* was dramatizing the historical friendship the marquis shared with Eliza, too. Given her father's role in military affairs, Eliza likely met the marquis when they were both twenty-year-olds in Albany in late 1777. If not then, they certainly would've met when both Alexander and the marquis were at the winter encampment at New Windsor. Indeed, it was the marquis delaying Alexander with conversation that piqued Washington's impatience and sparked the disagreement that ended in Alexander's resignation. Eliza saw Lafayette in 1784 when he returned to the United States for a four-month visit, and in 1795, she and Alexander took in Lafayette's son, Georges, when Adrienne Lafayette sent the boy to the United States for safety. In 1824, Eliza likely had an even greater organizational role in Lafayette's reunion tour than the one we depicted in *My Dear Hamilton*. In reality, Eliza and Lafayette were friends in their own right and it was a friendship that lasted most of her life.

## The Maria Reynolds Affair

There's no disputing that Alexander Hamilton became embroiled in a sex scandal—because he did, quite literally, write it down *right there*. In excruciating detail. With appendices. The musical's timeline presents a wonderful spiral of loss and forgiveness as Eliza learned of the affair with the 1797 publication of the *Reynolds Pamphlet*, and then has her and Alexander largely estranged until Philip Hamilton's death by duel. Their reconciliation out of grief over their son occurs before the election of 1800.

*My Dear Hamilton* asserts a number of differences here. Historically, the affair is documented to have occurred in 1791–92. And Hamilton published the *Reynolds Pamphlet* in 1797 in an attempt to clear his name of charges of speculation. Philip Hamilton died by duel in November 1801, *after* the election of 1800.

Even so, the big question remained: when did Eliza know?

We think it's highly likely that she already knew before the *Reynolds Pamphlet*. When James Monroe and others first confronted Hamilton about possible financial impropriety, rumors Eliza would've heard spread thereafter. In August of 1793, Eliza and Alexander nearly died of yellow fever, and the next year, Alexander tendered his resignation from public office. Though he remained a public figure, he appears to have become more focused on his family. His letters to Eliza are tender, devoted, appreciative, and seemingly apologetic. To us, the timing of all that felt more than coincidental, leading us to posit that Eliza learned of his infidelity in 1792. We like to believe their near-death experiences and reconciliation led Hamilton to reevaluate his priorities and dedicate himself to Eliza and their growing brood.

## Aaron Burr

Aaron Burr is the narrator for most of the musical in which he makes a sympathetic villain and delightful foil. But Burr posed a special challenge for us in writing *My Dear Hamilton*. ▶

**Telling Her Story** *(continued)*

Eliza definitely knew him and his wife, Theodosia. They were, as described by a contemporary, in and out of each other's houses during those early years. Burr studied in Eliza's father's law library at the Schuyler Mansion in Albany, and socialized with the Hamiltons frequently when they all lived in New York City. But once the rivalry between the two men escalated, Eliza saw less and less of Burr. Though Alexander continued to have occasion to interact with and correspond with Burr, Eliza had far less reason.

In *My Dear Hamilton*, we were telling *her* story, so Burr was rarely central to it, even though his actions would change the whole course of her life one fateful day at Weehawken.

## Another Fifty Years

In the last song of the musical, Eliza briefly but emotionally summarizes some of her accomplishments during the fifty years after her husband's death.

From the beginning, we wanted to tell Eliza's *whole* story. Just as Eliza was someone before she met Alexander, she was also someone after he died, and she was a widow for far longer than she was a wife. Indeed, this was one way we wanted *My Dear Hamilton* to stand out. The source material for Eliza's later years is scarce, scattered, and therefore time-consuming to track down. But once we did that work, we found that there was *so much* that we couldn't begin to include it all. Thankfully, it did give us the opportunity to tell Eliza's story as it's never been told before! ∽